COURTESY OF AMERICAN LOCOMOTIVE WORKS

ENGINEMEN'S MANUAL

INTENDED FOR THE

Engineer, Fireman or Mechanic who wishes
to extend his knowledge of the
Locomotive or Air Brake

QUESTIONS AND ANSWERS FOR INSTRUCTIONS AND EXAMINATION

BY W. P. JAMES

ILLUSTRATED

W. P. JAMES PUBLISHING COMPANY
Louisville, Kentucky
1919

Copyright, 1916
BY W. P. JAMES PUBLISHING COMPANY
Louisville, Ky.

Copyright, 1917
BY W. P. JAMES PUBLISHING COMPANY
Louisville, Ky

Copyright, 1918
BY W. P. JAMES PUBLISHING COMPANY
Louisville, Ky.

Fifteenth Edition

This Book Has Been Digitally Watermarked to Prevent Illegal Duplication

This printing ©2008-2009 Periscope Film LLC
All Rights Reserved
ISBN #978-1-935327-82-0   1-935327-82-8
www.PeriscopeFilm.com

Table of Contents

	Page
Introduction	xi
Steam	1
Combustion	4
Definition of Technical Terms	14
Handy Rules in Arithmetic	16
British Thermal Unit	17
Classification of Locomotives	18
What Constitutes an Engine Failure?	19
Pounds in Locomotives	20
Mikado Type Locomotives	24
Schroeder Electric Headlight	28
Mallet Locomotives	38
Triplex Articulated Compound Locomotive	45
Electric Headlights	49
Lubricators	64
Injectors	67
Slide Valves	71
Walschaert Valve Gear	73
Baker Valve Gear	103
Southern Valve Gear	122
Superheaters	127
Engine Failures and Breakdowns:—	
The Locomotive and Adhesion	136
Boilers	140
Draft Appliances	147
Injectors	150
Lubricators	157
Frames, Trucks, Tires, Wheels, and Axles	161
Valves and Valve Gear	172
Progressive Examinations:	
First Year	192
Second Year	205
Third Year	226
Handling of Freight Trains	292
Reasons for Air Pumps Running Hot	294
Definition of the Terms "Piston Travel," "Running Travel," and "Standing Travel"	296
"PC" Passenger Brake Equipment	298
No. 6 "ET" Locomotive Brake Equipment	322
B-3 Locomotive Brake Equipment	382
"K" Triple Valve	397
Westinghouse Eleven-inch Pump	409A
Rules and Instructions for Inspection and Testing of Steam Locomotives and Tenders	410
Safety Appliance Standards for Locomotives, as fixed by order of the Commission Dated March 13, 1911	435

Introduction

My object is to make this Manual so clear and simple that the youngest fireman can comprehend what is dealt with.

It is not pretended that it treats of every particular kind of locomotive appliance or breakdowns, nor does it go into details.

On all railroads it's the practice to examine enginemen; such examinations differ on various roads, and it is needless to say that it would be sufficient to memorize the answers to questions given herein. They are simply given to be used as a guide in preparing for examinations, and to familiarize himself with the details of the mechanism and construction of the locomotive.

With enginemen many methods have been employed to increase their knowledge so that they may better serve themselves and the railroads with which they are connected.

In order to pass the examinations, experience, careful study, preparation and ability are required. No book, of course, can directly supply all those qualities. But indirectly such book knowledge may contribute much to the enginemen in the hour of emergency.

It is essential that the fireman and engineer should be familiar with the construction and operation of the subsidiary machines and devices that form the modern locomotive if he hopes for success in his profession, and the aim of this work is to help him achieve success.

I take the pleasure of extending public thanks to those who have contributed articles in the preparation of this work; and to the manufacturers who have so kindly rendered their assistance.

This book is respectfully submitted, but not without consciousness of its many imperfections, to the enginemen for their approval.

W. P. J.

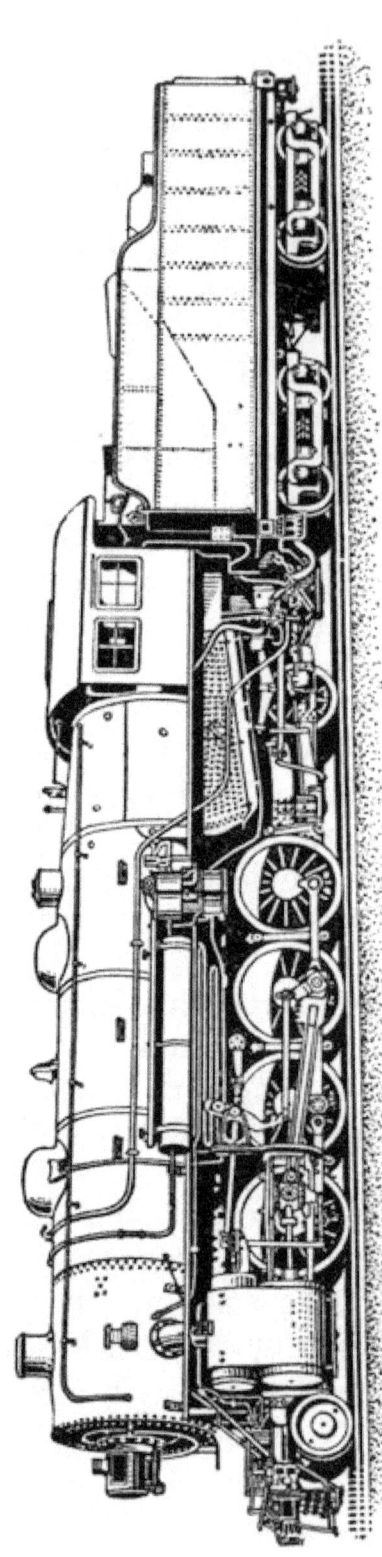

Steam

Records show that steam was used for heating purposes back to the year 150 B. C. To James Watt, more than any other man is due the honor of first controlling and utilizing steam for power, and perfecting the steam engine, though others had used steam for power before Watt.

Steam is the vapor of water generated by heating water above the boiling point, hence steam is water in a gaseous state and is colorless and imperceptible to the eye. The vapor seen escaping from a vessel of boiling water, or rolling in clouds from the exhaust of an engine, is only a modification, or diluted agent of the mighty force that does so much of the world's work.

This vapor is steam that is resolving itself back into water, the change which is visible is caused by its contact with the cold air.

Saturated steam is steam either in contact with the water from which it was generated or, if separated therefrom, is kept at the same temperature and pressure. Wet steam is steam not only saturated, but also holding in suspension unevaporated water in the form of minute drops; it holds this water in suspension mechanically, due either to ebullition of the water from which it is generated or else from a rapid flow of steam from near the surface of the water.

Dry steam is the term usually used for saturated steam in distinction from wet steam. Superheated steam is steam removed from contact with water and heated above the temperature of the water from which it was generated; it is variously called steam-gas, surcharged steam, or anhydrous steam. Steam more closely resembles a perfect gas when superheated than in any other state, and it is for this reason that in the locomotive the attempt is made to superheat the steam. The boiler has a dome from which, and at quite a distance above the usual water level, reasonably dry steam is taken, passed through a pipe called the "dry pipe," and branching in the smoke-box or front end of the locomotive where the escaping hot gases have a tendency to superheat it, passes into the two cylinders in which its energy becomes useful.

In steam, as in other gases, there is a natural repulsion between its various particles, each particle trying to separate itself from the others, so that it will fill the receptacle in which it is placed, regardless of the quantity of steam or size of the vessel holding it. Its natural tendency is to expand and thus push out whatever resists expansion. If the steam is enclosed and superheated, therefore, as in the case of a locomotive boiler, the natural tendency of its particles to separate is intensified and we thus obtain, according to its quantity or volume, the steam pressure required.

Real steam is an invisible gas, or, rather, a transparent fluid, really water changed into gas by the action of heat. Accordingly, to make the steam that an engine requires water must be boiled. To hasten this and to lessen the cost, the boiler is permeated with tubes, or flues, connecting with the fire-box, into which the flames therefrom are drawn, thus multiplying the heating surface and, in so far as this is done, hastening the boiling of the water and the generation of steam. As the water is transformed into steam it rises into the dome. From there it is released by opening the throttle valve and is thence conveyed, through the dry pipe and steam pipes, through the steam chest, thence to the cylinders.

It is the expansive power of the steam operating through the mechanism of the cylinders that affords the propelling power of the locomotive.

THEORY OF SUPERHEATING

The theory of superheating contains several important points, and without going into the realm of thermodynamics we may glance at the advantages which are claimed for superheated steam. In the first place, superheated steam contains a greater amount of energy per pound than dry, saturated steam does if both are at the same pressure. This increased energy is in the form of heat units, which enables the superheated steam to do more work in the cylinders than saturated steam could do if both were exhausted at the same pressure.

The reason for this is that dry, saturated steam is always on the point of giving up some of its heat and turning into water. Such a loss not only reduces the volume and pressure in the cylinder, but it gives up the store of latent heat contained in the particles of steam which are thus turned to water, and as the latent heat of steam is 970.4 British thermal units, it is evident that the loss owing to condensation is very considerable. If now, by superheating, we give to the steam, which is so ready to fall back into the form of water, a temperature greater than that due to its pressure, condensation will not take place until the superheated steam has given up the whole of the heat represented by this extra temperature. There is, of course, a reduction in temperature when superheated steam strikes the comparatively cool walls of the cylinder, but there is no condensation. This is practically where the principle upon which the value of superheating depends.

The increase of temperature in superheated steam augments its volume, and all the moisture which is sure to be contained in saturated steam and any particles of water which may have been entrained as the steam entered the throttle valve are evaporated, and thus the action of the steam in the cylinders, that is, its expansion, follows the laws which apply to a perfect gas. Superheated steam also possesses a higher velocity than saturated steam at the same pressure, this results in the hotter steam more rapidly passing through the steam pipes and ports, and reaches the piston, if one may say, with increased striking force, which is an advantage in high-speed service.

In writing of this subject in their catalogue, No. 10,037, the American Locomotive Company says that "actual experience, as well as theory, proves that these advantages are obtained to the fullest extent only by the use of high degrees of superheat, by which is meant from 150 to 175 degrees Fahrenheit and above." The table published in connection with these remarks shows that for the lower ranges of superheat, such as 25, 50 and 75 degrees Fahrenheit, the economy is small.

A very satisfactory reduction in the amount of water consumed is evident when superheating is carried out. This amounts to from about 15 to 25 per cent for superheated steam receiving 150 to 200 degrees Fahrenheit of superheat. A reduction of the fuel used is also one of the advantages of superheating, which follows from the fact that less water has to be evaporated to do a given amount of work.

In describing the principle of superheating one might almost say that it is utilizing waste heat to change high pressure fog into a perfect gas.

Combustion*

Three things are essential to combustion or burning in a locomotive fire-box, as well as elsewhere. They are: The fuel to be burned; oxygen, the supporter of burning, and the igniting temperature of the fuel. Sometimes in our attempts to economize we apparently lose sight of two of these and regretfully watch the other disappear into the fire-box. One person's regret may be due to the fact that the fuel is costing him money, while the other may be thinking of the fuel only in relation to the performance sheet. What is needed just now among all railroad men who have any immediate connection with the consumption of fuel is a concentration of attention on the interdependence of fuel, oxygen and ignition temperature.

The fuel used on most of our locomotives is soft or bituminous coal, and for that reason it will receive sole consideration in this discussion. Let it be said that *coal, as such, does not burn*. Before any burning can occur the coal must be broke down, which process requires an expenditure of heat. The first products of this breaking down process are coke and gases. The coke is made up of carbon (technically known as "fixed carbon") and those substances which help to make the ash. The gases evolved are almost all composed of hydrogen (the lightest known gas) and carbon, therefore called hydro-carbons. These hydro-carbons must also be broken down into their components, hydrogen and carbon. Practically speaking, *the heat value of a ton of bituminous coal depends on the number of pounds of fixed carbon and number of pounds and relative composition of the hydro-carbon gases which will be produced upon heating it*. In general the hydro-carbons are in excess of the fixed carbon, and the two together will usually average from 1,600 to 1,700 pounds per ton of coal.

The real process of burning in a locomotive fire-box is the uniting of oxygen, a gas, with the fuel to be burned. In this *uniting process* heat is evolved and used in generating steam. If a sufficient supply of oxygen be present, a pound of carbon will burn to form a colorless gas, carbon dioxide, and enough heat will be evolved to convert 12.5 pounds of water into steam, the water to begin with being at the tank temperature, and the steam generated at a boiler pressure of 180 to 200 pounds. If, however, the supply of oxygen be restricted, then another colorless gas will be formed called carbon monoxide, and but 4 pounds of water will be evaporated under similar conditions of pressure, etc. That is, with the same carbon to be burned one may get its full heat value or *less than one-third*, depending solely upon the supply of oxygen. A

---
*From Mr. J. W. Shepherd.

pound of hydrogen burned will evolve heat enough to evaporate 54.5 pounds of water under the above conditions.

The igniting temperature of carbon is a little more than 900 degrees Fahrenheit; hydrogen about 1,200 and hydro-carbons from 940 to 1,230 degrees. There is no reason why these temperatures cannot be constantly maintained in a fire-box.

It need hardly be mentioned that in obtaining fuel we must take what nature has provided for us, but in supplying the oxygen —which is just as necessary—man's skill is called into play. This important gas, oxygen, is a part of the air, being about one-fifth of it, by volume. Since it may be had for the taking, the enginemen's source of supply is the atmosphere and by extraordinary demand is met by an induced draft. At present this draft is produced by shooting the exhaust steam into the stack. Objections to this method are back pressure in the cylinders and the almost absolute dependency of the strength of draft on position of reverse lever, or cut off. This latter objection frequently manifests itself to the discomfiture of the fireman and also in the loss of fuel. The economic considerations of the present warrant the prediction that another method must supplant this one.

Not only is oxygen necessary for burning, but it must touch whatever burns. Right here is where locomotive men's troubles begin in earnest. It is not enough that the requisite amount of oxygen pass through the fire-box in a given time, but its usefulness is largely determined by *just where* it is going through the box. To illustrate: Some time ago the writer had occasion to ride on a locomotive used in heavy freight service. This particular locomotive was known among the men as "the coal eater," and the reason was soon apparent, for practically all the oxygen was being pulled up through the forward two-thirds of the box and the fireman kept steam at the expense of fuel. Evidently the draft appliances were improperly adjusted. Other instances might be cited in which with apparently a proper adjustment of draft appliances similar results were temporarily produced on account of uneven firing. These illustrations are based on the improper utilization of grate area, and instances of "holes" in a fire and "clinkers" belong in the same category.

In an earlier part of this chapter it was stated that of the two heat-producing factors from coal the hydro-carbons usually weigh more than the fixed carbon. About one-fifth of the weight of the hydro-carbons is the weight of the hydrogen which they evolve when broken down. And a pound of hydrogen, it will be remembered, is worth more than 4 pounds of carbon for heating purposes. It must be evident, therefore, that more than half the fuel consumed in a locomotive is consumed as gases. In this connection it is well to remember that when these gases are evolved *they do not loiter,* in order to be burned, but hasten at once toward the stack. One or two seconds' delay in burning them means their loss. If they remain intact they, being colorless, escape unnoticed. This is the condition that generally obtains when a fire is badly clinkered and the fireman longs for black smoke while his pointer continues to drop backward. No wonder the pointer goes back. Heat is expended in breaking down the coal, and then the best part of the fuel is simply thrown away. When a fireman produces black smoke he does so because he is partially, but only partially, burning the hydro-carbon gases, and thereby is getting *something* in return for the heat used in evolving them and breaking them down. Such a smoky fire will generate more steam per pound of coal than the smokeless, *cindery* one cited, but that does not justify the belief prevalent among some enginemen that a smoky fire is the best kind of steam. *Black smoke is unburned carbon from the hydro-carbons.* It is unburned usually because of the lack of sufficient oxygen. In this dearth of oxygen some of the carbon is partially burned to form carbon monoxide. Therefore the black smoke by no means represents the fuel loss from a smoky fire. *It is simply an indicator pointing to a loss.* In general a smoky fire is produced by putting the coal into the box in such a way and in such quantity that the hydro-carbons upon being evolved are not in contact with sufficient oxygen for their complete burning. Fires that roll out dense clouds of black smoke are not the only ones that waste fuel. A given amount of hydro-carbons requires a certain amount of oxygen for complete burning. But suppose there is an insufficiency of oxygen, then some of the carbon may be but partially burned, forming carbon monoxide, which is perfectly colorless. There is always danger of a loss of fuel in heavy firing, because of the large amount of hydro-carbons evolved in a given time.

Too much stress cannot be laid on the consideration of the hydro-carbon gases in locomotive combustion, for they are either the friend or the foe of the fireman just as he chooses to make them. If properly handled, they are worth more than all else he can get from his coal, or if improperly handled he may lose almost any portion of them and obtain black smoke besides. To secure proper combustion of these gases then, immediately upon being evolved they should be mixed with sufficient oxygen for their complete burning. On some roads a brick arch is used to assist in this mixing.

No stress has been laid on the burning of the carbon in the coke, because it simply lies on the grates and waits for the oxygen to come along. A fireman doesn't lose fuel from that source.

Since oxygen must touch whatever burns it is evident that coal should be finely broken in order to insure proper contact. At present too much coal is put into fire-boxes in large chunks, and the hydro-carbons evolved do not have the chance to come in touch with oxygen as they *must* in order to be burned.

A word might be said regarding the influence of moisture in

coal—also the practice of wetting coal—aside from the fact that it takes heat to evaporate this moisture. The steam generated from a quantity of water occupies about 1,800 times the volume of the water at atmospheric pressure. At a reduced pressure and high temperature, such conditions as one would find in a fire-box, the volume would be correspondingly larger. Therefore water introduced into a fire-box through any medium, upon becoming steam (and if not dissociated) occupies space that would otherwise be filled with other gaseous products. That is, the efficiency of the draft is impaired. This same effect manifests itself in firing on damp or rainy days.

As a concluding statement, permit the prediction that inherent objections to the present method of draft and the present form of fuel make a change in both necessary.

QUESTIONS AND ANSWERS ON COMBUSTION

Q.—What in your opinion is the simplest method by which engineer and fireman can save fuel?

A.—First, be sure that the engineer knows how to direct the work of the fireman. Second, that the fireman is willing and intelligent enough to see and do as he is instructed, then it becomes merely a matter of getting them to co-operate in their work, after which good results are bound to follow. Any plan that ignores the absolute authority of the engineer must fail. Much unsatisfactory service of the power as well as many absolute failures may be directly traced to the want of a directing head on the engine.

Q.—What is combustion, or burning?

A.—It is the union of that element of the air known as oxygen with the hydrogen and carbon of the coal, this union forming a gas.

Q.—What are the elements of fire, as considered in locomotive practice?

A.—Quality of fuel, composition, distribution and application of air through the burning fuel to produce the greatest possible degree of heat with the smallest possible consumption of fuel.

Q.—Is there such a thing as perfect combustion?

A.—No.

Q.—What is perfect combustion from a theoretical standpoint?

A.—It is combustion that supplies just the required number of heat units to furnish a given amount of steam at all times to perform the required work without a fuel waste.

Q.—Why can it not be attained?

A.—The manner of supplying the fuel to the fire at irregular intervals and in varying quantities; the loss that is continually taking place from imperfect combustion, which will be spoken of later; the variation of grades, load and speed, with consequent variation in cut-off and fuel consumption. While a heavy train means more money earned than a light one to offset the increased fuel consumption a higher rate of speed increases the amount of coal consumed without any increase in the earnings; so that it is evident from an economical standpoint fast trains are not a success. For these reasons perfect combustion is impossible in locomotive practice, and is not attained with stationary boilers where the engine load and speed is not variable.

Q.—What is meant by the term heat unit?

A.—The amount of heat necessary to raise one pound of water one degree Fahrenheit.

Q.—What is its equivalent mechanically expressed?

A.—The power exerted to raise 772 pounds one foot high.

Q.—How many heat units does a pound of coal burned represent?

A.—It varies with the quality of coal burned, but about 14,000 may be considered a fair average with the different grades of coal. With an excellent grade of coal where there was but very small loss from unburnable material it would run much higher, and with a poor grade the opposite condition would prevail in a similar degree. A good grade of coal that cost much more than a poor one is often the cheaper when the relative amount of heat units in the two are considered.

Q.—What is the amount of water evaporated for each pound of coal consumed?

A.—Seven to eight pounds of water to one pound of bituminous coal burned; about one pound less water is evaporated per pound of anthracite coal.

Q.—What are the two most important elements in the production of combustion?

A.—The carbon of the fuel and the oxygen of the air. These two elements have a strong natural affinity for each other, which fact aids greatly in the process of combustion and producing both light and heat amid violent evolution of the gases, within the fire-box.

Q.—What is the composition of soft coal?

A.—About 80 per cent carbon, 5 per cent hydrogen, and the remainder may be classed as waste material, that is, incombustible matter.

Q.—What is the amount of air required to consume one pound of soft coal?

A.—The exact amount can not be given in locomotive practice, owing to the varying conditions of the fire and the work and the quality of the coal used, but from 12 to 18 pounds is a fair average. The rate of air admission must be proportionate to the coal consumption. Too much air, especially if admitted above the fire, cools it and causes a fuel waste; too little air supplied causes imperfect combustion with a consequent fuel waste.

Q.—How much space does a pound of air occupy?

A.—Thirteen cubic feet. Taking 12 pounds of air, the lowest rate of air consumption per one pound of coal, multiplied by 13 cubic feet, gives 156 cubic feet of air used for each pound of coal burned; allowing 20 pounds for a shovel of coal gives 3,120 cubic feet of air consumed for each shovel of coal burned, and on that basis 31,200 cubic feet of air for each ton burned. *The necessity of unrestricted air admission through the grates is obvious* to any one who cares to give the matter any consideration whatever.

Q.—How can the amount of carbon and hydrogen in coal be determined?

A.—Only by chemical test. Therefore the comparison of coal sheets of parallel lines of road with varying grades and qualities of coal is no fair comparison in any sense of the locomotive performance.

Q.—Which is the lighter gas, carbon or hydrogen?

A.—Hydrogen. It raises first and is first consumed of the gases of any given piece of coal, and a certain amount of moisture is consumed with it. The carbon is next burned, but the two burnings are so rapid as to be practically one and the same. Nothing in nature is destroyed. Its form only is changed. Coal by combustion is changed into heat and waste material; the oxygen of the air changes its form, and water is converted into a gas called steam, to be later vaporized and changed back to water by cooling. Always changed but no destruction of matter.

Q.—Is oxygen necessary for combustion?

A.—Absolutely: It must also come in contact with whatever is to be burned, so that the admission of air is the important matter in combustion.

Q.—What change must occur with coal before it is burned?

A.—It must be broken down, that is, the heat properties must be separated from the waste material, and heat is required to do this and by its application gas and coke are produced. Coke is known as the fixed carbon of the coal, and the waste material is designated as ash. The gas is carbon and hydrogen. The hydrogen and carbon in a ton of coal is equal, as before stated, to about 85 per cent of the whole, or 1,700 pounds for one ton of coal.

Q.—What gas is formed by the proper mixing of oxygen with the gas from the coal?

A.—Carbon dioxide. A colorless gas.

Q.—What result as to loss of heat does insufficient air admission to a fire-box have?

A.—A pound of carbon turned to carbon dioxide will convert 125 pounds of water into steam at a high boiler pressure, but with too small an admission of oxygen only about one-third as much water will be evaporated under similar conditions, so that the fuel waste is enormous; therefore, the restriction of the draft area by reason of bad damper arrangement or handling, or from clinkered or heavy fire are expensive matters for the railroad companies financially, and physically for the fireman who makes the steam.

Q.—What three important things are to be considered as most essential in combustion?

A.—The kind and quality of the fuel to be burned; the admission or furnishing of sufficient oxygen—the supporter of burning—to the fire, and the igniting temperature of the fuel burned.

Q.—What usually controls the kind and quality of coal burned?

A.—Natural availability. Often a soft coal is used that shows a poorer rate of heating power than some other coal that must be hauled from a distance. However, it will make the steam by using more of it, and its availability over the other coal makes it cheaper per 100 ton mile even with a higher consumption.

Q.—What is the igniting temperature of bituminous coal?

A.—Carbon 900 degrees. The two gases united as hydro-carbons 950 to 1,250 degrees Fahrenheit. These are only approximate figures for the different grades of soft coal, the kind most commonly used in locomotive service.

Q.—What part of the air is oxygen?

A.—About one-fifth part. The source of supply is unlimited, but the same is not true concerning the source of admission. To meet this demand for abundant air admission and to meet the extra demand by the use of large locomotives various plans were tried.

Q.—Explain some of these plans.

A.—At first by increasing the length of the fire-box to such a degree that it was found to be impractical for efficient firing and combustion. To give the required grate area and shorten the box to reasonable proportions the shallow fire-box extending out over the frame and rear drivers; or trail wheels on some types of locomotives with high drive wheels.

Q.—Has any other method of admitting air other than through the grates been tried, and with what result?

A.—Admission by hollow stay bolts and by flues running from the atmosphere through the fire-box sheets above the fire, and known as combustion flues. The all-hollow stay bolt is not used as much as formerly and the combustion flues are used in a milder degree.

Q.—Why are combustion flues used to a less extent than formerly?

A.—The admission of air above the fire through a number of two-inch tubes was found to be more detrimental than beneficial, on account of such large currents or air cooling the fire and sheets and tubes of the fire-box. Where the grate area is deficient, air admitted in small jets above the fire would be of benefit, as it would mix readily with the gases without cooling them to such an extent as is done by combustion tubes.

Q.—Why is air that has passed through the grates to the fire-box preferable for the purpose of combustion?

A.—Because in passing through the fire it becomes heated and is more ready to unite with the coal gases and take its part in combustion than that which is admitted above the fire. A certain amount of air admitted above the fire can be used without noticeable loss, but the heat loss is considerable when it is admitted in such quantities as to cool the gases below the igniting temperature. All firemen know what the result of holding the firedoor open is on the fire.

Q.—What regulates the openings between the grate fingers in addition to the air admission?

A.—The openings must not be so large as to allow coal to drop unburned in the ash pan. They should rock enough to shake small cinders and pieces of slate through readily.

Q.—How can the necessity for the immediate burning of the gases be illustrated?

A.—As before stated, at a high temperature with plenty of oxygen admitted to the coal gases, carbon dioxide is formed with a heat value three times as great as where the supply of oxygen is reduced or the temperature is too low, and carbon monoxide is formed; they do not *wait* to be burned, but are at once carried forward through the flues and escape unobserved out of the stack to the atmosphere.

Q.—Why is escaping gas from a smokestack not noticeable?

A.—Because it is colorless. Turn on a gas jet and watch if you can see the escaping gas.

Q.—Will gases be burned after once they have entered the tubes?

A.—To no great extent.

Q.—Why?

A.—Because of the low temperature within the tubes and the amount of heavy gas they contain. A light lowered into a well where there is a carbonic acid gas immediately dies, and so the blaze from the fire-box enters the flues but a short distance and dies. That the temperature of the flues is low is demonstrated by the fact that flues seldom, if ever, leak in the smokebox end, evidence that they are not subjected to the great temperature variations that they are in the fire-box end.

Q.—Is a fire that gives off plenty of black smoke evidence that all the gases are being consumed and that it is the best kind for steam?

A.—No. A fire that is in good condition will always give off some black smoke when a fresh supply of coal is put on the fire, but this will only be for an instant, unless a large amount of green coal has been used. Light firing will do away with much black smoke, which is an indication of too little oxygen for the amount of coal supplied and represents unburned carbon and a loss of heat.

Q.—Does black smoke represent all the heat loss that may be taking place?

A.—No. Colorless gas may be escaping at the same time unnoticed.

Q.—Is there any difference in the amount of coal burned in either end of the fire-box under different conditions of service or cut-off?

A.—There is. When engine is first started and when getting under headway, the draft is strongest through forward end of grates. This is due to the presence of the baffle sheet in front end covering a large portion of the upper flues, while the lower ones are free to accommodate the violent circulation which takes place under such service; and the air to supply the circulation will naturally come from the most convenient source, which is at the point nearest the lower flues, the forward end of fire-box. When headway is gained and lever is cut back, the draft becomes less violent, giving time for a more equal circulation through all the grate surface, and all the flues as well.

Q.—What effect, if any, does the regulation of draft have on the life of flues?

A.—Theoretically speaking, there would perhaps be little, if any difference, assuming that the grate surface be amply supplied with fuel to meet the variations of draft, as already explained in the foregoing answer; but the difficulty of meeting these changes by the average fireman is apparent to any practical man. So, if the front end of grates is not properly supplied with coal at times when the draft is strong there, holes will be pulled through fire, permitting cold currents of air to strike the flues, which may cause them to leak. It requires the greatest skill on the part of the fireman to prevent this, for if he finds the fault only after the steam has gone back the damage to flues may have already taken place.

Q.—Why is it necessary that front-end doors and joints of cinder hoppers be kept tight?

A.—To prevent the vacuum creating action of the exhaust from being interfered with. Also to prevent admission of air that might fan fire created by sparks.

Q.—How does the size of exhaust tip affect the steaming and working of the engine?

A.—As all the steam from the cylinders must escape through the exhaust tip, its outward velocity will depend upon the size of the opening. The smaller the tip, the faster the steam must rush. When a tip is small some part of the steam will be prevented from escaping, and will remain in the cylinder, obstructing the return movement of the piston, causing back pressure.

Q.—What effect on fuel consumption has a small tip?

A.—When the tip is small the velocity of exhaust steam is high, which induces a fierce rush of the fire gases through the flues, thereby wasting fuel.

Q.—What is the effect of admitting less than sufficient air to the fire?

A.—The act of combustion produces a gas deficient in heat.

Q.—What is the effect of admitting an excessive supply of air to the fire?

A.—The volume of air in excess of that needed to supply oxygen to form carbon dioxide absorbs part of the heat that ought to be used for steam making. It also tends to depress the fire below the ignition temperature.

Q.—What is the ignition temperature of fuel?

A.—The degree of heat at which any kind of fuel begins to burn is called its ignition temperature. Different kinds of fuel have different igniting points. If one takes a piece of iron heated to a dim red and applies it to a gas jet, the gas will not ignite. Increase the temperature of the iron until it reaches a cherry red and it will ignite the gas jet. From this experiment it may be inferred that this ignition temperature of hydrogen gas is about the same as the cherry heat of iron, which is about 1,600 degrees Fahrenheit. As carbon requires still greater heat for ignition, it may safely be inferred that the heat of a fire-box performing active duty is considerably higher than the cherry heat of iron.

Definition of Technical Terms

Absolute pressure of steam is its pressure reckoned from vacuum; the pressure shown by the steam gauge, plus the pressure of the atmosphere.

Boiler pressure is the pressure above atmosphere; the pressure shown by a correct steam gauge.

Initial pressure is the pressure in the cylinder at the beginning of the forward stroke.

Terminal pressure is the pressure that would be in the cylinder at the end of the piston's stroke if release did not take place before the end of the stroke; it can be determined by extending the expansion curve to the end of the diagram, or by dividing the pressure at the cut-off by the ratio of the expansion.

Mean effective pressure is the average pressure against the piston during its entire stroke in one direction, less the back pressure.

Back pressure is the loss in pounds per square inch required to get the steam out of the cylinder after it has done its work. On a locomotive it is shown by the distance apart of the atmosphere and counter pressure lines.

Total back pressure is the distance between the lines of counter-pressure and perfect vacuum represented in pounds.

Initial expansion is shown by the reduction of pressure in the cylinder before steam is shut off.

Ratio of expansion would be the ratio of the fall in pressure between the cut-off and the end of the stroke, providing there was no exhaust.

Wire drawing is the reduction of pressure between the boiler and cylinder; it often causes initial expansion. It is caused by contracted steam pipes or ports.

Clearance is all the waste space between the piston and valve, when the piston is at the end of its stroke.

A unit of heat is the heat required to increase the temperature of one pound of water one degree Fahrenheit when the temperature of the water is just above the freezing point.

A unit of work (foot pound) is one pound raised a height of one foot. One unit of heat equals 772 units of work.

One horse power is 33,000 pounds lifted a height of one foot in one minute; or one pound lifted 33,000 feet in one minute or an equivalent force.

Indicated horse power is the horse power shown by the indicator. It is the product of the net area of the piston; its speed in feet per minute and the mean effective pressure divided by 33,000 pounds.

Net horse power is the indicated horse power less the friction of the engine.

Saturated steam, called dry steam, is steam that contains just sufficient heat to keep the water in a state of steam.

Superheated steam is steam which has an excess of heat which may be parted with without causing condensation.

A ton mile is a unit of measurement of train weight. It represents one ton hauled one mile.

A car mile is also a unit of measurement, when the rating is based on cars hauled, and a car mile represents a car hauled one mile.

Handy Rules in Arithmetic

To find the circumference of a circle multiply its diameter by 3.1416.

To find the diameter of a circle multiply its circumference by .31831.

To find the area of a circle multiply the square of its diameter by .7854.

To find the cubic inches in a ball multiply its cube of diameter by .5236.

To find the revolutions of drivers per mile divide 1680 by the diameter of the wheel in feet.

To find revolutions per minute multiply the speed in miles per hour by 28 and divide the product by the diameter of the driving wheel in feet.

To find piston speed in feet per minute multiply revolutions per minute by twice the stroke of piston in feet.

To find the speed of train per second multiply speed in miles per hour by 22 and divide by 15.

To find time when rate of speed and distance is given multiply distance by 60 and divide by rate of speed.

To find rate of speed when distance and time are given, distance multiplied by 60 and divided by the time in minutes.

To find the distance when the time and rate of speed are given, multiply the time by the rate of speed and divide by 60.

To find the number of tons of coal in a bin: Length, height and width of pile in feet multiplied together, divide by 30 for hard coal, by 35 for soft coal, by 128 for cords of long wood, and by 135 for cords of sawed wood.

British Thermal Unit

The British thermal unit, generally expressed in the letters B. t. u., is the quantity of heat required to raise the temperature of one pound of water one degree. As a gallon of water weighs $8\frac{1}{3}$ pounds, it requires $8\frac{1}{3}$ B. t. u. to raise the temperature of one gallon one degree, $16\frac{2}{3}$ B. t. u. to raise the temperature two degrees, and so on. Thus, when a given coal is said to have a heat value of 13,800 B. t. u. per pound, it is meant that if all the heat caused by the complete combustion of one pound of that coal could be transmitted to 13,800 pounds of water it would raise the temperature of that water one degree. Or, if all the heat could be transmitted to, say, 138 pounds of water, it would raise the temperature of that water just 100 degrees, because $138 \times 100 = 13,800$. The pounds of water heated multipled by the number of degrees the temperature has been raised equals the number of B. t. u. The standard method of finding the heat value of a fuel is to burn a small sample of it in a tight steel bomb under water. The heat caused by the burning of the sample is then all absorbed by the water and by multiplying the weight of the water by its rise in temperature and dividing by the weight of the sample, the heat value of the coal is calculated direct in B. t. u. per pound.

Classification of Locomotives
(WHYTE'S SYSTEM)

0-4-0	4 WHEEL SWITCHER
0-6-0	6 WHEEL SWITCHER
0-8-0	8 WHEEL SWITCHER
0-10-0	10 WHEEL SWITCHER
0-4-4-0	ARTICULATED
0-6-6-0	ARTICULATED
0-8-8-0	ARTICULATED
2-4-4-0	ARTICULATED
2-6-6-0	ARTICULATED
2-8-8-0	ARTICULATED
2-6-6-2	ARTICULATED
2-8-8-2	ARTICULATED
2-4-0	4 COUPLED
2-6-0	MOGUL
2-8-0	CONSOLIDATION
2-10-0	DECAPOD
4-4-0	8 WHEEL
4-6-0	10 WHEEL
4-8-0	12 WHEEL
0-4-2	4 COUPLED & TRAILING
0-6-2	6 COUPLED & TRAILING
0-8-2	8 COUPLED & TRAILING
0-4-4	FORNEY 4 COUPLED
0-6-4	FORNEY 6 COUPLED
0-4-6	FORNEY 4 COUPLED
0-6-6	FORNEY 6 COUPLED
2-4-2	COLUMBIA
2-6-2	PRAIRIE
2-8-2	MIKADO
2-10-2	10 COUPLED
2-4-4	4 COUPLED
2-6-4	6 COUPLED
2-8-4	8 COUPLED
2-4-6	4 COUPLED
2-6-6	6 COUPLED
4-4-2	ATLANTIC
4-6-2	PACIFIC
4-4-4	4 COUPLED DOUBLE ENDER
4-6-4	6 COUPLED DOUBLE ENDER
4-4-6	4 COUPLED DOUBLE ENDER
2-8-6	8 COUPLED DOUBLE ENDER

What Constitutes an Engine Failure

There is often controversy as to what constitutes an engine failure, especially when it comes to making out reports for failures to make time or haul full tonnage. What is generally regarded as an engine failure on most roads?

A.—The standard engine failure rules adopted by the Master Mechanics' Association cover the question completely. That part covering the engineer's report is as follows:

1. All delays on account of engine breaking down, running hot, not steaming well, or having to reduce tonnage on account of defective engine, making a delay at a terminal, a meeting point, a junction connection, or delaying other traffic.

2. Do not report cases where engines lose time and afterwards regain it without delay to connections or other traffic. In cases where a passenger or scheduled freight train is delayed from other causes and an engine (having a defect) makes up more time than she loses on her own account, should not be called an engine failure.

3. Do not report delays to passenger trains when they are less than five minutes late at terminal or junction points.

4. Do not report delays to scheduled freight trains when less than twenty minutes late at terminals or junction points.

5. Do not report delays if engine is given excess tonnage and stalls on hill if engine is working and steaming well.

6. Do not report delays on extra dead freight trains if the run is made in less hours than the total miles divided by ten.

7. Do not report engine failures on account of engines steaming poorly, or flues leaking on any run where the engine has been delayed on side tracks other than by defects of engine, on the road an unreasonable length of time, say fifteen hours or more per hundred miles.

8. Do not report delays for cleaning fires and ash pans on the road.

9. Do not report failures against engines coming from outside points to shops for repairs. There are more of these rules, but they practically mean that engine should not be charged with failure when the conditions of service are not normal; this includes everything affecting train movement as well as unusual delays.

Pounds in Locomotives

Pounds are generally caused by slack wedges or rod keys, or a loose driving binder. A broken frame or driving-box jaw will cause a pound, but quite often their breakage is due to a neglected pound in a rod or box.

A loose follower bolt or head, a piston loose on piston rod, or a main rod keyed too long and allowing piston to strike cylinder head will cause a pound, and if very bad will result in the breakage of the cylinder head itself. A pound of this kind is more pronounced when steam is shut off and engine drifting, as all the slack in the rod and connections is free to move to the limit, there being no steam pressure in cylinder to cushion and restrain. A pound of this kind is more noticeable when main rod is passing forward center.

If a pound is caused by a main rod being too long have it shortened; if by a loose piston head or any of its parts remove cylinder head and tighten the part.

With a main rod long enough so that packing rings can drop into counterbore, and yet not long enough so that piston will strike cylinder head, the sound will be much the same as a pound and is rather more difficult to locate. The mark will show on the edge of the counterbore if cylinder head is taken off and an examination made.

Little can be done for a pound caused by a broken frame or pedestal jaw except to work the engine lightly to the terminal and have the necessary repairs made there.

Pounds cause nuts to work loose and fall from bolts, binder studs to work out and be lost, and rod straps, pedestal jaws and frames to be broken.

A bad pound at the front end of the main rod is more liable to cause a breakage of a strap that any other pound, as the whole strain is thrown on the strap when the rod is in tension. In keying the front end of a main rod care must be exercised not to get the brasses too tight on the wrist pin, as front end brasses cut out easily if too tight. Key on lower eighth or quarter. The wear is greatest on the front and rear of the wrist pin, owing to the direct pull and push of the piston. In keying, the key should be driven a little at a time and the front end of the rod moved laterally on the wrist pin with a short chisel until the desired tightness of the brass to the pin is secured.

Owing to the peculiar motion of the front end of a main rod, which is a combination of the movement of the cross-head in the guides and the crank pin of the main driver to which the back end of the main rod is connected, the wear on a wrist pin is different than that to which the crank pins are subjected.

The keying of back end of main rods seems to be a matter of opinion or individual experience as to the best position of the crank pin when key is driven. If a pin is round it makes not the slightest difference as to its position when key is driven, or even if the pin is out of round and the man driving the key knows how to key at the position the pin is in, for in the other positions the crank pin will assume in its revolution no bad effects will result.

The man who keys the back end of a rod so there will be a thump in it at all—with a pin that is much out of round—when the engine is given steam and thumped will have trouble. Naturally the thump will come where the pin is the smallest, and driving the brasses tight at that point will result in a hot pin.

Where rod grease is used care should be taken to wait until the grease in the brasses is well worn out after screwing cup plugs down before keying rods, for if the brasses are full of rod grease they will not move freely on the pin and one gets the impression that the brasses are tight on the pin, when in fact they are not. In case one starts the babbitt in a brass it should all be thrown out before stopping. Babbitt is seldom thrown out where grease cups are used. A pin might become hot from brasses being too loose—that is pound hot. If a pin runs hot it is not advisable to slacken the rod key at that connection unless key has been recently driven and is too tight. Look for some other cause for the trouble.

The side rods should be keyed on the center, as at that point the length of the rods will not be changed so as to interfere with the revolution of the crank pins. Side rod brasses will not pound, but will click if run too loose. If, on keying, a rod is found to be too short or too long, the changing of a liner from the front to the back of the pin, or vice versa, as the case may require, will remedy the trouble. If the side rod is too short the outside brass will get the hottest; if the rod is too long, the end or outside brass will be the hottest. These troubles are not likely to occur unless rods have been down and not put up the proper length.

The keying of a double-keyed middle connection of a ten-wheel engine should be in the following manner:

Place engine on center and drive both keys clear out. Put one key in and drive it clear down, make a scratch on the key along the top of the strap and drive key out. Do the same with the other key. Start both keys and drive them down equally, that is, so that when brasses are keyed satisfactorily the lines on the keys will be equally distant from the top of the strap. The other ends of the side rods can then be keyed. Side rods are often put up with what are known as solid ends. Brass bushings are fitted into the enlarged ends of the rod. When put up they run very nicely, but as they wear, while they do not pound, they rattle and make a great deal of noise, and as there is no way of keying them up snug to the pin they are often allowed to run in this condition a long time before new bushings are submitted for the worn ones.

Properly the wedges should be adjusted before the rods are keyed, but on most any engine, except one recently from the shop or one that has been neglected, the wedges will be up and rods keyed, except as to ordinary wear one becoming loose requires them to receive attention. Under the pool system on most railroads the adjusting of wedges and, to a large extent, the keying of rods is left to the roundhouse force, and as a rule these things are not cared for as they should be.

No one can adjust wedges and key rods as successfully as the man running the engine, as he has the opportunity to note anything that is needed and can apply the remedy, but with pooled engines it is not reasonable to expect engineers to do this work, and the roundhouse having assumed it, should look after it more closely than it usually does, for the heavy class of power soon pounds itself to pieces when neglected.

A wedge should be so adjusted that the box can move up and down freely in the pedestal jaws without sticking and, at the same time, not allow room for the box to pound in the jaws. On smooth, well-ballasted track this is not difficult to accomplish, but over very rough track wedges will have to be run a little slack or else the box will stick and the engine ride very hard.

The engine should stand on level, straight track when wedges are being adjusted, as a curve in the track or an inequality in its surface will pinch the box and wedge together, or allow too much slack in the boxes on one side on a curve, and a proper adjustment can not be obtained. The wedge should be forced up as far as it will go and then pulled down a little, say from one-fourth to one-half inch, according to the track the engine runs over and the condition of the wedge. If the wedge is rough or has a shoulder worn on it, the more play will be needed. Taking into consideration the gradual taper of the wedge it will be seen that pulling one down one-half inch does not give a very large amount of play to the box.

Where wedges are set up by the roundhouse force, two pinch bars, one in front and one behind the wheel, may be used to pinch it up and down and show whether or not the box has the proper amount of up and down motion in the pedestal jaws.

When it is desired to get all the slack in a box against the shoe before setting up the wedge run the wheel to the box with a pound against a block on the wedge side or the wheel at the opposite end of the journal against a block on the shoe side.

After a wedge is set up it should be well oiled before starting out. If a wedge bolt breaks, block between the binder and bottom of the wedge and between the frame and top of the wedge. It may be held in place sometimes by putting washers on the binder and changing the set nut so that it will overlap the break, but blocking will usually be quicker and easier to accomplish.

When a wedge sticks, loosen the set nut on top of the binder and tighten nuts under binder, or run wheel over a good sized nut; this will pull the wedge down. It may be necessary to cool the box down before doing this. If in a hurry, oil the wedge and box good, loosen the set nut and go. This treatment ordinarily will result in the wedge being loosened and coming down without further trouble.

Stuck wedges are not only hard on the engine, but also on the roadbed, and are particularly liable to do damage to bridges, and an engine should not be run any distance in that condition, and more particularly at a high rate of speed.

Wedges need more oil in dry weather than in damp, as the dust dries up the oil on them the same as on guide bars or other parts of the machinery. The top quarter offers the best opportunity to work at wedges.

A loose driving binder will cause a pound similar to a loose wedge, and may be caused by loose bolts or the binder being poorly fitted to the jaws. The hollow binder with a large bolt through it and the binder jaws is preferable, as it is more easily kept tight than where the binder is fitted to the lower ends of the pedestal jaws and studs are used. These studs are continually working loose and getting lost, and causing extra work and expense to replace them.

Mikado Type Locomotives*

    The Mikado type of locomotive, as illustrated and described in the following pages, has been developed to meet the present requirements of heavy freight service. The hauling capacity of a locomotive is primarily dependent upon the weight carried on the driving wheels, and the locomotive must be so proportioned that the tractive force developed bears a suitable relation to this weight. High tractive force, however, cannot be developed for sustained periods of time unless sufficient steaming capacity is provided. This is especially true if speed is an element of consideration, since other things being equal, the higher the speed the greater the horse power required; and the maximum horse power that a locomotive can develop is directly dependent upon the steaming capacity of its boiler.

    The 2-8-2 wheel arrangement, as used in the Mikado type, permits the use of a long boiler barrel in combination with a wide and deep fire-box, which is placed back of the driving wheels and over the trailing truck. The additional weight involved by reason of the large boiler is carried on the trailing truck, so that the driving wheels are not overloaded thereby. This form of fire-box is specially suitable for burning high volatile coal, as there is sufficient furnace volume for the combustion of the gases before they enter the tubes. Cases are on record where Mikado type locomotives have successfully burned fuel of a quality too inferior for use in Consolidation type, engines of equivalent hauling capacity, but having smaller fire-boxes.

    With a given weight on driving wheels and equal ratios of adhesion, a Mikado type locomotive will show no superiority over a Consolidation as far as starting tractive force is concerned. As the speed increases, however, the tractive force of the Mikado type will fall off less rapidly than that of the Consolidation, because of the greater boiler power of the former locomotive. At a speed of thirty miles per hour the Mikado type develops fifty per cent of its maximum tractive force, as compared with thirty-five per cent for the Consolidation; an increase in favor of the Mikado type amounting to forty-three per cent. It should be understood, of course, that the curves represent average conditions, and that they are based on the assumption that the boilers of both locomotives are being worked at their maximum evaporative capacities.

    Mikado type locomotives, because of their wheel arrangement, are specially suitable for service in which it is frequently necessary to run backward. The rear truck, under such circum-

---

*Courtesy of Baldwin Locomotive Works.

stances, protects the driving wheels against flange wear, and guides the locomotive into sharp curves and switches without danger of derailment. It is largely for this reason that Mikado type locomotives have proved specially successful on short industrial lines, where powerful locomotives are needed for both switching and road service.

On Consolidation type locomotives having wide fire-boxes and comparatively large driving wheels, the depth of the furnace throat is necessarily restricted, and it is difficult to apply a satisfactory design of brick arch. This difficulty is avoided in the Mikado type, as there is ample space, between the grate and bottom row of flues, for an arch with its supporting tubes. The arch is an important addition to the furnace equipment, especially when burning high volatile coal.

The majority of the large Mikado type locomotives now in service and being built, are equipped with superheaters, and are making excellent records for capacity and economy. The superheater is of special value when making long, hard runs, requiring the locomotive to develop high power for sustained periods of time. Under favorable conditions Mikado type locomotives with superheaters, replacing Consolidation engines using saturated steam, are hauling thirty to forty-five per cent more tonnage per train with no increase in actual coal consumption.

The locomotive illustrated and described in the following pages is equipped with the Ragonnet power reserve mechanism. This device greatly lessens the amount of labor required to handle the engine, and saves valuable space in the cab, as the mechanism is controlled by a small hand lever.

With a weight limitation of 60,000 pounds per driving axle, which it is seldom advisable to exceed even with the best track conditions, a Mikado type locomotive can carry 240,000 pounds on driving wheels and can exert a tractive force of 60,000 pounds. Such engines, equipped with superheaters, represent the maximum tractive and steaming capacity thus far attained in eight-coupled locomotives.

Built by Baldwin Locomotive Works for Erie Railroad Company.

MIKADO TYPE LOCOMOTIVE

(Built by Baldwin Locomotive Works for Erie Railroad Company.)
Railroad Co.'s Class N-1   Baldwin Class 12-50¼-E, 22
Gauge 4' 8½"

GENERAL DIMENSIONS

CYLINDERS
Diameter ....28"
Stroke ....32"
Valves ....Balance Piston

BOILER
Type ....Straight
Material ....Steel
Diameter ....84"
Thickness of Sheets ....⅛"
Working Presure ......170 lbs.
Fuel ....Coal
Staying ....Radial

FIRE-BOX
Material ....Steel
Length ....120"
Width ....84"
Depth, front ....88½"
Depth, back ....72¾"
Thickness of Sheets..sides, ⅜"
  back, ⅜"; crown, ⅜"; tube, ⅝"
Water Space,
  front, 6"; sides, 6"; back, 6"

TUBES
Diameter ....5½" and 2¼"
Material ....5½", Steel
                   2¼", Iron
Thickness ....5½", No. 9 W. G.
             2¼", 0.125"
Number ....5½", 36; 2¼", 232
Length ....21' 0"

HEATING SURFACE
Fire-box ....188 sq. ft.
Tubes ....3936 sq. ft.
Firebrick Tubes ......31 sq. ft.
Total ....4155 sq. ft.
Superheating Surface.877 sq. ft.
Grate Area ....70 sq. ft.

DRIVING WHEELS
Diameter, outside ....63"
Diameter, center ....56"
Journals ....11" x 14"

ENGINE TRUCK WHEELS
Diameter, front ....33½"
Journals ....6" x 12"
Diameter, back ....42"
Journals ....8" x 14"

WHEEL BASE
Driving ....16' 6"
Rigid ....16' 6"
Total Engine ....35' 0"
Total Engine and
  Tender ....66' 10½"

WEIGHT
On Driving Wheels .236,950 lbs.
On Truck, front .....30,200 lbs.
On Truck, back .....54,900 lbs.
Total Engine ......322,050 lbs.
Total Engine and
  Tender, about ....485,000 lbs.

TENDER
Number of Wheels............8
Diameter of Wheels ....33"
Journals ....6" x 11"
Tank Capacity ......9,000 gals.
Fuel Capacity ....16 tons

Schroeder Incandescent Electric Headlight

INSTRUCTIONS FOR OPERATING

The lubricant to be used on the RE-2 is grease throughout. Three cups are provided, two for the main and end ball bearing and one for the governor ball. Grease spaces about the bearings are ample so that the machine will run ten days or more without application of grease and no trouble experienced. We recommend, however, that cups be given several turns twice a week. (Use Greoil B. B. grease or its equal.)

COMMUTATOR

Commutator should be kept smooth and running true. It can be readily smoothed with a strip of fine sand paper held to the surface while the machine is running. Should commutator become out of round, remove same and true it up in a lathe using small sharp tool and a fine feed. Mica should be cut below surface of copper occasionally with a three-cornered file. Keep commutator free from grease.

BRUSHES

Brushes should fit perfectly on commutator and just enough tension used on springs to prevent sparking.

SPEED REGULATING

The governing mechanism of the RE-2 generator can be inspected by removing one cap screw and opening cover. The speed of the machine is about 2,700 r. p. m. The governor is adjusted at the factory and rarely requires readjustment.

Should a change of speed be desired, it can be accomplished by loosening nut 640 and turning adjustment nut 639 to the right to increase and to the left to decrease the speed.

Should it be necessary to change the speed, we recommend that a volt meter be used.

VALVE

The governor valve is of the balanced piston type and is set at the factory for 3/16-inch travel, by means of adjusting stud 646. This, as with the governor, seldom needs to be reset, as there is practically no wear to the governing parts in service, so long as the governor ball is lubricated through grease cup 620. Be sure that valve stem moves freely through packing 619. This packing should be renewed occasionally.

Armature

Shaft

Governor

REMOVAL OF PARTS

Armature.—Unscrew cap No. 607 and nut 634 (L. H. thread), uncouple brush holder wires and end bearing housing can be removed after taking out cap screws. Unscrew lock nut No. 663 (L. H. thread), and armature can be drawn from shaft.

Governor.—Take out pin No. 647 and remove lever 645. Governor can then be unscrewed with special wrench supplied with each outfit.

Valve.—Back off valve screws about ⅛ inch, drive screw driver behind flange to loosen same, then remove screws and valve. Use just enough tension on spring 648 to open valve.

Turbine Wheel.—Take off lever 645, governor and turbine head 601, tap wheel lightly with hammer and remove.

Shaft.—Remove end bearing housing and wheel as instructed, unscrew bearing lock nut 633 and withdraw shaft.

Center Bearing.—Remove wheel, shaft and armature as instructed, take out screws and remove cap 605. Bearing can be removed without taking out housing No. 604.

Blue Print.—All parts of this equipment are made strictly interchangeable. When ordering repair parts give number and name of piece, also number of blue print.

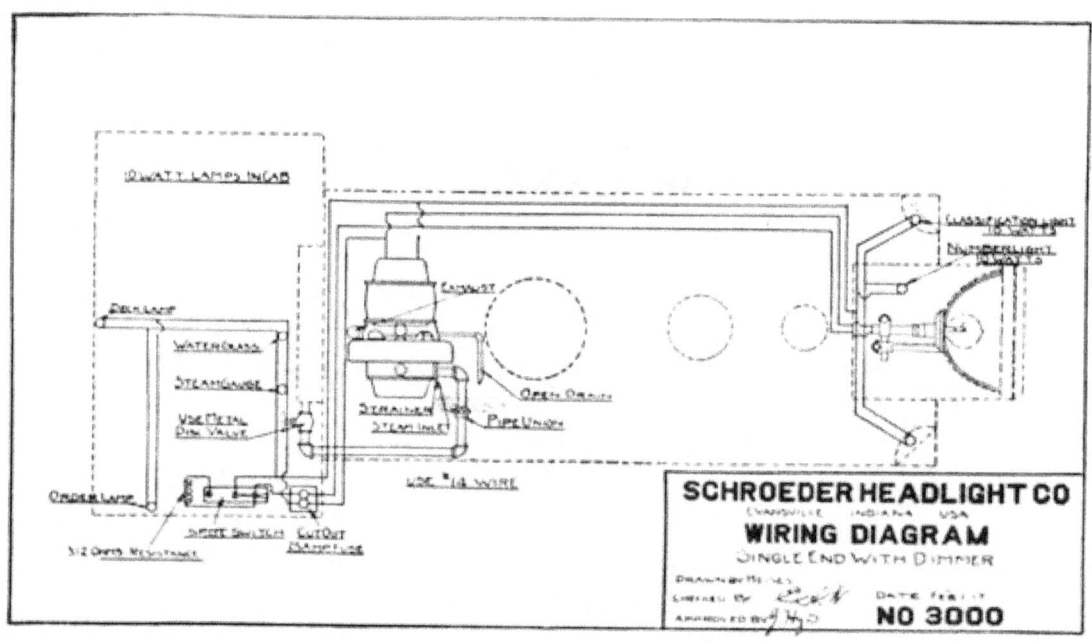

INSTALLATION

When mounting this equipment make platform or brackets level so that all standards rest firmly on same.

Use ½-inch pipe for steam line, with valve located convenient to engineer. A short 1½-inch pipe should be used for exhaust. Run a ¾-inch open drain from exhaust chamber to ash pan to prevent freezing. See that steam line is also properly drained.

Run ½-inch conduit from generator to head lamp and to cab. Conduit, moulding or open wiring may be used in the cab. Locate cut-out just inside the cab. Fuse headlight, cab and number light lines as shown in diagram.

When mounting case see that it stands square and plumb on the engine.

When installation is complete remove strainer plug at steam inlet, crack the throttle valve and while steam is flowing through strike the pipes with a hammer so as to remove all scale and sediment. This should be repeated after one trip has been made.

GENERAL DESCRIPTION OF SCHROEDER INCANDESCENT ELECTRIC HEADLIGHT

The Schroeder Incandescent Electric Headlight consists of a Turbo Generator and headlight case.

The principal parts of the Turbo Generator are the frame (which is cast in one piece), the turbine wheel, armature, commutator, field coils, governor, governor valve, shaft and ball bearings.

To produce electric current, it is necessary that the armature revolve between the field poles. The power for rotating the armature is obtained by a steam jet striking a row of vanes or buckets which are mounted on a cast steel wheel. The speed of the armature must be constant, so as to produce a uniform voltage or pressure of electric current. The governor and governor valve regulate the flow of steam striking the turbine buckets, keeping it at a constant speed through any practical working range of boiler pressure and from full load to no load.

The turbine wheel, armature and governor are mounted on the same shaft which revolves on two ball bearings, the main bearing and end bearing. The main bearing is the largest of the two and carries the greater part of the weight, while the end bearing carries some weight and also controls the end thrust.

The governor and governor valve with their simple mechanism can readily be inspected by loosening a cap screw and opening the turbine end cover. The commutator and brushes can be examined by raising generator end cover, which is held shut by a catch spring.

The lubrication of the ball bearings and governor ball is a soft grease, and will last ten days or more between applications as the spaces about the bearings hold a large supply.

The headlight case has a very simple focusing mechanism for the incandescent lamp. Either copper silver plated or mirror glass reflector can be used with the equipment.

QUESTIONS AND ANSWERS ON SCHROEDER INCANDESCENT ELECTRIC HEADLIGHT

Q.—What principal parts comprise the Schroeder Electric Headlight?

A.—The turbine engine, the generator and incandescent lamp.

Q.—What are the duties of the turbine engine?

A.—The turbine engine furnishes the mechanical power that operates the generator, the latter producing an electric current for the incandescent lamp.

Q.—What are the principal parts of the generator?

A.—The main frame, field poles, field coils, armature, commutator and brushes.

Q.—What are the duties of the amature?

A.—The armature induces an electromotive force in the copper wires wound upon it, and directs the flow of current.

Q.—What are the duties of the commutator?

A.—The duties of the commutator are to collect the current from the armature coils and cause it to flow in one direction.

Q.—How is the commutator constructed?

A.—The commutator is made up of a central brass ring or bushing upon which is mounted a series of copper bars which are separated from each other by pieces of mica which is a non-conducting material.

Q.—What is the duty of the field coils?

A.—To produce a magnetic field in which the armature revolves.

Q.—Define the pole pieces.

A.—The pole pieces are cast iron projections on the inner part of the main ring or casting. The field coils are mounted on them.

Q.—Give the first three measurements of electricity.

A.—The volt, the ampere and the ohm.

Q.—Define the volt.

A.—The volt is the unit of measurement of electrical pressure.

Q.—Define the ampere.

A.—The ampere is the unit of measurement of the rate of flow of current.

Q.—Define the ohm.

A.—The ohm is the unit of measurement of electrical resistance.

Q.—What produces the voltage?

A.—The voltage is produced in the armature wires by the armature revolving in the electrical field at a high rate of speed.

Q.—Does the rate of speed affect the voltage? If so, how?

A.—The rate of speed does affect the voltage. As the speed increases, the voltage increases proportionately, and as the speed decreases, the voltage decreases proportionately.

Q.—Should the voltage become too high, what will result?

A.—If the voltage is too high, the head lamp and cab lamps

will become very bright and if the voltage is still further increased, the lamps will burn out.

Q.—Should the voltage become low, what will result?

A.—The lamps will burn dim.

Q.—What is meant by a short circuit?

A.—A short circuit is a passage offered whereby a quantity of electricity may flow with less resistance than when flowing through desired points, such as lamps.

Q.—What is frequently the cause of a short circuit?

A.—Wearing away of insulation by wires chafing against each other or parts of the locomotive.

Q.—What damage will a short circuit do?

A.—If the generator is allowed to run a long time on a short circuit, the armature and field coils will burn out.

Q.—What kind of bearings are used?

A.—Ball bearings.

Q.—What kind of grease should be used?

A.—A good soft grade of grease having a high melting point which will not leave a sediment in the bearing housing.

Q.—How often should the cups be screwed down?

A.—The cups should be given several turns twice a week.

Q.—What kind of oil may be used in an emergency, if no grease is at hand?

A.—Cylinder oil.

Q.—Why are square threads used on the shaft next to the ball bearings?

A.—To keep the grease in the bearing housing.

Q.—Explain how the steam imparts mechanical power to the armature.

A.—The turbine wheel, which is fastened to the same shaft with the armature and governor, has mounted upon it a row of vanes or buckets which a steam jet strikes causing the wheel to turn.

Q.—How is the speed of the generator controlled?

A.—By a centrifugal governor which operates a balanced type governor valve.

Q.—Explain how this is done.

A.—When the machine is at rest, the governor valve is wide open. When it revolves at a high rate of speed, the governor weights fly outward from the center due to centrifugal force, and, being hinged by a governor pin, force the governor stem outward by the governor weight toe pressing against it. The pressure of the governor stem is then exerted on the governor ball which causes the lever, which is hinged at the top, to move outward at the bottom bringing the valve stem with it and closing the seats.

Q.—What is the function of the lever spring?

A.—To open the valve when the speed of the machine is reduced and to keep the governor ball touching the governor stem.

Q.—How can the speed of the machine be altered?

A.—By turning the governor adjusting nut. Turning this nut to the right increases the speed, turning it to the left, decreases the speed.

Q.—What is the function of the governor lock nut?

A.—To lock the governor adjusting nut in position when the speed is properly set.

Q.—What is the valve travel of a governor valve?

A.—The valve travel is the greatest distance over which the valve seats are allowed to move.

Q.—What is the proper valve travel for this machine?

A.—Three-sixteenths of an inch.

Q.—How is the valve travel set?

A.—By means of an adjusting stud at the top of the lever. Turning this stud to the right will decrease the valve travel, turning it to the left will increase the valve travel.

Q.—What are the duties of the deflector rings?

A.—The deflector rings are to prevent the steam from escaping from the housing at the point where the shaft enters.

Q.—Why is a steam strainer used with this equipment?

A.—To prevent boiler scale and pipe scale from entering the governor valve and interfering with the operation of it.

Q.—If a large quantity of scale enters the strainer what will happen?

A.—It will cause the machine to slow down and the lamps to burn dim.

Q.—When is this trouble most apt to occur?

A.—Immediately after the installation of the equipment or when a new set of piping has been installed.

Q.—Is the strainer self-cleaning under ordinary conditions?

A.—Yes; the scale drops into a hollow plug below it.

Q.—What care should be given the commutator?

A.—The commutator should be kept clean, running true, and

the mica between the bars should be filed below the surface of the copper with a three-cornered file.

Q.—What care should be given the brushes?

A.—The brushes should be kept clean and just enough tension used to prevent sparking.

Q.—If the light fluctuates what may be the cause of the trouble?

A.—The valve packing gland may be drawn too tight, the governor may not be working freely or the lever tension spring may be too weak.

Q.—If the light burns dim what may be the trouble?

A.—Brush tension may be too weak, commutator dirty, mica high between the commutator bars, machine running too slow, scale in strainer, a very weak lever spring or a short circuit.

Q.—What are the indications of a short circuit?

A.—Lamps burning very dim, machine running slow and a large quantity of steam coming from the exhaust.

Q.—If cab lamps burn normal when headlight is cut in and get very bright when headlight is cut out, what does this indicate?

A.—The machine is speeding on light load due to the governor valve becoming wire drawn.

Q.—What should be done in this case?

A.—Valve should be reground or renewed.

Q.—How is the governor ball oiled?

A.—Through channels in lever and lever stud from a grease cup at top of head.

Q.—When steam is turned on and turbine appears to be running at normal speed but lamps fail to light up, where should the trouble be looked for?

A.—Look for grease or dirt on the brushes, high mica between the commutators, loose connections at lamps, machine, or other points, or a broken wire.

Q.—What does sparking of the brushes on the commutator indicate?

A.—That brush spring tension is too weak or commutator is rough.

Q.—To produce best results how should headlight case be mounted?

A.—Case should be mounted level and square on the boiler.

Q.—What kind of lamp is used with this equipment?

A.—A Tungsten, gas-filled incandescent lamp known as Type C locomotive headlight lamp is used with this equipment.

Q.—Why is it necessary to provide a focusing device for an incandescent headlight?

A.—Because the lamp filaments are not uniform in length.

Q.—What is the focal point of a reflector?

A.—The focal point of a reflector is a point in space within the reflector, which, when a light is located in it, will cause the reflected rays to project from the reflector in a parallel direction.

Q.—When is the best time to focus a headlight?

A.—On a dark night when locomotive is standing on a straight track.

Q.—If the light projects from the reflector in rings and shows a dark spot in the middle of the track, what does this indicate?

A.—That the lamp is either ahead or back of the focal point.

Q.—If the light does not throw straight on the track, but deviates to left or right, how can this be remedied?

A.—By adjusting lamp to right or left until the proper direction is obtained.

Q.—If the light is too high or too low, what adjustment should be made?

A.—The lamp should be raised or lowered.

Q.—Is it necessary to keep the reflector clean?

A.—Yes; a dirty or tarnished reflector may reduce the efficiency of the headlight by as much as 75 per cent.

Q.—How is the headlight dimmed when meeting trains or pulling into terminals?

A.—By operating main switch which has the bright headlight connected to one side of it and the headlight with resistance unit in series to the other.

Questions and Answers on Mallet Locomotives, Breakdowns and Operating Rules

Q.—How would you start a locomotive of this type?

A.—Always open the cylinder cocks before opening the throttle. With the Baldwin type, if the train is heavy, open the starting valve. With the American type, try to start the train with the reverse lever down in the corner. If the engine can not start the train in this way, open the emergency operating valve in the cab by pointing the handle to the rear.

Q.—After the train is started, how would you handle the locomotive?

A.—After a speed has been reached of three or four miles per hour, close the starting valve, on the Baldwin type, and close the emergency valve, on the American type, as you would simply be burning more coal with these valves open without getting any more power out of the engine.

Q.—How would you proceed if you were about to stall on a grade?

A.—With either engine, if the speed is below three or four miles per hour, proceed the same as when starting a heavy train.

Q.—In what position would you carry the reverse lever when drifting?

A.—At about three-quarters stroke or more.

Q.—What attention should be given the power reversing gear?

A.—Keep the oil cylinder full of oil, and the piston rod packing on the oil and air cylinders tight. Always see that the latches of both reverse levers mesh in the teeth of the quadrant. Whenever they do not, report it.

Q.—What attention should be given by-pass valves?

A.—They should be reported to be cleaned periodically, in order to keep them from getting gummed up and sticky.

Q.—What would be the effect if a by-pass valve were stuck open or stuck shut?

A.—If stuck open, they will cause the engine to blow. If stuck shut, they will cause the engine to pound when drifting.

Q.—What attention should be given the relief valves on low pressure steam chests and cylinders?

A.—They should be tested about once a month, in order to see that they open at the proper pressure.

Q.—How would you handle the intercepting valve used in connection with the American type locomotive so far as lubricating it, etc., is concerned?

A.—Give it a liberal feed of oil for about one minute before starting, and occasionally during long runs where the throttle is not shut off for a considerable length of time. Except for this, one drop of oil about every four or five minutes, when running, is ample.

Q.—Beside the intercepting valve, what other parts of an articulated compound locomotive should be oiled that are not found on the ordinary locomotive?

A.—The sliding boiler-bearing on the front engine; the ball joint in front of the high pressure cylinder; the upper or rear ball joint of the exhaust pipe; the lower or front ball joint of the exhaust pipe (these ball joints need only be oiled before starting, as one oiling should be sufficient for the trip); the bolt in the flexible connection connecting the two engines; the ball bearing of the vertical suspension or trim bolts, which connect the upper rails of the front frames with the lower rails to the rear frames; the ball bearing of the floating columns, if any; the piston rod packing of the cylinders of the power reversing gear; the air cylinder of the power reversing gear, by means of the plug in the top of the cylinder; about once a week will be often enough for the air cylinder.

Q.—What is the arrangement of cylinders on Mallet compound engine?

A.—High pressure cylinders rigidly attached to the boiler and rear engine; low pressure cylinders rigidly attached to the frames of the forward engine, but not attached to the boiler.

Q.—Describe the make of valves used on high pressure engines and on low pressure engines.

A.—As a rule, piston valves are used on the high pressure engines and "D," or slide, valves on the low pressure engines. (The following questions and answers apply to American type engines only except as noted.)

Q.—Does the engine work simple or compound when first started?

A.—Simple.

Q.—When does the Mallet engine work compound?

A.—When the receiver pressure has reached the desired amount, which is about four-tenths boiler pressure, thereby closing the intercepting valve.

Q.—When the engine is working compound, what change is necessary to make the engine work simple?

A.—Open the emergency valve in the cab, which causes the separate exhaust valve to open. This takes the pressure off the end of the intercepting valve, allowing it to open and live steam to pass through the reducing valve direct to the low pressure cylinders.

Q.—How would you determine if the intercepting valve was stuck open? If stuck closed?

A.—If the intercepting valve was stuck open, the engine could not be converted from compound to simple, as, in this case, opening the separate exhaust valve would allow part of the steam from the receiver to pass out through the separate exhaust and, consequently, but a small portion would pass to the low pressure cylinders and the engine would lose power and, if on a hard pull, would probably stall. It might also be noticed by the high pressure engine slipping.

If the separate exhaust valve was stuck closed, the locomotive could not be converted from simple to compound and, unless the separate exhaust valve was opened, the pressure would bank up in the receiver until it balanced on both sides of the high pressure piston, and, in this case, as before, if the engine was on a hard pull it would probably stall. You could tell if the intercepting valve stuck closed by first opening the separate exhaust valve and noticing if the engine picked up speed, then closing the separate exhaust valve, by means of the emergency valve in the cab, and noting if the speed reduced quickly.

Q.—Describe how steam is conveyed from high to low pressure cylinders.

A.—As the steam is exhausted from the high pressure cylinders it passes on into what is termed the receiver pipe, which connects the exhaust chamber of the high pressure valve with the steam chamber of the low pressure valve, and when the engine is working compound the movement of the low pressure valve allows the steam from the high pressure cylinders to enter direct into the low pressure cylinders. When the engine is working in simple position the low pressure engines operate with live steam direct from the boiler, while the steam exhausted from the high pressure cylinders into the receiver passes by way of the separate exhaust valve direct to the nozzle.

Q.—In starting the locomotive, if the forward engine does not take steam, what is the trouble?

A.—The reducing valve is stuck shut, as, with this type of engine, unless the reducing valve is open there would be no steam in the low pressure cylinders until after the high pressure cylinders have exhausted.

Q.—What would you do if a by-pass valve was stuck open or stuck closed?

A.—If one of the by-pass valves should stick open it would cause a severe blow, and, if it could not be closed in any other manner, the cap on the end of the chamber should be removed and the valve forced into closed position with the handle of the coal pick. At the same time, while the cap is removed, see that the small port at the end of the by-pass valve chamber is open. If the valve is stuck shut the engine would not drift freely, and, if necessary to do considerable drifting before reaching the end of the terminal, it is advisable to take off the valve chamber cap, remove the by-pass valve, clean it with coal oil and replace. The sticking of the by-pass valves is generally caused by the smokebox gas being sucked into the cylinder, on account of the reverse lever being carried too high up when the engine is drifting. The reverse lever should always be carried at about three-fourths cut-off when the engine is drifting, as this will allow the engine to drift more freely and there will be less smoke and gas sucked into the cylinder.

Q.—Describe the course taken by the steam from the time it leaves the boiler until it is exhausted from the stack, when starting and when working compound?

A.—Ordinarily, when starting without the separate exhaust valve being open, steam, upon opening the throttle, passes from the throttle standpipe to the dry pipe and to the steam pipes leading to the high pressure steam chests, thence, as the high pressure valves open and close the steam ports, it passes to the high pressure cylinder and is exhausted into the receiver, from which, by the movement of the low pressure valves, it is admitted to, and exhausted from, the low pressure cylinder, the exhaust passing out through the exhaust nozzle the same as in an ordinary locomotive. At the same time, when starting, live steam is admitted to the low pressure steam chest through the reducing valve, this steam taking the same course into and out of the low pressure cylinder as the receiver steam, or exhaust from the high pressure cylinder. After the engine has made a few revolutions the exhaust steam from the high pressure cylinder will bank up in the receiver, causing the reducing valve to close, and thereafter the engine will work compound, the steam taking the same course as before, with the exception of the live steam passing through the reducing valve. If the engine is started with the separate exhaust valve open, however, the exhaust from the high pressure cylinder, instead of banking up in the receiver, is exhausted direct to the exhaust nozzle through the separate exhaust valve, the steam used in the low pressure cylinder and admitted through the reducing valve taking the same course as before.

Q.—How are the simple and compound features controlled in Mallet engine?

A.—In the Baldwin type, by means of an emergency valve in the cab, which, when opened, allows high pressure steam to flow direct from the boiler into the receiver and from the receiver into the low pressure cylinders. In the American type, by means of an intercepting valve and an emergency valve. When the emergency valve is opened it throws the intercepting valve in such a position as to allow high pressure steam to flow from the high pressure steam chests direct into the receiver pipe, and from thence to the low pressure cylinders.

Q.—Should the high pressure engine become disabled, how would you get the locomotive in?

A.—By opening the emergency valve in the cab, so as to allow high pressure steam to flow to the low pressure engine.

Q.—Under what conditions should the emergency or starting valve be used?

A.—Only when starting, and to prevent stalling on a heavy grade.

Q.—What are the duties of the intercepting valve?

A.—To supply steam to the low pressure cylinders when starting, and to cut off the supply when the reservoir pressure has reached the desired amount.

BREAKDOWNS

In case of any breakdown in which one or more of the cylinders can be disconnected and the locomotive run in with the remaining cylinders active, simply throw the emergency operating valve in the cab into the simple position and proceed as with a simple locomotive, namely, disconnect and block the disabled cylinder or cylinders. This is the only rule to follow and the only one to be remembered, and covers all cases of accidents which do not entirely disable the locomotive.

OPERATING RULES*

Always open the cylinder cocks in starting.

Usually the locomotive will start the train when the throttle is opened in the ordinary way with the reverse lever in the position required for the weight of the train or ordinarily in the extreme notch. If the locomotive fails to start the train when operated in this way, change it into simple working by turning the handle of the emergency operating valve in the cab so that it points to the *rear*. This same course should be followed if the engine is about to stall on a heavy grade. If the speed is over three or four miles an hour, no increase in power will be obtained by changing the locomotive into simple working.

---

*The American Locomotive Co.

When drifting, the reverse lever should be kept at ¾-stroke or more. As before stated, if this is done, the locomotive will drift freely.

The oil cylinder of the power reversing gear should always be kept full of oil. The piston and piston rod packing of the oil cylinder should be kept in good condition so as to prevent leakage. If the reversing gear operates too rapidly it indicates that there is not sufficient oil in the oil cylinder and this should be refilled and the leakages stopped.

If the reversing gear is not adjusted properly so that the latch of the main reverse lever does not engage with the teeth of the quadrant, the trouble should be remedied as soon as possible. If not properly adjusted, the locking of the reverse gear will be put almost entirely on the latch of the auxiliary lever, which is not designed for such duty and would, therefore, quickly wear.

The by-pass valves should be taken out and cleaned periodically to prevent them from being gummed and sticking. When the locomotive is first put into service, these valves should be cleaned quite frequently for a few times so as to keep them free from the core sand which is sure to work into them. Afterwards they will require only ordinary attention to work properly. When these valves are properly performing their functions, the locomotive will drift freely. If they stick open it will cause a severe blow, while if stuck in the closed position, it will cause a pounding in the low pressure engines.

The relief valves in the low pressure steam chests should be tested occasionally to see that they are correctly set at 45 per cent of the boiler pressure, as these valves relieve any excessive pressure in the steam chests.

Repairs to Flexible Joints. In renewing the packing of the flexible joints the same kind of packing should be used as that originally applied. Also care should be taken to keep it arranged, trouble from leaky joints will be avoided.

The brass ring of the receiver pipe joint at the high pressure cylinder may be removed in order to insert new packing, but the original arrangement of the joint packing should always be preserved.

Lubrication. Give the intercepting valve a liberal feed of oil for a minute before starting and occasionally during long runs, when the throttle is not shut off for a considerable length of time. Except for this, one drop of oil to the intercepting valve every four or five minutes is ample when running.

Besides the intercepting valve, the other parts of the articulated compound locomotive which should be oiled, which are not found on the ordinary locomotive are:

Sliding boiler bearings on the front engine.

The ball joint in front of the high pressure cylinder (*before starting on a trip*).

The upper or rear ball joint of the exhaust pipe (*before starting on a trip*).

The lower or front ball joint of the exhaust pipe (*before starting on a trip*).

The bolt connecting the two engines.

The ball bearings of the vertical suspension or "trim" bolts which connect the upper rails of the rear frames with the lower rails of the front frames.

The ball bearings of the floating columns (if applied).

The piston rod packing of the cylinders of the power reversing gear.

The air cylinder of the power reversing gear, by means of the plug in the top of the cylinder (*about once a week*).

Blows. To test for blows in the valves or pistons, throw the emergency operating valve in the cab to the simple position, namely, with the handle pointing to the *rear*. Spot the locomotive and test the same as a simple locomotive.

Triplex Articulated Compound Locomotive

The Baldwin Locomotive Works has completed for the Erie Railroad a locomotive for pusher service, which develops a tractive force of 160,000 pounds and is by far the most powerful locomotive yet built. This capacity is secured not by using excessive wheel loads or a rigid wheel base of unusual length, but by placing driving wheels under the tender, and thus making the weight of the latter available for adhesion. In heavy grade work especially the weight of the tender detracts materially from the net hauling capacity of a locomotive of the usual type; while in this case the tender is used as a means for increasing hauling capacity.

This locomotive is built in accordance with patents granted to George R. Henderson, Consulting Engineer of the Baldwin Locomotive Works. The wheel arrangement is 2-8-8-8-2, the third group of driving wheels and the rear truck being placed under the tender section. The cylinders are all of the same size, two acting as high pressure. The two high pressure cylinders drive the middle group of wheels. The right-hand high pressure cylinder exhausts into the two front cylinders, and the left-hand high pressure cylinder exhausts into the two rear cylinders. This arrangement is therefore equivalent to a compound engine, having a ratio of cylinder volumes of one to two. The boiler has a conical connection in the middle of the barrel, and is fitted with the Gaines type of furnace. The fire-box has a total length of 13 feet 6 inches, and of this the grates occupy 10 feet. A combustion chamber 54 inches long extends forward into the boiler barrel and the tubes have a length of 24 feet. The brick arch is supported on six 3½-inch tubes; and heated air is delivered under the arch by seven 3-inch pipes which are placed vertically in the bridge wall. There are two fire doors, placed 32½ inches between centers; and a Street mechanical stoker is applied. The barrel of this boiler measures 94 inches in diameter at the front end and 102⅛ innches at the dome ring. The center line is placed 10 feet 7 inches above the rail. The circumferential seams have sextuple riveted butt joints, which are welded at the ends, and have an efficiency equal to 90 per cent of the solid plate. The dome is of pressed steel, 33 inches in diameter and 13 inches high. It contains a Chambers throttle, which is connected with the superheated header, in the usual manner by an internal dry pipe. The superheater is composed of 53 elements, and is the largest ever applied to a locomotive; the superheating surface being 1,584 square feet, the header is divided, separate casings being used for saturated and superheated steam sections. The front end contains a single exhaust nozzle with ring blower.

The size of the nozzle can be varied by a simple adjustment device placed outside the smoke-box. The stack is 22 inches in diameter, and it has an internal section which extends down to the center line of the boiler.

The superheated steam is conveyed to the high pressure cylinder through outside pipes, and the high pressure distribution is controlled by 16-inch piston valves, arranged for inside admission, similar valves are applied to the low pressure cylinders. These valves are all driven by Baker Valve Gear, and the three sets of motions are controlled simultaneously by the Ragonnet power reverse mechanism.

All six cylinders are cast from the same pattern, and the valve motion and driving gear details used with the three groups of wheels are as far as possible interchangeable. A large number of these details also interchange with those of the Mikado type locomotives in service on this road.

Among the details of the driving gear may be mentioned the pistons, all six of which are alike. The piston heads are steel forgings of the dished shape; and each is surrounded by a cast iron bull ring. The bull ring carries three packing rings and is secured to the piston head by a retaining ring which is electrically welded. The packing rings, both for the cylinders and valve chambers are of Hunt-Spiller Metal.

The efficiency of a locomotive used in slow, heavy service is largely proportional to the percentage of total weight available for adhesion. In this respect the Triplex excels all previous designs, having 89 per cent of the total weight of the Engine and the tender on the drivers. In large Mallets of the 2-8-8-2 type this ratio is not above 65 per cent.

TRIPLEX ARTICULATED COMPOUND LOCOMOTIVE

(Built by Baldwin Locomotive Works) (The Most Powerful Locomotive in Existence)

DIMENSIONS OF THE TRIPLEX LOCOMOTIVE

Cylinders, high pressure, two	36 x 32 in.
Cylinders, low pressure, four	36 x 32 in.
Driving wheels, diameter	63 in.
Steam pressure	210 lbs.
Boiler diameter	94 in.
Tubes, length	24 ft.—0 in.
Tubes, number	53—5½ in.
Tubes, number	326—2¼ in.
Heating surface, tubes	6,418 sq. ft.
Heating surface, fire-box	272 sq. ft.
Heating surface, combustion chamber	108 sq. ft.
Heating surface, arch tubes	88 sq. ft.
Heating surface, total	6,886 sq. ft.
Heating surface, superheated	1,584 sq. ft.
Fire-box	162 x 108 in.
Length of grate	120 in.
Grate area	90 sq. ft.
Wheel base, rigid, each group	16 ft.—6 in.
Wheel base, driving	71 ft.—6 in.
Wheel base, total	90 ft.—0 in.
Weight, driving	753,600 lbs.
Weight, front truck	32,050 lbs.
Weight, rear truck	54,000 lbs.
Weight, total	845,050 lbs.
Tender capacity, water	10,000 gals.
Tender capacity, coal	16 tons
Maximum tractive power	160,000 lbs.

48 ENGINEMEN'S MANUAL

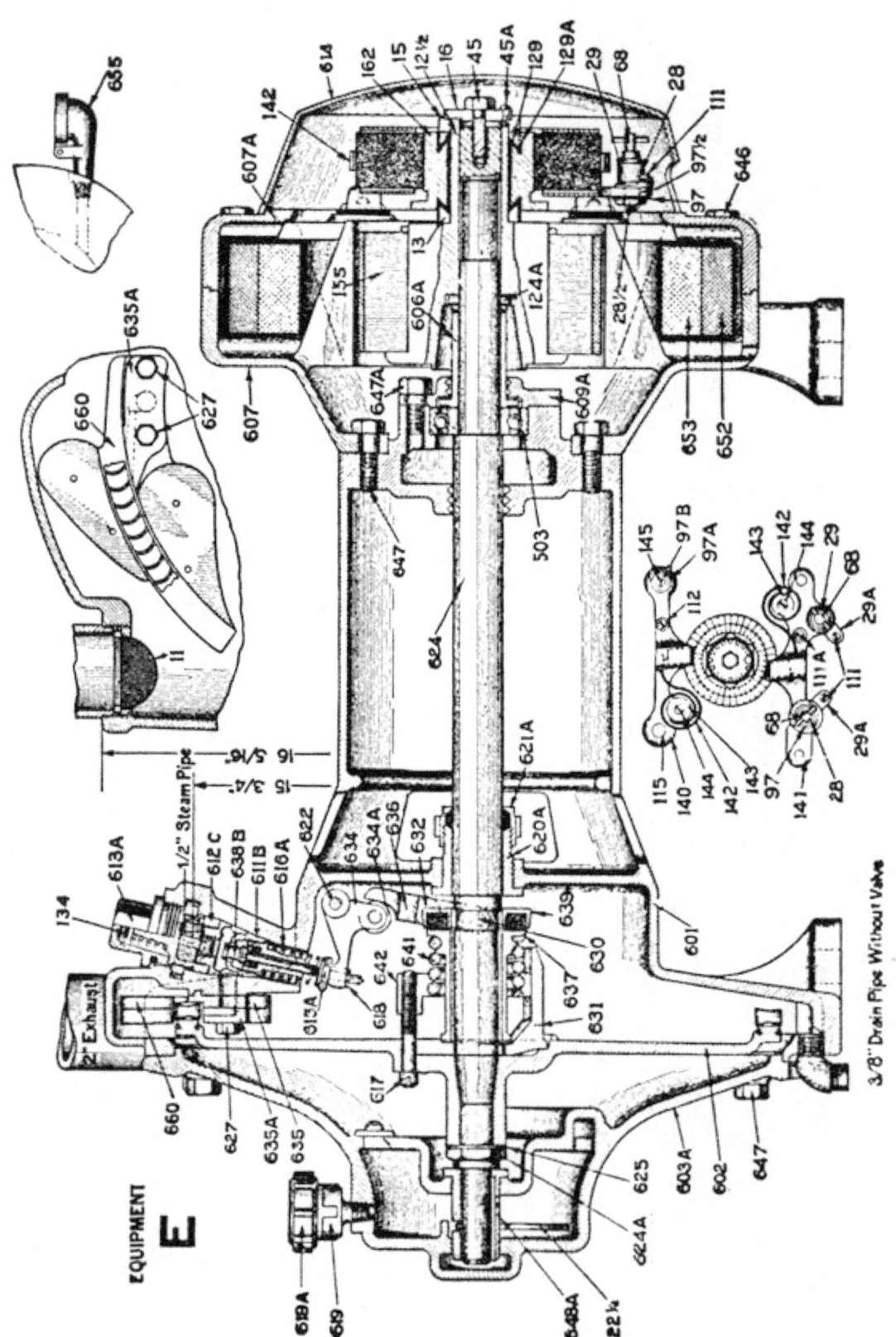

The Pyle-National Electric Headlight

NAMES AND NUMBERS OF PARTS, EQUIPMENT "E"

11	Exhaust Screen.
12½	Armature Spider.
13	Commutator Ring.
15	Commutator Nut.
16	Outside Washer.
28	Binding Post, large hole with Nut.
28½	Binding Post Nut.
29	Binding Post, small hole with Nut.
29A	Incandescent Terminal.
45	Armature Lock Screw.
45A	Small Lock Screw.
68	Binding Post Screw.
97	Insulation Washers.
97A	Small Fibre Washer.
97B	Brush Holder Iron Washer.
97½	Fibre Bushing.
111	Binding Screw.
111A	Shunt Field Connecting Screw.
112	Field Screw.
115	Bushing.
124A	Shaft Pin.
129	Mica Taper Ring.
129A	Mica Band Ring.
130	Winding Ring.
140	Top Brush Holder.
141	Bottom Brush Holder.
142	Brush Spring.
143	Brush Spring Adjuster.
144	Brush Adjuster Screw.
145	Brush Holder Screw.
146	Top Brush Holder, complete.
147	Bottom Brush Holder, complete.
155	Armature.
162	Commutator, complete.
503	Ball Bearing.
600	Turbine, complete.
601	Turbine Casing.
602	Turbine Wheel.
603	Turbine Cover.
604	Turbine Cover Cap.
606A	Armature Sleeve.
607	Rear Field Frame.
607A	Front Field Frame.
609A	Ball Bearing Cap.
611A	Valve Cage.
612A	Valve Seat.
613A	Valve Cap.
614	Dynamo Door.
614A	Dynamo Name Plate.
614B	Dynamo Door Pin.
614C	Dynamo Door Latch.
615A	Valve Adjusting Nut.
616A	Governor Valve Spring.
617	Governor Adjusting Screw.
618	Valve Lock Nut.
619	Oil Cup.
619A	Oil Cup Cover.
620A	Turbine Case Bushing.
621A	Packing Gland.
622	Governor Link Screw.
624	Shaft.
624A	Wheel Retaining Nut.
625	Wheel Retaining Washer.
627	Nozzle Screw.
630	Anti-Friction Ring. Holder Screw.
631	Governor Weight.
632	Governor Arm Screw.
633A	Oil Cup, complete.
634	Governor Link with Roller.

THE PYLE-NATIONAL ELECTRIC HEADLIGHT

NAMES AND NUMBERS OF PARTS, EQUIPMENT "E"—Continued

634A	Governor Link Roller.	647A	Ball Bearing Cap Screw.
635	Guide Passage Plate.	648	Turbine Bearing, complete.
635A	Steam Nozzle.		
636	Governor Arm.	649	Oil Ring.
637	Governor Sleeve.	650	Governor Valve and Cage, complete.
638A	Governor Valve.		
639	Anti-Friction Ring Holder.	651	Dynamo Field Coil, complete.
641	Governor Spring.	652	Shunt Field Coil.
642	Governor Yoke.	653	Series Field Coil.
646	Field Frame Screw.	660	Nozzle and Guide Passages, complete.
647	Turbine Screw.		

THE PYLE-NATIONAL ELECTRIC HEADLIGHT

NAMES AND NUMBERS OF PARTS, HEAD LAMP "D"

28	Binding Post, large hole.	88A	Contact Brushes, set.
28A	Washer 5-16.	90	Solenoid Plunger Yoke.
29	Binding Post, small hole.	90A	Solenoid Yoke Pivot Pin.
40	Reflector Clamp, bottom.	90C	Solenoid Yoke Cotter Pin.
40½	Reflector Clamp, top.	90C	Spring Cotter.
41	Reflector Support.	91	Carbon Holder Spring.
44	Carbon Clutch.	92A	Clutch Spring.
49	Extension Lamp Base.	93	Tension Spring.
50½	Lamp Base.	93A	Tension Spring Screw and Thumb Nut, complete.
51½	Lamp Column.		
52	Large Bottom Clamp.		
53	Small Bottom Clamp.	96	Bottom Clamp Insulation.
54	Hand Nut.	96½	Top Bracket Insulation.
55	Hand Nut Washer.	97	Insulating Washers (large).
57	Top Bracket.		
58	Tension Spring Screw.	97A	Insulating Washers (small).
58½	Tension Spring Screw Nut.		
		97½	Insulating Bushing.
59	Top Lever.	98	Vertical Adjusting Screw.
60	Small Lever.	99	Vertical Adjusting Screw Nut.
61	Dash Pot, complete.		
62	Insulating Link.	100	Top Carbon Holder Slide.
63	Solenoid Plunger Connecting Link.	100A	Top Carbon Holder Stud.
		100C	Washer.
63½	Solenoid Plunger Yoke Link.	102	Clutch Foot.
		106A	Lower Electrode Holder Shank.
64	Solenoid Plunger.		
64A	Link connecting Nos. 64 and 90.	106B	Lower Electrode Clamp.
		106C	Electrode Holder Pin.
65	Solenoid.	109A	Lower Electrode.
67	Top Positive Conductor.	112A	No. 6 Tinned Iron Burrs.
67½	Beaded Conductor.	115	Insulating Bushing.
67½A	Screw for Beaded Conductor.	120	Solenoid Screw.
		121	Reflector Clamp Screw.
68	Binding Post Screw.	122	Clutch Weight Shoulder Screw.
69	Top Lever Screw.		
74	Set Screw.	132	Reflector Support, complete.
78A	Clutch Weight.		
78B	Clutch Weight Rod.	145A	No. 3 Tinned Iron Burrs.
79	Thumb Nut.	200A	Lower Electrode Holder, complete.
79A	Chain and Link.		
81B	Thumb Screw.	300	Upper Carbon Electrode Holder, complete.
87	Carbon Clamp, male.		
88	Carbon Clamp, female.		

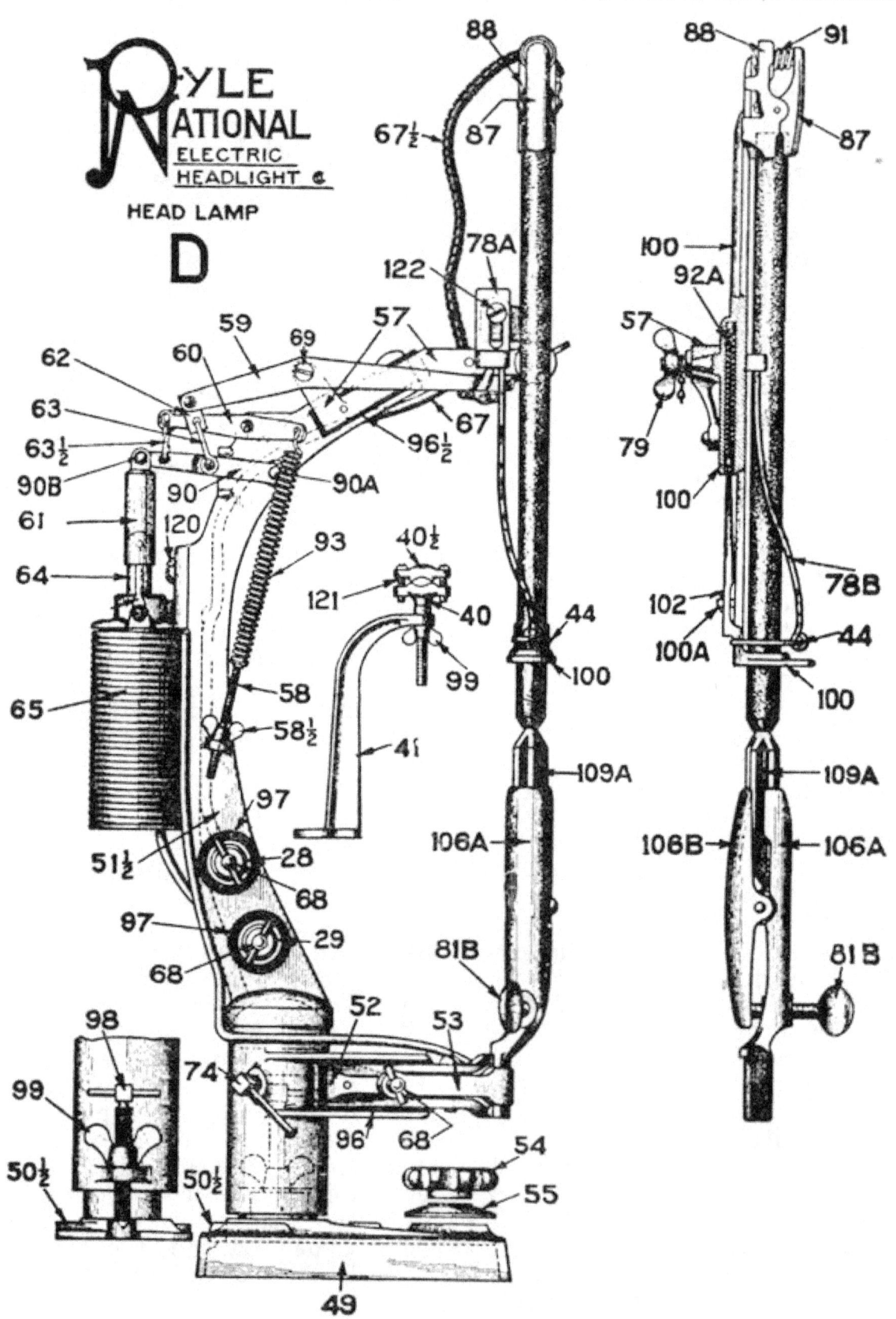

THE PYLE-NATIONAL ELECTRIC HEADLIGHT

NAMES AND NUMBERS OF PARTS, HEAD LAMP "D"—Continued

MISCELLANEOUS SCREWS.

207	Connecting Nos. 67 and 57.	212	Connecting Nos. 61 and 90.
208	Connecting Nos. 57 and 51½.	215	Connecting Nos. 88A and 88.
209	Connecting Nos. 60 and 51½.	157	Lamp, complete.
210	Connecting Nos. 90 and 51½.	197	Bottom Clamp, complete.
211	Connecting Nos. 61B and 65.	199	Carbon Contact Holder, complete, comprising Nos. 87, 88, 91.

TO FOCUS LAMP

First.—Adjust back of reflector so front will be parallel with front edge of case.

Second.—Adjust lamp to have point of copper electrode as near center of reflector as possible.

Third.—Have carbon as near center of chimney hole in reflector as possible.

Fourth.—Have engine on straight track and move lamp until you get best results on track. The light should be reflected in parallel rays and in as small a space as possible.

To lower light on track, raise lamp.

To raise light on track, lower lamp.

If your light throws any shadows it is not focused properly.

If light is focused properly and does not then strike center of track do not change focus, but shift entire case on base board. Point of copper electrode should be about one inch above top of holder. If it is higher than this, there will be too much heat on clutch.

QUESTIONS AND ANSWERS ON THE PYLE-NATIONAL ELECTRIC HEADLIGHT

Q.—What is an electric headlight?

A.—A device applied to the front of a locomotive and used to illuminate the track by means of a light produced by a current of electricity.

Q.—What principal parts comprise the Pyle-National Electric headlight?

A.—The turbine engine, the dynamo and the arc lamp.

Q.—What are the duties of the turbine engine?

A.—The turbine engine furnishes the mechanical power that operates the dynamo, the latter producing the light.

Q.—What are the principal parts of the dynamo?

A.—The armature, the commutator (which is attached to the armature shaft), the two field magnets and the pole pieces.

Q.—What are the duties of the armature?

A.—The armature induces an electromotive force in the copper wires wound upon it, and concentrates and directs the flow of current.

Q.—What is the function of the commutator?

A.—The function of the commutator is to collect the currents produced by the armature wires and cause them all to concur to a desired result.

Q.—At what point is the commutator attached to the armature?

A.—The commutator is attached to the end of the armature shaft in such a manner as to rotate with it.

Q.—Give the formation of the commutator?

A.—The commutator is composed of copper bars, to which the armature wires are attached at one end. These copper bars are separated from each other by pieces of mica, which is a nonconducting material.

Q.—What is the duty of the field coils or magnets?

A.—To produce a magnetic field, in which the armature revolves.

Q.—Define the pole pieces and give their requirements?

A.—The end portion of the field magnet are called the pole pieces; they form the armature chamber in which the armature revolves.

Q.—Give the first three measurements of electricity?

A.—The volt, the ampere and the ohm.

Q.—Define the volt.

A.—The practical unit of measurement of *electrical pressure* is the volt.

Q.—Define the ampere.

A.—The practical unit of measurement of the *rate of flow of current* is the ampere.

Q.—Define the ohm.

A.—The practical unit of measurement of *electrical resistance* is the ohm; a resistance that would limit the flow of electricity under an electro-motive force of one volt to a current of one ampere.

Q.—What produces the electro-motive force, or voltage?

A.—The electro-motive force, or voltage, is produced in the armature wires by the armature revolving in its chamber at a very high rate of speed.

Q.—What causes the electrical pressure, or voltage, to become too high?

A.—By increasing the speed of the armature beyond the point desired.

Q.—Then the speed at which the armature revolves determines the amount of voltage produced?

A.—Yes.

Q.—Should the electrical pressure become too great, what would result?

A.—If the electrical pressure, or voltage, becomes too high, the wires conducting the current will be heated so hot that the insulation wound upon them will become charred.

Q.—When the insulation on the wires becomes charred, does it lose its virtue?

A.—Yes. When the material covering the wires becomes charred, it is no longer a good insulator, and the current will leak through from layer to layer of the coils.

Q.—What is this called?

A.—A burned out coil.

Q.—Does the volt represent any electricity?

A.—It does not. It represents only the pressure that acts upon the electricity.

Q.—What effect has the volt upon a current of electricity?

A.—It forces a quantity of current to flow through the wires at a certain rate per second.

Q.—How is this rate of flow measured?

A.—In amperes.

Q.—What is meant by a short circuit?

A.—A short circuit is a passage offered whereby a quantity of current of electricity may flow with less resistance than is offered by its passage to points desired, such as lamps, etc.

Q.—What is the cause for most of the short circuits found in this device?

A.—Distorted insulation of wires, brought about by chafing.

Q.—What style of governor is used?

A.—A centrifugal governor.

Q.—Is there any other means employed within this turbine to prevent the speed attaining a velocity beyond the point desired?

A.—Yes. There is a centrifugal brake applied to the turbine wheel and set so that it will act at about 150 revolutions higher speed than the point at which the governor is set to act.

Q.—Why is this centrifugal brake not adjusted so that it will act at the same speed as the governor?

A.—There are two reasons why the brake is not set so that it will act in conjunction with the governor. First, the brake will not act as quick as the governor weights, and would therefore interfere seriously with the speed at the critical time. Second, it was designed and applied to prevent any possibility of the turbine wheel running away and being thrown to pieces by centrifugal force at times when the governor plungers have been neglected.

Q.—How many governor weights are there in this device?

A.—Four in number.

Q.—How many sets of governor springs are used and what is their duty?

A.—There are four sets of governor springs used, and their duty is to offer the proper amount of resistance to the movement of the governor weights and to cause them to act quickly.

Q.—How many governor valves, and where are they located?

A.—There are two governor valves, and they are placed within the governor stands.

Q.—If governor is set so that the plungers are seated when the governor weights are drawn at right angle position to face of turbine wheel, will it become necessary to change them again; and why?

A.—The action and position of the governor plungers are determined by the position of the governor weights, the latter's position being determined by the speed at which the turbine wheel revolves. If the plungers are set so that they are carried to seat of steam supply when weights are thrown to point of least resistance, it will be found when the plunger valves have worn so they must be faced off, that they will not seat when these governor weights are drawn to position stated above, and it will now be necessary to bend the ends of the crossarm until the plungers will seat.

Q.—When it is found that the governor weights will overtravel, that is, may be drawn beyond a position that is at right angles to face of turbine wheel before the plunger valves may be seated, in which direction must the ends of crossarm be bent to cause plunger valves to seat firmly when governor weights are drawn to critical service position?

A.—The ends of crossarm must be sprung out—away from the wheel—until the valves will seat firmly when weights are drawn to position stated above.

Q.—How should this work be done so that both plunger valves may have the same travel?

A.—Pull governor weights until they stand straight out from face of turbine wheel, hold in this position with one hand, place rule or scale on top of governor stand, move plunger into seat—and out, and note amount of travel shown. The ends of crossarm must be bent back away from face of wheel half the distance of measurement shown to insure the correct travel to both plungers.

Q.—How often should the governor plungers be examined to insure ideal service?

A.—The governor plungers should be examined by a competent inspector once each month.

Q.—Should a record be kept of such inspection?

A.—Yes.

Q.—When the governor has been properly set, how long will this device run before the plunger valves may need facing?

A.—At least six months.

Q.—Why then is it necessary to remove the engine cap and examine these plunger valves once each month?

A.—This governor being of the centrifugal form is set so that it will act at the maximum speed it is desired this engine shall attain, which is at point of maximum output of dynamo desired. Oftentimes the locomotive boiler may foam, or the engineer get a little too much water in boiler; some of this water is sure to pass through the turbine engine and would have a tendency to cause the plunger valves to stick. If they should stick open, the copper electrode and holder might be destroyed, hence the necessity of the monthly inspection.

Q.—Is it not possible to ascertain whether the plunger valves are stuck or not without removing the engine cap?

A.—No, not in all cases, though if one of the valves is stuck "wide open," or "entirely shut," it can be determined by taking the speed with the load on, then with turbine running without the load.

Q.—If one of the plungers is stuck "shut," how can it be determined by the speed recorder?

A.—If the governor has been handling the load, that is, if the latter has been set on a wide-open throttle, when one plunger is stuck shut, the speed will be very low with light burning, but when load is taken off speed will go up to usual maximum speed.

Q.—How may it be known if plunger should stick "open?"

A.—Should the governor plunger stick open, the copper electrode will be fused almost instantly, and when the load is taken off the speed of turbine will become very great. A constant and heavy flow of steam out of the exhaust pipe can also be noted.

Q.—What lubricates the centerpiece and face of crossarm?

A.—The "graphite" ring.

Q.—Describe this ring and its location.

A.—The ring known as the graphite ring is a flat bronze ring that is drilled full of holes and these holes are filled with graphite. This ring is held in a small recess in the centerpiece by the crossarm.

Q.—How often do these rings have to be renewed?

A.—There is no actual time limit to the life and wear of these rings. They wear indefinitely.

Q.—How can the speed of the turbine and dynamo be increased when all ports are normal?

A.—The speed of this device can be increased by moving all of the governor spring adjusting screws to the right.

Q.—How may the speed be reduced?

A.—By moving all governor spring adjusting screws to the left.

Q.—To increase the speed of dynamo 100 revolutions per minute, how far should the screws be turned?

A.—To increase speed of dynamo 100 revolutions per minute, all of the adjusting screws must be moved one-half turn to the right.

Q.—To decrease the speed?

A.—One-half turn to the left.

Q.—Is there any reason why the adjustment of the governor spring screws will not cause the engine to respond to the speed desired at all times?

A.—Yes, there are several things that will, at certain times, prevent the regulating of speed by movement of the adjusting screws.

Q.—Give one cause that will interfere with this regulating of speed with adjusting screws.

A.—When bushing in engine cap becomes worn from lack of lubrication. It will also be found that the edge of the bottom governor stand has been worn off by the turbine wheel, which has slowly dropped down by this bushing wear until it came in contact with the governor stand. In a short time the space between the governor stands and turbine wheel will be increased until the steam will not have to pass through the turbine wheel to gain the atmosphere, but can pass around on either side of wheel to the exhaust. In this case adjustment of regulating screws could not be effective.

Q.—Is there another cause why adjustment of regulating screws will not be effective?

A.—Yes. If the bearings are not properly lubricated and the end thrust maintained too close. Since the steam is directed against the buckets of the wheel by the governor stands, the latter suspended to the main casting; in a short time the flange of bushings and the cast iron washer in engine will be worn so badly that the turbine wheel will be carried out and away from the main casting and governor stand, when now a considerable amount of steam will pass around to back side of turbine wheel to the exhaust instead of passing through wheel.

Q.—Can you give another cause that might occur wherein the adjustment or the governor spring screws would not be effective?

A.—If one of the plunger valves should stick either closed or open, it would be impossible to regulate speed as desired while in such condition.

Q.—What should always be done just before engine cap is removed?

A.—The end thrust should always be adjusted to 1-32 of an inch before the engine cap is removed.

Q.—Why?

A.—If it is found that some changes are necessary in governor, such as changing crossarm, etc., unless the end thrust is adjusted *before* such changes are made, there is great danger that the travel of the plunger valves might be cut off, perhaps entirely closed.

Q.—How is adjustment of end thrust made?

A.—When facing the dynamo by first loosening screws in the end-thrust casting, then tapping same on left side will take up end movement, and by tapping on right side will increase end movement.

Q.—When it is found that the turbine wheel has been carried too far away from the governor stands (due to end-thrust movement), to direct the steam against the center of the bucket in wheel, what is the cure?

A.—It will require a new bushing in engine cap and a new cast iron washer.

Q.—If there are no new parts at hand to make repairs what may be done?

A.—If no new parts are at hand temporary repairs can be made in this way: First loosen screws in end-thrust casting and move the latter to the right, then move the wheel towards the main casting as far as it will go; now place a metallic washer of some kind between the flange of bushing in engine cap and the cast iron washer, being careful that this washer is only of sufficient thickness to take up the lost motion between the flange of bushing and cast iron washer.

QUESTIONS AND ANSWERS PERTAINING TO THE CARE OF THE ELECTRIC HEADLIGHT IN GENERAL

Q.—How would you inspect an electric headlight equipment before going out? How should the light be started?

A.—See that the commutator is clean, that the brushes are properly adjusted, that all screws are tight, that the point of the copper electrode is clean and the proper distance above the holder, that the headlight is properly fitted with carbon which will fall freely through the holder, and that the oil wells are properly filled before starting the engine; see that the casing is properly drained, and then turn on a little steam so as to allow time for condensation to get out of the engine, after which steam can be turned on full. The headlight should always be started slowly.

Q.—How can you tell when the turbine is running too fast?

A.—By the light burning green.

Q.—Can you tell when the governors are not working properly, and have you any way to test governors before engine leaves the terminal?

A.—Yes, you can tell by the manner in which the light burns, as, for instance, if upon giving the turbine a full head of steam your light burns green, you will know the engine is running too fast. If the light burns dim, it is not running fast enough. The speed of the governor in a Pyle-National Electric headlight can be regulated by turning the adjusting screws, to the left if running too fast, and to the right if running too slow, being careful to adjust all screws the same as near as possible; one-half turn of these screws will change the speed about one hundred revolutions per minute. On a Schroeder headlight the speed is regulated by adjusting the governor tension spring, which is done by means of a nut on the end of the spring; turning the nut clockwise, that is, to the right, tightens this spring and increases the speed, while turning it to the left reduces the speed; one-quarter of a turn on this nut in either direction will make a marked difference in the speed.

Q.—What kind of oil should be used for dynamo and turbine bearings, and why?

A.—For the bearings use valve oil, except in extremely cold weather, when engine oil can be used. This because, owing to the high speed at which the turbine runs, if engine oil is used in warm weather the bearing may run hot, while if valve oil is used in cold weather the oil may become too thick to feed. There is a plug in the top of the engine for the purpose of introducing oil to cut away any lime or scale that may have formed about the governor plungers. Engine oil or coal oil should be used for this purpose, as it is not necessary to lubricate the governor plungers to prevent any frictional wear, but simply to cut away the scale. This should be done each trip before starting out.

Q.—Do you ever put oil in hole at top of the turbine, and for what purpose?

A.—Yes, engine oil should be put in each trip for the purpose of cutting out the scale or sediment that may have formed around the governor plungers.

Q.—How can you tell when the main bushing is worn?

A.—By the brushes sparking, wearing out rapidly and the headlight not throwing a steady light but flickering.

Q.—What effect does a worn-out bushing have on the working of a lamp?

A.—The lamp does not burn steadily but the light flickers.

Q.—When the dynamo sparks, and small pin-point sparks runs around commutator, what is it an indication of? How would you remedy it?

A.—It is due to the carbon brushes not being adjusted properly or having a poor contact on the commutator. It is usually an indication that the tension springs are too loose, and can be remedied by increasing the tension. A little judgment must be used in this case, however, for if the brushes are not in proper condition, or if the commutator is not smooth and true, there will be sparking at the brushes regardless of how much pressure is used; therefore, before adjusting the tension springs see if the commutator is clean and runs true.

Q.—If the dynamo sparks badly and commutator is blistered and rough, and by pressing hand on the brushes the sparking becomes less, what is indicated and how could it be remedied.

A.—This usually is an indication that the commutator is getting out of round and requires truing up. Where it is not too much out of round or too rough, it can be trued up by removing the brushes and holding a strip of No. 0 sandpaper, about the width of the brushes, by the ends of the commutator while the same is running. After the commutator has been smoothed up, file the mica strips between the copper strips down a trifle below the surface of the copper, being careful not to get them too low, as this would allow them to collect dirt, etc., and cause a short circuit. If the commutator is very rough or out of round it should be trued up in a lathe and the tool used should be very sharp and very light cuts taken, then polish it with fine sandpaper, examining it carefully to see that no two sections of the copper touch. In fact, it is better after the commutator has been trued up to polish and cut or file the mica between each section a little below the surface, as it does not wear away as rapidly as the copper, and if the mica is not cut away it may lead to sparking. After doing this be sure that no ragged edges of the copper stick up, as this will cut away the brushes rapidly.

Q.—When the brushes spark badly in one place and pressing down on brushes does not help matters, and on shutting off the machine the mica between two bars is found to be burned and copper bars burned also, how could this be remedied?

A.—This is an indication of a short circuit at that particular point, caused either by dirt or by the coppers coming in contact; to remedy it, clean out the slot where the mica strip fits between the two copper bars, and if any copper has been dragged over from one bar to the other file away.

Q.—What damage is a worn bushing likely to cause to the dynamo?

A.—It is liable to injure the armature by allowing it to come in contact with the field coils.

Q.—When the lamp goes out while the engine is running and burns O. K. while engine is standing what is the indication?

A.—It is due to the tension spring number 93 in the Pyle-National headlight being adjusted too tight, which prevents the solenoid from separating the carbon sufficiently to form a proper arc, or the carbon clutch spring 92A in the Pyle-National headlight being too loose, allowing the back edge of the clutch to be jarred up and release the carbon. On the Schroeder headlight it is an indication that the clutch spring is too weak.

Q.—When the wires are wrongly connected at either dynamo or lamp, what occurs when the light is started?

A.—It will cause a short circuit and put the light out. When this occurs the dynamo will be generating a heavy current, the speed will be quite low and there will be but a small light at the lamp, or else the light will burn green. When this occurs the dynamo should be stopped at once, the trouble located and remedied.

Q.—If the lamp goes out when turbine is running and the carbon is found to be held off the electrode, what is wrong?

A.—It is generally due to the tension spring 93 in the Pyle light being very loose, so that the magnet is drawn down too far. It may also be due to a deposit of scale on the point of the copper electrode, which prevents the top carbon touching the copper.

Q.—When the light flashes badly and the bars of the commutator have a reddish color resembling copper after having been heated, what is indicated?

A.—It would indicate that the tension spring is so tight that the magnet is unable to separate the carbons, giving a poor light, and if run too long in this condition it will result in burning out the armature or the fields, owing to the heavy current generated.

Q.—When a carbon is put in, what precautions should be taken to be sure that it will work satisfactorily?

A.—After putting in a new carbon always push down on lever 90 Pyle light, and notice if the carbon lifts and falls freely. If it does not fall down freely, turn it partially around and find the freest place, as these carbons are moulded and sometimes there is a little more stock at one point than the other, and when very rough it is advisable to smooth them up so as to insure their feeding properly.

Q.—After copper electrodes have been in service for some time what often happens to them to affect the light, and how remedied?

A.—A crust is frequently formed on the end of the copper electrode which prevents the current from passing through it, consequently the light fails. This is remedied by removing the crust.

Q.—How should a copper electrode be sharpened? Why?

A.—Remove it, put it in a vise and sharpen or point it with a file. It should be kept pointed in order to insure better contact with the carbon.

Q.—What effect does the burning off of the copper electrode, or filing it off, have on the lamp?

A.—It has the same effect as lowering the lamp, in that it raises the light on the track.

Q.—If the light moves from one side of the track to the other and would not remain focused for any length of time, what would you look for?

A.—Look for a loose hand nut at the bottom which secures the foot or stand to the lamp base.

Q.—If the copper electrode and clutch melted, how should the lamp be fixed so as to have a light without delaying the train?

A.—Remove the electrode from the bracket and substitute an iron bolt, securing the same in the bracket where electrode holders were removed; be sure that the end of the bolt comes up in the center of the reflector. This bolt will fuse slowly, but it will give you a good light. An ordinary carbon can also be used in such emergencies but it will burn away faster, which would necessitate its being moved up quite frequently.

Nathan Three-Feed Type Bull's-Eye Lubricator

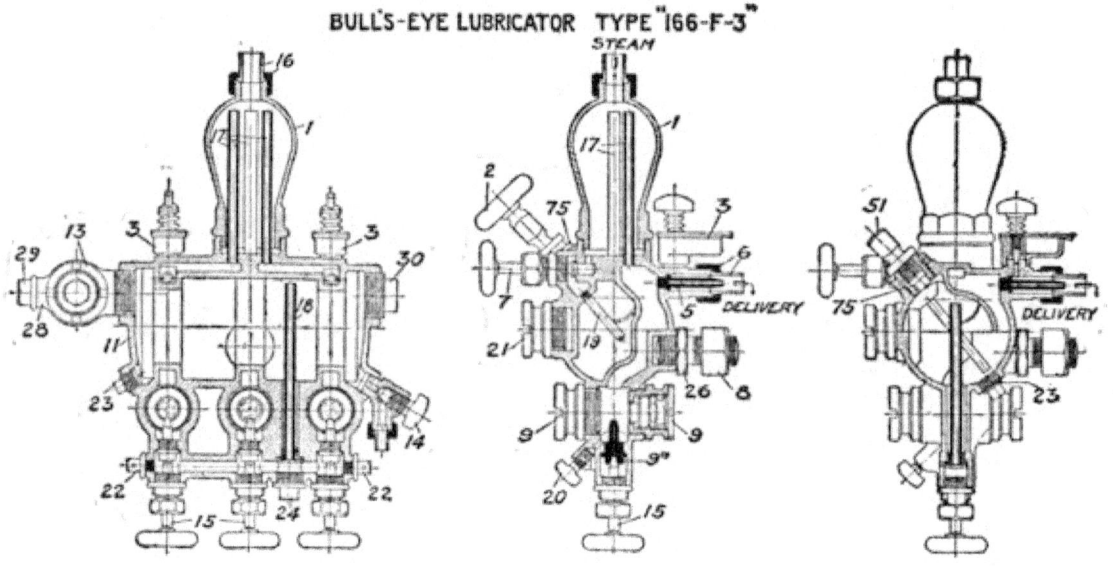

BULL'S-EYE LUBRICATOR TYPE "166-F-3"

NAME OF PARTS

- 1 Condenser.
- 2 Filling Plug.
- 3 Hand Oiler.
- 5 Reducing Plug.
- 6 Delivery Nut and Tailpiece.
- 7 Water Valve.
- 8 Stud Nut.
- 9 Sight Feed Glass and Casing.
- 9a Feed Nozzle.
- 11 Body.
- 13 Gauge Glass and Casing.
- 14 Waste Cock.
- 15 Regulating Valve.
- 16 Top Connection.
- 17 Equalizing Pipe.
- 18 Oil Pipe.
- 19 Water Pipe.
- 20 Sight Feed Drain Valve.
- 21 Reserve Glass and Casing.
- 22 Cleaning Plug (Body).
- 23 Body Plug.
- 24 Oil Pipe Plug.
- 28 Gauge Glass Bracket.
- 29 Cleaning Plug (Gauge Glass).
- 30 Gauge Glass Cap.
- 51 Plug for Filling Hole.
- 75 Removable Seat for Filling Plug.

SPECIFIC CHARACTERISTICS

The lubricator is provided with two filling plugs, one near each end of the lubricator, so that either one may be used as is found most convenient. The filling plugs do not seat on the body, but on removable bushings. In case the seats on the bushings wear out only the bushings need replacement. These bushings are provided with left-hand threads in the body.

GENERAL DESCRIPTION

The body of the lubricator 11 is made of one single cylindrical casting, with the sight feeds 9 and the regulating valves 15 located at the bottom of the lubricator, all being in one casting. An oil pipe 18 extends from the oil channel connecting with the regulating valves nearly to the top of the reservoir, and supplies the oil to each of the regulating valves as long as there is any oil in the reservoir. The water pipe 19 extends from the water valve 7 to the bottom of the oil chamber, so that when the water valve is open, water from the condenser passes freely into the oil chamber and transmits to the oil the pressure due to the head of water in the condenser.

The condenser 1 is kept filled with water up to the top of the equalizing pipes 17 which are contained in the condenser, by the condensation of steam from the boiler. Any excess of water passes down these tubes with the live steam. These equalizing pipes are screwed into the passages connecting with the outlets from the lubricator and supply live steam to these passages, which keeps them full of condensed water up to the level of the reducing or choke plugs 5, from which point the excess of water, oil and steam leaves the lubricator to pass through the oil pipes to the steam chest and cylinders. This supply of steam from the equalizing pipes also balances the steam pressure on the water in the condenser and on the water in the sight feed and outlet passages, and the duty of the choke plugs is to restrict the flow of steam from these passages so that the steam pressure back of the choke plugs is equalized with that in the condenser, whether the engine is working steam at full boiler pressure or whether steam is shut off.

Three openings are provided to clean out the oil passages to the regulating valves, which openings are covered by the plugs 22 at the ends of the oil channel, and plug 24 underneath the oil pipe 18.

Hand oilers 3 are provided, one for each oil pipe leading to the cylinder or steam chest, which hand oilers are provided with spring covers to keep out foreign matter.

The steam chest oil plug is not furnished with the lubricator, for any standard plug of this character is adaptable. It must be provided at its lower end with a bore of not less than 3-32" or more than 1/8" in diameter. This is absolutely necessary for the proper function of the lubricator.

OPERATION

The lubricator is first filled with clean strained oil through the filling plug 2, and when the oil chamber is full, the plug is replaced and the water valve 7 opened immediately, irrespective of whether or not the lubricator feeds are started. This opening of the water valve immediately after the cup is filled is very important in order to prevent the bursting of the oil chamber through the force of expansion of the oil as it becomes heated. The steam valve of the lubricator is then opened, which operation fills the sight feed chambers with water. The lubricator may then be started feeding by opening the regulating valves 15 more or less, according to the feed desired.

To renew the supply of oil after it has been fed from the lubricator, first the regulating valves, then the water valve is closed. If the water valve is tight, then it is not necessary to close the steam valve at the boiler. The drain cock 14 is then opened and the water removed from the reservoir, after which the filling plug is opened. When the water is entirely out of the cup, the drain cock is closed and the reservoir filled with oil, after which the filling plug is replaced and the water valve opened immediately.

To use the hand oilers, which should be done only when the engine is running on a down grade with the throttle closed, steam is shut off from the lubricator by closing the steam valve at the boiler, then the valve of the hand oiler is opened, the cover turned to one side and the oil poured in. When the oil has run out of the hand oiler, the valve of the same is closed and the steam turned on from the boiler to the lubricator. This at once carries the oil to the steam chest.

The steam valve at the boiler should always be opened before the engine begins to work, whether the feeds are started or not, and should be kept open as long as the engine is doing service of any kind, whether steaming or drifting, unless using the hand oilers as described before.

The water valve should be open at all times except when filling the cup as described.

In making the steam connection from the boiler to the lubricator, the valve should connect at a point where dry steam can be obtained, since when water gets from the boiler into the lubricator it interferes with its proper performance, and muddy water soon cuts the valves and their seats, causing leaks. The type of steam valve as represented in the illustration is provided with a pipe ring 32, to which the dry pipe may be attached, leading from the point on the boiler where the valve is attached to a point inside of the boiler above the highest water level.

Nathan Simplex Injector Type "R"

DESCRIPTION

This type of injector meets the most severe requirements of modern locomotive practice. It is simply constructed and contains only a few operating parts. It is self-regulating, that is, after being started at the highest operating pressure, the latter may drop down to about forty pounds before there is any waste at the overflow. It is also restarting, that is, if from any cause the supply of water should be temporarily interrupted, the injector restarts automatically as soon as the water supply is restored. The reducing capacity is 50 per cent of the maximum capacity under ordinary variations of lift and feed water temperatures.

The action is as follows: Steam from the boiler is admitted to the lifting nozzle 22 by drawing out the starting lever 4 slightly, and without withdrawing the plug on the end of the steam spindle 11 from the steam nozzle 21. Steam then passes through the small openings around the steam nozzle, and discharges into the overflow chamber, lifts the heater cock check 26, and issues from the overflow nozzle 34 to which the overflow pipe is attached.

When water appears at the overflow, the lever 4 is drawn back as far as it will go, which opens the steam nozzle 21 and allows the full supply of steam to enter the intermediate nozzle forcing the water through the delivery nozzle 25 into the boiler.

At high steam pressure a vacuum is produced in the overflow chamber which draws an additional supply of water into the nozzles through the inlet valve 19, and through the supply openings between the nozzles, which additional water is forced into the boiler, thereby increasing the capacity of the injector under ordinary conditions of operation.

In other injectors provided with the inlet valve, the injector does not prime properly, or not at all, if for some reason this valve leaks, but in the Simplex Injector the cut-out or emergency valve 35 is provided, which in such cases enables the inlet valve to be cut out and the injector to be operated until there is an opportunity to grind or otherwise repair the defect.

The quantity of water needed is regulated by means of the water valve 13.

The heater cock arrangement is made either in the form of a cam motion, as represented by parts 26 to 31, or in the form of a screw motion, as represented by parts 46 to 48. This check is closed down only when it is desired to warm the water in the tank, in which case it is accomplished either by means of the cam 30, or the screw spindle 47. At all other times the heater cock check 26 must be allowed to open to its full extent.

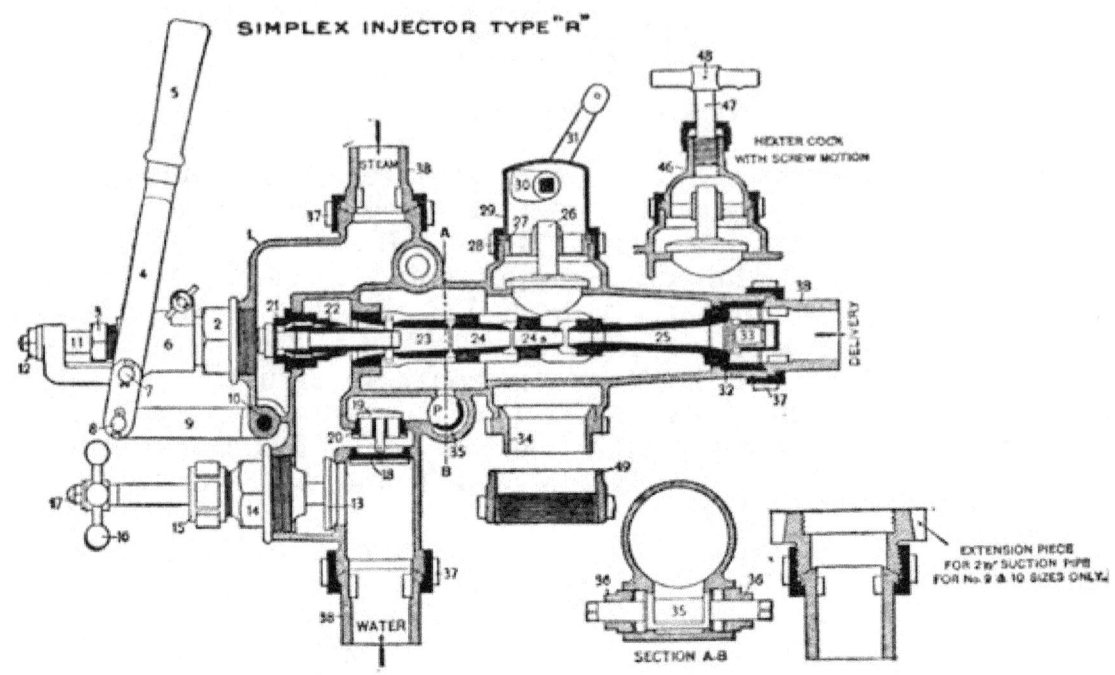

NAME OF PARTS

1. Body.
2. Steam Bonnet.
3. Steam Packing Nut.
4. Lever.
5. Lever Handle.
6. Guide for Steam Spindle.
7. Guide Pin.
8. Lever Pin.
9. Fulcrum Bar.
10. Fulcrum Pin.
11. Steam Spindle.
12. Lock Nut.
13. Water Valve.
14. Water Valve Bonnet.
15. Water valve Nut.
16. Water Valve Handle.
17. Water Valve Topnut.
18. Inlet Valve Cap.
19. Inlet Valve.
20. Inlet Valve Seat.
21. Steam Nozzle.
22. Lifting Steam Nozzle.
23. Intermediate Nozzle.
24. Combining Nozzle.
24a. Combining Nozzle.
25. Delivery Nozzle.
26. Heater Cock Check.
27. Guide for Heater Cock Check.
28. Nut for Cam Casing.
29. Cam Casing.
30. Cam.
31. Cam Lever.
32. Nozzle Holder.
33. Linecheck Valve.
34. Overflow Nozzle.
35. Emergency Valve.
36. Packing Nut for Emergency Valve.

Steam, Water or Delivery (Specify):
37. Coupling Nut.
38. Tailpiece.

For Heater Cock with Screw Motion:
46. Guide For Heater Cock Check.
47. Heater Cock Spindle.
48. Heater Cock Handle.
49. Overflow Pipe Sleeve.

SELLERS' CLASS "N" IMPROVED SELF-ACTING INJECTOR

This injector is simply constructed and contains few operating parts. The lever is used in starting only, and the water valve for regulation of the delivery. It is self-adjusting with fixed nozzles and restarts automatically. All the valve seats that may need refacing can be removed; the body is not subject to wear and will last a lifetime.

The action is as follows: Steam from the boiler is admitted to the lifting nozzle by drawing the starting lever 33 about one inch, which does not withdraw the plug on the end of the spindle 7 from the central part of the steam nozzle 3. Steam then passes through the small diagonal-drilled holes and discharges by the outside nozzle, through the upper part of the combining tube 2 and into the overflow chamber, lifts the overflow valve 30, and issues from the waste pipe 29. When water is lifted the starting lever 33 is drawn back, opening the forcing steam nozzle 3, and the full supply of steam discharges into the combining tube, forcing the water through the delivery tube into the boiler pipe.

At high steam pressures all injectors having side openings in the combining tube, produce a vacuum in the overflow chamber. In the Improved Self-Acting Injector this is utilized to draw an additional supply of water into the combining tube by opening the inlet valve 42; the water is forced by the jet into the boiler, increasing the capacity about 20 per cent.

The water-regulating valve 40 is used only to adjust the capacity to suit the needs of the boiler. The range is unusually large (see page 70).

The cam lever 34 is turned toward the steam pipe to prevent the opening of the overflow valve when it is desired to use the injector as a heater or to clean the strainer. The joint between the body 25 and the waste pipe 29 is not subject to other pressure than that due to the discharging steam and water during starting; the metal faces should be kept clean and the retaining nut 32 screwed up tight.

To tighten up the gland of the steam spindle, push in the starting lever 33 to end of stroke, remove the little nut 5 and draw back the lever 33. This frees the crosshead 8 and links 15, which can be swung out of the way, and the follower 12 tightened on the packing to make the gland steam-tight.

METHOD OF OPERATING

To Start—Pull out the Lever.
To Stop—Push in the Lever.
Regulate for quantity with the water regulating valve.

Self-Acting Injector, Class N Improved.

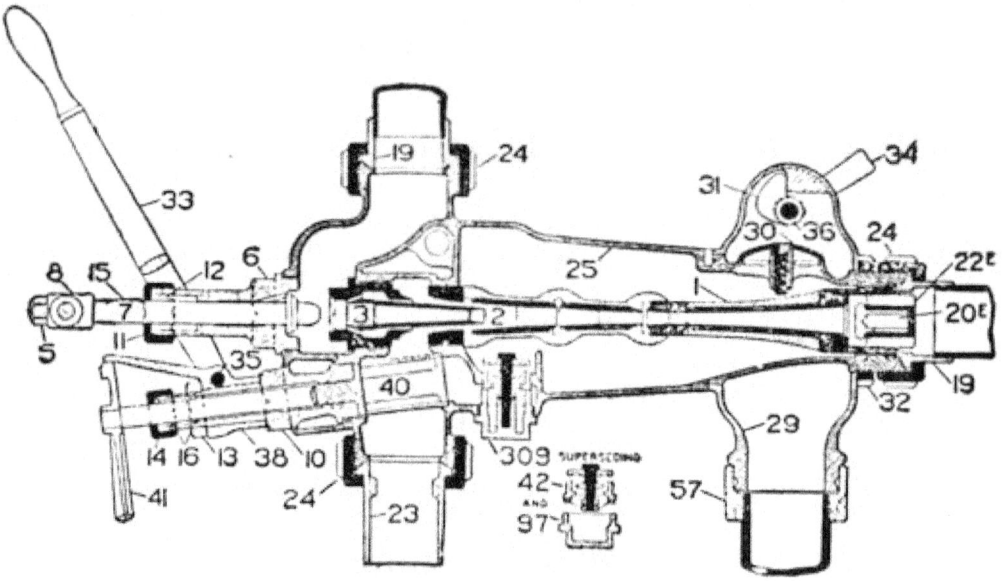

LIST OF PARTS, SELF-ACTING INJECTOR, CLASS N IMPROVED

1	Delivery Tube.	24	Coupling Nut.
2	Combining Tube.	24d	Coupling Nut, Overflow.
3	Steam Nozzles.	25	Injector Body.
5	Spindle Nut.	27	Wrench for No. 24.
6	Steam Stuffing Box.	29	Waste Pipe.
7	Spindle.	30	Waste Valve.
8	Crosshead.	31	Waste Valve Cam.
10	Water Stuffing Box.	32	Jam Nut for No. 29.
11	Follower.	33	Starting Lever.
12	Packing Ring.	34	Cam Lever.
13	Lock Nut.	35	Pin, Nos. 33 and 38.
14	Follower for No. 10.	36	Cam Shaft.
15	Links.	37	Washer on 36.
16	Packing Ring.	38	Collar and Index.
19	Plain ⎫ Rings for	40	Plug Water Valve.
19a	Reduc. ⎭ Copper Pipe.	41	Regulating Handle.
20e	Check Valve.	42	Inlet Valve.
22e	Guide for No. 20e.	55	Tube Wrench.
23	Plain ⎫ Unions for	57	Waste Pipe Connection.
23a	Reduc. ⎭ Iron Pipes.	97n	Cap under No. 42.
23d	Union, Overflow.	309	Inlet Valve (Vertical).

The Allen-Richardson Balanced Slide Valve

The Allen Valve is designed to at least partially prevent the wire-drawing of steam, when high speeds are maintained, with the valve cutting off early in the stroke. In the Allen ports, an additional passage for the intake of steam is furnished at such times, and consequently when the steam port is open one-half inch in the ordinary manner, the port of the cored passage is also open to a like extent on the other side of the valve, and consequently the effective area of the steam port is doubled, and the actual equivalent of a single port with a one inch opening.

The wire-drawing incident to running at high speeds with the valve cutting off early in the stroke, is thus greatly diminished with a resultant economy of steam and fuel. A reduction of wire-drawing carries with it a higher average pressure on the piston when working at a similar cut-off, consequently the usual average pressure can be maintained with a shorter cut-off, resulting in an appreciable economy. While the unbalanced Allen Valve therefore secures a better and more economical distribution of steam, its use entails certain disadvantages.

On the face of a slide valve, the area of bearing surface is never sufficient to secure its wearing well under a heavy steam pressure; and this wearing surface is yet further reduced in the Allen Valve, owing to its internal steam ports. This internal passage actually divides the valve into two parts, and the steam pressure, acting on the outer part, springs and bends its working face below that of the internal or exhaust port of the valve. The available wearing face is consequently reduced to a space about one-half as wide as the outside lap of the valve, and this fully accounts for the rapid wearing of the unbalanced Allen Valve, and, for the trouble and expense of constantly refacing valves and seats, and the loss of the steam blown through leaky valves, quite offsets the advantages gained by a reduction of wire-drawing.

These manifest disadvantages are entirely overcome by a proper balancing of the valve, which secures all of the advantages of the Richardson device, plus an increased steam economy resulting from using the Allen ports.

To secure the best possible results from the employment of the Allen Balanced Valve, its ports and bridges should exceed the full travel of the valve by at least one-eighth of an inch, and the radius of the link should always be as long as permissible to escape an excessive increase of lead when cutting off early in the stroke.

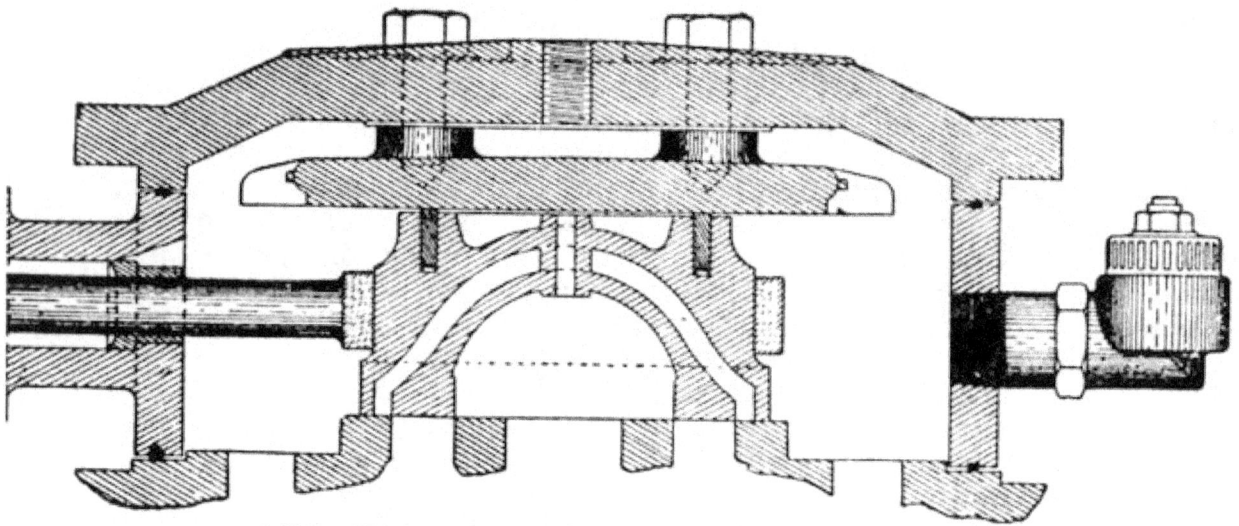

Allen-Richardson Balanced Slide Valve.
Longitudinal Section.

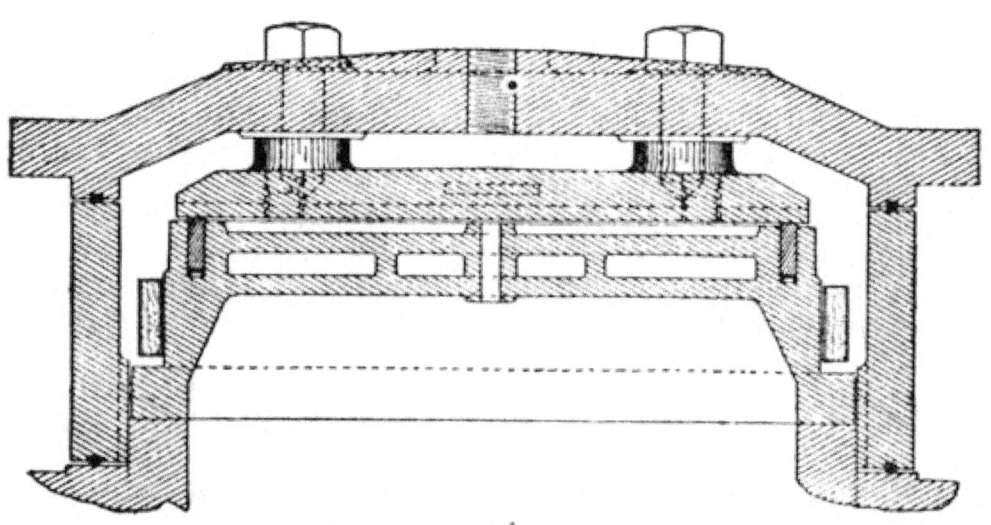

Allen-Richardson Balanced Slide Valve.
Transverse Section.

The Walschaert Valve Gear*

The Walschaert valve gear has been for many years the standard for locomotives on the State Railways of Belgium, and it is also extensively used in Germany and France. In the latter country it has been given preference over all others for the high-speed balanced compounds, which have made such remarkable records.

In this gear the two motions, one derived from the crosshead and the other from a crank arm or eccentric, are so combined as to produce a resultant motion similar to that obtained from the stationary link, and it is therefore classed as a radial valve gear. The revolving element is usually derived from a return crank on the main pin, with the center at right angles to the crank arm. The angular advance becomes zero, and so far as this part is concerned the valve has neither lap nor lead. The link oscillates about a fixed axis and its arc has a radius equal to the length of the radius rod. A short arm is bolted to the crosshead, and from its lower end extends a hinged connector, with the other end pinned to the combination lever. The lever so combines the crank and crosshead motions that the angular advance is restored and the valve is given a constant lap and lead. The equalization of the cut-off with the Walschaert motion is a much simpler matter and is made with greater ease than with the shifting link. This is due to the constant relation of the valve and piston motions, which is obtained by the combination lever.

The chief difference between the Walschaert and the link motions is the constant lead with the former when the valve travel is changed. This is due to the fact that at the end of the stroke the crosshead alone is responsible for the position of the valve, and as the crosshead always has the same position at the end of the stroke the valve will also have a definite location, and the travel may be decreased, but the lead remains constant. For high-speed locomotives, of the ordinary simple two-cylinder type, the constant lead may not be regarded as desirable, as early cut-offs are then used, and it is necessary to have greater preadmission, when the cut-off is so short, in order to permit the steam to enter the cylinder without excessive wire-drawing. With the four-cylinder balanced compound the cut-off need not be short. The record of the indicator cards taken from a locomotive of this kind on the Northern Railway of France, as given by M. Sauvage, shows that at 77 miles per hour the cut-off in the high pressure cylinder was 45 per cent, and in the low pressure cylinder 67 per cent. The Joy valve gear has a constant lead and it is used frequently in England in connection with inside cylinders, and it has not been found objectionable on account of this peculiarity. So far as the distribution of steam is concerned, the Walschaert valve motion will produce results as good as, if not better than, the link motion, and it has also mechanical advantages which recommend it.

---

*From Railway Magazine, London, Eng.

A valve gear outside of the frames is conveniently inspected and repaired, while one inside of the frames is certainly in an awkward position for either operation. With inside cylinders and crank axles there is little room for eccentrics and links, and if all this be removed it allows ample length for main pin bearings, and it is then possible to have an inside bearing for the crank axle.

A point worth consideration, however, is the great contrast in the weight of the moving parts and the size of the bearings when this Walschaert outside gear is compared with similar parts of the link motion driven by eccentrics. A well-known American locomotive superintendent says: "I consider that the increased complication and weight of the valve motion is an exceedingly serious matter in giving distorted steam distribution, due to the destructive effect of the valve motion in causing wear and tear." According to a paper issued about a year ago, the weights of parts of the link motion valve gear for large locomotives are as follows, in pounds: Eccentric, 212; eccentric strap, 225; eccentric rod, 125; link, 148; rocker arm, 248; transmission bar, 128; valve rod, 66; valve yoke, 90; valve, 211. These figures indicate that the link valve gear, including the eccentrics and straps, as found on some modern locomotives, has become a very ponderous affair. Some attention has been given to the valve pattern in the effort to make it as light as possible, but the same care has not been taken with the moving details connected with it, which easily become a disturbing factor at high speeds if made too heavy.

The principal load which comes on the eccentrics and straps, causing them to heat, is not the friction of the valve, but it is that due to the inertia of the reciprocating parts of the valve gear whose motion is reversed twice for every revolution. If we include the rocker arm, the weight, as found above, of the moving parts from valve to eccentric strap for one cylinder is 1,052 pounds, and at high speeds the energy of this moving mass must impose a heavy load on the eccentrics. The eccentrics and straps are the most difficult details in the locomotive machinery to keep properly lubricated, and it requires constant vigilance to prevent them from heating. When they do heat and cut, and the straps are taken down, their location inside the frames is the most inconvenient one possible, and with the increasing weight of the machinery this part of the locomotive repairs has become very laborious and expensive. More attention should be given to the reduction of the weight of the moving parts of the link valve gear, or some other type should be used. The Walschaert gear located outside the frames is easily accessible and very convenient for inspection, lubrication, and repairs. The main driving bearings are two small pins with bushed bearings, and the contrast with the heavy cumbersome eccentrics and straps which are their equivalent in a valve gear system is very striking. This gear is simple and light throughout, and it has much to recommend it which would overcome the objectionable features of the shifting link motion driven by eccentrics.

Having described the Walschaert valve gear, an account of the career of its inventor is of interest.

Egide Walschaert was born in 1820 at Mechlin, then a little retired village in the vicinity of Brussels. The railway line from Brussels to Malines was opened in 1835, and that decided the career of young Walschaert, who entered the railroad shops of the State Railways at Malines in 1842. He became chief superintendent of the shops of the Brussels Southern line, and at the early age of twenty-four had already acquired to an eminent degree all the qualities which go to make the successful engineer, which ought to have secured to him in a few years the position of technical director of the locomotive service of the system. It is humiliating to state that he remained chief shop superintendent all the remaining active years of his life.

On October 5, 1844, M. Fisher, engineer of the State Railways at Brussels, made an application in the name of Egide Walschaert for a patent of an invention relating to a new valve gear for locomotives. This Belgian patent was accorded by royal decree on November 30, 1844, for a term of fifteen years. The rules of the railway did not allow the foreman of shops to advertise a patent in Belgium to his profit, which explains, perhaps, the mediation of M. Fischer, who never claimed to have any part in the invention. The mechanism described in the patent of 1844 presents a strong resemblance to that which we are now familiar with, and the inventor constructed in 1848 a similar valve motion for application to locomotive No. 98. At this time the valve gear in use was that of Sharp, with two eccentrics and the usual forked rods. The shifting link attributed to Stephenson had been invented by Williams and Howe in 1842, and it is doubtful if Walschaert had ever seen it. The problem which to-day seems very easy was at that time an intricate one, and to Walschaert, who then gave the correct and most elegant solution, is certainly due unreserved admiration. He also invented a valve gear for stationary engines, somewhat on the Corliss or Sulzer principle, and he built at Brussels a shop for the manufacture of such engines, and this was managed by his son.

At the Paris Exposition of 1878, a gold medal was awarded him for his engine, and in 1883 the exposition at Antwerp awarded him a diploma of honor, in which his locomotive valve gear was given merited praise.

Walschaert died on February 18, 1901, at Saint Lilles, near Brussels, at the age of eighty-one years. His reputation, however great, was accepted with singular modesty, and his business relations were met with absolute disinterestedness. He gave his remarkable inventions to the world at a time when the study of steam distribution and valve gears was in its infancy, and he was deprived of the resources of a science which was not yet developed. On account of his great merits, which are here imperfectly recited, it is unfortunate that proper justice has not always been accorded Walschaert, for the ingenious mechanism which originated in his brain has been purloined through long years in the greater part of Europe.

ENGINEMEN'S MANUAL

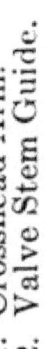

NAMES OF PARTS.

1. Main Crank Pin.
2. Eccentric Crank.
3. Main Rod.
4. Crosshead.
5. Link.
6. Eccentric Rod.
7. Radius Bar.
8. Valve Rod.
9. Combination Lever.
10. Union Link.
11. Crosshead Arm.
12. Valve Stem Guide.
13. Reach Rod.
14. Lifting Arm.
15. Reverse Shaft Arm.
16. Piston Rod.
17. Valve.

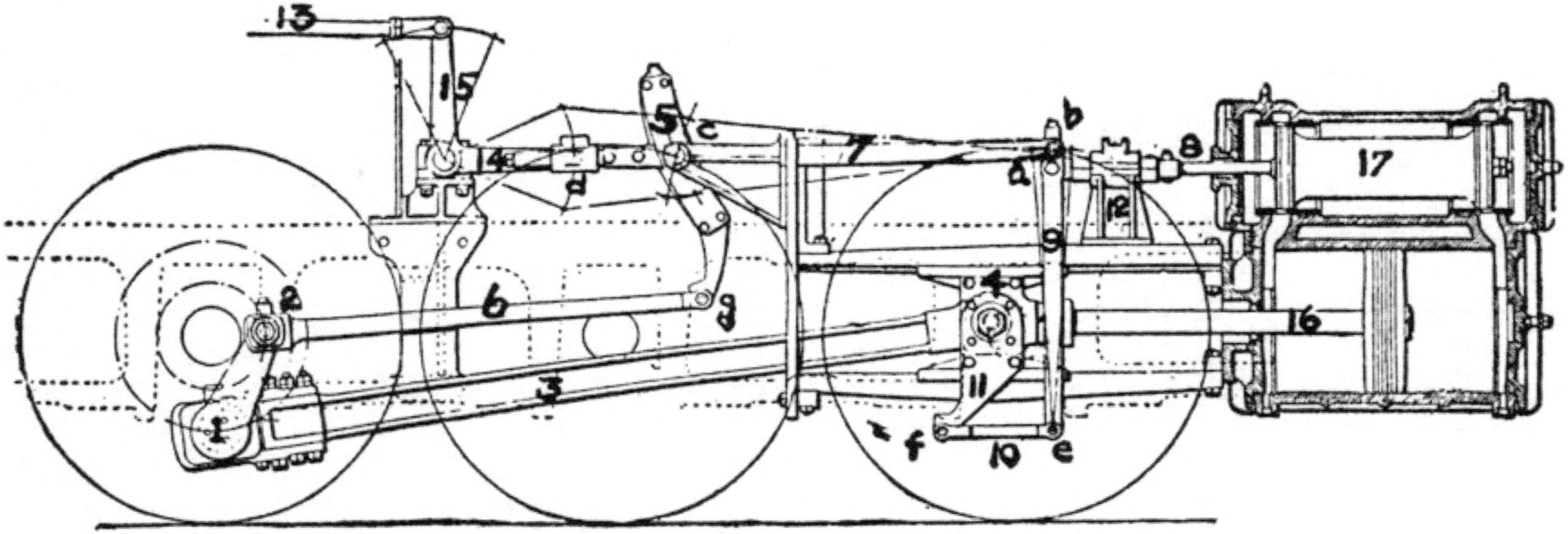

The Walschaert Valve Gear, with piston valve of inside admission, and list of names of different parts.

GENERAL INSTRUCTIONS FOR THE WALSCHAERT VALVE GEAR.*

In setting the Walschaert valve gear it must be borne in mind that two distinct motions are in combination, viz: The motion due to the crosshead travel, and the motion due to the eccentric throw.

The crosshead motion controls the lead, by moving the valve sufficiently to overcome its lap, by the amount of lead in both front and back positions. The eccentric throw controls the travel and reversing operations. It will be seen that the movement due to the eccentric, without the crosshead motion, would place the valve centrally over the ports when the piston is at the extreme end of the stroke. The combined effect of these two motions, when the parts are properly designed, gives the required movement of the valve, similar to that obtained by the use of a stationary link. To reverse the engine the link block is moved from end to end of the link, instead of moving the link on the block. This operation is accomplished by means of a reversing shaft connected with a reversing lever in the cab.

Walschaert gears should be correctly laid out and constructed from a diagram, as the proportions can not be tampered with by experimental changes without seriously affecting the correct working of the device.

The only part capable of variation in length is the eccentric rod, which connects the eccentric with the link. This rod may be slightly lengthened or shortened, to correct errors in location of the link center, from center of driving axle which carries the eccentric.

The eccentric usually assumes the form of a return crank on one of the crank pins, and its center is at right angles to the plane of motion, viz.: At ninety degrees to a line drawn from the point on the link at which the eccentric rod is attached, through the center of the driving axle. This eliminates the angular advance of the eccentric, and allows the use of a single eccentric for both forward and backward motion. The throw, as specified, must be correctly obtained, and great care taken that the position shown in the design be adhered to. The crank representing the eccentric is permanently fixed to the pin, and the slightest variation will be detrimental.

When the engine is assembled, the throw of the eccentric should be checked up by the specifications, and any error should be at once reported in order that the mistake may be rectified by either correcting the position of the eccentric, or by a change in the design of the other parts to compensate for the error.

In case of accident, if any of the rods or connections are broken, it is advisable if possible to disconnect the eccentric rod. The combining lever should be uncoupled from the crosshead and securely

---

*Formulated by the Baldwin Locomotive Works.

fastened in forward position. If for any reason the eccentric rod can not be taken down, the radius rod must be removed in order that no motion may be imparted to the valve. The valve can then be placed in central position and held either by suitable blocking or by clamping the valve rod. This seals both steam ports and cuts out the cylinder on the damaged side.

INSTRUCTIONS FOR ERECTING AND SETTING THE VALVES.

1.—Check carefully the dimensions of the following parts, rejecting any that are not exactly to drawing:
    a. Valve.
    b. Valve stem.
    c. Valve crosshead or slide.
    d. Combining lever.
    e. Crosshead link.
    f. Link radius rod.
    g. Reverse link.
    h. Location of combining lever on crosshead.
    k. Length of eccentric crank.

2.—Check eccentric throw to see that it is exactly as specified.

3.—Be sure that guide bearer is correctly located from center of cylinder, as the reverse link is usually attached to it, and variations in the location of the link can not be allowed. If the link is attached to separate crosstie, similar precautions must be taken to insure its correct location.

4.—Exercise great care in the location of the link so that the trunnion center is exactly to dimensions from the center of cylinder.

5.—See that the reverse shaft center is correctly located to dimensions given, and that the lifting arm and link are of the exact lengths as specified.

6.—Connect crosshead gear to valve, and radius rod to link, without connecting eccentric rod to link.

7.—Hook up radius rod to exact center of link, and then revolve driving wheels, seeing that crosshead gear gives correct lead as specified for both front and back admission ports.

8.—Connect link to return crank by eccentric rod, and obtain full travel front and back, and in both forward and backward motions, correcting any errors by lengthening or shortening eccentric rod, as previously noted.

The valves may now be considered as definitely set, and may be tested to any cut-off points in the usual manner.

A simple additional check should be made as follows:

Set one side of the engine so that piston is at its extreme forward position in cylinder, and check lead on admission port.

In this position it should be possible to move the link block through its entire travel in the link, without in any way disturbing the movement of the valve.

This operation should then be reversed, and the other side of the engine similarly tried with the piston located at its extreme backward position in the cylinder.

HELMHOLTZ MODIFICATION.

Among the various modifications of the Walschaert gear the one made by Helmholtz is probably of some advantage. This modification consists in making the link straight and the radius bar is connected to the lifting link instead of the link block. The curving of the link is compensated for by the reversing shaft or lifting arm fulcrum being located in a given position above the link so that the locus of the suspension point of the lifting link forms an arc of a circle with its chord perpendicular to the center line of the radius bar in its center position. The radius of this arc bears the same relation to the length of the radius bar as the distance of the radius bar connection above the link block bears to the length of the lifting link, which results in that this connection is moving in an arc with a radius of the length of the radius bar and the same motion of the valve is obtained as in the direct Walschaert gear.

Two advantages may be claimed for this modification, of which one is the straight link being simpler to make than the curved one, and the other is that on large piston valve engines with inside admission the link fulcrum can be lowered by the amount the radius bar connection falls over the link block, whereby the eccentric rod connection can be brought closer to the center line of the axle with less length of link and eccentric throw. It has, however, the disadvantage that there is little choice in the location of the reversing shaft or lifting arm fulcrum, a proper position for which is hardly obtainable on all types of engines and admits of no other method of lifting the radius bar in linking up or reversing the engine.

QUESTIONS AND ANSWERS ON THE WALSCHAERT VALVE GEAR

Q. 1.—What is meant by valve motion?

A.—Valve motion, or valve gear, refers to the system of rods, levers, etc., that tansmits motion to the main valve that is used to admit steam to, and exhaust it from, the cylinder of an engine; it is the action of the steam in the cylinder that empowers the piston.

Q. 2.—What are the principal parts of the Walschaert valve gear, and how do they act?

A.—First, the eccentric crank, attached to the main crank pin, which imparts motion to the valve through the connecting rods and levers, but one crank being used for both forward and backward motion instead of two eccentrics, as with the Stephenson gear; the eccentric rod, connecting the eccentric crank to the bottom of the link; the link, by means of which the engine is reversed and steam cut off as desired; the radius rod connecting the link to the combination lever; the union link connecting the crosshead to the combination or lap and lead lever; the combination or lap and lead lever connecting the union link to the valve stem and radius rod; the valve stem connecting the combination lever with the valve; the lifting arm connecting the radius rod with the tumbling or reverse shaft; the reach rod connecting the tumbling shaft with the reverse lever; the reverse lever and the quadrant. The action of the reverse lever, tumbling shaft and lifting arm is exactly the same with the Walschaert as with the Stephenson gear; the eccentric crank likewise acts the same as the eccentric on the Stephenson gear, in that the wheel as it rotates causes this crank to impart a forward and backward movement to the link through the eccentric rod. With the Walschaert gear, however, the link is not raised and lowered as with the Stephenson gear, the movement of the reverse lever simply moving the link block up and down in the link, the radius rod being connected to the link block; neither does the eccentric crank overcome the lap or impart lead to the valve as with the Stephenson gear, the lap being overcome and the lead imparted by means of the combination or lap and lead lever which is operated by means of the crosshead.

Q. 3.—What are the principal differences between the Stephenson and Walschaert valve gears, and what are the advantages of these?

A.—As explained above, the principal points of difference are that with the Stephenson gear two eccentrics are necessary on each side of the engine in order to impart forward and backward movement, while with the Walschaert gear but one eccentric crank is necessary. Also with the Stephenson gear the link is raised and lowered when the cut-off is to be altered and engine reversed, while with the Walschaert gear the link block is raised and lowered. Again, with the Stepehson gear the lap of the valve is overcome and lead is given by the eccentric, while with the Walschaert gear the lap is overcome and lead is given by means of the combination or lap and lead lever; also with the Stephenson gear the lead varies or increases as the lever is hooked up, while with the Walschaert gear the lead remains constant. Another advantage is, that the Walschaert gear is all outside, where it is easily inspected, lubricated, or repaired. The weight of the Walschaert gear is considerably less than that of a Stephenson gear for the same size engine. The Walschaert gear has less wearing parts and consequently is not so liable, as these parts wear, to produce an uneven steam distribution as with the Stephenson gear.

Q. 4.—What advantages has the Walschaert valve gear over the Stephenson link motion, aside from those generally known, such as convenience for inspection and repairs, reduced first cost, and greater durability?

A.—One of the chief advantages of the Walschaert gear is its wide range of adaptability. It may be applied to any design of locomotive without the aid of the usual accessories, such as transmission bars, unwieldy eccentric blades, and other features that tend to make the Stephenson gear expensive and cumbersome, as well as less durable than the other gear. It also permits of more substantial frame bracing, as the space between the drivers is free for any kind of bracing desired.

Q. 5.—Is the bottom of the link always used for the forward motion with Walschaert gear?

A.—The lower part of link usually is where the link block is placed with the lever in forward motion. The upper part of link is sometimes used for forward motion.

Q. 6.—With Walschaert gear how can one tell if engine has outside or inside admission valve?

A.—If the valve is inside admission, the radius rod is connected to top of combination lever, above valve stem, or valve stem crosshead connection with combination lever. If outside admission, the connection of combination lever with radius rod is below the point of its connection with valve stem crosshead. This change reverses the movement of valve with relation to the piston movement.

Q. 7.—What is meant by the "expansive force" of the steam?

A.—For the production of power, matter must first be changed in form or state, and its effort to return to its original form or state creates a force that may be employed and controlled. Through the action of heat, water in a locomotive boiler is changed to compressed steam, and in its effort to expand—to fill a larger space—this force is created; when the steam is being released through the cylinders of an engine its expansion, to make more room for itself, forces the piston from it; as it expands its pressure lessens, but if steam is continually admitted to the cylinder during the whole stroke of the piston its power continues undiminished, because the comparatively small cylinder is receiving the expansive effort from the whole boiler, and in this case expansion really drives the piston, but the term is not made use of. If the admission of steam from a boiler pressure of 100 pounds to a cylinder with a piston stroke of 24 inches should be closed after the piston has traveled, say 12 inches, the pressure against the piston at the instant of cessation of boiler supply would be, approximately, 100 pounds per square inch, but thereafter, as the piston was forced to advance in its travel, the pressure of the steam in the cylinder would decrease in inverse ratio to the increase in its volume—the increasing space between the piston and the pressure head of the cylinder—until, when the piston had completed its twenty-fourth inch of stroke, and if the exhaust had not yet commenced, the steam would have a pressure approximating 50 pounds per square inch, for the volume of the steam would then be twice what it was at the time of the cut-off of its supply. If the closure of steam supply had been earlier in the stroke than 12 inches the expansion would have been carried further, and the steam finally released from the cylinder at a still lower pressure; but in a locomotive cylinder steam is never expanded down to a pressure lower than that which will produce the required power. In starting a heavy train expansion, as we term it, is not made use of, while the lighter the train and the faster it is run, the shorter will be the duration of steam admission to the cylinder, with a consequent increase in the length of expansive effort of the steam at each stroke of the piston. Steam is capable of doing work until it has expanded down to an equivalent of atmospheric pressure, and at that stage will still exert a force of nearly 15 pounds to the square inch if a vacuum be produced on the opposite side of the piston by complete condensation of the exhaust steam. The engine that shows the greatest economy in the use of steam is the one in which there is the widest difference between the cylinder pressures at the times of steam admission and release.

Q. 8.—From where does valve gear, of any type, receive its actuation?

A.—As the valve controls the action of the piston its phases must be coincidental with certain regularly reoccuring phases of the piston's operation; therefore, the valve must receive its motion from some point or combination of points in the machinery that is actuated by the piston.

Q. 9.—What type of valve is required in association with the Walschaert style of gear?

A.—As with the common link motion, any type of valve that is in favor may be used with the Walschaert gear. The valve is not regarded really as a part of the valve gear.

Q. 10.—How many general types of valves are there in locomotive use?

A.—There are many styles of valves, but all are embraced within two general types—slide valves and piston valves. A slide valve, or "D-slide valve," so called because in sectional side elevation it has the appearance of a reclining capital letter D, has a flat, plane face bearing on its seat, and the admission of steam to the ports to each end of the cylinder is past the ends of the valve, while the exhaust is through the inside cavity, and a slide valve is, therefore, of "outside admission." If the total area of the top side of the slide valve was exposed to the full steam pressure from the boiler, it would cause the valve to work very hard on account of its high frictional resistance, but slide valves now have a large portion of the steam area balanced, causing them to work quite easily. Piston valves are in the form of a spool, the wide ends being really pistons similar to the main piston in the cylinder joined by the narrower tube of the spool, which is generally hollow, so that both ends of the valve chamber are in communication with each other, although some motive power officials use closed spools, as both ends of the valve chamber are otherwise in communication with each other. When piston valves are of outside admission the live boiler pressure occupies the ends of the valve chamber and the intermediate space between the pistons is open to the exhaust, so that the action is not unlike that of the D-slide valve. But most piston valves are of inside admission, wherein the ends of the valve chamber are open to the exhaust and the middle space holds the live steam; this balances the valve, fore and aft, perfectly, as the areas inside of the valve are equal, while outside end pressures on the valve are unequal, due to the space occupied by the valve-stem; with inside admission, also, there is no pressure against the valve stem packing, except that of the exhaust steam. When outside admission valves start to open an admission port to the cylinder, either regularly or for lead, they must move in the same direction the piston will move, while an inside admission valve must go in an opposite direction to the resulting travel of the piston, so that the live steam can pass from the inside of the valve to the admission port; and while it is doing this the port from the opposite end of the cylinder is open to the opposite end of the valve chamber and the exhaust.

Q. 11.—What is the theoretical position of the valve in relation to the piston, with either of the common types of locomotive valve gear?

A.—With outside admission the valve is always one-fourth of a cycle of motion, or double stroke, ahead of the piston; inside admission valves follow the piston by that distance.

Q. 12.—What is meant by direct or indirect valve motion?

A.—Valve motion is direct when there is no reversion in the line of motion between the eccentric and valve; indirect when there is such reversion, as by the double rocker arms of the Stephenson link motion, etc.

Q. 13.—What is lead?

A.—It has been stated that a valve of outside admission should travel one-fourth of a cycle in advance of the piston, and to obtain this result with direct motion the eccentric that actuates the valve must be located at a point on the axle, or wheel, just 90 degrees ahead of the main crank pin—in respect to the direction in which the engine is to run under the influence of that eccentric—and with indirect motion the location of the eccentric is 90 degrees behind the crank pin; but, with the eccentric so placed, when the crank pin was on either dead center, at the beginning of a stroke—the valve would be exactly centered on its seat with both steam admission ports widely covered—"widely," for the valve is considerably longer than the distance between the outer edges of the two admission ports—and as the wheels began to turn from the action of the engine on the other side the piston on this side would have been carried some distance in the cylinder before the valve would have moved far enough to uncover the admission port. In common practice, however, an alteration is effected in the gear whereby the valve—of either inside or outside admission—is advanced slightly further than its theoretical position, with the result that as the piston is nearing the end of its stroke, in either direction, the admission port will start to open. This gives a preadmission of steam against the piston that is expected to cushion the sudden stoppage of the motion work, and to provide a full opening for steam admission earlier in the course of the piston's stroke. This preliminary opening of the admission ports is referred to as the lead.

Q. 14.—Does lead have any further effects than those just stated?

A.—Yes; all of the regular events of the valve are hastened, and while steam will be admitted to the cylinder earlier in the course of the piston's stroke, it will be closed off correspondingly earlier; there is nothing in the matter of lead that can make the steam push against the piston during a longer part of the stroke than it would if lead were not present; in either case steam is admitted to the cylinder during the time that the crank is describing a certain number of degrees on the wheel's circle, and lead brings those degrees of force back to a point where the crank is effective—the dead center—with a consequent loss of power. Lead also causes an earlier closing of the exhaust, which in turn creates an undesirably high degree of compression between the piston and the cylinder head toward which it is advancing.

Q. 15.—Does not compression take place even though the valve should not be advanced for the purpose of securing lead?

A.—Yes; with any valve having lap, if it should be exactly central on its seat when the piston has arrived at the end of its stroke, there would be compression, for the reason that as the piston is nearing the end of the cylinder the valve is commencing to cover the exhaust opening, and before the piston has completed its stroke the exhaust is so strictured by the constantly lessening area of opening that even if the exhaust port is not entirely closed when the valve is on center there will be a certain amount of compression between the piston and cylinder head. But with the mere absence of lead opening of the admission port there will be a considerable amount of compression, for after the exhaust has closed the valve will have to travel the distance of its lap before the admission port is edge-and-edge with the valve, and while the valve is doing this distance the piston is moving through an equal proportion of its stroke, but toward the finish, with the exhaust port covered. So, in almost any conceivable case there is enough back pressure toward the finish of the piston's stroke to cushion its stop and the sudden reversal of the motion work, without the preadmission of live steam as lead for that purpose.

Q. 16.—What is it that causes this inevitable compression?

A.—It is due to the lap of the valve.

Q. 17.—What is the lap of the valve?

A.—As stated before, when the valve is centered exactly on its seat its front and back edges extend beyond the outside edges of the admission ports, and the distance that the valve so "overlaps" the ports is called the outside, or steam, lap, this with outside admission valves; with any kind of valve it is the distance the valve must be moved from an exactly central position on its seat until the admission port starts to open. With inside admission valves the steam lap is to the inside; the inner edges of the valve pistons overlap the admission ports by the same distance as do the outer edges of a slide valve of the same moments. The expansive strength of steam could not be obtained in an engine cylinder if its valve was without lap, for the lap of the valve extends the time between the completion of the cut-off of steam admission to the cylinder and the commencement of the exhaust opening from the cylinder.

Q. 18.—Then in order to secure preadmission of steam to the cylinder, or lead, the valve must be advanced in its direction of travel a distance equal to the lap plus the decided amount of lead opening?

A.—Yes; this should always be remembered.

Q. 19.—What is the method of securing this valve advance with the Stephenson link motion?

A.—It is accomplished by moving both the "go-ahead" and "back-up" eccentrics in the proper direction on the main shaft, or axle.

Q. 20.—How is lead obtained by the Walschaert gear?

A.—The device of the combination lever is employed in the Walschaert gear to produce the secondary motion of the valve by which it is advanced to overcome the delay in its movement due to the lap, and also to give the port opening for lead when such is desired; and to do this is the sole function of the combination lever. While in either type of gear the motion of the piston must eventually furnish every motion of the valve. The Stephenson plan must change the straight-line motion derived from the piston into the circular motion of the wheel and axle, and back again to the straight-line motion of the valve for each of its several functions, and this introduces errors impossible to entirely overcome. The Walschaert gear, however, takes the straight-line motion of the piston right at the crosshead and, through the combination lever, a short, diverting motion is imparted to the valve stem that most accurately shifts the position of the valve the required amount for lead.

Q. 21.—Then, if an engine with the Walschaert gear was standing with crank pin on the forward dead center, with cylinder cocks open, and the throttle should be opened if no steam should blow from the forward cylinder cock it would prove that this engine had no lead to the front admission port, would it not? And if the valve gear was correctly set up, would not the one foregoing test prove the amount of or absence of lead to the back admission port as well? And would not such test have the same result if made with the crank on either dead center?

A.—Yes to each question, because the combination lever gives exactly equal results at the finish of each stroke of the piston.

Q. 22.—And if an engine standing should prove to have no lead because no steam blew from the cylinder cock, would it still be necessary for a combination lever to be used?

A.—Yes. In the Walschaert gear the combination lever is a necessity whenever the valve has any steam lap, and all locomotive valves have.

Q. 23.—Does the amount of lead supplied by the Walschaert gear remain the same at all points of the cut-off?

A.—Yes; the lead is permanent for all points of cut-off, does not change, and can not be changed.

Q. 24.—In the Stephenson link motion does the lead vary?

A.—It does. The position of each eccentric is adjusted on the axle to a certain amount of lead when in full gear, but as the reverse lever is hooked up toward the center the lead increases in amount.

Q. 25.—Are there not different ideas held concerning the real meaning of the term "lead"?

A.—Yes. Many engineers refer to the shift in position of the Stephenson eccentrics, or the presence of the Walschaert combination lever, as simply for the purpose of securing lead, when, as explained, the valve may be set blind—without lead—yet still the valve should not be centered with the crank pin on a dead center.

Q. 26.—How may it be known from outward appearance whether with the Walschaert gear a piston valve is of inside or outside admission?

A.—This depends upon the individual design of the reversing gear principally, but in the strictly American style of construction, whereby the radius rod is lowered when the reverse lever is thrown forward and raised by throwing it back, and assuming an engine to be running forward, for the sake of distinction, with outside admission valves of either the D-slide or piston type, the eccentric is located 90 degrees ahead of the main crank pin, and the valve stem is connected to the upper end of the combination lever, with the radius rod connection to the combination lever beneath it; with inside admission valves the eccentric is located 90 degrees behind the crank pin, and the radius rod is connected to the upper end of the combination lever with the valve stem connection beneath it.

Q. 27.—Is the Walschaert valve gear of the type referred to as of "direct motion"?

A.—The Walschaert motion is either direct or indirect, according as to which direction the engine is running. When the radius rod is working below the center, or fulcrum, of the link there is a single direction of motion from the eccentric to the valve and the motion is direct; but with the radius rod working above the center of the link, the motion is indirect, for the reason that the link then acts as a double rocker-arm, and when the eccentric throws the lower end of the link in one direction the upper end of the link moves the valve the opposite way.

Q. 28.—In referring to "shorter cut-off," and "hooking-up," do not both expressions mean the same?

A.—"Shorter cut-off" is an effect with "hooking-up" as the cause. With the Walschaert gear, if the reverse should be set in either extreme end notch of the quadrant, it will cause the radius rod to be carried at either the extreme upper or lower end of the link, thus giving the valve its longest travel and admitting steam to the cylinder during the greater part of the piston's stroke. Hooking-up, means changing the position of the reverse lever to a notch nearer the center of the quadrant in either forward or back gear, and as this brings the radius rod and link-block correspondingly nearer to the center of the link, a shorter motion is imparted to the valve, and the admission of steam to the cylinder and the exhaust therefrom are cut off—cease—at earlier periods in the course of the piston's stroke. Hence the expression of "shorter cut-off."

Q. 29.—What further effects are produced in advancing the valve to create the lead opening, that can not be regarded as beneficial?

A.—The advance of the valve causes an earlier closing of the exhaust of the used steam from the cylinder, thereby creating higher compression ahead of the piston—between the piston and the cylinder head toward which it is traveling; the cut-off of live steam that is being admitted to the cylinder occurs sooner during the piston's stroke, and this detracts from the turning power of the main crank when the engine is working in full gear with a heavy load; and, as giving lead hastens all of the valve events, the steam that is driving the piston is retained in the cylinder during a shorter part of its stroke, and this earlier steam release is a loss of a certain per cent of the steam's expansive force.

Q. 30.—The Stephenson link motion may be either "direct" or "indirect." How about the Walschaert gear in this respect?

A.—The Walschaert gear is of direct motion when the reverse lever is forward of the central notch of the quadrant and the radius rod below the center of the link, for there is then a direct, or unreversed line of motion from eccentric to valve, the link acting as a single-arm rocker; it is of indirect motion with the reverse lever in any back-up notch, as then the radius rod is carried above the link center and the motion produced by the eccentric and transmitted to the lower end of the link by the eccentric rod is reversed by the oscillation of the link, and the motion it delivers to the radius rod and valve is in an opposite direction, therefore, to that received from the eccentric, the link in the latter case acting as a double-arm rocker.

Q. 31.—Will the eccentric of the Walschaert gear give any movement to the valve when the engine is running if the reverse lever is standing in the center notch of the quadrant?

A.—No; for then the radius rod is being carried at the center of the link and will receive no motion; but the valve will have the short travel derived from the crosshead, through the combination lever, a travel equal to twice the length of the valve's lap and lead added together. The pin in the forward end of the radius rod at this time acts as a fixed fulcrum to the combination lever which is receiving no motion except from the crosshead.

Q. 32.—When the reverse lever is forward of the center of the quadrant the radius rod is working in the lower half of the link, and with the lever back of the center the radius rod is in the upper half of the link—is it not?

A.—Such is common American practice; but if it will simplify the reversing gear the radius rod may work above the link center in the forward motion, and many European engines with Walschaert gear are so designed.

Q. 33.—Is it easier to secure equal cut-off of the admission of steam to each end of the cylinder with the Walschaert gear than with the Stephenson link motion?

A.—Yes; in the Walschaert gear the opening and closing moments of the ports are accomplished with equal precision in each direction of the valve's travel and can not be otherwise, for, as the piston moves in either direction from the center of the cylinder it causes the combination lever to move the valve in an opposite direction with outside admission, and in the same direction with inside admission valves of the piston type, but in either case the distance the valve is moved exactly equals a certain and fixed proportion of the distance of the piston's travel, this being the leverage proportions of the combination lever.

Q. 34.—The curve of the Stephenson link is from a backward radius. Why is the curve of the Walschaert link on a radius from ahead?

A.—As the radius rod, by its attachment to the link-block, may be carried at any point in the link according to the direction of motion and the point of cut-off, raising or lowering the radius rod from the center would put it at an untrue angle with the link if the curve of the link were not toward the radius rod and of a radius equal to the length of the radius rod from its pin connection with the combination lever to the link-block pin. Setting the engine on either dead center, for instance: The reverse lever may be brought from one end of its sector clear over to the farthest opposite notch without shifting the position of the valve in the slightest degree if all parts of the motion work have been correctly designed and properly set up, for, while the link-block is being moved from one end of the link slot to the other it is at all times equidistant from a fixed point represented by the location of the pin connecting the radius rod and combination lever when the radius rod is at the center of the link; to enable this to occur, the radius and direction of curve of the link must conform to the radius rod; and it is called the radius rod because its length determines the radius of the link's curvature.

Q. 35.—Is the eccentric rod always connected directly with the link foot?

A.—No; but it must have the same effect. Sometimes the valve chest lies so far in toward the center line of the engine that the link, to be in line, is also too far in for direct connection with the eccentric rod, and in such cases it is common for the link to have a supporting and carrying fulcrum pin on but one side—the outer side—and this fulcrum pin attached to the outer link bracket is lengthened to form a shaft working in a journal box, and extended outward far enough to have an arm attached to it in line with the eccentric rod; this arm reaches down as much farther than the lower end of the link as the link foot would extend, for the connection of the eccentric rod. When this method of connecting the eccentric rod with the link is employed there is, of course, no link foot, the link having exactly the same lengths above and below its central trunnion.

Q. 36.—Does the length of the radius rod hanger, and the location of its point of suspension, have any material effect on the action of the Walschaert gear?

A.—It does, to a remarkable degree. There is but one correct location for the point of suspension, and that point can only be determined by an expert designer of the gear, and any variation from the true focus will introduce serious error in the motion. As to the length of the suspension bar, that also has considerable influence on the action, but there is a variance of opinion as to the length of suspension bar that should give the more nearly correct results. On one of the earlier Mason engines the suspension bar extended from the radius rod to a lifting arm on a reversing shaft that was carried across the top of the boiler, while in a much later design of the Walschaert gear by the same builders the height of suspension above the radius rod was only equal to one-half the length of the link. The former was an extreme case, but the latter was not.

Q. 37.—Does the Walschaert gear admit of experimental changes or readjustments in the roundhouse or on the road, such as seem to be required with the common link motion?

A.—No; there is no portion of the Walschaert gear that can be lengthened or shortened, outside of the general repair shop, nor will there be any necessity for alterations in the motion work. Formerly it was the practice to fit the Walschaert eccentric rod with screw adjustments in order to correct through it any little variation in the proportions of other parts of the gear or slight errors in fixing the location of permanent positions of the gear forward of the eccentric. Such a screw take-up is impractical with the very heavy rods now used, but its length may be slightly changed by adjusting the bearings at the eccentric end on some engines. Even were it possible to do so no change should ever be made in the motion work of this gear ahead of the eccentric rod except in the "back shop."

Q. 38.—Does lost, or slack, motion appear in the Walschaert gear from wear at the connections or other sources as rapidly as it does in the Stephenson gear?

A.—No; and one of the greatest recommendations for the Walschaert gear is the almost entire absence of slack due to wearing away of the bearing parts, thus insuring continuous regularity in the distribution of steam to the cylinders. Under ordinary conditions an engine will run from shopping to shopping without having had any part of the Walschaert gear closed on account of worn looseness, and the engine will re-enter the shop with the valve gear cutting off the steam, often, with no perceptible loss in economy; this is largely due to the fact that all connections are made with pins working in bushings, all case-hardened, and no large eccentrics with the enormous frictional surfaces of their sheave and strap.

Q. 39.—The Walschaert eccentric is always referred to as being located 90 degrees from the main crank pin. Is this correct?

A.—Actually measured in degrees the Walschaert eccentric will usually be found to be located somewhat nearer to the crank pin than the nominal 90 degrees when outside admission valves are used, and an engine with exactly the same set-up of gear except in having inside admission valves would have the eccentric placed just the same number of degrees more than 90 away from the crank pin.

It must be remembered that the link is so centered with the valve as to impart to it a motion free from the result of incorrect angles, and in order to obtain that result the link is hung so high that there is an undesirable angle in the transmission of motion from the eccentric to the link. The ideally correct design of the Walschaert gear locates the connection of eccentric rod to link exactly on the center line through the axle, and when so placed in actual construction the eccentric will be located exactly 90 degrees from the crank pin; but, as explained, this location is not commonly obtained on modern locomotives; if the link foot was extended down to receive the eccentric rod connection at the theoretically correct location its length would shorten the throw of the link to an impossible extent, so a compromise is effected; the link foot is extended as low as may be permissible, and to correct the error still existing, due to the angularity of the eccentric rod's position, the location of the eccentric is slightly shifted in the indicated direction.

Q. 40.—While an engine is running the bounding up and down due to the spring action affects the proper working of the Stephenson gear, causing imperfect steam distribution. What effect does the rough carriage of the engine have on the Walschaert gear?

A.—It has no discernable effect, and when the link is set low enough that with the crank pin on the dead center the pin connecting the eccentric rod with the link foot will be on the horizontal center line through the axle—its theoretically correct location—the rise and fall of the engine will then have absolutely no effect on the motion imparted to the valve.

Q. 41.—By reason of the return crank projecting the Walschaert eccentric out and further from the driving box than the Stephenson eccentrics are usually placed, is it not the case that lost motion in the driving boxes will introduce greater irregularities in the action of the Walschaert valve gear?

A.—Not at all; for, while the Walschaert eccentric may be deflected slightly further than those of the Stephenson type, lost motion in the boxes is largely dissipated by the very great lever length between the suspension pins of the link and the eccentric rod connection with the link foot, and through which any motion engendered by the eccentric is reduced by a certain and considerable proportion when transmitted to the radius rod and valve. Loose driving boxes should not be permitted, however, as the general effectiveness of an engine with any style of valve gear is seriously impaired when the driving boxes are in such condition that setting up the wedges will not remove the lost motion at those points.

Q. 42.—Do the connections or other bearing parts of the Walschaert gear have a tendency to heat in service?

A.—No. This valve gear is peculiarly free from any disposition toward heating; there have been certain cases where it has not been designed to meet the unusual conditions of track and service, and the eccentric rod pins have heated on account of the twisting effect, on rough track, between the parts carried by the driving wheel and the parts carried by the main frame. Such troubles are not constitutional, are easily cured and never need to have existed.

Q. 43.—In connection with the Walschaert gear, how may the valve be exactly centered upon its seat so that with open throttle steam will not blow from the open cylinder cocks?

A.—With valves of either inside or outside admission, when the crosshead is at the exact center of its travel with crank pin on the upper or lower working quarter, reverse lever in center notch of the quadrant and the combination lever standing—as it must—in a plumb, vertical position, its two upper connection pins on the same vertical line—then the valve is at the perfect center.

Q. 44.—What is the meaning of the above reference to the crank pin as being on the "working quarter"?

A.—As explained in answer to a previous question, when the crank pin is on the perfect quarter it is on a vertical line through the hub center, either above or below it, but owing to the angularity of the main rod the piston is not then at the exact center of its stroke; but when the piston is at the true center of the cylinder—as outwardly indicated by the crosshead lying at the center of its travel in the guides—the crank pin is then a few degrees forward of the true quarter, but is usually referred to as being on the quarter at that time—therefore the working quarter. This difference sometimes causes confusion, and in alluding to the placing of an engine "on the quarter" it should be stated whether the quarter is to be fixed in reference to the position of the crosshead or crank pin.

Q. 45.—If an engine with the Walschaert gear is standing on the working quarter, the piston at the exact center of the cylinder and the reverse lever in the center notch of the quadrant, suppose that the valve was not truly centered—steam would blow from one of the cylinder cocks with the throttle open. What would be the cause, and how could the cause be detected and remedied?

A.—With the gear in this position there would have to be an extensive error indeed to allow steam to blow from a cylinder cock, as this would indicate a false movement of the valve more than equaling the length of its lap, and might be caused by a piston valve loose on the stem, or a broken yoke with a slide valve. However, if error is indicated in the position of the valve, first be sure that the reverse lever is in the center notch; if the notch is indicated there may have been a mistake in laying out the notches or in setting up the quadrant, but if the link trunnion and link block pin coincide exactly that is what we want and the reverse lever is centered all right, and in that case if the piston is also truly centered and the valve is not, probably the link bearer, which is commonly attached to the guides, varies a little in its position, fore or aft, and should be moved far enough to correct the error; or the valve valve stem can be lengthened or shortened, but as this induces other minor errors the other method would be preferable.

Q. 46.—If the link bearer should be moved, thus shifting the fulcrum of the link, would not other variations in the gear be introduced thereby?

A.—The resetting of the link fulcrum might be just what was needed to perfect the whole valve motion if it had been set up untrue; but it might be that while adjusting the location of the link fulcrum would square the valve, by the radius rod at the link center, with the reverse lever in a working notch, there would be unequal cut-off by the valve still, for the difference made by this change would have to be borne by the eccentric rod and to finally true up the motion it might have to be lengthened or shortened as required.

Q. 47.—Give directions for adjusting the length of the eccentric.

A.—Set the engine with the crank pins on the forward dead center, and have the reverse lever moved from the corner notch in forward gear up to the center of the quadrant, and if the valve stem is moved forward at all while the radius rod is rising the eccentric rod should be lengthened; or, if the valve stem is drawn backward as the radius rod is guided upward by the link the eccentric rod needs shortening. In either case, of course, the alteration should be by degrees, each one very slight and tests constantly repeated, until drawing the reverse lever from the corner up to the center notch will impart no movement whatever to the combination lever and the valve stem. For a general test try in the same manner and alter if necessary the eccentric rod on the other side of the engine, but starting the test with the crank pin on the back dead center.

It is a fundamental principle of the Walschaert gear that the motion work forward of the link, including the link bearer, is permanently set up and supported by rigid attachments to the guides, guide yoke and cylinder casting; the eccentric rod, however, represents the unstable distance between the rigidly carried gear and the main driving wheel, and as this distance will vary from wear in the driving boxes, the length of the eccentric rod should be tested as directed, occasionally, and if necessary, shortened or lengthened.

Q. 48.—Why is it so important that the Walschaert motion work should be supported by attachments in rigid connection with the cylinder casting?

A.—Any style of valve motion is designed to simply furnish a sort of reciprocating action between the piston and the valve; both work in practically the same body casting and are in permanent alignment, and the motion of one will be transmitted without error to the other if the associated arrangement of gear that develops the transmission is solidly attached to the body occupied by the piston and valve; in the common erection of the Walschaert gear the motion work is borne at but three supporting points—the link fulcrum, the reversing shaft, and the valve stem slide; the first two are carried on brackets attached to the guide bearer, or yoke, and the valve stem slide is either mounted on the upper guide bar or the slide bar is connected to the cylinder body at one end and to the guide yoke at the other. Therefore the accuracy of the Walschaert gear is not affected by the roll and twisting effect of an engine in motion.

Q. 49.—Besides furnishing a practically perfect locomotive valve motion, is not the Walschaert gear more desirable in other ways?

A.—Yes; in many ways; the absence of heating is a great feature, and as the whole motion work is outside of the engine frame a chance for perfect inspection is furnished, every part can be easily and economically oiled, and in case of breakdowns in the gear repairs can be most quickly made, as there will be no necessity for getting under the engine; and the removal of the gear from inside the frame offers a fine opportunity for better frame bracing, and at the point where most needed on the large engines now in service.

Q. 50.—When an engine equipped with the Walschaert gear becomes disabled on one side while on the road, is there any considerable difference in the methods employed in getting the engine in condition to proceed than if the Stephenson motion was employed?

A.—A great deal of difference. Enough to make it worth while taking up the several points of possible derangement. Some details are the same, however, in all cases—blocking the valve, for instance, may be done in the same way whenever necessary, and in the same way whether either type of valve gear is used, etc., and while a breakdown in the Stephenson motion work is quite common it doesn't frequently happen to the Walschaert gear, and engine failures are seldom charged to that account, but when a breakdown does occur repairs can be much quicker made to the Walschaert gear, exposed as it is, outside the frame.

Q. 51.—"Blocking the valve" has been mentioned; what is meant, and when and how should it be done?

A.—In almost every case of an engine becoming disabled so that the cylinder power can not be used on one side, if the engine is to proceed under her own steam by the power of the other side the valve on the disabled side should be placed in an exactly central position on its seat; the words "exactly central position" are to be taken literally, for it is not only to have both admission ports covered so that no steam can enter the cylinder, but because in that position both ends of the cylinder will be in communication with each other through the exhaust cavity of the slide valve, or through the passage in the spool of the piston valve of inside admission—this, of course, with valves having exhaust lead.

After the necessary disconnections of the motive and valve gear have been made the valve on the disabled side of the engine must be centered by moving on the valve stem and judging from its travel when correctly centered; a better way, with the Walschaert gear, however, is if the radius rod is not damaged have it placed at the center of the link—by putting the reverse lever in its center notch, if possible, and then fixing the combination lever in its central position so that its two upper connection pins are on a vertical line with each other; the valve will then be exactly centered.

After it is seen that no steam will blow from the opened cylinder cocks on the broken-down side with the throttle slightly opened, however, the valve is practically centered, but in any case it is best to disconnect the cylinder cock rigging on that side so that the cocks can be left permanently open and permit those on the other side to be worked at will, in order to afford relief against compression in the cylinder from the travel of the piston if the main rod is left up, in place, and also for detection in case the valve should get shifted off center by showing steam at one of the cocks; some engineers prefer to unscrew and remove the cocks entirely. When the cylinder is fitted with plugs for indicator connections their removal will obviate the necessity of disconnecting the cylinder cock rigging.

On many roads a clamp is carried on each engine to secure the valve stem immovably with and fix the valve on the correct center in case of breakdowns, but where such clamp is not at hand it has been generally the custom to raise the steam chest cover, where a D-slide valve is concerned, and place retaining blocks in front and behind the valve, wedging them in, and so secure it in position; but it is out of the question to try to raise the cover of the steam chest on one of our big, modern engines and it is safe enough, under the charge of a watchful, competent engineer, to omit the actual blocking, for, after the valve has been centered, when steam is used its pressure on the unbalanced area of the slide valve will be great enough to hold it beyond any danger of moving, except in case of bumping up against cars, and then the engineer will be warned by the steam from one of the open cylinder cocks. An advantage in not permanently securing the valve is that, where the main rod has not been taken down, if the live side should stop on the dead center the valve on the disabled side could be moved by the stem off center, to open the proper admission port, and steam then used to move the engine just far enough to get the working side off the center, stopping at the right moment with the air brakes, and then with steam shut off the valve can again be centered.

Piston valves of inside admission are perfectly balanced, fore and aft, and without blocking will usually remain centered by the pressure of the steam setting out the packing rings against the walls of the valve chest.

In times past engineers have been disciplined for not disconnecting the main rod on the disabled side of the engine and allowing the piston to churn in the cylinder; now, however, the weight of the main rod makes taking it down on the road prohibitive, and it has been found that no trouble need result from leaving it up if the engineer understands his business; if he does, he will let the lubricator feed to the steam chest on the disabled side as usual and at certain stops, if the valve is not blocked inside the steam chest, he will move it far enough to uncover one of the admission ports (even if not necessary to do so to work the other side off the dead center) and open the throttle slightly to blow the accumulated oil into the cylinder.

Q. 52.—With the Stephenson gear when the main rod is left up on the disabled side of an engine its motion can not affect any part of the valve gear, but with the Walschaert type of gear would it not give impulse to the combination lever, and should not the combination lever then be taken down?

A.—Through the crosshead motion would be imparted to the combination lever, but it need not be taken down, for its motion should not affect the valve, on account of disconnections made elsewhere in the gear.

Q. 53.—Whenever a valve is "blocked" or centered, it must be disconnected of course, from any part of the gear that would impart motion to it, and with the Stephenson link motion the valve stem is the general point of disconnection; would that be the recommended practice in connection with the Walschaert gear?

A.—No; it is inconvenient and unnecessary to disconnect the Walschaert valve stem—inconvenient, because there is no joint between the valve and the slide that carries the end of the valve stem, and unnecessary, for the reason that the radius rod must always be disconnected when the valve is blocked, and that removes the fulcruming point of the combination lever. For a lever to transmit motion it must have three points for the reception and transmission of power, and with the radius rod removed the combination lever is left with only the crosshead connection at the lower end and its upper end connected to the valve stem slide, the latter acting as a fixed suspension point for the pendulum-like swing of the combination lever in unison with the strokes of the piston.

Q. 54.—As the disconnection of the radius rod takes the place of, and with the same effect, as disconnecting the valve stem of the Stephenson link motion, it will be frequently referred to in the following answers to questions relating to breakdowns, and to avoid repetitions explain once for all, in detail, how it should be done.

A.—In many cases the radius rod will not need to be removed; where there is but a short distance for the engine to go, or it may be run slowly, remove the pin from point of radius rod and combination lever and raise the front of the rod above any chance of interference with the lever, suspending the front end of the rod by strong rope or wiring of a length that will permit it to swing freely to the motion of the link without striking anything; then just center the valve in the manner already described and proceed slowly. This method, of course, is only to be resorted to where it is merely desired to get to the nearest siding with the engine, which must be run very slowly or the radius rod will kick-off the running board.

If it is desired to so fix up the disabled side of an engine that she can use the power of the other side to finish the run and make the time with what she can pull in safety, set the reverse lever in the center notch in order to center the link block, in which position the link can give no motion to the radius rod; then fit a block of wood within the link slot and under the link block to support the latter, and disconnect the suspension bar from the radius rod, and also from the lifting arm if it will be in the way of the swing of the link; disconnect the front end of the radius rod from the combination lever and raise and secure it as before mentioned, but with a shorter suspension, as there will be no swing to it now. The slot above the link block should also be filled in with a piece of wood to prevent the link block from jumping up from the center and giving a thrust to the radius rod. It is not absolutely necessary to block within the link slot, as wooden pieces may be fitted under and over the radius rod, between its jaws and the ends of the link bracket, but in this case the ends of the pieces that are in contact with the radius rod must be rounded to roll against it as the link swings.

The radius rod having been disconnected from the combination lever, the motion of the lower end of the lever will have no effect on the valve, which may now be centered and secured—or trusted to "stay put" as heretofore explained. As the engine starts to move watch closely the motion of the combination lever during the first revolution of the driving wheels, to see that it does not strike the pin connecting the main rod with the crosshead, as the relative positions assumed by this pin and the combination lever are changed by the removal of the influence of the radius rod.

Q. 55.—If the eccentric rod of the Walschaert gear should break, what should be done?

A.—Remove the broken parts, and drop the reverse lever to the go-ahead corner notch; then disconnect the suspension bar from the radius rod on the disabled side of the engine, permitting the link block to rest at the bottom of the link, and disconnect the radius rod from the combination lever, raising the front end of the radius rod above any chance of interference and securing it there in order to keep the link from swinging. Center the valve in the prescribed manner and proceed.

Q. 56.—What should you do in case of a broken valve stem?

A.—The radius rod should be centered securely in the link, disconnected from hanger and combination lever and wired up at the front end as previously explained; then center the valve in the recommended manner and block, or otherwise secure, the valve stem slide against any movement on the slide bar that might be caused by the swing of the combination lever, as it has not the frictional resistance of the valve to hold it in a fixed position, now, but be sure to place the slide at a point where the combination lever will be carried without striking the pin that connects main rod and crosshead.

Q. 57.—How would you get along with a case where the radius rod was broken forward of the link?

A.—Would remove all parts of the broken rod, disconnecting same from the suspension bar and combination lever, and also from the link block, unless there was a long enough piece left attached forward of the link to permit of wiring it up and securing the link block in the center of the link, which could be done in that case. Center the valve in the manner referred to and go on. But under any circumstances in which the radius rod has been disconnected always remember the importance of seeing that the combination lever will swing clear of the wrist pin in the crosshead, and that the suspension bar will be out of the way of the swing of the link.

Q. 58.—If the suspension bar should break, or, where it is connected to an extension of the radius rod beyond and back of the link if that extension of the radius rod should break, what should be done?

A.—In either case place the reverse lever in a notch of the quadrant that will give the valve an average cut-off, or in which it may be continuously worked—forward or back gear, according to the direction in which the engine is to run—raise the radius rod with the broken piece, or hanger, until the link block is at the same height in the link as the one on the other side of the engine, and insert a piece of wood in the link slot under the link block to hold it up, and another piece above the link block to keep it from slipping up. Remove the broken parts and proceed, remembering not to reverse the engine nor to change the reverse lever to another notch.

Q. 59.—What should be done in case the combination lever, or the vibrating link that connects it with the crosshead, should be broken?

A.—If the combination lever is broken disconnect and remove all pieces that are not in connection with the valve stem slide; if it be the long arm of the combination lever that is broken, or the vibrating link, take down the vibrating link also, and if the piece of lever remaining attached to the valve stem slide is long enough to be in the path of the pin in the crosshead, either remove the piece or draw it out of the way and secure it there. Center the valve and disconnect the radius rod, both as heretofore explained, and go on.

Q. 60.—In all of the cases so far it has been understood that the main rod has been left in place; suppose, however, that the main rod should be broken, compelling its removal—what ought to be done?

A.—After taking down the broken parts of the main rod and disconnecting the radius rod, if the valve is of inside admission, push it to the forward end of the steam chest and clamp the valve stem or block the valve stem slide to secure it in that position; with a valve of outside admission draw it to the back end of its travel and secure it there; the idea is to hold the forward port open for steam admission against the front of the piston, and the back port open from the opposite side of the piston to the exhaust; the crosshead should then be drawn back until the piston is against the back cylinder head. This is called "steam blocking," for when steam is used it will hold the piston in its fixed position. Then you can go on, but after drifting any distance, shut off, use steam carefully at first for fear the piston may have also drifted forward a little way in the cylinder and will be pounded back to the head too severely; it is better, therefore, to fasten a piece of wood to fit in the guides ahead of the crosshead.

Q. 61.—Engines with the Stephenson link motion are totally unfitted to run under their own steam if but one section of side rod should break when it happens that the eccentrics are mounted on a different axle than the one worked directly by the main rod, and if the broken side rod is the one connecting the wheels of the eccentrics' axle with the wheels carrying the main rod on either side of the engine. Could the breaking of any section of side rod, only, have the effect of completely disabling an engine equipped with the Walschaert valve gear?

A.—No; the eccentric of the Walschaert gear is always mounted on the main pair of wheels—the wheels worked directly by the main rod—and therefore the removal of all sections of side rods on both sides of the engine could in no way affect the valve motion. If, however, any one section of the side rod should break, the corresponding section of rod on the other side of the engine should be taken down; the only result from doing so will be to make the engine more slippery and very hard to hold to the rail—if equipped with the Walschaert valve gear.

Q. 62.—If the piston should be broken, or loose from the piston rod in the cylinder, what repairs are required?

A.—Commonly the result of this accident is to tear off, or break, the front cylinder head, but the head should be removed whether injured or not, and the piston extracted from the cylinder; if the piston rod is not bent disconnect the radius rod and center the valve in the prescribed manner—except that of course the cylinder cocks will not need to be fixed open nor taken out on the disabled side—and move on.

Q. 63.—In case of a bent piston rod, what should be done?

A.—Take down the main rod, disconnect the radius rod in the regular manner and center the valve securely. Use your own judgment as to blocking the crosshead—the piston and rod will usually be so cramped as to make blocking unnecessary.

Q. 64.—In the too common case of blowing out a front cylinder head, what should you do?

A.—Disconnect the radius rod and center the valve, both by the instructed method, except that in this case if the fixed-open cylinder cocks will not afford relief for the compression from the piston's back stroke it is only necessary to remove one—the back—cylinder cock; or better still, where there is one, unscrew the indicator plug from the back end of the cylinder. In this case of running with the main rod up one of the objectionable features in doing so is removed—the general lack of facilities for oiling the piston in the cylinder—for with the front head off oil can easily be introduced.

When the back cylinder head is broken, it is best to proceed as directed in the case of bent piston rod.

Q. 65.—If disconnection of the radius rod in the Walschaert gear has the same effect as disconnecting the valve stem of the common link motion, then the radius rod will have to come down whenever the engine is so disabled on one side that the valve must be blocked; so you will explain in detail how one should go about it.

A.—The radius rod need not be *taken down* in all such cases of disability, but will always have to be, at least, disconnected.

Remove the pin from the joint of radius rod and combination lever and raise the disconnected end of the radius rod just above any chance of interference with the combination lever, suspending the rod by strong wiring or rope of such length as to permit it to swing freely to the motion of the link, taking particular care that the suspended end of the radius rod will not strike anything else. This method should only be resorted to, however, when the engine has only a short distance to go to reach its terminal and can be run at a moderate speed only. In answer to subsequent questions on breakdowns, the following instructions for disconnecting the radius rod should be observed:

If the engine is to be run any considerable distance, or may be speeded up at times, with one side disabled, a safer and more commendable method is, first, place the reverse lever in the center notch of the quadrant in order to get the back end of the radius rod and the link block in the exact center of the link; then saw a couple of pieces of wood to fit, and insert them between the bottom of the link and the link block, and secure them in position in order to support the back end of the radius rod at the center of the link; now disconnect the hanger between lifting arm and radius rod and take out the pin from the front end of the latter at its connection with the combination lever, wiring the radius rod up, as previously directed, or suspending it by anything that will support its weight, as there will be no motion imparted to it now. After centering the valve, and blocking it or clamping the valve stem—or trusting that the pressure of the steam will hold it in its central position— it will not be necessary to do anything with the combination lever, as the motion imparted to its lower end will not be likely to affect the valve, even if not clamped; but,—after disconnecting the radius rod from the combination lever, always watch the first movement of the crosshead *to see that the combination lever does not strike the wrist pin*—the pin by which the front end of the main rod is connected to the crosshead—as the motion of the lever is altered by the disconnection and pause of its upper end. Blocks of the proper size to hold the radius rod in the center of the link, and with their upper ends shaped half round, should be carried on all engines equipped with the Walschaert valve gear.

Q. 66.—What is meant by the above expression of the mainpin being on the "working quarter"?

A.—When the mainpin is on the *actual* quarter—either the upper or lower—it is on a perpendicular line through the center of the axle, but the piston will not be in the exact center of the cylinder, owing to the angularity of the main rod. On the other hand, if the piston *is* at the true center of the cylinder—as was supposed in the foregoing question—the mainpin will be a slight distance away from the perpendicular line through the center of the wheel, or axle, but it is now on the *working* quarter because, technically, it has half completed a single stroke; if the back end of the main rod should now be disconnected from the mainpin and dropped, or raised, as the case demands, until it was on a horizontal line, the opening for the mainpin in the sub end of the main rod would center, exactly, over the center of the wheel hub, proving that it was half-way in its stroke. The longer the main rod the less its angularity, and the lesser will be the difference between the actual and the working quarter positions of the mainpin.

Q. 67.—Describe the Walschaert link in detail.

A.—The reversing links used in connection with the Walschaert gear by different engine builders, and on locomotives of different types, vary somewhat in design; some are open links nearly like those of the Stephenson link motion, but generally they are very similar to the one illustrated.

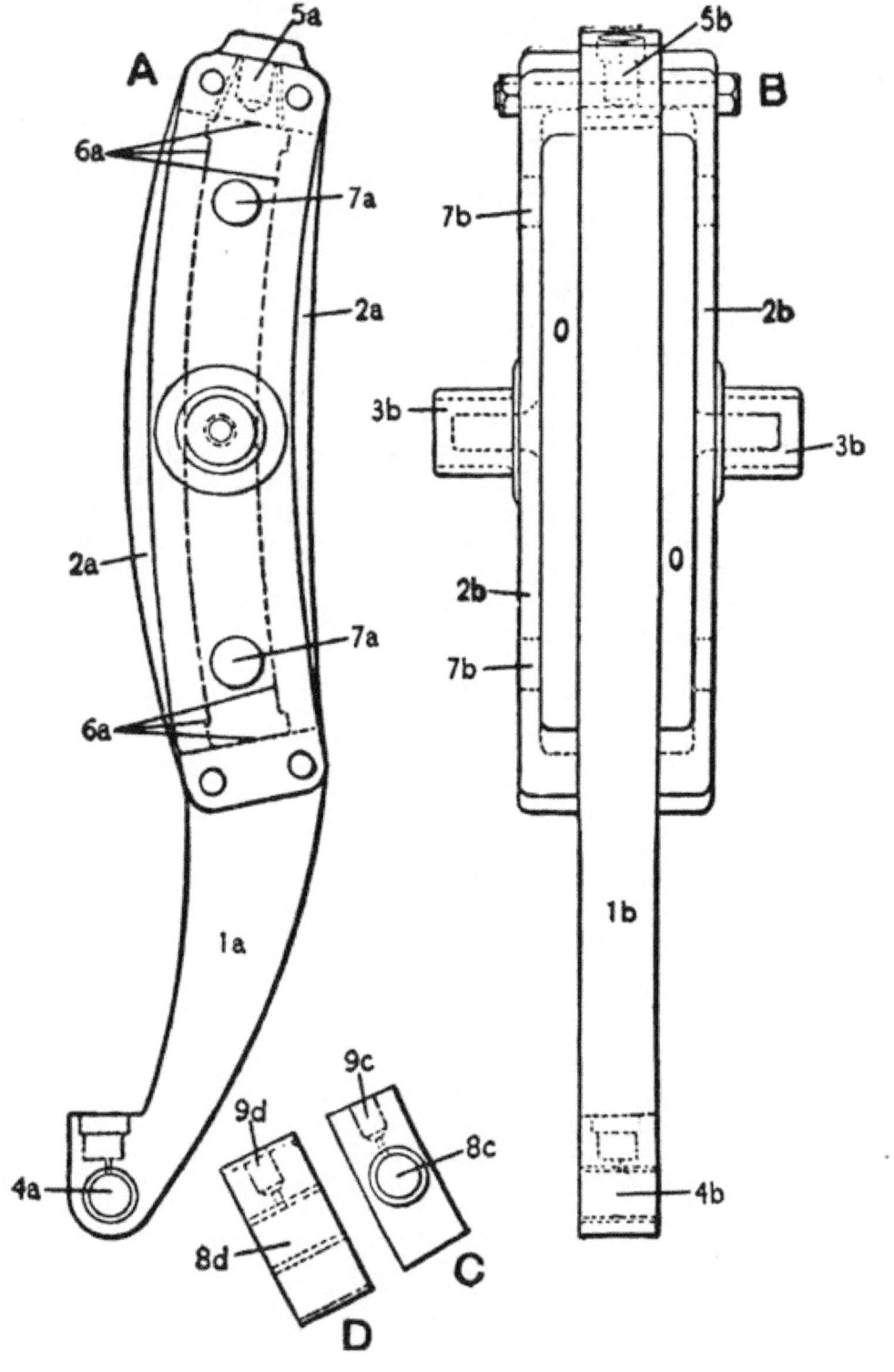

The piece that forms the link proper, and has the slot that holds the link block, is extended down much further than the slot, in order to take the eccentric rod connection as near as possible to the horizontal line through the wheel's center, this lower extension forming the link foot; the link piece is shown in side elevation A as $1a$, and in end view B as $1b$; it is forged from wrought iron and case-hardened. The frame that carries the link piece is composed of the two bracket pieces $2b$, in view B, one on each side, with their ends bolted to the link piece; they are of cast steel, each including the fulcrum pin $3b$ by which the link is suspended and which are designed to be even with the center of the link slot, both vertically and horizontally; a case-hardened bushing of wrought iron is pressed onto these link trunnions, or fulcrum pins, in order to prevent any lost motion from wear. The pin hole in the link foot, $4a$, $4b$, to which the eccentric rod is connected, is also fitted with a wrought iron, case-hardened bushing. In view A, the slot in the link piece in which the link block operates is in dotted outline, as indicated by $6a$, $6a$, and the link block is shown in the views C and D; C is the side of the block and as it would appear if raised to its position in the link slot in the view A, and the edge of the block is shown in view D as it would lie in the link turned to the endwise view B, and when in place in the slot the sides of the block are almost flush with the sides of the link piece to afford room for the jaws of the radius rod to pass inside of the brackets; the hole $8c$, $8d$, is for the pin by which the radius rod is attached to the link block, and this hole, like the others, is also bushed with case-hardened wrought iron.

The Baker Valve Gear*

The Baker Valve Gear is an outside radial gear, *i. e.*, it has no links or sliding blocks. The movement is derived from the crosshead and the eccentric crank. The crosshead moves the valve the amount of the lap and lead each way, and the eccentric crank gives the remainder of the movement. In the short cut-offs the actual effect of the eccentric crank is reduced, while the crosshead movement is constant.

The bearings are all pins and bushings, the latter being ground inside and out to a standard gauge. The pins are case-hardened and ground to size on both the bearing and tapers.

No loose oil cups are employed; each bearing has an oil reservoir or cup which is made integral with the part. These cavities can be filled with waste or curled hair to retain the oil, obviating the danger of a bearing running dry on the longest runs. All these bearing pins and bolts are exposed to view so that they can be got at to be removed by the engineman or repairman. Three pins, or two pins and a bolt, remove the hardest piece to be taken down. The heaviest piece, the bell crank, weighs only 86 pounds.

Standardization of Parts. This has been reached to some extent in the Baker Gear as all the outside admission gears of this make are alike and all the inside gears are the same, no matter what the type or class of engine upon which used. The yokes and radius bars are also the same for both admissions. The combination lever must suit the stroke of the engine and the lap and lead. Since there is not enough difference in the power it takes to operate a valve on different modern engines it does not warrant different sized gears. With other gears there is not much, if any, difference in the cross-section area of the same part on the different engines. All parts are interchangeable, and the castings, including the frame, are the same for both sides of the engine, except the gear connection rod. The combination lever has rights and lefts, but they are drop-forged.

The frame is one piece cast steel, the same casting on both sides of the engine; one type for inside admission and another type for outside admission. The frame is designed with an extension so that the same frame will go on a variety of engines. This reduces to the minimum the number of kinds of frames that any road may have. So far two designs of outside and one design of inside admission frame have been used.

Alignment. Every part of the gear is symmetrical with respect to the center line of the gear, and all pins are supported on each end. This makes a straight line motion, and prevents the possibility of a twisting effect on any part. This construction is claimed to increase the strength of the gear and also the wearing quality of the bearings.

---

* By courtesy of the Pilloid Co.

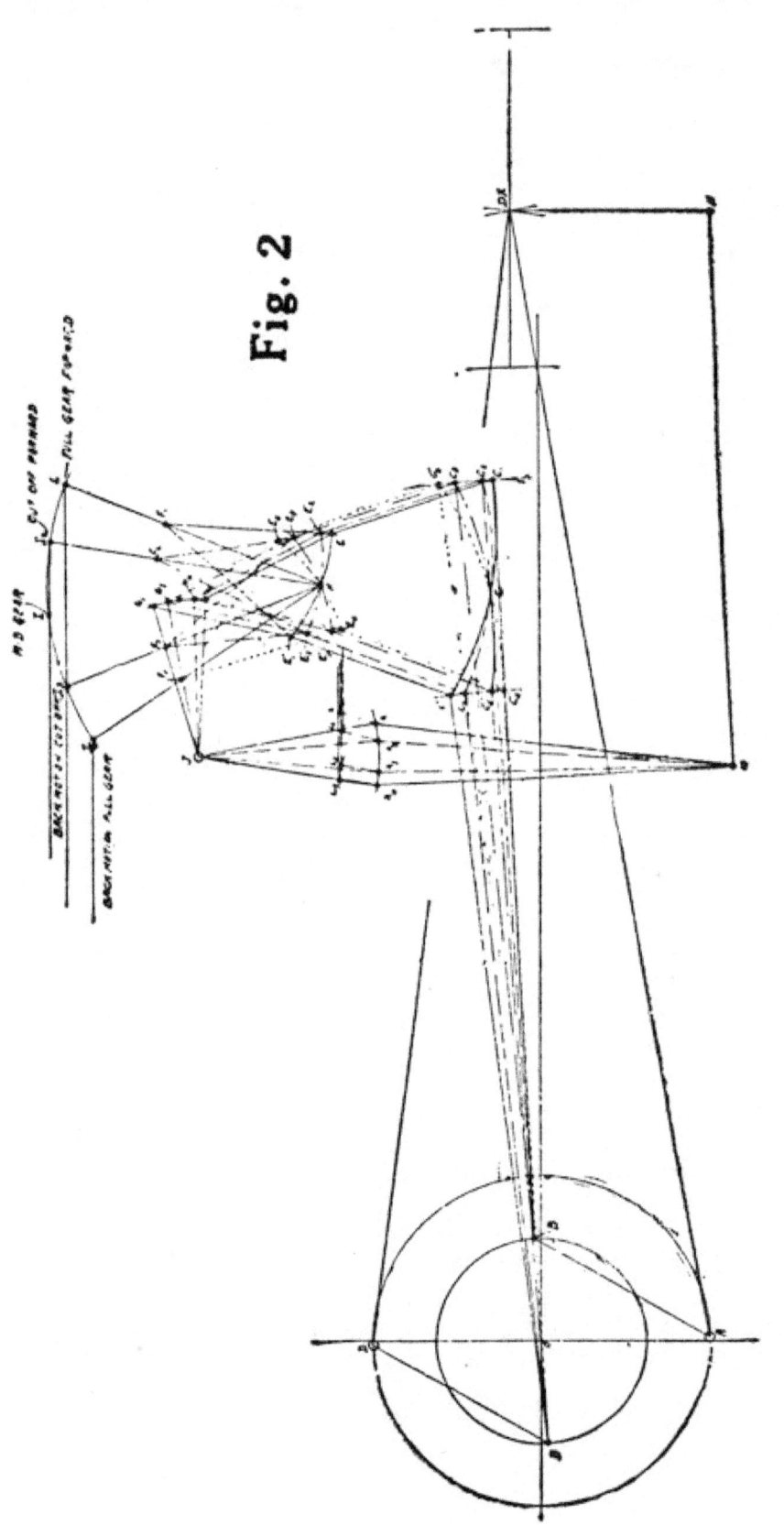

Lead and Preadmission. The Baker Gear has a constant lead with a variable preadmission. The objections to a constant lead have been that it retarded the engine while running in full gear and did not give compression enough in the short cut-offs.

It makes no difference what lead there is in full gear so long as there is not preadmission, which is the factor in compression. In full cut-off the Baker Gear has practically no preadmission and the indicator cards show a low compression line. This means a "quick" engine.

As the cut-off is shortened, the preadmission increases, and at 25 per cent there is from ¾-inch to ⅞-inch preadmission.

Fig. 2 shows in a general way the action of the Baker Gear for outside admission. On an inside admission gear the bell crank stands ahead of the reverse yoke, and point L for the connection of the valve rod is below point K instead of above. The eccentric crank follows in both cases.

The circle AD is the path of the crank pin. Circle BB' is the eccentric crank circle. ADX is the main rod. DX is the crosshead. DXN is the crosshead arm. MN is the union link. MKL the combination lever. KJG the bell crank. The gear connecting rod is GEC. EF shows the radius bar. HI is the reversing yoke.

The two movements of the gear are as follows: One from the eccentric crank B which follows the main pin at about 90 degrees. The other motion from the crosshead through the combination lever. The eccentric crank moves the radius bar and the action the radius bar has on the valve is controlled by the reverse yoke. The radius bar and yoke take the place of the link and block of a link motion. The combination lever throws the valve the amount of the lap and lead, the same as in the Walschaert Gear. This makes the lead constant and independent of the cut-off. Having a constant lead, the valve should show lead opening in all cut-offs when the engine is on either dead center.

The cut-off, release, and compression is done by means of the eccentric crank and controlled by the reversing yoke. The yoke controls the length of the cut-off and also reverses the engine. The action is as follows: Eccentric crank in going from B' to B moves point C from C'_{-1} to C''_{-1}. By this movement it moves pin E'_{-1} through H to E''_{-1}. The particular path of E is an arc whose radius is $E'_{-1}F_{-1}$. Thus it will be seen that EF causes point E to rise. This rising movement moves G from G_{-4} to G_{-1} which, by means of the bell crank, moves K from K_{-4} to K_{-1}. This, it can be seen, will move the valve forward. The valve is moved backward to its original position in the next half turn of the wheel. The peculiar action of the combination lever is not shown. As the combination lever does its important work near the dead center of the engine, and when the engine is in the position as shown in the diagram the combination lever is as shown on the diagram.

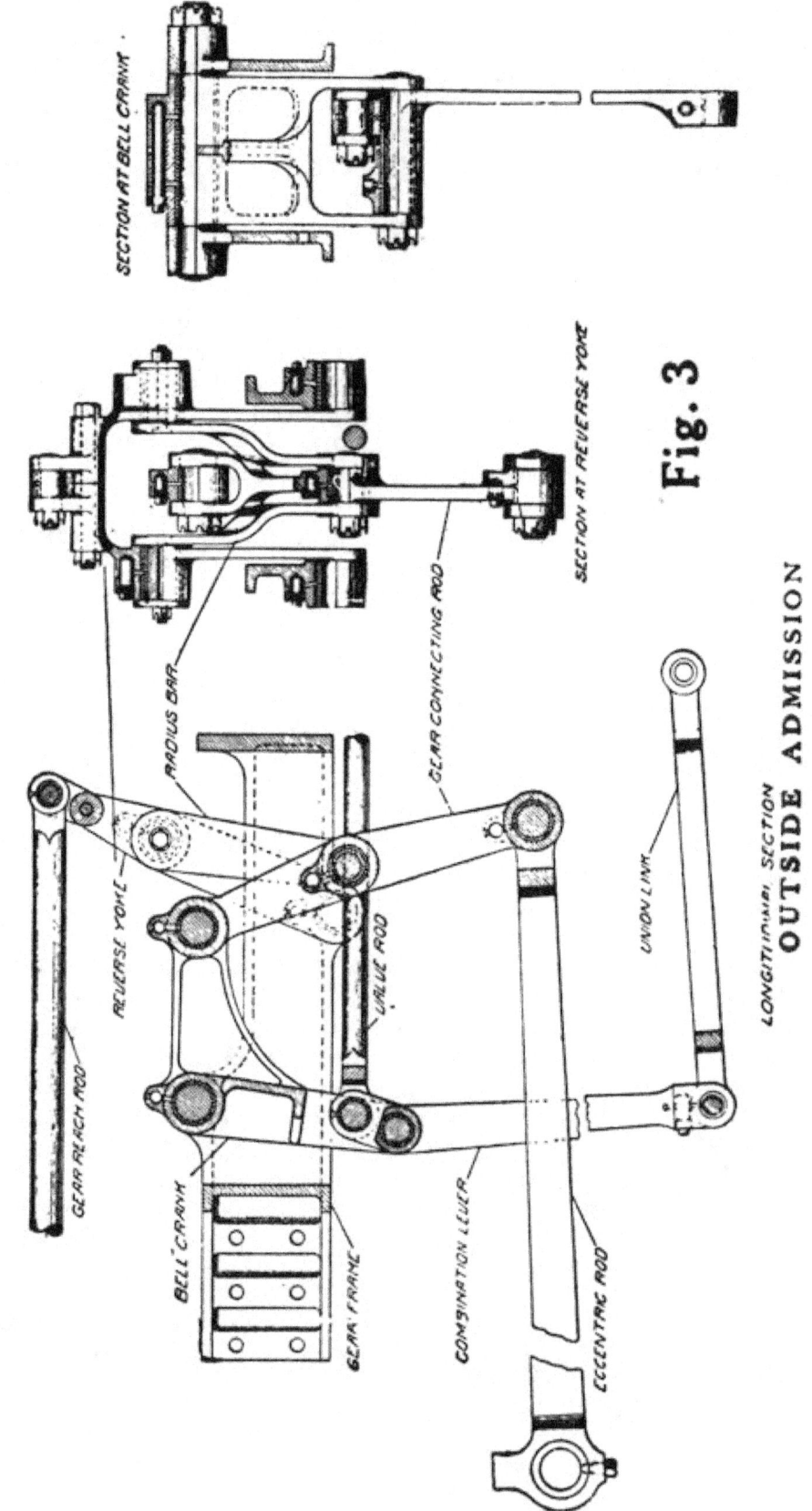

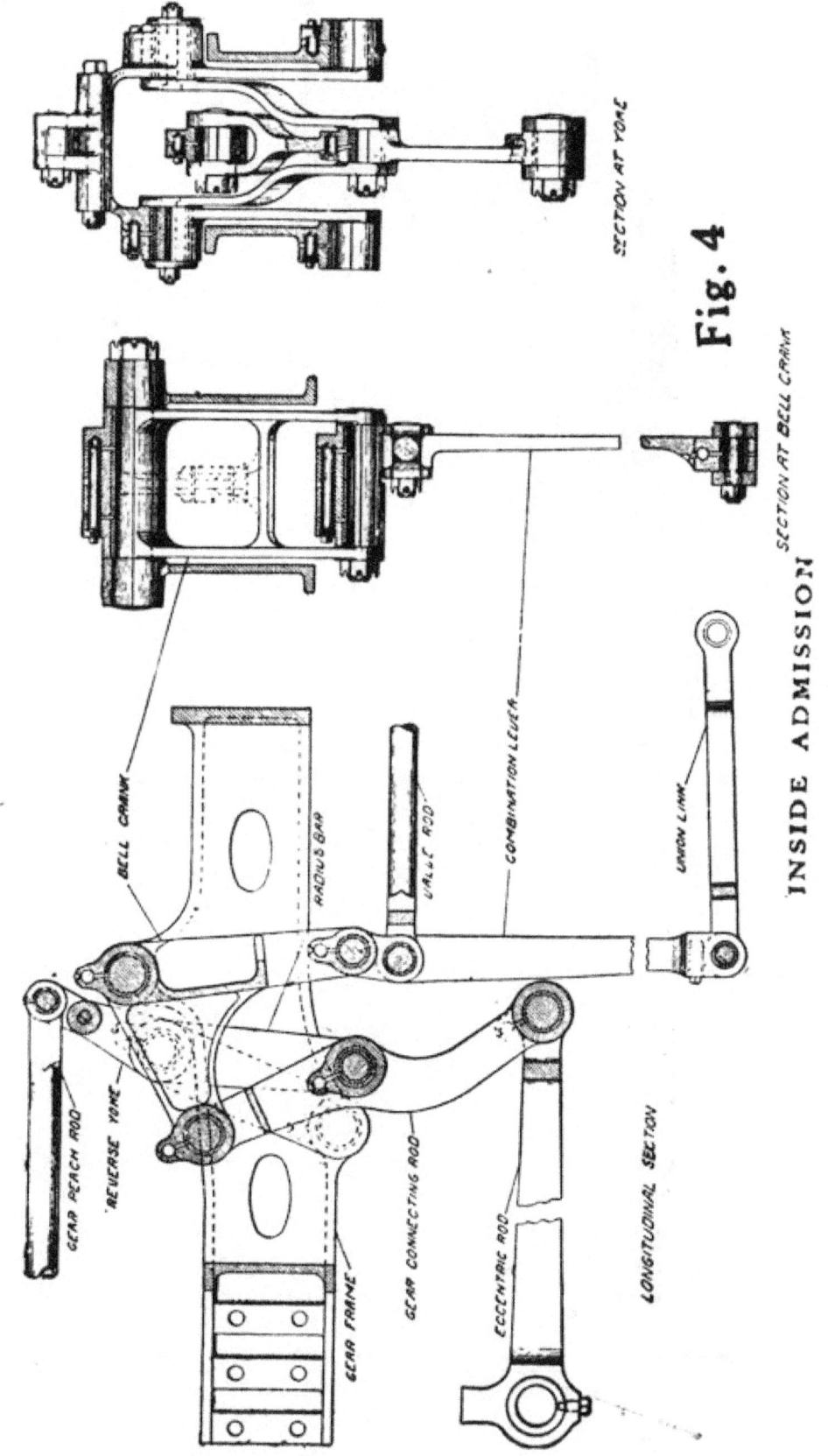

Fig. 4

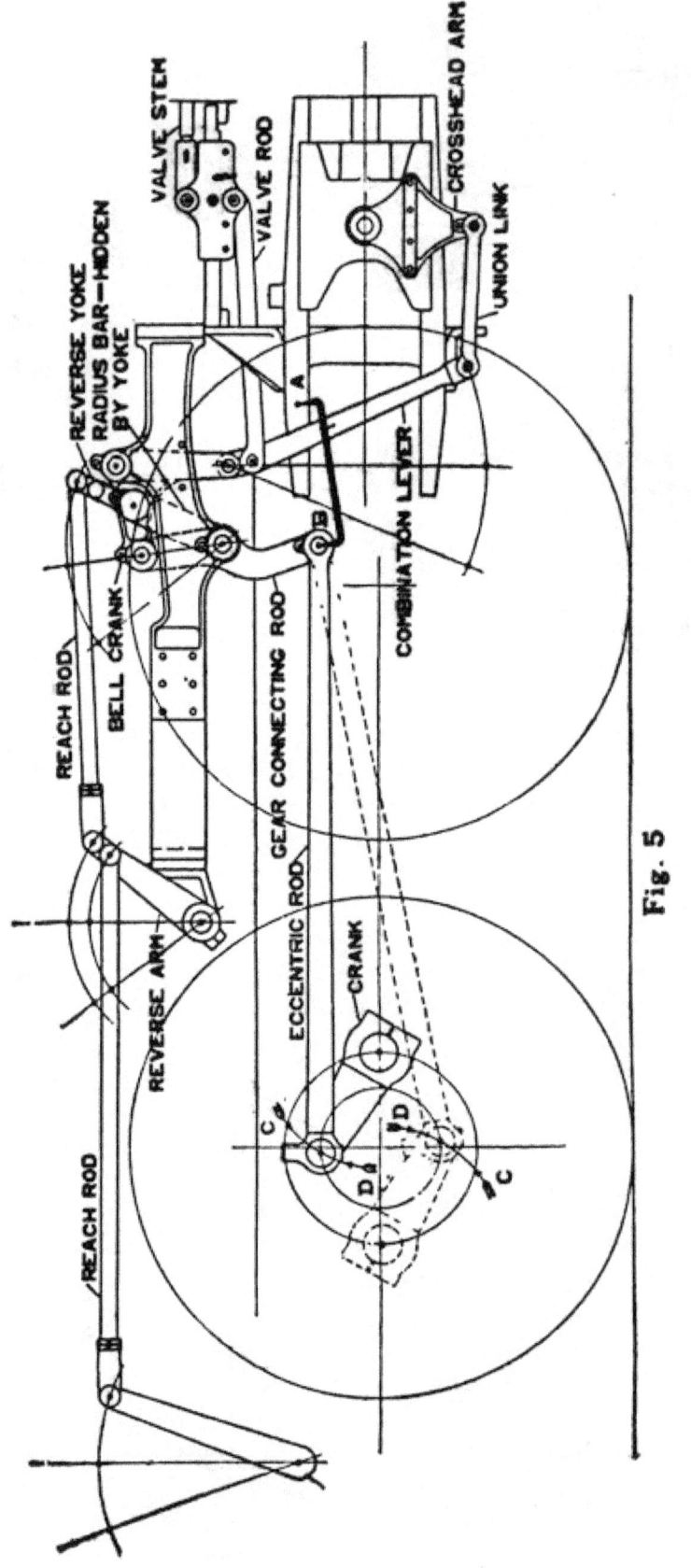

Fig. 5

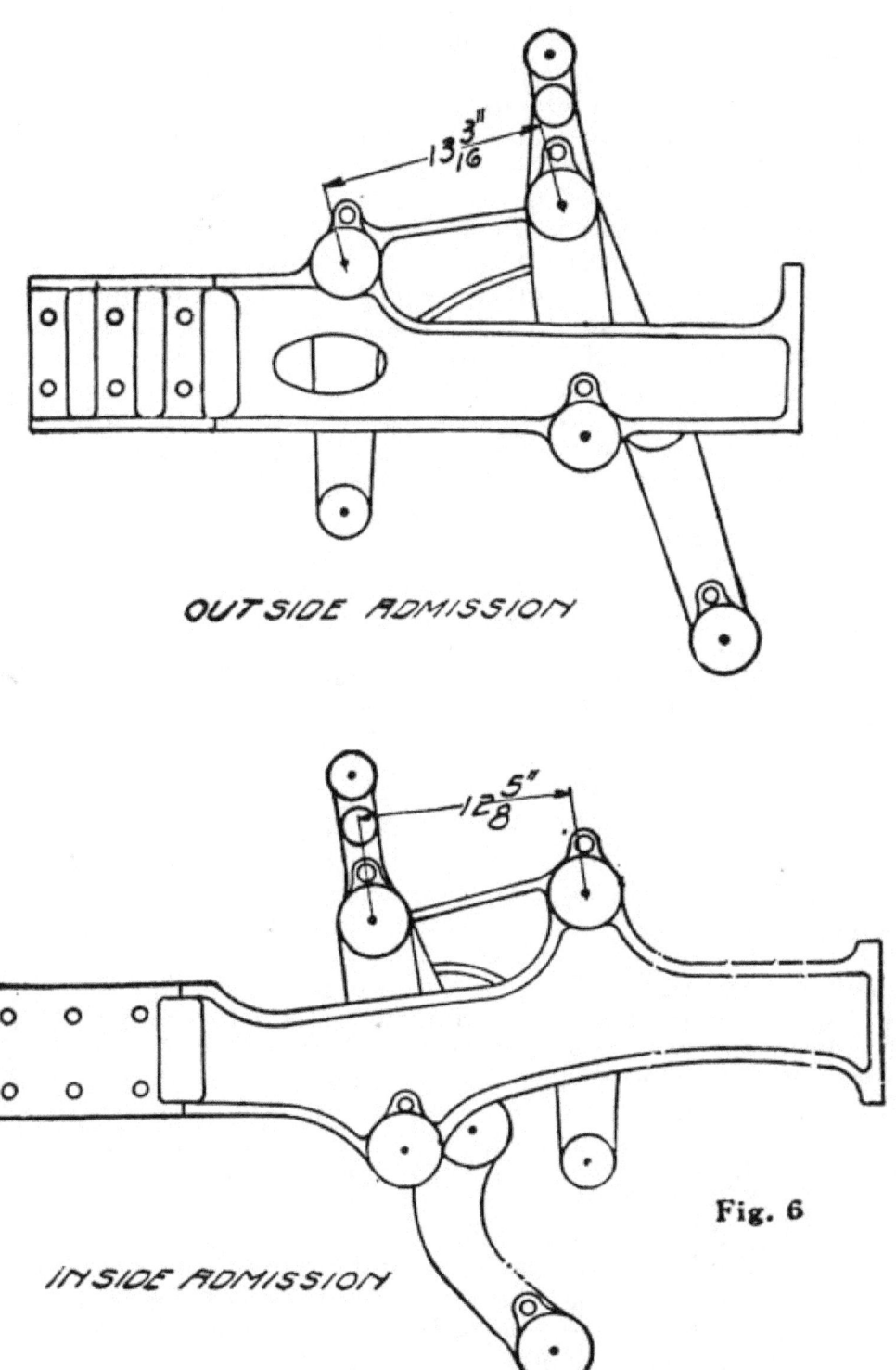

Fig. 6

From the diagram it will be noticed that E has a rising and falling movement, caused by the radius bar EF. If the yoke is changed from I_{-1} to I_{-2}, it would change the center of the radius F. So that E will move from E'_{-2} to E''_{-2}; in other words, the rising and falling movement is cut down, which would move G from G_{-3} to G_{-2} and K from K_{-3} to K_{-2}. Thus it will be seen that with the varying position of the yoke I the amount of movement of the valve varies. When I is in the mid-gear position E would not move up and down at all, but simply swing back and forth in an arc. If I is put in full backward motion, the same motion of the eccentric crank that caused the rising movement before would cause the falling movement in the back motion, and E would go from E''_{-4} to E'_{-4}. The full motion backward is shown by a dotted line and the short cut-off in backward motion by dash and three dots.

Instructions on Setting the Baker Gear. Connect up the gear and check the throw of the reverse yoke, also clearance at all points, with the eccentric crank clamped temporarily to the main pin, but as near as possible to the specified throw. Locate the dead centers in the usual way.

Eccentric Crank. With the engine on the front dead center, tram from the center of the pin in front end of eccentric rod to any stationary point, such as the guide yoke or guides, as shown by tram points A and B, Fig. 5. (In most cases the wheel tram can be used for this work.) After scribing a line across the side of the main guide with the A end of the tram, revolve the wheel to the back dead center and scribe the guide again; if these two lines are together the crank setting is correct. If they are not, knock the eccentric crank in or out until they do. The position of the reverse lever is not important while finding the eccentric positions. After the valve setter has had sufficient experience, the location of the eccentric can be determined while obtaining the dead centers.

Valve Travel. Put the reverse lever in full forward motion position and test the full travel. If there is a difference between the right and left sides of the engine, lengthen the gear reach rod on the side of the engine where the short travel exists. After obtaining the same travel on each side of the engine in this manner, the reverse lever should be put in its central position and the main reach rod adjusted until the dimensions shown on Fig. 6 are obtained for mid-gear position; then the quadrant length should be tested for the desired travel in both full forward and back motions.

Eccentric Rod Length. The inside admission gear is direct in the forward motion and indirect in the back motion and the ratio of the gear is 4 to 1, therefore the valve will move forward $\frac{1}{16}''$ if the eccentric rod is lengthened $\frac{1}{4}''$ *with the lever in the extreme forward motion and the engine on dead center.* If the lever is in the extreme back motion the valve will move back $\frac{1}{16}''$ when the rod is lengthened $\frac{1}{4}''$. Having taken the port marks with your standard valve stem tram, take the lead openings in both motions as shown by Fig. 7, which shows eccentric rod $\frac{1}{4}''$ too long for inside admission

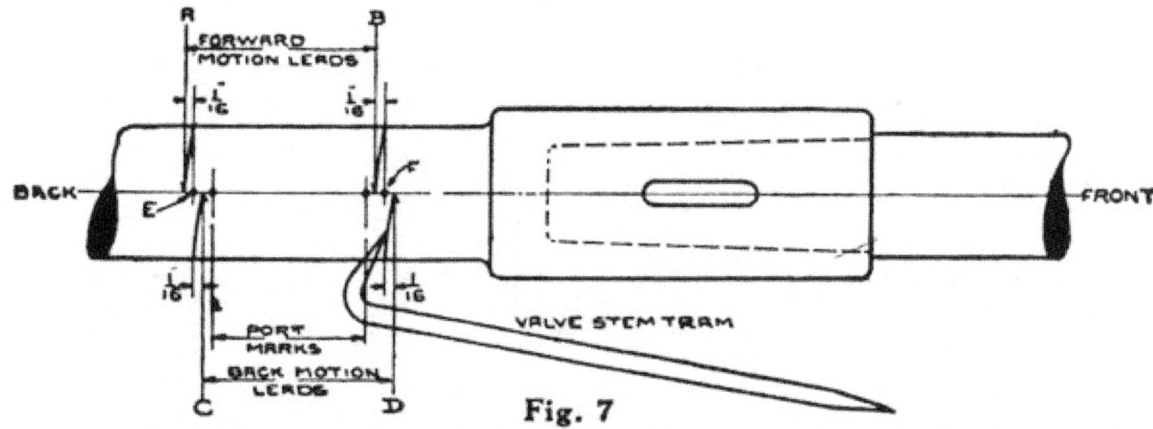

Fig. 7

If you shorten the rod ¼" and take the lead points again, the valve will be shifted back in the forward motion until lead line *A* is at *E* and lead line *B* is at *F*, and in the back motion the valve will be shifted ahead until the lead line *C* will be at *E* and lead line *D* will be at *F*, which will make the condition as shown by Fig. 8.

After obtaining leads as shown by Fig. 8, the length of the valve rod should be adjusted, making *G* and *H* equal. After the setter

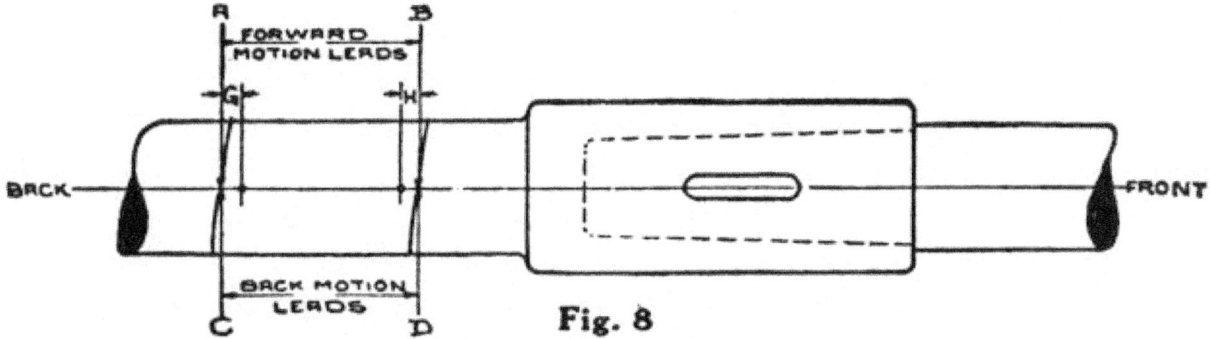

Fig. 8

has had some experience the valve rod and eccentric rod alterations can be made after one revolution of the wheels. Referring back to the paragraph on Eccentric Crank Setting, which can be checked from the stem (see Fig. 7), on which the distance between *A* and *B* on the horizontal line of the stem is equal to *C* and *D*, this will always be the case when crank setting is correct, whether the eccentric rod shows long or short.

If the eccentric rod is ⅛" too short and the crank setting correct, the full gear lead lines will come as shown by Fig. 9.

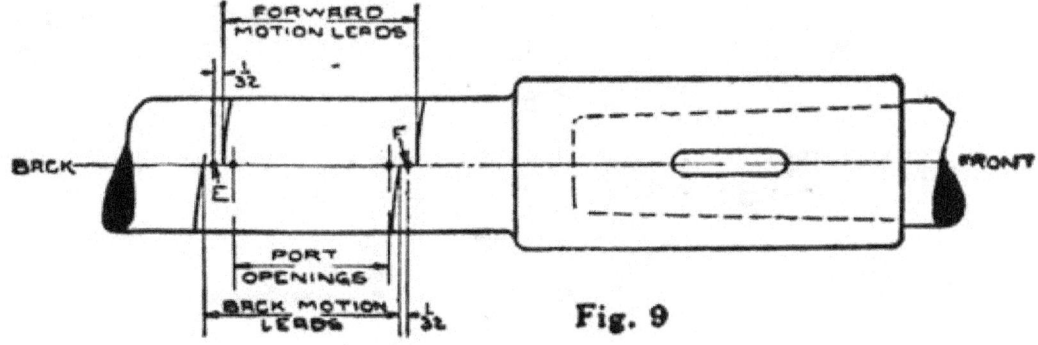

Fig. 9

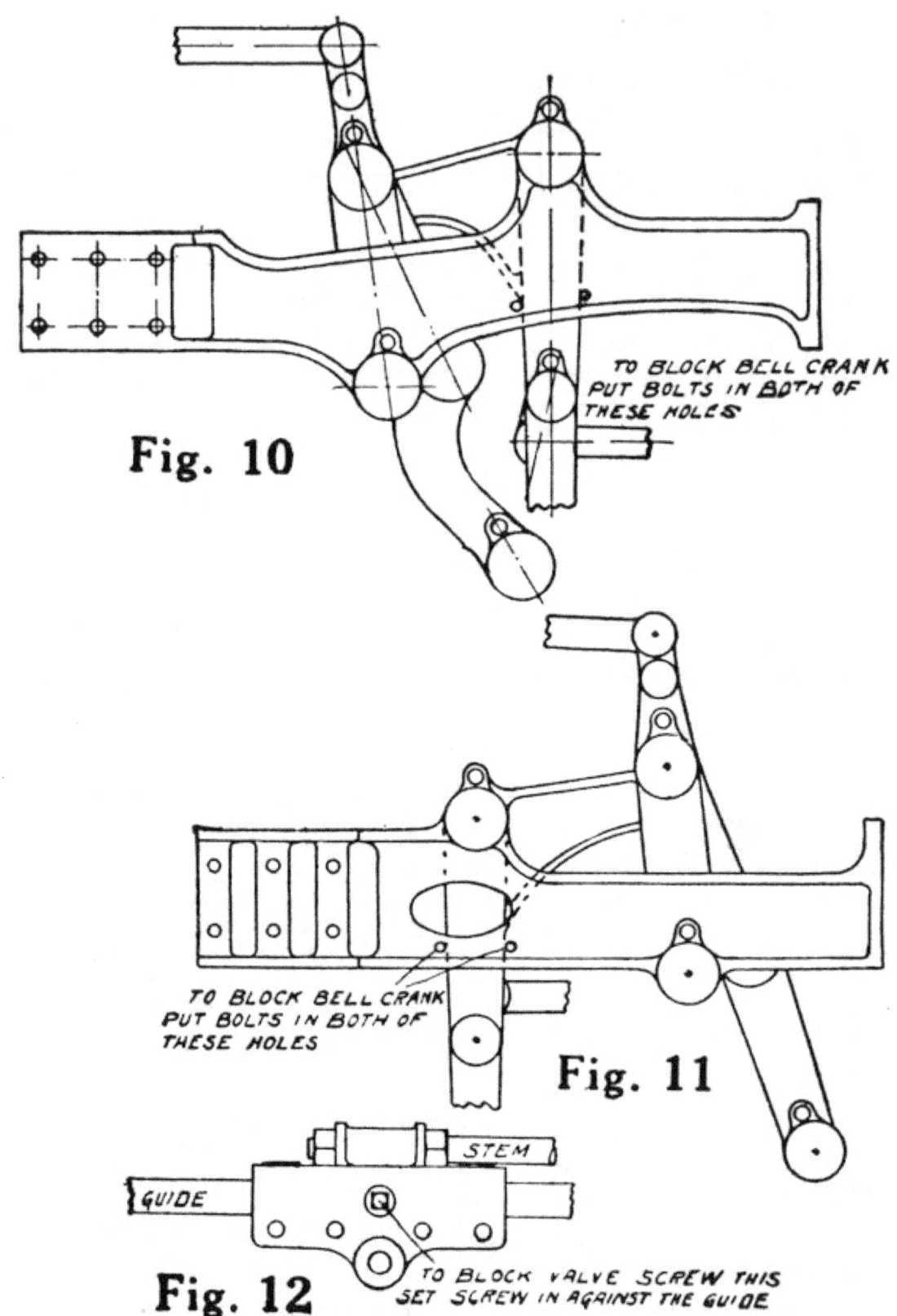

Fig. 10

Fig. 11

Fig. 12

After lengthening the rod ⅛" you will have the condition shown by Fig. 8.

The foregoing includes inside admission only and alterations in the eccentric rod length should be opposite for outside admission valves.

Valve Movements; General Information. The Baker Gear gets its motion from two points: the eccentric crank and the crosshead. The eccentric crank moves the radius bar and the action the radius bar has on the valve is controlled by the reverse yoke. The radius bar and the yoke take the place of the link and block of a link motion.

The crosshead moves the valve the amount of the lap and lead each way. This makes the lead constant and independent of the cut-off.

Having a constant lead, the valve should show lead opening in all cut-offs when engine is on either dead center.

Eccentric Crank Setting. With the Baker Gear the eccentric crank always follows the crank pin. It stands the same for both inside and outside admission.

Cut-off and Eccentric Rod. If the eccentric rod is off in length, you can tell it by the following rule: If cut-offs are long on front end in forward motion and long on the back end in backward motion, the rod is too long. If the cut-offs come just the opposite of the foregoing, then the rod is too short.

Breakdowns. Two means are provided for blocking the gear and valve in case of a breakdown. The valve stem crosshead is provided with a set-screw so that the valve can be blocked central over the ports by clamping the valve stem crosshead to its guide. This is done in case the breakage on the gear or engine disables one side. (See Fig. 12.)

The other way of blocking is by bolting the lower arm of the bell crank fast to the side of the frame. After the valves have been set, the reverse lever is put in mid-gear and two holes are drilled through the frame. Any bolt that will go through the hole can be used. (See Figs. 10 and 11.) With the gear bolted in this manner the valve will get the lap and lead movement and a port opening equal to the lead for all cut-offs. This allows the following parts to fail and yet get the lap and lead movement: eccentric crank, eccentric rod, connection rod, radius bars, reverse yoke, short reach rod and horizontal arm of bell crank.

In case the union link or crosshead arm fails, it will be necessary to block the valve over the ports, tie the combination lever fast, and disconnect the valve rod; unless the construction of the engine is such that the combination lever can be secured in practically a plumb position. If the combination lever can be fastened, the valve will get the eccentric movement. The port opening would be reduced and be closed in any cut-off shorter than 50 per cent.

In case the combination lever fails, close up the bell crank, block the valve over the ports, disconnect the valve rod and tie the loose parts to keep them from doing damage.

In case of engine breakage do the same as with any other gear.

The Baker Valve Gear, like the Walschaert and other radial gears, readily lends itself to any change in design that may be necessary to suit the construction of the locomotive to which it is applied.

In order that the action of this gear may be clearly understood with reference to the different types of valves used, we must first consider those with the gear illustrated as in Figs. 3 and 4. The fulcrum point of the combination lever is its connection to the lower end of the bell crank, while on the later type of gear the fulcrum point of the combination lever is where it is connected to the valve rod. In both instances this fulcrum is movable; in other words it does not occupy the same position at all points of the stroke. As explained previously, the combination lever gives the lap and lead travel; that is, it moves the valve so that it has traveled the amount of the lap and the lead at the beginning of each end of the stroke.

Referring to Fig. 3, as the combination lever obtains its movement from the crosshead, it is evident that when the crosshead is traveling forward carrying the lower end of the combination lever with it, the upper end of the combination lever must be traveling back, and the proportions of the combination lever are so arranged that when the crosshead is at its extreme forward position, the upper end of the combination lever has been pulled back the amount of the lap and the lead of the valve, thereby placing the valve in position to admit steam ahead of the piston to force the piston back. When the crosshead is at the other end of its travel, that is, at the back end of the guides, the upper end of the combination lever would be moved forward the amount of the lap and the lead, thereby placing the valve in position to admit steam back of the piston. In the view shown, the valve rod makes a direct connection with the valve stem and consequently imparts to the valve the same movement, that is, a movement in the same direction as that imparted to the valve rod.

If, still referring to Fig. 3, the valves were of the inside admission type, and the valve rod connected as before, it is plain that with the crosshead at its extreme forward travel, which would throw the top end of the combination lever back, the back steam port would be open instead of the front one, consequently the engine would not move. For this reason where inside admission valves are used, the valve rod must be coupled below the fulcrum point as shown in Fig. 4, in order that when the crosshead is at the extreme forward end of its travel, the connection point of the valve rod will also be carried forward, thereby moving the valve forward and uncovering the front steam port.

With the later type of the Baker Gear, as previously explained, the forward end of the valve rod, which in this case corresponds with the radius rod of the Walschaert Gear, forms the fulcrum point of the combination lever same as the combination lever connection to the bell crank as shown in Figs. 3 and 4; while the valve stem proper is connected direct to the combination lever, same as the valve rod is connected in the figures mentioned. A study of this motion, therefore, shows that the first movement imparted to the valve is that given by the crosshead through the combination lever, the remainder of the movement being imparted by the eccentric crank through the bell crank. To make this clear imagine in Fig. 3, which shows the reverse lever in forward gear, that the reach rod was pulled back so the reverse lever would occupy the center of the quadrant; this would then throw the reverse yoke connections in line with the bell crank connection and the only effect that the eccentric crank would have would be to oscillate the radius bars forward and back without imparting any material movement to the bell crank, and as the valve obtains its movement from the movement of the bell crank and the combination lever, it is clear that the only material movement imparted to the valve under these conditions would be that given by the combination lever, which would be equal to twice the lap and twice the lead.

Throwing the reverse lever into forward gear places the radius bars in an angular position and therefore they can not oscillate as before without rising up and down; as they are so connected, however, as to prevent any up and down movement, it follows that the movement of the eccentric crank instead of being imparted to the radius bars only, in this instance would be imparted to the bell crank, causing the forward end of the bell crank in Fig. 3, and the back end in Fig. 4, to move up and down. This would cause the lower end of the bell crank to move forward and back, thus imparting additional motion to the valve through the valve rod.

This explanation is deemed necessary in order that engineers will clearly understand the different movements, so that in case of failure of any one of the parts of this gear, they would know how to disconnect, what to disconnect, and how to block the remaining portion of the gear to get a valve travel on the disabled side. On the later type of Baker Gear there is practically nothing that could break which would prevent obtaining some valve travel, with the exception of a valve stem. On the type of gear herein illustrated there is practically nothing that could break which would prevent obtaining a valve travel with the exception of the valve stem, valve rod, or lower end of bell crank.

Breakdowns. Beginning at the rear end; in case the eccentric crank, eccentric rod, or the lower end of the gear connecting rod should break, the only movement that could be imparted to the valve would be that of the combination lever, and as the combination lever is fulcrumed to the bell crank, it is plain that the bell crank must first be secured in a rigid position so that all the movement imparted by the crosshead to the combination lever would be imparted to the valve, as otherwise were the bell crank not secured, the chances are the bell crank would move instead of the valve rod. On the type of gear herein illustrated you will notice two holes through the gear frame, Figs. 10 and 11; these holes are for the purpose of fastening the bell crank in case of failure of any of the parts previously mentioned, the bell crank being secured to the gear frame by means of a U-bolt placed in these holes.

The short reach rod connecting the reverse or tumbling shaft arm to the reverse yoke should also be disconnected at one end and the reverse yoke thrown forward against the gear frame in order to get it out of the way. This would then give the full valve travel on the good side of the locomotive but only a travel equal to the lap and the lead on the disabled side and a port opening on the disabled side equal to the lead opening.

With an engine disconnected in this manner, you should be careful not to stop with the good side on the dead center as, if the good side is on the dead center, the disabled side would necessarily be on the quarter and in this case the combination lever would be straight up and down, and the ports covered on the disabled side, making this side powerless, and as the good side of the engine would be on the dead center, that side would naturally be powerless also and the engine would not move. Should you happen to stop in this position, however, the engine could be gotten off the center on the good side without the necessity of pinching by disconnecting the lower end of the combination lever from the union link, and moving the combination lever in the right direction to uncover the port that would allow the engine to move in the direction desired, as for instance, if the engine stopped with the good side on the forward dead center with the other side on the upper quarter, and it was desired to move in a forward direction, the combination lever should be swung so as to uncover the back steam port on the disabled side. After the engine had been moved off the dead center on the good side, the combination lever should be coupled up again.

With the new type of gear there are no holes provided in the gear frame for the purpose of fastening the bell crank, but the bracket is so cast that wooden wedges can be driven on either side of the bell crank to hold it in position.

If the gear connection rod should break below the pin where it is fastened to the gear frame, it would of course be necessary to disconnect the eccentric rod, then block same as for broken eccentric rod or crank. If the gear connection rod should break above the pin, the eccentric rod could be left up, proceeding with the balance of the operation same as for broken eccentric rod, etc.

In case the union link or the combination lever should break, two methods could be employed. The combination lever together with the union link could be removed and in many instances the valve rod could be connected direct to the bell crank at the point where the combination lever was formerly connected. If this could not be done and the failure was of the union link or of the combination lever at a point below its connection with the bell crank, the union link, if broken, should be removed, or the union link and that portion of the broken combination lever should be removed, the remaining part of the combination lever placed so it would hang straight down and then either wedged or clamped in such a position that it could not move on its fulcrum point on the bell crank. This would then allow the eccentric crank to impart a motion to the valve equal to the difference between the motion imparted by the eccentric crank only and that imparted by the combined movements of the eccentric crank and the combination lever. The port openings would naturally be reduced and it would be necessary to work the engine in practically full stroke in order to get any opening on the disabled side. With an engine disconnected in this manner no port opening would be obtained on the disabled side at the beginning of the stroke.

With the type of gear herein illustrated, in case of failure of the valve rod, the engine would naturally be disabled on that side; it would not be necessary to disconnect anything, however; simply remove the broken parts if they are liable to interfere, clamp the valve central on its seat and make the usual provision for lubricating the cylinder. This can be done by either taking out cylinder relief valves, in case the cylinder is provided with them or slacking off on the front cylinder head. With the newer type of gear, however, even in case of a failure of the valve rod you could still obtain a port opening and work steam on the disabled side by first removing the engine so that the crosshead on the disabled side would be at the center of its stroke, that is, with that side on the quarter, then disconnect the disabled valve rod and cut a piece of plank long enough to reach from the back end of the steam chest to the guide yoke; cut a notch through this plank that will fit over the upper end of the combination lever; fasten it securely in place. This will act as a fulcrum point for the combination lever and give you the lap and lead travel. There would be no need of disconnecting any other portions of the gear.

QUESTIONS AND ANSWERS ON BAKER VALVE GEAR.

Q.—What portion of the travel of valve is controlled by the crosshead movement on a Baker Valve Gear?

A.—The movement of valve controlled by the crosshead motion amounts to the combined lap and lead of the valve. This movement is constant, regardless of position of lever.

Q.—When the position of reverse lever is changed with engine working, what part of the motion of Baker Gear is affected?

A.—That part which receives its motion from the eccentric crank, which may be cut out altogether by placing reverse lever on center. The position of lever has no effect whatever on the motion of valve imparted to it by the crosshead movement.

Q.—Is the Baker Valve Gear a direct or indirect motion?

A.—That depends on whether the valves are inside or outside admission. With inside admission valves the gear is direct in forward motion and indirect in back motion, and is the opposite when outside admission valves are used.

Q.—If an eccentric rod or crank on a Baker Gear should break, what could be done on the road to still use part of engine on disabled side?

A.—The thing to do is cut out that part of the gear to which the eccentric rod is connected. The eccentric rod is connected to the gear connection rod at bottom, and the motion given to this rod is imparted to the bell crank, which is connected at the upper end of this rod, when the reverse yoke is in any but its dead center (vertical) position. If the bell crank is to be cut out it must be placed in the dead center position and blocked there. The modern Baker Gears have two holes in gear frame which register with holes in bell crank, and a couple of bolts put through these holes will hold the bell crank. After this is done the valve will be operated only by the crosshead movement, which moves the valve the amount of the lap and lead only. The next thing to do is disconnect back end of short reach rod; there being no further use for the reverse lever on the disabled side (which, with the bell crank locked, would prevent the use of the lever anyway) and move the reverse yoke over against gear frame out of the way.

You are then ready to go. The power on the disabled side will not be much, but it is a "fix up" quickly done and permits the proper lubrication of valve and cylinder, which in itself is worth while.

Q.—In what does the Baker gear differ from the Walschaert?

A.—In the manner in which the cut-off is regulated and the engine reversed.

Q.—How is this accomplished in the Baker gear?

A.—By means of a reverse yoke instead of a link.

Q.—Through what parts does the valve obtain its movement with the Baker gear?

A.—Through the combination lever from the crosshead and through the eccentric crank connected to the main crank pin.

Q.—What movement is imparted to the valve by means of the combination lever?

A.—That necessary to overcome the lap of the valve and give the lead desired.

Q.—Is the lead given by the Baker valve gear constant or variable?

A.—It is constant.

Q.—What do you understand by preadmission?

A.—It is the act of admitting steam or having a port open before the piston reaches the end of its stroke.

Q.—With the Baker gear is the preadmission constant same as the lead?

A.—No; preadmission is variable, increasing as the cut-off is shortened.

Q.—What would be the effect of preadmission with an engine in full gear?

A.—It would have a tendency to retard the movement of the engine; also in a measure decrease its starting power.

Q.—Does this same objection obtain when an engine is worked in a short cut-off?

A.—No; preadmission in this case acts as a cushion for the reciprocating parts.

Q.—How can you tell at a glance whether an engine equipped with a Baker gear has an inside or outside admission valve?

A.—By the manner in which the valve rod is connected to the combination lever; an engine having an inside admission valve has the valve rod connected below the point at which the combination lever is attached to the bell crank, and one having outside admission valves has the valve rod connected above this point.

Q.—Is there any difference in the setting of the eccentric crank for the inside and outside admission valve?

A.—No; the eccentric crank always follows the main pin.

Q.—How should the different bearings of the Baker gear be lubricated? What kind of oil should be used?

A.—Bearings should be lubricated by filling the pockets or cavities cast in all the movable parts and connecting with the bearings; these pockets should preferably be kept full of curled hair in order to assist in retaining the oil and to prevent grit and other abrasives getting into the bearings. Engine oil only should be used.

Q.—Why not use valve oil in lubricating these bearings?

A.—Because owing to the limited movement of the bearings there is no tendency on their part to run hot, and valve oil being thicker than engine oil would not flow around the bearings as readily and consequently might cause the bearings to seize.

Q.—What would you do in case of failure of the eccentric crank, eccentric rod, or lower end of gear connection rod?

A.—Disconnect broken parts and remove such portions as are liable to interfere; disconnect the short reach rod; fasten the bell crank in its central position and proceed on both sides.

Q.—With an engine disconnected in this manner, what port opening would you get on the disabled side?

A.—A port opening equal to the lead.

Q.—With an engine disconnected in this manner what precautions should be taken in stopping?

A.—To see that the engine did not stop with the good side on the dead center.

Q.—Why is this precaution necessary?

A.—Because in this case, the good side being on the center would be powerless, and the disabled side being on the quarter would place the valve in its central position covering both ports, consequently no steam would be admitted to the cylinder on the disabled side and the engine would not move.

Q.—In case an engine disconnected in this manner, did stop with the good side on the dead center, could the engine be moved without pinching? If so, how?

A.—Yes; by disconnecting the lower end of the combination lever and moving the valve so as to obtain a port opening.

Q.—With an engine disconnected in this manner and the disabled side on the quarter, why could not a port opening be obtained by placing the reverse lever at full gear either forward or back?

A.—Because in the first place the reach rod is disconnected on that side, and in the second place, if the reach rod were not disconnected, the reverse lever would have no influence on the valve movement as the only movement given to the valve would be that imparted by the crosshead.

Q.—What should be done in case the gear connection rod broke above the point where it was fulcrumed to the gear frame?

A.—Proceed same as for a broken eccentric rod or crank, except in this case it will not be necessary to disconnect the eccentric rod.

Q.—What should be done in case of a broken radius bar?

A.—Handle same as for broken eccentric rod or crank.

Q.—What should be done if the upper or horizontal bell crank arm should break?

A.—Handle same as for broken eccentric rod.

Q.—What should be done in case the lower or vertical arm of the bell crank broke?

A.—With the type of gear here illustrated this failure would totally disable the engine on that side. All that would be necessary to disconnect, however, would be the combination lever, union link and valve rod; then clamp the valve to cover the ports and make the usual provision for lubricating the cylinder. With the later type of gear, disconnect the valve rod, then fasten the top of the combination lever by means of a plank extending from the steam chest to the guide yoke.

Q.—What would you do in case you broke the crosshead arm, union link or lower portion of the combination lever?

A.—Remove the broken parts that are liable to interfere. If in case of a broken union link or crosshead arm, the combination lever can be fastened so that it can not move, do this and proceed with a full train. If the combination lever is broken near its connection, however, or can not be fastened, connect the valve rod direct to the bell crank in place of the combination lever if possible; if not, wedge or clamp the upper end of the combination lever to the bell crank in such a manner that it can not move and proceed with a full train.

Q.—With an engine disconnected in this manner, how much valve travel will be obtained on the disabled side?

A.—About two-thirds of the usual travel.

Q.—With an engine disconnected in this manner at what cut-off should the engine be worked to secure any power on the disabled side?

A.-The engine should be worked at practically full stroke, if cut back to less than half stroke no port opening would be obtained on the defective side.

Q.—What do you do in case of a broken valve rod?

A.—Where the valve rod is connected from the combination lever direct to the valve stem crosshead, the engine would be disabled on that side and should be handled accordingly. There would be no need to disconnect anything however, except the valve rod. Where the valve rod forms a connection between the bell crank and the combination lever, and the combination lever is attached to the valve stem crosshead, a lead opening could be obtained by fastening the top of the combination lever.

Q.—What would you do in case of a broken reverse yoke?

A.—In case the yoke is broken at the short reach rod connection, take down the short reach rod and block the yoke securely at the cut-off in which it is necessary to work the engine. If the break in the reverse yoke is below the suspension point or lugs, proceed the same as with broken eccentric rod or eccentric crank.

Southern Locomotive Valve Gear*

While it is a radical departure from all previous outside gears, it is a gear that can be adapted to any class of locomotives, both inside and outside admission, and is designed with the view of eliminating roundhouse repairs and delays to power incident thereto. It is a well-known fact that there is a derangement in the valve movement on all outside radial gears, due to the change in the angularity of the main rod as the engine settles. This valve gear has been so designed as to practically eliminate this objectionable feature.

Transferring from a rotary motion to a reciprocating motion is accomplished by direct movements and on straight lines, doing away with strains and distortions found in other valve gears in common use to-day. The links being located in a horizontal position and being stationary, entirely does away with wear at this point, as the block only moves in the link when the reverse lever is moved to adjust cut-off or reverse gear. The link being stationary also eliminates what is known as the slip in the link block, found in some outside gears. There are but eight possible points of wear on each side of an engine or a total of sixteen points of wear per locomotive, this being less than half contained in other gears.

This gear will practically do away with engine failures due to breakage of valve gear parts. The different parts are so balanced as to reduce the wear on the pins and bushings to a minimum. The forward end of the eccentric rod is supported by bell crank hanger, which has at its top two bearings spaced widely apart, thus absolutely preventing any side slap on eccentric rod.

This valve gear is designed to eliminate all stress and strains on reverse lever and reach rod connections. The reverse lever is easily handled with one hand while engine is working under full steam pressure. This feature appeals very strongly to the engineer as it enables him to adjust his cut-off without fear of the reverse lever getting away from him and will induce him to work as short cut-off as possible, resulting in the saving of fuel. This valve gear will stand hard usage that it is bound to get under heavy freight service, as has been proven in a series of dynamometer car tests.

Directions for Setting and Adjusting Southern Locomotive Valve Gear.—The dead centers are found in the usual way, and the valve gear assembled according to elevation, with eccentric crank of proper length and set so that the pin travels in an 18-inch circle and the

---
* By courtesy of Southern Locomotive Valve Gear Co.

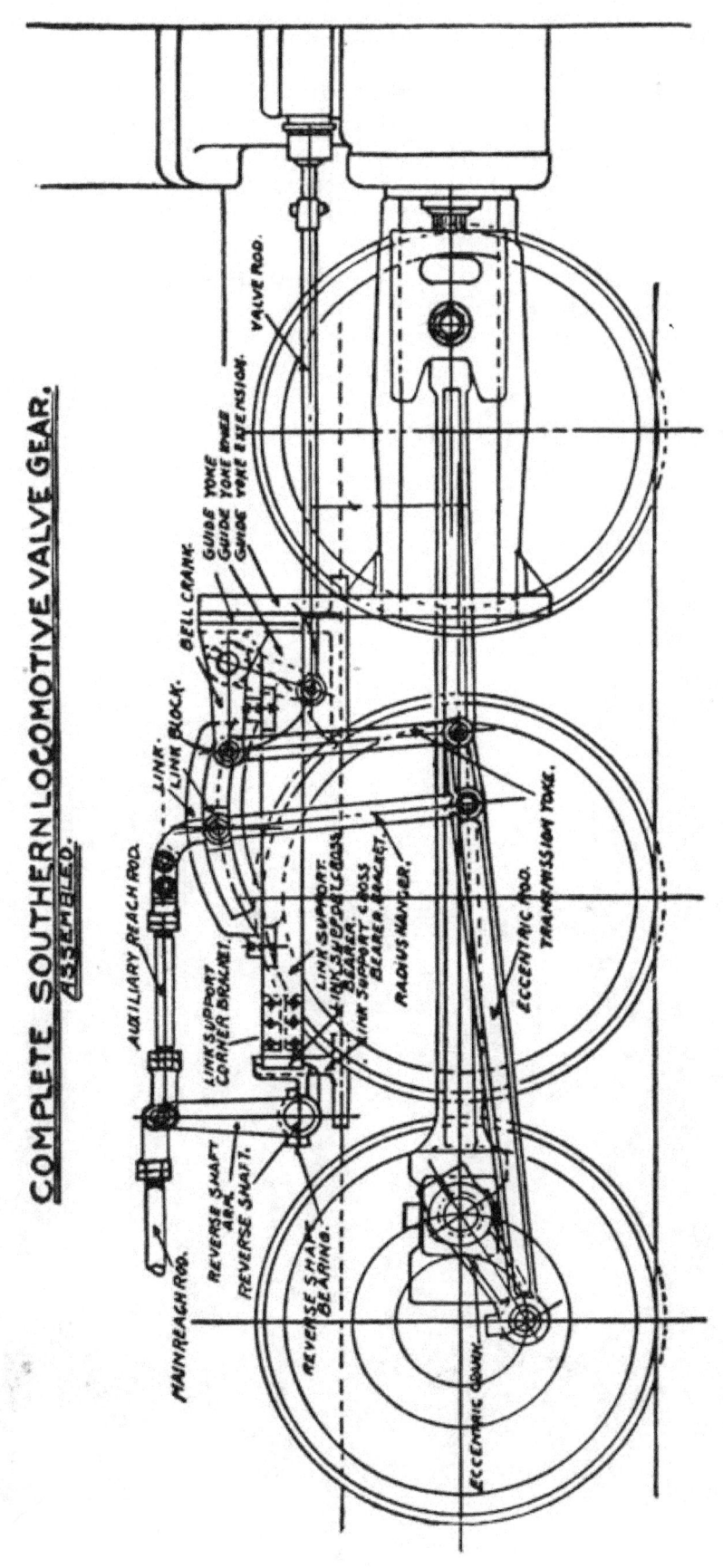

reverse shaft arms stand vertical while the reverse lever is in center position of quadrant and the link set in position shown on the elevation, and securely clamped; also that the auxiliary reach rods have been adjusted to bring the link block in the center of the link while the reverse lever is in middle position.

Diagram shows an ideal valve gear, with all parts of proper dimensions and properly located and adjusted. This gear will have a uniform lead at both front and back ports.

Full lines show the position of eccentric crank for outside admission, and dotted lines show the same for inside admission.

For outside admission, the eccentric crank leads the main crank pin, but for inside admission, it follows the main crank pin.

QUESTIONS AND ANSWERS ON SOUTHERN VALVE GEAR

Q. 1.—Give a brief description of the Southern Valve Gear.

A.—This is an outside valve gear; the valve receives its motion from an eccentric crank, or main pin, and differs from other outside gears, in that the valve receives its motion direct from the eccentric rod and has no crosshead connections.

Q. 2.—In what particular way does this valve gear differ from other outside valve gears?

A.—By reason of its having no crosshead connection and the link being stationary.

Q. 3.—What would you do in case of a broken main reach rod?

A.—Block the link blocks both sides at suitable cut-off to start and handle train, using a block on each side of the link block in link.

Q. 4.—What should be done for a broken auxiliary reach rod, or tumbling shaft arm?

A.—Block the link block on the disabled side at a suitable cut-off to handle train.

Q. 5.—How would you disconnect for a broken eccentric crank or rod?

A.—Remove the broken parts, block the valve with ports covered, secure the radius hanger and transmission yoke and proceed on one side.

Q. 6.—What disconnection should be made in case of a broken bell crank?

A.—If valve rod connection, remove broken parts; if transmission yoke connection, remove the transmission yoke; block the valve with ports covered in both cases.

Q. 7.—What should be done in case of a broken radius hanger?

A.—Remove the eccentric rod, secure the transmission yoke from swinging and block the valve with ports covered.

Q. 8.—What provision should be made for lubricating cylinders, where valves are blocked with steam ports covered, with main rod not connected?

A.—If indicator plugs are provided, would remove them and lubricate through openings; if no indicator plugs, would slack off on cylinder head and secure it in position to lubricate through opening.

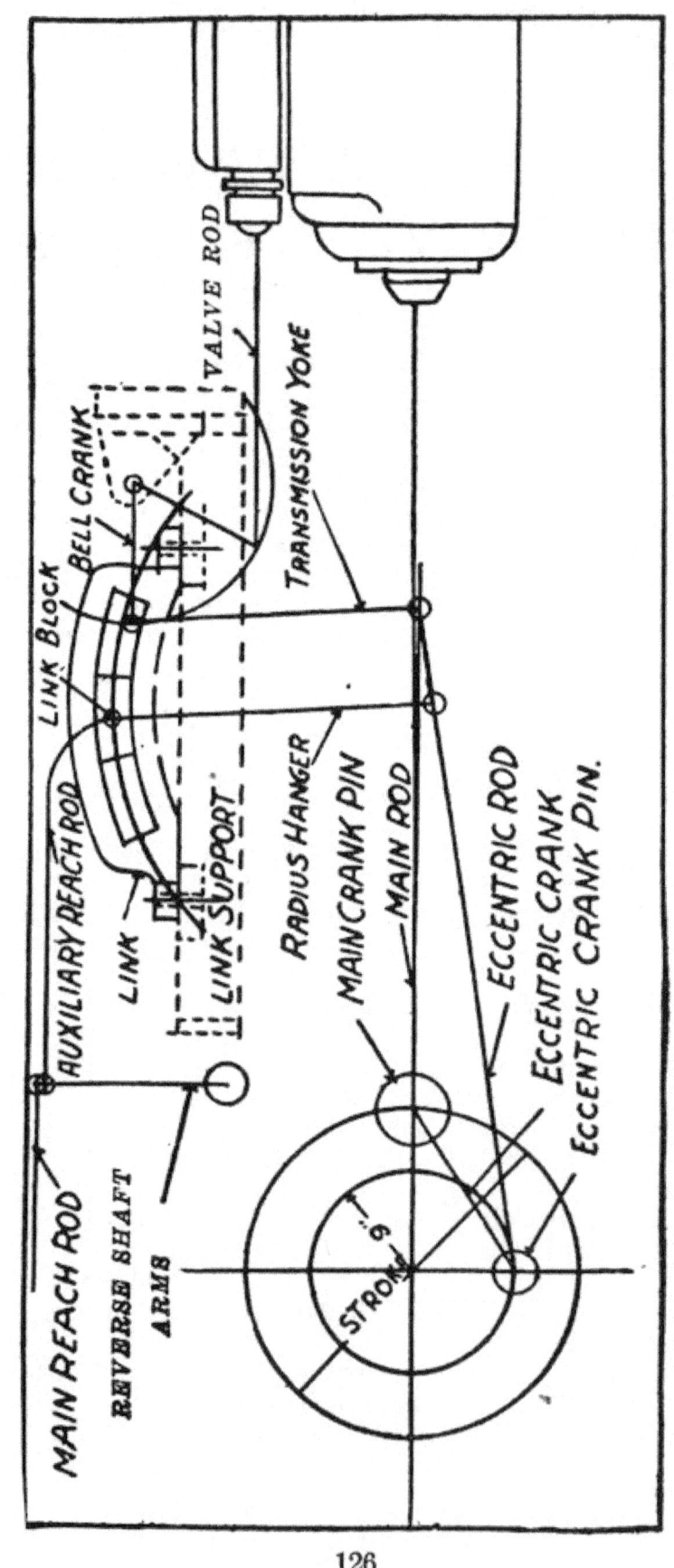

NAMES OF THE DIFFERENT PARTS OF THE SOUTHERN VALVE GEAR

The Schmidt Top Header Type Superheater

Which is in most general use on railroads in the United States. We will illustrate and explain this type as it will probably be of more value to my readers than any other. Referring to Fig. 2 it will be seen that the superheater proper consists of a number of superheater units, each unit being made up of four pieces of seamless steel tubing about 1½ inches O. D., and all of which are located in the upper portion of the boiler, having their back end swaged down to 4½ inches O. D., to secure better circulation of water next to the tube sheet. The seamless steel tubes are connected by cast steel return bends to form a continuous tube, as shown in Fig. 4. To insure the proper flow of steam through these units, the special Superheater Header, shown in Fig. 5, is provided, which takes the place of the ordinary "Tee" or "Nigger" Head.

This header is so designed with internal walls that the steam entering it from the dry pipe must pass through the passages marked "W" to the tubes of the superheater units where it is superheated. On leaving the units, the superheated steam is returned to the header, on the opposite side of the partition walls, to the passages marked "S," connecting it with the steam pipes and steam chests.

The direction of the steam flow in a superheater locomotive is indicated by arrows in the dry pipe, header, superheater units, and steam pipes of Figs. 2 and 3 and in the header, Fig. 5.

The Ball Joint Connection between the superheater unit and the lower face of the header is made with a single bolt centrally located, as shown on Figs. 2, 3, and 4. In making these ball joints, the ends of the superheater tubes are machined, and the bored collars which form the ball joints driven out. They are then welded and turned to their spherical form. The ball joints and their seats in header are ground steam tight.

To protect the ends of the superheater tubes next to the fire against overheating when there is no steam flowing through them, especially when the blower is on, it is necessary to stop the flow of hot gas through the large flues. This result is secured by separating the front end of the superheater units from the rest of the smoke box by means of a vertical partition plate located just in front of the superheated body, extending across the smoke-box and from the top of the smoke-box down to the back edge of the table plate. From the bottom edge of this partition a horizontal plate, reaching across the smoke-box, extends back to the tube-sheet just below the large flues.

This horizontal plate contains an opening which is closed by the superheater damper, Fig. 6.

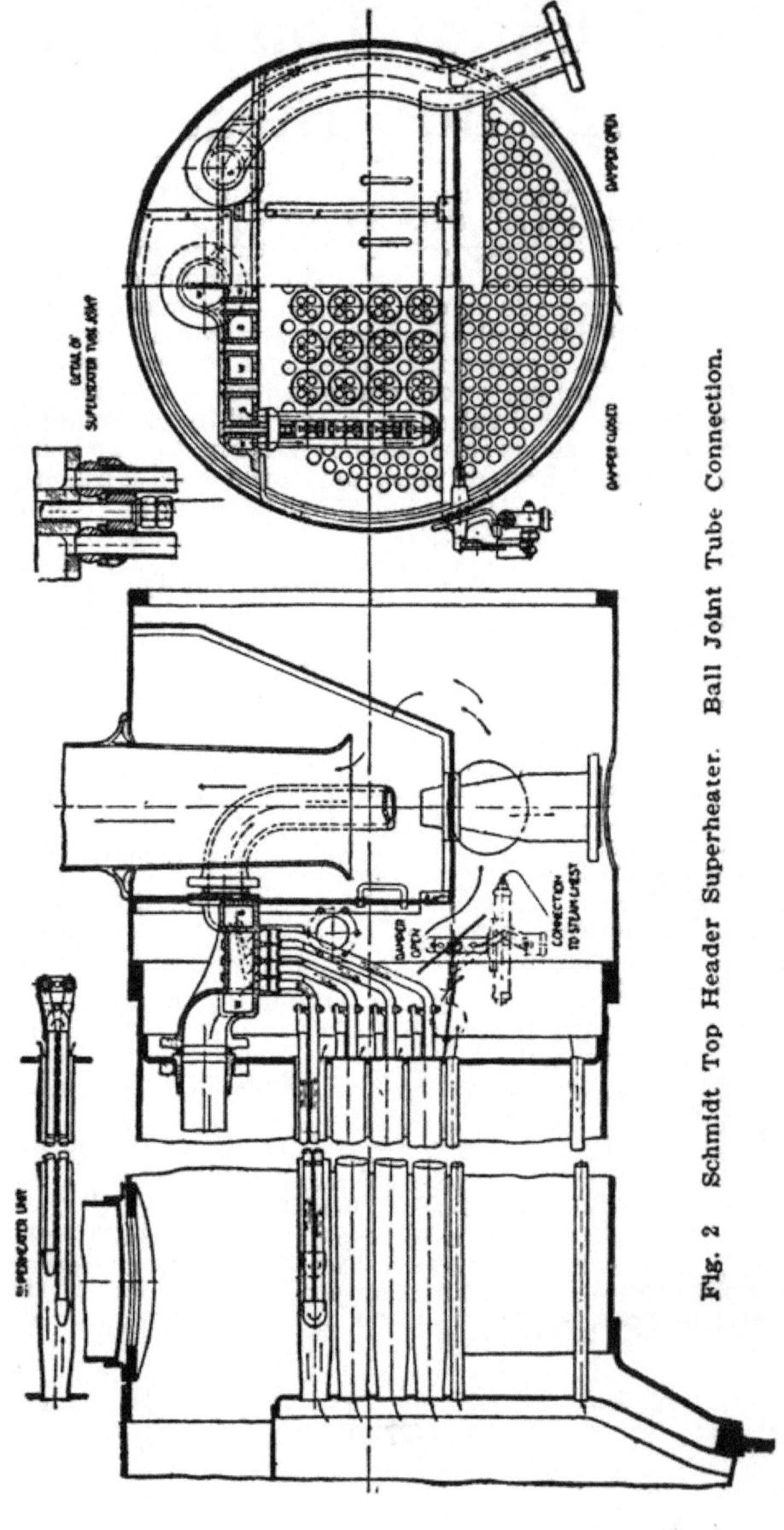

Fig. 2 Schmidt Top Header Superheater. Ball Joint Tube Connection.

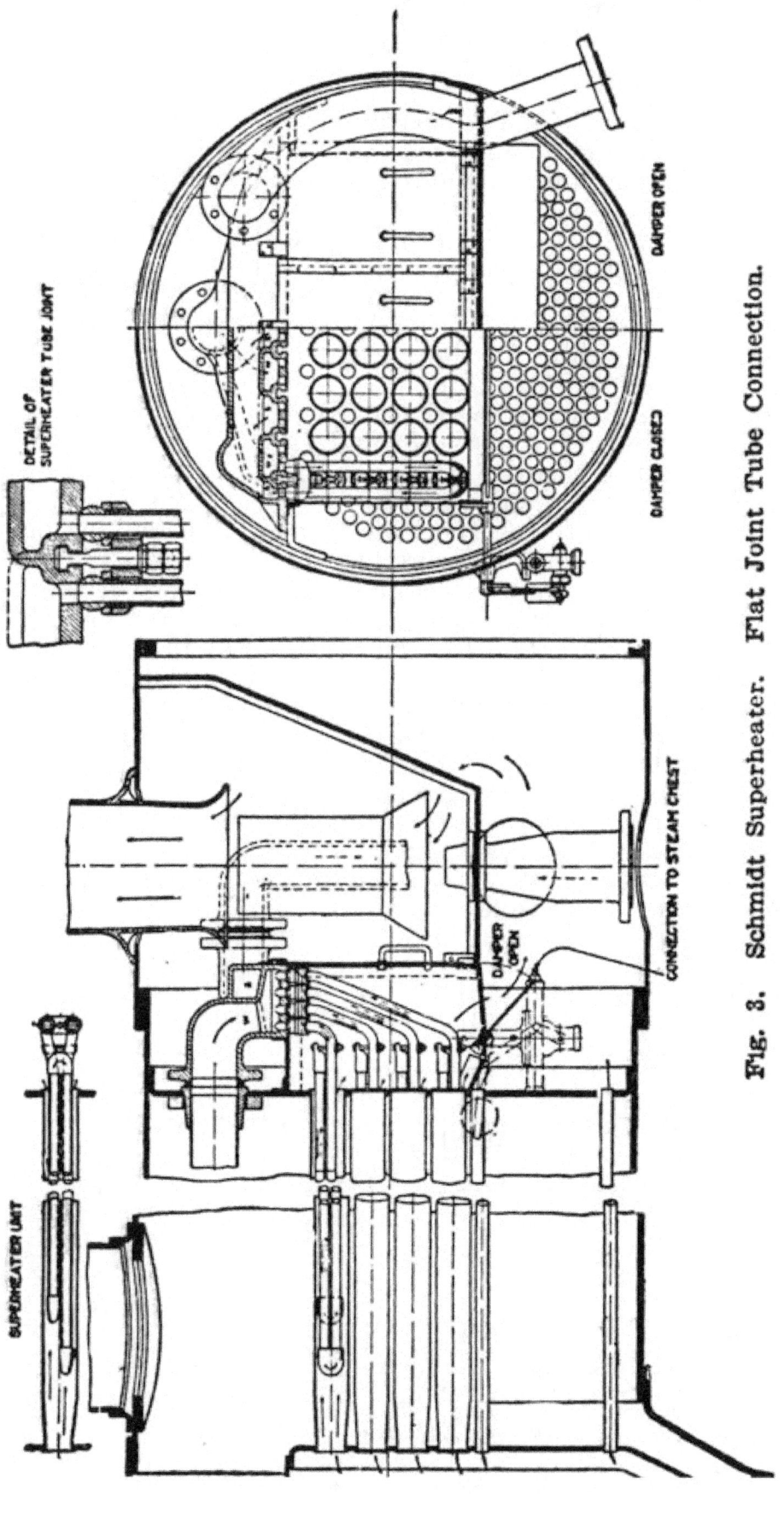

Fig. 3. Schmidt Superheater. Flat Joint Tube Connection.

The vertical partition is so designed that the portion between the header and table plate consists of three or four plates. These plates are equipped with handles, and by raising them slightly they may be removed and thus permit free access to the superheater units and header. Hand holes are also provided in the sides of smoke-box for inspection of superheater parts from the outside without opening the smoke-box door.

The superheater damper is held open by pressure of steam from the steam chest acting on the piston in the damper cylinder, and permits hot gases to flow through the superheater flues. It is closed by a weight or a spring as soon as the steam is out of the steam chest, and stops the flow of hot gases through the large flues.

On opening the throttle, the steam passes through the dry pipe and, on reaching the header, is forced through the passage "W" to the various units forming the superheater. On leaving the superheater units the steam is delivered to the passages "S," from which it passes to the steam pipes and steam chests. On reaching the steam chests, it passes automatically to the superheater damper cylinder through the connecting pipe. The steam pressure acting on the piston of the superheater damper cylinder opens the damper, and this permits the free flow of hot gases from the fire to the smoke-box through the large boiler flues which contain the superheater tubes.

A part of the heat of the gases flowing through the large flues is absorbed by the surrounding water. Another portion is absorbed by the tubes of the superheater units and transmitted by them to the steam passing through them and superheating it.

In order that the gases with the cinders which they carry with them may meet with the minimum of obstruction in their flow through the large flues, the return bends of the superheater units are provided with lugs which raise the tubes of the superheater units from the bottom of the flues and permit a practically free and unobstructed flow of the gases under and between the tubes forming the unit.

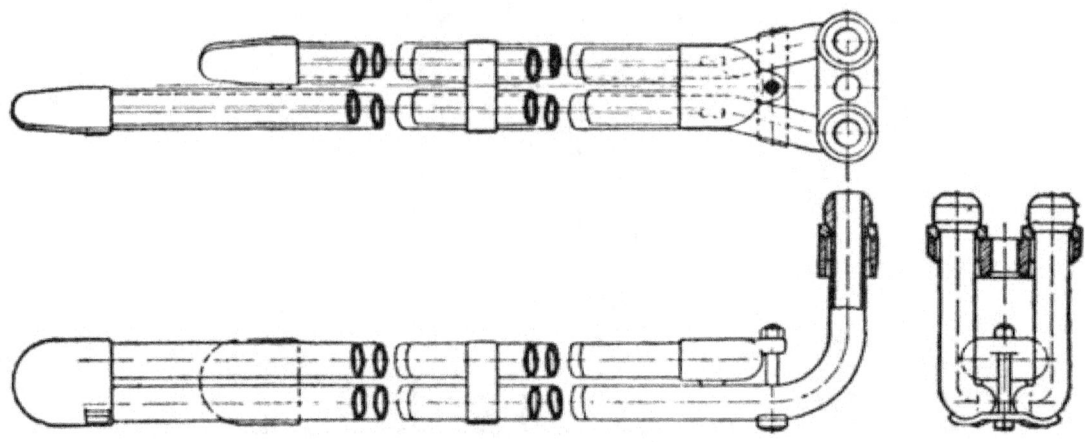

Fig. 4. Schmidt Superheater Unit.

On closing of the throttle the steam passes from the steam chest and at the same time from the superheater damper cylinder through the pipe connections, allowing the weight on the damper shaft arm to automatically close the damper, thus stopping the flow of hot gases through the large flues when there is no steam passing through the superheater units.

Under certain conditions of service, such as switching, etc., where service is intermittent, another form of the automatic acting superheater damper cylinder is sometimes used. This form permits the superheater damper to remain open at all times except when the blower is on, when it is closed by steam from the blower pipe.

The amount or degree of superheat is the increase of the final temperature of the steam leaving the superheater over that of the steam and water in the boiler. For example, steam at 200 pounds gauge pressure has a temperature of 387.5 degrees F. on entering the dry pipe. On leaving the superheater suppose it has a temperature of 600 degrees F. In that case it has been superheated in its passage through the superheater by an amount equal to the difference of 600 and 387½, i. e., 212½ degrees F.

To secure the best results the quantity of heat absorbed by the superheater units should be sufficient to superheat the steam to an average temperature of 600 degrees F.

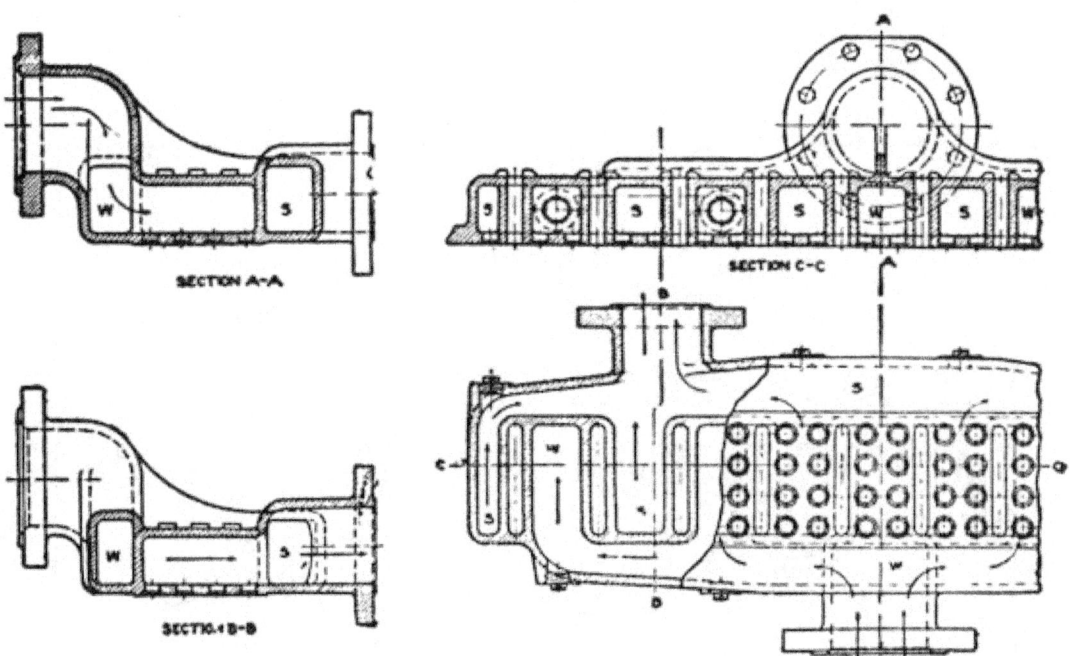

Fig. 5. Schmidt Superheater Header.

For cleaning the flues the use of air of at least 100 pounds pressure should be used. It should be applied through a 3-inch gas pipe, which is inserted at the back end of the flue and gradually worked forward under the superheater unit, blowing the dirt out of the front end of the flue. The use of air for blowing out the boiler flues is recommended in preference to steam or water.

In case steam is used instead of air for blowing out the flues, the boiler should be under steam to avoid the condensation of water in the flue, as it would be liable to mix with the ashes, etc., and form a coating on the inside of the large flues. The superheater damper should be open in all cases while cleaning the flues.

The superheater units and header are in the top portion of the boiler, symmetrically located, and will not interfere with work in the smoke-box.

The design of the unit and arrangement of the front end presents the least obstruction to the free flow of gas from the fire through the smoke-box to the stack.

The design permits the use of external steam pipe connections to the cylinders, and this reduces the obstruction offered by the ordinary type of saturated engines.

When necessary to remove the small flues in the bottom portion of the boiler they may be taken out without removing the superheater parts.

No extra joints are required in the steam pipes and the existing joints are rendered more accessible than on a saturated engine.

Each individual unit can be disconnected from the header by loosening a single bolt.

The joint between the unit and header is the ball joint, which permits easy removal and replacement of units.

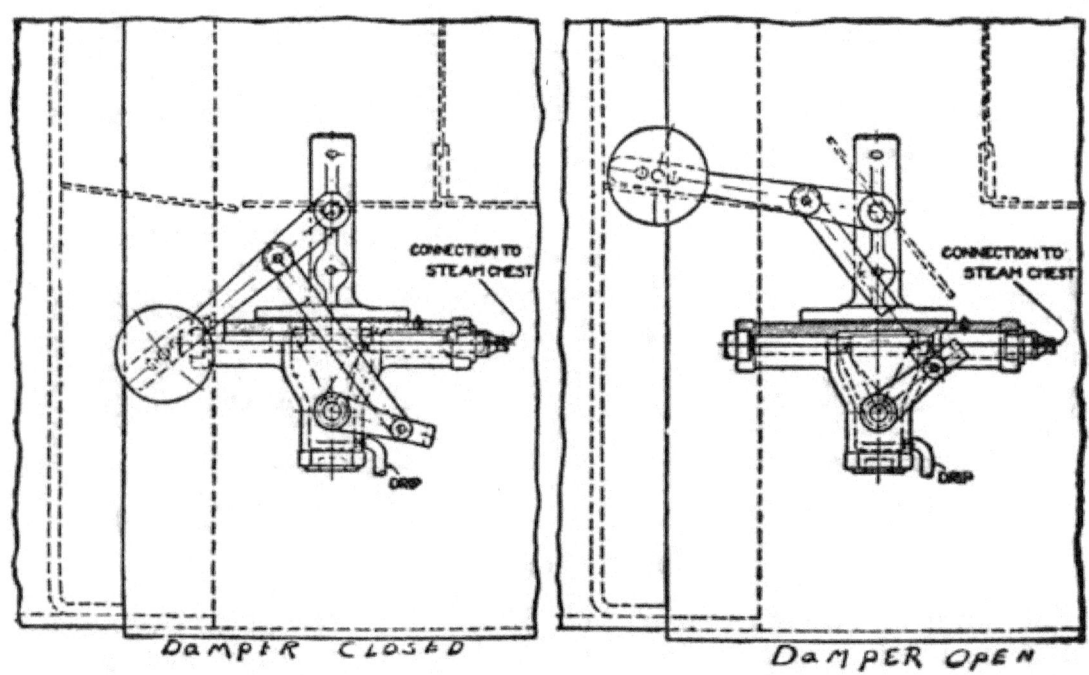

Fig. 6. Schmidt Superheater Damper.

The minimum number of shapes of superheater tubes is required, as every unit in each horizontal row is exactly alike.

The usual stresses in the cylinder casting, due to difference in temperature between the live and exhaust passages, are reduced through the use of external steam pipe connections, which remove the hot steam from the saddle.

Inspection of the superheater tubes and joints, boiler flues and front tube sheet, which can be made without removal of any of the superheater parts, should cover examination for air and steam leaks in front end, for any accumulation of cinders and ashes or deposits on return bends in boiler flues.

All air and steam leaks should be stopped. In the case of steam leaks between the header and the superheater units, joints should be immediately tightened, if necessary regrinding ball joints or applying a new gasket to flat joints. In case a new gasket is applied the joint should be tightened again after the gasket has been under steam heat the first time.

Suitable handholes are provided in the sides of the smoke-box so that the superheater can be inspected by means of an electric flash light without opening the smoke-box door.

The flues can be easily inspected from the front while a light is held at the fire-box end.

At regular intervals the boiler flues should be blown out the same as the boiler tubes are blown out, and thoroughly cleaned of all ashes, cinders, and soot. At the same time any deposit which may have accumulated on the return bends nearest the fire-box should be broken off and removed.

Every two months the superheater, the steam and exhaust pipes should be tested with warm water of about working pressure to make sure that all joints, etc., are tight in front end. The return bends at fire-box end should be examined from fire-box end at this test. In setting the flues the prosser is used in preference to the roller whenever possible in working over the superheater flues. The prosser should not have less than twelve sections, and the rollers not less than five rolls. Inserting plugs in the regular tubes surrounding superheater flues when using roller has proved good practice.

The superheater damper and rigging should work freely, and the damper should be wide open when the throttle is open and there is steam in the damper cylinder. With no steam in the damper cylinder the damper should be closed.

The damper should be closed when the blower is used for firing up.

The piston rod extension should be inspected at regular intervals, and have extension guide adjusted to maintain the piston central in the cylinder.

When handling the engines about the engine house, yards, etc., before the cylinders are warmed, the cylinder cocks should be kept open until dry steam appears.

Operation. The general operation of the superheated steam locomotive is the same as the ordinary saturated steam locomotive.

Cylinder cocks should be kept open when starting until dry steam appears.

In starting, the reverse lever should be put in full gear to insure oil distributing the full length of the valve bushing.

In general, superheated steam locomotives should be operated with full throttle and short cut-off, when working conditions will permit.

On account of the larger diameter of cylinders used in superheater engines, the throttle must be opened slowly and special care taken to prevent slipping of the drivers.

The firing should be light and regular to produce as high a flame temperature and as perfect combustion as possible in the fire-box.

A smoky fire has a lower flame temperature, reduces the degree of superheat, and uses more coal.

The engineer should know that the superheater damper is open while using steam and closed when steam is shut off.

If the engine does not steam freely make sure that the superheater damper is open.

Leaks in the front end or superheater units, flues stopped up, and derangement of draft appliances not only affect the steaming of the engine, but reduce the degree of superheat and should be reported and corrected at once.

Blows in cylinder and valve packing should be reported and receive proper attention, as they will cause scoring, due to removal of oil from wearing surfaces.

Repairing. When the engine is in for general repairs the superheater parts should be carefully cleaned, examined, and all defective parts should be repaired or replaced.

The superheater units should be painted with a thin coat of hot tar as soon as cleaned to prevent rusting.

The ball joints should be reground and joint should show a good continuous bearing all around the ball.

With the flat gasket type of joint between header and superheater units the flange on the unit should come up parallel to the face of header so that the gasket has only to make the joint and does not have to take care of any angle between the flange and header.

In replacing the superheater units it is essential that they be properly located in the top of the flue to prevent obstruction to the flow of gases through the flue.

In locating the superheater header, its face for superheater unit joints should be square with the tube sheet, parallel to the top row of flues and the correct distance above them to insure correct position of the superheater unit in the flue. It should be firmly supported at the ends by Header Supports securely fastened to the sides of the smoke-box.

The Joint Ring between the header and dry-pipe should have a flat and ball face to permit free adjustment of the header.

On reassembling, the superheater should be subjected to same water tests as boiler.

DON'TS ON SUPERHEATERS

Don't expect too much of the superheater; it is not intended to overcome blows or stop steam leaks or square valves, and it is like some children—won't keep itself clean.

Don't forget when switching that there is more steam between the throttle and cylinders with the superheater than with the saturated steam engine—the superheater holds some.

Don't carry water too high just because you don't hear any in the smokestack. You might be using your superheater to boil water instead of heating steam.

Don't think because your engine steams that you are getting the full value of the superheat; your engine may not be calling for the capacity of your boiler.

Don't close your throttle entirely on road engines until you get to going quite slow; your cylinder lubrication will be much better.

Don't fire your coal too wet; it won't clinker so badly if reasonably dry. The more you rake the fire the more the flues will stop up. There are only two reasons why a fire should be raked; one, because too much coal is used, and the other because it is not put in the right place.

While there is a great difference in coal, there is not as much difference as in what YOU are able to get out of it. They tell us of the high number of heat units or B. T. U.'s in certain coal; what does that amount to, to us, if we are not able to catch them, harness them up, and use them to our advantage?

These don'ts apply with equal force to the handling of engines that are not equipped *with superheaters.*

Engine Failures and Breakdowns

THE LOCOMOTIVE AND ADHESION

Q.—What is a locomotive engine?

A.—A locomotive is two steam engines placed on wheels, equipped with the mechanism necessary to move itself on rails and to haul trains of cars.

Q.—What are the principal parts of a locomotive?

A.—The principal part of a locomotive is the boiler which is carried on substantial frames that also carry two cylinders that transmit power generated in the boiler, as steam to the driving wheels secured in the frames. With an eight-wheel engine there are two pairs of driving wheels coupled together by side rods and a four-wheel truck supporting the front end of the engine. The cranks of the driving wheels are set at right angles with each other so that when one crank is on the dead center the other will be transmitting the maximum power. Power is transmitted to the driving wheels by main rods that extend from the piston connection in the crossheads to the crank pins. Nearly all road locomotives have a tender attached which carries the necessary supply of fuel and water.

Q.—What would you do should your engine become disabled while out on the road?

A.—In case a locomotive becomes disabled while on the road, proceed at once to protect your train in accordance with the rules and regulations, then notify the proper officials and prepare the engine as far as possible with the means at hand, to be towed in.

Q.—Can a train be handled with one side of locomotive disabled?

A.—That depends on the physical characteristics of the road and the nature of the disablements of the engine, as well as the class of locomotive to which the injury occurs. With the lighter class of locomotives and level roadbeds, with the side rods up, 50 per cent or more of a train can be handled, but with an unfavorable grade or with side rods down the engine will do no more than to handle itself. The heavy modern locomotive will do no more than handle itself without side rods up, as with only one pair of drivers to furnish the adhesion to propel the whole weight of the locomotive it will stand and slip and will not handle itself to a terminal.

Q.—How do the engines of a locomotive transmit their power to the driving wheels?

A.—The power exerted by the steam pressure on the piston head is transmitted by medium of the piston rod, crosshead, wrist pin, and main rod to the crank pin, which is located on the outside of the driving wheel between the hub and the outer edge of the wheel. This arrangement makes a crank lever of the pin and gives a rotary motion to the wheels, propelling the locomotive and its load in the direction indicated by the position of the reverse lever.

Q.—When is there the greatest danger of damage to the machinery from an engine slipping, when running at a high or low rate of speed?

A.—At a low rate of speed, because at a high rate of speed the revolutions of the wheels are not increased so much over normal as when slipping at a low rate of speed.

Q.—Upon what is the power of a locomotive to do work dependent?

A.—On the energy it can exert to produce motion without the driving wheels slipping, and is dependent on the adhesive power of the locomotive. This power is proportional to the weight on the driving wheels.

Q.—How may adhesion be increased or diminished?

A.—Increased by the use of sand, which makes the friction greater, and lessened by a wet or frosty rail, which reduces the friction. Sand on a wet rail will give about the same adhesion that a dry rail would have without the use of sand. If the sand lever is opened wide and too heavy streams of sand are run on the rail, friction will be greatly increased on the train wheels and a train "stalled," that could have been pulled with a lighter use of sand, besides exhausting the supply sooner than necessary, which is limited to the none too great capacity of the sand box. The frequent opening and closing of the sand valves will give the best result on a hard pull, for if the valves are left open just a little, to run fine streams of sand, they will speedily close up and the wheels will slip. The quantity of sand that will give the requisite adhesion with the least train friction is what is desired.

Q.—Is there anything aside from a "bad" rail that will cause wheels to slip?

A.—Yes. Too great cylinder power for the adhesion of the wheels. This condition is not intended to exist. A small driving wheel will slip with the same cylinder power more easily than a larger wheel, because greater leverage is exerted.

Q.—On what is the tractive power dependent?

A.—The length of the stroke, area of piston, average mean effective steam pressure and diameter of driving wheels.

Q.—Are you acquainted with the rule used for calculating the tractive power of a locomotive?

A.—I know the rule that reads: Square the diameter of one cylinder in inches, multiply the product by length of stroke in inches, multiply that product by 85 per cent of the boiler pressure in pounds and divide the product by the diameter of the driving wheels in inches.

Q.—Put that problem into figures.
A.—22 × 22 = 484 × 28 = 13,552 × 170 = 2,303,840 ÷ 72 = 31,998, the tractive power from which 10 per cent is subtracted for friction.

Q.—What do you understand the expression tractive power to mean?
A.—The power which the engine exerts upon the drawbar to haul a load.

Q.—Is the whole tractive power of a locomotive exerted in ordinary working?
A.—No. The figures given represent the haul the engine would be capable of exerting while starting a train or hauling on a slow heavy pull.

Q.—When that engine is pulling a heavy train at a speed of 60 miles an hour, about what would be the tractive power exerted?
A.—Running at 60 miles an hour, that engine whose drivers are 72 inches diameter would make 284.5 revolutions per minute and would open the ports for steam admission and exhaust 569 times, which would leave about one-tenth of a second for steam to enter the cylinder. Under these circumstances the mean effective pressure, as it is called, inside the cylinder would be about 40 pounds per square inch instead of 170 pounds available in starting. So then the problem of that engine power would be 22 × 22 = 484 × 28 = 13,552 × 40 = 542,080 ÷ 72 = 7,528.8 pounds: As a passenger train running at 60 miles on a level track offers resistance of about 16 pounds per ton of entire train, this engine ought to be capable of moving 470 tons, including the engine and tender at the speed named.

(Figuring out these particulars for engines having different proportions is excellent practice for a person trying to learn the principles of locomotive engineering.)

Q.—What is reckoned by engineers as one horse power?
A.—The power applied in raising 33,000 pounds one foot per minute.

Q.—How would you calculate the horse power of the locomotive whose tractive power has just been demonstrated?
A.—By the following process:

380.15 square inches of piston area of one cylinder.
40 pounds mean effective pressure on piston.
———
15,206.00
4.66 feet piston travel each revolution.
———
70,859.96
2 cylinders.
———
141,719.92
284.5 revolutions per minute.
———
40,318,317,240 ÷ 33,000 = 1,221 horse power developed.

Q.—What is the difference between the maximum and minimum power of a locomotive, and how can same be ascertained; also the difference between maximum and minimum weight on driving wheels?

A.—The maximum power of an engine is its greatest power, or highest drawbar pull it can develop. This is found by the aid of the dynamometer, an instrument connecting the tender of engine to be tested to the train. The dynamometer indicates the drawbar pull or tractive power just the same as scales indicate the weight of anything. The minimum power is never considered in the performance of an engine.

The difference between maximum and minimum weight on driving wheels is the difference between the greatest and least weight on driving wheels of the different classes of engine.

Q.—What is friction?

A.—Friction is the resistance to motion offered by the surfaces of bodies in contact in a direction parallel to these surfaces. The action of friction is illustrated in railway work by the operation of brake shoes on wheels to stop trains; the friction between driving wheels sufficiently loaded and the surface of the rails enables the locomotive to exert much tractive force without slipping the wheels. Friction also resists the turning of an axle on its journal and makes tractive force necessary to move a train of cars.

Q.—Upon what does the amount of friction between two bodies depend?

A.—The amount of friction between two bodies in contact, depends on pressure, temperature, speed, kind of material, and the quality and quantity of lubricant used. Friction is nearly independent of the area of surface of an article to be moved. A brick will move as freely on a board or incline while resting on its side as when resting on its face.

Q.—What is meant by the co-efficient of friction?

A.—The proportion which the resistance to sliding motion bears to the force pressing the substances together. A smooth iron casting loaded to weigh 100 pounds will require a force of 15 pounds or 15/100 of the weight to slide the plate upon another smooth plate. The co-efficient of friction is therefore said to be 0.15.

Q.—What effect has the introduction of oil or other lubricant between rubbing parts?

A.—It renders friction in proportion to the quantity and quality of the lubricant used. Tests with different lubricants showed that with tallow the co-efficient of friction was 0.1; with lard oil, 0.07; with olive oil, 0.064; with lard and graphite, 0.055, which proves that the amount of frictional resistance is greatly influenced by the lubricants used.

Q.—What effect has pressure between the rubbing parts upon lubrication?

A.—High pressure between, say, bearing and journal, has a tendency to prevent the lubricant from being efficient. The lighter the load the easier it is to apply lubricants to advantage.

Q.—What effect has speed upon lubrication?

A.—When frictional parts, such as journals, crank pins, or eccentrics move at high velocity, lubricating the parts effectually is much more difficult than it is when the speed is low or moderate.

BOILERS

Q.—What are the principal parts of a locomotive boiler?

A.—The shell or cylindrical part to which is attached the firebox in the rear and the smoke-box in front. The fire-box is a square or oblong box with outside and inside sheets forming a water space on all parts except the bottom, where the fire grates are situated. The sides and back sheets are secured to each other by stay bolts and the crown sheet is generally supported by radial stays secured to the outside shell. Sometimes the crown sheet is supported by crown bars that extend across the fire-box and rest upon the sheet seams at each side of the box. From the front of the fire-box an equipment of flue-tubes, each about two inches in diameter, conveying the products of combustion to the smoke-box, thence to the atmosphere.

Q.—What are the principal strains endured by a locomotive fire-box?

A.—First, to the strains due to the high pressure of steam; second, to the strains that result from varying temperatures with the hot water on one side of the sheets and a hot flame or, perhaps, cold air on the other side. These changes of temperature act to lengthen or shorten the steel sheets, putting immense strains upon the material. Varying temperature of feed water also puts strains upon the fire-box.

Q.—Why is the fire-box surrounded by water?

A.—To prevent the hot fire from burning the sheets. The surface of the fire-box sheets, being exposed to the direct heat from the fire, forms a valuable steam making area.

Q.—How is the bottom of the fire-box secured?

A.—By a heavy ring made to conform to the shape of the fire-box. The outside and the inside sheets are riveted to this ring, which is generally called the mud-ring, because the mud that drops from the evaporated water settles there.

Q.—What is below the mud-ring?

A.—Attached to the mud-ring is a frame which supports the grates, and beneath the grates is the ash pan to catch the ashes that drop through.

Q.—How many forms of boilers are in common use?

A.—The straight boiler, which has the top of the fire-box flush or on line with the top of the cylindrical part; the wagon top boiler, in which the top of the fire-box is raised considerably above the line of the cylindrical top; the Bellpaire boiler, which has the top of the fire-box flat.

Q.—For what purpose is a dome placed on a boiler?

A.—To provide the exit for steam at a point considerably above the level of the water level, thereby tending to supply steam free from mixture of water. It also provides a convenient place for the throttle valve, for safety valves, and other attachments.

Q.—In operating a locomotive, what is the most important duty concerning the boiler?

A.—To keep a proper supply of water.

Q.—What would happen if the crown sheet becomes bare of water when the engine was working?

A.—If it became sufficiently hot, the crown sheet would be forced away from the stay bolt and an explosion might result.

Q.—Would it be advisable to put water into a boiler after the sheets had become bare and red hot?

A.—It would not. The fire should be killed at once.

Q.—What part of the boiler has the greatest pressure? Why?

A.—The bottom, because the weight of the water is added, in addition to the steam pressure.

Q.—What results from many of the flues becoming stopped up?

A.—Every flue stopped up takes away an important part of the heating surface, with the result that when many flues are stopped up the steaming capacity of the boiler is impaired.

It has been found on some roads that removing one or two of the bottom rows of flues has improved the steaming of engines.

Q.—What is the purpose of placing the injector check valves near to the front end of the boiler?

A.—The front end of the boiler is considerably cooler than the back end, and the coal gases keep cooling as they approach the front end. When the feed water is injected close to the front end it presents a heat absorbing medium to the cooling gases.

Q.—How is the flat surface of the flue sheets prevented from collapsing under the great pressure upon them?

A.—The flues, which are expanded or beaded at the ends, act as stays to strengthen the flue sheets.

Q.—How is the boiler secured to the frames?

A.—At the front end of the smoke-box, which is an integral part of the boiler, it is substantially secured to the cylinder saddle casting, preventing any movement at that end. Then there is a cross brace at the back end of the crosshead guides which secures the boiler to the frames. The fire-box end of the boiler is secured to the frames in such a manner that there is fore and aft motion, but no side motion.

Q.—What is the purpose of giving the boiler fore and aft motion?

A.—To provide for the expansion and contraction of the boiler. It is longer when hot than it is when cold.

Q.—What must be the condition inside the boiler to give the best results in steam making?

A.—It must be kept as clean as possible, and as free from mud and scale as circumstances will permit.

Q.—What is meant by an engine priming or foaming?

A.—It is water mixed with the steam passing into the cylinders.

Q.—What is the cause of priming?

A.—Impurities passing into the boiler with the feed water. When an engine first leaves the shop priming may be caused by oil and grease left inside the boiler by workmen.

Q.—What is meant by circulation in the boiler?

A.—The water inside the boiler is always moving from one point to another, due to the action of the heating gases. That movement is called circulation. Circulation tends downward at the cooler parts and upwards close to the heating surfaces. It is strongest about the fire-box and arises from the steam rushing away from the sheets where it has been generated.

Q.—What is the leg of a fire-box?

A.—The parts extending down to the mud-ring.

Q.—What happens when the leg of the fire-box gets filled with mud?

A.—The sheets exposed to the fire get burned, so that they bulge between the stay bolts and are likely to crack.

Q.—If the water became low in the boiler and the injectors failed to work, what should be done?

A.—Quench the fire or smother it with earth or slack coal.

Q.—Why is it necessary to provide extra support to a crown sheet?

A.—The crown sheet, being flat or nearly so, has little resisting power to the steam pressure on top that tends to push it downward.

Q.—In what way is the crown sheet generally supported?

A.—Generally by stay bolts that tie it to the outside shell of the boiler. Some boilers have the crown sheets supported by crown bars that extend across the crown, with stay bolts securing the sheet to the bars. The bars are double, set on edge, with space between, through which the stay bolts pass.

Q.—What objection is there to using crown bars instead of radial stays?

A.—The crown bars add considerable weight where it is not wanted, and cause accumulation of mud and scale difficult to remove.

Q.—How are the side sheets and the front and back sheets of a fire-box, which are all flat, prevented from bulging under the pressure of steam and water inside?

A.—By being bound to the outside sheets by stay bolts.

Q.—Can you tell when a stay bolt is broken?

A.—No. To find broken stay bolts is the duty of a boiler inspector or boilermaker, who has acquired special skill in doing that work.

Q.—For what purpose are small holes drilled in the outside of stay bolts?

A.—To detect breakage of the stay bolt. When a stay bolt so drilled breaks water will leak through the hole.

Q.—What are the principal causes of leaky flues?

A.—Rapid changes of temperature is the most fertile cause of leaky flues. That may be produced by irregular boiler feeding or by defects of firing, such as leaving holes in the fire that admit cold air direct to the flues. This is made worse by reckless use of the blower when the damper is open. The rapid change of temperature that is most destructive to flues generally happens upon the cinder pit. When drawing the fire the blower is frequently kept on at full force, drawing a great volume of cold air into the fire-box, causing leakage of flues and fire-box sheets.

Q.—How would you act to make the best of an engine having leaky flues?

A.—Keep up as bright a fire as possible, feed the boiler regularly, and avoid the use of the blower, and keep the fire door closed as much as circumstances would permit.

Q.—What causes scale to form upon the heating surfaces of a boiler?

A.—Generally the solid matter held in solution in the feed water. Muddy feed water may also increase the scale.

Q.—What is the effect on the economical operation of a locomotive to have the heating surfaces coated with scale?

A.—Scale on the heating surfaces prevents the hot fire gases from imparting full vaporing service to the water inside the flues and the fire-box sheets, so that they pass into the smoke-box at a higher temperature than they would if the heating surfaces were clean. In short, scale leads to waste of fuel.

Q.—How much water should be in the boiler when an engine is given up at the engine house?

A.—Three gauges or more.

Q.—When should the boiler be filled with water at the finish of a trip?

A.—While the engine is working its train. Rushing water into the boiler when engine is running from train to engine house is bad practice.

Q.—What is the effect of leaky steam pipe joints inside the smoke-box?

A.—Leaky steam joints in smoke-box are very detrimental to free steaming.

Q.—How should the water be suppled to the boiler?

A.—As nearly as possible at the rate it is being used, which can be found by keeping the water at the same level. Sometimes it is wise to have extra water to be prepared for a long, hard pull. At other times the injector may be freely used to prevent steam blowing off.

Q.—What is the difference between priming and foaming of a boiler?

A.—Priming and foaming both mean that water is being carried by the steam from the boiler to the cylinders, a dangerous condition. Priming generally results from the water level in the boiler being carried too high, or through forcing the engine to its full power; foaming is caused by impurities, such as grease, soap, or alkali, causing an aggregation of suds or bubbles that mix with the steam. Boilers that need washing out generally cause annoyance by foaming.

Q.—Explain the difference between a "wide" and a "narrow" fire-box engine.

A.—A wide fire-box engine has the fire-box widened out and set on top of the frames and extends out over the rear driving wheels, while with a narrow fire-box engine the fire-box is long and deep and fits in between the frames.

Q.—Has the more recent or wide fire-box type any advantages over the narrow fire-box? If so, what are the advantages?

A.—Yes. The wide fire-box provides a much larger grate area than can be obtained with the narrow fire-box fitting between the frames, thus allowing a poor grade of coal to be burned. It is also easier to fire properly than a long, narrow fire-box.

Q.—Describe in a general way the construction of a locomotive fire-box.

A.—The fire-box is rectangular in form and consists of the back tube sheet (in front), the crown sheet (on top), the two side sheets, the door sheet (in back), and the grate at the bottom. It is secured to the back part of the boiler, and its sheets are surrounded by water, being separated on all sides from the outside shell by a distance of from $3\frac{1}{2}$ to $4\frac{1}{2}$ inches; this space is called the water leg. The fire-box sheets are secured to the outside shell by means of stay-bolts screwed through both sheets. The bottom of the water leg is formed by a wrought iron or cast steel ring, called the mud-ring, to which the outside and the inside sheets of the fire-box are riveted. Below the grate is the ash pan, which is provided with dampers to regulate the supply of air admitted to the fire-box from underneath. The crown sheet is supported either by means of crown bars or radial stays.

Q.—What is a stay bolt?

A.—A stay bolt is a bolt, generally made of wrought iron, $\frac{7}{8}$ to 1 inch in diameter. In some cases the bolts are threaded their whole length, and in others the threads are turned off the central portion. These bolts are screwed through the outer and inner sheets of the fire-box and the ends riveted cold.

Q.—Approximately how many stay bolts are required in a fire-box of average size?

A.—Considering the stay bolts proper, there are usually from about 800 to 1,100, depending upon the size and shape of the fire-box.

Q.—What is the purpose of using stay bolts in a locomotive fire-box?

A.—They form a support for the fire-box sheets by fastening them to the main shell of the boiler, and enable them to resist the strains to which they are constantly subjected when under pressure.

Q.—(a) What would you do in case of a throttle becoming disconnected while closed?

(b) If while open?

A.—(a) Would be governed largely by conditions; if on a busy main line, would be prepared to be towed in, while if on some branch line or at some isolated place, would reduce all pressure, remove the dome cap, and connect up throttle. If for a short distance, no preparations would be necessary for towing; if long distance and cold weather, the choke plugs could be removed from the lubricator and sufficient lubrication conveyed to the steam chest and cylinders without disconnecting; however, if it is the wishes of the road, the valve rods can be disconnected and the cylinders lubricated through the relief valves by blocking the valves in one end of the steam chest.

(b) In the event of the throttle becoming disconnected while open, the pressure can be reduced to where the injectors will work properly and the engine and a few cars handled by means of the reverse lever and brakes, or, if it is so desired, where we have a clear road the crew and despatcher may be notified and the full train handled into the terminal.

Q.—Suppose you shut off and the water in the glass dropped out of sight, what would you do?

A.—In the first place, when an engine is foaming badly, the throttle should not be closed entirely until the proper location of the water is ascertained. However, in the event of the water passing out of sight, the lever should be hooked up on the center, throttle opened, gauge cocks tested in an effort to locate the water. If the water cannot then be located, I would protect the fire-box by knocking or banking the fire.

Q.—What would you do if, while out on the road, the blow-off cock would not close or should become broken off, or in case a washout plug should blow out?

A.—The first thing to do is to prevent the burning of your fire-box sheets, as the boiler will be emptied of water very quickly, and no time must be lost. Start your injectors and get your fire out in the quickest way possible, either by dumping it or smothering it. After the fire has been dumped or smothered and the pressure has all blown off from the boiler, there are two things that may be done: Either prepare to be towed in, or else, if the time permits and conditions are such as to make it possible, fit a plug into the washout hole or the hole where the blow-off cock screwed in, refill your boiler, and get in under your own steam.

Q.—What would you do in case the grates should be burned out or broken while out on the road?

A.—If the grates are only partially burned out, the hole formed can be stopped up with old fish-plates, bricks, or something similar, if any such material can be found. Sometimes it is possible to get hold of some ties and put them in the fire-box in such manner as to cover over the hole made in the grates long enough to get into clear.

If there is no other means at hand and the ash pan is a shallow one, gravel or stones can be shoveled into the hole until a bank is made extending up to the grates. However, in case the grates are completely out, there is no use of attempting to come in, and the fire should be dumped to prevent burning the ash pan completely up.

Q.—What would you do in case a tube should burst or start leaking very badly?

A.—It should be plugged, if practical. To plug a bursted flue, the pressure must be reduced sufficiently to allow working at it, and it may be necessary in some instances to cool off the fire-box sufficiently so that it can be entered. Some engines are provided with iron plugs and a plugging bar, which should be used if possible. Flues have been successfully plugged with a 2 x 4 scantling driven in from the fire-box door and left to burn off even with the sheet. The back end should be plugged first and then the front end.

Q.—What would be the best method of testing for a leaky exhaust pipe joint or nozzle joint?

A.—It is hardly practical to make a good test for leaky exhaust pipe joints or nozzle while on the road. However, the front end may be opened while the engine is working slowly, and it is possible that the leaks will show themselves or that the absence of any sparks around the joint at the bottom of the nozzle stand will indicate leakage at that point. To make a thorough test, the exhaust tip must be plugged and then, with the throttle open, the reverse lever should be moved from the forward to the back corner several times, using water pressure when available.

Q.—Is there any difference in effect from a leaky dry pipe and a leaky throttle?

A.—A leaky dry pipe will permit water to flow from the boiler to the cylinders, while a leaky throttle valve merely allows dry steam to escape from boiler, it being above water line.

Q.—Do the gauge cocks indicate the true water level in boiler as accurately as the water glass? Why?

A.—No, the gauge cocks are not as reliable as a perfect working water glass, because boiling water will rise the moment the pressure is relieved even a little, therefore, when the gauge cock is opened it relieves the pressure on water below it and the globes of steam in water begin to burst beneath the surface of the water and throw it up to opening in gauge cock, many times showing water at a gauge cock an inch or two above the true water level, while the water glass having the pressures perfectly equalized in it, the same as they are in boiler, the water in glass is at exactly the same level as it is in boiler.

Q.—Suppose the whistle or one of the safety valves blew out, what would you do?

A.—Put on both injectors and endeavor to hold the water to a safe level and, if the surrounding conditions permitted, place a wooden plug in the hole, holding it down by a timber across the hand rails, tying it down.

Q.—What would you do if one of the safety valve springs broke?

A.—Screw down the adjusting screw and put that safety valve out of business, if possible. If this is not successful, reduce all the pressure, remove the adjusting screw and drop a small nut or bolt and then replace the adjusting screw, screwing it down until the safety valve is out of commission.

Q.—How can a locomotive boiler without steam be filled with water by towing?

A.—That can be done by pumping the air out of the boiler and permitting atmospheric pressure to force water into the boiler from the tender. The procedure is this: All openings where air could enter the boiler must be closed. These include relief valves, gauge cocks, cylinder cocks, the whistle valve, and air pump steam valve. When these have been closed, place the reverse lever in full gear in the direction the engine is to be hauled, and open the water supply valve and injector throttle. A good supply of engine oil should be fed through the auxiliary oil caps to valves and pistons. The movement of the pistons in the cylinders will pump the air out of the boiler and the atmospheric pressure on the surface of the water in the tank will force a supply into the boiler.

Q.—If a throttle valve leaks, what should be done?

A.—This is annoying but not dangerous, and, as a rule, results from wear, or from the seat or valve cutting from wire drawing. The main thing to provide for is to keep the cylinder cocks open always and the reverse lever in the central notch when at a standstill In order to determine whether it is the throttle or dry pipe leaking, it should be observed whether the steam is dry or wet. Steam leaking through the throttle valve would be dry, because the valve is some distance above the water level, but the dry pipe is below the water level, indeed, is sometimes submerged, and, therefore, more or less water would leak through.

DRAFT APPLIANCES

Q.—Of what does the front end, or smoke-box, consist, and what does it contain? Describe the general arrangement of the parts.

A.—The extended front end consists of an extension to the front end of the boiler, and contains the steam pipes, the exhaust nozzle, and the draft appliances. The front part of the extended front is fitted with a door, which can be opened and the parts inspected inside. The front end door must be kept air-tight, for if air were allowed to enter the smoke-box it would partially destroy the vacuum and would affect the draft through the fire. The different parts consist of a deflector plate, which extends diagonally from the flue sheet to the nozzle, where it joins a horizontal piece of netting; the netting also extends at an angle up to the top of the smoke arch; the lower end of the deflector passes the exhaust pipe and the steam pipes and has attached to it, extending diagonally downwards, a movable apron. Across the front end and a little above the middle is a horizontal plate that may be perforated or made of netting. There is also a petticoat pipe attached to the smoke-box at a certain distance above the nozzle. The steam pipes and exhaust nozzle are located in the smoke-box, and the smokestack is placed on top of the smoke-box.

Q.—State briefly the purpose of each separate part going to make up the front end arrangement.

A.—The deflector plate deflects the gases and cinders downwards; the netting stops the sparks and cinders on their way to the stack and also acts to break the cinders up; the adjustable apron on the end of the deflector plate serves to equalize the draft through the flues and to clean the cinders out of the bottom of the smoke arch; the petticoat pipes, where used, also serve to equalize the draft through the flues and to direct the exhaust steam centrally up the stack. The exhaust pipe and nozzle conveys the steam from the cylinders and directs it centrally up the stack, and gives force to the steam when leaving the nozzle. The smokestack carries off the products of combustion above the engine and train, and serves as an instrument to enable the exhaust steam, in escaping, to create a draft through the fire. The steam pipes form a connection between the dry pipe and the steam passages in the cylinder saddle.

Q.—How should a displaced petticoat pipe be readjusted?

A.—The purpose of a petticoat pipe is to obtain an even draft over the whole of the tubes. If too high, the most of the draft would pass through the lower rows of the tubes and pull upon the front end of the fire. If too low the draft would be strongest through the upper rows of tubes and the pulling would be at the rear end of the fire-box. Therefore the displacement of the petticoat pipe may be readily detected by the action of the fire. Where there is the least draft the tubes will also be choked with ashes and cinders. Therefore, if there be an excessive draft through the lower rows of tubes, the petticoat pipe should be lowered; if through the upper rows, it should be raised.

Q.—Should a diaphragm or deflector plate on the smoke-box become misplaced, how may it be readjusted?

A.—The purpose of the diaphragm in the front end of an engine is the same as that of the petticoat pipe. Uniformity of draft is obtained by the adjustment of the lower edge of the diaphragm, which is a separate sheet from the main body. Originally this lower sheet was movable and could be raised and lowered by a system of levers under the control of the engineer. Now it is bolted to the main plate in such a way as to permit of a limited amount of motion.

Diaphragm displacement is indicated by the uneven action of the draft upon the fire, and a possible collection of cinders in tubes having an insufficient current of gases to keep them clear. If the diaphragm be too high, it would cause an excessive draft through the top rows of tubes, if too low, the same with the lower rows.

For an excessive draft through the upper rows and at the rear end of the fire-box, the diaphragm should be lowered. If through the lower rows and at front of fire-box the plate should be raised.

General directions for the adjustment of this plate, or for the petticoat pipe that would make it possible to set either to the desired position without trial, can not be given. It depends upon the type of engine, the service it may be called upon to perform, and also the quality of coal to be burned.

Q.—If the netting should become clogged or broken, what should be done?

A.—Should the netting become clogged it is apt to seriously interfere with steaming, besides the danger of causing the fire to blow back into the cab.

Clogging is usually caused by an excessive quantity of oil in the cylinders. Where an automatic oiler is used, it does not occur so frequently as where the cylinders are lubricated from cups in the cab. With this form of lubricator, the opening of the throttle immediately after the oil has been introduced is apt to throw it out at the exhaust nozzle and spatter the netting.

There is danger of throwing out large sparks and starting fires if the netting has been cut or worn away so that there are holes in it. When this happens on the road, the engine should be worked as easily as possible when traversing districts where there is danger of starting a fire. The netting should be replaced with new when the terminal is reached.

Q.—With a broken front, what should be done?

A.—This rarely happens. When it does it is usually the result of a blow, such as a collision, and as a rule is accompanied by other damages. A broken front should be repaired by replacing it with boards which can be held by the studs and nuts which were used to hold the front. This, however, is but a temporary makeshift, owing to the liability of the boards being burned by the heat and cinders of the smoke-box. However, it would serve until the terminal could be reached provided the engine worked easily.

Q.—What are the probable causes when exhaust is apparently coming out of one side of stack?

A.—The exhaust nozzle may be set so high that the steam could not properly fill the stack. Or, if either petticoat pipe or nozzle were out of line the same result would be effected.

Q.—What would be the effect if the steam did not properly fill the stack?

A.—It would lower the steaming efficiency of the engine and the vacuum in the smoke-box would be irregular in its formation and action, because the blast produces a partial vacuum in the smoke-box by induction, just as a jet of steam in an injector lifts the water from a tank. If the jet does not fill the stack, the unfilled space permits a sluggish flow of the gases, resulting in the vacuum being lowered considerably. Hence it is important that there should be a proper adjustment of the size and position of the exhaust nozzle relative to the height and diameter of the stack.

Q.—What should be done when the hopper of deep ash pan is burned or broken in a drop grate?

A.—The fire should be pulled about three feet from the front of the remaining grates; then (if near a section house) the opening should be bridged over with a splice laid lengthwise. If unable to obtain a splice, anything available to serve the purpose may be used, because it would be impossible to proceed with the train any distance with the drop grate down. If a space the size of the drop grate were open, all the air that the exhaust draws would pass through it, and the fire on the remaining grates would not burn enough to maintain steam, even with a "light" engine.

Q.—What precaution should be taken to prevent the locomotive from throwing fire?

A.—See that the spark arresting appliances are kept in perfect order, ash pan kept clean, and side dampers kept closed.

Q.—What is the result of having leaky steam pipe joints in the smoke-box?

A.—It interferes very seriously with the steaming of the engine.

QUESTIONS AND ANSWERS ON INJECTORS

Q.—What are the main working parts of an injector?

A.—The steam nozzle, combining tube, delivery tube, and the overflow nozzle.

Q.—What is the use of each of these parts?

A.—The steam nozzle directs the steam to the combining tube, where it unites with the water. The combining tube is that which its name implies, the tube where the water and steam combine; the steam is condensed and imparts its velocity to the water, moving into the delivery tube, where the greatest velocity is attained, and passing through the delivery tube and branch pipe, forces the boiler check valve from its seat and enters the boiler.

Q.—How are the tubes arranged in regard to each other?

A.—They are in exact line with each other.

Q.—What is the shape of the tubes?

A.—Tapering. The small ends of the steam nozzle and the combining tube all face toward the small end of the delivery tube.

Q.—What three kinds of injectors are commonly used on locomotives?

A.—The non-lifting, the lifting, and the restarting injectors.

Q.—Explain the meaning of the different names.

A.—The non-lifting injector is one so located on the engine that the supply of water flows to it. A lifting injector is one where a jet of steam discharges, by opening an overflow valve through a waste pipe, thus creating a vacuum. This causes a suction through the overflow pipe and water flows from the pipe. The steam throttle being opened, the water is forced through the delivery tube into the boiler. Closing the overflow valve stops the flow of steam from the waste pipe after the injector has been started to work.

A restarting injector is one that, if the supply of water is stopped temporarily, it will resume work as soon as the supply of water comes back to it, as in the case of an injector breaking from low water in the tank or on account of rough track.

Q —Why will not a lifting injector restart when it breaks?

A.—On account of the injector having a closed overflow the steam flows back through the tank hose into the tank when the injector breaks, and the water in the tank is thus kept from reaching the injector so that it could restart.

Q.—Why will the restarting injector go to work automatically when it breaks?

A.—Passages are provided for the escape of the steam to the atmosphere when the injector breaks, and the water still being furnished to the injector it goes to work automatically.

Q.—What tube measures the capacity of the injector?

A.—The delivery tube, it being the smallest tube in the injector.

Q.—Explain how the water delivered at the boiler check overcomes the boiler pressure at the boiler check and enters the boiler.

A.—Because the water moving through the branch pipe has pressure, velocity, and weight, while the pressure within the boiler is at rest and is in this manner overbalanced.

Q.—About what is the ratio of water and steam combining in the ordinary injector?

A.—About fifteen parts of water to one of steam.

Q.—Why is the delivery tube made small at the end where it receives the water and then expands?

A.—To give the water greater velocity when it escapes from the tube.

Q.—What causes the lifting effect in the lifting injector?

A.—The vacuum being in front of the water supply from the tank, the air pressure on the water in the tank forces the water up into the injector.

Q.—If an injector had been working in a satisfactory manner and suddenly stopped working, where would be the first place to search for trouble?

A.—In the water supply. The tank valve might have become disconnected. The strainer might be stopped up or fine coal or cinders might have gathered about the tank valve.

Q.—In any of these cases how would you remove the obstruction without stopping engine and taking hose down?

A.—Close overflow valve and blow a heavy jet of steam back through the tank hose from the injector steam throttle; if this does not suffice it will be necessary to take the hose down at the first opportunity. If air sucks into feed pipe at any point injector will break, so look out for this trouble also.

Q.—What will cause an injector to fail to prime?

A.—Low water in the tank, leaky boiler check valve or other leak of steam to injector that would destroy the vacuum, or an overflow pipe stopped up.

Q.—In case an injector was not used for some time what might occur?

A.—Boiler check valve might become corroded and stuck fast to seat so that injector would not work, and tubes might also become corroded and partly stopped up.

Q.—If a boiler check valve would only partly lift when injector was started to work what would be the result?

A.—Water would be thrown out on the ground through the overflow pipe.

Q.—Under either of these conditions can anything be done to remedy or help them?

A.—Open cock to frost pipe and tap boiler check valve cage and try to work the injector; this will sometimes loosen the valve from its seat and injector will go to work properly.

Q.—What effect has loose tubes on the working of an injector?

A.—It will cause the injector to break.

Q.—If the steam furnished by the injector steam throttle is not all condensed what is the result?

A.—Injector will not work or will only partly take up the water. Either reduce the supply of steam or increase the supply of water.

Q.—Will variation of steam pressure on boiler have any effect on the working of an injector?

A.—Yes. If the steam pressure falls considerably the supply of water must be decreased or the injector will not take it all up, or the boiler will be oversupplied with water.

Q.—What effect has bad water on injectors?

A.—It corrodes or limes them up and they soon get in a condition where they will not work, and a bath in muriatic acid will be necessary to restore them to a good working condition.

Q.—Which injector will corrode the more quickly, a lifting or a non-lifting injector?

A.—The lifting injector, on account of steam being continually in the body of the injector. In some localities where the water is quite bad and injectors corrode quickly, only the non-lifting injectors are used to avoid changing and cleaning injectors so often.

Q.—Must air enter tank above water as fast as the water is taken out by the injector?

A.—Yes. In all cases.

Q.—What depends on the good condition of the injectors?

A.—The safety of the boiler and the proper handling of the train.

Q.—How should a boiler be pumped on a through train where stops are infrequent?

A.—The injector must be worked hard enough to maintain the water level in the boiler.

Q.—How should a boiler on a local train be pumped?

A.—So that the water level will fall some between stations. The supply can be replenished while doing station work and the pops thereby kept from blowing off steam, and a brighter fire be kept burning on the grates.

Q.—Is it desirable or not to have a good supply of water in the boiler when pulling out of town with a train?

A.—Yes. The injector need not be put to work where there is plenty of water in the boiler until fire is in good shape and steam pressure at maximum.

Q.—What should an engineer know about the injectors on the engine he is taking out before starting on a trip?

A.—That both work in a satisfactory manner. If only one injector is used all the time the chances are that the other one will fail when most needed.

Q.—Why will an injector not prime with hot water in feed pipe as we know it will not? What action takes place to prevent its doing so? Also, why is it that if injector is thrown back it will usually prime all right immediately after?

A.—To prime the injector a vacuum must be formed in the feed pipe above water level. The water in feed pipe may not be hot enough to make steam rise against the normal atmospheric pressure but when priming valve is opened the pressure of atmosphere above water in feed pipe is reduced, so that steam may rise from the hot water and thus prevent the formation of vacuum sufficient for the water to be forced into the injector. By blowing the water back into the tank in such cases the contact of hot steam with the feed water would seem to make matters worse, yet the fact is the water which flows again into feed pipe, after having blown back, is usually of low enough temperature to not generate steam in the vacuum necessary to raise the water to injector as in priming.

Q.—Some of the late injectors will not drop the water with a lowering of boiler pressure. What is the reason for that?

A.—One of the injectors most efficient in operating with changes of boiler pressure is the simplex. It is really a double injector. When the steam pressure is high both its supply features are in operation; when the pressure falls, one of the features is automatically cut out. The principle on which it works is briefly stated as follows: When the steam has imparted its full propelling force to the water where the steam and water join in the combination tube, the water is driven not directly into branch pipe, but into another nozzle from which the water is again discharged into a receiving tube joined to branch pipe. There is as open space between the ends of the discharging nozzle and receiving tube, and the rapid flow of water over this open space when injector is working at or nearly full capacity induces a vacuum at that point where means are provided for water to be supplied when this vacuum is created. The effect of this auxiliary feature is to take up some of this feed water, which is carried to the boiler by force imparted to the current of water by the steam in the combining tube. It is at once apparent that this principle affords a maximum supply of water with a minimum quantity of steam, which represents a considerable measure of economy, and when the boiler pressure varies there is no danger of waste at the overflow, as the effect of the reduced pressure would be to automatically cut out the water taken up by the auxiliary feature referred to. The small amount of steam needed to operate the original supply being such that it is not weakened enough by change of pressure to drop feed water at overflow, as the ordinary injector does.

Q.—Will a leak in feed pipe have same effect on injector capacity, no matter where leak may be?

A.—There is much difference in a leak in feed pipe on the capacity of the injector. The nearer it is to the injector the worse effect it has. One reason is that in being above water line it tends to prevent the formation of the vacuum needed for priming. Another reason is that owing to the constant presence of a partial vacuum in feed pipe above the feed water level the same size of leak will admit more air than if same leak is at point below water line.

Q.—What is the principle on which an injector works?

A.—An injector works upon the principle of induced currents coupled with velocity; a jet of steam flowing through the injector first creates a vacuum, allowing the atmospheric pressure acting on the water in the tank to force the water into the injector and out the overflow; the injector is now said to be primed. When the steam valve is opened wide the increased jet of steam meets with the body of water in the injector, with which it combines and imparts sufficient velocity to the water to force it through the delivery pipe and open the boiler check valve and enter the boiler against the pressure that is in there.

Q.—What are the various parts of a lifting injector?

A.—A lifting injector consists of two different parts: the lifting part for lifting the water and the forcing part to force the water into the boiler. It consists of the injector body, a steam nozzle, a lifting tube, a combining and condensing tube and a delivery tube, also the various steam and water valves to operate it.

Q.—How would you start an injector?

A.—To start the injector, first open the water valve and then open the steam valve slightly until water appears at the overflow; the injector is now said to be primed; then open the steam valve wide and the injector will start to work.

Q.—What are the most common causes for injectors failing to work?

A.—The most common causes are the suction pipe or strainer wholly or partially stopped up; tank valve closed or partly closed; loose hose lining; leaks in the suction pipes; leaky steam valve in the injector or leaky boiler check and line check valves; or the boiler check stuck shut; overflow valve stuck shut with a double tube injector; obstruction in the injector tubes; or in cold weather the tank may be frozen up air tight.

Q.—What would you do if a check valve should stick open?

A.—Go out on the running board and with a block of wood tap lightly on the check valve case and the delivery pipe; this will usually cause the check valve to be seated again. This can futher be assisted by opening the small pet cock in the branch pipe and reducing the pressure there. If the check valve cannot be seated, close the overflow valve and the water regulating valve to prevent the water from the boiler passing back through the injector. In case the injector has no water regulating valve or it will not close tight, reduce the steam pressure in the boiler, disconnect the hose from the feed pipe and plug the end of the pipe with a wooden plug, couple up the hose again to hold in the plug and use the other injector.

Q.—How would you make sure whether it was the check valve or the steam valve that was leaking?

A.—Shut off the steam supply from the boiler; if the steam stops flowing from the overflow the trouble is in the steam valve to the injector; while if steam and hot water continue to flow from the overflow the trouble is in the boiler check.

Q.—How would you remedy the trouble?

A.—In either case the water in the suction pipe will be too hot and the injector will not prime; however, it can be started to work by turning on the priming jet and closing the overflow valve so as to blow steam back into the suction pipe and force the hot water into the tank, then open the overflow valve and the cold water entering the suction pipe will rise and pass out through the overflow, when the steam valve can be opened wide. The water regulating valve should be kept closed when the injector is not working, to prevent the water in the tank from being heated. At the end of the trip the check valve and steam valve should be reported so that they may be ground in.

Q.—If an injector refuses to work on account of an obstruction in the combining tube, what should be done?

A.—The combining tube should be taken out and the obstruction removed.

Q.—How would you know if there was a leak in the suction pipe, and how could it be located?

A.—If the suction pipe is leaking the injector will work noisily. A leak in the suction pipe can be located by closing the overflow valve and the tank valve and opening the steam valve of the injector slightly; if there are any leaks steam will be seen escaping through them.

Q.—Does the steam valve of an injector, whether a lifting or non-lifting kind, always take the steam from a dry pipe? Is this provision made merely to protect against carrying water too high?

A.—All injectors, however designed or attached to boiler, must take the steam from the highest point in boiler, as through a dry pipe. The principle of the injector makes it impossible to operate it unless the steam is dry, and however much care may be exercised in keeping water in boiler at a proper level there are effects of grade and shifting of water due to motion of engine that will carry enough water into steam pipe to break the injector. To make the injector reliable steam used to operate it must be all condensed at the moment a combination of the steam and water in combining tube takes place, which can not be done if water be carried into steam pipe.

Q.—What would be the reason for injector failing to take up water when the pressure drops?

A.—When the injector fails to "take up" all the water, as we say, as when the pressure of steam gets low, it shows the injector is designed for high pressure, and too much water is being supplied for the volume of steam supplied to drive it into boiler. If one injector will deliver more water at low pressure than another, it is because of its being proportioned so as to prevent an excessive amount of water being supplied to injector, or more at any time than the steam pressure within a certain range can handle cleanly. The latter is best suited for varying service, but where the demand for engine power is continually at or near the maximum the range of injector is less important than its ability to supply boiler.

Q.—In pumping an engine what would you consider the proper amount of water to carry in boiler with engine working hard?

A.—The proper water level is enough to protect the crown sheet and not so high as to be liable to be carried over into cylinders. Any height between these extremes is all right. The successful handling of engine is best managed when the water level is made to vary to suit the steaming of engine. If the engine be a poor steamer, or the fireman not skilled, it is well to start out with all the engine will carry so you can trade water for steam to make the next stop without blowing up. The fellow who pumps his engine according to some vague theory not in accord with this plan of loading up before you start may call you a poor pumper, and you may overdo the job at times, especially if the water is not of good quality or the boiler dirty; but in the long run you will leave the other fellow miles behind in point of performance and economy. Holding a fixed water level is all right if conditions permit it. They seldom do.

Q.—How about the practice of supplying water to boiler only when engine is working? Is there any advantage in that way of pumping, either as to economy of fuel or life of flues?

A.—The practice you mention is theoretically correct in so far as its tendency is to prolong the life of the flues, but it is impossible to follow it out in a practical way, in general service, for obvious reasons. As to its effect on coal consumption, it is evident that if the engine is pumped only while working the supply must always equal the consumption. This would naturally tax the steaming capacity of engine to the limit quite often, which would be more wasteful of fuel than if the supply of water at starting would permit favoring the engine by pumping lightly between stops.

QUESTIONS AND ANSWERS ON LUBRICATORS

Q.—Explain how the oil gets from the cup to the steam chest and cylinders.

A.—Steam from the boiler is connected to the top of the cup, which keeps the condenser or ball at top of cup full of water. This steam also passes down steam pipes, sometimes located inside the cup, sometimes outside the cup, to top arms over sight feed glasses, and thence through oil pipes to steam chest. A water pipe leads from the bottom of condenser to bottom of oil tank, so oil will not come up this pipe, but water can pass down under the oil. The head of water in condenser forces oil out through feed valves and it rises through water in sight feed glass to where it mingles with the current of steam from top arm into oil pipes and then to steam chest. To bring the oil from top of oil tank to sight feed valve there is a pipe running up to top of tank which takes oil to feed valve till it is fed out, and water rises to top of this pipe. It requires a head of water in condenser to force oil through feed valves and a full boiler pressure of steam in the cup to make it feed regular at all times, whether working steam or with throttle shut off.

Q.—What about the small check valves over sight feed glasses; what are they for?

A.—They are put in by the makers to close down in case a glass bursts, and prevent the escape of steam from that side of cup, so the other side of cup can be used. They become gummed up after they are used, so they do not always operate. If they stick shut, the cup won't feed, as oil can not pass up by these valves.

Q.—Are there any other valves between the lubricator and the steam chest? Why not?

A.—Not in the lubricators that have these check valves. The oil pipe, after leaving the cup, should have a clear passage without any valves in it to obstruct the passage of oil or steam. The later style of cups have a very small nozzle or "choke" put in the passage where the current of oil and steam leaves the cup. This is to maintain a steady boiler pressure in the cup, so it will feed regularly, either shut off or pulling a train. If the openings in these nozzles are too large the cup will commence to feed faster as soon as you close throttle so steam chest pressure falls.

Q.—After filling the cup, which valve do you open first? Why?

A.—Steam valve should be opened first, then the valve admitting water from condenser to bottom of oil tank, and when you want to set cup to feeding, with old Detroit No. 1, open auxiliaries next, about one-eighth of a turn or less; then feed valves. With new cups the auxiliary oilers do not regulate the steam feeds; the nozzles do this.

Q.—If you should fill the cup with cold oil while in the house, would you open the water valve or leave it closed?

A.—Open it and also open the valve on boiler enough so steam pressure would be in cup, unless engine was cold. This steam valve must be open whenever engine is working steam. If engine is cooling off, leave steam valve on boiler closed, if you think there is any danger of oil siphoning over into boiler when steam in boiler condenses.

Q.—How often should lubricator be cleaned out? Why?

A.—If oil is good quality and kept free from dirt while in cans on engine, every two or three months is enough; if gummy oil is used, whenever it does not work freely.

Q.—Should sight feed glass or feed valve on one side become broken or inoperative, can the sight feed on the other side be used?

A.—Yes, if you can shut the steam out of top of broken glass, and oil off at bottom of glass, the other side can be operated.

Q.—Will any of the lubricators in our service "cross-feed"—that is, feed to the opposite side of the engine? Why or why not?

A.—Yes; some of the old style cups will. The manufacturers say none of the new style cups will. A cup can be tested by closing the escape of oil and steam from one side of cup—say to the *right* cylinder. Then if the *right* side sight feed will operate regularly, the oil must be going across and coming out on left side. In this test we expect the left sight feed valve is to be shut off. Then test the other side in like manner.

Q.—Explain the cross-feeding difficulty as experienced in some of the lubricators in service.

A.—With most of the old cups and some of the new ones, if the steam and oil outlet from cup to steam chest gets stopped up, the oil will rise up through the steam pipe and cross over, going down the other steam pipe to other outlet, so one steam chest gets all the oil intended for both of them. If when the outlet from cup is stopped up or shut, the water fills up this steam pipe or "equalizing tube" till it stands higher than the head of water in the condenser, it can not cross-feed, as the low head of water in condenser will not force the oil through feed valve against a higher head of water in the equalizing tube. This is the reason the equalizing tube is coupled to the lubricator at a higher point than the pipe bringing steam from the boiler. Such lubricators will not cross-feed if steam pipe can drain the surplus water from condenser back to boiler.

Q.—When will lubricator lose the oil remaining in it at time it is shut off? What action takes place and how can it be avoided?

A.—When oil leaves lubricator at shutting off it is the result of not doing it right. The water valve should always be closed before the steam valve. When the steam valve is shut off first there is a sudden reduction of pressure in condenser and sight chambers and oil pipes. The pressure in body of lubricator or oil reservoir, due to the presence of the heat retained in the oil and water stored there, does not immediately reduce, as in the other parts named, with the result, that as the pressure lowers in other parts the greater pressure in the old reservoir causes the oil and water there to rush to the parts in which the pressure has become less. This action will sometimes empty lubricator and is what is known as siphoning.

When the water valve is shut off first, and the steam valve after, the same reduction of pressure takes place as before, but with water valve shut there is no connection between the oil reservoir and other parts, so the siphoning action can not take place.

Q.—What is a good way to lubricate cylinder in a case where one side of engine is cut out, say by blocking valve on center of seat, leaving main rod up and piston connected? Also in a case where engine is towed dead with both rods up and pistons connected?

A.—There are many rules offered to provide for lubrication of cylinder, such as blocking valve so as to leave one steam port open a little, or to oil through indicator holes in cylinder, and in some places it is the practice to slack off forward cylinder head to give cylinder oil, but it is usually not necessary to go to so much trouble. There is rarely a valve so tight as to prevent some steam, if even but condensed steam, to get to cylinder on side valve is blocked centrally on seat, and if the lubricator is feeding oil will surely get to cylinder.

Where the engine is dead it is different, for the lubricator is not working. In this case it is not alone the cylinder but the valves also that need attention, and the best way to care for them is to feed oil through relief valves, making it thin enough so it will flow and spread easily over the bearing surfaces in the cold cylinders.

Q.—Does a cold draft affect the working of a lubricator? Why?

A.—Yes. Because it cools the oil so it will not flow freely and affects the equalization.

Q.—Name the different causes for irregularity in lubricator feeding.

A.—Steam pipe leading to condensing chamber too small, or steam valve only partially opened; equalizing tubes stopped up or too small; choke plug openings worn too large, or the choke plug loose.

Q.—When and in what order should you close the steam and water valves on a lubricator?

A.—At the completion of a trip, or when necessary to fill lubricator, the water valve should be closed first and then the steam valve may be closed. At the beginning of a trip or after filling lubricator, the steam valve should be opened first and then the water valve may be opened.

Q.—What will result from filling a lubricator with cold oil?

A.—Oil will be wasted and the lubricator will be strained, because the cold oil will expand and exert a great pressure on the walls of the oil reservoir, and when the water valve is opened some of the oil will be forced back into the condenser, and in some types of lubricators oil will be forced into the boiler.

Q.—If the sight feed is stopped up, how would you clean it out on the different styles of lubricators?

A.—Close all feed valves but the one affected, open check valve in top feed arm, then open the drain plug and steam from the equalizing tube will blow out the dirt and sediment from the glass and feed tip. On some of the modern types drain cocks are provided in lower feed arm, and a plug valve controls the opening from top feed arm to feed glass, to be used when necessary to blow out.

Q.—How would you clean out chokes on different style lubricators in use on this road?

A.—On most lubricators the chokes can be cleaned by closing the main steam valve and draining a little water out of oil cup and condensing chamber, then open engine throttle and the steam coming up through oil pipe will blow out the obstruction. Another way is to close the main steam valve, open the check valve in top feed arm, open sight feed drain, then open throttle and blow dirt into feed glass. On others it is necessary to disconnect the oil pipes and clean them by hand.

Q.—Which is the better practice, to close the feed valves or the water valves while waiting on a siding?

A.—It is better to close the feed valves.

Q.—How can you tell when the equalizing tubes become stopped up?

A.—With equalizing tubes partly stopped up, the oil will run in streams from the feeds when the throttle is eased off, and if they are entirely stopped up, the oil will squirt from the feed tips.

FRAMES, TRUCKS, TIRES, WHEELS, AND AXLES

QUESTIONS AND ANSWERS

Q.—What defects in a tender or engine truck wheel would, in your opinion, render same unsafe?

A.—A bad tender or engine truck wheel is one that is cracked, that is slid flat or has the tread shelled out, or that has a sharp or broken flange.

Q.—What would be the proper thing to do in case of a broken engine truck wheel or axle?

A.—If a forward engine truck wheel or axle breaks it is impossible with the means usually at hand to do anything except send for help to put in a new pair of wheels. If the broken wheel or axle is at the back of the truck, however, the back end of the truck can be chained up to the frame of the engine by jacking up the front end of the engine to take the weight off the truck, raising the axle so that a block can be put under it to hold it up, then jacking up the journal box and truck frame and putting a chain around it that extends around the frame and is so fastened that it will hold it up. A second chain should also be placed from the truck to the opposite side of the engine to prevent the back end of the truck swinging far enough to allow the good wheel to drop off the rail. A block should then be placed between the frame of the engine and the front end of the equalizer on the disabled side to take the weight off the broken wheel. A broken wheel can be skidded for a short distance if necessary to clear the main line.

Q.—In case you find it necessary to raise a wheel while out on the road where jacks were not available, how would you accomplish it?

A.—A wheel can be raised when jacks are not available by running it up on a wedge.

Q.—What would you do with a broken frame if the break should occur back of the main driver?

A.—If the frame is broken back of the main driver, it is not advisable to try to handle any part of the train, but the engine can be brought in light without doing any damage.

Q.—How do you block up an engine for a broken driving spring or hanger?

A.—If engine was raised with jacks, would block up the end of equalizer that had been connected to broken part, so it was a little higher than before, to allow for settling. It is customary to also block up between driving box and frame at the box where spring is broken. If this is a forward box, it puts the load on that box, which may be too much; it is better to block up over back driving box, whichever spring is broken; the weight is carried there best. If engine was raised by running up on blocks or wedges, would put a block on top of box under broken spring first, if possible, run that wheel up on wedge till the engine was raised up so equalizer could be blocked up level again; then put block over back box also, to carry what weight of engine the spring still at work on that side would not hold up; take out the broken spring or hanger if necessary. If equalizer is under frame and boxes, block under the end that will hold it in proper place.

Q.—With a broken equalizer?

A.—If on a standard eight-wheel engine, do the same work as for broken driving spring on that side. Take out broken parts, if necessary. If an engine truck equalizer, block on top of truck oil boxes and under top bar of engine truck frame. If it is the cross equalizer on a four-wheel switch engine, block up between top of forward boxes and engine frame; some of these equalizers are located under the bottom rail of frame, with the hangers going up outside of frame, in which case you can block between hanger and frame. For broken cross equalizer between the forward drivers of a mogul, it will be necessary to block on top of forward driving boxes; if equalizer going to center pin is broken or disabled, a block can be put over cross equalizer and under boiler, and thus get the use of the forward driving springs.

Q.—With broken engine truck spring or hanger?

A.—If it is a four-wheel engine truck, block over the equalizers and under top bar of engine truck frame close to band of spring, high enough so engine will ride level with other side; with mogul, over the truck box. If engine truck center casting breaks on a standard engine, block across under truck frame and center casting and over the equalizers, from one side to the other; a couple pieces of rail four and one-half to five feet long come handy for this. Or you can put a solid block under the engine frame next to cylinder saddle and on top of truck frame on each side; this plan will give you the use of the engine truck springs, although it does not always hold the center casting up against male casting under smoke arch, so engine will track straight.

Q.—With broken intermediate equalizer on mogul?

A.—Block over driving boxes if necessary, as with the cross equalizer broken; under the boiler and over cross equalizer, if engine truck equalizer is disabled.

Q.—With broken engine truck center pin on mogul, what is to be done?

A.—Block up same as for broken equalizer, except that a block is needed over truck axle and under front end of equalizer; a truck brass comes handy for this purpose.

Q.—What should you do when a tire breaks and comes off the wheel on a standard engine?

A.—If it is a main tire, raise that wheel center up off the rail a little higher than the thickness of the tire to allow for engine settling when blocked up; take out oil cellar so journal would not get cut on the edges of cellar, put a solid block of wood between pedestal brace and journal, to hold wheel center up clear of rail, and block up over back driving box, so engine could not settle or get down to allow cast iron wheel center to strike the rail. It will take considerable strain off the pedestal brace to put a block under spring saddle and on top of frame. Taking out this driving spring makes a sure job. Take off all other broken or disabled parts; if rods are still in good order, leave them up. If a back tire, block up in the same manner as for main tire, except that blocking comes next other journals and boxes. If engine is very heavy, it may be necessary to carry part of the weight of back end of the engine on tender. This can sometimes be done by wedging up under chafing block on engine deck and over coupling bar; at other times it may be necessary to lay a solid tie or short rail on top of deck, the end against the fire-box, extending back into tender. Chain around this tie or rail and to the frame at back driving box pedestal, and block up under end that is on tender, so weight of engine will be carried on rail or tie back on tender. This plan of blocking leaves three good tires on the rails, and the disabled wheel carried away from the rail. Run wheel on blocks to raise it clear of rail when possible.

Q.—With main tire on mogul?

A.—Block up under main journal and over back driving box. If with either tire broken on mogul or ten-wheel engine, side rods have to be taken off, it may be necessary to be towed in if crank pin in forward wheel does not clear crosshead when side rods are uncoupled. Some mogul and ten-wheel engines have the main tires without flanges, others have the forward pair "bald," which makes a little difference in keeping them on track when blocked up.

Q.—With the back tire on mogul?

A.—Same as for back tire on any other engine, taking off all broken parts. To hold flanges of the good tire against the rail when running, chain from end of engine frame and deck (the step casting is handy for this) across to corner of tender, behind the good tire; this will hold flange over and tender will be used to hold back end of engine on rail.

Q.—With both back tires on mogul?

A.—Raise both wheel centers up to clear the rail and block under journals to hold them up. Arrange to carry part of weight of back part of engine on tender; chain back end of engine each way to tender frame, so main wheels will have no chance to get off track. Or a shoe or "slipper" having a flange on one side can be fastened to center wheel—a piece of old tire will make a good one—the wheel center blocked so it will slide, and bring engine in that way. Another way is to take out the back wheels, as in the case of a broken axle, and put in a car truck, blocking up under engine deck; this is a job for the wrecking car. With a four-wheel switch engine with front tire broken, if engine is still on track, front end of engine can be chained to a flat car, which will carry the weight and steer front end of engine. In all cases of broken tire, it is understood that other parts of the engine that are damaged must be removed; the tire generally removes itself.

Q.—With back tire or back driver broken off, how do you fix engine so you can back around curves when necessary?

A.—Chain across from step on engine deck on disabled side to tender frame on other side, or put a block from cab casting or chafing iron on deck across where the block can brace against tender frame; this will hold good flange against rail. Look out when going through frogs, as there is nothing to keep flange from leading into point of frog.

Q.—At what fixed points is the weight of engine carried when springs and equalizers are in good order?

A.—On a standard engine the "permanent bearings" or fixed points are the equalizer centers, one on each side of fire-box, and the center bearing of engine truck; with moguls, where equalizer centers are fastened to frame and to center of cylinder saddle. With most all four-wheel switch engines the weight is also distributed to three points, which are the back driving boxes and middle of equalizer, which extends between the forward ends of front driving springs. Engines are designed to carry their weight on three points, so all wheels will bear evenly on the rails; equalizers are then used to distribute the weight to all the driving wheels evenly.

Q.—Where is the weight carried when blocked up over the forward driving box?

A.—If blocked up over forward driving box *solid*, this box takes all the weight that was carried on both boxes on that side, and a little more, as the block comes more nearly under the center of the engine than the equalizer post does. If the block over driving box carries the weight which was carried by equalizer before, it will have a double load on it. When blocked up solid over a driving box, as in the case of a broken tire, the weight of the entire engine comes on engine truck center, the equalizer post on good side of engine, and on the block over driving box on disabled side of engine.

Q.—When blocked up over the back driving box?

A.—On that box, on the equalizer post on opposite side of engine, and engine truck center casting. A block over back box carries less of the weight than a block over forward box, as the engine truck carries a larger share of the load. The nearer the center of the weight of an engine the blocking is located, the greater proportion of the total weight the block carries. As, for instance, if a standard eight-wheel engine balances, or has half her weight ahead of and half behind the main axle, if blocked up solid over main axle, in case of a broken axle on both back tires, these blocks over main axle carry the entire weight of the engine. If all wheels are bearing on the rail and springs still in service, the springs take some of the strain off the blocking.

Q.—What is the best material to use to block between driving box and frame?

A.—Wood or an old rubber spring is most elastic, but it will not hold up a heavy engine; it is liable to get in the oil holes and stop them up. An iron block made for that purpose, or extra large nuts are the best for heavy engines.

Q.—If driving box or brass breaks so it is cutting the axle badly, what can you do to relieve it?

A.—Block between spring saddle and top of frame, so as to take the strain of driving spring off the disabled box; or take out the driving spring entirely. This last is a very sure way; the block may work out from under spring saddle.

Q.—Do you consider it an engineer's duty to have suitable hard wood blocks on his engine to use in case of a breakdown?

A.—Yes; he should have a set of crosshead blocks for each side of the engine; two blocks of straight grained hard wood that can be split to proper size for blocking under driving wheels or over engine truck equalizers with broken truck springs and bell cord to use in tying up disabled parts. He should have suitable wedges or blocks for running driving wheels up on in case of broken springs, tire, etc.

Q.—How do you block up or get to a sidetrack with a broken engine truck wheel or axle?

A.—If a piece is broken out of wheel, it can be skidded to next side track by laying a tie in front of that pair of wheels. If axle is broken or wheel broken off outside of box, you can chain that corner of engine truck up to engine frame, being careful to chain so as to crowd good wheel against the rail.

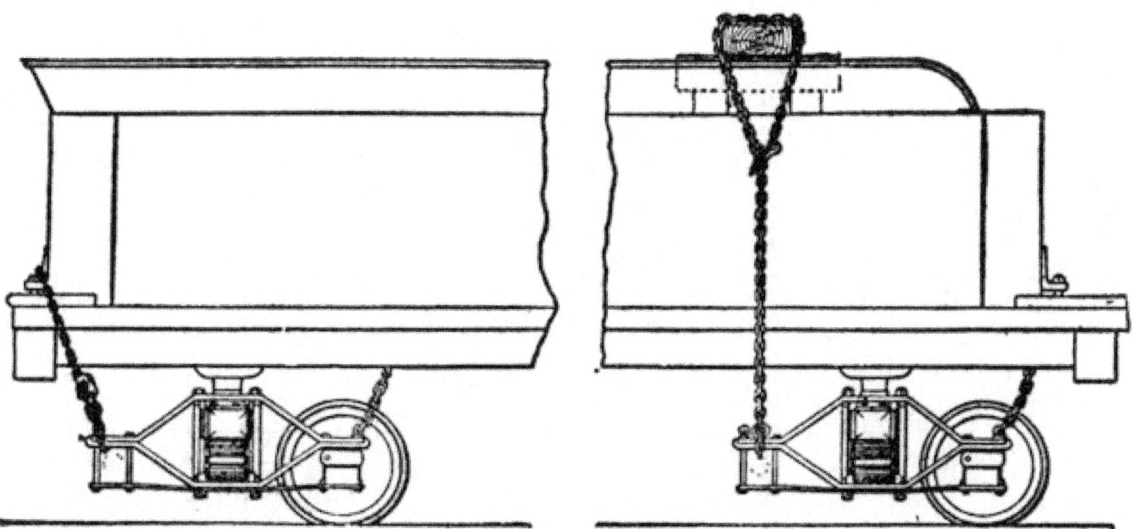

Two Methods of Chaining up Truck for Broken Wheel or Axle

Q.—With mogul, with broken engine truck wheel or axle, what would you do?

A.—Take it out if necessary. Chain engine truck to engine frame; block up on top of forward driving boxes.

Q.—With broken tender truck wheel or axle, what would you do?

A.—If with broken wheel, try and skid it to the next station, so as to clear main line. With broken axle, take disabled wheels out and suspend that part of truck to tender. Block over the good wheels in this truck and under tender frame.

For Broken Engine Truck, Wheel or Axle

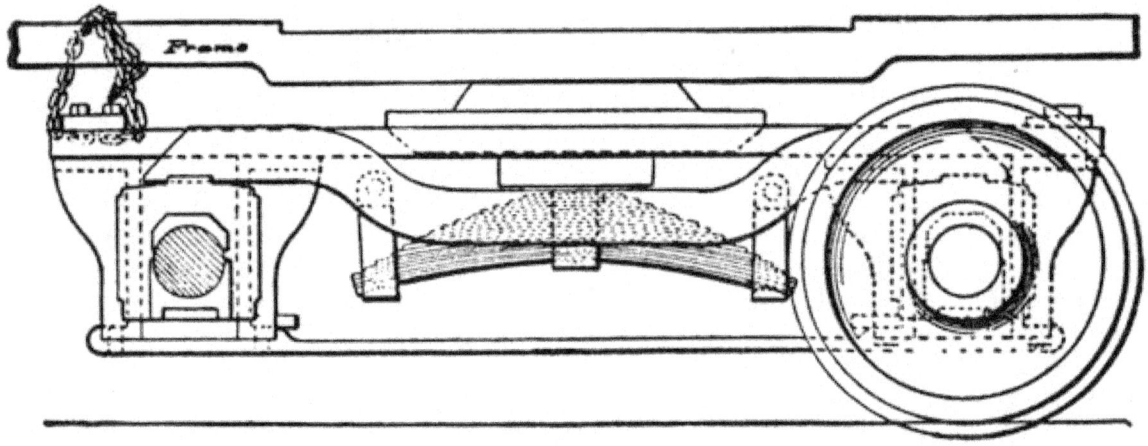

Q.—Is it necessary to take down the main rod if the frame is broken between the cylinder and forward driving box?

A.—Yes, if crack opens up when engine is working steam, and it generally does. Don't let any other engine pull on you while frame is broken.

Q.—Would you take down either rod if the frame is broken between forward and back driving boxes?

A.—If broken badly, take down side rods.

Q.—Where is the frame fastened solid to the other part of the engine?

A.—At the cylinder saddle, solidly; at side of fire-box, loosely, so as to allow of expansion of boiler in length when under steam; at the guide yoke, to keep sides parallel, and solidly at the deck casting. Some engines also have belly braces from cylinder part of boiler to frame.

Q.—What should be done if a main wheel breaks off its axle?

A.—Would disconnect on broken side and remove all the side rods and the broken wheel. The eccentrics would serve to prevent the other wheel from leaving the rail. Even though a blind tire, would use a jack to raise the axles on the broken side. Remove the oil cellar and fit a hardwood block between the driving axle and the pedestal jaw or binder. Old rod-keys or any kind of iron could be used to block between the spring saddle and the top of the frame to keep part of the weight off the axle at that point. Then the jack should be removed. Would next slightly raise the engine on the broken side and block between the top of the driving box or the boxes nearest to the main wheel on the broken side, using hard wood or iron. If an eight-wheeled engine, would also block between the engine truck equalizers and the truck frame on both sides, because additional weight would be imposed upon the truck. If a consolidated engine, would block on top of the two boxes nearest the main box only. The engine should then be let down and run slowly.

Q.—If a main wheel is cracked, what should be done?

A.—If possible, would run engine slowly to the first side-track, provided the wheel were not too badly broken, but would watch it closely. Then would disconnect broken side and remove all the side rods so as to take the strain off the crank pin on the broken wheel, and it might then be possible to proceed. But, if the break were bad enough to render it unsafe to proceed "light," would block the wheel up to clear the rail the same as for a broken tire. Then would run very slowly and carefully.

Q.—If a main driving axle breaks, what should be done?

A.—If an eight-wheel engine with the axle broken off outside of the driving box, would remove the spring over the broken axle and jack up the broken axle to free the driving box cellar. Would next remove the cellar and fit a solid block of wood between the axle and the binder brace and nail a strip across each side to prevent it from falling out. All the side rods would have to be taken down and the engine run slowly, using only one side.

QUESTIONS AND ANSWERS ON GUIDES AND RODS

Q.—What is the use of the crosshead?

A.—It is a medium of connection between the piston rod and the main rod, by means of which the pressure exerted on the piston head by the steam is transmitted to the crank pin of the main driving wheels.

Q.—Why can not the main rod be connected directly to the piston rod?

A.—The strain on the piston rod, stuffing box, and packing gland would be too great for obvious reasons, and to overcome this the crosshead working in guide bars is employed.

Q.—Describe the crosshead at piston end.

A.—It has a horizontal tapering socket at this end, through which a tapering key-way is cut at right angles perpendicularly to the socket. This socket receives the tapering end of the piston rod, and a key is driven in the key-way, which draws and holds the piston rod firmly in the crosshead.

Q.—What is the result if this key becomes loosened or broken, or the piston rod breaks?

A.—If key becomes loosened it will result in a bad pound. If piston rod or key become broken the front cylinder head will be destroyed, and it will be necessary to disconnect the valve stem and cover ports.

Q.—How is the main rod end of the crosshead equipped?

A.—With a wrist pin extending across the extended sides of the crosshead. The forward end of the main rod is connected to this wrist pin by a strap and bolts holding brasses that fit around the wrist pin and are adjusted by means of a tapering key, which is held tight by means of a set screw through a keeper at the bottom of the strap.

Q.—If this key is not properly adjusted, what is the result?

A.—A pound that may result in a broken rod strap and other consequent damage.

Q.—In case of a broken wrist pin, front end strap to main rod or crosshead, what is to be done?

A.—Take down the main rod and such other parts as may be necessary from breakage by the accident, block crosshead back in guides, disconnect valve stem and cover ports.

Q.—Why should crosshead be blocked in back of guide bars?

A.—Because front cylinder head is more easily and cheaply replaced in case of damage from crosshead getting loose in guides through blocking working loose.

Q.—Where will the wrist pin become the smallest through wear?

A.—At the front and back side, owing to the direct pull and push of the piston. For this reason keying the front end of a main rod on the eighth will give the best result, although care must be taken not to get the brasses too tight, as no brasses will cut out more quickly if improperly keyed.

Q.—How are the sides of crosshead equipped?

A.—With wings or slides that work between the guides and bear the weight of the crosshead and a portion of that of the piston and main rods.

Q.—Why are crosshead wings equipped with gibs?

A.—To receive the wear where the crosshead travels in the guides. They can be replaced more easily and cheaply than a new crosshead could be put in.

Q.—Why is a wrist pin made heavy?

A.—To withstand the strain to which it is subjected, and which is especially heavy on curves where it is subjected to a twisting motion.

Q.—What causes this twisting motion on curves?

A.—The lateral play, or, more plainly speaking, the side motion between the hubs of the driving wheels and the inside of the driving boxes. This side motion will not amount to a great deal in a new engine, but will be considerable in one about ready for general repairs.

Q.—Driving boxes will slip back and forth on the journals where there is straight track; why is the twisting motion any greater on a curve?

A.—Owing to the cramped condition of the rods, boxes, and wheels on one side and their drawn condition on the other. The wheels on the outside of the curve travel the farthest, so it is evident those on the inside must slip to keep them in unison.

Q.—How are guide bars put up?

A.—Parallel with the axis of the cylinder.

Q.—Is there more than one type of guide bars?

A.—Yes, the single bar, which passes through the crosshead and has piston and main rods attached to under side; the two-bar type, with one bar under and one above the crosshead; and the four-bar type, two bars above and two below the crosshead.

Q.—What are guide blocks?

A.—Blocks which are attached at one end of the guides to the back cylinder head, and at the other end of the guides to the guide yoke by studs. The guides are bolted to these blocks. These blocks are subjected to great vertical strain.

Q.—What is done to reduce guide wear to a minimum?

A.—They are made as hard and smooth as possible. The crosshead gibs are made softer than the guide bars to take the wear, as they can be renewed more cheaply and quickly.

Q.—How is the wear of the gibs compensated for to avoid lost motion before gibs are worn out?

A.—By liners placed between the end of the guide bars and guide blocks, which are removed as the gibs wear and the guides closed. When new gibs are put in liners can be replaced.

Q.—Is the wear equal on all guide bars?

A.—No; it is more uniform on yard or suburban passenger engines because they run more evenly in both directions, while the majority of locomotives do the greater part of the work running ahead. With them the upper guide bars receive the most wear, because when the stroke is toward the crank pin and the main rod is below the crosshead, the pressure on the piston head makes compression on the crosshead and pushes it up against the guide bars, and on the return stroke the main rod is in tension and is above the crosshead, and pulls it up against the guide bars. Running backward, the main rod, being in tension, pulls the crosshead down on the guide bars, and on the return stroke the main rod, being in compression above the guide bars, pushes the crosshead down on the lower guide bars.

Q.—At what point is the greatest strain exerted on the guide bars?

A.—At their centers, as this point is farthest from the point of support, and also at that point the angularity of the main rod is the greatest.

Q.—Explain the difference in the motion of the different ends of the main rod?

A.—The main rod and crank pin receive the pressure exerted against the piston by the steam and convey it to the wheel. This pressure gives to the front end of the main rod a reciprocating motion that corresponds to the motion of the crosshead. The back end of the main rod has a rotary motion that corresponds to that of the crank pin, and parts of the rod intermediate to these points have a combination motion of the two, varying from a reciprocating to a rotary, according to their distance from the crosshead or the crank pin.

Q.—Is there any loss of power owing to the varying angle at which the main rod transmits power to the crank pin?

A.—None, except that which is lost through friction.

Q.—In what portion of the crank pin circle is the greatest power exerted on the pin?

A.—When pin is on the quarter and piston is at the center of its stroke.

Q.—What are the dead points of an engine?

A.—When the centers of the wrist pin, main rod, crank pin, and main driving axle are in a straight line on one side, then the engine on that side is practically powerless and must be carried by these points by momentum previously gained, or by the engine on the opposite side, which is then working at its maximum power.

Q.—What is done in case of a broken main rod?

A.—Take off broken parts. Block crosshead, disconnect valve stem and cover ports.

Q.—Define compression and tension of a main rod.

A.—Compression is when rod is pushed toward crank pin, and tension when pulled from the crank pin.

Q.—What are main rods?

A.—Flat bars of wrought iron, larger at the crank pin than at the wrist end. Some of them are fluted, as are side rods, to make them lighter and stronger.

Q.—Why are main rods made larger at the crank pin end than at the wrist pin end?

A.—Because of the greater size of the crank pin. It has also been found that more main rods break at the crank pin end.

Q.—How are rod brasses made?

A.—They are made in pairs, cored out to fit the pin, and dressed slightly less than a half circle to allow for keying when brasses become worn. They are held in place by U-shaped straps that surround the grooved sides of brasses, and slipping over the end of the main rod are held in place by bolts.

Q.—Is there any other form of brass used?

A.—Yes, what is known as solid brass. It is a round bushing of brass forced in the hole at the enlarged end of the rods. The objection to this brass is that when worn it can not be tightened to the pin by keying, and so is often worn loose to save putting in new bushings.

Q.—Do driving rod-keys alter the length of the main rod?
A.—With one key ahead of crank pin and the other ahead of wrist pin the length of the rod will not be visibly altered.
Q.—If the edges of the rod brasses meet and the key is tight, and the brasses are still too loose on the pin, what must be done?
A.—The brasses must be reduced.
Q.—When should rod brasses be keyed where grease cups are used to lubricate pins?
A.—After the locomotive has been run some distance, and after cups have been screwed down so that the grease between the pin and the brasses will be worn out, otherwise the brasses will appear tight on the pin when in reality they are loose.
Q.—Why is babbit put in grooves in inner side of rod brasses?
A.—Because they run cooler, and as babbit will fuse at a lower degree of heat than brass, a warning will be given by its melting that would save more serious damage.
Q.—Why is it necessary to keep rod brasses keyed up properly?
A.—To avoid their pounding. A pounding brass will heat the same as one keyed too tight.
Q.—Where should the back end of a main rod be keyed?
A.—On the center, which should be the largest part of the crank pin.
Q.—What are the rods called that unite the driving wheels?
A.—Side rods, connecting rods, and parallel rods.
Q.—Explain these different terms.
A.—Side rods are so called because they are placed on the sides of the driving wheels. Connecting rods, because they connect the driving wheels; and parallel rods, because the one on one side is parallel to the one on the other side and also to the rail.
Q.—Where should side rod brasses be keyed?
A.—With engine on center on side that is being keyed, to avoid changing the length of the rod.
Q.—Should wedges be properly adjusted before side rods are keyed?
A.—Slack wedges will cause more wear on recently keyed rods than would occur in natural wear many times over.
Q.—Should a rod-key be slackened if a pin runs hot?
A.—No, not unless it has been recently keyed and is found to be keyed too tight. Look for the trouble from some other source.
Q.—How should a middle connection be first keyed on a ten-wheel engine?
A.—Drive both keys out and then drive one down, mark it, when clear down, with a knife, scratch even with top of strap and drive it out. Drive the other one down and mark it in like manner and drive it out. Start both keys and drive them down, and when brass is tight enough to suit, have marks on both keys equally distant from **rod strap.**

Q.—How can it be determined if there is a pound in rod brasses or a driving box?

A.—Put engine on quarter on side to be tried and have fireman give cylinders a little steam and throw lever back and forth, "chug" her, it is termed. A pound will readily be found by this means. Do not key brasses so they will not yield a bit under "chugging" or there will be a hot pin.

Q.—What is to be done in case of a broken side rod or crank pin?

A.—Take down side rods on both sides on an eight-wheel engine, and if a main pin the main rod on that side must come down.

Q.—Why must opposite side rod come down?

A.—With nothing to guide it when it reaches the center it is as apt to go up as down, in the wrong direction instead of the right one, and then there will be more damage. On consolidated engines, when rod in front or back section breaks take down the same rod on the opposite side, as they have the same relation to each other as the side rods of an eight-wheel engine. If in middle section, all side rods must come down. On six-wheel connected engines, if back side rod breaks take down back side rods; if a front side rod breaks all side rods must come down, because knuckle joint back of pin would turn with crank pin and without rest of side rod.

Q.—Why are knuckle joints used on side rods on engines with more than two pairs of driving wheels, instead of a one-piece rod?

A.—To allow the wheels to adjust themselves to the inequalities of the track.

Q.—Where should knuckle pins be located?

A.—As near the crank pin as possible, to lessen the strain on it. When one breaks it is to be dealt with the same as a broken back side rod.

Q.—Why are side rods made heavier in the center?

A.—To make them stiffer in the vertical plane.

QUESTIONS AND ANSWERS ON VALVES AND VALVE GEAR

Q.—What controls the admission and exhaust of steam to and from the cylinders of a locomotive?

A.—The valves and their gears.

Q.—Name the parts of the valve gear.

A.—The reverse lever, reach rod, reversing arm, tumbling shaft, lifting arm, link hammer, link saddle, link saddle pin, link, eccentrics, eccentric straps and blades, top and bottom rocker arms, valve rod, yoke, and, lastly, the valve.

Q.—Describe the common slide, or D, valve.

A.—The unbalanced common slide valve is so little used as to be not worthy of special description, the balanced slide valve or piston valve having taken its place. On top of the cylinder is a flat ported surface called the valve seat. Over the surface of this seat the valve plays, alternately filling or exhausting the steam from the ends of the cylinders. A yoke surrounding the valve forms the steam chest end of the valve rod, and the other end of the rod being attached to the top rocker arm receives its motion back and forth from it as it in turn receives its motion from the eccentrics. The body of the valve is hollow and has lips projecting from its base.

Q.—Why was the balanced slide valve adopted?

A.—The unbalanced slide valve, owing to the steam pressure on its top, rode too heavy on the seat, thus lessening the power of the locomotive. To overcome this, a plate, called the pressure plate, was fastened to the steam chest cover parallel with the valve seat. The top of the valve was faced off and metal strips fitted in grooves were run around the top of the valve. Springs were placed under these strips to force them up against the pressure plate when the cover was put on, thus preventing steam from getting on top of valve and pressing it down on seat. A hole is drilled down through the top of the valve to allow any steam that might leak past the valve strips to escape through the exhaust port.

Q.—Describe the piston valve.

A.—It is a cylinder or spool-shaped valve, and is designed to travel in a cylinder-bore steam chest with the same ports of admission and exhaust as are employed with the slide valve. It derives its name from its form of construction. Each end of the piston valve has two or more packing rings which form the exhaust and admission edges of the valve.

Q.—Is the piston valve one solid piece?

A.—As a rule it is not. Usually it is made in two parts held together by a hollow rod.

Q.—What is the effect of the ends of the piston valve being near the ends of the cylinder?

A.—The amount of steam used at each stroke of the piston for filling the clearance is lessened.

Q.—What was the piston valve designed to do?

A.—To balance the pressure in steam chest and thereby reduce the friction on high pressure locomotives and lessen the amount of lubrication required with their use. The wear on piston valves is not great under normal conditions.

Q.—Is it best for valves and cylinders to work a little steam when running down a hill?

A.—It is, for two reasons, principally to lubricate the valves and cylinders and cushion the piston at the end of the stroke. When a locomotive has drifted down a hill some distance with steam shut off, upon first opening the throttle the valves will be noticeably dry and will not work smooth again for some distance. When an engine is running with throttle shut off the strain of stopping and starting the pistons twice at each revolution of the wheels falls on the piston rod and its connections, which the steam cushion at the end of the stroke avoids.

CYLINDER AND ITS APPURTENANCES

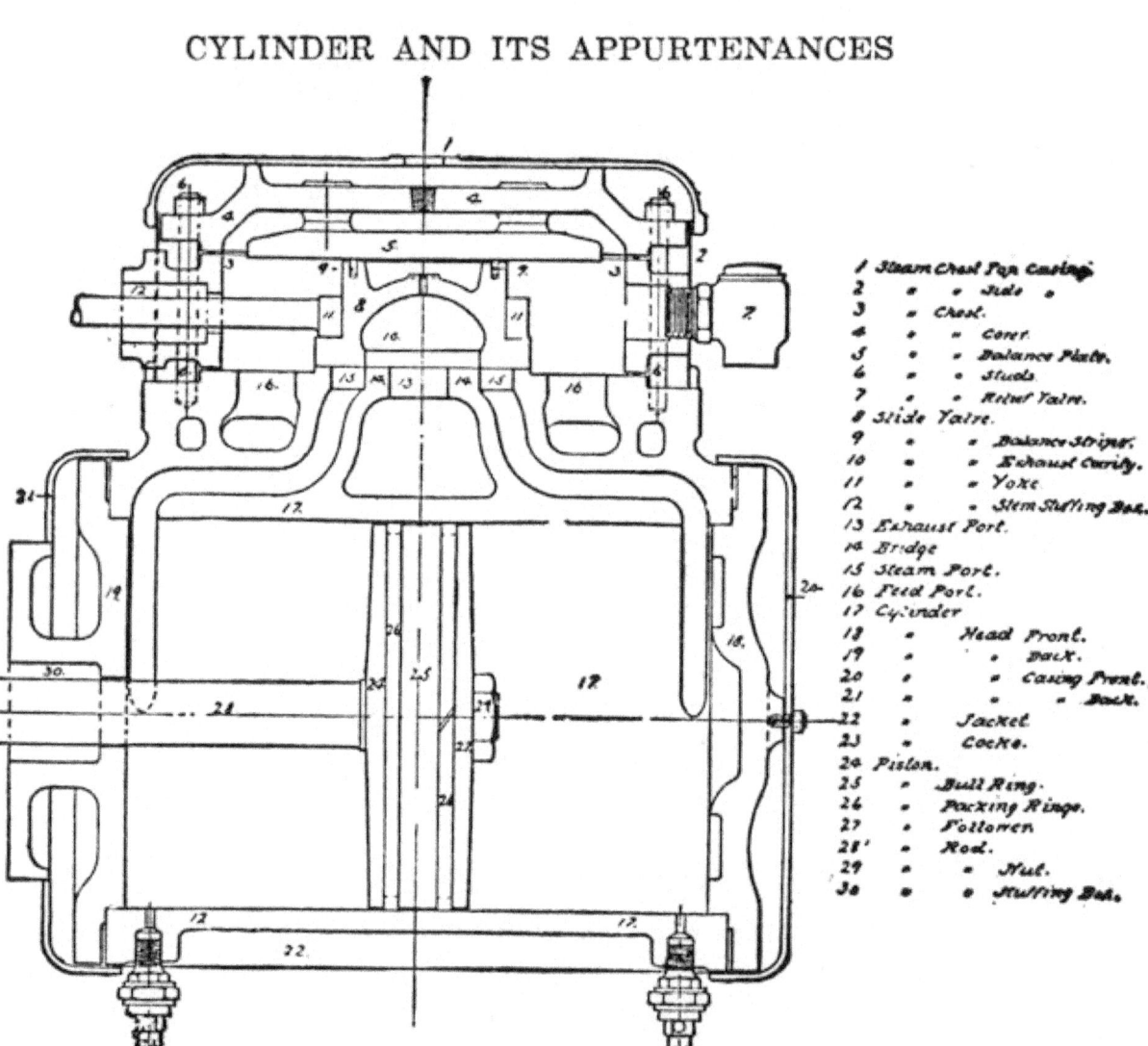

1 Steam Chest Top Casing.
2 " " Side "
3 " " Chest.
4 " " Cover.
5 " " Balance Plate.
6 " " Studs.
7 " " Relief Valve.
8 Slide Valve.
9 " " Balance Strips.
10 " " Exhaust Cavity.
11 " " Yoke.
12 " " Stem Stuffing Box.
13 Exhaust Port.
14 Bridge.
15 Steam Port.
16 Feed Port.
17 Cylinder.
18 " Head Front.
19 " " Back.
20 " Casing Front.
21 " " Back.
22 " Jacket.
23 " Cocks.
24 Piston.
25 " Bull Ring.
26 " Packing Rings.
27 " Follower.
28 " Rod.
29 " Nut.
30 " Stuffing Box.

Q.—Should the reverse lever be dropped in full gear when steam is shut off at high speed or even moderately high speed.

A.—No. The whole load is practically put on the one eccentric and the lever will jerk. The locomotive will run more smoothly and there will be less danger of a hot eccentric if the lever is dropped down but a short distance on the quadrant.

Q.—Are all piston valves alike as to the manner in which they admit steam to the cylinders?

A.—No. Some are inside admission and others outside admission valves.

Q.—What is an inside admission valve?

A.—One that takes the steam from the boiler supply into its central cavity and from there passes it to the steam ports of the cylinder, and the exhaust steam from the cylinder comes out at the ends of the valve and passes through the exhaust passages in the cylinder saddle to the stack and atmosphere.

Q.—Describe the outside admission valve?

A.—One that uncovers the ports the same as the D slide valve. The outside ends of the valve uncover the ports for steam admission to the cylinder, and the exhaust steam passes through the cavity of the valve before escaping through the exhaust passages to the nozzles and stack.

Q.—How does the piston, piston valve, and valve motion compare on an outside and inside admission valve?

A.—With the inside admission valve the motion of the valve is in the opposite direction to the motion of the piston at the beginning of the stroke, while with the outside admission valve the movement of the valve is in the same direction as that of the piston at the commencement of the stroke. The inside admission valve is the one more commonly employed.

Q.—How can one tell whether a piston valve is of the inside or outside admission type?

A.—Watch the valve rod and note if it moves with the piston at the commencement of the stroke; if so, it is an outside admission valve; if in the opposite direction, it is inside admission.

Q.—Define direct and indirect-motion valve gear.

A.—Direct-motion valve gear is that in which the motion of the eccentric is direct to the valve and is not reversed by means of a rocker arm, or is one having a rocker on which both arms are either hung down or stand up and move in the same direction. An indirect-motion valve gear is one in which the motion of the eccentric is reversed by means of a rocker, the lower arm of which moves in the opposite direction to the upper arm and also of the valve.

Q.—At what point in its travel is the piston valve most perfectly balanced?

A.—At mid travel with all ports closed.

Q.—What are by-pass valves; why are they necessary with piston and not with slide valves, and what duty do they perform?

A.—They are merely relief valves. When an overpressure occurs in a cylinder from any cause the D slide valve would lift and allow it to escape, but as this could not obtain with a piston valve the by-pass valve connecting the steam pressure chamber of the valve with the cylinder is employed. The valve chamber end of the by-pass valve is the larger, so that the pressure in the cylinder must exceed that in the valve chamber before the by-pass valve will open and let the excess pressure blow into the valve chamber. A relief, or pop, valve is used on some locomotives in place of a by-pass valve.

Q.—What is cut-off as applied to valve motion?

A.—The point where the steam admission from the chest is cut off from the cylinder by the valve travel. This point is determined by the position of the reverse lever in the quadrant in cab, and should be the one where the engine is doing its work most satisfactorily and economically.

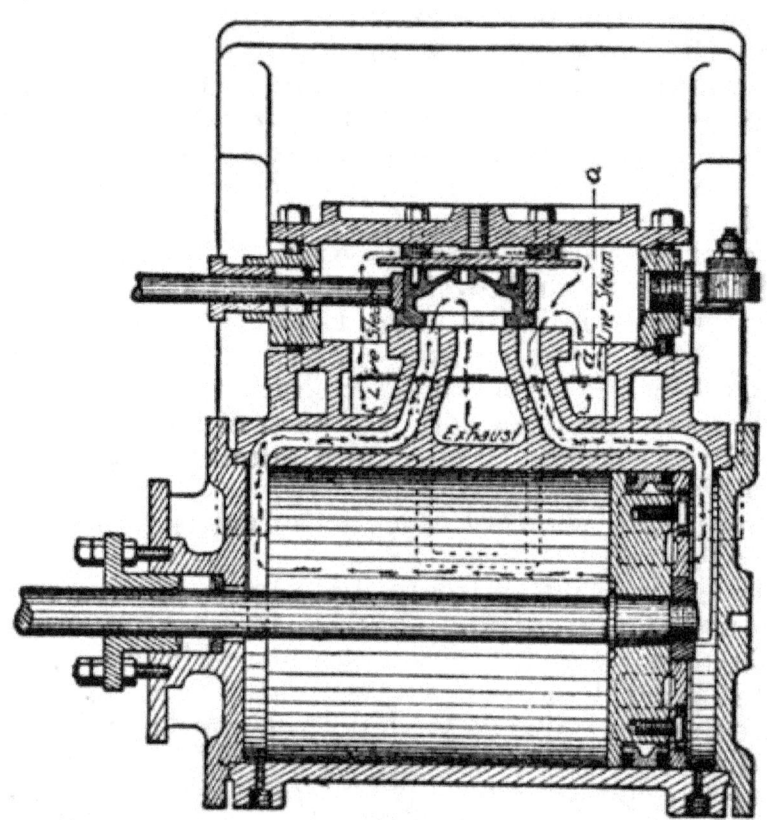

Section Showing Action of Steam in Single Expansion Cylinder. Piston Shown in Section

Q.—How is steam used expansively?

A.—After the valve in its travel has closed the steam admission ports to the cylinder the steam still continues to exert a pressure against the piston head by reason of its elasticity and expansibility until the exhaust port allows it to escape. This pressure on the piston lessens in a degree proportionate to the piston travel after the steam supply is cut off. Thus, if the steam was cut off with a mean effective pressure of 100 pounds per square inch of piston surface when the piston had traveled 10 inches, at 20-inch piston travel the mean effective pressure would be 50 pounds per square inch. The distance the valve travels through the expansion of the steam equals the total inside and outside laps of the valves.

Q.—What is compression?

A.—The confining of any portion of the exhaust steam in one end of the cylinder by closing the exhaust port before all the steam in the cylinder has had time to escape, which is done by means of inside (exhaust) lap on the valve. This might be sufficient to cause back pressure, and thus hurt the efficiency of the engine, or it might be only enough to cause a cushion.

Q.—What is meant by a cushion, and how is it obtained?

A.—The presence of a small amount of steam in the clearance space to ease the stoppage of the piston at the end of its stroke. This steam may be admitted by valve lead just prior to the piston completing its travel, or, as before shown, may be retained in the cylinder also by exhaust lap.

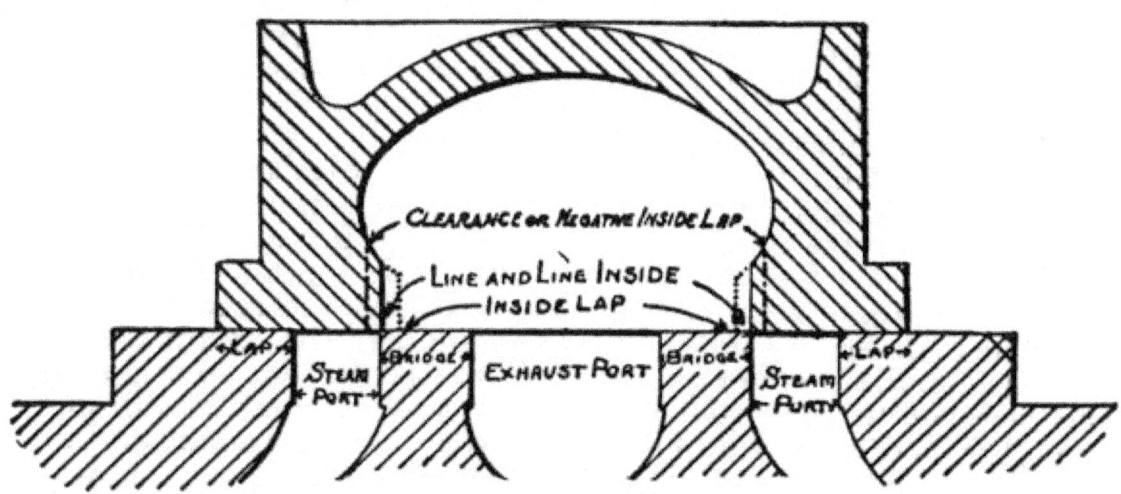

Graphic Definitions of Valve Dimensions

Q.—What is clearance?

A.—The free space between the piston head at the end of the stroke and the cylinder head, and including the steam ports between cylinder and lower face of valve.

Q.—Of what use is it?

A.—To guard against the possibility of the piston head striking the cylinder head and breaking it out by reason of wear of any connecting part or change in adjustment of the same, and to cushion the piston as stated in answer to previous question. Water is often carried over into the dry pipe by the rush of steam from the boiler and into the cylinder. As it is not compressible, the result would be a broken cylinder head if there were no provision made for its disposal.

Q.—Can compression in a cylinder exceed steam chest pressure?

A.—Yes. For this reason pop or by-pass valves are provided to relieve the cylinder of excess pressure.

Q.—What will do away with compression?

A.—Inside clearance.

Q.—What is exhaust?

A.—The escape of the steam from the cylinder by way of the exhaust ports and ways, standpipe, and smokestack after its work in the cylinder has been completed.

Q.—What else might cause back pressure beside the valve construction?

A.—Nozzles too small to allow free escape of the steam before piston reached the end of its stroke. This is more often the cause of back pressure than is too much inside lap. An engine will be steaming poorly, and other changes not having bettered the condition, the nozzle tips will be bushed, causing a greater coal consumption and often lessening the engine's power to do work.

Q.—What is lap?

A.—Outside lap is the amount the valve projects over the edges of the ports when the valve is placed centrally on the valve seat. Inside lap is the amount the inside edges of the valve project over the ports with the valve placed in the same manner. This is sometimes called exhaust lap.

Q.—What is inside clearance?

A.—The amount the exhaust port is open with the valve placed centrally on its seat.

Q.—Explain the difference between inside lap and inside clearance.

A.—Inside lap is given the valves to delay the escape of steam from the cylinders up to the point of back pressure, and is desirable on all locomotives not employed in fast train service. Inside clearance is given to valves to allow the early escape of steam from the cylinders, and is used on engines in extra fast train service where speed is desired without regard to economy.

Q.—What is meant by the expression in regard to valves of "line and line?"

A.—That the inside edges of the valve line with the edges of the exhaust port.

Q.—How can a cylinder packing blow be distinguished?

A.—It will be intermittent with each revolution of the wheels, ceasing as piston nears end of stroke and recommencing as steam pressure is applied to piston head. The blow has a roaring sound. This blow can be located by putting crank pin on quarter on side to be tested and giving engine steam with both cylinder cocks open. If the cylinder packing blows, steam will escape from both cylinder cocks in good volume.

Q.—How does a valve blow sound?

A.—Sharp. Something like a whistling sound.

Q.—If a blow is caused from a cocked valve, how could it be seated?

A.—Move reverse lever back and forth several times until valve is seated. This defect will not occur with a balanced valve.

Q.—How can a steam or standpipe blow be located as such?
A.—The blow is more noticeable with fire door open. Fire burns red and is inclined to come out at fire door. Engine will not steam free and is worse on a hill when working hard.

Q.—How can a blow caused by a valve traveling too far be determined as such?
A.—The blow will occur with lever in full gear and cease when it is hooked up a little.

Q.—With a balanced slide valve, of what is a steady blow the indication?
A.—Of a broken strip or a weak or broken spring.

Q.—How can a test be made for a strip blow?
A.—Put the crank pin—on the side where the blow is thought to be—on the forward center and reverse lever in center notch of quadrant with valve covering ports. Open the cylinder cocks. Move the reverse lever ahead a little bit; not enough, however, to open forward admission port. Set brake and give engine steam. If a strip or spring causes the blow, steam will enter the exhaust cavity of the valve and pass down and out of back cylinder cock. Repeat the operation with the reverse lever slightly back of center and steam will come from front cylinder cock. This proves that steam comes out of cylinder cocks from above the valve and not from under it. The valve and cylinder on the side where there is a strip blow will become very dry on account of the oil going out with the exhaust steam before it has had an opportunity to lubricate the valve and cylinder.

Q.—What can be done for an engine with a broken valve seat?
A.—The place and kind of breakage has much to do with the remedy. If it was a forward port that was broken, place the valve so as to cover the back steam port and the exhaust port. Disconnect and clamp valve stem. Take down main rod and block crosshead at rear of guides. The main rod is taken down because steam having free admission to the front end of the cylinder would cause engine to work against itself on forward stroke of piston on disabled side. For a broken back port, place valve over front steam port and exhaust port and disconnect and block the same as for a broken front port, except that it would be best to block crosshead at front of guides. A valve seat breakage will usually result in broken or bent rocker arms, valve stem or eccentric blade, and the valve gear should be examined for trouble of this kind. If bridge is broken between steam port and exhaust port, disconnect valve with ports covered and clamp it. Leave main rod up. Unless all broken pieces can be located, examine cylinder for them and avoid another breakage.

Q.—What is the remedy when a valve breaks on the road?
A.—Take up chest cover, in case of a slide valve, or head off with a piston valve. Put the broken parts of the valve together so as to cover ports if it can be done. Block the valve firmly in place and put the cover or head on, as the case may be, and disconnect and

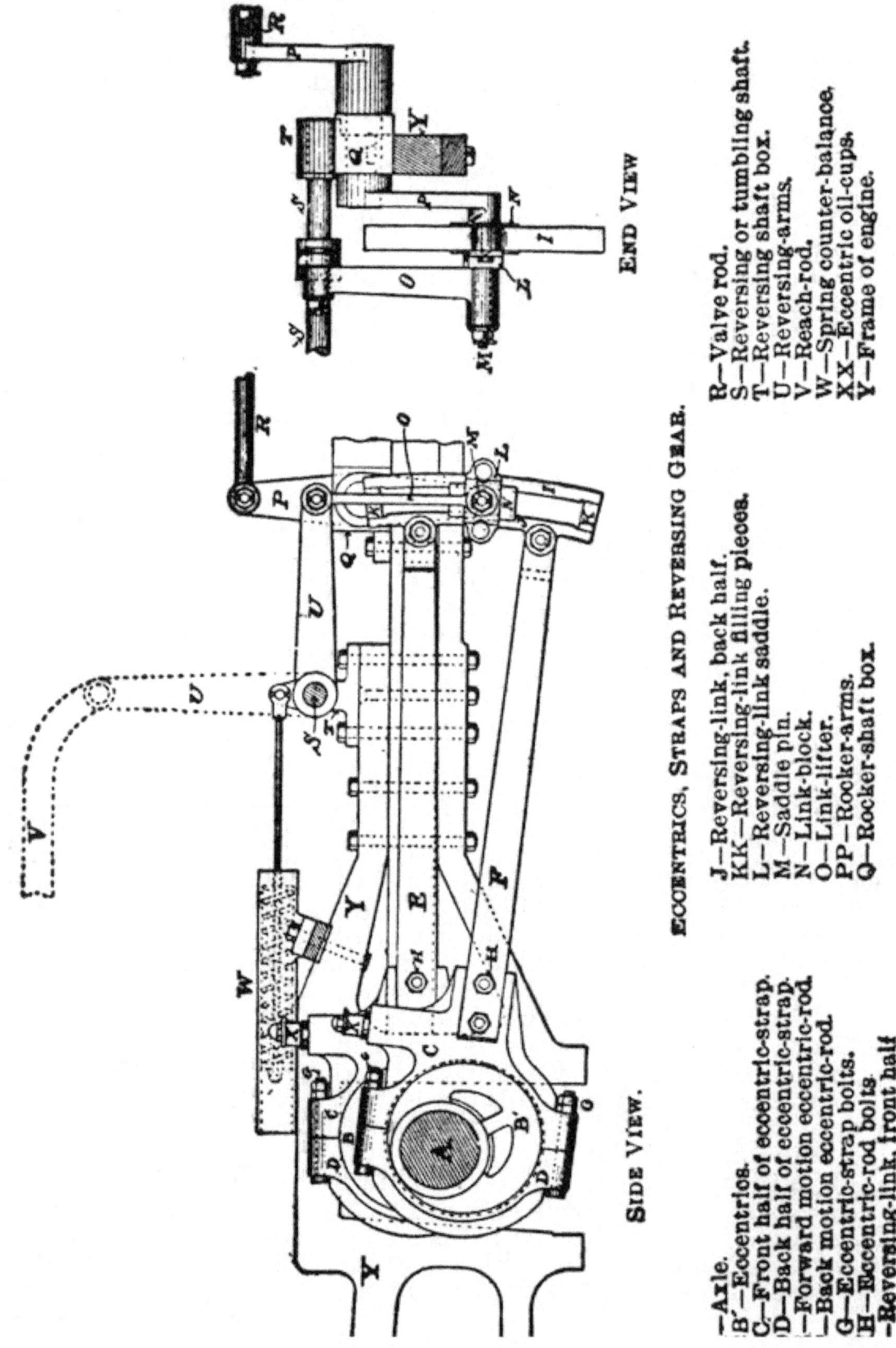

ECCENTRICS, STRAPS AND REVERSING GEAR.

SIDE VIEW. END VIEW.

A—Axle.
B'—Eccentrics.
C—Front half of eccentric-strap.
D—Back half of eccentric-strap.
E—Forward motion eccentric-rod.
F—Back motion eccentric-rod.
G—Eccentric-strap bolts.
H—Eccentric-rod bolts.
I—Reversing-link, front half.
J—Reversing-link, back half.
KK—Reversing-link filling pieces.
L—Reversing-link saddle.
M—Saddle pin.
N—Link-block.
O—Link-lifter.
PP—Rocker-arms.
Q—Rocker-shaft box.
R—Valve rod.
S—Reversing or tumbling shaft.
T—Reversing shaft box.
U—Reversing-arms.
V—Reach-rod.
W—Spring counter-balance.
XX—Eccentric oil-cups.
Y—Frame of engine.

clamp valve rod. If valve is broken so it can not be put together and blocked, a block must be used in place of it to keep steam out of cylinders. In case of a balanced slide valve a piece of short metal, if available, is very serviceable.

Q.—How would you proceed with a broken steam chest?

A.—If chest is only cracked, remove casing and wedge between studs and body of chest to close crack and hold the sides in place. If badly broken, it is best to send for an engine to take train and disabled engine in. Going in to front end and putting a blind gasket in steam pipe to keep steam out of steam chest is a rather difficult proposition on the road. The fire must be low, or out, and no steam admission to front end, so that one can work in there. The delay is too great to be tolerated on a busy line.

Q.—How can the blow from a broken valve yoke be located and repaired?

A.—When a valve yoke breaks off the engine will stop on the forward center on that side, if valves are of outside admission, and will stop on the back center on that side if valves are of inside admission, as the valve with the broken yoke will go to the front of the steam chest and remain there and can not be shifted by moving reverse lever. Take out relief-valve cage and move the valve with a small bar so it will cover the ports. Disconnect valve stem and clamp it. Put a plug of wood through relief-valve cage opening firmly against valve and screw relief-valve cage in place to hold plug against valve. If yoke is only cracked, drop lever ahead and work a light throttle. Engine will be lame but it may hold until a terminal is reached, and a greater delay avoided than would occur otherwise.

Q.—If a valve rod breaks outside of steam chest, what can be done?

A.—Cover ports, clamp valve stem and take off the broken piece. Leave main rod up.

Q.—What are the main causes of an engine going lame?

A.—A slipped eccentric or blade, a loose eccentric strap bolt, a cracked valve yoke, a difference in the size of nozzle tips on a double nozzle engine, or anything that would change the regularity of the exhaust sound.

Q.—If a nozzle tip was gone on a double nozzle engine, how would the exhaust sound?

A.—Two heavy and two light exhausts.

Q.—What is the position of the eccentric cams on the axle relative to the crank pin?

A.—This depends on the type of valve used, and also the kind of rocker.

Q.—How can a slipped eccentric be located?

A.—By its position on the axle in reference to the crank pin, by the sound of the exhaust, and by the keyways cut in the cam and axle.

Q.—What are the chief causes of eccentric slipping?

A.—Deficient lubrication or strap too tight on eccentric, causing it to bind, or so loose as to allow dust to pass freely in between cam

LINSTROM'S IMPROVED ECCENTRIC

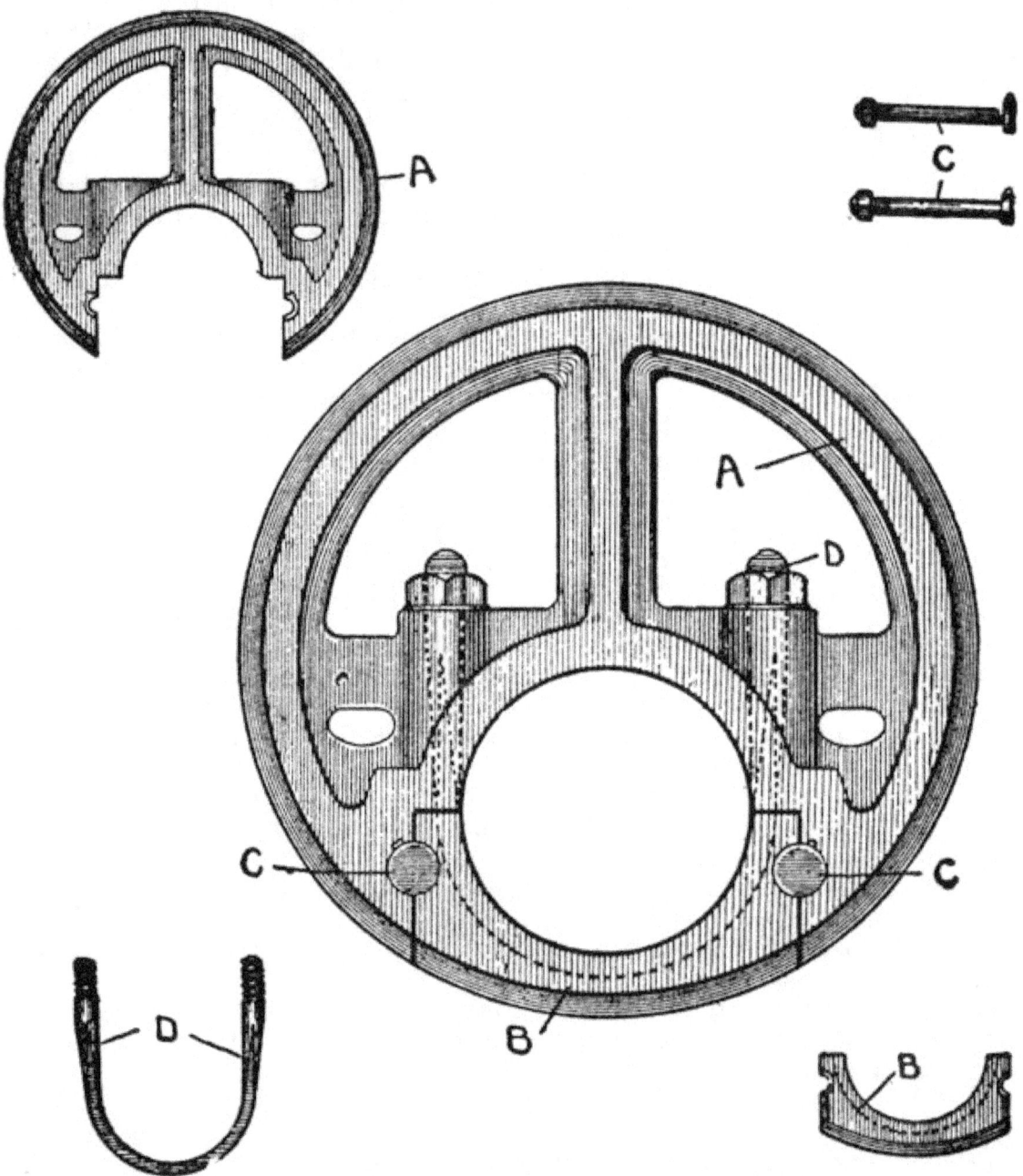

The eccentric set screw is done away with, the U-shaped bolt D not only holding the two segments A and B together, but also clamping them to the shaft.

The two bolts C C serve as dowel pins to hold the two halves of the eccentric rigidly together, even if nuts on U-bolt D should become loosened.

and strap. Dry valves, caused by lack of oil or water being carried over on them from dry pipe. Lack of oil on eccentric may be caused by oil hole being stopped up, insufficient packing in eccentric strap oil cellar, or plug gone out of the bottom of the same.

Q.—How can the trouble be remedied?

A.—See that oil hole is open. If stopped up, it will probably be necessary to take strap down to get it open. If the strap has been recently closed and is too tight, loosen the strap bolts and put in a liner. If strap is too loose, give it plenty of the best oil you have frequently, and have the strap closed when the terminal is reached. Do not put water on a hot eccentric unless you are looking for trouble.

Q.—Is it advisable to drop the reverse lever down when an engine goes suddenly lame?

A.—No. A change in valve travel might break something. Leave the lever up until train is stopped or until satisfied that it is only a dry valve causing the trouble.

Q.—How can a slipped blade be located?

A.—There will usually be a break in the grease and dust where the blade enters the strap. If not, put engine on forward center on lame side, set the brake, and give the engine steam with cylinder cocks open. Throw the lever back and forth, and if forward blade is slipped in but little steam will come from front cylinder cock, and if slipped out steam will blow strong from it. Reverse the movement of the lever and the opposite condition will prevail. If there is too much steam at the front of the cylinder, shorten blade; if too little, lengthen it. This is for indirect motion gear. With direct motion, where rocker arms move in the same direction, if there is too much steam at front end of cylinder, lengthen blade; if too little, shorten it. In other words, move the valve toward the heavy exhaust. This applies when squaring valves.

Q.—How can a slipped eccentric be set?

A.—If a go-ahead eccentric has slipped, put the engine on center on disabled side; next put reverse lever in extreme back notch and mark steam valve stem at gland, then put reverse lever in extreme forward notch and turn eccentric on axle until mark made on stem shows at gland. Tighten set screws. This is setting the slipped eccentric by the one not slipped on that side. For the back-up eccentric, put the lever in the extreme forward notch when marking the valve stem, then put lever in extreme back notch and turn eccentric on axle until mark on stem shows at gland. Another plan is to place the engine on either center on the side having the slipped eccentric. For a go-ahead eccentric that has slipped, put reverse lever in full forward gear, block the wheels and open cylinder cocks. Admit just a little steam to the cylinder, sufficient to show at the cylinder cocks. If engine is indirect, and standing on front center, move eccentric toward crank pin until steam escapes from front cylinder cock and tighten set screws. If standing on back center, move eccentric toward crank pin until steam escapes from back cylinder cock and tighten set screws. For a direct connected engine, outside admission piston valves, engine standing on forward center, if go-ahead eccentric has slipped, move the eccentric away from the crank pin until steam escapes from front cylinder cock. If engine is direct and has inside admission piston valves, the position of the eccentrics is the same as on an indirect engine having D slide valves. If the slipped eccentric is next the frame and a long delay will be caused through it being necessary to take the other one off to get at it, it may be best to send for an engine. Or the cam may be wedged on the key, or be so hot that it can not be moved on the axle, when it will also be best to send for another engine. Where engines are regularly assigned it may save time to mark the blades and eccentrics.

Q.—What can be done in case a cam or cam bolt breaks?

A.—For a broken cam, take off broken parts. Disconnect valve rod, cover ports and clamp valve rod. For a broken cam bolt, replace it. If it is a back-up cam bolt and there is no key, or key can be removed, loosen set screws to this cam, oil good between cam and axle and with lever well ahead on quadrant, proceed with the train.

Q.—What is done in case of a broken eccentric strap?

A.—Disconnect on that side is the safest and best way.

Q.—What is to be done in case of a broken piston valve rod?

A.—Plumb rocker arm. Take off front steam chamber head and push valve over ports until broken stem is together. Clamp valve stem and take off broken piece to rocker arm. Replace chest head. Leave main rod up. In all cases where main rod is left up arrangements must be made to lubricate the cylinder.

Q.—In case of a broken transmission bar, what is the remedy?

A.—Remove the broken parts. Cover ports, disconnect and clamp valve stem. Leave main rod up.

Q.—If transmission bar hanger is broken, how is it repaired?

A.—Take off broken parts. Block link at top and bottom at point of cut-off desired. To reverse engine, blocks must be changed in link.

Q.—What happens if inside piston valve packing ring becomes broken?

A.—The corresponding end of the cylinder receives too much steam and the exhaust from that end will be too heavy.

Q.—If a piston valve ring is weak or broken, how does it differ in result from a leak caused by a by-pass valve?

A.—With a piston valve ring leak, engine is lame but does not blow; where leak is caused by a by-pass valve, engine is lame and blows also.

Q.—What causes a broken cylinder head?

A.—A front head breakage may be caused by a broken main rod or main rod strap, or broken crank pin, crosshead, wrist pin, piston rod or loose follower bolt. Back head by anything getting in guides and blocking crosshead, broken main pin, or back main rod strap. Weak metal or anything getting in cylinder will cause a breakage of either cylinder head.

Q.—How remedied?

A.—Disconnect valve stem, cover ports and clamp valve rod. Take off broken parts. If front head is only cracked, a brace may be put from pilot beam against head to hold it. If it is a back head, the guides must come down with main rod and crosshead. The piston must be removed from the cylinder so it will not slide about and do more damage.

Q.—Where is the proper place to block crosshead?

A.—At rear of guides ordinarily. In case of a broken back steam port it should be blocked at the front end of the guides. The reason for blocking at the rear of the guides is that in case the blocking should give way less damage would follow than if it were blocked at the front.

Q.—What is done in case of a broken top or bottom rocker arm or link-block pin?

A.—Cover ports, disconnect and clamp valve stem. Remove loose or broken parts. Leave main rod up.

Q.—What can be done in case of a broken link hanger, saddle pin, tumbling shaft or tumbling-shaft arm?

A.—Put a block on top of link block to work engine about half stroke and a short block under link block, allowing some room for slip of link, for a broken link-hanger pin or tumbling-shaft arm. For a broken tumbling shaft, block both links. To reverse engine, shift blocks. Remove broken parts.

Q.—What is to be done in case of a broken reach rod or reach-rod arm?

A.—Block the links top and bottom, or support the tumbling-shaft arms by means of a bar placed across the top of the frames.

Q.—If a main rod, main rod strap, crosshead, wrist pin, or piston rod breaks, what is to be done?

A.—Cover ports, disconnect and clamp valve stem. Remove broken parts.

Q.—What valve gears are used on locomotives you are acquainted with?

A.—The shifting link motion, usually known as the Stephenson valve gear; the Walschaert valve gear, the Joy valve gear, the Pilliod, the Baker-Pilliod.

Q.—What description can you give of these different valve gears?

A.—The Stephenson valve gear is actuated by two eccentrics secured, generally, to the main driving axle. These eccentrics or sheaves are provided with straps to which rods are attached that connect with a radial movable link. By means of a sliding block the link connects with the lower end of a rocking shaft. The upper end of this rocking shaft is attached to a valve rod which transmits the motion of the eccentrics to the slide valve. The movement of the valve is regulated by the position of the sliding block in the link. When that block is near the top of the link, it gives full movement to the valve in forward gear. When the block is near the bottom of

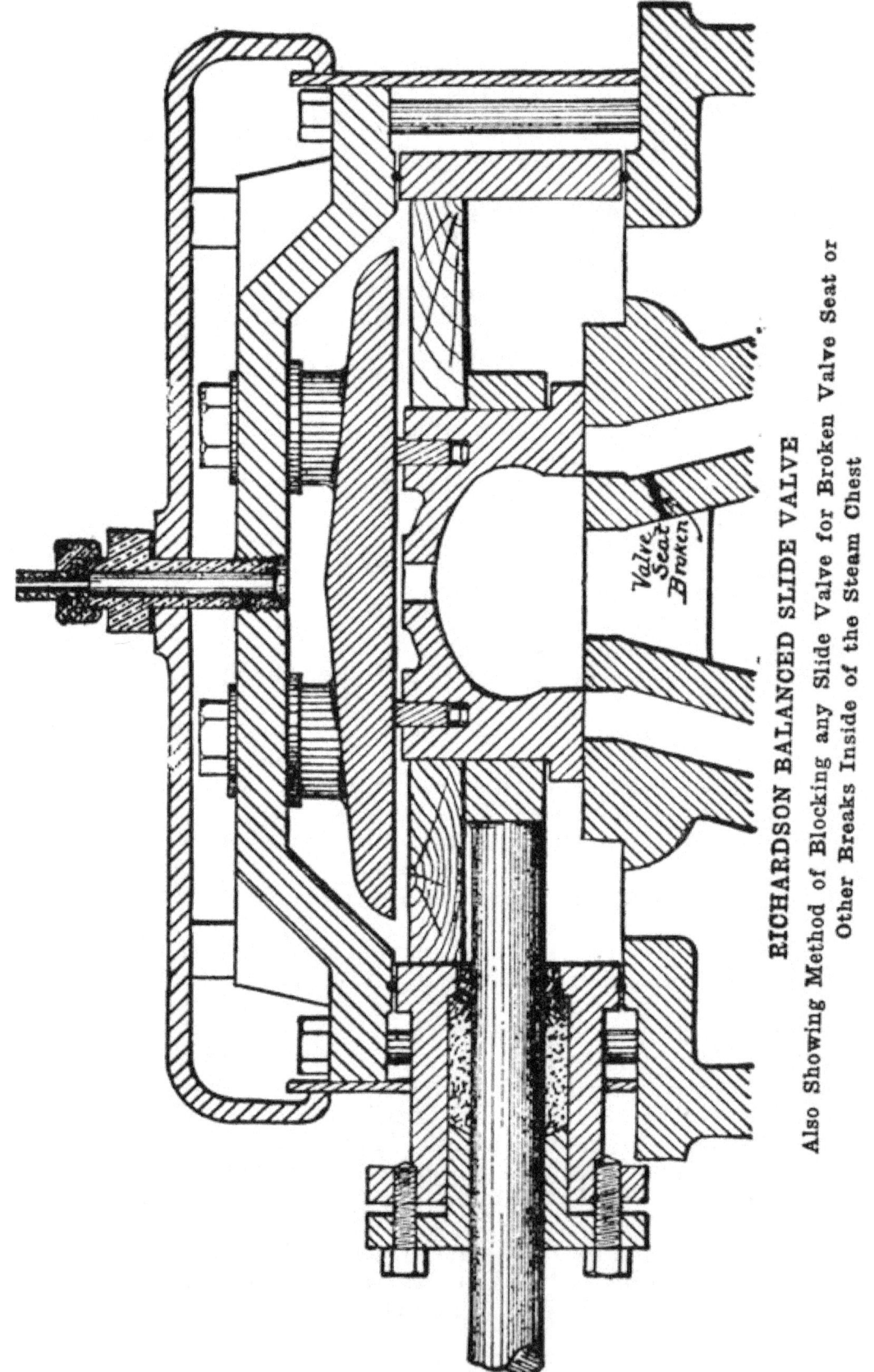

RICHARDSON BALANCED SLIDE VALVE

Also Showing Method of Blocking any Slide Valve for Broken Valve Seat or Other Breaks Inside of the Steam Chest

the link it produces full motion to the valve in back gear. The Walschaert is of the type known as a radial valve gear, has a single crank arm attached to the main crank which performs the functions of the two eccentrics in a link motion. The crank arm has a rod connecting it to an oscillating link traversed by a movable block. A radius bar conveys the motion of the block to the valve rod. There is a combination lever attached to the crosshead at its lower end and to the valve rod at its upper end. This combination lever moves the valve a sufficient distance from the central position to provide for the lap or lead.

Q.—What are the chief features of the Baker-Pilliod valve gear?

A.—It resembles the Walschaert valve gearing in having a single crank attached to the main crank, which by a connecting or eccentric rod transmits the motion to the valve, and also by the addition of a combination lever which modifies the motion, but it does not transfer the motion from the main crank through a movable or oscillating link, but through a system of bell cranks the motion of which is modified by a suspended radius bar attached to the reach rod. The lower arm of the bell crank is attached to the valve rod by suitable connections.

Q.—What are the principal features of the Joy valve gear?

A.—In this form of valve gear the eccentrics and their equivalents, such as the eccentric crank are dispensed with. The motion for the valve is taken directly from the connecting rod. By utilizing the backward and forward motion of the main rod and combining this with the vibrating action of the rod up and down, a movement results which is employed to actuate the valves of engines using any combination of lap and lead desired.

Q.—What is an Allen valve?

A.—A valve having an extra port that extends over the valve cavity from one side to the other.

Q.—What is the purpose of the Allen valve?

A.—To increase the steam port opening so that steam may be admitted into the cylinder more rapidly than with the plain slide valve.

Q.—Is the travel of the valve always of the same extent?

A.—No. The travel of the valve is regulated by the position of the reverse lever. When the reverse lever is set in full gear, the valve will travel its full stroke. As the reverse lever is notched back the extent of valve trave is gradually diminished.

Q.—What effect on steam distribution results from shortening the travel of the valve?

A.—Its tendency is to accelerate the events of the piston stroke.

Q.—What are the events of the stroke?

A.—Admission, cut-off, release, compression.

Q.—Describe these events.

A.—Admission is the act of steam entering the cylinder through the steam port opened by the valve. Cut-off is the act due to the valve closing the port opening and preventing the admission of more steam. Release is the act of opening the exhaust port and permitting the steam to escape. Compression begins when the valve closes the admission port permitting the advancing piston to squeeze into small bulk any steam or air left in the cylinder.

Following these events of the piston stroke on a valve motion model is the proper way to understand them. Ten minutes' study with the aid of a model is worth a whole day's study without that graphic help.

Q.—What is the variable lead? What is a fixed lead? Why are there two kinds?

A.—Variable lead is that which varies according to the cut-off being regulated by position of reverse lever, as in the Stephenson link motion. A fixed lead is that which is the same at all positions of lever, as in the Walschaert's and some other gears.

The variable lead was a desirable feature of the Stephenson link motion, but it had to be dispensed with when outside gears were adopted. The adoption of the fixed lead was not a matter of preference, but we had to have the outside valve gears, as the modern engines did not afford room enough for the Stephenson link motion, and the loss of the variable lead was one of the sacrifices made with the change, as the outside valve gears give same lead for all cut-offs.

Q.—What is the difference between preadmission and lead?

A.—Preadmission is the admitting of steam to cylinder for one stroke of piston before the opposite stroke of piston has been completed, while lead is the admitting of steam after either stroke of piston has been completed, but before the return stroke has begun.

Q.—What is the difference between inside lap and exhaust lap?

A.—The exhaust lap is on the inside on an outside admission engine, and on the outside on an engine having inside admission valves. Whatever the type of valve the exhaust lap is the lap on that part of valve which controls the exhaust.

Q.—Will a blow from balance strips of D valve show at the cylinder cocks, or will it only show at top of stack when testing engine standing?

A.—It depends upon the position of valve having the defective strips. If the engine stands with valve (line and line) on center of seat, steam blowing through strips will blow through top of valve into exhaust cavity and out through exhaust passage to stack. If valve be moved ahead of a central position the inside edge of valve will uncover forward port, through which some of the steam blowing through strips will pass into cylinder, which will show at forward cylinder cock. The same is true of rear cylinder cock if valve is moved back of a central position, but the passage through exhaust way is most free, permitting most of the steam to go that way.

Q.—What would one be able to tell by the exhaust as to whether an eccentric was not set right or a blade not the right length?

A.—The sound of exhaust can be relied upon to indicate whether the lameness is due to the eccentric or a blade. If it is the blade that is too long or too short there will be an uneven distribution of steam at each end of cylinder on that side, making one exhaust stronger than the other. If the lameness is due to the eccentric the amount of steam admitted to each end of the cylinder will be the same on the defective side, but will be either weaker or stronger than the exhausts on good side. They will be weaker if the eccentric is advanced on the axle too much, and will be stronger if the eccentric is not advanced enough. When advanced too much the port opening takes place too early, also the cut-off, for any position of lever. If not advanced enough the valve events will all take place too late and difference in amount of steam used in the defective side as compared to the other side will make the difference in the exhaust force, which indicates the course of lameness. When the fault is with the setting of eccentric, the exhausts will not be spaced the proper distance from those on opposite side, both coming too close to them, while in the case of a wrong length of blade one exhaust, the weaker one, will take place too soon, while the other will take place too late.

Q.—What causes piston valve engines to pound or hump when shut off, with lever hooked up?

A.—There is much difference of opinion as to the cause of that. Many claim it is due to the absence of compression, saying there is none when no steam is admitted to cylinder to compress. A more reasonable solution of the problem seems to be that instead of no compression taking place with engine shut off, the fact is, it becomes greater, since all the air drawn in through relief valves can not escape through exhaust. That portion which remains in cylinder when the exhaust is closed is compressed, and, owing to the greater density of air, even if the volume was not great at time compression began, the pressure would run up much higher than if steam were confined in the cylinder instead of air, the latter being less dense and more compressible. This fact is no secret, as there are by-pass valves on some of the modern engines that provide for relief from the very trouble caused by the compression of air in locomotive cylinders when engine is drifting.

Q.—In what way does the eccentric motion impart the desired movement to the valve on a Southern valve gear?

A.—The motion of the eccentric is imparted to the valve in the simplest and most direct manner through the medium of the eccentric rod, which has two connections at its forward end, one to the radius hanger, the other one at the extreme end of rod connects with the transmission yoke. The radius hanger is connected to link block, serving as a swinging fulcrum, which, in response to the different positions of link block in the stationary link, imparts to the transmission yoke and through it to the bell crank and valve rod in a practically perfect manner all the variations of the cut-off, and this without the lost motion due to slip of link found in other inside as well as outside valve gears in use today. The Southern valve gear has no crosshead connections, and there are but eight points of wear on each side of engine, which is much less than in many other gears.

For the purpose of particularizing the various positions of the driving wheel crank (when occasion requires), the 360 degrees through which it passes are divided into eight parts; the "upper

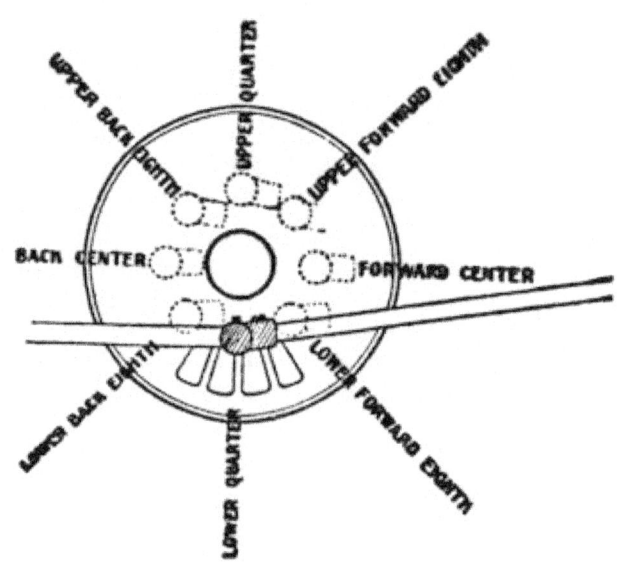

quarter" represents the crank pin when directly above the main axle; the "lower quarter" when directly below it; the "forward center" locates the crank pin on a straight line between the main axle and the cylinder, the "back center" 180 degrees from there. The "eighths" are the upper, lower, forward, and back as shown by diagram.

Progressive Examination for Firemen—Questions and Answers in Detail

It is the policy of railroads to employ men as locomotive firemen, who will be capable in time to become locomotive engineers. This requires that a man should have at least a common school education, good habits, and be in good physical condition. He should also be quick and alert and a man of sound judgment. Having these qualifications, advancement will come to those who are conscientious in the discharge of their duties and who devote some of their leisure hours to study. As an aid to this end, and in order that there may be derived the highest efficiency from a man engaged as a locomotive fireman, there is placed in the hands of every man who is employed as a fireman, a code of questions and it is expected that in the preparation necessary for correct answering of the questions a course of study will be necessary, which shall fit him for the work which he is expected to perform. His answers to the questions will indicate how well he has progressed.

When a man is employed first as a fireman, he will be given the questions on which he will be examined at the end of the first year. Having answered these questions satisfactorily he will then be given the questions for the following year. Having passed this one, he will be given a third and final set of questions on which he will be examined before being promoted to engineman.

The following describes the method and time of holding these progressive examinations:

When a man is employed as a fireman he shall be given the First Series of questions and notified that at the end of the first year of service he will be required to pass a written and oral examination thereon, under the direction of the division mechanical officer and air-brake supervisor (or air-brake instructor).

After passing the First Series of questions, he will be given the Second Series of questions and notified that at the end of another year of service he will be required to pass a written and oral examination thereon, under the direction of the division mechanical officer and air-brake supervisor (or air-brake instructor).

When he has passed the Second Series of questions he will be given the Third Series of questions and notified that before being promoted and within not less than one year he will be required to pass a written and oral examination before a general board of examiners.

It should be borne in mind, however, that the wording of the answers is not, as a rule, considered of much consequence as long as the candidate shows that he understands the subject, and any engineer or fireman who can give an intelligent answer to the majority of these questions is very liable to obtain the position he seeks, or pass his examination for promotion. The form of the question is not always the same, the wording often being different, but when stripped of all surplus words, mean the same and are susceptible to the same answer, and the examiner as a rule makes sure that the candidate has not merely committed the questions and answers to memory, but that he really and truly understands the various matters they cover.

It will always happen that conditions on different railroads vary, as, for instance, compound engines are not in service on all roads, oil burning locomotives are restricted to those properties where that fuel can be economically used, electric headlights have not been universally adopted, and so on. For this reason the questions and answers on these subjects are given under separate headings, but are available in case of need.

FIRST YEAR'S EXAMINATION

Q. 1.—What are the obligations of the fireman to the company employing him?

A.—The fireman should always be ready for duty when needed, and should be at his home or place of residence ready for a call unless given the privilege of a certain time to be away, and he should be sure to be back at his calling address when his leave of absence has expired.

Note.—The importance of this lies in the fact that in case of emergency, where a man is needed on short notice, he will be available, and the company assumes that he can be relied on at all times when he is given employment.

Q. 2.—What are the duties of the fireman when called for a run?

A.—He should get to the roundhouse as soon as possible, making sure that he is there in ample time to prepare his engine for the run without delay.

Q. 2½.—What are the duties of the fireman on arrival at the roundhouse previous to going out on a trip?

A.—He should report to the engine despatcher or foreman in charge, and find out which engine he is to get, see that all firing tools are on the engine and in good condition, draw the necessary supplies for the trip (such as oils, waste, packings, extra water glasses and lubricator glasses with gaskets, etc.), see that the fire is in good condition and ready for the trip, and while examining fire note the condition of the fire-box sheets and flues, examine the grates and the ash pan, see that there is a full supply of coal, water, and sand, and that lights are in proper condition for use and in their proper place, see that the necessary flags, fusees and torpedoes are on the engine, and read all bulletins.

Q. 3.—Upon arriving at the engine what are your first duties?

A.—To see that the boiler has plenty of water in it to protect the crown sheet, by trying the gauge cocks and comparing them with the water glass, then see that the fire is in proper condition.

Q. 4.—Have you acquired the habit of comparing time with the engineer's time and do you insist on seeing all train orders?

A.—Yes.

Note.—The importance of seeing all train orders is that it is a protective act; not only do you protect yourself, but others as well, when you know where the meeting points are, and it enables you to handle the fire in the most economical and scientific manner.

Q. 5.—What is the most important duty of the locomotive fireman?

A.—To produce the greatest amount of steam with the least possible amount of fuel.

Note.—The cost of fuel on the railroad is one of its greatest expenditures, and the fireman who can produce the necessary heat to evaporate the greatest amount of water with the least amount of fuel consumed is the most valuable man—his economy will more than pay his salary.

Q. 6.—Does a knowledge of the principles of combustion, from a scientific point of view, aid in fuel economy? Why?

A.—Yes, because if a fireman knows just the conditions necessary (and how they are obtained) in fire-box to produce the greatest amount of heat, he will be able to produce the heat many times when conditions are not the best.

Q. 7.—What is the composition of "bituminous" coal?

A.—Bituminous coal is composed of carbon (fixed and free), hydrogen, water, oxygen, nitrogen, and ash.

Note.—The fixed carbon is what we call coke and the free carbon is the part that goes away as black smoke if not consumed in the fire-box, the hydrogen is a gas and produces great heat, the ash is the residue of combustion, and if clinkers are formed it shows that the coal had some iron and sulphur in it, which is called by the chemist "iron perides."

Q. 8.—What are the heat producing substances in the bituminous coal?

A.—Carbon and hydrogen.

Q. 9.—What is combustion or of what does burning consist?

A.—Burning or combustion is the chemical combination of a fuel element with oxygen.

Q. 10.—What three things are essential to produce combustion?

A.—To produce burning or combustion it is necessary to have the oxygen, the fuel and the temperature at which they will combine.

Q. 11.—From what source do we get the oxygen that combines with and burns the carbon and the gases?

A.—We get the oxygen from the atmosphere.

Note.—The oxygen is one-fifth part of the air we breathe, the other four-fifths being nitrogen.

Q. 12.—Are we liable to get too much oxygen for perfect combustion of the fuels? Why?

A.—No, we are not liable to get too much oxygen, because the fuel elements will not take more than they need to make the right combination.

Q. 13.—In what proportions do the oxygen and carbons combine and what are the results?

A.—The proper proportion of oxygen to combine with carbon is two parts of oxygen to one part carbon, but carbon will combine with one part of oxygen to one part of carbon, and in this combination it will produce only one-third the heat that results from the proper combination.

Q. 14.—How does the hydrogen combine with the oxygen?

A.—Hydrogen requires but one part oxygen for two parts hydrogen and will not combine in any other way.

Note.—Hydrogen is one-sixteenth the weight of the air and being very light will escape to the atmosphere unconsumed unless the oxygen is in fire-box to combine with it.

Q. 15.—Is it a good plan to have more oxygen in fire-box than is used? Why?

A.—Yes, because the excess amount will be used when the fresh fuel is first placed in fire-box and the gases are being rapidly given off.

Q. 16.—How is forced draft created in the fire-box? Why is it necessary?

A.—The forced draft is created by the exhaust forming a partial vacuum in the front end (smoke-box) and the air, which will flow into any space which is not already filled with something as dense as the air, will flow up through the fire and furnish the oxygen for burning. It is necessary to create the forced draft in order to get the required amount of oxygen into the fire-box for the rapid burning of the fuel to produce the heat and steam for the cylinders.

Q. 17.—Describe the condition in which your fire should be when ready for the trip, and say what you would do to get it in that condition with either bituminous or anthracite coal?

A.—The fire should be level and burning brightly and free from clinker or any dead spots. To get the fire in proper condition, I would clean out all ashes and clinkers, put fresh fuel in the light spots, adding a little at a time until the fire was level and of the proper thickness.

Q. 18.—State how you would fire the engine while running along, to obtain the best results, with either bituminous or anthracite coal?

A.—I would supply the fuel to the fire as it was being consumed, keeping the fire of an even depth and burning at a dazzling white heat all over, by firing into the lightest spots in small charges, in that manner producing all the heat possible and wasting none of the fuel.

Note.—The coal should be broken up into small pieces for best results.

Q. 19.—What would you do with the coal to prepare it for the fire so that best results would obtain in heat and economy?

A.—I would break the coal up into pieces about the size of an apple to prepare it for the fire.

Q. 20.—Why is it very important that bituminous coal should be broken up so that the pieces will not be larger than an apple before being thrown into the fire-box?

A.—Because the oxygen must be in actual contact with the fuel for burning, and by having the coal broken up into small pieces it exposes a larger surface to the oxygen, consequently getting more of the fuel burning at once, creating greater heat.

Q. 21.—In what condition should the fire be maintained in regard to its depth and thickness with either bituminous or anthracite coal?

A.—The fire should be kept at a proper thickness and even all over, to prevent any holes being torn in it which will allow cold air to reach the flues, and at the same time thin enough to admit sufficient air to furnish the oxygen to combine with the fuels that are in the form of gases above the fire.

Q. 22.—Does the amount of air admitted to the fire-box have any influence on the amount of fuel consumed or heat produced? State why it does.

A.—Yes, unless the necessary amount of oxygen is present in the fire-box to combine with the gases as fast as they are given off, they will go out through the flues (helped by their lightness and the forced draft) unconsumed and a total loss, and all the heat we will get is from the fixed carbon which will be only about one-third or one-fourth of what we should have gotten from the fuel placed in the fire-box.

Q. 23.—Why is it important that the fire be kept at an even depth all over and free from clinkers and ash?

A.—It is important that the fire be of an even thickness all over to insure the air, of which the oxygen is a part, be admitted in the same volume at all points so that the oxygen will come in actual contact with the fuel and keep the fire burning brightly over its entire surface, and the temperature high enough for the combination of the oxygen with the fuels.

Q. 24.—At what temperature do the fuels combine with the oxygen?

A.—Best results obtain with a temperature of not less than 1,800 degrees.

Q. 25.—What is the temperature in the fire-box when the fire is burning brightly all over its surface.

A.—It is from 2,200 to 2,800 degrees Fahrenheit.

Q. 26.—Does the nitrogen which enters the fire-box benefit the fire? If not, what is the effect of it?

A.—No, the nitrogen is a dead loss, but must be passed through the fire-box to get the oxygen that is mixed with it in the air, and it uses up some of the heat in the fire-box.

Q. 27.—In what manner does the condition of the fire with regard to depth, holes, banks, or clinkers affect the admission of air?

A.—If the fire is too thick the air can not get through it in sufficient quantity; if there are holes in the fire the air will take the line of the least resistance and enter the fire-box in large quantities and pass through the flues cooling them as well as the temperature of the fire-box, and the air does not come up through the fire where it will touch the fuels with the oxygen and there can be no burning. Banks and clinkers force the air to come up through the thinner parts of the fire so the fuel on top of the bank or clinker gets no oxygen and produces no heat.

Q. 28.—What are the effects of too strong a draft?

A.—Too much air will be drawn up through the fire, reducing the temperature in fire-box, and the gases which are very light will pass out through the flues before they have time to burn.

Q. 29.—What bad effects would follow carrying too heavy a fire.

A.—Air could not get through the fire in sufficient quantities to furnish the oxygen to burn the gases, and the best part of the fuels would be lost.

Q. 30.—What bad effects would follow carrying too light a fire?

A.—Too much air would enter the fire-box and cool the gases below the igniting point and they would be wasted.

Q. 31.—If while the engine is standing the fire becomes very light and thin, what effect would starting a heavy train have on the fire?

A.—It would tear holes in the fire.

Q. 32.—What harm would result from putting more than three or four scoops of coal on the fire at one time, under working conditions, with bituminous? with anthracite?

A.—With bituminous coal it will start a bank which will turn into a clinker and cut out part of your grate surface; with anthracite coal it would cause holes to be torn in the fire.

Q. 33.—What are the advantages of utilizing the entire grate surface?

A.—You have more fuel burning and will produce more heat and steam.

Q. 34.—How can you prevent coal from being forced through the flues and out through the stack?

A.—By keeping the fire free from banks and clinker, of an even depth and sufficiently heavy to meet requirements.

Q. 35.—Is there a serious loss from this cause? If so, what conditions tend to increase it? what conditions will decrease it?

A.—Yes, having the fire too light, having holes in the fire, clinkers and banks in the fire or the exhaust too sharp will increase the waste.

Having the fire of proper thickness, free from clinkers and banks and even all over with plenty of oxygen being supplied through the fire, will tend to decrease the waste.

Q. 36.—What causes a pull at the fire-box door when the engine is working?

A.—By having the fire too heavy, badly clinkered or banks in it, or with the dampers to ash pans closed or draught openings shut off so there is not sufficient air entering through the fire, to fill the vacuum formed by the exhaust, atmospheric pressure on the fire-box door causes the pull.

Q. 37.—What will cause the engine to tear holes in the fire?

A.—By having the fire lighter in spots than it should be, or by allowing clinkers and banks to form, compelling the air to come through the free spots with great force.

Q. 38.—What will cause dead spots in fire, with bituminous or anthracite coal?

A.—Dead spots are formed in a bituminous or anthracite coal fire by neglecting to fire evenly and supply fuel as it is burned, or by clinkers keeping the air from furnishing the oxygen to keep up the burning in that spot.

Q. 39.—Will improper firing cause banks and clinkers to form in the fire-box? What are the bad results from this?

A.—Yes, clinkers and banks are formed by not firing evenly at all times, and the bad results from clinkers and banks are fuel wasted, grate surface not all being used, dead spots formed, low steam pressures, flues and fire-box seams caused to leak.

Q. 40.—What is the cause of the drumming in the fire-box when engine is shut off? How can you avoid it?

A.—Drumming in the fire-box is caused by the oxygen and gases in the fire-box mixing in proper proportions to explode. To stop it either admit more air by opening the fire-box door, or reduce the supply of air by closing the dampers to ash pan openings.

Q. 41.—What are the effects, good or bad, of raking the fire when the engine is working?

A.—Bad; it will cause clinkers and holes to form in the fire.

Q. 42.—Describe the ash pan and say what its duties are.

A.—The ash pan is box like in shape, made of iron or steel, and is suspended under the grates. The duty of the ash pan is to catch ashes and cinders as well as live coals that fall through the grates and prevent setting fires; it also provides a means of controlling the flow of air through the fire.

Q. 43.—Why is it important that ash pan dampers and slides be kept closed while on the road, especially in dry, hot seasons?

A.—The dampers and slides should be kept closed to prevent live coals from falling out of ash pans and setting fires.

Q. 44.—Why are the damper and netting openings provided in ash pans?

A.—To furnish openings for the air to enter the ash pan under the fire, and the dampers provide a means for controlling the admission of air to the ash pan and in that manner control the draft on the fire.

Q. 45.—Why are grates made to shake?

A.—The grates are made to shake so that clinkers may be broken up and ashes shook through them into the ash pan.

Q. 46.—When should the grates be shaken? Why?

A.—The grates should be shaken when the engine is not working steam, because to shake the grates when engine is working will cause holes to form in fire.

Q. 47.—Does any loss occur from shaking the grates too frequently or too severely?

A.—Yes, the fire is made too thin and much good coal is shaken into ash pan.

Q. 48.—What would you do in case of a disconnected grate?

A.—I would try to connect it up, if impossible to do that would straighten it up so that the fingers would not be burned off.

Q. 49.—What would you do in case of a broken grate?

A.—I would cover the opening with pieces of iron or stone to keep the coal from dropping into ash pan, and keep the cold air from entering fire-box.

Q. 50.—If clinkers form on the grates, what will be the effect on the fire, and how would you avoid it?

A.—Clinkers on grates shut off heating surface of the fire, and cause dead spots, and will cause the exhaust to tear holes in the fire. I would avoid this by keeping the fire clean and firing evenly all the time.

Q. 51.—What will be the effect of allowing the ash pan to become filled with ashes and clinkers?

A.—With the ash pan filled, the draft is shut off and air can not enter in sufficient quantities through the grates to furnish the oxygen for burning, and the grates are liable to burn.

Q. 52.—Do you consider it beneficial or otherwise to admit air above the surface of the fire?

A.—No, it is not good practice to admit air above the fire, because it cools the gases below the igniting temperature and much of the best heat producing part of the fuel is wasted; it also tends to cause the flues to leak.

Q. 53.—What effect does opening the door have on the fire?

A.—It deadens the fire, because the oxygen is not coming up through the fuel nor getting in contact with it.

Q. 54.—Is it good practice to leave the fire-box door open longer than is absolutely necessary while the engine is working? Why?

A.—No, because the forced draught will cause large quantities of cold air to be drawn through the flues, contracting them and causing them to leak.

Q. 55.—What is black smoke and is it combustible?

A.—Black smoke is small particles of carbon going away unconsumed. It is combustible and will produce great heat if it has the oxygen present to combine with and the proper temperature for combination at the time it is given off as free carbon from the fire.

Q. 56.—Why does the black smoke clear up so quickly when fire-box door is opened?

A.—Because the oxygen for its burning is admitted in sufficient quantity to combine with the gases and consume them, resulting in a colorless gas.

Q. 57.—What effect has the stoppage of a number of the boiler flues?

A.—It reduces the heating surface and causes the draft on the fire to be unequally distributed.

Q. 58.—What harm may follow if a bank be allowed to form and remain against the flue sheet?

A.—The lower flues are cooled off and will be weakened and will begin to leak, besides a clinker will form and cold air will pass up between it and the flue sheet.

Q. 59.—Has improper firing a tendency to cause the flues to leak? How?

A.—Yes, by causing the temperature in fire-box to vary, the continual expansion and contraction of the sheets and flues weakens them and makes them leak.

Q. 60.—In descending a long gradient where it is necessary to inject water into the boiler, how should the fire be regulated?

A.—In such cases the fire ought to be maintained sufficiently active to keep the incoming water up to the temperature of the steam. When that is not done the comparatively cool water inside the boiler may have disastrous effect upon flues and fire-box sheets.

Q. 61.—Is it possible for the water inside of the boiler to have a lower temperature than the steam?

A.—That is possible and it happens frequently. There is so little circulation inside the boiler when an engine is drifting that the incoming water may not be affected by the steam heat. When this condition exists the stream pressure will drop suddenly when the throttle is opened when the end of the grade is reached. Keeping the fire active while the engine is drifting has the effect of converting the incoming water into steam, thereby maintaining the water and steam at the same temperature.

Q. 62.—What is the force most active in stimulating the fire for generating steam in a locomotive boiler?

A.—The exhaust steam passing through the smokestack.

Q. 63.—Explain the draft-creating action of the exhaust steam.

A.—The exhaust steam rushing through the smokestack at great velocity induces a movement of the gases in the smoke-box toward the atmosphere so that steam acts to some extent as a piston pumping out the gases, the combined action producing a partial vacuum in the smoke-box. This partial vacuum draws the gases through the flues and fire-box, while the pressure of the atmosphere forces air through the grates, thereby stimulating the fire.

Q. 64.—What is a spark arrester?

A.—A spark arrester consists of an obstruction placed in the smokestack or in the smoke-box on which the sparks strike before they get outside. There is also a wire netting to arrest the sparks that otherwise would escape into the atmosphere.

The spark arrester formerly consisted of a cone and netting placed in the smokestack. The modern practice is to use a plate of iron sloping in front of the flues which projects the sparks into an extended smoke-box. A wire netting for stopping the emission of sparks is spread between the flues and the smokestack opening.

Q. 65.—What are locomotive draft appliances?

A.—These consist of an exhaust nozzle and the plate already mentioned as extending from above the upper row of flues. This plate, called a diaphragm, is also employed to make the gases pass uniformily through the different rows of flues. It is also used to make the fire burn evenly, which results from the flues drawing the gases evenly from the fire-box.

Some engines have a petticoat pipe or lift pipe interposed between the exhaust nozzle and the smokestack. That pipe is sometimes used to regulate the draft through the flues.

The diamond-stack form of engine has a petticoat or lift pipe in the smoke-box set above the exhaust nozzle and extending within a few inches of the base of the smokestack. Some lift pipes have a movable sleeve which is used to regulate the draft through the flues.

Q. 66.—What is a boiler flue?

A.—It is a plain iron or steel pipe about two inches in diameter, extending the length of the boiler secured to tube plates. The flues are surrounded by the water in the boiler and transmit the greater part of the heat generated in the fire-box.

The invention of the multi-tubular boiler—that is, putting a multitude of flues in a boiler—first made a high speed locomotive possible.

Q. 67.—What is the most common causes of leaky flues?

A.—Abrupt changes of temperature, such as injecting much water when the fire is low; permitting cold air to strike the flues and using the blower after the fire is drawn.

Q. 68.—How would you fire a boiler that had leaky flues?

A.—Fire so that the fire would be kept uniform and avoid opening the door more than was positively necessary.

Q. 69.—When there are indications that steam would begin to blow off, how would you check the heat?

A.—By closing the dampers and putting the fire door upon the latch.

Q. 70.—As a fireman would you be interested in watching the water level, and why?

A.—Certainly. It is only by watching the water level that I could co-operate with the engineer.

Q. 71.—What is the purpose of a brick arch in the fire-box?

A.—A brick arch lengthens the journey of the gases from the fire to the entrance of the flues promoting the admixture that produces the maximum possible heat; it maintains an intensely hot body where the gases have to pass, with the result that gases are frequently ignited that without the arch would pass into the flues without heating vitality. The brick arch is an excellent spark arrester, and it also prevents cold air from passing directly into the flues, thereby preventing leakage of the flues and fire-box sheets.

Q. 72.—When and for what purpose is the use of the rake upon the fire desirable?

A.—When the surface of the fire is caking and obstructing the passage of air through the mass.

Q. 73.—What would you consider to be abuse of a boiler?

A.—Heaping a heavy load of coal into the fire-box at one firing, cooling the boiler by running with the fire door open, irregular use of the injector and operating the injector when steam is shut off.

Q. 74.—Are there any advantages for a boiler to have large grate area?

A.—Under certain limitations a large grate area permits of slow combustion and promotes economy of fuel. The grate surface may, however, be so large that the intensity of heat necessary to consume all the fuel gases will not be reached. Some railroad companies find it economical to put dead grates in some classes of engines having very large grate areas.

Q. 75.—Why is it necessary to provide for a liberal supply of air to promote combustion in a locomotive fire-box?

A.—Because the oxygen in the air is essential in the act of combustion, which is a chemical combination of oxygen and carbon, the latter being the principal element in the fuel.

Q. 76.—Is it possible to use too much air in promoting combustion, and what is the result?

A.—Using more than the necessary quantity of air is wasteful for the superfluous air has to be heated to the same temperature as the vital gases, thereby wasting heat.

Q. 77.—What results from the fire receiving a supply of air inadequate to effect complete combination?

A.—A form of gas is generated from the fuel which is of inferior heating quality.

Q. 78.—Are you familiar with any simple experiment that will illustrate the effect of too little and of too much air in promoting combustion?

A.—That can be shown by a common kerosene lamp. The admission of too much air will make the flame smoke and the same result will come from restricting the air supply.

Q. 79.—In what condition must a fire be kept in order to prevent smoke.
A.—As bright as possible.
Q. 80.—In what way would you act to maintain a fire bright?
A.—Fire frequently and in small quantities.
Q. 81.—What effects upon the working of the fire has a small nozzle?
A.—With a small nozzle the exhaust steam escapes with such violent shocks that it tends to tear up the fire. A small nozzle also causes back pressure in the cylinders.
Q. 82.—How would you prevent the fierce exhaust due to small nozzle from tearing holes in the fire?
A.—By firing heavily.
Q. 83.—Is the pressure inside the boiler uniform over the whole surface?
A.—The steam pressure is uniform all over but the weight of the water adds pressure on the lower part in proportion to the height.
Q. 84.—Do you recognize any rule concerning the dumping of ashes?
A.—I do understand that ashes should not be dumped close to stations or among switches, road crossings or places where they might start fires.
Q. 85.—Is there any rule covering the filling of the water tank?
A.—See that it is filled at the usual water stations. Avoid permitting the water to overflow as that is a dangerous practice, especially in frosty weather.
Q. 86.—Do you consider it your duty and to your interest to study how the engine you are firing may be handled in such manner as will result in its performing the full service it is equal to without accident or delay, at the lowest possible cost, as respects the fuel, oil, and other supplies furnished for its maintenance and use in service?
A.—Yes, it is my duty to perform my duties in the most economical manner.
Q. 87.—Do you consider it to your interest to cheerfully comply with all the orders issued by your superiors?
A.—Yes.
Q. 88.—Do you realize that your service as a fireman is merely a period of apprenticeship for the position of locomotive engineer, and that it is necessary for you to familiarize yourself with all the parts of an engine, and the duties of an engineer, so that when needed you will be prepared for promotion and the successful performance of the duties of an engineer?
A.—Yes.
Q. 89.—Will you make a conscientious effort to learn the locomotives on this road and the modern methods pertaining to the successful and economical management of them?
A.—Yes.

Q. 90.—How can you best learn the latest and most modern methods in handling and care of the locomotive and its attachments?

A.—By studying the best books written on the locomotive and its attachments and studying the engine from what I learn in the books, and by helping the engineer do his work on the engine while out on the road.

AIR BRAKE QUESTIONS AND ANSWERS—FIRST YEAR'S.

Q. 1.—Name the different parts of the air brake on a locomotive.

A.—The air pump, discharge pipe, main reservoir, main reservoir pipe, automatic brake valve, independent brake valve, equalizing reservoir, feed valve, reducing valve, duplex air gauge number one, duplex air gauge number two, pump governor, distributing valve, inducing valve, brake pipe, double-heading cock, brake cylinders, brake cylinder pipe, brake cylinder cut-out cocks, distributing valve supply pipe and cut-out cock, non-return check valve with strainer, air signal pipe, reducing valve pipe, feed valve pipe, dead engine feature with cut-out cock and non-return check valve and strainer, release pipe, application cylinder pipe, angle cocks and the necessary hose connections for the various pipes, and the pipe connections to governor, gauges and the equalizing reservoir, and the choke fittings in pipes to the equalizing reservoir, engine truck and tender brake cylinders, brake beams, brake heads, brake shoes or liners, brake levers, and the rods connecting them.

Q. 2.—What is the air pump for?

A.—To compress air for use in the air brake and air signal systems.

Q. 3.—What is the main reservoir for?

A.—To store the compressed air for use in the air system as it is compressed by the pump.

Q. 4.—Why are the main reservoirs on most locomotives in two parts?

A.—For convenience in storing a large volume of air without having the reservoir in the way, and to cool the air as much as possible before it passes into the air system.

Q. 5.—What other air brake parts are used on engines not equipped with the E. T. brake?

A.—An auxiliary reservoir and triple valve, with the necessary pipe connections.

Q. 6.—What does the triple valve do?

A.—It charges the auxiliary reservoir, applies and releases the brake.

Q. 7.—What is the auxiliary reservoir for?

A.—To carry a supply of air sufficient to apply the brake on the vehicle to which it is attached.

Q. 8.—Where is the air taken from that is used in the brake cylinders on engines equipped with the E. T. brake?

A.—It is passed from main reservoir into the brake cylinders by the distributing valve.

Q. 9.—What other type of brake is used on many locomotives, besides the automatic brake?

A.—The straight air brake.

Q. 10.—For what purpose is the cut-out cock placed on a branch of the brake pipes in the back cab of the double cab locomotives?

A.—To be used by the fireman to stop the train, in case of emergency when it is impossible to communicate with the engineer, and a stop is necessary to avoid an accident.

Q. 11.—How should an engine be handled on the ash pit to avoid or prevent injury to the fire-box and flues?

A.—The air pump throttle should be closed and the blower worked just enough to keep the gases from coming back out of the door, and the fire cleaned as quickly as possible, fresh fuel added, and the door closed at once, the injector should not be worked while cleaning the fire nor until the fire is burning brightly again.

Q. 12.—Why should the air pump throttle be closed and the pump stopped while cleaning the fire?

A.—To avoid the forced draft which would draw cold air through the flues and to prevent cinders and dust from the ashes being drawn into the air cylinder of the pump, where it would do harm.

Q. 13.—Do you understand that the engineer is responsible for the work done by the fireman, and that the fireman is to be instructed by his engineer?

A.—Yes.

Q. 14.—In case of an emergency, such as a bursted flue or hole in the boiler which will let the water out, or failure of injectors and water becoming low, what should be done?

A.—The fire should be drawn or killed.

Q. 15.—How can you kill the fire quickly?

A.—By covering the stack, closing the dampers and door, and putting the blower to work.

Note.—By covering the stack the draft will be stopped and no oxygen be drawn up through the fire. By putting the blower to work the gases in front end, resulting from combustion, will be forced back into the fire-box, where they will be deadly to the fire, for without oxygen there can be no fire.

Q. 16.—What is an injector? What is it used for?

A.—An injector is a device for forcing water into a steam boiler against a pressure greater than that which is affording the power. It is used to supply water to the boiler as it is needed.

Q. 17.—What two different kinds of injectors are used on locomotives?

A.—The non-lifting type, which is placed below the water supply and has the water running into it from the force of gravity, or the natural tendency of a fluid to seek a lower level. The lifting type, which is placed above the body of water and is so constructed that it raises the water up into it.

Q. 18.—What is a lubricator and its use?
A.—The lubricator is a device used to feed oil to the steam chests and the steam cylinders uniformly as it is needed.

Q. 19.—What should the fireman be sure to do after taking water each time?
A.—He should be sure to close the manhole to tank so that cinders and fine coal cannot get down into the water tank and perhaps stop the feed pipe to injector, or damage the injector itself.

Q. 20.—Why should the fireman accompany the engineer while he is making the inspection of engine, reporting the work needed, registering arrival and making out the time tickets for trip?
A.—Because he will learn the names of the parts of the engine during the inspection, learn how to properly report the necessary work, register his arrival in the proper manner, make out time ticket and delay reports as they should be, receiving the practical education necessary for his future vocation in life as a locomotive engineer.

SECOND YEAR'S EXAMINATION

Q. 1.—What, in your opinion, is the best way to fire a locomotive?
A.—To fire as lightly as is consistent with the work required; to avoid smoke trailing back over the train; to avoid popping; to endeavor to maintain a uniform steam pressure under all circumstances, and to carry a nice, level fire on the grates, a little heavier at the sides and corners, to keep the air from coming through it near the sheets as rapidly as in the center of the fire-box.

Q. 2.—What are the advantages of superheated steam over saturated steam in locomotive service?
A.—Economy of water consumption; economy of fuel; increased boiler capacity and a more powerful locomotive. Superheated steam contains a greater amount of energy per pound than dry, saturated steam. It does away absolutely with condensation in the cylinders, while saturated steam, coming in contact with passages in cylinder saddle and walls of cylinder, is immediately cooled, and, therefore, part of it is changed back into water, which affects the pressure and its capacity to do the work.

Q. 3.—How is the saving in water produced?
A.—By eliminating all cylinder condensation present in saturated steam, and the increase in volume of a given weight of steam.

Q. 4.—How is the saving in coal accomplished?

A.—Because less steam is required to do a given amount of work, therefore, less water is evaporated, and consequently less coal is required to evaporate the water.

Q. 5.—How is the increased boiler capacity obtained?

A.—A boiler will evaporate a certain amount of water into steam, which is always on the point of giving up some of its heat and turning into water, thereby reducing the volume and pressure. Superheating eliminates the loss owing to condensation, and increases the available useful steam. It also increases the volume of a given weight of steam, thereby reducing the consumption of steam required to develop a certain power, and, therefore, increases the capacity.

Q. 6.—How is a more powerful engine obtained?

A.—The increased boiler capacity permits working the engine at a longer "cut-off" before a steam failure occurs.

Q. 7.—What type of fire tube superheater is in most general use in locomotive service?

A.—Schmidt, top header, superheater, which consists of a system of units located in the large flues, through which the steam passes on its way from the dry pipe to the steam pipes. A damper mechanism controls the flow of gases through the large flues.

Q. 8.—Describe the construction and location of the header.

A.—The header is a casting divided by partition walls into saturated and superheated steam passages. It is located in the top portion of the smoke-box so as not to interfere with work in the smoke-box, and is connected to the dry pipe at one end, and the steam pipes at the other. In locating the superheater header, its face for superheater unit joints should be square with the tube sheet, parallel to the top row of flues, and the correct distance above them, to insure correct position of the superheater units in the flues. It should be firmly supported at the ends by header supports, securely fastened to the sides of the smoke-box.

Q. 9.—Describe the construction of superheater units and their connection to the header.

A.—The units consist of seamless steel tubing, four in number, connected by three return bends. Of the four pipes, two are straight and two are bent upward and connected to the header by means of a clamp and bolt. One end of the unit is in communication with the saturated steam passage, and the other with the superheated steam passage in the header.

Q. 10.—Trace the flow of steam through the top header fire tube type superheater.

A.—On opening the throttle the saturated steam passes through the dry pipe into the saturated steam passage end of the header casting. From this passage it goes into one end of the unit, passing backward toward the fire-box, forward through one of the straight pipes and the front return bend, backward through the other straight pipe to the back return bend, and forward through the bent pipe and upward into the superheater steam passage of the header, from which

Q. 11.—What should be the position of throttle valve when running a superheater locomotive?

A.—Superheater locomotives should be operated with as full a throttle as working conditions permit, regulating the steam admission to the cylinders in accordance with the work to be performed.

Q. 12.—What should be the position of throttle while drifting?

A.—The position of the throttle while drifting should be slightly open, so as to admit a small quantity of steam to the valve chamber and cylinder above atmospheric pressure, to prevent the inrush of hot air and gases, which destroy lubrication, and also to avoid excessive wear to valve, cylinder, and piston rod packing.

Q. 13.—How should the water be carried in boiler of superheater locomotives?

A.—Water should be carried in boiler of superheater locomotives as low as conditions will permit. This practice reduces the tendency to work water into the dry pipe and units, as the superheater locomotive will use one-third less water than the saturated locomotive.

Q. 14.—What care should be exercised in lubricating a superheater locomotive?

A.—The engineer should watch very closely the supply of oil to the steam chests and he should know that the lubricator is feeding constantly and evenly over the entire division, and in accordance with the work to be done.

Q. 15.—Describe the general form of a locomotive boiler.

A.—It is cylindrical in form. It has usually a rectangular shaped fire-box at one end and a smoke-box at the other end. Flues run through the cylindrical part, which, like the fire-box, are surrounded by water.

Q. 16.—How does the wide fire-box type of boiler differ from the ordinary boiler, and what are its advantages?

A.—The ordinary "deep" fire-box is limited in width to the distance between the frames; the "shallow" fire-box sets on top of the frames, and over the driving wheels. The wide fire-box is not only above the frames, but extends out on each side of the driving wheels. The advantage is to obtain a larger grate area in the same length fire-box so as to cause slower combustion per square foot of grate surface.

Q. 17.—Why have two fire-box doors been placed in the large type of locomotive boilers?

A.—Owing to the greater width of the fire-box, two doors have been placed in the large type of locomotive boilers so that the coal can be more conveniently distributed to all parts of the fire-box.

Q. 18.—Describe a locomotive fire-box.

A.—The modern form of locomotive fire-box is a rectangular shaped structure located at the back end of the boiler. It has a door and is composed of two side sheets, a crown sheet, a back sheet, and a flue sheet from which the flues extend to the smoke-box at the other end of the boiler.

Q. 19.—To what strains is a fire-box subjected?

A.—To the crushing strains of the steam pressure and the unequal expansion and contraction of plates, stay bolts, etc.

Q. 20.—How are the sheets of a fire-box supported?

A.—They are supported by means of stay bolts, screwed through the inside and outside sheets with their ends riveted over.

Q. 21.—In what manner is a crown sheet supported?

A.—By means of crown bars or radial stay bolts.

Q. 22.—What are the bad features about crown bars?

A.—They are hard to keep clean and frequently cause "mud-burned" crown sheets.

Q. 23.—What are the advantages of radial-stayed crown sheets?

A.—They are comparatively easy to keep clean and cheaper to repair.

Q. 24.—How are the inside and outside sheets of a fire-box secured at the bottom?

A.—They are riveted to a wrought iron ring, called a mud-ring.

Q. 25.—Describe the ash pan and its use.

A.—The ash pan is a receptacle secured to the bottom of the fire-box, and is provided with two or more dampers designed to regulate the admission of air to the fire. It collects the ashes dropped from the fire-box and thus prevents their setting fire to bridges, cattle guards, and other property elsewhere along the road. Enginemen should see that the ash pan slide and hopper bottoms are closed before leaving engine house.

Q. 26.—What is a "wagon-top" boiler?

A.—It is a boiler which has the fire-box end made larger than the cylindrical part, in order to provide more steam space.

Q. 27.—Why are boilers provided with steam domes?

A.—To furnish more steam space, to obtain drier steam and to provide a place for the steam pipes, throttle valve, safety valves, and whistle.

Q. 28.—What must be the condition of a boiler to give the best results?

A.—It must have a good circulation, flues and seams tight, no flues stopped up and no leaks at other places, and must be clean and free from mud and scale.

Q. 29.—What is meant by "circulation" in a boiler?

A.—The free movement of the water so that it may come in contact with the heating surfaces and after being converted into steam be immediately replaced by fresh supplies of water.

Q. 30.—What would be the effect if a "leg" of the fire-box became filled with mud?

A.—There would be no water in contact with the fire-box sheets and they would, in consequence, become blistered or "mud burned." (The narrow water space between the inside and outside sheets of the fire-box is termed the "leg" of a boiler.)

Q. 31.—What would be the result if the fire-box sheets became overheated?

A.—They would be forced off the stay bolts and an explosion would occur.

Q. 32.—Would it be advisable to put water into a boiler after the sheets had become bare and red hot?

A.—It would not. The fire should be killed at once.

Q. 33.—What effect has the stoppage of a large number of flues?

A.—The heating surface and draft are decreased by just so much area.

Q. 34.—Why are boiler checks placed so far away from the fire-box?

A.—In order to introduce the water into the boiler at as great a distance from the fire-box as possible. This permits the water to become heated to a high temperature before coming in contact with the fire-box and also tends to better circulation.

Q. 35.—What part of the boiler has the greatest pressure? Why?

A.—The bottom, because the weight of water is added, in addition to the steam pressure.

Q 36.—What are the advantages of the extension front end?

A.—To provide room for suitable draft and spark appliances.

Q. 37.—What is the purpose of a netting in a smoke-box or front end?

A.—To crush the cinder and prevent the large ones from passing out of the front end, through the stack.

Q. 38.—What is the object of hollow stay bolts?

A.—To immediately indicate that the stay bolt is broken by the escape of steam through the small (detector) hole.

Q. 39.—What will cause the engine to tear holes in the fire?

A.—Working hard, or slipping with dampers open and doors closed, or too thin a fire.

Q. 40.—Name the various adjustable appliances in the front end by which the draft may be regulated.

A.—The exhaust nozzle, the diaphragm, and the draft pipes or petticoat pipe.

Q. 41.—What object is there in having the exhaust steam go through the stack?

A.—To produce a forced draft on the fire.

Q. 42.—How does this affect the fire?

A.—The exhaust steam passing through the stack tends to empty the smoke-box of gases, producing a partial vacuum there. Atmospheric pressure then forces the air through the grates and tubes to refill the smoke-box, thus causing the fire to burn more rapidly, producing a much higher temperature than could be obtained by natural draft.

Q. 43.—Explain what adjustments can be made and the effect of each adjustment on the fire.

A.—Larger or smaller nozzle tips cause less or greater draft on the fire; angle and position of the diaphragm does the same, and raising or lowering it burns the fire more at the rear or front end of the fire-box. The size and position of the petticoat pipe increases or decreases the draft through the top or bottom flues. These latter adjustments should always be attempted before reducing the nozzle.

Q. 44.—What does it indicate when the exhaust issues strongest from one side of the stack?

A.—The stack, exhaust pipe, or petticoat pipe are out of plumb.

Q. 45.—What is the effect of leaky steam pipe joints inside the smoke-box?

A.—Engine will not steam freely.

Q. 46.—What causes "pull" on the fire-box door?

A.—The partial vacuum in the front end; excessive "pull" indicates dampers closed, fire clinkered or grates stopped up.

Q. 47.—If, upon opening the fire-box door, you discover there what is commonly called a red fire, what might be the cause?

A.—That the grates have become clogged with ashes and clinkers so that sufficient air could not pass through them to the fire.

Q. 48.—Is it not a waste of fuel to open the fire-box door to prevent pops from opening? How can this be prevented more economically?

A.—Yes, sometimes. By putting the heater into the tank, or starting the injector, or by more careful firing.

Q. 49.—Describe the principle upon which the injector works.

A.—The action of the injector is due, first, to the difference between "Kinetic" or moving energy and "Static" or standing energy; second, to the fact that steam at a pressure travels at a tremendous velocity and if placed in contact with a stream of water, imparts to the latter much of its velocity and, besides, is condensed to water itself. By imparting this velocity to the water it gives it sufficient energy to throw open the check valves and enter the boiler against high pressure.

Q. 50.—What is the difference between a lifting and a non-lifting injector?

A.—A lifting injector will create sufficient vacuum to raise the water from the level of the tank. The tubes in a non-lifting injector are shaped differently and will not raise the water, but merely force it into the boiler. It is necessary to place a non-lifting injector below the level of the water in the tank so the water will flow to it by gravity.

Q. 51.—Will an injector work with a leak between the injector and tank? Why? Will it prime?

A.—Not if a bad leak. It will not prime because the air admitted through the leak destroys the vacuum necessary to raise the water to the injector level. A non-lifting injector will often work, as the water will escape from the leak instead of air being drawn into it, as with a lifting injector.

Q. 52.—If it primes well, but breaks when the steam is turned on wide, where would you look for the trouble?

A.—Insufficient water supply, due to tank valve not open, strainer stopped up, hose kinked, injector tubes out of line, limed up, or delivery tube cut, or wet steam from throttle.

Q. 53.—If it would not prime, where would you expect to find the trouble?

A.—Insufficient water supply, or priming valve out of order. With the lifting injector the trouble might be due to a leak between injector and tank.

Q. 54.—Will an injector prime if the boiler check leaks badly or if it is stuck up? If the injector throttle leaks badly?

A.—Not if either leak badly.

Q. 55.—If steam or water shows at the overflow pipe when the injector is not working, how can you tell whether it comes from the boiler check or the injector throttle?

A.—Close the main steam valve at the fountain. This will stop the leak if it be from the injector throttle.

Q. 56.—Will an injector prime if primer valve leaks? Will that prevent its working?

A.—The injector will prime, but not so readily as with priming valve in good condition. It will not prevent its working, but there may be some waste from the overflow.

Q. 57.—Will an injector work if air cannot get into the tank as fast as the water is taken out?

A.—It will not.

Q. 58.—If you had to take down a tank hose, how would you stop the water from flowing out of the tank that has the syphon connections instead of the old style valves?

A.—Open the small pet cock at the top of the syphon.

Q. 59.—Is any more water used when the engine foams than when the water is solid?

A.—Very much more—one cubic inch of water is equal in weight to one cubic foot of steam.

Q. 60.—How would you prevent injector feed pipes or tank hose from freezing in winter when not in use?

A.—The steam valve should be opened slightly to allow a slight circulation of steam through the feed and the branch pipes. The heater cock closed, and the drip cock under the boiler check or on the branch pipe opened to insure circulation of steam through the branch pipe.

Q. 61.—How would you prevent the overflow pipe from freezing with a lifting injector?

A.—By keeping the overflow valve slightly open to permit some steam to escape from the overflow pipe.

Q. 62.—Name the various parts of the injector.

A.—It consists of the injector body, with a steam valve, a steam nozzle, a primer, a combining and condensing tube, a delivery tube line check valve, overflow valve, and water valve. A lifting injector has a lifting tube.

Q. 63.—What may be done if a combining tube is obstructed?

A.—Remove the steam valve bonnet and with a stiff piece of wire force out the obstruction, or uncouple the delivery pipe from the injector, unscrew and remove the tubes, then clear the obstruction and replace the tubes.

Q. 64.—How is the greatest injury done to a boiler when cleaning or knocking the fire?

A.—By using the blower excessively, thus drawing cold air through the fire-box and flues.

Q. 65.—Why does putting a large quantity of cold water into a boiler when the throttle is closed cause the flues to leak? When is this most dangerous?

A.—When steam is not being used there is little circulation of water in the boiler and water entering the boiler at about 150 degrees temperature is heavier than the water in the boiler. As the colder water will go to the bottom, the temperature will be reduced in that part of the boiler, and cause the flues to contract in length as well as in diameter. This will have a tendency to pull them out of the sheet, thereby loosening them. After the fire has been knocked this tendency is much greater; hence, cold water should never be put into the boiler after the fire is knocked out. The boiler should always be filled before the fire is knocked out.

Q. 66.—Is warm water in the tank of any advantage in making steam rapidly?

A.—It is. Careful experiments have shown that a locomotive boiler will generate 1 per cent more steam for every 11 degrees that the tank water is heated. Thus heating the water in the tank from 39 to 94 degrees would effect a saving of 5 per cent.

Q. 67.—Then why not heat the feed water to the boiling point (212 degrees)?

A.—If the feed water is heated much above blood heat (about 100 degrees) it will not condense enough steam in the injectors to cause them to work properly. Some injectors will take hotter water than others. It would also ruin the paint and varnish on the tank.

Q. 68.—At 200 pounds pressure per square inch, what is the pressure per square foot on the sheets of a boiler?

A.—About fifteen tons.

Q. 69.—What is the total pressure on the fire-box of a large locomotive?

A.—Over three thousand tons.

Q. 70.—Give a practical definition of heating surface.

A.—The heating surface of a boiler includes all parts of the boiler that are directly exposed to fire or heat from the fire and surrounded by water.

Q. 71.—Should an engine be slipped to get water out of the cylinders or steam passages?

A.—Never. Open the cylinder cocks and start the engine slowly.

Q. 72.—What does it indicate when the smoke trails back over the train and into the coaches after shutting off?

A.—Either poor firing, or else a lack of understanding between the engineer and fireman as to where the engine was to be shut off.

Q. 73.—Before shaking grates or dumping the ash pan, what should be observed?

A.—That the locomotive is not passing over bridges, cattle guards, crossings, switches, interlocking fixtures, or in yards. Promptly extinguish fire on the track where ash pans are cleaned.

Q. 74.—Which is easier and more satisfactory on a long run, to stop and clean the fire if necessary, or to continue to the end of a long, hard trip with a dirty fire?

A.—Stop and clean the fire and thus save fuel and labor for the remainder of the trip. Very often an engine failure will be saved by so doing.

Q. 75.—Should you examine the flues to see if they are stopped up and leaking, and inspect the grate and grate rigging carefully before leaving the engine at a terminal?

A.—Yes, so they can be reported if necessary. Clean flues and grates working well, make a vast difference in the success of a fireman. By keeping the flues and grates in proper condition engine failures can be avoided.

Q. 76.—How should cab lamps, signal lamps, oil cans and lanterns be cared for?

A.—They should all be kept clean, free from leaks, and filled before starting any trip.

Q. 77.—About how many drops are there in a pint of valve oil when fed through a lubricator?

A.—About six thousand drops.

Q. 78.—Assuming that five drops per minute are fed to each of two valves and one drop per minute to the air pump, how many hours would be required to feed one pint of valve oil?

A.—About nine hours.

Q. 79.—Assuming that the engine is running twenty miles per hour, how many miles per pint would be run?

A.—About one hundred and eighty miles per pint.

Q. 80.—How many drops per minute should ordinarily be fed?

A.—This will vary according to the size of the locomotive and the work to be done. One drop per minute for each cylinder, and one drop for the air pump every two or three minutes is usually sufficient on small yard engines. This depends on the condition of the pump and the service being performed. Four or five drops per minute should be fed large engines in slow freight service, and from five to seven drops per minute for large engines in heavy fast passenger service. Where the brake pipe is in moderately good condition, air pumps in freight service can usually be run with one or two drops per minute when handling long trains of cars equipped with air brakes.

Q. 81.—Will any bad results ensue from filling the lubricator full of cold oil?

A.—Yes, when the oil becomes hot it will expand and may bulge or burst the lubricator.

Q. 82.—If a sight feed gets stopped up, how could you clean it out?

A.—Close the water valve and the regulating valves to other feeds. Open the drain cock, draw out a small quantity of water so as to bring the oil in the top part of lubricator below the top end of oil pipe leading to the feed arm, then open wide the regulating valve to the feed which is stopped up. The pressure from the equalizing tube will force the obstacle out of the feed nozzle and up into the body of the lubricator. Close this regulating valve until the feed glass fills with water and then open water valve and start feeds.

Q. 83.—How would you clean out chokes?

A.—Shut off boiler pressure and condenser valve, remove feed valve bonnet and open main throttle valve. The steam from the steam chest will blow back through the choke plug, clearing it.

Q. 84.—What is superheated steam?

A.—It is the saturated steam separated from the water from which it is generated by adding more heat, increasing its temperature from 100 to 250 degrees Fahrenheit above saturated steam temperature.

Q. 85.—What is the advantage of superheating or increasing the temperature of the steam?

A.—The increase of temperature in superheated steam augments its volume and all the moisture which is sure to be contained in saturated steam, and any particles of water which may have been entrained as the steam entered the throttle valve are evaporated. This results in a reduced steam consumption, a saving in coal and water, and increased boiler capacity.

Q. 86.—How is the increased temperature obtained by the use of the superheater?

A.—The saturated steam is admitted into a partitioned receiver which has a number of 1½-inch pipes attached to it. These are located in and extend nearly the full length of the large flues. The steam in passing through these 1½-inch pipes on its way back to the receiver absorbs the heat from the gases passing through the large tubes, causing its temperature to rise—to become superheated.

Q. 87.—How much is the volume of steam increased by superheating?

A.—At temperatures ordinarily used in locomotive practice, for each 100 degrees of superheat added to saturated steam the volume of a given weight is increased approximately from 16 to 17 per cent.

Q. 88.—Why is the superheated steam so much more economical on coal and water than the saturated steam?

A.—By superheating, the reduction in the amount of water consumed is from about 15 to 35 per cent for superheated steam receiving

150 to 250 degrees Fahrenheit of superheat. If less water has to be evaporated to do a given amount of work, it follows that less coal has to be used.

Q. 89.—Which is the better practice, to close the feed valves or water valve while waiting on sidings, etc.?

A.—Close the feed valves. There may be a leak in the water valve.

Q. 90.—How can you tell if equalizer tubes become stopped up or broken?

A.—The stopping of the tubes would destroy the equalization and when the steam chest pressure was less than the boiler pressure the feed would work too fast and nstead of forming into drops the oil would enter the feed glass in a stream; if broken the lubricator could not be used and the auxiliary oilers would necessarily have to be used to lubricate the cylinders.

AIR BRAKE QUESTIONS AND ANSWERS—SECOND YEAR'S.

Q. 1.—Name the operating parts of the 9½-inch pump? the 11-inch pump?

A.—Steam piston and air piston connected to same piston rod, reversing plate, reversing stem, reversing valve, main steam valve, differential piston, receiving valves and discharge valve. The parts of the 11-inch pump are the same as those of the 9½-inch pump.

Q. 2.—Explain the operation of the air end of pump on the up stroke? the down stroke?

A.—When the air piston starts on the up stroke the air that is in the upper end of the air cylinder is compressed and forced out by the discharge valve and through the discharge pipe into the main reservoir, and in the lower end of the air cylinder there is being formed a vacuum which causes the atmospheric pressure to raise the receiving valve from its seat and the air will flow into the cylinder until the piston completes its stroke, filling it full of air at atmospheric pressure, then the receiving valve drops to its seat of its own weight. The piston starts on its down stroke and the air present in the lower end of the air cylinder is compressed and forces the lower discharge valve from its seat and passes through discharge pipe into the main reservoir, and a vacuum is formed in the upper end of the air cylinder that causes the air entering receiving strainer at atmospheric pressure to raise the upper receiving valve from its seat, and air flows into the upper end of the air cylinder until at the completion of stroke the cylinder is filled with air at atmospheric pressure and the receiving valve drops to its seat of its own weight.

Q. 3.—Explain the operation of the steam valve gear of the 9½-inch pump on both strokes.

A.—The first stroke of the pump is generally the up stroke; all parts being at the lower end of stroke, the reversing valve will be in position to connect chamber back of large head to differential piston with the exhaust and the steam in the main valve chamber moves the differential piston to the right, and it moves the main steam valve with it to a position where the admission port to the lower end of the steam cylinder is opened and live steam is flowing into the cylinder and moving the piston on the up stroke. The hollow or exhaust cavity in the main steam valve is connecting the admission port to the upper end of the steam cylinder with the exhaust and any pressure present in the upper end of the cylinder is permitted to escape to the atmosphere. As the piston nears the completion of the up stroke, the shoulder on reversing stem engages the reversing plate on piston head and is moved upward, moving the reversing valve up to a position where the live steam is admitted to chamber back of the large head of the differential piston, and pressures are equalized on each side of large head to differential piston, neutralizing it, and the steam pressure on small head of differential piston moves the piston to the left and the main steam valve is moved with it to a position where the admission port to the upper end of the steam cylinder is opened and live steam enters the cylinder, pushing the piston on its downward stroke. At the same time the admission port to the lower end of the cylinder is placed into communication with the exhaust through the exhaust cavity in main steam valve, and the steam used in the up stroke is exhausted to the atmosphere. As the piston completes the down stroke, the reversing plate engages the button on the lower end of the reversing rod and pulls it and the reversing valve down to a position where the steam will be exhausted from back of the differential piston and the parts move to position for the up stroke.

Q. 4.—How many strokes (single) per minute should pumps run to give best results?

A.—120 strokes per minute; never more than 140 at any time.

Q. 5.—What should govern speed of pumps on heavy grades?

A.—The length of train and the amount of train line leaks.

Q. 6.—What is the duty of the pump governor, and how is it adjusted?

A.—To control the main reservoir pressure by stopping the pump when the pressure reaches the maximum. It is adjusted with the regulating spring and regulating nut.

Q. 7.—Does the governor control the speed of the pump? How is the speed controlled?

A.—No. The speed is controlled by the throttle valve regulating the amount of steam admitted to the pump.

Q. 8.—What is the duty of the triple valve?

A.—To apply and release the brakes, and to charge the auxiliary reservoir. Or another explanation is that it controls the flow of air from brake pipe to auxiliary reservoir, from auxiliary reservoir to brake cylinder, and from brake cylinder to the atmosphere.

Q. 9.—Explain the duty of the triple piston, slide valve, graduating valve, emergency valve and check valve.

A.—The triple piston controls the feed groove and the movements of the graduating and slide valves. The slide valve controls the flow of air from auxiliary to brake cylinder, and from brake cylinder to exhaust; it also controls the emergency port. The graduating valve controls the graduating port. The emergency valve controls the flow of air from train line to brake cylinder in an emergency application of the brake. The check valve prevents the flow of air from the brake cylinder to brake pipe when brake pipe pressure is reduced below brake cylinder pressure.

Q. 10.—How many different types of triple valves are used on this road?

A.—Four: Plain; quick action, style H; quick action, style K, and "L" triple.

Q. 11.—What is the duty of the engineer's brake valve?

A.—To control the air from main reservoir to brake pipe, and to control the flow of air from brake pipe to atmosphere.

Q. 12.—Name the different positions of the brake valves: (G-6), (H-6).

A.—(G-6) full release, running, lap, service, and emergency. (H-6) full release, running, holding, lap, service, and emergency.

Q. 13.—Name the two different types of independent brake valves used.

A.—(S-6) independent, and the straight air brake valve (S-3-A).

Q. 14.—Where does the main reservoir pressure begin and end? Where does the brake pipe pressure begin and end?

A.—The main reservoir pressure begins at the top side of the discharge valves in pump and ends at the rotary valve in the brake valve. The brake pipe pressure begins at the rotary valve in the automatic brake valve and ends at the triple piston.

Q. 15.—What is the duty of the feed valves?

A.—To control brake pipe pressure.

Q. 16.—In what positions of the brake valve is the feed valve in operation?

A.—The running and holding positions.

Q. 17.—Describe the operation of the feed valve.

A.—Main reservoir air enters the supply valve chambers and forces the supply valve piston over, compressing the spring and opening the supply port, so the main reservoir air can flow direct into the feed valve pipe until the pressure in the feed valve pipe compresses the diaphragm and regulating spring, allowing the regulating valve to seat and cut off communication between the chamber, back of the supply valve piston and the feed valve pipe, so that the small volume of main reservoir air flowing by the piston head will soon be equalized with main reservoir pressure, and the supply valve piston spring moves the piston and supply valve to the closed positions.

Q. 18.—What is the purpose of the hand wheel and stops on (B-6) feed valve?

A.—So that the brake pipe pressure may be changed accurately by the engineer, through moving the hand wheel from one stop to the other.

Q. 19.—What is the difference between a feed valve and a signal reducing valve?

A.—The principles of operation are the same, but, while the feed valve controls brake pipe pressure and is adjusted for that pressure, the reducing valve is adjusted for a pressure of 45 pounds generally and controls the air signal and independent brake valve pressures.

Q. 20.—For what purpose and where are safety valves used on locomotives?

A.—The safety valves are used with the (S-W-A) and (S-W-B) brakes, and are connected with the brake cylinder to prevent the brake cylinder pressure being excessive; they are adjusted at 53 pounds. Safety valves are also used with the (E-T) brake attached to the distributing valve and are in communication with the application cylinder in all positions of the brake except the service lap, and by keeping the application cylinder pressure at a safe limit they prevent the brake cylinder pressure being excessive; they are adjusted at 68 pounds.

Q. 21.—When should the feed valve be cleaned and lubricated?

A.—On the first indication of sluggish action, and at least once in three months; some will not run over one month.

Q. 22.—What is the purpose of auxiliary reservoirs on locomotives and tenders?

A.—To carry a supply of compressed air to be used in the brake cylinders on an engine in an automatic application of the brakes.

Q. 23.—Are engines with the E-T type of brake equipped with auxiliaries?

A.—No.

Q. 24.—Can the driver brakes and tender brakes be released with the (S-6) independent brake valve after an automatic application? With the (S-3-A) independent valve?

A.—Yes, the brake can be released with either brake valve, after an automatic application has been made.

Q. 25.—What pressures do the red and black hands of the air gauges indicate?

A.—The red hand on duplex gauge No. 1 indicates main reservoir pressure, and the black hand indicates the pressure above the equalizing piston, or, as it is termed, chamber D pressure. The red hand on duplex gauge No. 2 indicates the brake cylinder pressure, and the black hand indicates brake pipe pressure.

Q. 26.—Does the black hand of gauge indicate brake pipe pressure at all times?

A.—No, only at the time when brake pipe and chamber D pressures are equalized.

Q. 27.—What pressures are indicated on the small gauge?

A.—Brake cylinder by the red hand, and brake pipe by the black hand.

Q. 28.—At what pressures are the safety valves set when used with the standard equipment (A-1)? With (E-T) equipment?

A.—At 53 pounds with standard (A-1), and at 68 pounds with the (E-T).

Q. 29.—Why is a cut-out cock placed on each engine in the brake pipe close to the brake valve? When is it cut out? When is it cut in?

A.—To be used in double heading service, on engine which is second in the train or does not have control of the brakes, to close communication between brake pipe and the main reservoir or other apparatus on the engine. It is cut in when brakes on train are being handled by the engineer in charge of the engine. It is cut out when the brakes on train are being handled from another engine.

Q. 30.—Explain the difference between an angle cock and a cut-out cock, and where used.

A.—An angle cock has the body turned at an angle of 45 degrees for the convenience in making the hose connections; and the body of the cut-out cock is straight, and is used in pipe connections. The angle cock is used at the end of the brake pipe, where the brake pipe hose connections are attached; the cut-out cock is used in pipe lines leading to various parts of the brake apparatus on engines and cars.

Q. 31.—What is the duty of the pressure retaining valve? How many different kinds in use?

A.—The pressure retaining valve's duty is to retain pressure in brake cylinder on long grades while recharging the auxiliaries. There are two different kinds of pressure retaining valves.

Q. 32.—Would the absence of a retainer render the brake on a car inoperative?

A.—No.

Q. 33.—What is the proper piston travel for driver brakes?

A.—About four inches for driver brake, and seven inches for tender brake.

Q. 34.—Can a plain triple valve on driver or tender brake cause train brakes to go into quick action when a service application is being made? Why?

A.—No. Because it cannot cause any sudden reduction of train line pressure, and has no quick action parts.

Q. 35.—Trace the air through the air brake system.

A.—Air enters the pump through the receiving ports, and it passes by the receiving valves into the air cylinder. There it is compressed and forced out by the discharge valves and discharge ports, and through the discharge pipe into the main reservoir, and passes from main reservoir through the main reservoir pipe to the feed valve; then through the feed valve pipe to the feed valve port in rotary valve seat and up into cavity in rotary valve face; then down through brake pipe port in rotary valve seat to brake pipe, and through brake pipe and cross-over or branch pipe to the triple valve, it enters the triple piston cylinder through the ports in cylinder cap, then passes through feed groove to slide valve chamber and into the auxiliary reservoir, charging it to an equalization with brake pipe pressure. In response to a brake pipe reduction the auxiliary pressure moves the triple piston; this opens the graduating port and moves the slide valve to service position, so the graduating port registers with brake cylinder port and air flows from the auxiliary reservoir through graduating and brake cylinder ports into the brake cylinder applying the brake. In response to an increase in brake pipe pressure the triple piston is moved to the release position and the exhaust cavity in slide valve connects the brake cylinder port with the exhaust port, allowing the air which was used in the brake cylinder to pass out to the atmosphere.

OIL-BURNING LOCOMOTIVES.

Q. 1.—What are the fireman's duties on arrival at the engine house previous to going out on an oil-burning locomotive?

A.—The fireman should observe the condition of draft pans and arch, of burner and dampers; try the regulating valve, and see that the burner is delivering fuel oil properly to the fire. He should see that the fuel oil is heated to a proper temperature; that the oil heaters are in working order, and that there is a proper supply of fuel oil, sand and water on hand, as well as the necessary tools for handling an oil fire. He should also perform such other duties on the engine as may be required of him.

Q. 2.—How warm should the oil be at all times in the tank?

A.—The best results are obtained when the oil is heated to such a temperature that the hand can be held on the tank, or to about 110 degrees Fahrenheit.

Q. 3.—If the oil is too warm, what happens?

A.—Some of the qualities of the oil are lost by keeping it too warm, and the burner does not work so well and will make it more difficult to operate. If the oil is too warm it will give off too much gas which is liable to cause an explosion in the oil tank.

Q. 4.—What tools are necessary for firing purposes on an oil-burning locomotive?

A.—The necessary tools include a sand horn, brick hook, and a small iron bar for cleaning carbon from the mouth of the burner.

Q. 5.—What is liable to happen if the heater valve is open too much?

A.—It is very apt to burst the heater hose, as well as to heat the oil to too high a temperature, placing an unnecessary strain on all the heater connections, causing them to leak.

Q. 6.—What should be done on approaching stations where additional supply of fuel oil is to be taken?

A.—Shut off the fire, close safety and main oil valves and see that there are no lamps or lights on the tender.

Q. 7.—What care must be exercised in the use of lamps, torches, or lanterns about oil tanks whether hot or cold?

A.—Do not carry, nor permit anyone to carry oil lamps or oil torches within a distance of ten feet of the tank opening. Pocket flash lights or incandescent lamps only should be used around oil tank manhole when taking oil.

Q. 8.—How can oil in the tank be measured without taking a light to the manhole?

A.—By the use of the stick or rod made for that purpose, carrying it to the light to find the number of inches of oil in the tank.

Q. 9.—What precautions must be taken before entering tanks that have been used for oil to clean or make repairs?

A.—Oil tanks should not be entered until thoroughly steamed and cooled. For safety they should be steamed from six to nine hours.

Q. 10.—How should the fire be lighted in an oil-burning locomotive?

A.—See that no one is working under the engine, that the boiler is properly filled with water and that it will flow through the gauge cocks, and that there is no accumulation of oil in the ash pan or fire-box, or existing leaks throughout. Steam connection can be made to the three-way cock on the smoke arch which will act as blower and atomizer. If there are 20 or 30 pounds of steam in the boiler it can be operated with its own blower. See that the front of the fire-box is free from carbon or anything that would obstruct it from burning; it must have free passage so oil can get to burner. Open the front damper, put on the blower strong enough to make the necessary draft, open the atomizer valve long enough to blow out any water which might be in steam pipe or burner; next close the valve and throw a bunch of lighted old waste in front of the burner, then open the atomizer sufficiently to carry oil to the waste and open the regulator slowly until the oil is known to be ignited—this you can see through the fire-box door. Be sure that no oil is wasting below the burner or an explosion may result.

Q. 11.—Should the fire go out and it is desired to rekindle it while bricks are hot, is it safe to depend on the hot bricks to ignite the oil without the use of lighted waste?

A.—No; always use waste in rekindling the fire as the bricks are not very reliable and apt to do damage from explosive gases formed.

Q. 12.—What is termed an atomizer, and what does it perform?

A.—The atomizer is a casting divided into two long ports, with an extension lip. The upper port is for oil and the lower one for steam. The lip aids the steam in atomizing and spreading the oil, which, when properly mingled with the air and ignited, will produce combustion. The atomizer is located just under the mud-ring, pointed a little upward, so the stream of oil and spray of steam will strike the opposite wall a few inches above the bottom if it were to pass clear across the box.

Q. 13.—In starting or closing the throttle of the locomotive, how should the fireman regulate the fire, in advance or after the action of the engineer?

A.—In starting an oil-burning engine, bring the oil up gradually as the throttle is opened, and keep the movement and amount of oil slightly in advance of the action of the engineer, so as to prevent the inrush of cold air as the engine is working, which would result in injury to the fire-box and flues. Reduce the fire very slightly in advance of closing the throttle. This will prevent the engine from popping and black smoke trailing over the train.

Q. 14.—Is it necessary that the engineer and fireman on an oil-burning locomotive work in perfect harmony and advise each other of intended action at every change of conditions?

A.—Yes, they should work in harmony with one another and while the fireman should watch every move the engineer makes it is also the duty of the engineer to advise the fireman of every change of the throttle so that he can operate his valves according therewith and thus save fuel, and avoid black smoke.

Q. 15.—What is the effect of forcing the fire on an oil-burning locomotive?

A.—It will cause the flues to leak. Always keep an even temperature in the fire-box.

Q. 16.—Is a careful regulation of steam and oil valves and dampers necessary to obtain the most economical results?

A.—Yes, the firing valve should be opened sufficiently to make it certain that enough oil is being fed to produce a good fire, but not enough to cause a waste of oil or a great volume of black smoke.

Q. 17.—How can you judge whether the combustion is good or bad, so the valve may be regulated accordingly?

A.—When the fire is a dull red color it indicates that the temperature is less than 1,000 degrees, combustion is incomplete and dense black smoke will be emitted from the stack. When the fire is a bright red color, it indicates that the temperature is more than 1,800 degrees, combustion is very good and no smoke will issue from the stack.

Q. 18.—How should the flues be cleaned from soot when running, and about how often is this necessary?

A.—A small quantity of sand should be placed in an elbow-shaped funnel, and inserted through an aperture provided in the fire door; while engine is working hard, the exhaust drawing the sand through the flues, carries with it the accretions of soot, discharging them from the stack. The flues should be cleaned of soot after leaving terminals, or after the engine has been standing for some time, and as often as found necessary to aid the engine in steaming. Just prior to entering points where engine is to be put in roundhouse or otherwise detained, attention should be given the flues in order to leave them clean, as this will aid in putting the engine under steam with little delay where the blower alone is to be relied on for draft.

Q. 19.—Is the injudicious use of the blower particularly injurious on an oil-burning locomotive?

A.—Yes, the frequent use of the blower is injurious to a boiler and the cold air drawn in through the fire-box injures the sheets and flues and will cause them to leak.

Q. 20.—Is the blower more injurious when a light smoke is emitting from the stack or when a dense black smoke is emitting?

A.—It is more injurious when a light smoke is emitted from the stack.

Q. 21.—In drifting down long grades, should the fire be shut off or burned lightly? Why?

A.—The fire should be burning lightly, yet it should not be permitted to get too low, allowing the fire-box to lose its temperature and thus contracting the flues and causing them to leak.

Q. 22.—How should the fire be handled when switching?

A.—The fire must be regulated according to the work the engine performs on each move, and to protect against the possibility of the fire being drawn out by the exhaust.

Q. 23.—Would not some fuel be wasted in this way?

A.—Very little will be wasted if the fireman watches closely, when switching as well as when running.

Q. 24.—How should the fire be handled when leaving stations?

A.—It should be burning brightly and sufficiently strong to keep the draft from putting it out when the throttle is opened. A little smoke should show up at the stack, indicating that the fire was being forced a little ahead of the working of the engine.

Q. 25.—Which is desirable, to use as much or as little steam jet atomizer as possible?

A.—Use as little atomizer as possible at all times.

Q. 26.—What is the result of too little steam jet atomizer when standing at stations or when the engine is working light?

A.—The oil will not be carried far enough into the fire-box or arch and not properly atomized and the fire is very apt to go out. The oil will drop from the mouth of the burner into the draft pan to the ground and is liable to start a fire under the engine.

Q. 27.—If too much steam jet atomizer is used with a light fire?

A.—A disagreeable gas will be formed, causing the fire to burn with a succession of light explosions and kicks. It will use too much steam and reduce the temperature of the fire-box.

Q. 28.—When the fire kicks and smokes, what should be done?

A.—Adjust the atomizer. If this does not eliminate the trouble, start the heater, as the oil may be too cold to flow freely. Water being mixed with the oil will also cause the fire to kick and smoke. In this case drain the water out of the oil tank immediately.

Q. 29.—How should the dampers be used on an oil-burning locomotive?

A.—They should be opened just enough to admit sufficient air to produce perfect combustion, but not enough to cool the fire-box. When drifting they should be closed to prevent cold air being drawn in, causing flues and stay bolts to leak.

Q. 30.—About how much smoke do you consider an oil-burning locomotive should make under adverse conditions, when the engine is steaming weak, but is being crowded by the engineer?

A.—No more than when an engine is working ordinarily.

Q. 31.—What color is most desirable at peep-holes in the fire-box?

A.—A bright red color is most desirable.

Q. 32.—What will produce the bright red color?

A.—Feeding only the amount of oil that is properly burned and properly manipulating the regulating valves, with no leaks and fire-box in good condition.

Q. 33.—How does the water in the oil affect the fire?

A.—It will produce popping or kicking with the fire in the fire-box. At times the fire will almost go out entirely and then suddenly flash up as the oil appears at the burner, and the water disappears. Water in the oil produces a very dangerous condition and should be prevented by immediately draining it from the oil tank.

Q. 34.—Do you consider it advisable to keep the burners clean, and how often?

A.—When furnished with steam blow-out pipes, the burners should be blown out before commencing trip so they will distribute oil evenly to each side of the fire-box.

Q. 35.—What position should burner be with reference to level and in line with center of fire-box?

A.—It is very necessary that burners be level and throw flames just to clear floor of arch that the full benefit of the heating surface may be derived, as the draft has a great tendency to elevate flames at opposite end of the fire-box.

Q. 36.—Are you aware that in course of time the atomizer port will become worn too large and will discharge too large a volume of steam to properly atomize, and the remedy?

A.—Yes. In order that the oil may be atomized properly, and not flow out in quantities against flash walls before it has time to ignite, the lip or bushing should be properly regulated so the steam will be restricted at the nozzle and escape with a bursting effect.

Q. 37.—What is the real object of having the fire-box lined with bricks, and will engine steam without them?

A.—The engine will not steam as well without, as with brick. The sheets being in contact with water are too cold to flash the oil readily. Hence the use of the "flash wall," which, heated to a very high temperature, very materially aids combustion.

Q. 38.—Do you consider it your duty to keep close inspection of brick work as to need of repairs, such as air entering between brick and side sheets?

A.—Yes. Plaster should be kept between walls and sheets to prevent the cold air from being drawn in.

Q. 39.—Will engine steam if brick falls in front of burners or in path of flame, and what may be done?

A.—No. The bricks should be removed by pulling them out with a brick rod or hook through damper of draft pan.

Q. 40.—Where engine is equipped with an oil-reheater or oil line, do you consider it a help to engine's steaming qualities when used?

A.—Yes. This heater should be used at all times.

Q. 41.—Why use second heater? Why not heat it to a high temperature in oil tank with oil heater?

A.—Too much gas generates. Continually boiling the oil destroys some of the higher qualities and it is more difficult to control the flow through regulation valve.

Q. 42.—Do you consider a vent hole in oil tank advisable, and why?

A.—I do. To permit the gas which accumulates to escape and to admit air so the oil will flow freely.

Q. 43.—Do you inspect your oil pipes and report all leaks? What other bad effect has a pipe leak aside from waste of oil?

A.—Yes. A leak in the pipe will cause oil to feed irregularly.

Q. 44.—Are you aware that keeping the flues clean is the greatest one thing that you can do in regard to fuel economy, and how often should they be cleaned?

A.—Yes. At least every ten miles if the engine has to be smoked hard.

Q. 45.—Do you know that the engine should be working hard and at a speed not less than twenty miles per hour when sanding flues, to avoid the sand falling to floor of the fire-box and accumulating in front of them?

A.—Yes.

Q. 46.—Do you realize that on first closing throttle you should not adjust fire too low? Explain best method.

A.—Yes. The steam pressure should be allowed to fall back some fifteen pounds before the throttle is closed, and when closed a good fire should be left in the box and allowed to cool gradually, to avoid leaky flues, broken stay bolts, and cracked sheets, all of which are caused by a sudden fall of temperature.

Q. 47.—How is the flow of oil controlled?

A.—By valves in tank and pipe connections.

Q. 48.—Name these valves, their location and purpose.

A.—The safety valve, the main oil valve, and firing valve. The safety valve controls the flow of oil from the fuel oil tank through an opening in the bottom sheet of tank to pipes leading to burners. This valve is forced to its seat by a heavy spring and held off its seat by a key in the upright rod extending above the top of the tank. A rope or chain is attached to this key and also to the cab to cause the pin in rod to be pulled in case of a separation between engine and tank, and permit the valve to be seated by its spring and avoid a waste of oil. The main oil valve is situated in oil pipe under deck leading to burner, usually of the plug-cock pattern, connected by bell crank, and this connected to some part of the engine by chain, in which case it also acts as a safety valve in case of separation between engine and tender. In other cases it is connected by an operating rod extending above deck of tender, and in case of safety valve's failure it can be operated by hand to shut off the flow of oil. The firing valve is usually situated between heater box and burner and regulates the flow of oil desired to reach the fire. It has an upright rod extending into cab, where it is provided with a handle or lever in position to be handled conveniently by fireman when seated in cab.

Q. 49.—When shutting out fire, which valve should be closed first? Why?

A.—The safety valve. So the oil in the pipe may be consumed and to see that this valve is in working order.

THIRD YEAR'S EXAMINATION

Q. 1.—What are the duties of an engineer on being called, preparatory to attaching to train?

A.—He should report at the roundhouse on time required by rules, or earlier if possible. Inspect the bulletins and sign for those requiring acknowledgment. Compare his watch with standard time and register result in seconds slow or fast, or O. K. Find out the number of engine he takes out, and register out. Examine work report for work reported and work done at that point while engine was in. Go to engine, inspect condition of crown sheet and fire-box and flues, and note condition of fire. Try gauge cocks to ascertain water level and compare water glass with the try cocks, blowing out the water glass and trying stop cocks in upper and lower mountings to know that they are free and will close properly when needed, then open each stop cock the same to insure a perfect equalization and a true water level indicated in the glass. Try both injectors and know that they are O. K. See that you have the necessary supplies of coal, water, sand, firing and hand tools and other tools and extras required, signal lamps and flags and safety devices. Fill lubricator, start air-pump working slowly with drain cocks open, inspect engine and tender thoroughly, starting at a given point and examining ash pans and all parts underneath engine and tender, and connections between engine and tender, as well as all parts outside, noting especially that parts having work done on them are properly replaced, adjusted, and secured with split-keys when necessary. Examine headlight and tail-light to know that they are in perfect condition, and finish inspection at starting point where it began.

Climb up on engine and increase speed of air pump, take engine oiler and oil around, furnishing lubrication to all parts requiring it, adjust oil feeders in cups having feeders, open angle cocks to train and signal lines at pilot and rear of tender to free them of cinders, dirt and moisture. Separate hose connections between engine and tender for same purpose.

When proper air pressures are accumulated try automatic brakes, noting piston travel and whether they apply properly and hold on at least three minutes, then try the independent or straight air brake in the same manner and note whether the brakes release in proper manner, being sure that brakes are operative on both engine and tender and piston travel properly adjusted. Try the air sander device to be sure that sand flows freely on both sides. Try the other devices operated by compressed air, such as bell ringer, fire doors, etc., to know they work right, start cylinder feeds to lubricate about ten minutes before attaching engine to train.

Note.—It takes a drop of oil about seven minutes to reach steam chest after it leaves sight feed glass.

Q. 2.—What tools and supplies do you require starting on trip?

A.—Name the necessary hand and firing tools, classification lamps, hand lamps, markers, flags, and so forth, that your rules prescribe, being sure to name coal, oil, water, sand, extra brasses, headlight wick and chimney or carbons (depending on kind of light in use), water glass and gaskets, lubricator glasses and gaskets, colored plates for markers, replacers, cable chain, pinch bar, sledge hammer or maul, and all such necessary appliances as the rules pertaining to road requirements may call for as a complete complement for service.

Note.—The higher officials of different roads determine the necessary complement of tools and safety devices required to meet conditions obtaining on that system or part of system, and issue rules relative to the kind and number of each needed to promote safety and facilitate movement of trains.

Enginemen are responsible for having the proper equipment leaving terminals.

Q. 3.—Should an engine break down while on the road in your care, what are your first duties?

A.—*Whistle out the flag*, and see that the train is protected at once.

Q. 4.—What are your next duties?

A.—Clear the main line as soon as possible and report exact conditions to the proper officials (the master mechanic and superintendent).

Note.—"Clearing the main line" means ascertaining extent of damages and making such temporary repairs as will enable you to get on siding out of way of other trains, after which more extensive repairs can be made as the occasion may require to enable you to proceed safely to terminal.

Q. 5.—Do the gauge cocks indicate the true water level in boiler as accurately as the water glass? Why?

A.—No, the gauge cocks are not as reliable as a perfect working water glass, because boiling water will rise the moment the pressure is relieved even a little, therefore, when the gauge cock is opened, it relieves the pressure on water below it and the globes of steam in water begin to burst beneath the surface of water and throw it up to opening in gauge cock, many times showing water at a gauge cock an inch or two above the true water level, while the water glass, having the pressures perfectly equalized in it, the same as they are in boiler, the water in glass is at exactly the same level as it is in boiler.

Q. 6.—Is the water glass safe to depend on for water level in boiler if water does not move up and down in it when engine is in motion? Why?

A.—No. If the water does not oscillate in glass when engine is in motion, one of the stop cocks in mountings is partially closed or the opening leading from boiler is stopped up with corrosion or piece of gasket so the pressures are not equalized and water in glass does not respond to movements of water in the boiler, consequently it does not show the true water level and is not reliable.

Q. 7.—How should all water and steam valves and cocks be handled at all times to prevent them becoming defective?

A.—They should be opened and closed gently, using only the pressure of the hand in manipulating them.

Note.—A wrench or other force used causes serious damage to seats and is liable to break the body of fitting off where it enters boiler, resulting in personal injury.

Q. 8.—How do you inspect an engine?

A.—Thoroughly. Beginning in the cab, inspect all fittings and appliances there, examining the fire-box sheets and tubes, then get down and inspect connections and parts between engine and tender; going ahead, examine all parts of frame, ash pan, wheels, boxes, valve gear, spring rigging, bolts, nuts, rods, keys, levers, etc.; passing around front end of engine, noting conditions there, work back to rear of tender, thoroughly inspecting every part; passing around back of tender, finish the inspection at place where you started, having noted every defective part.

Q. 9.—What work on the engine should be done by the engineman?

A.—Setting up wedges, keying rods, tightening nuts if necessary, adjusting oil cup feeds, securing pipe clamps, adjusting brake shoes that may have become loose by wearing, tightening valve stem packing, and any other necessary work while on the road to insure a successful trip and avoid engine failures.

Q. 10.—What are the duties of the slide or piston valves?

A.—The main valves (slide or piston) control the admission of steam to the cylinders and the exhaust of steam from cylinders to atmosphere after the steam has done its work in cylinder.

Q. 11.—What is steam lap?

A.—Steam lap is the amount or distance the steam edge of valve face overlaps the steam edge of admission port, when the valve is in mid-position (or on center of its seat).

Note.—The edge of valve face or ring by which the steam flows on its way to cylinder is termed the steam edge of valve, and the edge of admission port over which steam flows as it passes into cylinder is called the steam edge of admission port. The edge of valve face or ring by which steam flows from cylinder to the exhaust is called exhaust edge of valve, and the edge of admission or steam port over which steam passes from cylinder is termed the exhaust edge of port.

Q. 12.—What benefits are derived from the steam lap feature of valve?

A.—Steam lap enables us to get an early cut off of steam entering the cylinder and to retain the steam in cylinder, getting work from the expansion of the steam.

Q. 13.—What is meant by lead?

A.—Lead is the amount the admission port is open for admission of steam to cylinder at time piston is ready to begin its stroke.

Q. 14.—What is the object of lead?

A.—To admit steam to cylinder just as piston completes its stroke, in that manner cushioning piston and bringing it gradually to rest, relieving reciprocating parts of excessive strain and wear. It also gets the power into cylinder to push piston on return stroke the moment crank pin passes the dead center.

Q. 15.—Is lead beneficial on all classes of engines?

A.—No.

Q. 16.—On what class of engines is it invaluable?

A.—On engines running at a high speed.

Q. 17.—Why is lead not good for engines at slow speeds?

A.—Because steam is admitted to cylinder before piston completes stroke and acts as a resistance to piston's movement, overcoming its equivalent in power exerted on opposite side of piston.

Q. 18.—Is the lead the same at all points of cut-off on all engines? Explain.

A.—No. The Stephenson valve motion has the amount of lead increased as cut-off is shortened, account of influence of the eccentrics. The Walschaert and Baker-Pilliod valve gears give a constant lead at all points of cut-off because the lead is controlled by connection to crosshead, the movements of which do not vary.

Q. 19.—How much lead is generally given on Stephenson valve geared engines, and about what is the amount of its increase at shortest cut-off?

A.—On most of the modern engines the valves are set line and line at full stroke, or if any lead is given it is merely the width of a line and the increase from this to the short cut-off is about three-sixteenths of an inch on the average engine, and it may vary some on account of difference in methods of construction and adjustment of parts.

Q. 20.—How much steam lap is generally given in construction of valves?

A.—This depends entirely on the ideas of heads of mechanical departments on different roads and varies from five-eighths of an inch on some roads to one and one-fourth inches on other roads and classes of service. The amount of lap being determined by experiments and calculations to obtain best results.

Q. 21.—What is exhaust lap?

A.—Exhaust lap is the amount the exhaust edge of valve's face overlaps the exhaust edge of admission port when valve is in mid-position or on center of its seat.

Q. 22.—On what class of engines is exhaust lap considered a benefit?

A.—On engines in very slow speed service handling heavy trains on long grades.

Q. 23.—What is the effect of exhaust lap and why is it beneficial in slow speed service?

A.—Exhaust lap delays the exhaust getting greater expansion of steam and consequently saves water and fuel. It also hastens compression and makes the engine loggy.

Note.—Exhaust lap is only beneficial at a speed where exhaust has ample time to escape from cylinder through the restricted port opening.

Q. 24.—What is exhaust clearance?

A.—It is the amount the admission ports are open to the exhaust when valve is in mid-position.

Another Answer.—It is the distance the exhaust edges of valve lack of touching the exhaust edges of the admission ports when valve is on center of its seat.

Note.—"Exhaust clearance" is often called "exhaust lead."

Q. 25.—What is the object in giving valve exhaust clearance? What does it do?

A.—To reduce resistance to movement of piston in cylinder on high speed engines making them smarter and more speedy.

Exhaust clearance gets exhaust open earlier and keeps it open longer, in that manner reducing the back pressure and delaying compression.

Q. 26.—Is "exhaust clearance" a benefit or detriment from economical point of view? Why?

A.—It is a detriment and sacrifices water and fuel that speed may be gained.

It is an expensive feature from economical standpoint because it does not get the expansion of the steam, account of allowing it to be exhausted while still at high pressure in cylinder.

Q. 27.—What is the approximate amount of lead given engines equipped with the Walschaert and Baker-Pilliod valve gears?

A.—It is from about three-sixteenths to seven thirty-seconds of an inch on most engines, although many roads are still experimenting to determine the proper amount of lead to get best results in different classes of service.

Q. 28.—Name the events (different actions or occurrences taking place) during stroke of piston.

A.—Admission, cut-off, expansion, exhaust or release (during which time we have back pressure), and compression.

Note.—The resistance of exhaust steam called "back pressure" obtains during the release and is so considered an "event" of the stroke, because it is co-relative with exhaust.

Q. 29.—What is back pressure?

A.—"Back pressure" is the resistance of exhaust steam to the piston during time the exhaust is open.

Note.—This resistance is caused by friction of current of exhaust steam on walls of channels and restricted openings in nozzle tips through which it passes.

Q. 30.—What is compression?

A.—"Compression" is the resistance (to the piston) of steam confined in the cylinder after the exhaust closes.

Note.—"Compression" begins at point where "back pressure" ends, that is, at time the opening from cylinder to exhaust is closed, trapping some steam in cylinder ahead of piston.

Q. 31.—Name and describe the two general classes of main steam valves in use.

A.—The "outside" admission valve, which may be either a piston or slide valve, is one which admits steam to cylinder by its outer edges and exhausts steam from cylinder by its inner edges.

The "inside" admission valve is a piston valve which admits steam to the cylinder by its inner edges and exhausts steam from the cylinder by the outer ends or edges of the valve.

Q. 32.—What is a balanced slide valve?

A.—A balanced slide valve is one which has the pressure kept off the greater portion of its upper surface.

Another Answer.—A balanced slide valve is one so constructed that the pressures on top of valve are about equalized with the pressures on under side of valve.

Note.—About 65 per cent of the upper surface of valve is protected from the pressure—the pressure allowed on the balance of 35 per cent of its upper surface being necessary to overcome the influence of the exhaust and steam pressure against face of valve over admission port at end of where steam is present.

Q. 33.—How is a slide valve balanced?

A.—It is balanced by placing strips of metal in suitable grooves cut in top of valve near its outer edges. These metal strips are held up by elliptical or coil springs (and by steam pressure in chest) against the pressure or balance plate (which is attached to or cast on the cap of chest), forming a steam-tight joint excluding steam from top part of valve enclosed by the balance strips.

Q. 34.—What is small hole drilled in crown of valve for and what is it called?

A.—This hole is to allow any steam which might get on top of valve by defective balance strips, to pass to exhaust and atmosphere, in that manner maintaining the balanced feature of valve, and it is called the "release port."

Q. 35.—Why are valves balanced?

A.—To reduce friction.

Q. 36.—How does the Allen valve differ from the plain D type slide valve?

A.—The Allen valve has a supplementary port extending from one face of the valve up and over through crown of valve to the other face.

Q. 37.—What is the object of the supplementary port in the Allen valve?

A.—It is to get a more rapid admission of steam to the cylinder at the beginning of stroke of piston and it gets the full port opening in about one-half the time the plain D type valve would give it.

Q. 38.—Describe the piston valve.

A.—The piston valve is a cylindrical spool-shaped device, with metallic packing rings fitted in suitable grooves cut in the outer surface of the heads at each end, these packing rings forming a steam-tight joint with walls of bushing in valve chamber and determining the steam and exhaust edges of valve face.

Q. 39.—How many ports in steam chest for an outside admission valve, and what are the names and duties of these ports, naming them as arranged?

A.—Five ports. The two outer end ports are called supply ports, because the supply of steam from boiler to steam chest comes through them; the next two ports are called admission ports because steam is admitted to the cylinder through them; the central port is called the exhaust port because steam is exhausted to atmosphere through it after being used in cylinder.

Q. 40.—How many ports in valve chamber for an inside admission valve? Name them in order of arrangement.

A.—Five. The two outer ports are the exhaust ports, the next two are admission ports, the central port is the supply port.

Q. 41.—Trace the flow of steam from the boiler to the atmosphere in a saturated steam locomotive.

A.—The steam passes from dome, through throttle box, standpipe, dry pipe, tee or nigger head, steam pipes, steam channels or ways in cylinder saddle casting, supply ports, steam chest, and admission ports to cylinder, after it has done the work in cylinder it passes from cylinder through admission port, exhaust cavity in valve, exhaust port, exhaust channel in cylinder saddle casting, nozzle base, or nozzle box, nozzle tips, petticoat pipe and stack to the atmosphere.

Q. 42.—Trace the flow of steam from boiler to atmosphere in a superheated steam locomotive.

A.—The steam passes from dome through throttle box, standpipe, dry pipe, top or saturated steam header, superheater return pipes in large tubes or flues, lower or superheater header, thence through the supply pipes and supply ports to valve chamber or steam chest, then it enters admission ports to cylinder. After performing work it passes from cylinder through same admission port it entered cylinder through, by end of valve (for inside admission valve) or through exhaust cavity of valve (for outside admission), to exhaust ports, exhaust channels, exhaust base, exhaust nozzles or tip, petticoat and stack to atmosphere.

Q. 43.—Explain how the power of the steam is transmitted from cylinder to driving wheels in a locomotive.

A.—The movement of valve admits steam to one end of cylinder where it exerts its influence or power on the piston head and the power is transmitted through the piston head, piston rod, crosshead, wrist pin, main rod and main crank pin to main driving wheel, causing it to revolve.

Q. 44.—What is a valve motion?

A.—Any mechanism that will control the movement of valve, so as to admit steam to the cylinder and exhaust steam from the cylinder at proper intervals, is a valve motion.

Q. 45.—What are the parts of valve motion and connections to valve for the Stephenson valve motion?

A.—The eccentric (sometimes called cam or pulley), eccentric strap, eccentric blade, link, link saddle, saddle pin (suspension stud), link hanger, link block, link block bolt, lower rocker arm, rocker shaft, upper rocker arm, rocker box, valve rod bolt, valve rod, valve stem, valve yoke, and on some engines a transmission bar is used between link block and rocker arm.

Q. 46.—What are the parts of the Walschaert valve motion and connection to valve?

A.—Eccentric crank, eccentric rod, link foot, radial link, trunnion pins, trunnion pin brackets, link blocks, link block bolt, radius rod (or radius bar), combination lever, union link, crosshead arm, valve rod, or valve stem, valve yoke, valve stem crosshead, valve stem guides, suspension link.

Q. 47.—What is a balanced valve?

A.—A balanced valve is one which has the greater part of the pressure kept off the top of the valve.

Note.—Generally about 65 per cent of the pressure is removed from the upper surface of the valve, leaving a pressure sufficient to overcome the influence of the exhaust and working pressure in one end of the cylinder.

Q. 48.—How are valves balanced?

A.—By keeping the pressure off the top surface of the valve; this is accomplished by fitting strips of iron (called "balance" strips or valve packing strips) in grooves cut in the top of valve near its outer edges and supporting these balance strips on coil or elliptic springs, which hold them up against the pressure plate attached to the cap of steam chest; these balance strips form a steam-tight joint with the pressure plate, excluding the steam from the portion of the top of the valve which they enclose.

Q. 49.—Why are valves balanced?

A.—To reduce friction between valve and its seat.

Q. 50.—What is the small hole drilled in the top of the valve for, and what is it called?

A.—It is to release any small volume of steam which may get by slightly defective balance strips, allowing it to pass out to the exhaust, in that manner maintaining the balanced feature of the valve. It is called the release port.

Q. 51.—What is the vacuum valve for, and what is it generally called?

A.—It is to relieve the vacuum formation in the steam chests and cylinders when drifting. It is commonly called the relief valve.

Note.—Many of the most up-to-date railroads are doing away with the relief valve, believing that it destroys lubrication qualities of the valve oil by admitting the oxygen, and to relieve the vacuum formation they either have a drifting valve, which admits a small amount of steam to the cylinders while the throttle is closed, or they instruct the enginemen to leave the throttle open a slight amount for the admission of sufficient steam to prevent the vacuum formation.

Q. 52.—What is a transmission bar?

A.—A transmission bar is a bar of steel or iron used to connect the link block to the rocker arm or valve rod connection, on engines where the rocker is placed some distance ahead of the link.

Q. 53.—What are the two different valve motions most common on our locomotives today?

A.—The Stephenson and the Walschaert.

Q. 54.—In what way do these valve motions differ in construction of the parts?

A.—The Stephenson valve motion has two eccentrics and the reversal is accomplished by changing the controlling eccentric, which is possible because the eccentrics are attached to the shifting link.

The Walschaert valve motion has but a single eccentric, which has a connection with lower end of radial link, which is suspended at its center, and the reversal is accomplished by changing the manner in which the motion is transmitted to the valve, which is possible because the link block can be moved to point above or below the point at which the link is suspended.

Q. 55.—How many ways are there of transmitting motion from eccentric to the valve? How are these different methods designated?

A.—There are two ways of conveying motion from the eccentric to the valve, and they are called the "Direct" and the "Indirect" valve motions.

Q. 56.—What is a direct valve motion?

A.—A direct valve motion is one in which the valve moves in the same direction as the throw of the eccentric which is controlling it.

Note.—The connection from eccentric which is in control of valve is direct or straight from eccentric to valve.

Q. 57.—What is an indirect valve motion?

A.—An indirect valve motion is one in which the valve moves in the opposite direction to the throw of the eccentric which is controlling it.

Note.—On engines having the indirect valve motion we have the upper and lower rocker arms and rocker shaft (or the equivalent) between the eccentric and valve, as a consequence, a reversal of the motion given off at the eccentric will obtain at the valve.

Q. 58.—In the Stephenson valve motion, what is the relative position of the eccentrics to the main pin for the direct valve motion with outside admission valve?

A.—The throw of the controlling eccentric will lead the main pin in the direction in which the wheel will turn, at right angles to the main pin plus the angle of advancement from the main pin necessary to get the lap of the valve out of the way and give the desired lead.

Q. 59.—In the Stephenson valve motion, what is the relative position of the eccentrics to the main pin for the indirect valve motion, outside admission valve?

A.—The throw of the controlling eccentric will follow the main pin in the direction in which the wheel will turn, at right angles to the main pin minus the angle of advancement toward the main pin necessary to get the lap of the valve out of the way and give the desired amount of lead.

Q. 60.—What is the relative position of the eccentrics to the main pin with the Stephenson valve motion, with the inside admission valve and the direct motion gear?

A.—The throw of the controlling eccentric will follow the main pin in the direction in which the wheel will turn, at right angles to the main pin, minus the angle of advancement toward the main pin necessary to get the lap of the valve out of the way and give the desired amount of lead.

Q. 61.—With the Stephenson valve motion, what is the relative position of the eccentrics to the main pin for the indirect valve motion, with the inside admission valve?

A.—The throw of the controlling eccentric will lead the main pin in the direction in which the wheel will turn, at right angles to the main pin plus the angle of advancement from the main pin necessary to get the lap of the valve out of the way and give the desired amount of lead.

Q. 62.—How is the Stephenson link carried or suspended?

A.—By the saddle pin (suspension stud) and link hanger to the lifting arm of the tumbling shaft.

Q. 63.—Why is the link saddle pin (suspension stud) placed to one side of center of link?

A.—To overcome the effect of the angularity of the main rod and harmonize the travel of the valve with the travel of the piston.

Note.—The effect of the angularity of the main rod can be overcome by the manner in which the tumbling shaft is placed, but on account of the limited space on the ordinary locomotive this method is not possible, although considered the better way to get the proper distribution of steam.

Q. 64.—To what is the link block attached in the Stephenson valve gear?

A.—To the lower rocker arm or to the transmission bar which is used to carry the motion ahead to the rocker arm.

Q. 65.—How is the Stephenson geared engine reversed?

A.—The eccentrics have their blades attached to the shifting link, the go-ahead blade is connected with the top end of the link, and the back-up blade to the lower end of the link; the link may be moved up and down on the link block, in that manner accomplishing the reverse by changing the controlling eccentric.

Q. 66.—How is the eccentric placed in relation to the main pin on a Walschaert geared engine having outside admission valve and direct motion, when going ahead?

A.—The eccentric will lead the main pin at nearly right angles or be a little less than one-fourth of a turn ahead of the pin when engine is going ahead.

Q. 67.—How is the eccentric placed in relation to the main pin on a Walschaert geared engine having outside admission valve and indirect motion, when going ahead?

A.—The eccentric will follow the main pin at a little greater angle than a right angle or be a little more than one-fourth of a turn back of the main pin when the engine is going ahead.

Q. 68.—How is the eccentric placed in relation to the main pin on a Walschaert geared engine, having inside admission valve and direct motion, when going ahead?

A.—The eccentric will follow the main pin at a little more than one-fourth of a turn when engine is going ahead.

Q. 69.—How is the eccentric placed in relation to the main pin on a Walschaert geared engine, having inside admission valve and indirect motion when going ahead?

A.—The eccentric will lead the main pin a little less than one-fourth of a turn when the engine is going ahead.

Q. 70.—Is the Walschaert eccentric ever placed at exactly right angles to the main pin? If so, when?

A.—Yes, on engines where the connection between eccentric rod and the link foot is made on the dead center line of motion.

Q. 71.—Why is the eccentric on most Walschaert geared engines placed more than a quarter of a turn back of the main pin when following the main pin, and less than a quarter of a turn ahead of the main pin when leading the main pin?

A.—To overcome the effect of the angularity of the eccentric rod.

Note.—On most modern engines the link is suspended so high that it is necessary to make the connection between the eccentric rod and link foot above the center line of motion. As a consequence of this condition in the construction of the engine the distance between the eccentric crank and point of connection with link foot when link was standing perpendicular (as it should be when main pins are on the dead centers) would be greater when eccentric was below the center line of motion than when the eccentric was above the center line of motion if the eccentric was placed at exactly right angle to the main pin. This is on account of the angularity of the eccentric rod, and would cause a distortion in the movement of the valve and an unequal distribution of the steam. To overcome this effect the eccentric is so placed that with main pins on either dead center, the distance between link foot connection, to eccentric rod, and eccentric will be equal, when link stands perpendicular and the eccentric is either above or below the center line of motion.

Q. 72.—How is the effect of the angularity of the main rod overcome with the Walschaert valve motion?

A.—The combination lever establishes a connection between the piston and valve which will harmonize the travel of the valve with the travel of the piston, in this manner eliminating the effect of the angularity of the main rod.

Q. 73.—How is the link of the Walschaert valve gear carried or suspended?

A.—It is hung on trunnion pins at its exact center as regards width and length, and the trunnion pins rest in boxes formed in the trunnion pin brackets so the link may rotate about the centers of the trunnion pins.

Q. 74.—How is the eccentric connected to the link on the Walschaert valve gear?

A.—By the eccentric rod which connects the eccentric to an arm which extends down from the lower end of the link (called "the link foot"), and as the eccentric rotates it gives the link the action of the upper and lower rocker arms in the Stephenson gear.

Q. 75.—What is the object of the "link foot" in the Walschaert gear?

A.—To extend the lower end of the link down as near as possible of the center line of motion for connection with the eccentric rod.

Note.—The link foot is merely a convenience to perfect the point to connection with the eccentric rod and reduce the angularity of the eccentric rod as much as it is practicable.

Q. 76.—To what is the link block in the Walschaert gear connected?

A.—To the radius rod which establishes a connection with the valve through the combination lever and valve stem.

Q. 77.—Why is the "radius rod" so-called?

A.—Because the length of the radius rod, from center of point of connection with link block to center of point of connection with combination lever, is the exact length of the line used to describe the circle of which the link is an arc.

Q. 78.—What duties are performed by the combination lever?

A.—The combination lever gets the lap of the valve out of the way for admission of steam, gets the port open the desired amount of lead at the beginning of stroke of piston, and eliminates the effect of the angularity of the main rod by harmonizing the travel of the valve with the travel of the piston.

Q. 79.—How is the Walschaert geared engine reversed?

A.—By changing the manner of transmitting the motion from eccentric to the valve—changing it from direct motion to indirect motion or vice versa.

Note.—The manner of changing manner of transmitting motion is made possible through having the link suspended at its center and the link block moved above or below the point of suspension.

Q. 80.—Why is there a difference in manner of placing eccentric in relation to the main pin on different engines?

A.—Because there is a difference in the construction of the valve or on account of a difference in manner of transmitting the motion from the eccentric to the valve.

Q. 81.—What is the difference in manner of placing the eccentric where the valves are the same but the manner of transmitting motion is different, or where the valves are different and manner of transmitting motion is the same?

A.—Just one-half of a turn difference, or 180 degrees.

Q. 82.—How far will the Walschaert eccentric move the valve without any other influence brought to bear on movement of valve?

A.—When in full control it will move the valve built line and line (that would be a valve without any lap) just far enough to give the full port opening each way and no more, or we might say that it will move the valve just the width of the port each way from the center of its seat.

Q. 83.—How far will the combination lever move the valve?

A.—Just twice the lap plus twice the lead of the valve during one complete stroke of the piston.

Note.—Without any eccentric connection, and with the link block placed in the center of the link so as to give a positive fulcrum for the combination lever on forward end of radius rod, the combination lever will move the valve far enough to have the port open the amount of lead when piston is at end of stroke.

Q. 84.—How is the proper location of the Walschaert eccentric found?

A.—When the connection between eccentric rod and link foot is made above or below the center line of motion (at which time the angularity of the eccentric rod would affect the distribution of steam), the engine is placed with main pin on forward dead center so that center line of motion will cut the center of main pin and center of main axle, the link is placed exactly perpendicular and the eccentric is set at right angles to a line drawn from the center of the point of connection with link foot to the center of main axle.

Q. 85.—How much clearance is given the piston at each end of the cylinder and why is it necessary?

A.—The piston is given from one-fourth to one-half of an inch clearance, generally about three-eighths of an inch at each end of the cylinder to allow for the wear of the connections of the reciprocating parts and wear on shoes and wedges, to prevent knocking out cylinder heads.

Q. 86.—What results obtain when the combination lever on a Walschaert gear is broken and the radius rod is connected to the valve stem as is possible on some classes of engines?

A.—The valve is moved far enough each way (with reverse lever in the extreme end of quadrant) to open the port the width of port less the lap of the valve, and this opening will occur when the crank pins are passing the top and bottom quarters.

Q. 87.—What causes the cylinder to be ruptured or burst on engine equipped with Walschaert's valve gear and having piston valves?

A.—When the union link breaks it will allow the valve to move to the center of its seat and confine pressure in the cylinder which will be compressed by the piston until the walls of cylinder or the cylinder head gives out under the great pressure.

Q. 88.—What generally causes steam chests to burst?

A.—Compressed air, account of reversing the engine with cylinder cocks and throttle closed.

Note.—By reversing the engine you immediately change the engine's cylinders into air compressors, and with the throttle closed this compressed air is confined in the steam chests and steam pipes until they burst. By opening the throttle the compressed air would pass into the boiler and the safety valves would relieve the excessive pressure.

Q. 89.—Where does this air get into the cylinders and steam chests?

A.—It comes down through the stack, nozzles and exhaust channels.

Q. 90.—If the exhaust gets out of square on the road, what does it indicate?

A.—It indicates an improper distribution of steam, caused by some defect in valve motion or lack of lubrication, causing friction to take up all the slack in worn parts of valve motion. Where the double exhaust tip is used, a bushing lost out of one tip will cause the exhaust to be out of square.

Q. 91.—How would you block a crosshead?

A.—Securely, blocking it at the back end of the guides where the construction of the engine will permit, or at the front end when necessary.

Note.—We block at the rear end when possible so that if the blocking should accidently give way and the crosshead move, the front cylinder head will be damaged in preference to the back head, as the cost of replacing it is far less.

Note.—Block the crosshead at the travel mark at the rear end of the guide bars, in that manner preventing the cylinder packing ring from getting down into the counterbore and causing delay in making repairs at the terminal; secure the crosshead by placing a block of wood between crosshead and guide block to hold it at the travel mark, then lash block to lower guide bar between crosshead and front guide block or the back cylinder head; this applies to the "Locomotive" type crosshead and the "Underhung" type of crosshead; but where you have the "Alligator" type crosshead, and desire to block the crosshead ahead, loosen one of the guide bolts with the "plow bolt" head, which holds the lower guide bar to yoke; drive the bolt up so head will be about three-fourths of an inch above the bar; cut the block about one-half inch longer than the distance from bolt head to crosshead; sink bolt head into end of blocking and lash the blocking down on guide bar; this will prevent the bolt from working out and hold the crosshead secure.

Note.—Whenever crosshead is blocked remove both cylinder cocks or fasten them open, except when the steam edge of valve seat is broken so that steam will be present in cylinder, which case you will remove the cylinder cock at end where piston head rests and block the cylinder cock open at end of cylinder, where steam is present, to allow condensation to pass out of cylinder—this is to protect cylinder, especially in freezing weather.

Q. 92.—What kind of a blow is a valve blow?

A.—A steady, constant blow at the exhaust during time the throttle is open.

Q. 93.—Is there more than one defect that will cause a valve blow?

A.—Yes, two different defects cause a valve blow.

Q. 94.—What are these defects?

A.—Broken valve packing strips or springs, and the face of the valve or its seat cut or worn hollowing, and in the piston valve the packing rings broken give the same result.

Q. 95.—Is there another defect which will cause the steady blow at the exhaust when the throttle is open? And what is this defect?

A.—Yes, a sand hole or crack in the cylinder saddle casting between the live steam channel and one of the exhaust channels will cause the steady blow at the exhaust while the throttle is open, but this blow is generally much more pronounced than the valve blow.

Q. 96.—How can you tell the difference between the valve face blow and the defective valve packing strip, so that you will make the proper test?

A.—The defective valve packing strip, or as it is called, the balance strip, in addition to the constant blow while throttle is open, will have the reverse lever jerking severely in the rack while the engine is in motion, because the balanced effect is lost for that valve and the friction on its seat is excessive.

The cut valve, or one of the piston type, having broken rings, will have the blow, but does not handle hard nor does the reverse lever jerk in the rack, because it still has the balanced effect.

Q. 97.—How do you test for valve packing strip blow?

A.—Place the engine on the quarter on side to be tested, set the brake, open throttle a little and handle reverse lever, moving it from one corner to the other, noting manner in which the reverse lever handles, whether hard or easily, test the other side in same manner and on the side where the lever handles the harder you will find the defective valve packing strips.

Q. 98.—Why do you place the engine on the quarter on side to be tested?

A.—So as to move but the one valve which is to be tested.

Note.—If both valves were moved, you could not tell which valve moved hard, so it is necessary to place the engine on quarter on side to be tested so that the other side will be on the dead center, in which position the valve will not move any with the Walschaert gear, and with the Stephenson gear it moves very little.

Q. 99.—How do you test for a valve face or seat blow?

A.—Place the valve on the center of its seat, on side to be tested, open cylinder cocks, set brake and open throttle; if steam shows up at one or both cylinder cocks it indicates a defect in face of valve or its seat.

Note.—If the defect does not show with valve on center of its seat, it is advisable to move the reverse lever a little, in that manner moving the valve a little on its seat so that if the cause of blow is seat worn hollowing, the valve will be raised as it comes out of the hollowed place and show the defect.

Note.—Valve may be gotten on center of its seat by placing the engine on the quarter and reverse lever in the center of the rack, or you can get the valve located centrally by getting the rocker arm at right angles to the valve rod.

Note.—With the Walschaert gear the valve is central on its seat when the link block is placed in center of link and the combination lever is at right angles to the valve rod.

Q. 100.—What would be the first thing you would do if the exhaust got out of square on the road?

A.—Ease off on the throttle a little, and see that the lubricator was working all right and feeding properly.

Q. 101.—Why is it necessary to ease off on the throttle to get the proper lubrication to valves and cylinder sometimes while on the road?

A.—Because the steam pressure in chest becomes greater than the pressure in the feed arms, and the current of steam flowing up through the oil pipes holds the oil back from entering the steam chest; easing off on the throttle reduces the chest pressure below that in the feed arms, and allows the oil to flow into the chest.

Note.—This trouble may be caused by the main steam valve to lubricator being only partly open, by the equalizing tubes being partially closed by corrosion or lime deposit, or it may be caused by the main steam pipe to lubricator being too small, and not maintaining the high pressure necessary in the feed arms to equalize with the chest pressure.

Q. 102.—What are the different causes of improper distribution of steam, or of an engine going lame on the road?

A.—Lost motion in valve gear and insufficient lubrication, sprung valve yoke, cracked valve yoke, sprung vale rod, sprung rocker arm, loose rocker box, badly worn rocker shaft or rocker box, worn link block, link sprung or cracked, sprung tumbling shaft, link lifting arm bent, link hanger too long or too short, blade bolts badly worn, sprung eccentric blade, slipped blade, badly worn straps or cam, strap bolts loose, cylinder saddles loose and working in frame, and engine frame broken between main driving box and cylinder saddles.

Q. 103.—What would you do if valve yoke was cracked?

A.—Work the engine full stroke with light throttle, handling full train.

Note.—By having the steam follow the piston the entire length of stroke you get the power to handle the train, and by using the light throttle you reduce the steam pressure on top of valve, and, consequently, the friction on seat and face of valve, therefore the liability of breaking the yoke entirely off is less.

Q. 104.—How do you tell when a valve yoke is cracked?

A.—The exhaust will be normal when the main pin is passing the front center, and it will be light when passing the back center.

Standing test.—Place the engine on the top quarter on side to be tested, with the reverse lever in front corner or quadrant, set the brake, open cylinder cocks, open throttle wide and pull reverse lever back, noting position of reverse in relation to center of quadrant when steam ceases to flow from the back cylinder cock; if the lever is back of center of rack when steam ceases to flow from back cylinder cock it indicates that the yoke is cracked or defective.

Note.—The friction between valve and seat causes the crack in yoke to open, and the valve is pulled back diagonally on its seat;

therefore, the back port will not be closed at the proper time, and many times the front port will be opened and steam be showing at front cylinder cock before the back port is closed.

Q. 105.—What would you do if the valve yoke was broken entirely off, or the valve stem was broken off the yoke?

A.—Disconnect the valve rod and remove the vacuum valve, then with a stick or bar push the valve as far back in the chest as possible, replace vacuum valve, open cylinder cocks, admit a little steam to chest, and with the valve rod push the valve back slowly until a little steam shows at the back cylinder cock, clamp the valve stem in that position, remove the vacuum valve and fit stick of wood in it that will reach the valve when the vacuum valve is screwed back in place; in that manner you will hold valve in position with back port open a little; remove the cylinder cocks, and you are ready to proceed. *Do not take down the main rod;* you will lubricate the cylinder and piston rod by having the little current of steam flowing down through the cylinder and out of the back cylinder cock opening; use the lubricator as when the engine is all right.

Note.—There is no need of disconnecting a main rod, the main rod or its connections are not damaged, and no large volume of steam is entering cylinder, and proper lubrication can be provided.

Note.—Where the cylinders are provided with indicator plugs, they may be removed to establish free circulation of air in cylinders instead of removing the cylinder cocks.

Note.—Some heads of mechanical departments desire the valve blocked in central position at all times when it is blocked at all; in that case lubrication may be provided by pouring oil into the indicator plug openings, or by slacking off the front cylinder head and putting a small piece of wood in at the top, then tightening up on the studs, pour oil in at the opening thus provided.

Note.—Whenever valve is blocked for any cause, except for the broken outer or steam bridge of seat, or the piston is gone entirely from the cylinder, remove both cylinder cocks or both indicator plugs, to avoid the vacuum formation and compression in cylinder, which would be caused by the movement of piston to and fro in the cylinder, and the vacuum and compression, if allowed to form, would cause serious resistance to the movement of piston in cylinder, causing the cylinder to heat and cut.

The old method of disconnecting for broken valve yoke or stem: Get the rocker arm at right angles to the valve rod, clamp the valve stem in that position, remove the valve rod or secure it to clear rocker arm, remove the vacuum valve, and with rod or stick push the valve back against end of valve stem, fit block into vacuum valve that will reach the valve when vacuum valve is in place, securing valve in mid-position in this way; then disconnect main rod, block crosshead securely in guides, remove the cylinder cocks, and put collar on main pin.

Q. 106.—What would you do if valve to the exhaust cavity were broken?

A.—Remove cap of chest, disconnect valve rod, and remove the valve from chest, then fit pieces of wood into the admission port where face of the valve was broken, fit blocking into the exhaust port, place valve back on center of seat, using the good part of face to cover its admission port, put cap back on chest, and clamp valve stem to hold valve central, provide for free circulation and lubrication, and proceed.

Another way.—Remove cap of chest, disconnect valve rod, take out valve, put block of hard wood over seat to cover all ports, having it reach from one side of chest to the other; nail another piece of blocking crossways on the seat block, which will reach from the forward end of chest to the back end of chest so that it will hold the block over the ports; drive nail hole or bore small hole through seat block into back port, for the steam to carry lubrication into cylinder through; leave valve stem in chest and put cap back on; remove the indicator plugs, and you are ready to go. The steam pressure will hold blocking on the seat.

Q. 107.—Can you tell whether valve yoke is cracked or eccentric strap bolts are loose? How?

A.—Yes, with the valve yoke cracked you will have the normal exhaust as the main pin passes the forward center and the light exhaust as the main pin passes the back center, and with the loose strap bolts the normal exhaust will be as the main pin passes the back center and the light exhaust as the main pin passes the forward center, if the valve motion is indirect, but with the direct valve motion the effect of loose strap bolts is about the same as the cracked valve yoke.

Q. 108.—What would you do if body of piston valve or its heads were broken?

A.—Put blind gasket in joint of live steam pipe.

Another way.—Cut large, round stick of wood that would fill valve chamber, put piece of sheet iron around it to keep steam from cutting it away, and put it in valve chamber in place of valve, then in either case it would be necessary to disconnect valve rod and provide for free circulation of air in cylinder and for lubrication.

Q. 109.—How would you test for broken packing rings in an inside admission piston valve?

A.—In practically the same way as with a slide valve, but as the rings determine the steam and exhaust edges of the valve, you may be able to tell which ring is defective by placing the engine on the quarter on side to be tested, and the reverse lever in center of rack-open the cylinder cocks, admit steam; if you get a blow through to the exhaust at end where steam will show at cylinder cock, both rings are defective; if you get no blow with valve on center of seat, move the lever so that steam ring will open admission port a little, and if you get a blow through to the exhaust it will indicate that the exhaust ring is defective at end of valve where steam port is opened, and steam is showing at the cylinder cock; if you get no blow, move the lever so that the valve will be moved to position where exhaust ring will uncover exhaust edge of admission port; if you get a bowl through to the exhaust in that position it indicates that the steam ring at that end of valve is defective; testing both ends of valve in this way, you can locate the rings which are defective.

Note.—The broken steam rings are generally located when valve is placed on the center of seat, and steam is admitted to chest, because, with cylinder cocks open, the steam will show at end of cylinder where steam ring is defective. The test merely proves it to you.

Q. 110.—How can you locate a slipped eccentric or blade quickly, and know whether it is the back-up motion eccentric or the forward motion which is gone wrong?

A.—By knowing that, with the reverse lever placed in either corner of the rack, one eccentric practically controls the valve movements, but between the corners both eccentrics have an influence on the valve, and that the exhausts occur when crank pins are crossing the centers; if engine goes lame while running along, on account of slipped eccentric or rod, you may move the lever towards the corner, and if valve motion squares up as the go-ahead eccentric is placed more in control of the valve, it indicates that the go-ahead eccentric is all right, and by pulling the lever up toward the center you will place the back-up eccentric more in control, and the engine will get lamer the nearer the center you get, the lever indicating that the back-up eccentric is wrong, but if she gets lamer as you drop the lever down, placing the go-ahead in control, it shows that the go-ahead is wrong, and as you hook her up toward center she will square up; watching the crank you can locate which side has the uneven exhaust.

Note.—By placing the engine on the dead center on the defective side, and having the reverse lever in center of rack, you can tell whether the blade has slipped too long or too short, because with the engine in this position, when eccentrics are right, the link will stand straight up, or perpendicular; so, by noting which way the defective blade causes the link to incline from the perpendicular position, you will know whether to shorten or lengthen the blade.

Q. 111.—How would you set a slipped eccentric?

A.—Place the engine on the dead center on disabled side, place the reverse lever in the extreme corner of quadrant which will place the good eccentric in control of the valve, mark the valve stem flush with the face of the gland, place the reverse lever in the opposite extreme corner of quadrant, go under the engine and turn slipped eccentric on axle until the mark on valve stem comes back flush with the gland, being sure to have the throw (web) of eccentric on the opposite side of the main pin from the one that is solid on the axle.

Another way.—Knowing that the left main pin is one-fourth of a turn back of the right main pin (if a right lead engine) and on the left lead engine the left main pin is one-fourth of a turn ahead of the right main pin, and that the eccentrics bear the same relative position to their respective main pins; no matter what position the engine is standing in, you may go under the engine and turn the slipped eccentric on the axle until the throw (web) is one-fourth of a turn ahead or back of the corresponding eccentric on the opposite side of engine, as the construction of the engine may require, and the eccentric will be approximately right. This is called the **quartering the axle method**.

Another way.—Knowing that, with the engine standing on the dead center and reverse lever in either extreme corner of the rack, the admission port at end of cylinder where piston rests will be open the amount of the lead, and that, with indirect motion and the outside admission valve, or the direct motion and the inside admission valve, the throw or web of the go-ahead eccentric follows the main pin at right angles less the lap and lead angle of advance toward the pin, and the back-up eccentric is ahead of the pin at the same angle. Know also that the direct motion for outside admission valve and the indirect motion for the inside admission valve, have the go-ahead eccentric leading the main pin at right angles plus the lap and lead angle of advance from the pin, and the back-up eccentric is following the pin at a corresponding angle. With this knowledge, you will place the engine on the dead center on disabled side, with reverse lever in corner of rack which will place the slipped eccentric in control of the valve, go under the engine and turn the disabled eccentric until the throw (web) is at right angles to main pin, being sure to have it on opposite side of main pin from web of one that is solid on the axle, then, with the cylinder cocks open and a little steam admitted to chest, incline the eccentric towards or from the main pin, as the construction of the valve movement requires, until a little steam shows at the cylinder cock at end of cylinder where the piston rests; secure it there, and proceed.

Q. 112.—What is a right lead engine?

A.—A right lead engine is one having the right main pin one-fourth of a turn ahead of the left main pin.

Q. 113.—What is a left lead engine?

A.—A left lead engine is one on which the left main pin leads the right main pin one-fourth of a turn.

Q. 114.—Are most engines right or left lead?

A.—Most engines are right lead, but the Pennsylvania R. R. has the left lead engine as a standard.

Q. 115.—How are the eccentrics kept in place on the axle?

A.—They are secured by keys and set screws, and some roads have the eccentrics fastened to each other by bolting them together.

Q. 116.—What would you do if steam chest were cracked?

A.—Disconnect oil pipe, remove the casing, slack off on all cap studs and wedge between wall of chest and studs to force the cracked sides together, tighten down on cap studs, connect up oil pipe, and proceed.

Note.—Where the studs are put through the walls of chest, it will be necessary to sling a chain around the chest and wedge between the chain and walls of chest to make it tight.

Q. 117.—What would you do if steam chest were so badly broken that it could not be repaired?

A.—Remove the broken parts, disconnect the valve rod, and take valve and valve yoke and rod out of the way, then drive pieces of wood into the supply ports and fit piece into top of supply ports, then build up on top of supply ports with blocking, place cap of chest on blocking and tighten down on studs to hold blocking in place on face of supply ports.

If the cap of chest is broken so it cannot be used, take a brake lever from a box car and put it from one stud to another across top of blocking on supply ports, and tighten down on blocking.

If the studs are gone or useless, sling a large chain around the cylinder and chest, passing it outside the guide bars at back end of cylinder and in next the frame of engine at front end of cylinder, place a heavy block on blocking to ports and use jack under chain to make the blocking solid on ports.

Q. 118.—What would you do when top rocker arm breaks?

A.—Disconnect valve rod from broken part, clamp valve with back port slightly open, remove cylinder cocks or indicator plugs, and proceed.

Another way.—Disconnect broken part, clamp valve centrally on the seat, provide for lubrication and free circulation of air in cylinder, and proceed.

Note.—Some people desire to have the main rod disconnected for an accident of this kind; in that case disconnect the valve rod, clamp the valve central on its seat, remove cylinder cocks, disconnect the main rod, clamp the crosshead securely at the back end of the guides when it is possible, but if the construction of the engine requires it you may have to secure the crosshead at forward end of guides, put collar on the main pin, and proceed.

Note.—It is not necessary to take down the main rod, so long as you provide for proper lubrication in the cylinder, and for free circulation of air in cylinder so that the cylinder will not heat and cut.

Note.—There are several good ways of providing for lubrication in the cylinder when the piston is left connected up to the main rod; one way is to leave the back admission port open slightly, then, with the cylinder cock removed, the steam will pass through port and out of cylinder cock, taking the oil, which the lubricator feeds, along with it and distributing it on the piston rod and walls of the cylinder; the steam in itself is a lubricant and, when saturated with oil, protects the cylinder for the engine to run any distance.

Another way is to pour the oil into the indicator plug openings when the valve is blocked centrally, or you may slack off on the studs to the front cylinder head and place a small wedge of wood in between head and end of cylinder, then tighten up on the studs so the head will not loosen off, and pour oil in at the opening thus afforded.

Q. 119.—What would you do if the bottom rocker arm became broken?

A.—Follow either of the above methods, being sure to make the link on the disabled side clear lower end of broken rocker arm. This may be done by lashing the rocker arm parallel with the frame of the engine, or by lashing the link hanger on the disabled side to the one on the good side of the engine, making the good link hold the disabled link away from the rocker arm, and when the link hangers are lashed together it will not be necessary to disconnect the valve rod from top rocker arm.

Another way which is absolutely safe is to take down both eccentrics and lash the disabled link to link hanger, but this takes time, and is not necessary, unless required by those in authority.

Q. 120.—What would you do if link block bolt (pin) were broken?

A.—Substitute another bolt if possible; if you have no suitable bolt, disconnect valve rod from top rocker arm, lash rocker arms parallel with the frame rail of engine, block valve with back port slightly open, remove the cylinder cocks or indicator plugs and proceed.

If it is not possible to lash the rocker arms parallel with frame and have them clear rods, either lash the link hanger on disabled side to the one on the opposite side to hold link clear of lower end of rocker arm, or take down the eccentrics and lash link to the hanger.

Q. 121.—What would you do if the bolt that attaches the valve rod to top rocker arm lost out or became broken?

A.—Substitute another bolt, or use the knuckle pin out of front draw bar and secure it in place. Do not disconnect anything.

Q. 122.—What would you do if link saddle pin (suspension stud) broke?

A.—Raise the link to the height where it will give you the desired cut-off to handle train, block between link block and top of link, remove the broken parts and proceed, keeping the disabled link well oiled. Do not reverse the engine.

Note.—It is permissible and practical to place block in lower end of link, but it must be cut about one inch shorter than distance from link block to end of link to allow for the slip of the link.

Note.—When you desire to back up, the longer block must be placed in top end of link to raise link high enough to place the back-up eccentric in control of the valve, and get the proper distribution of steam.

Q. 123.—What would you do if the link hanger was broken?

A.—Block the link at the desired point of cut-off to handle the train, remove the broken parts necessary, and proceed.

Q. 124.—What would you do if the lifting arm was broken?

A.—Block the link at the desired point of cut-off to lift and handle the train, remove the broken parts necessary, and proceed.

Q. 125.—What precaution must be taken when you have one link blocked up for broken saddle pin or link hanger?

A.—You must guard against reversing the engine without first changing the blocking, because if engine were reversed without placing the link to the same position the good side would be after reversal, you would have one side working against the other, and if reversed while in motion might cause wheels to lock and slide. You must also guard against dropping the good side any lower than you have the disabled side blocked at, unless you know that the lifting arm will clear the head of link on disabled side.

Note.—To get the proper length of block to place on link block to hold link up to the desired point of cut-off on the disabled side, place the reverse lever at point in rack where you will want to work engine the hardest to handle train, cut the block to fit on top of link block in good side and place it in link on disabled side.

Note.—To guard against dropping the lever below point at which you have disabled side blocked, put block in quadrant.

Q. 126.—What would you do if the tumbling shaft breaks?

A.—Where the construction of engine will permit, place bar across top of frame under the lifting arms and lash it there, also lash the lifting arms to the bar: where this is impossible it will be necessary to block both links at the desired point of cut-off by placing block on top of link blocks under the head of links.

Note.—When both links are connected to the same part of shaft, block in one link only, because when one link is slipping up the other one is moving down on its link block at each vibration of the links, consequently blocking in both links would be liable to cause further damage.

Q. 127.—What would you do if the reverse lever or reach rod breaks?

A.—If vertical arm to tumbling shaft extends up through the running board, you can raise the links up to the desired point of cut-off and block the vertical arm in that position in slot in running board, otherwise you can support the links (where construction of engine will permit) by placing a bar across top of frame under lifting arms, or by placing block in top of one link only, making it carry both links at the desired height.

Q. 128.—What would you do if the vertical arm to tumbling shaft broke?

A.—Place bar across top of frame under lifting arms, or block in top of one link only, to hold links at desired point of cut-off.

Q. 129.—What is a quick way to get valve central on seat when engine stops on dead center, and it is necessary to block valve to cover ports?

A.—Knowing that the port at end of cylinder where piston rests is open the amount of lead, and that the valve has about seven-eighths of an inch steam lap with outside admission valve engine standing on forward center, mark valve stem about one inch from valve stem packing case and disconnect valve rod, move it ahead until mark is flush with face of packing case. With inside admission valve, engine on forward center, mark valve stem flush with face of packing case, disconnect valve rod and pull it back until mark is about one inch away from face of packing case.

With outside admission engine standing on back center, mark valve stem at face of packing case, disconnect valve rod and pull back until mark is about one inch away from face of packing case. With inside admission valve, engine on back center, mark valve stem about one inch from face of packing case, and disconnect valve rod and move it ahead until mark on valve stem is flush with face of packing case.

Note.—This method will not get the valve exactly in center of its seat, but will place it near enough to center to cover the ports, and if you know the exact amount of lap and lead, by moving valve in this manner the amount of lap plus the lead, you will get valve on exact center of seat.

Note.—Another method of placing the valve in center of seat when engine is standing on dead center, if a Stephenson gear: place reverse lever in center of rack, disconnect one eccentric blade from link and move the link until the rocker arm is at right angles to the valve stem, clamp valve there, disconnect valve rod and connect up eccentric rod again.—If a Walschaert valve gear, place reverse lever in center of rack, disconnect lower end of combination lever and move it until valve rod forms a right angle with its upper end, clamp valve there and disconnect radius bar from combination lever, suspend it up and connect up the lower end of combination lever to union link.

Q. 130.—How would you locate side on which valve yoke or valve stem was broken off inside of steam chest?

A.—Open the cylinder cocks while engine was in motion and throttle open, and would get a steady blow from the back cylinder cock on the disabled side if an outside admission valve, or from the front cylinder cock if an inside admission valve.

Note.—When valve yoke breaks or valve stem breaks it will leave the valve at the forward end of steam chest, and with the outside admission valve the back admission port would be wide open, and the inside admission valve would have the front admission port wide open.

Note.—On an engine having an outside admission valve, if working steam when engine stops, or attempting to spot engine after breaking valve yoke or stem, the engine will stop on the forward dead center, because the steam in back end of cylinder would move the piston to forward end of cylinder and hold it there. An inside admission valve will sometimes move to center of seat on account of perfect balance and close port so engine might be moved, but generally it would stop on the back dead center on the disabled side.

Note.—In either case after engine had stopped on dead center, you can test for disabled side by opening cylinder cocks, admitting steam and moving reverse lever from one corner to the other; if you are able to shift steam from one cylinder cock to the other it shows that you have control of valve on side where engine is on the quarter and the other valve must be the one that is disabled.

Q. 131.—What would cause you to think valve yoke or stem was broken?

A.—The loss of two exhausts and peculiar rocking motion of engine, caused by one side working against the other side during half the revolution.

Q. 132.—What would you do if valve yoke were cracked or sprung?

A.—Work reverse lever down at long cut-off, and light throttle, handling full train.

Note.—By working light throttle you reduce the pressure on valve and the friction being less the yoke will hold to complete trip. By allowing the steam to follow piston nearly entire length of cylinder, you will have power to handle train to terminal.

Q. 133.—How would you locate the cracked or sprung valve yoke?

A.—By engine going suddenly very lame and having a heavy exhaust when the crank was passing the front center and a light exhaust when pin was crossing back center, account of valve not giving much port opening at front end of the cylinder.

Standing test.—Place engine on top quarter on side you desire to test, have reverse lever in forward corner, open cylinder cocks, set the brakes, open the throttle so as to admit heavy steam pressure to steam chest, pull reverse lever back and note where lever is in relation to center of rack when steam ceases to flow from back cylinder cock. If lever is back of center of rack before valve closes the back admission port it indicates a defective valve yoke.

Note.—When the valve is being moved ahead the stem and back of the yoke will move it squarely on its seat and give the back port full opening, but as valve is being pulled back, the friction will cause crack to open up and valve will move back diagonally on seat and open the forward port but a little, and will not close the back port as soon as it should.

Q. 134.—What would you do if relief (vacuum) valve in steam chest broke?

A.—Would remove cap and clamp it on seat with block of wood or iron placed on valve and cap screwed down on it.

Note.—Many grease plugs will fit opening in steam chest where the vacuum valve screws into chest.

Q. 135.—What would you do if cap to vacuum valve blew out and was lost?

A.—Would remove vacuum valve cage from chest and plug it on inner end and screw it back in place.

Q. 136.—If, when throttle was closed, steam showed at cylinder cocks, what might be the cause?

A.—It might be a leaky throttle or a leaky dry pipe.

Q. 137.—How would you test to determine whether throttle or dry pipe was leaking?

A.—Close the lubricator valves, and the air pump throttle if the exhaust from pump were tapped into cylinder saddles, fill boiler with water so I would have the dry pipe covered with water, have cylinder cocks open, and if dry steam showed at cylinder cocks the throttle would be leaking; if water showed with a little steam, would report dry pipe leaking.

Q. 138.—What would you do if the transmission bar hanger became broken?

A.—Support it with a chain or several strands of wire; if necessary would fit block above bar between strands of the chain or wire to prevent bar from raising up when lever was hooked up.

Q. 139.—What would you do if transmission bar were broken?

A.—It would depend on where bar was broken; if broken near rocker arm connection, would block valve central, support front end of bar with chain or wire, provide for lubrication and free circulation of air and proceed. If broken near link, would take down broken parts necessary, clamp valve centrally provide for lubrication and circulation and proceed.

Q. 140.—Why is the throttle placed as high as possible in the dome?

A.—To get the steam at as high a temperature and as dry as possible.

Q. 141.—What are the cylinder cocks for?

A.—To free the cylinders of condensation.

Q. 142.—Why is it necessary to keep the cylinders free from condensation?

A.—To prevent knocking out cylinder heads, breaking packing rings, and washing off lubrication from walls of cylinder.

Note.—Water is not compressible and if left in cylinders when the piston moved toward the head, the water not being able to get out and being solid, would damage the head or packing rings.

Q. 143.—In what manner can both valves be placed on center of seat at the same time?

A.—Place engine on either quarter on one side and reverse lever in center of quadrant, go to the other side and disconnect lower eccentric blade from link, move the link until rocker arm is at right angles to valve rod, and you will have both valves central.

Note.—The above applies to the Stephenson gear; with the Walschaert gear you will get the same results by placing engine on quarter and reverse lever in center of rack, then on the other side disconnect combination lever and move it until its upper end is at right angles to valve rod, and both valves will be central.

Q. 144.—Name the various causes for pounds.

A.—Loose or lost cylinder key; piston head loose on piston rod; loose follower bolts; piston rod loose in crosshead; main rod too long or too short; cylinder bushing loose and a little short; wrist pin loose in crosshead; rod brasses loose on pins or not keyed properly; pedestal binder loose; wedge down on binder or not properly adjusted; wedge not right taper; axle worn out of round; driving box brass worn large for axle; driving box broken; engine frame broken; crosshead loose in guides; knuckle pins or their bushings in side rods worn.

Q. 145.—When does the loose follower head pound the most?

A.—When drifting with throttle closed.

Q. 146.—When does the main rod too long or too short pound?

A.—When drifting with throttle closed, because the weight of piston will take up all the slack in main rod and its connections and cause piston to strike the head of cylinder.

Note.—If main rod is too short, piston will strike back head of cylinder as crank passes back center, when drifting with throttle if closed; too long, the piston will strike front cylinder head as crank passes front center, when drifting with throttle closed. To protect cylinder heads, open throttle and the steam admitted to cylinder account of the lead will cushion piston and take up all of the lost motion in rod and connections, preventing piston head striking cylinder head.

Q. 147.—When does the loose piston head on rod, or piston rod loose in the crosshead pound hardest?

A.—When working steam, and crank pins are passing centers.

Q. 148.—How do you locate the loose piston head or rod?

A.—It can be located when running along working steam; you will get a heavy pound when crank pin on defective side is crossing back center and a lighter pound when crank is crossing front center.

Standing test.—Place engine on top quarter on side you desire to test, open the throttle and work lever from one corner to the other of quadrant; if piston is loose you will get a heavy pound when lever goes toward the front corner, and a lighter pound when lever goes toward the back corner.

Note.—The piston head is taper fitted on end of rod and rod is taper fitted into crosshead, consequently when steam is admitted back of piston, the piston moves away from the taper, and the farther it moves the less resistance it has, and it strikes the nuts on end of rod a hard blow; but when the steam is admitted ahead of piston it goes against the taper and is slowed down by friction so that it loses force so that it strikes the shoulder a very light blow.

Q. 149.—How would you be able to detect the loose cylinder bushing?

A.—This defect can only be located while engine is in motion and working steam. The pound occurs at each end of stroke of piston, just after pin passes the center and generally before it reaches the eighth.

Note.—The cylinder packing rings are expanded by the steam against the walls of the bushing, and the friction moves the bushing until it strikes the cylinder head.

Q. 150.—How do you test for cylinder packing blow?

A.—It may be located while running along working steam; you will have an intermittent blow at the exhaust, the blow at exhaust occurring just after the crank on defective side leaves the center, getting stronger up to the eighth, and stopping as soon as valve closes communication between admission port and exhaust at other end of cylinder.

Standing test.—Place engine on top forward eighth, set brake and place reverse lever in forward corner of rack, block front cylinder cock open, admit steam to cylinder and if steam shows at front cylinder cock the cylinder packing rings are defective.

Note.—The reason for placing engine on the eighth for this test is that cylinder wears most from center to forward end and the rings might not show defective with piston back of center.

Note.—The old way for this test (and it is a good one). Place engine on top quarter on side you desire to test, reverse lever in front corner, set brake, open cylinder cocks, admit steam and if steam shows at front cylinder cock it indicates that packing is defective.

Q. 151.—Why is the link saddle pin (suspension stud) placed to one side of the center of link?

A.—To overcome the effect of the angularity of the main rod.

Q. 152.—Why have side (parallel) rods on mogul and consolidation types of engines knuckle joints?

A.—To allow for the free movement of the wheels over uneven track, without straining the pins and rods.

Q. 153.—What are the pedestal braces (binders) of locomotives?

A.—They are a detachable portion of the lower frame rail, made of bars of iron or steel to bind the lower end of jaws for driving boxes, after the boxes and wheels are in place.

Q. 154.—How is a locomotive boiler attached to engine frame?

A.—The boiler is solidly attached to cylinder saddles with bolts, and the cylinder saddles are solidly attached to frame with bolts and saddle keys, and at the rear end the boiler is supported on frame by expansion plates which are attached to boiler and rest on frame, or by hangers which are hinged on plates attached to boiler and frame.

Note.—The expansion plates are constructed so that they move backward and forward easily on frame, and still support rear end of boiler; this is a necessary arrangement because the boiler expands and contracts more than the frame does and these expansion plates or hangers guard against the strain on boiler and frame which would obtain if boiler were solidly attached to frame at rear end as well as at front end. It is well to observe that the bolts holding the expansion plates are properly fitted so that the expansion plate does not bind on the cap too hard.

Q. 155.—How would you handle a hot eccentric?

A.—See that all oil holes are clean and that the lubrication is getting to the bearing. If the strap is too tight on cam would loosen nuts on strap bolts and put in liners enough to make it free, then tighten the strap bolts. If the strap is too loose on the cam, causing it to pound hot, would loosen strap bolts and remove liners enough to make strap fit the cam.

Q. 156.—Would you use water on a hot eccentric?

A.—No.

Q. 157.—Why would you not use water to cool a hot eccentric?

A.—Because the strap is so much lighter than the cam that it would cool off faster than the cam and contract and tighten on cam until it bursted, and the cam would contract faster than the axle, causing the cam to burst.

Q. 158.—How would you handle a hot driving box to cool it down and prevent cutting the bearing?

A.—Would be sure that the bearing was getting the lubrication; if it did not cool down then, I would run the wheel up on a wedge and block on top of frame under the spring saddle, or under the ends of the arch equalizer to relieve the box of weight.

Q. 159.—Is it good practice to use water on a very hot bearing?

A.—No. It causes crystallization and weakens the metal, eventually resulting in a break.

Q. 160.—What will cause crystallization and weakening of metals used in bearings, besides sudden expansion and contraction?

A.—A continual bending of the metal or a constant hammering of the metal while it is cold will cause the molecules to crystallize, forming what we generally call a coarse grain (crystallization), and as the grains of the metal become coarser the metal grows weaker at that point.

Note.—This effect is clearly noticeable in driving pins which are broken in line with the boss of the wheel; the oil on the broken ends will show that the pin has been gradually separating until only a small portion of the pin is intact, then a sudden strain separates that portion so the break shows just how much of the metal was holding before the break.

Note.—When rod brasses pound on the pins, the hammer blow which the pin receives, when the piston starts backward and forward in the cylinder, taking up the lost motion in the brasses, causes the pin to bend at point in line with the face of the wheel, starting the weakening of the pin at that point through crystallization.

Q. 161.—What is the effect of leaky steam pipes or exhaust joints?

A.—It prevents forming a vacuum in the front end and stops the draught on the fire, causing the fire to burn a dull red color and engine will not steam.

Q. 162.—How would you test for leaky steam pipes?

A.—Place the reverse lever in the center of the quadrant, open the front end door, apply the brake, pull the throttle wide open to admit full steam pressure to the pipes, and with a lighted torch try around the joints for leaks—the leak will be shown by the flare of the flame.

Note.—The reason for opening the throttle wide is that the great pressure inside the pipe has a tendency to straighten it out and will develop a leak if one exists, and a lighted torch is the only sure way to locate the leak, because the escaping steam is not visible, and the old idea that the cinders will be blown away from the leaking joint is not reliable for the reason that chemical action takes place in cinders, causing them to form a porous mass solidly knitted together through which the steam will pass without moving the cinders.

Q. 163.—How would you test for a leaky exhaust joint?

A.—The best way is to get the engine on a clear straight piece of track, open the front end door and have the fireman start the engine moving; then apply the brake and open the throttle wide; take a lighted torch and try around the nozzle joints for the leak, testing both sides; the escaping steam will blow the flame of the torch and locate leak.

Another way.—Place the engine on the quarter (top or bottom), open the front end door, have the fireman set the brake, open the throttle and move the reverse lever back and forth from corner to corner of the rack, take the lighted torch and try the joint on that side of the exhaust for the leak; place the engine on the quarter on the other side and test it in the same manner.

Note.—It is necessary to get a strong exhaust from each side to locate the defective joint; the base of the nozzle is divided into two openings by a partition which comes over the joint between saddle castings, therefore the reason for moving the engine to the quarter on each side for the test.

Note.—Another way to test for leaky nozzle joint is to place the engine on the top or bottom eighths; having the front end door open, set the brake, open the throttle, and move the reverse lever from corner to corner of the rack, trying for the leak around joint with lighted torch; in this way both sides may be tested without moving the engine, but it is not very reliable, because the exhaust will not be strong.

The best way to test is with the engine moving slowly with brake set and throttle wide open, where it is possible to do it that way, and the next best way is to place the engine on the quarter.

Q. 164.—What would cause you to test for leaky steam pipes or exhaust joint?

A.—The fire dying down and burning a blood red color and the exhaust not working the fire as it should when you begin to work steam, and the engine not steaming while working steam, but the fire burns brightly and engine steams as soon as throttle is closed. Sometimes the blow may be heard when the fire-box door is opened.

Note.—When the air pump has an independent exhaust in the front end it gets disconnected or broken off, and it will affect the fire the same as the leaky steam pipes or exhaust joint, only the leaky air pump exhaust will affect the fire and steaming of the engine all of the time as long as the air pump is working, while the leaky steam pipe joint or nozzle joint will only affect the fire when working steam.

Q. 165.—How would you test for pounds in main driving box?

A.—Place the engine on top quarter on side you desire to test, have the fireman open throttle, and move reverse lever from corner to corner of rack; watch movement of box to locate pound.

Q. 166.—Why do you place engine on top quarter on side you desire to test for pounds in driving box?

A.—To get the power applied as near as possible to the point you desire to move.

Note.—With pin on top quarter, all of the lost motion in box will be taken up before there is any liability of the wheel slipping.

Q. 167.—What are the principal causes for pounds in main driving box?

A.—Loose or broken pedestal binder, improperly lined shoe or wedge, wedge loose or down on binder, journal badly worn out of round or small, brass badly worn too large for journal, driving box brass broken, driving box broken.

Q. 168.—What other causes for pounds have we besides those affecting the driving boxes?

A.—Loose or lost cylinder key, loose follower bolts, piston head loose on piston rod, cylinder bushing short and loose in cylinder, piston rod loose in crosshead, lost motion between crosshead and guides, wrist pin loose in crosshead, rod brasses too large for driving pins, rod brasses loose in strap, knuckle pins or their bushings badly worn, engine frame broken and main rods keyed too long or too short so that piston head strikes cylinder head.

Q. 169.—Are all wedges alike in the manner of adjustment? How do they differ?

A.—No. Some are forced up by having the wedge bolt screwed through the binders, others have the wedge bolt passed through hole in binder, and have to be pried or pinched up and are secured and held in place with nuts on wedge bolt on top of binder.

Q. 170.—When should wedges be reported to be lined?

A.—When the wedge has been moved up as far as it will go and the box still pounds.

Note.—The box is up as far as it will go when it strikes the top frame rail.

Q. 171.—When should wedges be set up?

A.—When the driving box is pounding between wedge and shoe.

Q. 172.—What work about the engine should be done by the engineer?

A.—Setting up the wedges, keying up rod brasses, and any other necessary work while on the road to insure a successful trip and prevent engine failure.

Q. 173.—At what time or place should wedges be set up to obtain the best results?

A.—Either on arrival at terminal at completion of trip or at some place on road after engine has been pulling train and working hard; then the frame and other parts are expanded so that the wedges can be properly adjusted under the right conditions.

Q. 174.—How do you proceed to set up wedges?

A.—Get the engine on a piece of straight level track, place her on the top quarter on side you desire to set up first, cut out driver brake and apply tender and truck brake, or block tender and truck wheels; admit a little steam with reverse lever in forward corner—this will pull the box away from the wedge—go under the engine and set the wedge up as far as it will go; then pull it down one-eighth of an inch for dope packed boxes and one-quarter of an inch for hard grease packed boxes, to allow for expansion of box and prevent the wedge and box from sticking; set up the main wedge first, then the other ones; handle the other side in the same way.

Another way.—Place the engine on the top back eighth on the side you desire to work on first, having engine on straight level track; put block on rail ahead of wheel on opposite side, with reverse lever in the forward corner; admit steam to pull box away from wedge, set up the wedge as explained above, set up the opposite main wedge in same way, then handle the others one at a time.

Another way.—Place the engine on top forward eighth on right side, then it will be on top back eighth on left side (if a right lead engine); set tender brake, place reverse lever in forward corner, admit steam to cylinders, pulling both sides away from wedges; go under engine, set up main wedges first, then the others, as explained above.

A good way where solid rods are newly fitted with bushings.—Place block on rail back of driver so that when wheel hits it the rods will be on dead center, start the engine moving back and let her drift onto the block; this will throw the box away from wedge so wedge can be set up to the box, and it prevents getting rods and boxes out of tram; handle each wheel in same manner, setting up main wedges first.

Another way.—Place engine on dead center on side you are to work at wedges, use pinch bar to throw wheels ahead, then set up wedges.

Note.—The last explanation is for the method generally used by mechanics on dead engines and new work, but it is always best to have the engine hot and parts expanded when wedges are to be adjusted.

Note.—Where engines have keyed side rods it is a good method to slack back the keys before setting up the wedges.

Q. 175.—What would you do if wedge bolt broke and the wedge came down on top of binder?

A.—Sometimes the broken wedge bolt can be spliced with a nut and then the wedge can be adjusted with the bolt. If this is impossible, raise the wedge to proper height and secure it there by blocking it top and bottom with nuts lashed to the jaws.

Q. 176.—How would you handle a stuck wedge to get it down?

A.—Strain down on wedge with wedge bolt, then run the wheel over a nut or coal pick placed on rail; this will generally bring them down; but if it does not, slack off on the binder bolts and run over the block on rail again; this failing, loosen up more on the binder and run the wheels ahead and back of the one with stuck wedge up on wedges, having both up at the same time; this will open the jaws of the box and the wedge will come down; tighten the binder and adjust the wedge so it will not stick again.

Note.—Sometimes a little signal oil or kerosene oil poured in between jaw and wedge and box and wedge will help to lubricate it so it will come down.

Q. 177.—How do you locate a stuck wedge, and what would cause you to think a wedge was seized or stuck?

A.—The engine would ride hard and every rail joint would cause a heavy jar, as though engine had no springs, when wedge is stuck.

To locate the stuck wedge, would go out on running board and note the movement of boxes in jaws; if a box was not moving up and down in the jaws when the engine was in motion, the wedge at that box is stuck.

Q. 178.—Why are side rods provided with knuckle joints?

A.—To allow for the free movement of the wheels over uneven track without bending or breaking the side rods.

Q. 179.—How would you proceed to key the side rods on a mogul or a consolidation engine?

A.—Have the wedges properly set up; place engine on dead center on side you are to key first, having engine on piece of straight, level track; on engines having but a single key at intermediate and front and back connections, drive the key at intermediate connection on side next main pin, first keying brasses so they are close to pin and still move freely on pin; then key the brasses at main connection, driving key in solid portion of rod first so as to get that part of the rod of proper length between main and intermediate pins; then drive the other pin at main connection to close brasses to fit pin closely, but move freely on pin; then key the forward and backward brasses, move engine to the other dead center, and try all brasses to be sure that they move freely at that point also.

Note.—When keying brasses on side rods, keys should be driven so rods will be as long as possible between pins and still move freely at all points of the revolution, and if there is any slack in the rods, it should be lengthways so there will be no strain on the rods when the wheels are moving up and down over the uneven track; this will make the knuckle joints and brasses wear longer without renewal.

Note.—Where there are two keys at the intermediate connection, the main connection may be keyed first, then drive the key nearest the main pin at the intermediate connection to get the solid portion of rod the proper length, using key on other side of pin to close brasses to fit pin, and if two keys are used at each of the forward and back ends of the rod, always drive the key on side towards main pin first so that the rods will be proper length between pins; then after you have the brasses all keyed, be sure to place the engine on the other center to make sure that brasses are free at that point, because a pin sprung or drivers out of tram might cause the rods to bind and run hot.

Q. 180.—Why place the engine on the dead center on side rods to be keyed when keying side rods?

A.—To prevent keying the side rods too long or too short, or out of tram.

Q. 181.—If side rods are keyed too long or too short, where will they bind?

A.—Passing the dead centers, because that is the rigid point, and all the relative wheel and pin centers must be equally distant from each other and are held rigidly in that position passing the dead centers.

Note.—The dead wedges or shoes are placed in the driving box jaws in front of the driving boxes, to determine the proper location for the wheel centers, and maintain the wheel centers in their correct relative positions (in tram) when the live wedges are properly adjusted.

Q. 182.—What is meant by "engine out of tram"?

A.—When the distance between wheel centers on one side of engine is greater or less than the distance between the corresponding wheel centers on the other side.

Q. 183.—What is meant by "rods out of tram"?

A.—When the rods are keyed or fitted up so that the distance between pin centers is greater or less than the distance between the corresponding wheel centers.

Q. 184.—When should rod brasses be reported to be closed or refitted?

A.—When they are keyed solidly brass to brass and pounding on pin.

Q. 185.—When should rod brasses be reported to be lined?

A.—When the key is driven as far as possible and the brasses are working in the strap.

Q. 186.—How do you place engine to locate pounds in main rod brasses and why in that position?

A.—Place engine on bottom quarter on side to be tested, set brake, admit steam to cylinder and work reverse lever back and forth, watch brasses. We place the engine on bottom quarter so as to have the pin between two rigid points, and then any lost motion in brasses will show before box would move or the wheel slip.

Q. 187.—Where do you place engine to key back end of main rod and why there?

A.—On dead center, so as to key brasses against largest part of crank pin.

Q. 188.—Where do you place engine to key front end of main rod brasses and why there?

A.—On top or bottom quarter. Generally bottom quarter so as to key against largest part of pin, and on bottom quarter because it is easier to get at set screw that holds front end key.

Q. 189.—What would you do if the main rod broke?

A.—Remove broken parts and disconnect valve rod and block valve to cover admission ports, block crosshead, remove cylinder cocks, put collar on main pin and provide for lubrication.

Q. 190.—What would you do if the piston rod broke off at crosshead?

A.—Remove broken parts, disconnect valve rod, block valve to cover the admission ports and proceed.

Note.—Most likely the piston would have gone out through the front cylinder head.

Q. 191.—What would you do if front cylinder head broke?

A.—Disconnect valve rod, block valve with back admission port slightly open, remove back cylinder cock.

Note.—Do not take down main rod.

Note.—If in dusty weather, would cover front end of cylinder with gunny sack or boards.

Another way:—Disconnect valve rod, block valve centrally on its seat, remove back cylinder cock, board up front end of cylinder, placing a swat of waste saturated with oil in cylinder.

Another way:—Disconnect valve rod, block valve centrally on its seat, disconnect main rod, put collar on main pin and block crosshead.

Q. 192.—With the Walschaert valve motion explain how you could disconnect for broken eccentric, eccentric rod, or link foot.

A.—Disconnect eccentric rod and remove other broken parts, disconnect back end of radius rod and block link block in center of the link.

Note.—When blocking link block in link of Walschaert's valve gear block above and below it in slot of link.

Q. 193.—What would you do if link trunnion pin broke?

A.—Take down eccentric rod, disconnect back end of radius rod and block link block in center of link, then wedge the link in place by driving wedge between trunnion pin bracket and link on side where the trunnion pin is broken.

Q. 194.—What would you do when link trunnion pin bracket breaks?

A.—Take down eccentric rod, disconnect both ends of radius rod and take link and radius rod out, block valve centrally on seat, provide for lubrication and free circulation of air on cylinder.

Note.—If link can not be readily removed, support forward end of radius rod and chain link so as it will carry, allowing back end of radius rod to carry with link block at bottom of link.

Q. 195.—What would you do with broken valve stem or valve yoke of Walschaert's valve motion?

A.—Block valve centrally on seat, disconnect forward end of radius rod and support it underneath the running board, provide for lubrication and free circulation and proceed.

Note.—With link block in center of link and combination lever (lap and lead lever) at right angles to it the valve will be centrally on its seat.

Note.—To secure the valve centrally where yoke or stem is broken locate the central position, clamp valve stem, then remove the vacuum valve and block it against the valve, or if it is a piston valve, remove the front head to valve chamber and cut piece of board (that is nearly as wide as diameter of valve chamber) to fit between valve in central position and head of valve chamber.

Note.—Some desire as an extra precaution to stop all motion of radius rod when front end of it is disconnected and supported up. To do this you may remove eccentric rod, or disconnect back end of radius rod and block link block in center of link.

Note.—When the forward end of radius rod is supported and eccentric rod is taken down, the link block does not always move freely in links and at times bothers in handling the reverse lever, consequently the better way to stop motion of radius rod is to disconnect back end of it and block link block in center of link.

Q. 196.—What would you do in case of broken reversing lever? Reach rod or reversing arm, or lifting shaft, Walschaert's valve gear?

A.—If reversing arm extended up through running board and was not broken, could block forward and back of it in slot in running board to hold link blocks at the desired point of cut-off, otherwise would have to block above and below both link blocks in slot of link to hold link blocks at the desired point of cut-off necessary to start and handle train.

Q. 197.—What would you do in case of a broken radius arm or radius arm hanger?

A.—Remove the broken parts and block link block in slot of link to get the desired point of cut-off to handle train.

Note.—With the Walschaert valve gear. Where one link block is blocked as above the other side may be worked at a longer or shorter cut-off as desired.

Q. 198.—What would you do in case of a broken radius rod?

A.—Remove the broken part from the combination lever—support the forward end of radius rod, secure valve centrally on seat, provide for lubrication and free circulation in cylinders and proceed.

Note.—Absolute safety is provided by disconnecting back end of radius rod and blocking link block in center of link.

Q. 199.—What would you do in case of a broken lap and lead lever, union link or crosshead arm?

A.—Remove broken parts necessary, block valve centrally on its seat, support front end of radius rod, provide for lubrication and free circulation and proceed.

Note.—Where lap and lead lever is not broken the lower end of it may be secured to back cylinder cock.

Note.—Many engines have the front end of radius rod constructed so it can be connected to back end of valve rod, when the lap and lead lever is taken down. On such engines it is a good plan in accidents of this kind to make the connection between radius rod and valve rod. This will give enough movement to valve to provide the lubrication to cylinder but will not aid much in handling the train because the eccentric only moves the valve far enough to open ports wide if the valve had no lap, and the engine working full stroke, and as the cut-off is shortened by hooking up of lever so is travel of valve shortened and with lever hooked up the lap of valve would prevent much port opening and the angularity of main rod would cause an unequal distribution, so the actions of steam on disabled side would be erratic at the best, and the ports would only be open a very little and for only an instant when cranks were passing the quarters on the disabled side.

Q. 200.—What would you do in case of a broken crosshead, crosshead pin, main rod or main rod straps or brasses, Walschaert's valve gear?

A.—Disconnect main rod and remove other broken parts necessary, put collar on pin, secure valve centrally on its seat, disconnect forward end of radius rod and support it. Block crosshead at back end of guides, remove cylinder cocks and proceed.

Note.—The motion of radius rod may be stopped if desired as explained before.

Q. 201.—What would you do if the main rod crank pin broke?

A.—Block valve centrally on its seat, disconnect and support forward end of radius rod, take down eccentric rod and remove straps and brasses at back end of main rod; block crosshead at forward end of guides and carry main rod in guides. Take down all side rods and remove cylinder cocks on disabled side.

Q.—What would you do if piston rod broke?

A.—Secure valve centrally on its seat, disconnect and support forward end of radius rod. Take off cylinder head and remove piston from cylinder. Motion of radius rod may be stopped, if desired.

Q. 203.—How would you handle a piston valve if stem were broken inside of valve chamber?

A.—Get valve rod at right angles to rocker arm, clamp valve stem, remove front valve chamber head and push valve back against stem, then cut piece of board or plank (that is nearly as wide as the diameter of valve chamber) to reach from valve head and screw head against it. Disconnect valve rod, provide for lubrication, free the cylinder and proceed.

Q. 204.—What is the necessity of keeping brasses keyed properly?

A.—To prevent pounding and to keep the rod the proper length.

Q. 205.—How should main rod brasses be keyed?

A.—They should be keyed as close as possible to avoid pounds and so they will move freely on pin at all points in the revolution.

Q. 206.—Describe a piston valve.

A. It is a hollow spool-shaped casting with packing rings (in the heads that form its ends) that make a steam-tight joint with the walls of the valve chamber.

Q. 207.—What is the relative motion of the piston and valve for inside admission valve? For outside admission valve?

A.—The inside admission valve moves in opposite direction to piston for admission and with the piston for cut-off, expansion and exhaust. The outside admission valve moves with the piston for admission and in the opposite direction for cut-off, expansion, and exhaust.

COMPOUND LOCOMOTIVES

Q. 1.—Wherein do compound locomotives differ from ordinary or simple ones?

A.—Compound locomotives differ from the ordinary type in that a simple engine has but one set of cylinders of the same diameter and uses the steam but once, while a compound or double expansion engine has either two or four cylinders of varying diameters, and the steam, after passing through the first cylinder and losing part of its energy, passes into the second cylinder, where a certain amount of its remaining energy is used. Simple and compound engines consist of two engines, coupled to the same set of driving wheels. Balanced compounds have four sets of main rods and crank pins, and Mallet compounds have two complete sets of engines under one boiler.

Q. 2.—Why is one cylinder on a compound locomotive called the high pressure cylinder and the other one the low pressure cylinder?

A.—Because the high pressure cylinder takes its steam directly from the boiler at nearly initial boiler pressure, while the low pressure cylinder, under ordinary conditions, receives the steam from the high pressure cylinder and works with a low pressure. It is always larger than the high pressure cylinder in order to get the same power from the low pressure steam.

Q. 3.—In the Schenectady two-cylinder compound, what is the duty of the oil dashpot?

A.—To insure a steady movement of the intercepting valve, without shock, which might damage the valve or seat, and in order to keep it working properly, the oil dashpot should be kept full of oil.

Q. 4.—Explain how a Schenectady two-cylinder compound may be operated as a simple engine?

A.—Place the handle of the three-way cock so as to allow air pressure to flow from the main reservoir to the cylinder of the separate exhaust valve. This will open the separate exhaust valve and let the steam from the high pressure cylinder exhaust to atmosphere. The intercepting valve will allow live steam to feed through the reducing valve at a reduced pressure to the low pressure cylinder when the separate exhaust valve is open. When starting a train or when moving slowly and about to stall on a grade, it should be operated as a simple engine. It should not be operated as simple when running at high speed.

Q. 5.—Explain how a two-cylinder compound is changed from simple to compound.

A.—Place the handle of the three-way cock in the cab so as to release the air from the cylinder of the separate exhaust valve. A coil spring will then close this valve, causing the exhaust steam of the high pressure cylinder to accumulate in the receiver until sufficient pressure is obtained to force the intercepting valve into compound position, thereby shutting off live steam from the main throttle to the low pressure cylinder and opening a passage so steam from the receiver will feed to the low pressure steam chest.

Q. 6.—How should a compound engine be lubricated?

A.—In lubricating a compound engine one-third more oil should be fed to the high than to the low pressure cylinder, and at high speed more oil should be fed than at low speed.

Q. 7.—Why feed more oil to high than to a low pressure cylinder?

A.—Because some of the oil from the high pressure cylinder follows the steam into the low pressure cylinder.

Q. 8.—How would you lubricate the valve of low pressure cylinder if the oil feed became inoperative on that side?

A.—Feed an increased quantity through oil pipe connecting to intercepting valve, then, by shutting engine off occasionally and cutting into simple position, oil will go direct from intercepting valve into low pressure steam chest and cylinder. This would avoid going out on steam chest and disconnecting pipe and oil by hand.

Q. 9.—How much water should be carried in the boiler of a compound locomotive?

A.—Not more than two gauges or about one-half of a water glass. In case of broken glass, do not allow water to drop below a flutter in top cock when working. No more than this amount should be carried, in order to assure the delivery of dry steam to cylinders, as wet steam is particularly injurious to compound locomotives.

Q. 10.—How should a compound locomotive be started with a long train?

A.—Always in simple position, with cylinder cocks open.

Q. 11.—When drifting, what should be the position of the separate exhaust valve, the cylinder and port cocks?

A.—Should be in open position.

Q. 12.—What will cause two exhausts of air to blow from the three-way cock or simpling valve in the cab when the engine is being changed to compound?

A.—Exhaust valve being sticky. When air is first discharged it does not move. When it does move, the second exhaust comes.

Q. 13.—What does steam blowing at the three-way cock indicate?

A.—The separate exhaust valve not seating properly, caused by stuck valves, weak or broken spring, and the packing rings of separate exhaust valve leaking.

Q. 14.—What can be done if the engine will not operate compound when the air pressure in the separate exhaust valve is released by the three-way cock?

A.—The cause of this is the separate exhaust valve failing to close. Try tapping it with hammer on the front of the saddle near the exhaust valve. In case this will not cause the valve to close, disconnect the air pipe connection to the separate exhaust valve, take the nuts off the center circle of studs around the separate exhaust valve, pull out the casting, and, if the valve is not broken, it can be closed and replaced.

Q. 15.—If the engine stands with high pressure side on the dead center and will not move when given steam, where is the trouble, and what may be done to start the engine? Why?

A.—Intercepting valve is stuck in compound position, so live steam cannot get to the low pressure cylinder. In a case of this kind, close the main throttle, open the cylinder and port cocks, and, when all pressure is relieved, use a bar to shove forward the rod that works through the oil dashpot; this will move the intercepting valve to the simple position, admitting steam to the low pressure cylinder as soon as the throttle is open. The engine will not start for the reason that with the low pressure piston on quarter, steam must be admitted to its cylinder to start the engine.

Q. 16.—In the event of a breakdown, how should one disconnect?

A.—Disconnect the same as with a simple engine and run with the separate exhaust valve open, working engine simple instead of compound.

Q. 17.—What may be done to shut off steam pressure from the steam chest and low pressure cylinder?

A.—Pull out as far as it will come the rod that runs through the oil dashpot and fasten it in this position, and open the separate exhaust valve.

Q. 18.—Is it important that air be pumped up on a two-cylinder compound before the engine is moved? Why?

A.—Yes, it is very important, because the separate exhaust valve is opened by air, and the engine will not operate as a simple engine until sufficient air pressure is obtained to open this valve.

Q. 19.—How are the blows in a compound located?

A.—Blows in a compound may be located the same as in a simple engine, with the exception that any blow on the high pressure side of engine will not be heard when the separate exhaust valve is closed. A blow on the high pressure side of the engine will cause the relief valves on the low pressure cylinder to pop when working the engine with full throttle compound.

Q. 20.—What should be done if high pressure piston of a cross compound is broken off the rod, or if the high pressure or low pressure cylinder head is broken?

A.—Cover the ports on that side, open the separate exhaust valve, and run in, using live steam in low pressure cylinder only.

If high pressure cylinder head is broken off, cover ports on that side, open separate exhaust and run in, using live steam on low pressure side only. Do not take down main rod, but take out pop valves, front and back heads of cylinder, and see that the cylinder is properly oiled. If low pressure cylinder head is broken off, cover the ports on that side, open the separate exhaust valve, and run in with high pressure side. Do not take down main rod, but see that the cylinder is well oiled.

Q. 21.—In the event of separate exhaust valves failing to work when throttle is wide open, what can be done to assist in opening?

A.—Ease the throttle off very fine, which in a moment or two will reduce the receiver pressure so that the separate exhaust valve will move. If this does not have the desired effect, shut off entirely, even at the risk of stalling, as in that event train can be started from a dead stand with engine cut into simple.

Q. 22.—If a transmission bar on a cross compound is broken, what would you do for the right side? For the left side?

A.—If on the right side, cover ports, fasten valve stem, take out pops from cylinder heads, open separate exhaust valve, and, leaving main rod up, run in with high pressure cylinder only, looking carefully to its lubrication; if on the left side, cover ports, fasten valve stem, take out pop valves from cylinder heads, open separate exhaust valve, and leave main rod up, run in with live steam on low pressure side only.

Q. 23.—How test for piston packing blow with balanced compound?

A.—To test the high pressure piston packing on a Baldwin balanced compound, the engine should be placed with the outside main pin on that side of the engine on the bottom quarter, the reverse lever in the forward notch, close starting valve, block drivers or set brakes solid, remove indicator plug in the front end of either the high or low pressure cylinder. Steam will be admitted to the back end of high pressure cylinder with the throttle thrown open. There will be a leak past the piston or the high pressure valve if steam escapes out of this plug opening. If in doubt, next test the high pressure valve by moving the reverse lever to the center notch. This should cover the ports, and if the valve is tight the blow will cease. Stand the engine in the same position, with the wheels blocked, in testing the low pressure piston, open starting valve, back indicator plug out. When throttle is opened, the leaky packing will be shown by steam escaping from the plug opening. If in doubt, test valve by bringing reverse lever to center of quadrant; this will spot valve over port and, if it is tight, the blow will cease. A blow past the high pressure packing tends to increase the pressure in the low pressure cylinder, in compound engines. A blow past the low pressure packing is heard at the exhaust, and is generally on both forward and back strokes, while a blow past the by-pass valves or valve bushings occurs only at a certain part of a complete revolution.

Q. 24.—In case it was necessary to disconnect on one side of a compound engine, how would you cover ports and hold valves in position?

A.—Clamp the valve stem to hold valve in central position. All ports should be covered by doing this. It may be necessary to remove head of piston valve chest and block in there.

Q. 25.—Is it a disadvantage to work a compound engine in short cut-off? Why?

A.—It is. If cut-off is too short, steam passing the throttle will not get to the low pressure cylinder in its proper proportion. The work should be divided between the two cylinders on the same side.

Q. 26.—In what way do the Mallet or articulated compounds differ from the other steam locomotives in the distribution of the steam?

A.—It differs both in construction and in steam distribution. It consists of two separate and independent engines under one boiler. The rear engine is rigidly attached to the back end of the boiler in the usual manner. The front engine is not attached to the boiler, but supports it by means of sliding bearings, so that it can move freely from side to side under the boiler and pass curves more easily. There is a hinged or articulated connection between the engines by which the front one is permitted a limited swing in relation to the rear one, and it is this feature which gives the name "articulated" to this type of locomotive. The rear engine takes boiler steam direct, the same as a simple engine, and exhausts it from both cylinders into a large pipe or receiver. The front engine takes exhaust steam from this receiver, works it in a larger set of cylinders, and then exhausts it to the atmosphere through the stack.

Q. 27.—How do you get the use of both engines when starting a train?

A.—In order that there may be steam in the low pressure cylinders before the high pressure engine has exhausted, on some types of the Mallet compound there is a live steam pipe, with a valve in the cab, which admits boiler steam to the receiver pipe. Thus the use of the front engine is secured in starting a train. In the American Locomotive articulated compounds there is an intercepting valve, similar to the one used in the Richmond cross-compound, and is placed between the exhaust passage of the rear engine and the flexible receiving pipe of the front one. When in *simple* position, this intercepting valve permits the high pressure cylinders of the rear engine to exhaust directly to the stack instead of into the receiver, feeding boiler steam at a reduced pressure into the receiver pipe for the low pressure cylinders, without giving any back pressure on the high pressure pistons. By this arrangement the power of the complete locomotive is increased twenty per cent. In compound position, the intercepting valve shuts off the supply of live steam to the receiver pipe and the exhaust steam is forced to the low pressure engine.

Q. 28.—How is the American articulated compound changed from compound to simple, and back to compound again?

A.—When working the locomotive simple, the handle of the operating valve in the cab should be placed to point toward the rear. Steam is admitted against the piston which operates the emergency exhaust valve and opens it. Exhaust steam from the high pressure engine, instead of passing to the low pressure engine, passes to the exhaust nozzle. The intercepting valve then moves over so that live steam reduced to forty per cent boiler pressure passes through the receiver pipe to the low pressure engine. When working the locomotive compound, the handle of the operating valve should be placed to point forward. This exhausts the steam, holding the emergency exhaust valve open; by means of a spring and the pressure of the steam exhausted from the rear engine, the emergency exhaust valve is closed, and a pressure built up against the intercepting valve, which opens it, so that steam from the rear engine goes to the forward one, and at the same movement closes the reducing valve so that the receiver gets no more live steam.

Q. 29.—When is it necessary to use the operating valve to change the locomotive from compound to simple, or from simple to compound?

A.—The intercepting valve should automatically go to simple position until exhaust steam from the rear engine builds up a receiver pressure that shifts the valve to compound, when giving the engines steam to start. Use the operating valve if it does not do so. The engine should be set working simple, when about to stall on a grade or if moving less than four miles an hour; when the danger of stalling is over, or speed is more than four miles an hour, change to compound. Open the starting valve to admit live steam to the receiver pipe and low pressure engine if there is no intercepting valve to furnish live steam to the forward engine.

Q. 30.—If in starting the locomotive the forward engine does not take steam, what is the trouble?

A.—On account of being dirty the reducing valve may be stuck shut or stuck on the stem of the intercepting valve. Should the reducing valve be stuck, take off the head of the dashpot and work the valve back and forth to loosen it. Oil the intercepting valve freely just before starting and occasionally during long runs to keep it from sticking.

Q. 31.—Why does the Mallet compound have more power when working simple than compound?

A.—If a starting valve is used to admit live steam to the receiver pipe and thence to the low pressure engine, it gives a higher pressure to the low pressure cylinders. If an intercepting valve is used the open emergency exhaust valve permits exhaust steam from the rear engine to go direct to the stack, taking away the back pressure of the receiver steam from the high pressure pistons about 30 per cent of the boiler pressure, thus adding to the power of the rear engine. The reducing valve when feeding live steam gives about 40 per cent of boiler pressure to the low pressure engine instead of the 30 per cent it gets from the receiver. The compound operation is about 20 per cent less than the power of both engines working simple with this added power.

Q. 32.—What is the duty of the by-pass valves on the sides of the low pressure cylinders? Should they be kept clean of gum and grit?

A.—They are connected to the steam ports at each end of the cylinders and open to allow air and steam to pass from one end to the other of the cylinder away from the moving piston when the engine is drifting. If not kept clean they may stick open, when working steam the engine will blow badly, and if they stick shut will cause the engine to pound when drifting.

Q. 33.—In what position should the reverse lever be when the steam is shut off and the engine drifting?

A.—Below three quarters of full gear, in order that the valves will have nearly full travel.

Q. 34.—Why should the power reversing gear of the Mallet compound always have its dashpot cylinder full of oil?

A.—To avoid the too rapid movement of the reverse gear piston and prevent damaging it.

Q. 35.—In what position should the engines stand to test for blows in valves and piston packing?

A.—The operating or starting valve should be in simple position. "Spot" the engine in the proper position and each engine should be tested for blows the same as for a simple engine.

Q. 36.—What power is used with Ragonnet or Baldwin power reverse gear?

A.—Air pressure.

Q. 37.—Can and should steam pressure be used?

A.—It can, but steam should never be used except in an emergency when air is not available.

Q. 38.—What precaution should be taken regarding steam check and throttle?

A.—They should be tight and check working properly to prevent the steam from entering main reservoir. Should this occur the steam would burn out the gaskets in the air brake equipment; moisture would accumulate which would result in freezing and bursting the equipment, besides being dangerous.

Q. 39.—What would cause the gear to fail to hold links in intended cut-off, and allow them to raise and lower without operating valve in the cab being changed?

A.—This would be caused by leaks in main valve and piston packing.

LUBRICATION.

Q. 1.—What produces friction, and what is the result of excessive friction?

A.—Friction, as considered in locomotive service, is the rubbing together of any two surfaces, when held in contact by pressure. The result is heat, and the destruction of the journal and its bearing, or the roughening of the sliding surfaces.

Q. 2.—What is lubrication and its object?

A.—The interposing of a thin layer of lubricant so that the surfaces do not actually touch each other, the oily surface of one part sliding with less heat against the oily surface of the other.

Q. 3.—What examinations should be made by the engineer to insure successful lubrication?

A.—Examine so as to know that the oil holes are open, cups filled and in proper working order, that packing in cellars is put in evenly and in contact with the journal. Also see that grease cups are filled, and that grease cellars contain enough grease for the next trip. The waste on top of driving or truck boxes should also be in proper shape.

Q. 4.—How should feeders of all oil cups be adjusted?

A.—They should be adjusted according to the work, oil should be fed regularly to give perfect lubrication, and as small a quantity as possible for perfect lubrication used.

Q. 5.—Why is it bad practice to keep engine oil close to boiler in warm weather?

A.—It gets too hot and will flow off the bearings too rapidly, a hot bearing very often being the result.

Q. 6.—In what manner would you care for a hot bearing if discovered on the road?

A.—Take as much time as possible in cooling the bearing, carefully lubricate all moving parts and be sure that they move freely before proceeding.

Q. 7.—What kind of oil should be used on hot bearings?

A.—If too hot to stand engine oil use valve oil while bearing is warm enough to make it flow. To avoid reheating, the valve oil must be removed as soon as the bearing cools.

Q. 8.—At completion of trip what is necessary?

A.—Shut off the lubricator and all bottom feed oil cups, feel of all bearings and pins and report any that are running hot.

Q. 9.—How would you determine what boxes to report examined? Why not report all boxes examined?

A.—Placing the hand on driving box, on hub of engine truck wheel and on top of tender truck boxes nearest the brass, shows which are too hot. Unless the temperature was above running heat would not report them examined.

Q. 10.—Why is it bad practice to disturb the packing on top of driving and engine truck boxes with spout of oil can when oiling engine?

A.—It stirs up the dirt, cinders and sand and is liable to get them down on the bearings, as well as feed the oil away too quickly. This packing is placed on top of boxes to help keep the dirt and dust out of oil holes, and to aid in gradual lubrication from the top.

Q. 11.—How do you adjust grease cups as applied to rods?

A.—By screwing down the compression plug until a slight resistance from the grease is felt. When grease shows between brass and pin, then stop. This should be sufficient over the division.

Q. 12.—Is it usual for pins to run warm when using grease?

A.—Yes. The grease must melt and become practically an oil in order to lubricate freely.

Q. 13.—What effect does too much pressure produce?

A.—It wastes the grease and increases the friction until the surplus amount is worked out so that the bearing can run free on its journal.

Q. 14.—Is it necessary to use oil with grease on crank pins?

A.—No.

Q. 15.—When an engine is equipped with Elvin driving box lubricator, how can you tell whether a sufficient amount of lubricant is in the grease receptacle?

A.—By the indicator wire fastened to the bottom of the grease cellar, which shows the amount of grease left in the cellar.

Q. 16.—Why should engine oil not be used on valves and cylinders?

A.—Because it will vaporize and become like a gas which has no lubricating qualities at such a high temperature as that of the steam.

Q. 17.—At what temperature does engine oil lose its lubricating qualities? At what temperature for valve oil?

A.—Either oil loses its lubricating qualities before reaching its flash point. The flash point of engine oil is from 250 to 350 degrees F., that of valve oil from 500 to 600 degrees F., depending on the quality of the oil. Steam at 120 pounds has a temperature of about 350 degrees F., which is above the flash test of engine oil; steam at 235 pounds has a temperature of about 431 degrees F., which is much below the flash test of valve oil. Where superheated steam is used and the temperature is 600 degrees F. and more, a higher grade of valve oil with a higher flash test is required.

Q. 18.—How and by what means are valves, cylinders and the steam end of air pumps lubricated?

A.—By hydro-static lubricator with sight feed.

Q. 19.—What is the principle on which a lubricator operates? How does the oil get from the cup to the steam chest?

A.—Steam being admitted to the condenser condenses, and the water of condensation flows through the water pipe, when the water valve is open, to the bottom of the reservoir; the oil being lighter than the water remains on top and at such a height that it can flow downward through the oil tubes to the regulating feed valves; when the feed valves are open, the oil passes out of the feed nozzles in the form of drops, flowing upward through the sight feed glasses, where it is met by a small current of steam from the condenser, through the equalizing pipes, which forces the oil through the choke plugs into the oil pipes and thence into the steam chests.

Q. 20.—How should the lubricator be filled?

A.—Close all valves connected with the lubricator, remove filling plug, open the drain cock and draw off the water only. Then close drain plug. Fill the oil tank in the regular way, taking care not to overflow it; replace filling plug. If there is not enough oil to fill the lubricator water may be used, as the lubricator will begin feeding sooner when full.

Q. 21.—After filling lubricator, what should be done?

A.—Open wide the steam throttle to the lubricator, then carefully open water valves. Open feeds as required but not until sure the chamber in the glasses is filled with water.

Q. 22.—How long before leaving terminal should the feed valves be opened? Why?

A.—About fifteen minutes. This should be sufficient time to allow oil to feed through the oil pipe to the steam chests.

Q. 23.—How many drops should be fed per minute?

A.—From one to seven drops per minute for cylinders, depending upon conditions, timed by the watch. Large cylinders require more oil than smaller ones. About one drop per minute should be fed to the air pump.

Q. 24.—If lubricator feeds regularly when working steam and too rapidly after shutting off, what is the trouble?

A.—This is due to too large an opening in the choke plug at the lubricator or through the steam valves at the steam chest. Reduce to proper size by applying new chokes or valves.

Q. 25.—When valves appear dry while using steam and the lubricator is working all right, what would you do to relieve these conditions?

A.—Ease off on the throttle a few seconds to reduce steam chest pressure and drop the reverse lever a few notches, giving the valve a longer travel. Oil held in the pipes will then flow down.

GENERAL QUESTIONS AND ANSWERS ON ELECTRIC HEADLIGHTS.

Q. 1.—Describe the passage of the current through the lamp and tell how arc light is formed.

A.—The current flowing from the dynamo is called the positive current and enters the lamp at the binding post; thence through a No. 8 insulated copper wire to the bracket; thence through connections to carbon; then down through the copper electrode and holder to a No. 8 insulated copper wire, through the solenoid; then to the binding post and back to the dynamo.

As soon as current passes through the solenoid, it attracts the armature which in turn is connected with the levers which clutch the carbon and separate it from the point of the copper electrode. The current jumping this space, from the carbon to the electrode, creates the light, the distance between the points being regulated by current flowing through the solenoid. A solenoid is a coil of wires and when energized by a current flowing through them, acts as a magnet.

Q. 2.—Why should sandpaper be used to smooth commutator instead of emery cloth?

A.—Sand under these conditions is a non-conductor while emery is a conductor of the electric current, and should a piece of the emery lodge between the bars of the commutator, it would result in a short circuit. Emery will embed in the copper and cut the brushes, while sand will not do so.

Q. 3.—State how you would go about to focus a lamp?

A.—(1) Adjust back of reflector so front edge will be parallel with front edge of case.

(2) Adjust lamp to have point of copper as near center of reflector as possible.

(3) Have carbon as near center of chimney hole in reflector as possible.

(4) Have locomotives on straight track and move lamp until you get best results on track. The light should be reflected in parallel rays and in as small a space as possible.

To lower light on track, raise lamp.

To raise light on track, lower lamp.

Q. 4.—If the light throws shadows upon the track, is it properly focused?

A.—No.

Q. 5.—If the light is properly focused, that is, if the rays are leaving the reflector in parallel lines, but the light does not strike the center of the track, what should be done?

A.—Shift entire case on baseboard.

Q. 6.—What can you do to insure a good and unfailing light for the entire trip?

A.—The entire equipment should be carefully inspected before starting on each trip to know that there are no wires with insulation chafed or worn off; see that all screws and connections are tight; that commutator is clean, and brushes set in holder in the correct way. Carbon of sufficient length to complete the trip should be in the lamp, the copper electrode cleaned and oil in both bearings.

Q. 7.—Why would you not fill the main oil cellar full of oil?

A.—It will be thrown out of the ends of the cellar by the motion of the engine and might ruin the armature.

Q. 8.—What is the most vital part of the dynamo?

A.—The commutator.

Q. 9.—What care and attention should be given the commutator?

A.—The brushes should be examined as to bearing, surface and tension, the mica between the copper strips should always be a trifle below the surface, and the commutator clean.

Q. 10.—How should you clean the commutator, and when?

A.—The commutator should be cleaned each trip with a piece of damp waste not wet, rubbing endwise so as to keep the creases clean where mica is filed out. Wipe dry.

Q. 11.—What kind of a bearing should the brush have on the commutator?

A.—They should fit perfectly on the commutator; with bearings covering no less than two, nor more than three of the commutator bars.

Q. 12.—How are the brushes fitted?

A.—Take a piece of fine O sandpaper and introduce between the brush and commutator and draw in the direction of the rotation of commutator until the brush fits perfectly. Do not saw sandpaper back and forth; pull it in one direction only.

Q. 13.—Is it advisable to ever try to fit a brush up with a file or knife?

A.—It is not.

Q. 14.—Why is it important to clean the scale off the point of the copper electrode each trip?

A.—The current will not pass through this scale, and to allow the point of the carbon and the electrode to touch to form a circuit, it must be removed.

Q. 15.—How should the copper electrode be trimmed at the point?

A.—Should be trimmed with a piece of emery cloth to a rounding point having about ¼ inch surface.

Q. 16.—How far should the copper electrode project above the holder?

A.—One inch.

Q. 17.—Should the electrode be raised up to 1½ inches, what might happen?

A.—So much heat would be generated on the clutch that it would result in a lamp failure.

Q. 18.—If the dashpot should be found stuck, would you put oil in it?

A.—Cut the dirt from out of the pot and off the plunger with coal oil, wiping off all oil after cleaning as it would cause the plunger to collect dirt and stick.

Q. 19.—If one carbon of lamp should "jig or pound," what can be done to stop it?

A.—This is caused by the iron armature being too far out of the solenoid, or speed too slow.

Q. 20.—Does the pounding of the lamp occur with the old series wound machines or with the new compound wound machines?

A.—Occurs more with the old series wound as the compound winding gives a steadier voltage.

Q. 21.—If the copper electrode were fusing, how would you know it?

A.—The rapid burning of the copper would change the color of the light to green, instead of a shaft of white light.

Q. 22.—What should be done when a green light is seen?

A.—Steam should be throttled at once, then opened slowly until a white light reappears.

Q. 23.—What is the cause of the copper electrode fusing?

A.—May be caused by speed of dynamo being too high or by the wires from dynamo to lamp being connected up wrong so that the positive current enters the copper electrode instead of the top carbon.

Q. 24.—What arrangements have been made so that you can not connect your wires wrong?

A.—The positive binding post both at the dynamo and lamp have been provided with a much larger hole to receive the wire than has been made in the negative binding post. The ends of the positive wire should always be bent or doubled back so they will just enter the receptacle in the positive binding posts, but can not be connected to the negative binding post.

Q. 25.—Should the copper electrode and holder become fused until no longer serviceable out on the road, what would you do?

A.—Remove the damaged holder from the lamp. Fasten a bolt or carbon in the bracket of the lamp with the end in the center of reflector and not touching the base of reflector or lamp.

AIR BRAKE QUESTIONS AND ANSWERS—THIRD YEAR*

AIR PUMP

Q. 1.—Explain how an air pump should be started and run on the road.

A.—It should be started slowly to permit the condensation to be drained off. The lubricator should be started carefully, and the pump worked slowly until about 40 pounds have been accumulated in the main reservoir to cushion the steam and air piston of the pump. Then the throttle should be opened wider, giving a speed of about 130 or 140 single strokes per minute. The amount of work being done really governs the speed of the pump.

Q. 2.—How should the steam end of the pump be oiled?

A.—By the sight feed lubricator, with a good quality of valve oil, and at the rate of about one drop per minute. This amount will vary with the condition of the pump and the work being done.

---

*See questions and answers on "ET" No. 6. Equipment

Q. 3.—How should air end of a pump be oiled, and what lubricant should be used?

A.—High grade valve oil, containing good lubricating qualities and no sediment should be used. A good swab on the piston rod will help out a great deal. Oil should be used in the air cylinder of the pump sparingly but continuously, and it should be introduced on the down stroke, when pump is running slowly, through the little cup provided for the purpose, and not through the air suction valves. An automatic oil cup, such as has recently come into practice, is preferable to hand oiling.

Q. 4.—When first admitting steam to the 9½-inch pump, in what direction does the main valve move?

A.—If the main piston is at the bottom of the cylinder, as it usually is after steam has been shut off and gravity controls it, the main valve will move to the position to the right.

Q. 5.—With the main valve to the right, which end of the cylinder will receive steam?

A.—The bottom, or lower end.

Q. 6.—When the main piston completes its up stroke, explain how its motion is reversed so as to make the downward stroke.

A.—When the main piston reaches and is nearly at the top of its stroke, the reversing plate catches the shoulder on the reversing valve rod, moving the reversing rod and valve to their upper positions, where steam is admitted behind the large head of the main valve, forcing this main valve over to the left, carrying with it the slide valve which admits steam to the top end of the cylinder and exhausts it from the bottom end, thereby reversing the stroke of the pump.

Q. 7.—Explain the operation of the air end of the 9½-inch air pump on an up stroke and on a down stroke.

A.—The air piston is directly connected with the steam piston, and any movement of the steam piston will consequently be transmitted directly to the air piston. When the steam piston moves up, the air piston will, of course, go with it, thus leaving an empty space or a vacuum in the lower end of the air cylinder, underneath the air piston. Atmospheric air rushes through the air inlet, raising the lower receiving valve, and filling the bottom end of the cylinder with atmospheric pressure. At the same time the air above the air piston will be compressed. The pressure thus formed holds the upper receiving valve to its seat, and when a little greater than the air in the main reservoir, the upper discharge valve will lift and allow the compressed air to flow into the main reservoir. When the piston reaches the top of the stroke its motion is reversed, and on the down stroke the vacuum in the upper end of the air cylinder is supplied by atmospheric pressure passing through the upper receiving valve. The main reservoir pressure is held by the upper discharge valve, and the air being compressed in the bottom of the cylinder holds the bottom receiving valve to its seat, and when compressed sufficiently, forces the lower discharge valve open and passes to the reservoir.

Q. 8.—Give some of the causes of the pump running hot.

A.—First, air cylinder packing rings leaking. Second, discharge valves stuck closed or the discharge passages so obstructed that the pump is working against high air pressure continually. Third, poor lubrication. Fourth, high speed. Fifth, discharge or receiving air valves leaking. Sixth, air piston rod packing leaking.

Q. 9.—If the pump runs hot while on the road, how would you proceed to cool it?

A.—First, reduce the speed of the pump, and look for leaks in the train line. Second, make sure that the packing around the piston rod is not too tight or in bad condition. Third, see that the main reservoir is properly drained. If the pump still runs hot it should be reported at the end of the trip.

Q. 10.—If the pump stops, can you tell if the trouble is in the pump or in the governor?

A.—Yes. It may be tested by opening the drain cock in the steam passage at the pump, and noting whether there is a free flow of steam; if so, there is a free passage through the governor and the trouble is not there.

Q. 11.—State the common causes for the pump stopping.

A.—There are several reasons. First, it may be stopped by the governor being out of order. Second, the valves may be dry and need lubrication. Third, nuts may be loose or broken on the piston rod or one of the pistons pulled off. Fourth, the reversing valve rod may be broken or bent, or the reversing plate may be loose, or the shoulder on the reversing valve rod or the reversing plate may be so badly worn as not to catch and perform their proper functions. Fifth, nuts holding the main valve piston may be loose or broken off. Sixth, excessive blow past the packing rings of the main valve.

Q. 12.—Should a pump make a much quicker down stroke than up, what effect does it indicate?

A.—An upper discharge air valve leaking, a lower receiving air valve stuck to its seat or broken.

Q. 13.—Should it make a much quicker up stroke, what defect does it indicate?

A.—The lower discharge valve leaking badly, or the upper receiving valve is probably broken, or stuck to its seat.

Q. 14.—Should an engineman observe the workings of a pump on the road, and report repairs needed, and do you consider yourself competent?

A.—Yes.

PUMP GOVERNOR.

Q. 1.—What is the duty of the pump governor?

A.—To properly regulate the air pressure in the main reservoir.

Q. 2.—Explain how the governor operates?

A.—The governor is an automatic arrangement for admitting and closing off steam to the air pump, and is actuated by air pressure. The steam valve, which shuts off and opens up the steam passageway to the pump, is controlled by an air piston and spring. When air pressure is admitted above the piston, it forces the piston down, closing off the steam to the pump. When the air pressure is exhausted from above the piston, the spring forces the piston up and allows steam pressure to pass to the pump. The admission and exhaust of the air to this piston is controlled by a diaphragm and spring. The air from the main reservoir enters the body of the governor underneath the diaphragm, which is held by a spring of given tension, depending on the pressure desired in the main reservoir. While the main reservoir pressure is less than the pressure the governor is set for, this diaphragm is held down by the spring, and the air can pass no farther than a small pin valve attached to it, but when the main reservoir pressure overcomes the tension of the spring, it raises the diaphragm, unseats the pin valve, and allows the air to flow to the top of the air piston, shutting off the pump. During the time the air is acting on this piston, some of it escapes through a leakage port or vent hole, which is always open. When the main reservoir pressure drops below that to which the spring is adjusted, the spring forces the diaphragm down, seating the pin valve and allowing the air on top of the piston to escape to the atmosphere through the small vent port.

Q. 3.—By what air pressure is the governor operated when using the D-8 brake valve? When using the G-6 valve? When using the New York brake valve?

A.—With the D-8 valve, by train line pressure. With the F-6 or G-6 valve, by the main reservoir pressure. New York, by the train line.

Q. 4.—By what pressure is the duplex governor operated in high speed service? By what pressure in ordinary service?

A.—The governor tops are adjusted for 90 and 110 pounds, and the two feed valves are set for 70 and 90 pounds. To operate the low, or ordinary, pressure feature, the handle of the reversing cock is turned to the left; this cuts out the 110-pound governor and 90-pound feed valve and renders operative the 90-pound governor and 70-pound feed valve. By reversing the position of the reversing cock handle, the low pressure parts are cut out and the high pressure parts cut in; but the small stop cock in the governor pipe must also be closed.

Q. 5.—What is the object of the relief port in the governor? Why should it be kept open?

A.—If this port is not kept open, the air pressure which holds the piston down can not escape when the diaphragm valve closes, and, consequently, the governor will not operate the pump properly.

Q. 6.—If the pin valve leaks, what effect will it have on the pump?

A.—It will allow a certain amount of air pressure to flow in on top of the air piston. If the leak is greater than the escape from the little leakage port, the under pressure will accumulate and cause the governor to slow down or completely stop the pump.

Q. 7.—How can you detect leaks in the governor?

A.—By disconnecting the upper from the lower section of the governor, then attaching the air pressure connection, turn the air pressure under the diaphragm. If it rises with the proper pressure and opens the port, the escape of air will be readily noticed. Should it not be raised, or the port be closed by dirt, it would be in that section; this will also show if the diaphragm leaks. I would then inspect the lower section.

Q. 8.—Where would you look for the cause if the governor allowed the pump to raise the pressure too high?

A.—The main reservoir pressure may not reach the governor, due to the stoppage in the pipe or in the union at the governor. This may also be due to the space on top of the diaphragm being filled with dirt. If the air is getting to the diaphragm valve, and is so indicated by the blow at the leakage port, the trouble must then be due to the drip pipe being stopped up or frozen, thereby preventing the air and steam, which leak in under the air piston, from escaping.

Q. 9.—Where, if the air pump stopped when the pressure was too low?

A.—If the pump were not getting steam it would probably be due to the pin valve being gummed up or dirt under it; the detector hole or leakage port in the side of the governor would then blow. Once in a great while the piston and steam valve have been known to stick closed, but very rarely.

ENGINEERS' BRAKE AND EQUALIZING DISCHARGE VALVE.

Q. 1.—Name the different positions of the brake valve and trace the flow of air through it in each position.

A.—Full release, running position, lap, service application, and emergency application. In full release there is a large direct communication between the main reservoir and the train pipe. In running position the air passes from the main reservoir indirectly to the train pipe, that is, through the ports and passages of the excess pressure valve or through the feed valve, as the case may be. In lap position all ports are closed. In service application, first the air from the equalizing discharge reservoir and cavity "D" escapes to the atmosphere, then, when the equalizing discharge piston rises, the air from the train pipe escapes to the atmosphere through the train line exhaust elbow. In emergency position a large direct opening is made between the train pipe and the atmosphere.

Q. 2—Where does the main reservoir pressure begin and end? Where does the train pipe pressure begin and end?

A.—The main reservoir pressure begins at the pump discharge pipe and ends at the connection to the brake valve. The train pipe pressure begins at the brake valve and extends to the rear cock on the train, with branches to the triple valve under each car, the tender, and the engine.

Q. 3.—Explain the effect of a cut rotary valve or seat.

A.—A leaky rotary valve or seat usually causes a loss of excess pressure in running position and releases the brakes in lap position.

Q. 4.—With the handle of the brake valve in either running or holding position, what defect will cause the black hand to equalize with the red hand?

A.—A leaky rotary valve, a lower body gasket, feed valve, or feed valve gasket.

Q. 5.—How do you regulate the excess pressure with each form of brake valve? How do you clean the valves?

A.—With the 1889 (D-8) brake valve, by the excess pressure spring; with the later forms of brake valves, by the spring in the feed valve attachment. Clean the valves and their seats by waste or friction from a soft piece of wood—never oil them when replacing.

Q. 6.—How do you apply and release the automatic brake?

A.—The automatic brake is applied by reducing the train pipe pressure below that in the auxiliary; it is released by increasing the train pipe pressure above that in the auxiliary. The brake valve is the valve to properly perform these functions, when everything is in working order.

Q. 7.—How can you tell which defect caused the hands to equalize?

A.—Reduce the brake pipe pressure below the adjustment of the feed valve, close the cut-out cock under the brake valve. If there is a leak at the service exhaust port, the rotary valve will be leaking. If there be no discharge, and the black hand rise, the body gasket is at fault. If the black hand remains stationary, the trouble will be found in the feed valve or its case gasket.

Q. 8.—What is the purpose of the equalizing reservoir, and what effect would a leak from this reservoir have?

A.—The purpose of the equalizing reservoir is to supply a larger volume of air above the equalizing piston, to enable the engineer to make a graduated reduction of the pressure above the piston. Leakage from this reservoir would be liable to cause the brakes to set when the brake valve is in lap position.

Q. 9.—If the pipe connecting the brake valve to the equalizing reservoir should break, what should be done?

A.—The pipe at the brake valve should be plugged, also the service exhaust port. Wishing to make a service application, move the handle carefully towards emergency position until the desired reduction is made, and then move back to lap very carefully.

Q. 10.—What can be learned by noticing the discharge of air from the train pipe exhaust?

A.—The length of the train line, that is, approximately the number of cars of air. By watching this exhaust it can also be determined if, in testing brakes, one defective triple sets quick action; third, in releasing brakes it can be told if you only have the lone engine.

Q. 11.—What is the duty of the small reservoir connected to the brake valve? If the pipe leading to this reservoir is leaking badly or broken off, what will you do?

A.—It is for the purpose of enlarging chamber "D" without making a great, bulky brake valve in the cab. Plug up this pipe or put in a blind gasket, also plug the train line exhaust nipple and use emergency position carefully, as with the old three-way cock.

Q. 12.—Where is the first air taken from in making a service stop? Where does it blow out? Where next?

A.—From chamber "D" and the equalizing reservoir. It blows out of the preliminary exhaust. Next, the train pipe pressure escapes from the train line exhaust nipple.

Q. 13.—Does air ever blow out of the train pipe exhaust when releasing the brake? Why?

A.—Yes, with a lone engine or very short train, in which case the train line charges more rapidly than chamber "D" and the equalizing reservoir, thus causing piston 17 to rise.

Q. 14.—What pressures do the red hand and black hand of the gauge indicate?

A.—Red hand—main reservoir; black hand—chamber "D" pressure.

Q. 15.—Does the black hand of the gauge also show the train pipe pressure at all times?

A.—No, only when chamber "D" and the train line are connected, as in full release and running position. On lap or in service positions, at the instant the train line exhaust starts or stops, they are also practically equal.

Q. 16.—What will be the result of leaving the handle of the brake valve in full release position too long, and then moving to running position?

A.—Brakes are likely to drag, due to temporarily shutting off all supply of air, to overcome the leaks.

Q. 17.—Following a straight air application, if the brake fails to release with the straight air valve in release position, where would you look for the trouble and what may be done to release the brake?

A.—This would indicate that the double-throw clutch valve was leaking and that the feed valve wanted cleaning. To release the brake, move the automatic brake valve to release and quickly return to running position.

Q. 18.—How is the train pipe pressure regulated with each type of brake valve?

A.—By the governor with the 1889 (D-8) brake valve; by the feed valve attachment with all later types of brake valves.

Q. 19.—In making a service application, what should the first reduction be?

A.—From 5 to 8 pounds, depending upon the length of the train.

Q. 20.—What reduction from 70 pounds train pipe pressure will fully apply the brake? Why?

A.—About 20 pounds; because that amount from the auxiliary reservoirs will equalize with the pressure in the brake cylinders at about 50 pounds.

THE TRIPLE VALVE.

Q. 1.—What is the duty of the triple valve?

A.—The duty of the triple valve is, first, to charge the auxiliary reservoir; second, to set the brakes by allowing auxiliary pressure to flow to the brake cylinder, and, third, to release the brakes by allowing the pressure in the cylinder to escape to the atmosphere.

Q. 2.—Why is the word "triple" used to designate this valve?

A.—Because it performs the three functions mentioned.

Q. 2 (a).—By what is it connected to the brake valve?

A.—By the branch pipe and the train line with hose.

Q. 3.—Explain the duty of the triple piston, the slide valve, and the graduating valve.

A.—The duty of the triple valve piston is, by variation of pressures on its two sides, to move the slide valve on its seat to the application, graduating, and release position, and to open and close the feed groove in the piston bushing. The function of the slide valve is, by its movement due to the triple valve piston, to make connection between the auxiliary reservoir and brake cylinder, applying the brake, and to make connections between the brake cylinder and the atmosphere, releasing the brake. The function of the graduating valve is, from its movement given by the triple piston, to admit pressure gradually from the auxiliary reservoir to the brake cylinder in response to reductions made in the train pipe pressure.

Q. 4.—How many kinds of triple valves are in use?

A.—Two, the plain type and the quick action type, or according to the fact.

Q. 5.—Describe how each kind operates.

A.—With the quick action type, a sudden reduction of pressure in the train pipe will cause the triple piston and its parts to be moved to quick action application position, which first throws into operation the emergency feature of the triple, admitting train line pressure to the brake cylinder, after which auxiliary reservoir pressure is permitted to pass to the brake cylinder, and consequently a higher pressure is obtained than in a full service application of the brake. With the plain type, any sudden reduction merely moves the parts to their extreme position, but allows no other than auxiliary reservoir pressure to flow to the brake cylinder.

Q. 6.—Explain where the air comes from that enters the brake cylinder in a service application. In an emergency application. With each kind of triple valve.

A.—In service application with either type of triple valve the air that enters the brake cylinder comes from the auxiliary reservoir; with the quick action triple only does part of the train pipe air first enter the brake cylinder quickly, later followed by the auxiliary pressure.

Q. 7.—How do you cut out a triple valve so its brake will not operate?

A.—The old style plain triple, by turning the handle down obliquely to about 45 degrees. With the later style and all quick action triples, by closing the stop cock in the branch pipe. Then bleed the auxiliary reservoir.

Q. 8.—If a triple valve does not apply the brake at the proper time, where will you look for the trouble?

A.—If the auxiliary is charged, the triple valve is probably frozen or stuck or the packing ring worn badly, or the brake cylinder itself leaking badly. If the auxiliary has not charged, the feed groove may be closed or the reservoir itself be leaking badly.

Q. 9.—If the brake will not release, where will you look for the trouble?

A.—Retainer turned up or its pipe stopped up; triple piston packing ring worn; triple strainer stopped up or triple frozen.

Q. 10.—Name the common defects of the triple valve and explain how you locate them.

A.—Triple valve frozen or stuck, packing ring leaking, etc., located as above. Emergency gasket leaking—cut the car out underneath and the brake will set quick action. Slide valve dirty or leaking—blows through the exhaust or retainer but will not cause emergency as last stated. Brake fails to release on long train—usually the piston packing ring or cylinder bushing worn badly.

NEW YORK AIR BRAKE—THE DUPLEX AIR PUMP.

Q. 1.—Describe the New York Duplex Air Pump and its operation in the steam end.

A.—It has four cylinders—two steam and two air; one air cylinder is double the area of any one of the other three, which are all the same size. The steam end is duplex, and the piston in each steam cylinder operates the slide valve which controls the flow of steam from the boiler into the opposite steam cylinder and out to the atmosphere. This is done by locating the slide valve for the right cylinder under the left cylinder, and for the left cylinder under the right one, and cross the steam ports from the left valve to the right cylinder and from the right valve to the left cylinder. The valves are D slide valves which admit steam to the cylinder by the outside edge of the valve and exhaust through a cavity in the center. The seat has three ports, two steam with the exhaust port between them. A reversing valve rod is attached to the steam valve and extends into the steam cylinder; the main piston rod is drilled to clear this valve rod within it and a plate is bolted on to the steam piston in such a manner as to strike a shoulder on the valve rod just before the stroke of the piston in either direction is completed, changing the steam valve to its opposite position in the steam chest. Both steam valves being down, when steam is turned on, the right piston makes a stroke up and at the completion of the stroke changes its steam valve, causing the left piston to make a stroke up, changing its steam valve at the completion of the stroke, and causing the right piston to move down, etc. The steam cylinders are the two bottom cylinders.

Q. 2.—Describe the operation of the air end.

A.—The large piston compresses air into the smaller cylinder and then the latter compresses it into the main reservoir.

Q. 3.—Is this a compound pump in both steam and air ends, or in the air end only?

A.—Only in the air end.

Q. 4.—What defects in the steam end will stop the pump? How do you locate them?

A.—Chiefly the reversing apparatus—the reversing plates and rods. Would investigate until the trouble was found, bearing in mind the main valve for one cylinder regulates the steam in the other.

Q. 5.—What defects in the air end will stop the pump? How do you locate them?

A.—Generally broken piston rods or loose nuts. Broken or defective valves cause the pump to go "lame" but seldom stop the pump unless broken parts get into the cylinder. Remove the top heads to get at the air cylinders and examine the valves through their caps.

Q. 6.—Explain how you will locate a blow of steam by the piston or main steam valves.

A.—It is difficult to distinguish between leaky packing rings, leaky slide valves and worn cylinder. These parts should be removed and examined carefully when there is a bad blow.

Q. 7.—What is the cause of the pump not exhausting square or working lame?

A.—Any one or more of the air valves stuck or broken or if they have much different "lift."

Q. 8.—What is the effect of leaky piston rod packing in the high pressure air cylinder?

A.—Any defective or leakage in the smaller or high pressure cylinder is more serious than in the low pressure cylinder because the pressure in the former is so much higher that the consequent loss is greater. This loss of compressed air to the atmosphere will cause the pump to run faster in order to maintain the same pressure.

Q. 9.—What is the effect of leaky piston rod packing in the steam cylinders?

A.—A waste of steam, obstructing the vision in the winter and causes the piston rods to cut and groove.

Q. 10.—Explain how you would locate a defective air valve.

A.—The general rule is this: The piston jumps toward a leaky or broken receiving valve and away from a broken or leaky discharge valve; also in the latter case the pump heats up more, as the compressed air is "churned," that is, pumped over and over again. Air blowing out of the low pressure receiving valves is readily detected.

Q. 11.—How should the air cylinders be oiled? The steam cylinders?

A.—In the air cylinders use good valve oil very sparingly. Always keep good, well oiled swabs on the piston rods, as it has been proven by many careful engineers that with these practically no oil need be put into the air cylinders. Valve oil in the steam cylinders and lubrication started directly after the pump has started. Remember the first steam admitted to a cold pump condenses and washes the surfaces clean of oil; hence oil should be supplied immediately thereafter.

Q. 12.—Which air cylinder requires the most oil?

A.—The smaller or high pressure cylinder, on account of the higher temperature.

Q. 13.—Explain the operation of the automatic oil cup used on the air cylinders.

A.—With the oil cup filled, the pump working and the stroke of the piston upward, air is forced up through a small passage in the center of the oil cup body and cap, down inside the extended cap nut sleeve, through the oil and forms a pressure thereon. When the piston is on its downward stroke, and there is a partial vacuum in the air cylinder, the air pressure formed on top of the oil in this cup forces the oil up inside the sleeve of the cap nut to the feed port and a small quantity of oil is then taken down through this port and sprayed into the air cylinders on each down stroke.

"LT" EQUIPMENT.

Q. 1.—What are the duties of the automatic control valve?

A.—The automatic control valve is designed to admit and exhaust air to and from all the brake cylinders on the locomotive and tender during an automatic application of the brakes, and to automatically maintain the desired brake cylinder pressure regardless of piston travel or leakage from the brake cylinders or their connections.

Q. 2.—Where would you look for the trouble if the locomotive brakes fail to apply or leak off after a service application is made?

A.—A leak in the control reservoir pipe or its connections or in the control cylinder cap gasket will cause this trouble, or the spring in the straight air brake valve may be weak or broken, permitting the handle of the valve to remain in the automatic release position.

Q. 3.—What should be done if the brake cylinder pipe breaks between the double chamber reservoir and the double check valves?

A.—Close the cut-out cock in the main reservoir supply pipe. If this occurs while train is in motion and brake applied, the loss of main reservoir pressure can be prevented by moving the handle of the straight air brake valve to the automatic release position.

Q. 4.—What should be done if the control valve release pipe breaks?

A.—If this pipe breaks, the holding feature would be lost. To hold the locomotive brakes applied when releasing train brakes, use the straight air brake valve.

Q. 5.—What should be done if the brake pipe cross-over pipe breaks? If the main reservoir supply pipe breaks?

A.—Close the cut-out cock in the pipe broken. Either pipe broken means the loss of the automatic brake on the locomotive.

Q. 6.—What should be done if the control reservoir pipe breaks?

A.—The locomotive automatic brakes can not be applied if this pipe is broken, but if plugged, it can be applied and released with automatic brake valve; therefore, the pipe should be plugged.

MISCELLANEOUS.

Q. 1.—Explain the operation of the quick action triple valve.

A.—In release position the auxiliary reservoir is charged from the brake pipe past the triple piston through the feed groove. A gradual brake pipe reduction causes auxiliary reservoir pressure to move the piston, slide and graduating valves to application position, admitting air from the auxiliary reservoir to the brake cylinder; when the pressure in the auxiliary reservoir becomes a trifle lower than the brake pipe pressure, brake pipe pressure moves the piston and graduating valve to lap, thereby stopping the flow of air from the reservoir to the brake cylinder.

A sudden reduction of brake pipe pressure causes auxiliary reservoir pressure to move the piston and slide valve to their extreme travel, which admits air above the emergency piston, forcing it and the emergency valve down, which then permits brake pipe pressure to raise the check valve and pass to the brake cylinder; auxiliary reservoir air also flows to the brake cylinder until equalized. By restoring brake pipe pressure the piston and slide valve are moved to release position, exhausting the air from the brake cylinder and recharging the auxiliary reservoir.

Q. 2.—What additional features are found in the "K" triple that are not found in the older types of triples?

A.—The venting of the brake pipe air to the brake cylinder in service application; retarded release and restricted recharge.

Q. 3.—What is meant by quick service?

A.—As a result of venting the brake pipe pressure to the brake cylinder, which increases the rate of reduction under each car, the application is hastened throughout the train.

Q. 4.—What is meant by retarded release? How is it obtained, and in what part of the train?

A.—By retarded release is meant the retarding or restricting the exhaust of brake cylinder air in the release of an application of the brakes. When rise of brake pipe pressure is rapid, the triple valve is moved to retarded release position; in this position the brake cylinder pressure is exhausted through a restricted port, thereby delaying the release. Retarded release may be had on about the first thirty cars in the train.

Q. 5.—Explain the operation of the high speed reducing valve?

A.—The construction of the high speed reducing valve is such that, when the pressure in the brake cylinder exceeds 60 pounds, it will automatically make an opening from the brake cylinder to the atmosphere and allow the air to discharge until the pressure has been reduced to about 60 pounds, when it will close, holding about 60 pounds in the brake cylinder. With an emergency application it is so constructed that it will reduce the pressure from the brake cylinder to the atmosphere from 85 pounds to 60 pounds in about 27 seconds.

Q. 6.—What are the essential parts of the "PC" brake as applied to a passenger car?

A.—One service reservoir and brake cylinder, one emergency reservoir and brake cylinder, and a control valve and its divided reservoir.

Q. 7.—In making a service application with the "PC" brake, how low can the brake pipe pressure be reduced before emergency application takes place?

A.—To one-half of the original brake pipe pressure.

Q. 8.—In making a service application what brake pipe reduction is necessary to insure the "PC" brake applying?

A.—Not less than 8 pounds.

Q. 9.—When should the brakes be released after an emergency application from any cause, and when should you proceed?

A.—After train has stopped and brake pipe pressure has been restored to within 10 pounds of the normal pressure.

Q. 10.—What is meant by an application of the brakes?

A.—The first and including all subsequent reductions until the brakes are released.

Q. 11.—How many applications of the brakes should be made when making a stop with a passenger train, and why?

A.—Two, to insure greater accuracy, and to avoid sliding of wheels and disagreeable back lurch.

Q. 12.—Explain how you would make an ordinary service stop with a long freight train. What should the first reduction be, and why?

A.—I would move brake valve from running to service position, making at least 7 to 10 pounds reduction, and would endeavor to make it so as to stop train at the desired point, but when about 40 feet from the stopping point would start another reduction in order to increase the brake power on the forward end of train but not on rear end and prevent slack stretching at time of stopping. Before releasing the brakes the total brake pipe reduction should be 20 pounds.

Q. 13.—Explain how a stop at a water tank or coal chute should be made with a long freight train.

A.—Make the ordinary service stop, not trying to "spot" the locomotive, but cutting off to obtain the supply.

Q. 14.—In making a stop with a freight train, why should the brakes not be released until stop is completed?

A.—Because the head brakes will release first and slack run out before the rear brakes release, resulting in a break-in-two or damage to equipment that will later on cause this trouble.

Q. 15.—In releasing brakes on a long freight train, what should the engineman do to be sure that all brakes are released?

A.—The brake valve handle should be placed in full release position and allowed to remain there until the brake pipe pressure has been restored to within 5 pounds of the normal.

Q. 16.—If the brakes are dragging, how can they be released from the engine?

A.—By making a reduction of brake pipe pressure, then placing the valve in full release position long enough to release all brakes, and then placing the valve in running position and leaving it there. With trains of 60 or more cars when moving at a speed of 15 miles or less per hour, come to a stop.

Q. 17.—Why is it dangerous to repeatedly apply and release the brakes on grades without giving time for the auxiliaries to fully discharge?

A.—As the feed ports in the triple valve are small, it requires considerable time to recharge the auxiliary reservoir, and if the brakes are repeatedly applied and released without sufficient interval of time to recharge, and braking power would be lost.

Q. 18.—What benefits are derived from the use of the retaining valve?

A.—When operated, it will retain a certain pressure in the brake cylinder, thereby assisting in retarding the movement of trains down grades while the brake pipe and auxiliary reservoirs are being recharged, and will give a higher braking power on second application with the same reduction.

Q. 19.—What does it indicate when making a service application, if the exhaust port closes quickly and the brakes go on hard?

A.—That the brakes have applied in emergency.

Q. 20.—When the brakes apply suddenly, what should engineman do?

A.—Immediately shut off steam and lap the brake valve.

Q. 21.—In case a hose should burst while on the road, what should the engineman do to assist the trainmen in locating it?

A.—After the train has come to a full stop, the engineer should occasionally move the brake valve to full release position for an instant, then return to lap position; by so doing there will be enough air permitted into the brake pipe to cause a blow at the point where the hose is burst.

Q. 22.—When double heading, which engineman should have full control of the brakes and what should the other one do?

A.—The head engineer should have full control of the brakes. The second engineer should have the cut-out cock closed under the brake valve.

Q. 23.—As a rule, how great a reduction of brake pipe pressure is necessary to insure the brake piston being moved by the leakage groove?

A.—This varies with the length of the train, but should never be less than 5 pounds.

Q. 24.—From a 70-pound brake pipe pressure, how much of a reduction will be required to apply the brakes in full, and why?

A.—About 20 pounds, after which brake cylinder and auxiliary reservoir pressure are equalized.

Q. 25.—What effect has the piston travel on the pressure developed in the brake cylinder?

A.—The distance the piston travels determines the space to be filled by the air that is permitted to flow from the auxiliary to the cylinder, and the pressure, therefore, developed in the cylinder will be inversely proportional to the space the air fills. If the space is small, the pressure will be higher than if space is large.

Q. 26.—When should the brakes be tested?

A.—Before leaving a terminal, after angle cock has been closed for any cause, and at all designated points.

Q. 27.—How should the brake valve be handled when making a terminal test of the brakes?

A.—Make a reduction of about 10 pounds and note the length of brake pipe service exhaust, then make a further reduction of about 15 pounds and hold the brake on until signaled to release, and do not go until signaled that all brakes have been applied and released.

Q. 28.—What is meant by a running test? How and at what points on the road should it be made?

A.—Apply the brakes lightly while the train is in motion, and note the blow that comes from the brake pipe exhaust; when the efficiency of the air brakes is known, the brakes should be at once released. It should be made approaching all railroad crossings, drawbridges, and all hazardous places, and within half a mile after standing test has been made.

Q. 29.—What is the proper brake cylinder piston travel on engine and tender?

A.—On engine and tender the piston travel should be such as to permit auxiliary reservoir and brake cylinder pressure to equalize at 50 pounds from a brake pipe pressure of 70 pounds.

On cars the piston travel should be adjusted to not less than 5 inches nor more than 7 inches.

Q. 30.—How is the slack taken up on engine and tender brakes?

A.—On engine by the adjusting screw and on tender by the dead lever on each truck and by adjusting the lower connecting rod.

Q. 31.—How often should the main reservoir be drained, and why?

A.—At the end of each trip, as an accumulation of water in the main reservoir reduces its volume and is liable to cause trouble in the brake system.

Q. 32.—What is the dead engine device, and when should it be used?

A.—The dead engine device consists of a three-eighth-inch cut-out cock and combined strainer and check valve with suitable choke connections between the brake pipe and main reservoirs. It is used for the operation of locomotive brakes when the engine is being handled "dead" in the train, or the air pump is disabled.

Q. 33.—Why is it important that piston travel be kept properly adjusted?

A.—To insure a prompt application or release of the locomotive brake, economy in the use of air, and also to provide proper braking power.

Q. 34.—What danger would there be from a leak of main reservoir air to the brake pipe, brakes applied, lap position?

A.—The brakes would release.

Q. 35.—Do you think it good practice to reverse the engine while the driver brake is applied, and why?

A.—No, on account of wheels sliding and reducing braking power.

Handling of Freight Trains

The secret of successful train handling is in knowing how to control the slack action; that is, in knowing how to prevent its running in or out quickly; and while this is at times difficult to do, yet by careful study of each train as we find it, it is possible to reduce to a minimum the pulling of drawbars. Time is a factor which enters largely into the successful control of the slack; slack can not be changed quickly without doing damage to the draft gear and the contents of the cars. It is therefore well to remember that when handling long trains, to give sufficient time for the gradual bunching or stretching of the slack, remembering again that the way to hurry is to go slow when handling these long trains. With the memory of our methods, when handling short trains, still before us, we are sometimes inclined to apply these methods when handling the long train, and this generally results in damage to the train, as the method used in handling a 50-car train would not be the proper method for handling a 100-car train. What we offer will simply be in the form of a suggestion. First, it may be said that, grade permitting, the "drift stop" is the most successful method of handling the big trains, and while in this more time is required to make the stop, yet if the time be taken from terminal to terminal and from one month's end to the other, it will be found that time is saved as well as the draft gear.

However, there are times when this method can not be used, as when making a stop on a favorable grade or where time will not permit; and it is then a question which brake is to be used, the automatic or straight air? Speaking generally, all stops made with the brakes should be made with the automatic brake, as experience has demonstrated that where the straight air is used, judgment is a thing forgotten; this to the man who closes the throttle with one hand and applies the straight air in full with the other. When making stops with trains of 90 to 125 cars, and the automatic brake used, steam should be shut off gradually, and ample time given for the slack to bunch, after which an 8 or 10-pound brake pipe reduction should be made and the automatic brake valve handle returned to lap position and left there until the train stops; as the speed decreases, the engine brake should be graduated off, having it almost fully released as the train comes to a stop. The reason for this method is, that in trains of this length it is practically impossible to obtain the maximum brake pipe pressure on the cars at or near the rear of the train, and it is no uncommon thing to find a variation of 20 pounds between the two ends of the train. With this variation of pressure it will be readily understood that a 10-pound reduction of the pressure at the head end of the train will not cause the brakes to set on the rear end, and this of course will cause a hard running in of the slack, with a tendency toward driving in of the drawbars on the cars found in the head portion of the train, and by the graduated release of the engine brake this is in a measure overcome. Now, to say that a train of this length can not be successfully stopped with the straight air brake would be to make a false statement, as it is done every day, and done successfully, many engineers using it exclusively in controlling their trains, even though the rules prohibit it. But then rules are created more particularly for those of us who lack in judgment, and the one rule of the many written is that which reads: "In case of doubt, take the safe side and run no risk;" and where in the judgment of the engineer the train can be handled more safely with the straight air than the automatic brake the straight air should be used. And in this he would not be infringing on any of the rules, as the above quoted rule would give him the right to use the straight air. That the time has arrived for the changing of the rule which prohibits the use of the straight air brake in the control of trains, and putting the matter entirely up to the judgment of the engineer, and holding him for the results obtained.

Changing the rule would be an easy matter if all engineers understood and *practiced* the proper method in the handling of this brake in the controlling of trains; but this condition does not exist. Suppose a train on an ascending or a level grade and a stop being made with the straight air brake; if the brake is held applied until the stop is completed, the result should be the pulling of one or more drawbars. The reason for this is, that when the brake was applied the slack running in caused compression of the draft gear springs, and when the train was finally brought to a stop these compressed springs, assisted by the grade, will cause the slack to again run out, and if the straight air is still applied when this run-out of slack reaches the engine it will be very easy to understand what pulled the drawbar. We might even go farther and say, that even though the engine brake was fully released just before the run-out of the slack reached the engine, the results, no doubt, would have been the same, as the severe jerk coming to the heavy engine would be more than the average drawbar could stand. Where a train is to be controlled, that is, a stop made by use of the straight air brake, ample time should be given after steam is shut off for the slack to bunch before the brake is applied, after which the brake cylinder pressure should be built up slowly until the desired or maximum pressure is reached. Then, shortly before the stop is completed, the brake should be graduated off, thus allowing the compressed draft gear springs to run the slack out gradually, thereby preventing severe strains on the draft gear. The thickness and fit of the driving tires is another point to remember when using the straight air for the control of trains, as only too often tires are loosened, which causes delays and sometimes calls for the assistance of the wrecking crew.

Reasons for Air Pumps Running Hot

There are several reasons for an air pump running hot, the principal ones are as follows: (1) Lack of lubrication; (2) air valves stuck open or shut; (3) running the pump too fast; (4) air piston packing rings worn; (5) air cylinder worn; (6) working against high pressure; (7) air passages in pump partially stopped up.

Lack of lubrication.—The amount of oil to be fed to the air end of the pump depends largely on the amount of work required of the pump, also its condition, as, where the packing rings and air valves are leaking, heat is generated, which destroys the oil. However, but little oil is needed, if given at the proper time. Where an air cylinder lubricator is used, it must not be treated as a continuous feed lubricator, but must be employed rather as a valve for use only when it becomes necessary to feed a few drops of oil to the pump.

Air valve stuck open or shut.—Where the air valves do not seat properly, the air will course back and forth through the air passages, causing the pump to heat quickly; where a receiving valve is stuck shut, the air will be unable to enter the pump at the end where is located the defective valve, and the pump will heat; if both receiving valves stick shut, the pump will work fast, heat quickly, and no air will be taken in, consequently no air delivered to the main reservoir. If a discharge valve sticks shut, the air can not leave the pump at the end where is located the defective valve, but must leak past the piston packing rings, thus creating friction, causing the pump to heat. If both discharge valves are stuck shut, the pump will work very slowly and will heat quickly, and no air will be delivered to the main reservoir.

Running the pump too fast.—When air is compressed, heat is created, and the faster the air is compressed the higher will be its temperature; also, the faster the pump is run the less time there is for the radiation of heat between the strokes. Therefore, since more heat is generated and less heat radiated at each stroke, it will be understood that the temperature of the pump will increase with its speed.

Air piston packing rings worn.—There is nothing that will cause a pump to heat more quickly than leaky piston packing rings, as where packing rings are badly worn, air can pass them in either direction, therefore less cool air is taken into the cylinder. For as the piston moves forward it compresses the air, causing its temperature to rise, and some of this heated air will leak past the piston and raise the temperature of the incoming air before it is compressed, resulting in a much higher temperature when it is compressed. There is still another reason why a pump will heat on account of leaky packing rings, and that is: As the pump neither takes in nor discharges as much air as it would if the packing rings were tight, it follows that the pump will have to work faster and for a greater length of time to compress the required amount of air.

Air cylinder worn.—The effect of a worn cylinder is much the same as though the packing rings were leaking, as here, too, air will leak past the piston.

Working against high pressure.—When air is compressed, heat is created, and the higher the pressure to which it is compressed, the higher will be its temperature. Therefore, where a pump is working for any great length of time against a high pressure, great heat will be created.

Air passages partially stopped up.—When the air passages on the discharge side of the pump, or the discharge pipe, is partially stopped up, the effect is much the same as when the pump is working against a high main reservoir pressure; as more work will have to be done to force the air through the choked opening, thereby causing the pump to heat.

Piston rod packing wearing or burning out.—To prevent the rapid wearing or burning out of the piston rod packing, it is necessary to maintain a clean and well oiled swab on the piston, and it must be remembered that it is useless to put oil on a swab unless it is first cleaned, as the oil will do no good unless it reaches the piston rod, which it can not do unless the swab be clean. Where packing is blowing bad, the oil will be blown from the swab about as fast as it is applied, and the piston rod and packing will become dry. Where this condition exists it will be found good practice to make a swab of hard grease. This may be done by taking, say a piece of an old flag, and wrapping up in it some hard grease, then tie around the piston rod. Never use signal or engine oil on the swab, as the temperature of the piston rod is above the flashing point of these oils.

Definition of the Terms Piston Travel, Running Travel, Standing Travel

The terms "piston travel," "running travel," and "standing travel" are quite commonly used in air brake discussions, and a definition of these terms may be given as follows: Piston travel, speaking generally, is the distance that the brake cylinder piston is moved outward when the brake is applied. To measure the travel, mark the piston rod close to the cylinder head when the brake is released, then noting the distance this mark is from the cylinder head when the brake is set. When taking such measurements the brake should be applied with a full service application. Standing travel: This is the distance the piston moves outward when the brake is applied upon a car that is not in motion. Running travel: This is the distance the piston moves outward when the brake is applied on a car that is in motion. The running travel is always greater than the standing travel, this increase of travel being due to the brake shoes pulling down on the wheels, slack in loose-fitting brasses, play between the boxes and pedestals and the lost motion throughout the brake rigging. To measure the running travel, mark the piston rod close to the cylinder head, then, with the train running at a speed that will allow for a full service application, apply the brakes in full, and hold them applied until the train comes to a stop; the distance the mark is from the cylinder head is the running travel. In studying the effects of piston travel, it must be remembered that in any application of the brakes the pressure developed in the brake cylinder depends on two things—the actual piston travel at the time the brake is applied and the amount of brake pipe reduction made. Therefore, when desiring to know the actual pressure developed in the brake cylinder for any given reduction, it is necessary to consider the running travel and not the standing travel; and as the running travel is always the greater, the cylinder pressure will be less. The reason for this, as no doubt is understood, is that brake cylinder volume depends on the amount of piston travel; if the latter is short, the volume is small, and the air coming from the auxiliary reservoir will create a higher brake cylinder pressure than if the piston travel were longer and the cylinder volume thereby greater. The running travel should be noted carefully on both driver and tender brakes, as where a standing travel of nine or ten inches is permitted it will be found that the brake pistons will be out against the cylinder heads and the brake power greatly reduced. This is especially true following an emergency application; when due to the high pressure, the pistons will be forced against the cylinder heads. There seems to be a tendency on the part of enginemen and roundhouse employes to neglect the brakes on locomotives equipped with either the "ET" or "LT" types of brakes on account of the brake cylinder pressure not being affected by piston travel. But it must be remembered that if the brake piston has traveled the full length of its cylinder, and is against the cylinder head, it matters not what pressure may be had in the cylinder, the brake power will be affected. In adjusting the brakes on locomotives having either the "ET" or "LT" equipment, just sufficient piston travel should be allowed as will give the proper shoe clearance, and where this is done, the brake will be more prompt in applying and releasing.

The Westinghouse "PC" Passenger Brake Equipment

With the introduction of heavy (125,000 pounds to 150,000 pounds) passenger equipment cars in steam road service, a greater braking force was required to control such heavy cars than was obtainable with a single brake cylinder using the highest brake cylinder pressure.

The increased speed and weight of trains, together with the increase in their length and consequently the much greater volume of air that must be handled through the brake pipe, have imposed conditions too severe to be met satisfactorily by the type of brake which met past conditions adequately.

Certain requirements essential in a satisfactory brake for this modern service demanded changes in the valve device used on the car, which led to the development of the equipment known as the Westinghouse Improved Brake Equipment, Schedule "PC," employing what is known as a control valve.

NOVEL FUNCTIONS CLAIMED.

First.—Graduated release and Quick recharge, obtained as with previous improved types of triple valves (*e. g.*, Type L). The air supply to assist in recharging and to accomplish the graduations of the release is taken from the emergency reservoir.

Second.—Certainty and uniformity of service action secured by insuring that the valve parts move so as to close the feed grooves on the slightest brake pipe reductions, the design of the valves being such as to then cause the necessary and proper differential to be built up to move the parts to service position as the brake pipe reduction is continued.

Third.—Quick rise in brake cylinder pressure, provided for by insuring a prompt movement of the parts and direct and unrestricted passages from reservoirs to brake cylinders during applications.

Fourth.—Uniformity and maintenance of service brake cylinder pressure during the stop, provided for in the same manner as by the application portion of the distributing valve.

Fifth.—Predetermined limiting of service braking power, fixed by the equalization of the pressure and application chambers of the control valve, which eliminates the safety valve feature of previous equipments. After such equalization has taken place, any further brake pipe reduction causes the moving parts of the valve to travel slightly beyond the service position to the "over-reduction" position. Air is then vented from the pressure chamber to the reduction limiting chamber until equalization takes place between these two chambers, if the brake pipe reduction is continued far enough. During this time the application chamber remains at the first equalization pressure and the brake cylinder pressure is maintained accordingly.

The maximum service brake cylinder pressure (service equalization) is fixed at 86 pounds. On this account it is claimed to be possible to use a much lower total leverage ratio (which is necessary if the required efficiency of the foundation brake rigging for the class of cars considered, is to be maintained). This equalization pressure corresponds to a reduction of 24 pounds from 110 pounds brake pipe pressure, which is the reduction required with the old style high speed brake equipment to give maximum service brake cylinder pressure (60 pounds, corresponding to the opening point of the high speed reducing valve).

Sixth.—Automatic emergency application on depletion of brake pipe pressure. If the brake pipe reduction is still further continued below the point at which the pressure and reduction limiting chambers equalize, the parts move to emergency position and cause both the quick action and emergency portions to operate, starting serial quick action throughout the train and obtaining emergency brake cylinder pressure.

Seventh.—Full emergency braking power at any time. As the operation of the emergency and quick action portions is dependent only upon the movement of the parts to emergency position and as this can be caused at any time by making an emergency application with the brake valve, conductor's valve, etc., it follows that full emergency braking power can be obtained at any time, irrespective of a service application previously made.

Eighth.—The service and emergency features being separated permits the necessary flexibility for service applications to be obtained.

Ninth.—A low total leverage ratio, with correspondingly greater overall efficiency, is made possible by the use of two brake cylinders per car, and also higher service equalization pressure.

Tenth.—Less sensitiveness to the fluctuations in brake pipe pressure, which tend to cause undesired light applications of the brake, which helps against brakes creeping on or dragging or burning of brake shoes.

Eleventh.—Maximum rate of rise of brake pipe pressure possible with given length of brake pipe. With non-graduated release equipments or previous graduated release equipments operating with graduated release feature cut-out, the recharging of the brake pipe toward the rear end of a train of any length may become very slow, due to the draining away of the air from the forward end of the brake pipe by the large reservoirs with large size feed grooves which take their entire supply from the brake pipe only. The quick recharge feature of the "PC" equipment is claimed to overcome this difficulty, either with or without graduated release cut in, by restoring the pressure to the pressure chamber on each car at as rapid a rate as the brake pipe pressure alone can be raised by the flow of air through the brake valve. Consequently, up to the point of equalization of the pressure chamber and the emergency reservoir under each car (about 5 pounds less than normal brake pipe pressure), no air is being drawn from the brake pipe. This makes possible a prompt and certain release of the brakes, and a rapid recharge and prompt response to successive reductions which may be made, because (1) practically no air is drawn from the brake pipe; (2) pressure chamber and brake pipe air pressure recharge at the same rate; and (3) with graduated release cut out, no air is supplied to pressure chamber except from brake pipe.

Twelfth.—Greatly increased sensitiveness to release tends to produce a very slow rate of rise of brake pipe pressure when releasing and recharging, especially toward the end of a long train of heavy cars having large reservoirs. It then becomes necessary to provide the maximum sensitiveness to an increase in brake pipe pressure, in order to insure all valves in the train responding as intended.

Thirteenth.—The elimination of the graduated release feature is provided for in the construction of the valve. During the transition period, when graduated release equipment is likely to be handled in the same train with cars not equipped with a graduated release brake, especially where long trains are handled and the air supplied from the brake pipe likely to be limited in any way from any cause, it is usually best to cut out the graduated release feature until all cars are furnished with this type of brake. All that is required to change the "PC" equipment from the graduated to a direct release brake or vice versa, is the loosening of a bolt and turning of the "direct and graduated release cap" on the front of the control valve head until the desired position is indicated, the bolt being then re-tightened.

APPARATUS—BRAKE CYLINDERS.

Two brake cylinders per car are used. Only one brake cylinder operates during service applications, but both are brought into play when an emergency application is made. This is claimed to give the necessary increased braking power for emergency applications, not by an increased pressure in one brake cylinder (as in previous equipments), but by bringing the same brake cylinder pressure to act upon the pistons of two brake cylinders instead of one. This means that double the maximum service braking is obtained in emergency applications.

A slack adjuster is used on each brake cylinder connected by a pipe to the proper slack adjuster hole in the service brake cylinder. In this way both slack adjusters are made to operate simultaneously and the slack is taken up equally for both cylinders, depending on the travel of the service brake cylinder piston.

RESERVOIRS.

Two supply or storage reservoirs are used, denoted as the *service* and *emergency* reservoirs, respectively, according to the brake cylinders to which they are related. The service reservoir is used to supply air only to the service brake cylinder. The emergency reservoir, in addition to supplying air to the emergency brake cylinder in emergency applications, is also the source of supply utilized in obtaining the graduated release and the prompt recharging of the equipment in service operation.

In addition to these reservoirs there is the control valve reservoir of three compartments, called the *pressure chamber*, *application chamber*, and *reduction limiting chamber*, respectively. This reservoir bears practically the same relation to the control valve that the distributing valve reservoir bears to the distributing valve of the "ET" locomotive brake equipment.

The valve portions of the control valve are supported upon this reservoir, which is bolted to the underframing of the car. All pipe connections are made permanently to this reservoir, so that no pipe connections need to be disturbed in the removal or replacement of any one of the control valve portions.

CONTROL VALVE.

The control valve, corresponding in a general way to the triple valve of the old style passenger equipment, or more closely to the distributing valve of the "ET" locomotive brake, consists of four portions:
    (1) Equalizing portion.
    (2) Application portion.
    (3) Emergency portion.
    (4) Quick action portion.
The *compartment reservoir* is made up of the following chambers:
Pressure chamber.
Application chamber.
Reduction limiting chamber.

The *equalizing portion* is similar, in a general way, to the equalizing portion of the distributing valve used with the "ET" equipment, or the plain triple valve of the old style brake. It is the portion which is directly affected by variations in brake pipe pressure and it controls (either directly or indirectly, through the medium of the other portions of the control valve), the desired charging of the reservoirs, the application of the brake, whether in service or emergency, and the release of the brake.

The *application portion* corresponds to the application portion of the distributing valve used with the "ET" equipment. It controls the flow of air only from service reservoir to service brake cylinder and the release of same, and has nothing to do with the emergency reservoir or the emergency brake cylinder.

The *emergency portion* contains a double piston and slide valve which controls the flow of air from the emergency reservoir to the emergency cylinder and the release of same to the atmosphere.

The *quick action portion* corresponds in general design and function to the quick action portion of a triple valve. It operates only when an emergency application of the brakes is made, vents brake pipe air to atmosphere locally on each car and closes the vent to the atmosphere automatically after the desired brake pipe reduction has been made.

GENERAL HINTS.

The brake should be handled by the engineers in the same manner as with cars equipped with quick action triples, the only difference being that an emergency application will be obtained should a service reduction of the brake pipe pressure be continued below 60 pounds when carrying 110 pounds pressure, or below 35 pounds with 70 pounds brake pipe pressure.

When it is found necessary to cut out the brake, close the cut-out cock in the cross-over pipe and bleed both the service and emergency reservoirs.

Should it become necessary to bleed the brake when the engine is detached, or air connection is not made, first bleed the brake pipe and then bleed both the service and emergency reservoirs.

The two sets of cylinder levers are connected to the same truck pull rods as stated above. Therefore, when a service application of the brake is made, the push rod end of the emergency cylinder lever will move the same distance as the push rod end of the service cylinder lever, but the crosshead being slotted, the piston of the emergency cylinder will not move. Consequently, the fact that the *emergency cylinder* crosshead is in release position does *not* indicate that the air brakes are released. To determine this, look at the push rod of the *service cylinder*.

Whenever it is necessary to change the adjustment of the automatic slack adjuster, it is imperative that the crossheads of the two adjusters be left at the same distance from their respective brake cylinder heads, in order that the piston travel of the two cylinders in emergency application will be the same.

The quick action exhaust is the one-inch opening in the bottom of the control valve reservoir. Should there be a continual blow at this opening, make an emergency application and then release; if the blow continues, remove the quick action portion and substitute a new or repaired portion or repair the quick action valve seat which will be found defective. The quick action portion is at the left hand when facing the equalizing portion.

There are three control valve exhaust openings, two on the equalizing portion and one on the side of the control valve reservoir, all tapped for $3/8$-inch pipe.

Should there be a blow at the application chamber exhaust ($3/8$-inch exhaust opening on the side of the control valve reservoir) with the brakes applied or released, make a 15-pound service reduction and then bleed both the service and emergency reservoirs. Should the blow continue, it indicates that the equalizing portion is defective and a new one, or one that has been repaired, should be substituted.

Should there be a blow at the reduction limiting chamber exhaust ($3/8$-inch exhaust on the left-hand side of the equalizing portion), make a 30-pound brake pipe reduction and lap the brake valve. If the blow ceases, it indicates that the application portion is defective and a new one, or one that has been repaired, should be substituted. This portion is located back of the equalizing portion, inside the reservoir. If the blow does not cease, it indicates that the equalizing portion is defective and a new one, or one that has been repaired, should be substituted.

Should there be a blow at the emergency piston exhaust ($3/8$-inch exhaust on the right-hand side of the equalizing portion), make a 15-pound brake pipe reduction and lap the brake valve. If the blow ceases, it indicates that the emergency portion is defective, and a new one, or one that has been repaired, should be substituted. If the blow does not cease, it indicates that the equalizing portion is defective and a new one, or one that has been repaired, should be substituted.

A hard blow at the service brake cylinder exhaust (tapped for $3/4$-inch pipe and located on the side of the control valve reservoir), with the brakes either applied or released, indicates that the application portion is defective and a new one, or one that has been repaired, should be substituted. This portion is located back of the equalizing portion inside the reservoir.

A hard blow at the emergency cylinder exhaust (tapped for $1/2$-inch pipe and located on the bottom of the control valve reservoir), with the brakes either applied or released, indicates a defective emergency portion, and a new one, or one that has been repaired, should be substituted.

If the trouble described in the five paragraphs preceding are not overcome by the remedies therein suggested, remove the application portion and examine its gasket, as a defect in same may be the cause of the difficulty.

When removing the application, emergency, and quick action portions, their respective gaskets should remain on the reservoir. On removing the equalizing portion, its gasket should remain on the application portion, except when the application portion is shipped to and from points where triple valves are cared for.

When applying the different portions the gaskets should be carefully examined, to see that no ports are restricted, and that the gasket is not defective between ports.

On the front and at the center of the equalizing portion is located the direct and graduated release cap (held by a single stud) on which is a pointer. The position of this pointer indicates whether the valve is adjusted for direct release or graduated release. This cap should be adjusted for either direct or graduated release according to the instructions issued by the railroad.

LUBRICATION OF No. 3-E CONTROL VALVE.

Equalizing portion.—All equalizing portions should be lubricated with dry graphite instead of oiling.

The following is a good method of lubricating the equalizing portion:—

After the bearing surfaces have been properly rubbed in by a free use of oil, this oil should be wiped off with a soft cloth or some soft material. All oil, gum, or grease should be thoroughly removed from the slide valves and seats. After this has been done, rub a high grade of very fine, dry (not flake) graphite, of the highest obtainable fineness and purity, onto the face of the slide valves, their seats, the face of the graduating valves, their seats, and the upper portion of the bushings where the slide valve springs bear, in order to make as much as possible adhere and fill in the pores of the brass and leave a very thin, light coating of graphite on the seats. When this is completed, the slide valves and their seats must be entirely free from oil or grease. Care must be taken when handling the slide valves, after lubricating, that the hands do not come in contact with the lubricated parts, as moisture will tend to remove the thin coating of graphite.

To apply the graphite, use a stick, suitable for the purpose about eight inches long, on one end of which a small pad of chamois skin has been glued. Dip the skin covered end in the dry graphite and rub the latter on the surfaces specified. A few light blows of the stick on the slide valve seats will leave the desired light coating of loose graphite. After the piston and slide valves have been replaced in the equalizing portion, they should be moved to release position and a little oil applied to the circumference of the piston bushings, and the pistons moved back and forth several times to insure proper distribution of this oil on the walls of the cylinders.

When oiling, as just directed or in the cases which follow, only a thin coating of oil is necessary, and care should be taken not to leave any free oil on the parts.

Application portion.—The exhaust valve and seat and the application valve and seat of the application portion should be cleaned, rubbed in and lubricated with graphite in a manner similar to that just explained for the equalizing slide valve and seat.

Before applying the piston to application portion, clean the application cylinder and piston. Lubricate the walls of the cylinder and piston ring, using a good grade of triple valve oil; apply a few drops of oil on the packing leather.

Emergency portion.—After the bearing surfaces have been properly cleaned, rubbed in and lubricated with graphite, as specified for the equalizing portion and before applying the slide valve to the emergency portion, remove the top cover and take out the loose fitting cylinder bushing. Lubricate the large piston with a few drops of a good grade of triple valve oil and apply the slide valve to the portion. Lubricate the slip bushing for the small emergency piston, applying a few drops of triple valve oil to inner circumference. Apply the bushing to the portion and bolt on top cover. Move the slide valve to *release position* and put a few drops of triple valve oil on the walls of large cylinder bushing. Move the slide valve and piston back and forth several times to insure a proper distribution of the oil. Apply the large cover to the emergency portion.

Quick action portion.—The only parts of the quick action portion requiring lubrication are the closing valve piston and cylinder bushing. A few drops of triple valve oil on these parts is all that is needed. After lubricating, work the piston a few times, making sure that it moves freely.

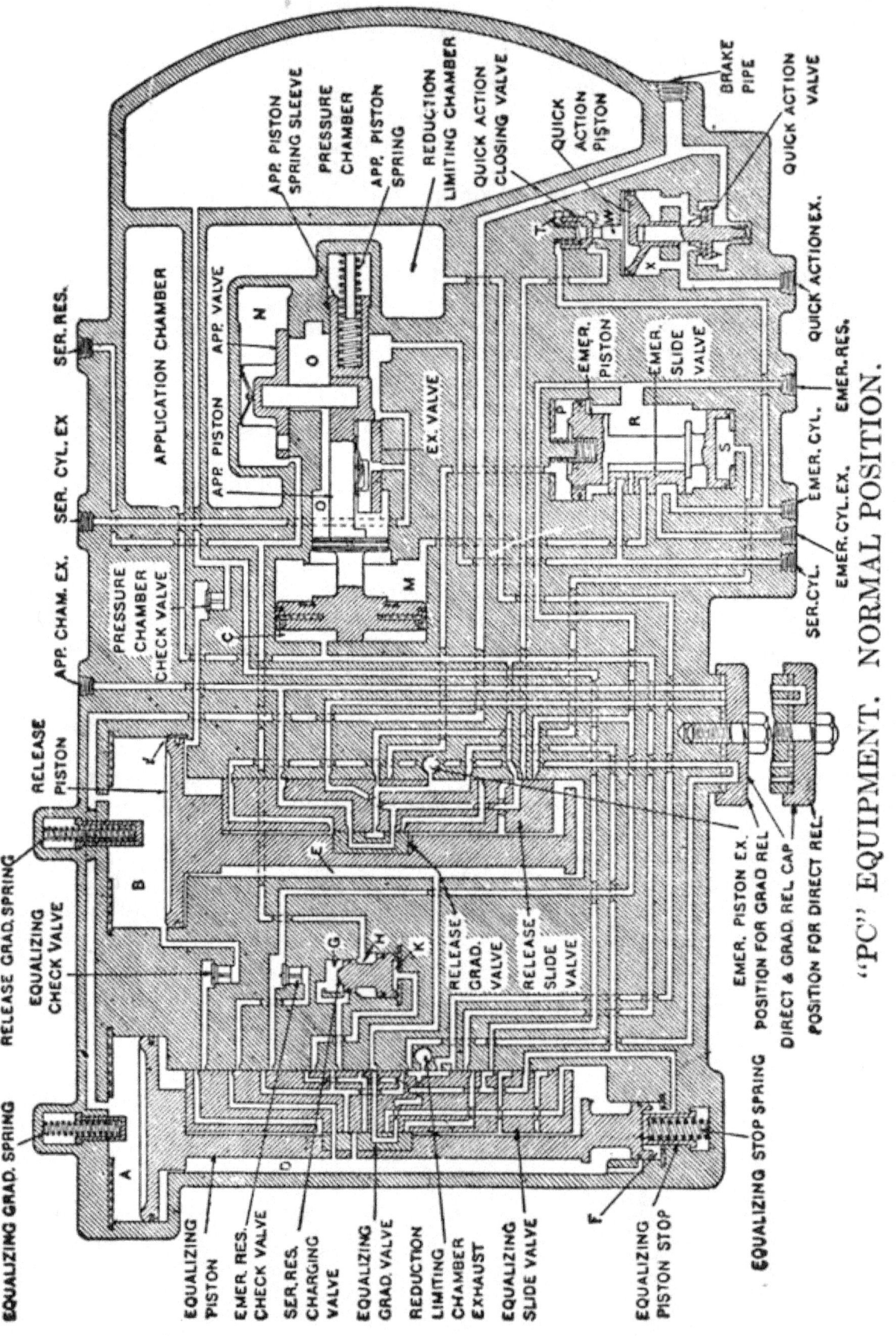

"PC" EQUIPMENT. NORMAL POSITION.

WESTINGHOUSE "PC" PASSENGER BRAKE EQUIPMENT.

QUESTIONS AND ANSWERS

Q.—On what is this type of brake designed to operate?
A.—On passenger equipment cars.

Q.—What made necessary this design of brake?
A.—With the introduction of heavy cars it was found that the older type of brakes was not able to meet the demands, as the brake force required to control the heavy cars was so great as to exceed the capacity of the triple valve and the apparatus used with it.

Q.—Is it to be understood from this that the "PC" equipment can not be applied to the lighter weight cars?
A.—No; the "PC" equipment may be applied to cars of any weight, the same size and type of control valve being used on all cars.

Q.—Name the different parts of the "PC" equipment.
A.—Control valve, control valve or compartment reservoir, service reservoir, emergency reservoir, service brake cylinder and emergency brake cylinder.

Q.—Can cars having this type of brake be run in trains with other cars equipped with the triple valve?
A.—Yes; the "PC" equipment has all the automatic features of the older types of brakes.

Q.—What additional features has the "PC" equipment not found in the older types of brakes?
A.—Brake cylinder pressure is not effected by piston travel or leakage in service applications; full emergency pressure may be obtained at any time, even though a service application has been made; brake will automatically apply in emergency, whenever the brake pipe pressure is reduced below a given amount; maximum brake cylinder pressure obtained in a much shorter time; braking power in emergency may be twice as great as that in service; quick recharge of brake pipe pressure and the use of graduated release when desired.

Q.—How is the service brake cylinder pressure maintained against leakage?
A.—This is taken care of by the application portion of the control valve in the same manner as the application piston and valve in the distributing valve of the "ET" equipment maintains the brake cylinder pressure on the locomotive.

Q.—How is full emergency pressure obtained after the brake has been applied in service?
A.—Full emergency braking power may be obtained at any time by making a sudden reduction of brake pipe pressure, as by moving the brake valve to emergency position, hose bursting, train parting, opening of conductor valve, in fact anything that will cause a sudden reduction of brake pipe pressure will cause the brake to work quick

action. Quick action may also be obtained by a gradual reduction of brake pipe pressure, where this reduction is made below a given amount. As the service and emergency features are separated in this equipment it follows that full emergency braking power may be had at any time, even though a service application has been made.

Q.—Explain how the brake will apply automatically in emergency when a gradual reduction of brake pipe pressure is made below a given amount.

A.—Owing to the construction and operation of the control valve the emergency features of the valve do not operate when a gradual reduction of brake pipe pressure is made until the pressure is reduced below a given amount, and this reduction may be made through the brake valve, or by brake pipe leakage while the brake valve is in lap position. However, when the brake pipe pressure is reduced sufficiently the parts in the equalizing portion of the control valve will move to emergency position, causing the emergency portion to operate and apply the brake in emergency.

Q.—What is meant by reducing the brake pipe pressure below a given amount; in other words, to what pressure must the brake pipe air be reduced, when making a gradual reduction before the brake will work quick action?

A.—Whenever the brake pipe pressure is reduced one-half in a single application the brake will apply to quick action. For example: If the brake is charged to 110 pounds, and in a single application is reduced to 55 pounds (one-half) the control valve should move to emergency position, and the brakes apply in quick action; if the brake were charged to but 70 pounds at the time the application was started, then it would be necessary when making a gradual reduction to reduce the pressure to 35 pounds (one-half) before the control valve would move to emergency position and apply the brakes in quick action; again, if the brake were charged to 90 pounds, drawing the pressure down to 45 pounds (one-half) would cause quick action. From this it will be seen that the point to which the brake pipe pressure must be reduced varies with the pressure with which the brake is charged at the commencement of the application.

Q.—How is the maximum brake cylinder pressure obtained in a much shorter time with the "PC" equipment than with older types of brakes?

A.—This is secured by a more prompt movement of the parts to application position when the required reduction is made, and by larger and more direct ports for the air to flow through.

Q.—Explain how the braking power may be twice as great in emergency as in a service application of the brake.

A.—As stated in answer to a former question, each car is equipped with two brake cylinders; one cylinder is used for service braking, while both are used when making an emergency application. Both cylinders may be the same size, and as the same pressure is obtained in both it follows that the brake power in emergency is double that obtained in service.

Q.—Explain how the brake pipe may be more quickly recharged with this than with the older equipment.

A.—With the older type of brakes, when the brake pipe is being recharged for the purpose of releasing the brakes as each triple valve moves to release position it commences to take air from the brake pipe for the recharge of its auxiliary reservoir, thereby keeping the pressure in the brake pipe from raising promptly. Whereas with the "PC" equipment, the quick recharge feature overcomes this trouble. A better understanding of this will be had in what is to follow.

Q.—How is the maximum brake cylinder pressure limited in service braking?

A.—This is brought about in the same manner as with the distributing valve in the "ET" equipment; when the pressure chamber and application chamber air equalizes, the maximum service braking power is obtained. For example: With a 70-pound pressure the pressure chamber and application chamber in the distributing valve will equalize at 50 pounds, while with a 110 pressure the pressure chamber and application chamber of the control valve will equalize at 86 pounds; therefore, with the distributing valve and 70 pounds pressure the service braking power is limited to 50 pounds, while with the control valve and 110 pounds pressure the service braking power is limited to 86 pounds. This eliminates the use of safety valves or high speed reducing valves as used with the older equipment.

Q.—What effect have fluctuations of brake pipe pressure due to the improper action of the feed valve on the control valve?

A.—The control valve is not affected by the variations of the brake pipe pressure, as it requires at least a 7-pound reduction of brake pipe pressure to move the control valve to application position, and it is seldom, if ever, that the feed valve allows such variation of pressure.

Q.—When should the graduated release feature be used? When should the direct release feature be used, and how is the control valve changed from graduated to direct release and vice versa?

A.—The graduated release feature should be used when the brakes on all cars in the train have this feature, or may be used with other types of brakes on short trains. Direct release to be used when other cars in the train are not equipped with graduated release brakes. To change from graduated to direct release or vice versa, all that is necessary is to loosen the nut on the direct and graduated release cap on the front of the control valve and turn the cap to the desired position as indicated on the control valve, then retighten the nut.

CONTROL VALVE.

Q.—What does the control valve compare with in the old style passenger equipment?
A.—With the triple valve, as it performs all the functions of the triple.

Q.—With what other device does it more closely correspond?
A.—With the distributing valve of the "ET" equipment, and may be said to be a modified distributing valve made applicable to cars.

Q.—How many parts or portions are there to the control valve?
A.—Four.

Q.—Name the different parts.
A.—Equalizing portion, application portion, emergency portion, and quick action portion.

Q.—What is the duty of the equalizing portion?
A.—The equalizing portion in a general way controls the charging of the emergency and service reservoirs, and the application and release of the brake in both service and emergency applications; in other words, the air that operates the other portions of the valve must first pass through the equalizing portion.

Q.—What is the duty of the application portion?
A.—The application portion controls the flow of air from the service reservoir to the service brake cylinder in both service and emergency applications of the brake, also exhausts the air from this cylinder; but neither admits or exhausts the air from the emergency brake cylinder.

Q.—What is the duty of the emergency portion?
A.—The emergency portion controls the flow of air from the emergency reservoir to the emergency brake cylinder in an emergency application of the brake, and exhausts this air when the brake is released.

Q.—What is the duty of the quick action portion?
A.—The duty of the quick action portion is similar to the quick action portion of the triple valve, that is, it operates only when an emergency application of the brake is made, when it vents brake pipe air to the atmosphere, causing a local reduction of this pressure on each car.

COMPARTMENT RESERVOIR.

Q.—How many compartments are there in this reservoir?
A.—Three.

Q.—Name them.
A.—Pressure chamber, reduction limiting chamber, and application chamber.

Q.—What is the purpose of the pressure chamber?
A.—The purpose of the pressure chamber may be compared to that of the auxiliary reservoir in the old equipment, or a still closer comparison may be made with the pressure chamber of the distributing valve of the "ET" equipment, as it is here that air is stored for the purpose of moving the parts to application position, when a brake pipe reduction is made.

Q.—What is the purpose of the reduction limiting chamber?
A.—It is to provide a chamber for the venting of a limited amount of pressure chamber air whenever a brake pipe reduction is made below the equalizing point of the pressure chamber and application chamber.

Q.—What is the purpose of the application chamber?
A.—It is into this chamber that air is admitted for the purpose of moving the application piston and valve to application position when applying the brake.

RESERVOIRS.

Q.—How many reservoirs are there on each car?
A.—Two.
Q.—Name these reservoirs.
A.—Service and emergency reservoirs.
Q.—Are both reservoirs the same size?
A.—No; the service reservoir is the larger.
Q.—What is the purpose of the service reservoir?
A.—To apply air to the service brake cylinder in both service and emergency applications of the brake.
Q.—What is the purpose of the emergency reservoir?
A.—The emergency reservoir supplies air to the emergency brake cylinder in an emergency application of the brake, and following the release of a service application its air is used to secure the graduated release feature and quick recharge of the pressure chamber.

BRAKE CYLINDERS.

Q.—How many cylinders are used on a car having this equipment?
A.—Two.
Q.—Name these cylinders.
A.—Service and emergency cylinders.
Q.—When is the service cylinder used?
A.—The service cylinder is used on all brake applications, that is, it operates in both service and emergency applications.
Q.—When is the emergency cylinder used?

A.—The emergency cylinder is used only when making an emergency application of the brake, and does not operate when a service application is made.

Q.—Are both cylinders the same size?

A.—Yes, both cylinders are generally the same size; however, where they differ in size, the emergency cylinder is the smaller.

PIPE CONNECTIONS.

Q.—Name the different pipe connections to the compartment reservoir.

A.—When facing the valve the upper pipe on the left leads to the service reservoir; the lower pipe on the left is the brake pipe connection; the upper pipe on the right leads to the service brake cylinder; the middle pipe to the emergency reservoir, and the lower pipe to the emergency brake cylinder.

OPERATION OF THE CONTROL VALVE.

RELEASE AND CHARGING POSITION.

Q.—Where does the air come from to charge this equipment?

A.—From the brake pipe, through the cross-over pipe and enters the control valve.

Q.—What pressure is found in these different chambers and reservoirs when fully charged?

A.—Brake pipe pressure.

Q.—When the control valve is in release or service position, to what is the reduction limiting chamber connected?

A.—To the reduction limiting chamber exhaust, which is the $\frac{3}{8}$-inch opening on the left side of equalizing portion.

Q.—When the control valve is in release position, to what is the application chamber connected?

A.—To the application chamber exhaust, which is $\frac{3}{8}$-inch opening on left side of reservoir.

Q.—When in release, to what is the service brake cylinder connected?

A.—It is connected to the atmosphere through the exhaust slide valve of the application portion, and the service brake cylinder exhaust port, which is the $\frac{3}{4}$-inch opening on the left side of the reservoir.

Q.—To what is the emergency brake cylinder connected when the control valve is in release position?

A.—To the atmosphere through the emergency slide valve and emergency brake cylinder exhaust port, which is the $\frac{1}{2}$-inch opening in bottom of the compartment reservoir.

SERVICE APPLICATION.

Q.—When the equipment charged equal to the brake pipe, what will be the result of a gradual brake pipe reduction?

A.—This will reduce the pressure on the top or brake pipe side of the release and equalizing pistons below that on the pressure chamber side below the piston, creating a difference in pressure on the two sides of the pistons.

Q.—How great a brake pipe reduction is necessary to move the control valve to service position?

A.—About 7 or 8 pounds.

Q.—Explain what takes place when the release piston moves.

A.—The first movement of the piston closes the feed groove i, also closes the opening from chamber B to the under side of the equalizing check valve, and its continued movement moves the release graduating and slide valve to what is called preliminary service position, in which the piston comes in contact with the release graduating spring sleeve.

Q.—Explain what takes place in preliminary service position.

A.—The movement of the release slide valve to preliminary service position closes the application chamber exhaust port, closes the port leading from Chamber F to the atmosphere and opens a port connecting chamber E and the pressure chamber with chamber F, thus balancing the pressure on both sides of the small end of the equalizing piston. Chamber E is now connected with chamber D past the equalizing check valve.

Q.—What effect has the balancing of the pressure in chambers F and D?

A.—This allows the equalizing piston to move.

Q.—Explain what takes place when the equalizing piston and slide valve first move.

A.—A connection is made from the emergency reservoir to chamber D through the equalizing slide valve and graduating valve. This is called secondary service position.

Q.—What is the object of this connection?

A.—It allows air from the emergency reservoir to restore the drop of pressure in chambers D and E caused by the movement of the equalizing and release pistons.

Q.—How far does the equalizing piston and valve travel?

A.—Until the piston comes in contact with the equalizing graduating spring sleeve, when the valve is said to be in service position.

Q.—Explain what takes place in this position.

A.—In this position the service port is open through the equalizing slide valve and its seat to the application chamber, allowing pressure chamber air, which is ever present in chamber D, to flow past the end of the equalizing graduating valve to the application chamber.

Q.—How long will the pressure chamber air continue to flow to the application chamber?

A.—Until the pressure in the pressure chamber becomes a shade less than that in the brake pipe, when the equalizing piston will move the graduating valve back just far enough to close the service port, or to lap position.

Q.—Explain what takes place when air is admitted to the application chamber.

A.—Pressure forming in the application chamber and chamber C in front of the application piston causes the application piston to move to application position, carrying with it the application and exhaust valve.

Q.—What takes place when these parts move to application position?

A.—Service reservoir air, which is always present in chamber N, will now be free to flow to chamber O and the service brake cylinder, also from the service brake cylinder port through the emergency slide valve to chamber M at the right of the application piston, thus bringing brake cylinder pressure on the right side of the application piston.

Q.—How long will the air continue to flow from the service reservoir to the service brake cylinder?

A.—Until the pressure in the service brake cylinder and chamber M equalizes with that in the application chamber.

Q.—When these pressures equalize what takes place?

A.—The application piston and valve will be moved to lap position, thus putting practically the same pressure in the service brake cylinder as that in the application chamber.

Q.—What moves the application piston and valve to lap position?

A.—The application piston spring at the back of the piston stem.

Q.—What effect will service brake cylinder leakage have on the application portion when the brake is applied in service?

A.—Any reduction of service brake cylinder pressure on account of leakage will be felt in chamber M at the right of the application piston, and when the pressure on this side of the piston becomes somewhat less than that on the application chamber side, the piston will move to application position, carrying with it the application valve, opening the application port, allowing a further flow of service reservoir air to the brake cylinder, and when the pressure is restored will again return to lap position.

Q.—When making a service application how much of a brake pipe reduction is required to set the brake in full, using 110 pounds brake pipe pressure?

A.—Twenty-four pounds.

Q.—At what pressure does the pressure chamber and application chamber equalize?

A.—At 86 pounds.

Q.—With 86 pounds in the application chamber, what pressure will be had in the brake cylinder?

A.—The same as in the application chamber, 86 pounds.

Q.—If the brake pipe pressure is reduced below the point at which the pressure chamber and application chamber equalize, what will result?

A.—The equalizing piston will move the full length of its cylinder, compressing the equalizing graduating spring and carrying with it its slide valve. The control valve is now said to be in over-reduction position.

Q.—What takes place in this position of the control valve?

A.—The service port in the equalizing slide valve is now connected to a port leading to the reduction limiting chamber, allowing pressure chamber air to flow to this chamber.

Q.—Does the release piston and valve move at this time?

A.—No.

Q.—What prevents their movement?

A.—The release graduating spring offers a much greater resistance to the movement of this piston than does the equalizing graduating spring to the equalizing piston, and as the pressure chamber air is now expanding to the reduction limiting chamber there will not be a sufficient differential created to move the release piston from service position.

Q.—At what pressure will the pressure chamber and the reduction limiting chamber equalize?

A.—At about 55 pounds from an original pressure of 110 pounds.

Q.—How much of a reduction is necessary starting with the equipment charged to 110 pounds to cause the control valve to move to over-reduction position, and for the pressure chamber to equalize with the reduction limiting chamber?

A.—About 55 pounds, or one-half the original pressure.

Q.—If a still further reduction of brake pipe pressure is made what will result?

A.—As there are no further means of continuing the reduction of the pressure chamber pressure, a differential pressure will be created on the two sides of the release piston, causing it to move the full travel of its cylinder, compressing the release graduating spring and carrying with it the release slide valve to emergency position, thus causing a full emergency application of the brake the same as though a sudden brake pipe reduction had been made.

Q.—What is the purpose of the reduction limiting chamber?

A.—It furnishes a limited space in which the pressure chamber air expands whenever an over-reduction of brake pipe pressure is made.

Q.—The above questions refer to full service and over-reduction positions; is it to be understood from this that a partial service application can not be made?

A.—No; with the "PC" equipment the brake may be graduated the same as with the triple valve.

RELEASING THE BRAKE.

Q.—How is this brake released?
A.—By an increase of brake pipe pressure.
Q.—Explain how this is done.
A.—When the pressure in chambers B and A increases above that in the pressure chamber, the equalizing piston will be the first to move toward release position, and it moves down until the lower end of its stem comes in contact with the equalizing stop spring, which momentarily stops it in its movement, and now the control valve is said to be in preliminary release position.

Q.—What takes place in preliminary release position?
A.—Chamber E and the pressure chamber are connected through the reduction limiting chamber exhaust with the atmosphere.

Q.—What is the object of connecting the pressure chamber with the atmosphere at this time?
A.—This causes a drop in pressure in chamber E below that in chamber B and the brake pipe, thus insuring the movement of the release piston and release slide valve to release position.

Q.—What takes place when the release piston and release slide valve move to release position?
A.—In this position, chamber F below the equalizing piston is connected through a port in the release slide valve, with the emergency piston exhaust port, dropping the pressure below the small end of the piston, causing a movement of this piston to its full release position.

Q.—With both pistons and their slide valves in release position, what takes place?
A.—When the release slide valve moves to release position, it connects the application chamber port with the application chamber exhaust, allowing the air to escape from this chamber and chamber C in front of the application piston. The air being exhausted from the left of the application piston, the service brake cylinder pressure on the right of the piston moves it to the left or release position, creating an opening through the exhaust valve to the service brake cylinder exhaust port and atmosphere, releasing the brake.

Q.—With the graduated release feature cut in, is there a direct opening from the application chamber to the atmosphere, when the control valve is in release position?
A.—Yes, but this opening is under the control of the release graduating valve.

Q.—With the graduated release feature cut out, does the release graduating valve control this opening?
A—No, it does not.

Q.—With both pistons in release as above stated, to what is the emergency reservoir connected?

A.—To chamber *G* above the charging valve, also to chamber *E* and the pressure chamber, through the direct graduated release cap.

Q.—How will the pressure in the pressure chamber and chamber *E* be affected by this connection?

A.—This will cause a prompt rise of pressure in these chambers.

Q.—If after making a service application of the brake the brake pipe pressure is only partially restored, what effect will it have on the release?

A.—The air coming from the emergency reservoir to chamber *E* and the pressure chamber will raise the pressure in chamber *E* above that in chamber *B*, and the release piston and release graduating valve will be moved up just far enough to close the port leading to the emergency reservoir, also the application chamber exhaust port. The closing of the application chamber exhaust retains a pressure in this chamber, and when the pressure in chamber *M* (service brake cylinder pressure) becomes somewhat less than that retained in the application chamber, the application piston and its valves will move back to lap position, retaining part of the service brake cylinder pressure, thus obtaining a graduated release of the brake.

Q.—How many graduations of the release may be made?

A.—Graduated release may be obtained each time the brake pipe pressure is increased until its pressure is restored to within about five pounds of the maximum pressure carried.

Q.—When air is first admitted in the recharge of the brake pipe, will the service reservoir be recharged?

A.—No, as now the service reservoir charging valve will be in its lower position, closing the port leading to the service reservoir; thus allowing the air coming to the brake pipe to cause a prompt rise of its pressure for the prompt release of all brakes. This feature is especially useful on long trains.

Q.—When will the charging valve rise, and the service reservoir be recharged?

A.—Not until the pressure chamber has been recharged to within about five pounds of the pressure in the emergency reservoir.

Q.—When the service reservoir charging valve lifts, where will the air come from for the recharge of the service reservoir?

A.—From the brake pipe, through chamber *D*, and from the emergency reservoir.

Q.—Explain how the air is released from the application chamber when the direct and graduated release cap is in direct release position.

A.—When the release piston and its slide valve moves to release position there is a direct connection through the release slide valve and direct and graduated release cap to the application chamber exhaust and the atmosphere; thus giving a direct release of the air in the application chamber and a straight-away release of the brake.

Q.—In direct release, does air from the emergency reservoir assist in the recharge of the pressure chamber and chamber *E*?

A.—No, the port through which the emergency reservoir air flowed to chamber E and the pressure chamber is closed when the direct and graduated release cap is in direct release position.

Q.—With the emergency reservoir air cut off, where does the air come from for the recharge of the pressure chamber and chamber E?

A.—From the brake pipe, through the feed groove I to chamber E and from this chamber to the equalizing slide valve, and through a port in this valve to a port in its seat, to the pressure chamber.

Q.—How is the operation of the control valve affected, in the release of the brake, by the emergency reservoir air being cut off from the pressure chamber and chamber E?

A.—With the emergency reservoir air cut off, the pressure in chamber E and the pressure chamber can rise no faster than that in chamber B and the brake pipe; therefore, when the release piston and slide valve and graduating valve once move to release position, they will remain there until the brake is fully released, which means a direct release of the brake.

EMERGENCY APPLICATION.

Q.—How is an emergency application of the brake obtained with the "PC" equipment?

A.—By a sudden reduction of brake pipe pressure; that is, whenever the brake pipe pressure is being reduced faster than the pressure chamber air can reduce itself to the application chamber or to the reduction limiting chamber, a differential pressure will be created on the equalizing and release pistons, and cause them to move the extreme length of their chambers, or to emergency position.

Q.—Can an emergency application be had in any other way than by a sudden reduction of brake pipe pressure?

A.—Yes; whenever the brake pipe pressure is reduced below the point at which the pressure chamber and reduction limiting chamber equalize the brake will apply in quick action, even though the reduction is made gradually.

Q.—With the equalizing and release pistons in emergency position, what takes place?

A.—In this position chamber E is connected to the chamber under the quick action closing valve, which allows air from chamber E to flow under this valve, raising it from its seat.

Q.—When the quick action valve is raised from its seat where can air from chamber E flow to?

A.—To chamber W on top of the quick action piston.

Q.—What effect will this pressure in chamber W have on the quick action piston?

A.—It will cause the piston to move down, unseating the quick action valve, thereby creating an opening from the brake pipe to the atmosphere, through the quick action exhaust port, causing a local reduction of brake pipe pressure, which will cause the control valve or triple valve on the following car to move to emergency position.

Q.—To what is chamber P above the emergency piston now connected?

A.—To the emergency piston exhaust port.

Q.—Explain what takes place when chamber P is connected to the exhaust.

A.—The emergency reservoir pressure in chamber R will force the emergency piston and its slide valve upward to emergency position.

Q.—What takes place when the emergency valve is moved to its upper position?

A.—The emergency reservoir is now connected to the emergency brake cylinder past the end of the slide valve.

Q.—What other connection has the emergency reservoir at this time?

A.—The emergency reservoir is also connected with chamber E and through this chamber to the application chamber and chamber C in front of the application piston.

Q.—How is the application piston affected by the pressure forming in chamber C?

A.—The piston and its valves are moved to application position, closing the service brake cylinder exhaust, and at the same time opening the application port, allowing service reservoir air to flow to the service brake cylinder.

Q.—What other connection is there to the service brake cylinder port?

A.—This port is also connected with chamber R in the emergency piston chamber, and through this chamber with the emergency reservoir and brake cylinder, thus allowing an equalization of pressure in both cylinders and reservoirs.

Q.—To what is chamber D connected?

A.—To chamber E and the reduction limiting chamber. From what has been said it will be seen that all reservoirs, chambers and brake cylinders are connected in emergency position, allowing an equalization of pressure in all the parts.

Q.—In replying to a former question it was stated that the quick action valve was opened by air coming from chamber E, and brake pipe air vented to the atmosphere for the purpose of causing a local reduction of brake pipe pressure; now how long will this valve remain open, and what will cause it to close?

A.—It will remain open until the pressure in the emergency brake cylinder which is present in chamber T above the quick action closing valve equals that in chamber W, when the quick action closing valve spring will force the valve to its seat, stopping the flow of air to the top of the quick action piston. The air entrapped above the piston will be free to escape through port X, thus relieving the pressure above the piston, when the spring under the quick action valve will force it to its seat, closing the opening from the brake pipe to the atmosphere.

Q.—How is the brake released after an emergency application?

A.—By recharging the brake pipe pressure above that in chambers D and E, when the equalizing and release pistons will be moved to release position.

Q.—To what pressure must the brake pipe be recharged for the release of the brake after an emergency application, when using 110 pounds brake pipe pressure?

A.—As all chambers are connected and pressure equalized at 86 pounds, it will be seen that the brake pipe pressure must be restored to a point above 86 pounds before the brake will release, where a 110-pound brake pipe pressure is used. However, where a 70-pound brake pipe pressure is used, the pressure of equalization is 54 pounds; therefore, when using this pressure the brake pipe pressure would have to be restored to a point above 54 pounds.

METHOD OF OPERATION.

Q.—When braking a train wholly or partially equipped with the "PC" equipment, how should the engineer handle the brake valve?

A.—The same as when braking a train equipped with quick action triple valves, only keeping in mind that the initial brake pipe reduction must be at least 7 or 8 pounds in order to move the control valve to application position.

Q.—In a train with mixed brakes, that is, part "PC" and part triple valves, will not the brakes, on cars having triple valves, apply with less than a 7 or 8-pound reduction?

A.—Yes.

Q.—What effect will this have on the slack action in the train?

A.—This depends on the location of the cars in the train having triple valves; if at the head end, and a 4 or 5-pound brake pipe reduction is made, the brakes on the triple valve cars will apply, while those on the cars having the "PC" will not, therefore the slack will run in; whereas, if the triple valve cars are at the rear, and a similar application is made, the slack will run out. From this it will be seen that in order to avoid the running in or out of the slack, as the case may be, the initial reduction must be sufficiently heavy to set all brakes in the train.

Q.—What other precaution is necessary?

A.—Should avoid an over-reduction of brake pipe pressure, to a point below one-half of the pressure in the brake pipe, at the time the application was commenced.

Q.—If, when making a service reduction, the pressure is reduced below one-half, what will follow?

A.—The brake will apply in quick action.

Q.—After making a service application, how should the brake be released?

A.—The same as on a train equipped with triple valves, when the control valve is cut into direct release; where graduated release is being used, the brake may be graduated off by raising the brake pipe pressure in steps.

Q.—How is this brake cut out?

A.—By closing the cut-out cock in the cross-over pipe and bleeding both service and emergency reservoirs.

Q.—Is there any movement of the emergency cylinder piston, when a service application of the brake is made?

A.—No; even though the cylinder levers are connected to the same truck pull rods, the emergency piston does not move.

Q.—Why is this?

A.—Because the crosshead of the emergency cylinder push rod is slotted, which allows the emergency cylinder lever to move without moving the emergency cylinder piston.

Q.—Do both service and emergency cylinders point in the same direction?

A.—The cylinders may be attached to the car, pointing in the same or opposite directions, depending on the construction of the underframing of the car.

The No. 6 "ET" Locomotive Brake Equipment

The No. 6 "ET" equipment, described herein, is a modification of the No. 5, to accomplish the same results by simpler means, as well as to embody certain additional operative advantages which railroad men suggested as valuable and desirable in a locomotive brake apparatus. The only difference in manipulation between No. 5 and No. 6 "ET" equipment is that on the second engine in double heading, the No. 6 brake valve handle remains in *running position*, as with the old standard G-6 brake valve, instead of in *lap position*, as with the No. 5 equipment.

ARRANGEMENT OF APPARATUS.

Fig. 1-A is a diagram of the No. 6 "ET" equipment, giving the necessary instructions for correctly piping up the equipment; Fig. 1-B is a similar diagram giving the designations of apparatus and piping as referred to in the following description:

PARTS OF THE EQUIPMENT.

1. *The air pump* to compress the air.
2. *The main reservoir*, in which to store and cool the air, and collect water and dirt.
3. *A duplex pump governor* to control the pump when the pressures are attained for which it is regulated.
4. *A distributing valve*, and small double-chamber reservoir to which it is attached, placed on the locomotive to perform the functions of triple valves, auxiliary reservoirs, double check valves, high speed reducing valves, etc.
5. *Two brake valves*, the *automatic* to operate locomotive and train brakes, and the *independent* to operate locomotive brakes only.
6. *A feed valve* to regulate the brake pipe pressure.
7. *A reducing valve* to reduce the pressure for the independent brake valve and for the air-signal system when used.
8. *Two duplex air gauges;* one to indicate equalizing reservoir and main reservoir pressures, the other to indicate brake pipe and locomotive brake cylinder pressures.
9. *Driver, tender,* and *truck brake cylinders, cut-out cocks, air strainers, hose couplings, fittings,* etc., incidental to the piping, for purposes readily understood.

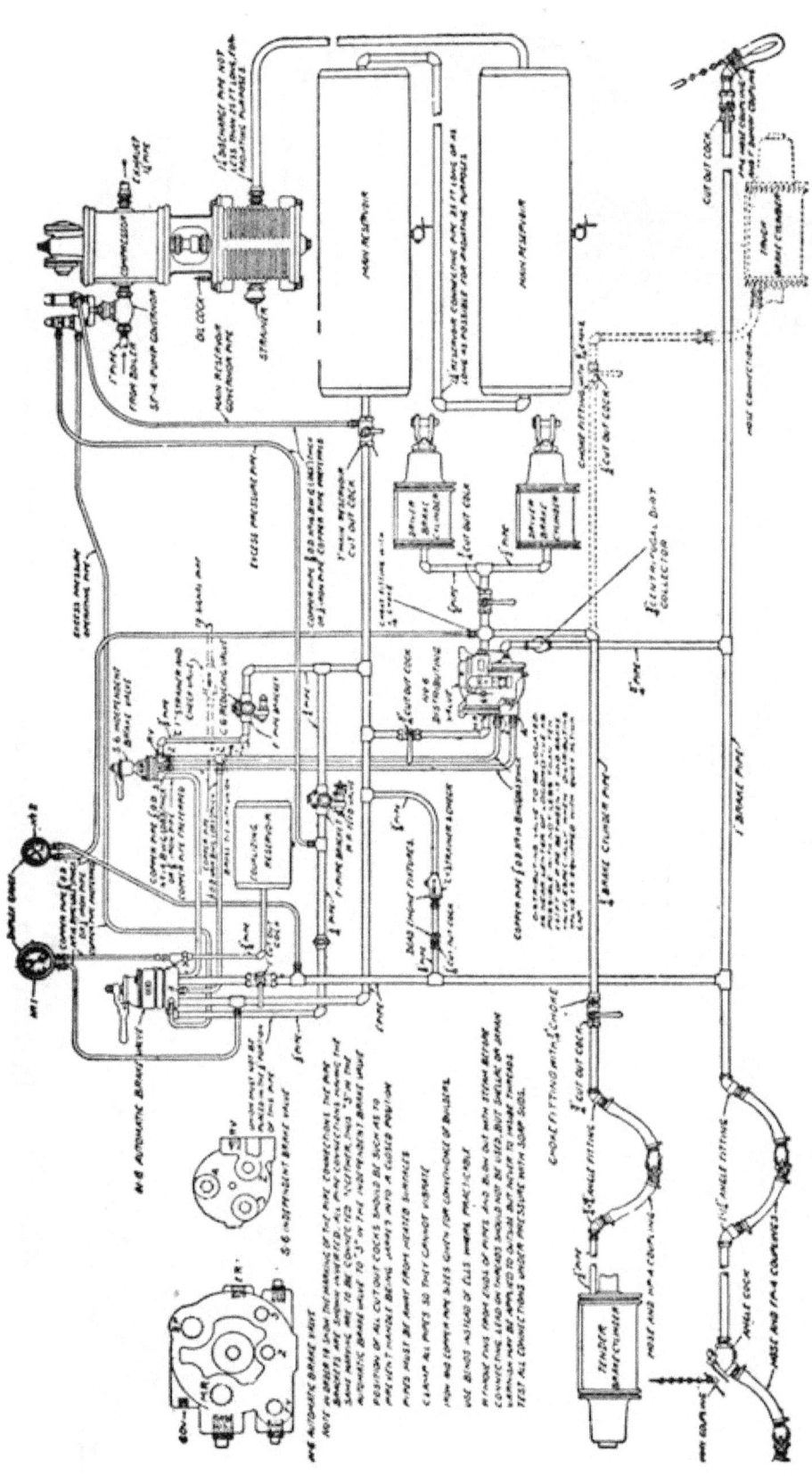

Fig. 1-A. Piping Diagram of the No. 6 ET Equipment

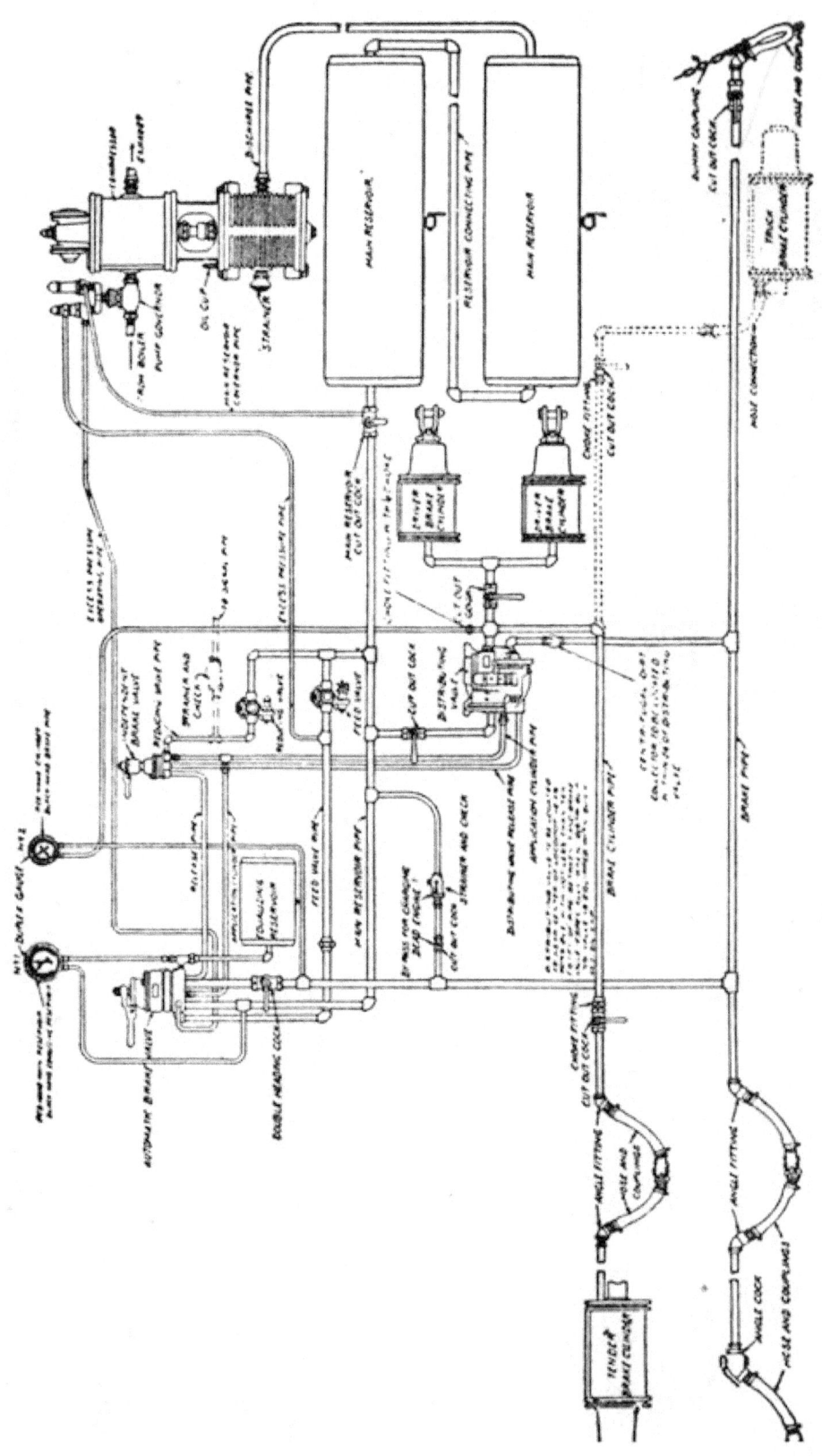

Fig. 1-B. Instruction Diagram of the No. 6 ET Equipment

NAMES OF PIPING.

Discharge pipe; connects the air compressor to the first main reservoir.

Connecting pipe; connects the two main reservoirs.

Main reservoir pipe; connects the second main reservoir to the automatic brake valve, distributing valve, feed valve, reducing valve, and compressor governor.

* *Feed valve pipe;* connects the feed valve to the automatic brake valve.

* *Excess pressure pipe;* connects the feed valve pipe to the upper connection of the excess pressure head of the compressor governor.

Excess pressure operating pipe; connects the automatic brake valve to the lower connection of the excess pressure head of the compressor governor.

Reducing valve pipe; connects the reducing valve to the independent brake valve, and to the signal system, when used.

Brake pipe; connects the automatic brake valve with the distributing valve and all triple valves on the cars in the train.

Brake cylinder pipe; connects the distributing valve with the driver, tender, and truck brake cylinders.

Application cylinder pipe; connects the application cylinder of the distributing valve to the independent and automatic brake valves.

Distributing valve release pipe; connects the application cylinder exhaust port of the distributing valve to the automatic brake valve through the independent brake valve.

PRINCIPLES OF OPERATION.

The principles governing the operation of it are just the same as those of previous automatic air brake equipments. The difference consists in the means for supplying the air pressure to the brake cylinders. Instead of a triple valve and auxiliary reservoir for each of the engine and tender equipments, the distributing valve is made to supply all brake cylinders. The distributing valve consists of two portions, called the *equalizing portion* and *application portion*. It is connected to a *double-chamber reservoir*, the two chambers of

---

* Note—In some installations the H-6 brake valve is provided with a pipe bracket to which the feed valve is directly attached, thus eliminating the feed valve pipe. The excess pressure pipe connection is then made to a pipe tap provided for this purpose in the pipe bracket.

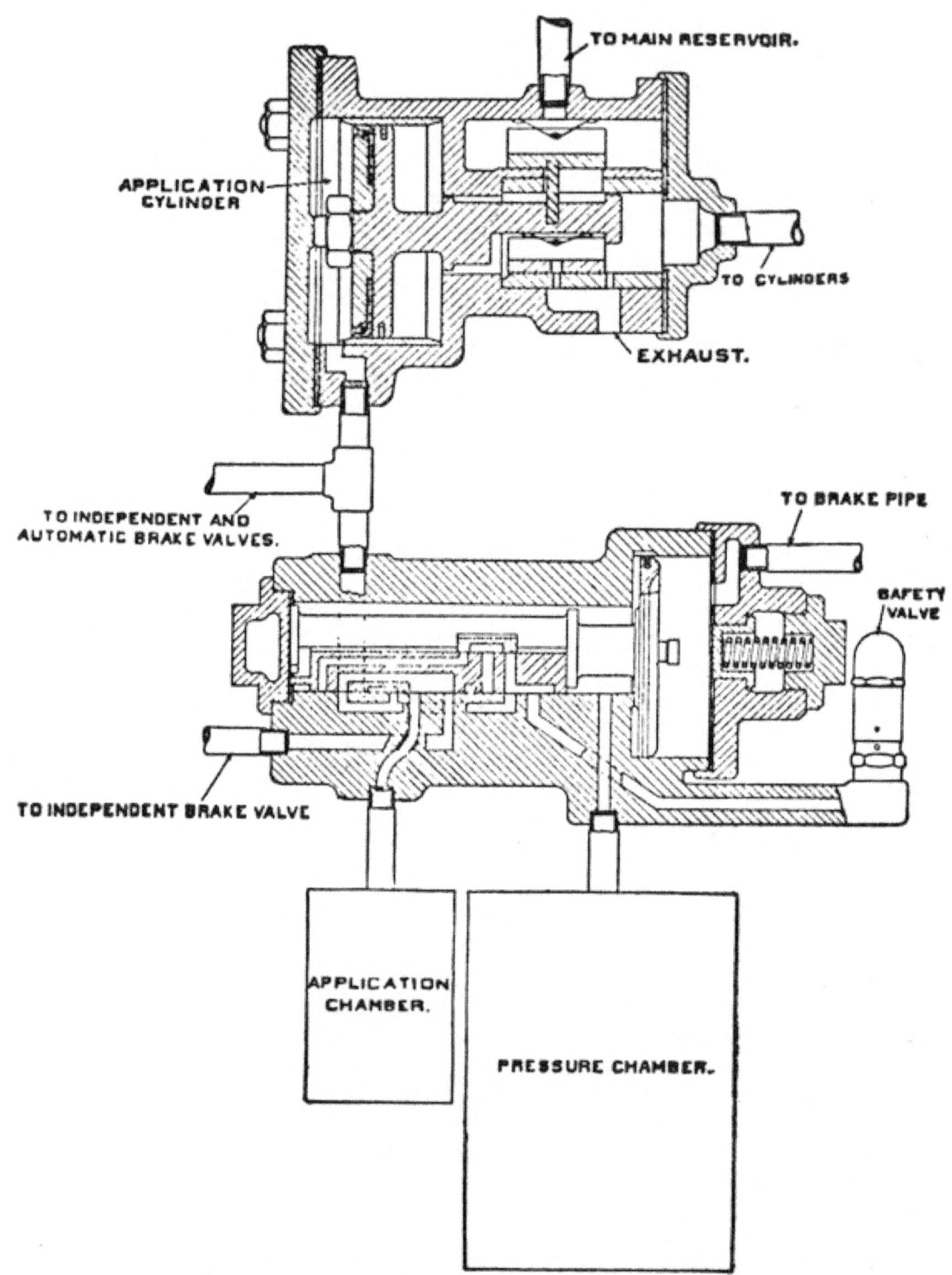

Diagrammatic View of the Essential Parts of the Distributing Valve and Double-Chamber Reservoir

which are called respectively the *pressure chamber* and the *application chamber*. The latter is ordinarily connected to the application portion of the distributing valve in such a way as to enlarge the volume of that part of it called the *application cylinder*. The connections between these parts, as well as their operation, may be compared with that of a *miniature brake set*—the equalizing portion representing the dummy triple valve; the pressure chamber, the dummy auxiliary reservoir; and the application portion (dummy cylinders) always having practically the same pressure in its cylinder as that in the real brake cylinders. For convenience, compactness and security they are combined in one device. The equalizing portion (dummy triple) and pressure chamber (dummy auxiliary) are used in automatic application only; reductions of brake pipe pressure cause the equalizing valve to connect the pressure chamber (dummy auxiliary) to the dummy cylinder, allowing air to flow from the former to the latter. The upper slide valve connected to the piston rod of the application portion, admits air to the brake cylinders and is called the *application valve*, while the lower one releases the air from the brake cylinders and is called the *exhaust valve*. As the air admitted to the brake cylinders comes directly from the main reservoirs, the supply is practically unlimited. Any pressure in the dummy cylinder will force the application piston to close the exhaust valve, open the application valve and admit air from the main reservoirs to the locomotive brake cylinders until their pressure equals that in the dummy cylinder; any variation of this (dummy) cylinder pressure will be exactly duplicated in the locomotive brake cylinders, and the resulting pressure maintained, regardless of any brake cylinder leakage. The whole operation of this locomotive brake, therefore, consists in admitting and releasing air pressure into or out of the dummy cylinder, in independent applications directly through the independent brake valve; in automatic applications, by means of the equalizing (dummy triple valve) portion and the air pressure stored in the pressure chamber (dummy auxiliary).

The well-known principle embodied in the quick action triple valve, by which it gives a high braking power in emergency applications, and a sufficiently lower one in full service applications, to provide a desired protection against wheel sliding, is embodied in the No. 6 distributing valve. This is accomplished by cutting off the application chamber from the application cylinder in all emergency applications. In such applications, the pressure chamber has to fill the small volume of the application cylinder only, thus giving a high equalization, and a correspondingly high brake cylinder pressure. In service applications, it must fill the same volume combined with that of the application chamber, thus giving a lower equalization and correspondingly lower brake cylinder pressure.

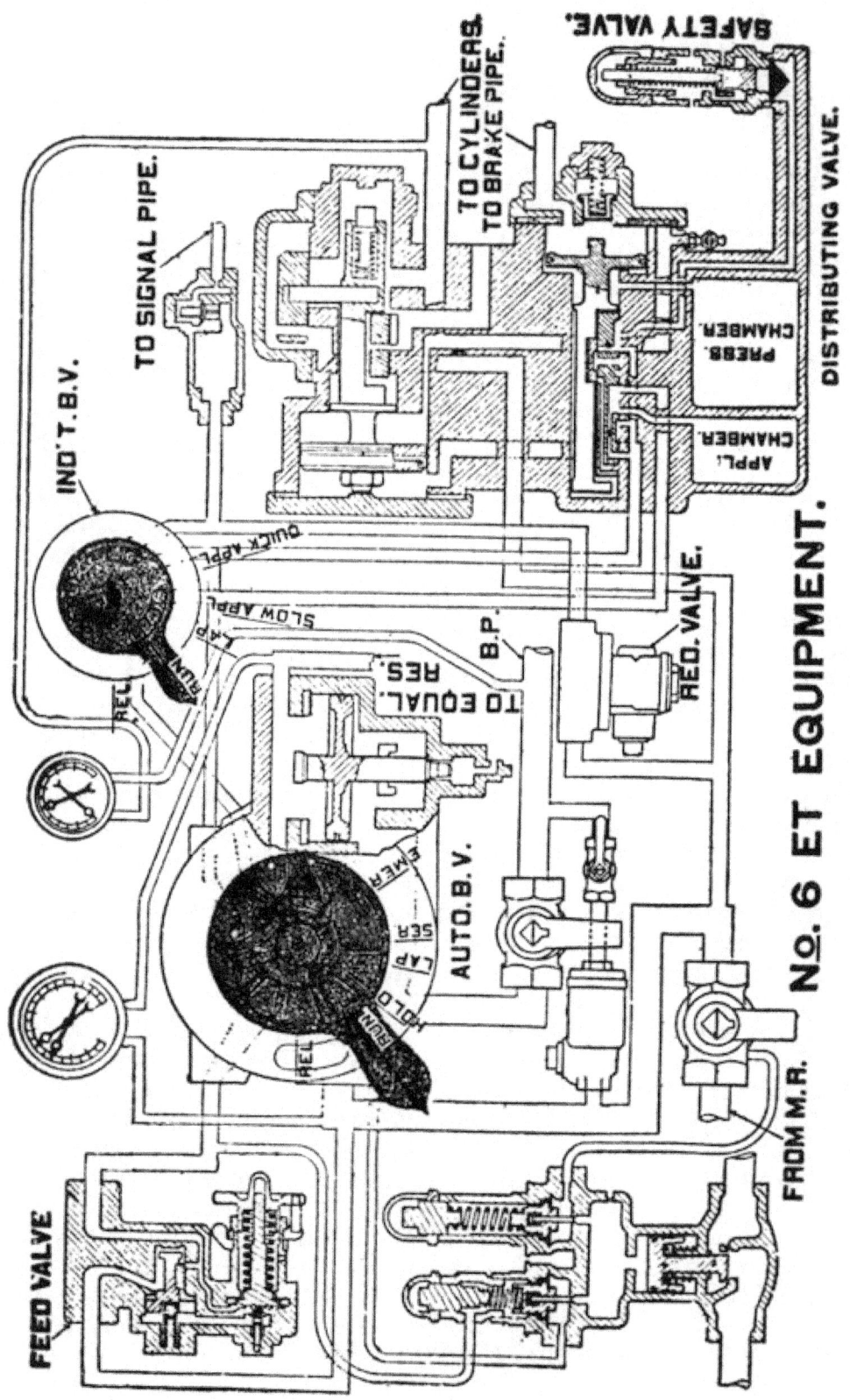

THE H-6 AUTOMATIC BRAKE VALVE.

This brake valve, although modelled to a considerable extent upon the principles of previous valves, is necessarily different in detail, since it not only performs all the functions of such types but also those absolutely necessary to obtain all the desirable operating features of the No. 6 distributing valve.

Figure shows two views of this valve, with the addition of a plan or top view of the rotary valve. The six positions of the brake valve handle are, beginning at the extreme left, *release*, *running*, *holding*, *lap*, *service*, and *emergency*. The names of the parts are as follows: 2, bottom case; 3, rotary valve seat; 4, top case; 5, pipe bracket; 6, rotary valve; 7, rotary valve key; 8, key washer; 9, handle; 10, handle latch spring; 11, handle latch; 12, handle latch screw; 13, handle nut; 14, handle lock nut; 15, equalizing piston; 16, equalizing piston packing ring; 17, valve seat upper gasket; 18, valve seat lower gasket; 19, pipe bracket gasket; 20, small union nut; 21, brake valve tee; 22, small union swivel; 23, large union nut; 24, large union swivel; 25, bracket stud; 26, bracket stud nut; 27, bolt and nut; 28, cap screw; 29, oil plug; 30, rotary valve spring; 31, service exhaust fitting; 35, governor union stud.

Referring to the rotary valve, a, j, and s are ports extending directly through it, the latter connecting with a groove in the face; f and k are cavities in the valve face; o is the exhaust cavity; x and t are ports in the face of the valve connecting by cored passages with o; h is a port extending from the face over cavity k and connecting with exhaust cavity o; n is a groove in the face, having a small port which connects through a cavity in the valve with cavity k. Referring to the ports in the rotary valve seat, d leads to the feed valve pipe; b and c lead to the brake pipe; g leads to chamber D; Ex is the exhaust opening leading out at the back of the valve; e is the preliminary exhaust port leading to chamber D; r is the warning port leading to the exhaust; p is the port leading to the pump governor; l leads to the distributing valve release pipe; u leads to the application cylinder pipe.

In describing the operation of the brake valve, it will be more readily understood if the positions are taken up in the order in which they are most generally used, rather than their regular order, as mentioned previously.

Charging and release position.—The purpose of this position is to provide a large and direct passage from the main reservoir to the brake pipe, to permit a rapid flow of air into the latter to (a) charge the train brake system; (b) quickly release and recharge the breaks, but (c) *not* release locomotive brakes, if they are applied.

Air at main reservoir pressure flows through port a in the rotary valve and port b in the valve seat to the brake pipe. At the same

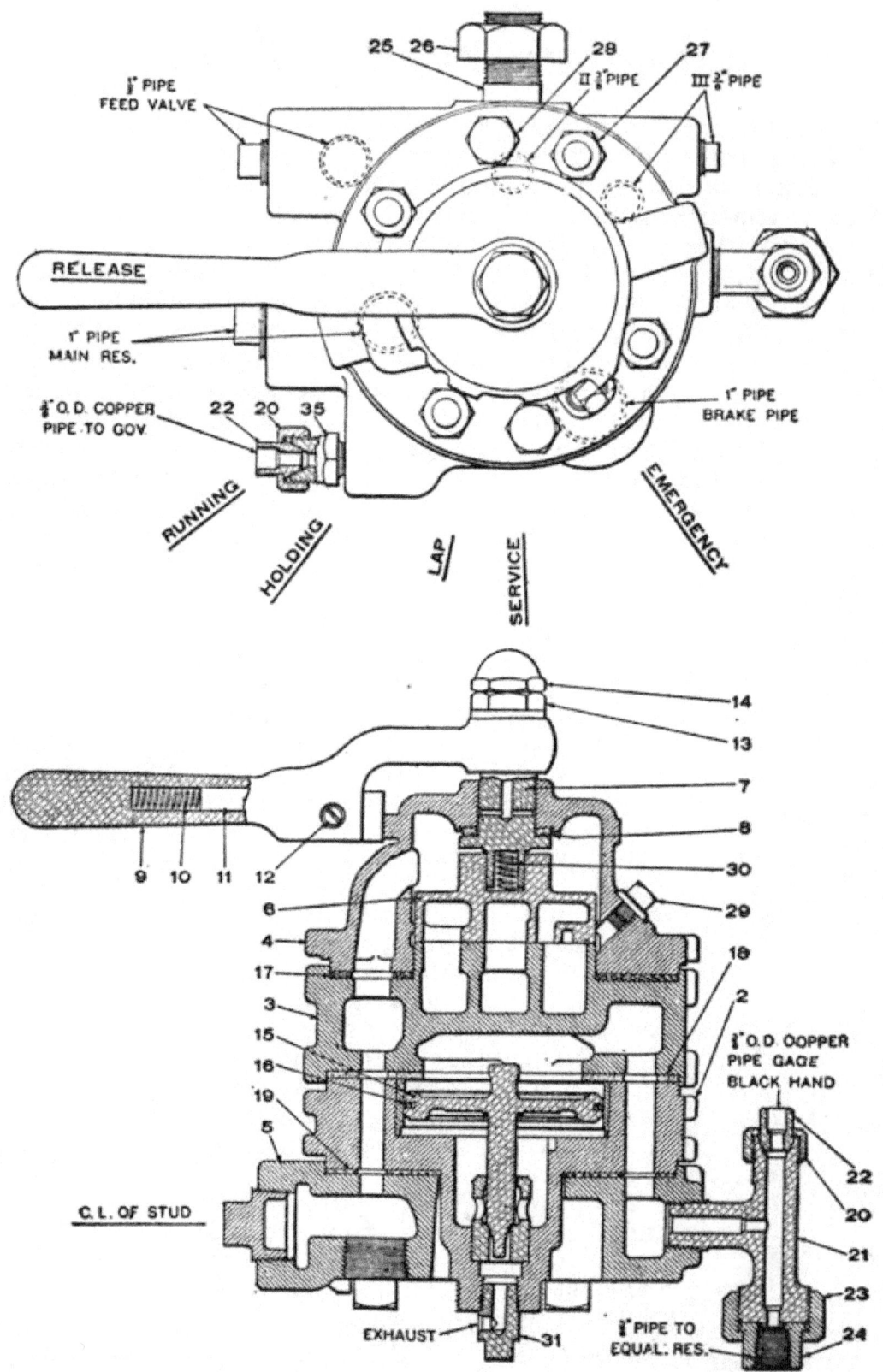

The H-6 Automatic Brake Valve

time, port j in the rotary valve registers with equalizing port g in the valve seat, permitting air at main reservoir pressure to enter chamber D above the equalizing piston.

If the handle were allowed to remain in this position, the brake system would be charged to main reservoir pressure. To avoid this, the handle must be moved to *running* or *holding* position. To prevent the engineer from forgetting this, a small port discharges feed valve pipe air to the atmosphere in release position. Cavity f in the rotary valve connects port d with warning port r in the seat and allows a small quantity of air to escape into the exhaust cavity Ex, which makes sufficient noise to attract the engineer's attention to the position in which the valve handle is standing. The small groove in the face of the rotary valve, which connects with port s, extends to port p in the valve seat, allowing main reservoir pressure to flow to the lower connection of the excess pressure head of the compressor governor.

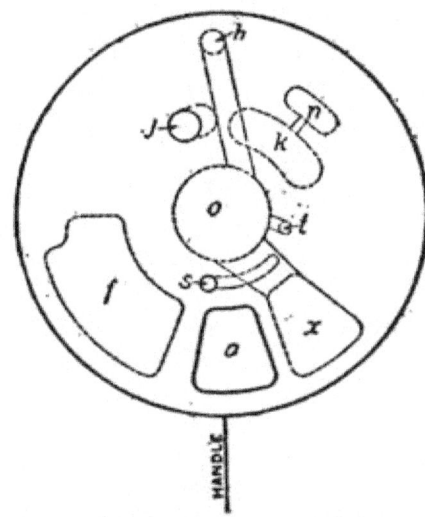

Rotary Valve, H-6 Automatic Brake Valve.

Running position.—This is the proper position of the handle (a) when the brakes are charged and ready for use; (b) when the brakes are not being operated; and (c) to release the locomotive brakes. In this position, cavity f in the rotary valve connects ports b and d in the valve seat, affording a large, direct passage from the feed valve pipe to the brake pipe, so that the latter will charge up as rapidly as the feed valve can supply the air, but can not attain a pressure above that for which the feed valve is adjusted. Cavity k in the rotary valve connects ports c and g in the valve seat, so that chamber D and the equalizing reservoir charge uniformly with the brake pipe, keeping the pressure on the two sides of the equalizing piston equal. Port s in the rotary valve registers with port p in the valve seat, permitting air at main reservoir pressure, which is present at all times above the rotary valve, to pass to the lower connection of the excess pressure head of the compressor governor. Port h in the rotary valve registers with port l in the seat, connecting the distributing valve release pipe through the exhaust cavity Ex with the atmosphere.

If the brake valve is in *running* position when uncharged cars are cut in, or if, after a heavy brake application and release, the handle of the automatic brake valve is returned to *running* position too soon, the governor will stop the compressors until the difference between the hands on gauge No. 1 is less than 20 pounds. The compressors stopping from this cause, calls the engineer's attention to the seriously wrong operation on his part, as *running* position results in delay in charging, and is liable to cause some brakes to stick. *Release* position should be used until all brakes are released and nearly charged.

Service position.—This position gives a gradual reduction of brake pipe pressure to cause a service application. Port h in the rotary valve registers with port e in the valve seat, allowing air from chamber D and the equalizing reservoir to escape to the atmosphere through cavities o in the rotary valve and Ex in the valve seat. Port e is restricted so as to make the pressure in the equalizing reservoir and chamber D fall gradually.

As all other ports are closed, the fall of pressure in chamber D allows the brake pipe pressure under the equalizing piston to raise it, and unseat its valve, allowing brake pipe air to flow to the atmosphere gradually through the opening marked $BP\ Ex$. When the pressure in chamber D is reduced the desired amount, the handle is moved to *lap* position, thus stopping any further reduction in that chamber. Air will continue to discharge from the brake pipe until its pressure has fallen to an amount a trifle less than that retained in chamber D; permitting the pressure in this chamber to force the piston downward gradually and stop the discharge of brake pipe air. It will be seen, therefore, that the amount of reduction in the equalizing reservoir determines that in the brake pipe, regardless of the length of the train.

The gradual reduction of brake pipe pressure is to prevent quick action, and the gradual stopping of this discharge is to prevent the pressure at the head end of the brake pipe being built up by the air flowing from the rear, which might cause some of the head brakes to "kick off."

Lap position.—This position is used while holding the brakes applied after a service application until it is desired either to make a further brake pipe reduction, or to release them. All ports are closed.

Release position.—This position, which is used for releasing the train brakes after an application, without releasing the locomotive brakes, has already been described under Charging and Release. The air flowing from the main reservoir pipe connection through port a in the rotary valve and port b in the valve seat to the brake pipe, raises the pressure in the latter, thereby causing the triple valves and equalizing portion of the distributing valve to go to release position, which releases the train brakes and recharges the auxiliary reservoirs and the pressure chamber of the distributing valve. When the brake pipe pressure has been increased sufficiently to cause this, the handle of the brake valve should be moved to either *running* or *holding* position; the former when it is desired to release the locomotive brakes, and the latter when they are to be still held applied.

Holding position.—This position is so named because the locomotive brakes are held applied while the train brakes are being released and their auxiliary reservoirs recharged to feed valve pressure. All ports register as in *running* position, except port l, which is closed.

Therefore, the only difference between *running* and *holding* positions is that in the former the locomotive brakes are released, while in the latter they are held applied.

Emergency position.—This position is used (a) when the most prompt and heavy application of the brakes is required, and (b) to prevent loss of main reservoir air and insure that the brakes remain applied in the event of a burst hose, a break in two, or the opening of a conductor's valve. Port x in the rotary valve registers with port c in the valve seat, making a large and direct communication between the brake pipe and atmosphere through cavity o in the rotary valve and Ex in the valve seat. This direct passage makes a sudden and heavy discharge of brake pipe air, causing the triple valves and distributing valve to move to emergency position and give maximum braking power in the shortest possible time.

In this position, main reservoir air flows to the application cylinder through port j, which registers with a groove in the seat connecting with cavity k; thence through ports n in the valve and u in the seat, to the application cylinder pipe, thereby maintaining application cylinder pressure.

At the same time port t in the rotary valve registers with port g in the seat, allowing the air in the equalizing reservoir to flow through the ports named to the exhaust o and atmosphere, thus reducing the pressure in the equalizing reservoir to zero during an emergency application of the brakes.

Leather washer 8 prevents air in the rotary valve chamber from leaking past the rotary valve key to the atmosphere. Spring 30 keeps the rotary valve key firmly pressed against washer 8 when no main reservoir pressure is present. The handle 9 contains latch 11, which fits into notches in the quadrant of the top case, so located as to indicate the different positions of the brake valve handle. Handle latch spring 10 forces the latch against the quadrant with sufficient pressure to indicate each position.

To remove the brake valve, close the cocks, and take off nuts 27. To take the valve proper apart, remove cap screws 28.

The brake valve should be located so that the engineer can operate it conveniently from his usual position, while looking forward or back out of the side cab window.

MANIPULATION AND TRAIN HANDLING.

The following instructions are general, and must necessarily be supplemented to a limited extent to fully meet the varying local conditions on different railways.

The instructions for manipulating the "ET" equipment are practically the same as those given for the combined automatic and straight air brake; therefore, no radical departure from present methods of brake manipulation is required to get the desired results.

The necessary instructions are briefly as follows:

When not in use, carry the handles of both brake valves in running position.

To apply the brakes in service, move the handle of the automatic brake valve to the *service position,* making the required brake pipe reduction, then back to *lap position,* which is the one for holding the brakes applied.

To release the train brakes, move the handle to the *release position* and hold it there until all triple valves are in release position; if locomotive brakes are to be released at once, use *running position;* but if they are to be held for a time, move to *holding position,* and then graduate them off by short, successive movements between running and holding positions. With all freight trains, and especially long ones, both release and holding positions must, of course, be used very much longer than with short trains, particularly passenger.

To apply the brakes in emergency, move the handle of the automatic brake valve quickly to emergency position and leave it there until the train stops or the danger is past.

To make a smooth and accurate *two-application passenger stop,* make the first application sufficiently heavy to bring the speed of train down to about 15 miles per hour at a convenient distance from the stopping point, then release train brakes by moving the handle to *release position,* then the locomotive brakes by moving it to *running position* for two or three seconds before re-applying. A little experience with the "ET" equipment will enable the engineer to make smooth and accurate stops with much greater ease than was heretofore possible.

When using *the independent brake only,* the handle of the automatic brake valve should be carried in *running position.* The independent application may be released by moving the independent brake valve handle to *running position.* Independent release position is for use only when the automatic brake valve handle is not in running position, as an example, when the engineer desires to release the engine brakes independent of the train brakes.

While handling long trains of cars, in road or switching service, the independent brake should be operated with care, to prevent damage to cars and lading, caused by running the slack in or out too hard. In cases of emergency arising while the independent brake is applied, apply the automatic brake instantly. The safety valve will restrict the brake cylinder pressure to the proper maximum.

The brakes on the locomotive and on the train should be alternated in heavy grade service, to prevent overheating of driving wheel tires and to assist the pressure retaining valves in holding the train while the auxiliary reservoirs are being recharged. This is done by keeping the locomotive brakes released by use of the independent brake valve when train brakes are applied, and applying locomotive brakes just before train brakes are released, and then releasing locomotive brakes after train brakes are applied.

When all brakes are applied automatically, to graduate off or entirely release the *locomotive brakes only*, use *release position* of the independent brake valve.

The red hand of gauge No. 2 will show at all times the pressure in the locomotive brake cylinders, and this hand should be observed in brake manipulation.

Release position of the independent brake valve will release the locomotive brakes under any and all conditions.

The train brakes should invariably be released before detaching the locomotive, holding with hand brakes where necessary. This is especially important on a grade, as there is otherwise no assurance that the car, cars, or train so detached will not start when the air brakes leak off, as they may in a short time where there is considerable leakage.

The automatic brakes should never be used to hold a standing locomotive or a train, even where the locomotive is not detached, for longer than ten minutes, and not for so much time if the grade is very steep or the condition of the brakes is not good. The safest method is to hold with hand brakes only and keep the auxiliary reservoirs fully charged, so as to guard against a start from brakes leaking off, and to be ready to obtain any part of full braking power immediately on starting.

The independent brake is a very important safety feature in this connection, as it will hold a locomotive with a leaky throttle or quite a heavy train on a fairly steep grade if, as the automatic brakes are released, the slack is prevented from running in or out (depending on the tendency of the grade), and giving the locomotive a start. To illustrate:—The best method to make a stop on a descending grade is to apply the independent brake heavily as the stop is being completed, thus bunching the train solidly; then, when stopped, place and *leave* the handle of the independent brake valve in application position; then release the automatic brakes and keep them charged. Should the independent brake be unable to prevent the train from starting, the automatic brakes will become sufficiently recharged to make an immediate stop; in such an event enough hand brakes should at once be applied as are necessary to assist the independent brake to hold the train. *Many runaways and some serious wrecks have resulted through failure to comply with the foregoing instructions.*

When leaving the engine while doing work about it, or when it is standing at a coal chute or water plug, always leave the independent brake valve handle in *application position*.

In case the automatic brakes are applied by a bursted hose, a break-in-two, or the use of a conductor's valve, place the handle of the automatic brake valve in lap position.

Where there are two or more locomotives in a train, the *doubleheading cock must be closed*, and the handle of the automatic brake valve must be carried in *running position* on each except the one from which the brakes are being operated.

Before leaving the roundhouse, the engineer should try the brakes with both brake valves, and see that no serious leaks exist. The pipes between the distributing valve and the brake valves should be absolutely tight.

QUESTIONS AND ANSWERS ON No. 6 "ET" LOCOMOTIVE BRAKE EQUIPMENT

Q. 1.—What is the No. 6 "ET" equipment?

A.—It is a brake equipment for engine and tender adapted to all kinds of engines and classes of service and combines the operative features of the standard automatic, straight air, high speed, and double pressure control brake equipments, with many additional features.

Q. 2.—Is the operation of the train brakes affected by the "ET" equipment?

A.—No; the operation of the train brakes is the same with this equipment as with former locomotive brake equipments.

Q. 3.—What is meant by the term *train* brakes?

A.—All brakes in the train except those upon the locomotive from which the brakes are being handled.

Q. 4.—What is meant by the term *locomotive* brake?

A.—The brake upon the engine and tender.

Q. 5.—What new features of operation are obtainable with the "ET" equipment?

A.—(a) Locomotive brake may be used with or independently of the train brakes, whether the train brakes are in use or not.

(b) Uniform and proper cylinder pressure is obtained, regardless of piston travel or leakage.

(c) Cylinder pressure is automatically maintained, regardless of brake cylinder leakage.

(d) Locomotive brake can be graduated on or off with either the automatic or the independent brake valves.

(e) Increased flexibility in service operations, with increased braking power in emergency applications.

(f) Brakes on second locomotive or helper can be released or applied without in any way interfering with any other brakes in the train.

PARTS OF THE EQUIPMENT.

Q. 6.—Name the essential parts of the "ET" equipment

A.—1, air compressor; 2, main reservoir; 3, duplex pump governor; 4, feed valve; 5, reducing valve; 6, automatic brake valve with equalizing reservoir; 7, independent brake valve; 8, distributing valve and double reservoir; 9, two duplex air gauges; 10, combined air strainer and check valve; 11, choke fitting; 12, locomotive brake cylinders; also various cocks and fittings.

Q. 7.—What special parts are sometimes used?

A.—(a) Quick action cylinder cap for distributing valve.

(b) Combined air strainer and check valve for train air signal system.

(c) Choke fitting for truck brake.

Q. 8.—What furnishes the compressed air for the brake system?

A.—The air compressor.

Q. 9.—What operates the air compressor?

A.—Steam from the locomotive boiler.

Q. 10.—After leaving the compressor, where does the air go?

A.—Through the radiating pipes to the main reservoir.

Q. 11.—What is the purpose of the radiating pipe?

A.—To cool the air after leaving the compressor.

Q. 12.—What is the purpose of the main reservoirs?

A.—The main reservoirs provide a place for the storage of an abundant supply of compressed air for use in promptly releasing the brakes on the locomotive and train and for recharging the brake system. They also assist in cooling the compressed air and collect moisture, oil or other foreign matter, allowing only clean, dry air to pass to the brake system.

Q. 13.—What controls the air pressure in the main reservoirs?

A.—The duplex pump governor.

Q. 14.—How does the pump governor control the main reservoir pressure?

A.—It automatically regulates the supply of steam to the compressor so as to maintain normal pressure in the main reservoirs.

Q. 15.—What connects the main reservoirs to the brake system?
A.—The main reservoir pipe.

Q. 16.—What provision is made for cutting off the main reservoirs from the rest of the brake system?
A.—A cock in the main reservoir pipe close to the main reservoir, known as the "main reservoir cut-out cock."

Q. 17.—Where do the pipe branches lead to from the main reservoir pipe?
A.—(a) To the duplex pump governor.
(b) To the main reservoir hand of the duplex air gauge.
(c) To the automatic brake valve.
(d) To the feed valve.
(e) To the reducing valve.
(f) To the distributing valve.
(g) To the dead engine fixtures.
(h) Other branches leading to various air-using devices on the locomotive, such as sanders, water scoop, etc.

Q. 18.—What is the purpose of the feed valve?
A.—To automatically maintain a predetermined pressure in the brake system, lower than that carried in the main reservoirs.

Q. 19.—To what does the feed valve pipe connect?
A.—To the automatic brake valve, and to the spring chamber of the excess pressure head of the duplex pump governor.

Q. 20.—What is the purpose of the reducing valve?
A.—It automatically reduces the air pressure from the main reservoirs to the proper pressure used with the independent brake and train air signal system.

Q. 21.—What is the purpose of the automatic brake valve?
A.—(a) To allow air to flow from the brake system for charging it.
(b) To discharge air from the brake pipe to the atmosphere to apply the brakes.
(c) To prevent the flow of air to or from the brake pipe when holding the brakes applied.
(d) To hold applied or release the locomotive brake as desired while releasing train brakes.
(e) To allow air to flow to the brake system for the purpose of releasing the brakes and recharging the system.
(f) To control the flow of air to the diaphragm chamber of the excess pressure head of the duplex pump governor.
(g) To allow main reservoir to flow to the application cylinder of the distributing valve in *emergency* position.

Q. 22.—What is the purpose of the independent brake valve?
A.—To operate the brakes on the engine and tender independent of the train brakes.

Q. 23.—State briefly the purpose of the distributing valve.
A.—(a) To automatically control the flow of air from the main reservoirs to the engine and tender brake cylinders when applying the brakes.

(b) To automatically maintain the brake cylinder pressure against leakage, keeping it constant, when holding the brake applied.

(c) To automatically control the flow of air from the engine and tender brake cylinders to the atmosphere when releasing the brake.

Q. 24.—What is the purpose of the locomotive brake cylinders?

A.—The brake cylinder is that part of the air brake equipment in which the force contained in the compressed air is transformed into a mechanical force, which is transmitted through a suitable combination of rods and levers to the brake shoes and applies them to the wheels.

H-6 AUTOMATIC BRAKE VALVE.

Q. 25.—How many positions has the H-6 brake valve?
A.—Six.

Q. 26.—Name the positions, beginning at the left.
A.—*Release, running, holding, lap, service* and *emergency*.

Q. 27.—Name and describe the purpose of the pipe connections to the H-6 brake valve.

A.—(a) Main reservoir pipe.—To connect the main reservoirs to the chamber above the rotary valve and permit a free flow of high pressure air into the brake pipe when the brake valve handle is in *release* position.

(b) Feed valve pipe.—To connect the feed valve to the under side of the rotary valve. When the brake valve handle is in *running* position this pipe is open to the brake pipe, thus permitting the feed valve to maintain a constant brake pipe pressure below that in the main reservoirs.

(c) Equalizing reservoir pipe.—This connects the chamber above the equalizing piston to the equalizing reservoir and the equalizing reservoir gauge.

(d) Brake pipe.—To connect the distributing valve on the locomotive and the triple valve on each car to the space underneath the equalizing discharge piston and the under side of rotary valve.

(e) Governor pipe.—This makes a connection from the rotary valve chamber (main reservoir pressure) to the under side of the diaphragm of the excess pressure governor head when the brake valve handle is in either *release, running* or *holding* positions.

(f) Distributing valve release pipe.—This makes a connection from the application chamber of the distributing valve (through the independent brake valve) to the under side of the automatic rotary valve, forming a connection to the atmosphere when both brake valve handles are in *running* position.

(g) Application cylinder pipe.—This connects the under side of the automatic rotary valve directly to the application cylinder of the distributing valve. In *emergency* position of the brake valve handle this pipe is open to the chamber above the rotary valve (main reservoir pressure) through the blow-down timing port.

Q. 28.—When is *release* position used?

A.—When it is desired to quickly charge the brake system and to release brakes on long trains.

Q. 29.—Explain the flow of air through the automatic brake valve when in *release* position.

A.—Air from the main reservoirs flows directly to the brake pipe, equalizing reservoir and pump governor. Air from the feed valve flows through the warning port to the atmosphere.

Q. 30.—When is *running* position used?

A.—When running along the road to maintain a predetermined brake pipe pressure lower than that carried in the main reservoirs, to release the engine and tender brakes and also to release the brakes on short trains.

Q. 31.—Explain the flow of air through the automatic brake valve when in *running* position.

A.—(a) Air from the feed valve flows to the brake pipe and to the equalizing reservoir.

(b) Air from the main reservoirs flows directly to the diaphragm chamber of the excess pressure head of the duplex pump governor.

(c) Air from the distributing valve release pipe flows to the atmosphere.

Q. 32.—When is *holding* position used?

A.—When it is desired to hold the engine and tender brakes applied by means of the automatic brake valve while releasing and recharging the train brakes.

Q. 33.—Explain the flow of air through the automatic brake valve when in *holding* position.

A.—The flow of air through the automatic brake valve when in holding position is the same as when in *running* position with one exception, namely, air from the distributing valve release pipe is prevented from flowing to the atmosphere.

Q. 34.—When is *lap* position used?

A.—When holding all the brakes applied after an automatic application. The handle should never be carried in this position except while bringing the train to a stop.

Q. 35.—Is there any flow of air to the brake system through the automatic brake valve when in *lap* position?

A.—No.

Q. 36.—When is *service* position used?

A.—When it is desired to make an automatic application of the brakes.

Q. 37.—Explain fully the flow of air through the automatic brake valve when in *service* position.

A.—In the automatic brake valve is a piston and valve called the equalizing discharge piston and valve, No. 15. The under side of this piston is directly connected to the brake pipe. The chamber

D, above piston 15, is directly connected to the equalizing reservoir ER and to a small port e in the rotary valve seat called the preliminary exhaust port. In *service* position the preliminary exhaust port is open to the atmosphere through port h and exhaust cavity o in the rotary valve, thus allowing air from the equalizing reservoir and the chamber D above the equalizing discharge piston to flow to the atmosphere. This reduces the pressure on the top of the piston below the brake pipe pressure on the under side, which raises the equalizing discharge piston 15 and permits brake pipe air to flow to the atmosphere through the service exhaust fitting $B. P. Ex.$ The flow of air from the equalizing reservoir to the atmosphere continues until the brake valve handle is returned to *lap* position. This closes the preliminary exhaust port e, and prevents further decrease of pressure in the equalizing reservoir and chamber D. Air will continue to discharge from brake pipe until its pressure has been reduced slightly lower than that remaining in chamber D. The higher pressure on the top of the piston then forces the valve to its seat and prevents further reduction of brake pipe pressure.

Q. 38.—What is the purpose of the service exhaust fitting?

A.—To fix the maximum permissible opening from the brake pipe to the atmosphere when making a service application.

Q. 39.—Is it important that all H-6 brake valves be provided with this fitting?

A.—Yes.

Q. 40.—When is *emergency* position used?

A.—When it is desired to make the shortest possible stop. In such case the handle should be moved to *emergency* position quickly and left there until the train stops.

Q. 41.—Should this position be used at any other time?

A.—Yes; this position should be used in case of an emergency application of the brakes from an unknown cause, such as the opening of a conductor's valve, bursted hose, etc., in order to prevent loss of main reservoir pressure and to insure a full application of the brakes, and the handle should be left there until signal to release is given.

Q. 42.—Why should *emergency* position be used as explained in the last answer instead of *lap* position?

A.—To insure the brakes remaining applied under all circumstances.

Q. 43.—Explain the flow of air through the automatic brake valve when in *emergency* position.

A.—A large and direct opening is made from the brake pipe to the atmosphere, through the rotary valve, causing a quick and heavy reduction of brake pipe pressure. At the same time the air in the equalizing reservoir escapes to the atmosphere through ports in the rotary valve. Connection is made from air at main reservoir pressure above the rotary valve through a restricted port in the rotary valve to the application cylinder pipe leading to the application cylinder of the distributing valve. This port is known as the blow-down timing port, and assists in building up and regulating application cylinder pressure during emergency application.

S-6 INDEPENDENT BRAKE VALVE.

Q. 44.—How many positions has the S-6 brake valve?
A.—Five.
Q. 45.—Name the positions, beginning at the left.
A.—*Release, running, lap, slow application* and *quick application*.
Q. 46.—Name and describe the purpose of the pipe connections to the S-6 brake valve.
A.—(a) Reducing valve pipe.—This is the only source of air supply to the valve and connects the reducing valve to the chamber above the rotary valve, and through the rotary valve when the independent brake valve handle is in either *application* position, to the application cylinder and chamber of the distributing valve and also through the warning port to the atmosphere when the handle is in *release* position.
(b) Distributing valve release pipe *to the distributing valve*.—Connects the application chamber of the distributing valve to the under side of the independent brake valve. When the brake valve handle is in *running* position, this pipe is connected through ports in the seat and cavities in the rotary valve to the automatic brake valve.
(c) Distributing valve release pipe to *the automatic brake valve*.—This pipe connects the under side of the rotary valve of the independent brake valve to the under side of the rotary valve of the automatic brake valve. With both brake valve handles in *running* position, free passage is made from the application chamber of the distributing valve to the atmosphere through this pipe.
(d) Application cylinder pipe.—Connects the application cylinder to the under side of the rotary valve of the independent brake valve. When the handle is in either *application* position air from above the rotary valve flows through this pipe to the application cylinder and chamber of the distributing valve. When the handle is in *release* position this pipe is connected to the atmosphere through ports in the rotary valve and seat.
Q. 47.—When is *release* position used?
A.—Whenever it may be necessary to release the brake when the automatic brake valve handle is not in *running* position.
Q. 48.—Explain the flow of air through the independent brake valve when in *release* position.
A.—Air from the application cylinder of the distributing valve flows direct through the application cylinder pipe and independent brake valve to the atmosphere. At the same time air from above the rotary valve (reducing valve pressure) flows through the rotary valve and warning port to the atmosphere.

Q. 49.—When is *running* position used?

A.—When running along the road and to release the locomotive brake after an independent application, the automatic brake valve handle being in running position.

Q. 50.—Explain the flow of air through the independent brake valve when in *running* position. (Automatic brake valve handle in *running* position.)

A.—Air from the application chamber of the distributing valve flows through the distributing valve release pipe and independent brake valve, then through the automatic brake valve to the atmosphere.

Q. 51.—When is *lap* position used?

A.—When holding the engine and tender brake applied after an independent application.

Q. 52.—Is there any flow of air through the independent brake valve when in *lap* position?

A.—No.

Q. 53.—When is *slow application* position used?

A.—When it is desired to apply the locomotive brakes lightly or gradually.

Q. 54.—Explain the flow of air through the independent brake valve when in *slow application* position.

A.—Air flows from the chamber above the rotary valve through the restricted service port and application cylinder pipe into the application cylinder and chamber of the distributing valve.

Q. 55.—When is *quick application* position used?

A.—When it is desired to apply the locomotive brakes promptly.

Q. 56.—Explain the flow of air through the independent brake valve when in quick application position.

A.—Air flows from above the rotary valve through a full open service port in the rotary valve and the application cylinder pipe to the application cylinder and chamber of the distributing valve.

Q. 57.—What prevents the independent brake valve handle from remaining in *release* position or in *quick application* position unless held there?

A.—A return spring.

Q. 58.—To what position does the return spring move the brake valve handle from *release* position?

A.—To *running* position.

Q. 59.—Why is this necessary?

A.—To prevent the possibility of the independent brake valve handle being left in *release* position, which would cause the engine and tender brakes to release whenever an automatic application was made.

Q. 60.—To what position does the return spring move the brake valve handle from *quick application* position?

A.—To *slow application* position.

Q. 61.—Why is the spring used for this purpose?
A.—To act as a stop, guarding against a quick application when only a slow application is intended, and to return the handle from *quick* to *slow application* position.

Q. 62.—Why is this latter necessary?
A.—In order to limit the flow of air to the application cylinder when the independent brake is to be left applied.

No. 6 DISTRIBUTING VALVE WITH PLAIN CYLINDER CAP.

Q. 63.—What controls the brake cylinder pressure on the locomotive with No. 6 "ET" equipment?
A.—The distributing valve.

Q. 64.—How does it do this?
A.—It permits air to flow from the main reservoirs to the brake cylinders when applying the brake, from the cylinders to the atmosphere when releasing the brake, and automatically maintains the pressure against leakage, keeping it constant, when holding the brake applied.

Q. 65.—Is the amount of air flowing from the main reservoirs to the brake cylinders limited by the distributing valve?
A.—Yes; the distributing valve acts as a reducing valve in supplying air from the main reservoirs to the locomotive brake cylinders.

Q. 66.—Facing the distributing valve, name the two pipes on the right-hand side of the reservoir and state to what each one connects.
A.—(a) The upper pipe on the right is the brake cylinder pipe. It connects the distributing valve to all the brake cylinders on the engine and tender.
(b) The lower pipe on the right is the brake pipe branch pipe. It connects the distributing valve to the brake pipe.

Q. 67.—Name the three pipes on the left-hand side of the reservoir and state to what each one connects.
A.—(a) The upper pipe on the left is the supply pipe. It connects the distributing valve to the main reservoir pipe.
(b) The intermediate pipe is the application cylinder pipe. It connects the distributing valve to both the automatic and independent brake valves.
(c) The lower pipe is the release pipe, which connects the distributing valve to the independent brake valve and through it to the automatic brake valve.

Q. 68.—How many chambers has the distributing valve reservoir?
A.—Two.

Q. 69.—Name them.
A.—Pressure chamber and application chamber.

Q. 70.—How many pistons has the distributing valve?

A.—Two.

Q. 71.—Name them.

A.—Application piston 10 and equalizing piston 26.

Q. 72.—How many slide valves has the distributing valve?

A.—Four.

Q. 73.—Name them.

A.—Application valve 5, exhaust valve 16, equalizing valve 31 and graduating valve 28.

Q. 74.—What valves are operated by the application piston?

A.—The application valve and exhaust valve.

Q. 75.—What valves are operated by the equalizing piston?

A.—The equalizing valve and graduating valve.

Q. 76.—With the brake released what pressures are present in the distributing valve?

A.—Main reservoir pressure, brake pipe pressure and atmospheric pressure.

Q. 77.—In what portion of the distributing valve is main reservoir pressure?

A.—In chamber a, above the application valve.

Q. 78.—In what portion of the distributing valve is brake pipe pressure?

A.—In the pressure chamber and in the chamber above the equalizing valve and graduating valve.

Q. 79.—In what portion of the distributing valve is atmospheric pressure?

A.—In chamber b above the exhaust valve 16 and on the right-hand side of the application piston 10; in chamber g on the left-hand side of the application piston (called the application cylinder), and in the application chamber and the ports and cavities connecting to them.

Q. 80.—How is chamber a charged with air at main reservoir pressure?

A.—Through the branch pipe leading from the main reservoir pipe to the connection marked MR on the distributing valve reservoir.

Q. 81.—Describe the operation of the distributing valve parts when an independent application of the brake is made.

A.—Air is admitted to the application cylinder g and the application chamber from the reducing valve through the independent brake valve and the intermediate pipe on the left (application chamber pipe). This pressure will force the application piston 10 to the right, lapping exhaust ports d and e with exhaust valve 16, and compressing graduating spring 20 and open supply port b through the application valve 5 to the brake cylinder chamber b, which is connected to the right of the application piston, obtaining a brake cylinder pressure slightly exceeding that in the application cylinder, when it and the graduating spring 20 then moves the piston 10 and the application valve 5 back to lap position. The exhaust valve 16 will remain lapped, as there is sufficient clearance between the shoulders of the piston stem and the exhaust valve to permit the application valve to return to lap without moving the exhaust valve. At the same time cavity s in the equalizing valve 31 registers with ports h and l in the seat, thus connecting the application cylinder port h to the safety valve. *The equalizing piston and slide valve do not move during an independent application of the brake.*

Q. 82.—Describe the operation of the distributing valve parts when an independent release of the brake is made.

A.—By a proper movement of the independent brake handle, air from the application cylinder g and the application chamber is allowed to flow to the atmosphere, which reduces the pressure in chamber g below that in chamber b, causing the application piston 10 to move to the left, carrying with it application valve 5 and exhaust valve 16, until ports d and e are open past and through exhaust valve 16, permitting the air in the brake cylinders to flow through port c into chamber b, thence through ports d and e, to the exhaust and atmosphere. *The equalizing piston and its valves do not move during an independent release of the brakes.*

Q. 83.—How is the pressure chamber charged with air at brake pipe pressure?

A.—Through the branch pipe leading from the brake pipe to the connection marked *BP* on the distributing valve reservoir leading into chamber p, then through feed groove v, around top of piston 26, into the chamber above the equalizing valve 31 and through port o to the pressure chamber, until the pressure on both sides of the piston is equal.

Q. 84.—From where do the application cylinder and chamber receive their air?

A.—From the *reducing valve* through the independent brake valve during independent applications, and from the *pressure chamber* during automatic service applications.

Q. 85.—Describe the operation of the distributing valve parts when an automatic service application of the brake is made.

A.—The brake pipe pressure in chamber p on the brake pipe side of equalizing piston 26 being reduced below that in the pressure chamber on the opposite side of the piston, results in piston 26 being moved toward the right. The first movement of piston 26 closes the feed groove v, and at the same time moves the graduating valve 28 until it opens the service port z in the equalizing valve and connects the safety valve ports r and s in equalizing valve through cavity t in the graduating valve. As the piston continues its movement, the "spider" on the end of the piston stem engages the slide valve 31, which is then moved to the right until the supply port z in the equalizing valve registers with the application cylinder port h and through cavity n in the equalizing valve with application chamber port w in the seat. This permits the air in the pressure chamber to expand into the application cylinder. At the same time the safety valve is connected to the application cylinder and application chamber by registering ports r and s in the equalizing valve with ports h and l in the seat and through the cavity t in the graduating valve. The amount of pressure obtained in the application cylinder and chamber depends upon the brake pipe reduction made. When the pressure in the pressure chamber is slightly reduced below that in the brake pipe, the piston and the graduating valve are forced to the left until the collar on the piston stem comes in contact with the equalizing valve. This position is known as "service lap." In this position the graduating valve has lapped port z between the pressure chamber and the application cylinder and has also lapped the safety valve port l. The air that expanded into the application cylinder and chamber will force the application piston 10 to the right, lapping the exhaust ports d and e with the exhaust valve 16, compressing graduating spring 20 and opening the supply port b through the application valve 5 to brake cylinder, as explained in answer to queston 81.

Q. 86.—Describe the operation of the distributing valve when the brake is released with the independent brake valve, after an automatic application.

A.—With the independent brake valve handle in *release* position, air in application cylinder g and the application chamber flows direct to the atmosphere through the application cylinder pipe. This reduces the pressure in chamber g below that in chamber b, causing supply valve piston 10 to move to the left, carrying with it application valve 5 and exhaust valve 16 to *release* position, thus releasing the brake.

Q. 87.—Do the equalizing parts of the distributing valve operate at this time?

A.—No.

Q. 88.—Describe the operation of the distributing valve parts when making an automatic release of the brakes.

A.—The brake pipe pressure in chamber p on the brake pipe side of equalizing piston 26 being increased above that in the pressure chamber on the opposite side of the piston, results in the piston being moved toward the left, carrying with it graduating valve 28 and equalizing valve 31 to release position. In this position cavity k in equalizing valve 31 registers with ports w, h, and i in the seat. This allows air from the application cylinder g and the application chamber to flow through the ports mentioned to the distributing valve release pipe IV and to the atmosphere. At the same time the reduction of pressure in chamber g below that in chamber b causes the supply piston 10 to move to the left, carrying with it exhaust valve 16 to release position, thus releasing the brake as described in answer to question 82.

Q. 89.—Describe the operation of the distributing valve parts when an automatic emergency application of the brake is made.

A.—Brake pipe pressure in chamber p on the brake pipe side of equalizing piston 26 is suddenly reduced below that in the pressure chamber on the opposite side of the piston. The considerable difference in pressure thus created on the two sides of equalizing piston 26 is sufficient to move it to its extreme position to the right, compressing graduating spring 46. In this position port h is open directly to the chamber above equalizing valve 31, past the end of the valve, so that air from the pressure chamber flows through port o, through the chamber above equalizing valve to port h and the application cylinder g. The application chamber port w is blanked by the equalizing valve 31 and the safety valve port l is connected through port r and restricted port q in valve 31 to port h of the application cylinder. The air that expanded into the application cylinder from the pressure chamber will force the application piston 10 to the right, opening the application valve 5, as in service application, and obtaining cylinder pressure equal to that in the application cylinder, when the application valve will lap.

Q. 90.—What brake cylinder pressure is obtained from a full automatic service application of the brake from a 70-pound brake pipe pressure? (Safety valve set at 68 pounds.)

A.—Fifty pounds.

Q. 91.—What brake cylinder pressure is obtained with and automatic emergency application from a 70-pound brake pipe pressure? (Safety valve set at 68 pounds.)

A.—About seventy pounds.

Q. 92.—How is the difference between service and emergency brake cylinder pressure obtained?

A.—With all automatic service applications the pressure chamber is connected to both the application chamber and application cylinder, the relative volumes of which are such that the air in the pressure chamber at 70 pounds pressure will equalize with the combined volumes of the application chamber and cylinder at 50 pounds pressure, which is, therefore, the maximum which can be obtained with an automatic service application. With all emergency applications the pressure chamber is not connected to the application chamber, but to the application cylinder only. The air in the pressure chamber then expands into the application cylinder, equalizing at about 65 pounds from a 70-pound brake pipe pressure. During emergency application air is admitted through a small port in the automatic brake valve (called the blow-down timing port) and the application cylinder pipe to the application cylinder. The size of the blow-down timing port in the brake valve is proportioned to the restricted port in the equalizing valve leading to the safety valve so as to give the proper time of blow-down of brake cylinder pressure.

Q. 93.—Will piston travel or brake cylinder leakage affect the brake cylinder pressure on the engine and tender?

A.—No.

Q. 94.—How is a predetermined brake cylinder pressure obtained and maintained in the engine and tender brake cylinder regardless of piston travel and leakage?

A.—As the brake cylinders receive their air from the main reservoirs, they have practically an unlimited supply to draw from. The distributing valve and its reservoir volumes are constant, so that with a given brake pipe reduction a given application cylinder pressure will be obtained (about $2\frac{1}{2}$ pounds application cylinder and chamber pressure for every pound brake pipe reduction). The air that is admitted to the application cylinder forces the application piston and its valves to the right, closing the exhaust ports and allowing air from the main reservoir branch pipe to flow to the brake cylinders until brake cylinder pressure becomes equal to that in the application cylinder, regardless of what the piston travel is, the number of cylinders, or the amount of leakage. When this pressure had been obtained, if brake cylinder leakage exists, the drop in cylinder pressure will reduce the pressure in chamber b on the right of piston below that in application cylinder g on the opposite side of the piston. This will cause application piston to again move to the right, opening application valve 5 and allowing air to flow from the main reservoirs to the brake cylinders until the brake cylinder pressure again equalizes with that in the application cylinder, when the application piston and supply valve will move to lap position. This action will continue indefinitely until the brakes are released.

SAFETY VALVE

Q. 95.—What is the purpose of the safety valve?
A.—To prevent abnormal brake cylinder pressure and to act as a high speed reducing valve for the locomotive brake cylinders.

Q. 96.—To what is the safety valve connected?
A.—To the application cylinder.

Q. 97.—When is the safety valve connected to the application cylinder?
A.—At all times except in automatic service lap position of the distributing valve.

Q. 98.—For what pressure is the safety valve adjusted?
A.—Sixty-eight pounds, except when the locomotive is transported light over the road, when it is ordinarily adjusted to 35 pounds.

Q. 99.—How does the safety valve act as a high speed reducing valve?
A.—When an automatic service application is made and the equalizing valve and graduating valve are in service position, the safety valve is connected to the application cylinder and chamber through large ports, and will, therefore, prevent the brake cylinder

pressure rising above that for which the safety valve is adjusted. During emergency application the connection between the application cylinder and the safety valve is smaller than during service application, so that the flow of air from the application cylinder to the safety valve is restricted, which, in conjunction with the blow-down timing port, regulates the time of blow-down of brake cylinder pressure.

QUICK ACTION CYLINDER CAP

Q. 100.—Where is the quick action cylinder cap located?
A.—On the brake pipe end of the distributing valve, replacing the plain cylinder cap.
Q. 101.—What is its purpose?
A.—To vent brake pipe air into the locomotive brake cylinders when an emergency position of the brake is made.
Q. 102.—Does it operate at any other time?
A.—No.
Q. 103.—Why is this cap used?
A.—To assist in obtaining an emergency application of the brakes in the train when double heading.
Q. 104.—Then the quick action cylinder cap performs the same function in actuating quick action as a quick action triple valve on the tender with other types of locomotive brakes?
A.—Yes.
Q. 105.—Does the air flowing to the brake cylinders through the quick action cylinder cap increase the brake cylinder pressure as is the case with the quick action triple valve?
A.—No; as the brake cylinder pressure is governed by the pressure in the application cylinder of the distributing valve.
Q. 106.—What advantage has this device over quick action triple valves on the tender?
A.—It is less liable to cause undesired quick action than a triple valve, as it is much less sensitive.
Q. 107.—Why is it possible to use a valve less sensitive to quick action than a triple valve?
A.—As the quick action cylinder cap is always located close to the automatic brake valve being operated; when an emergency application is made, the quick action cylinder cap is subjected to a more rapid brake pipe reduction than is the case with a triple valve located at a considerable distance from the brake valve, and consequently need not be so sensitive in order to accomplish its purpose.
Q. 108.—When the distributing valve is provided with a quick action cap, how should the automatic brake valve handle be **operated?**

A.—Exactly the same as when the distributing valve has plain cylinder cap.

Q. 109.—Describe the operation of the quick action cylinder cap.

A.—When the automatic brake valve handle is moved to emergency position, equalizing piston moves to the right, which movement causes the knob on the piston to strike the graduating stem 50, causing it to compress graduating spring 55, moving emergency valve 48 so as to open port j. Brake pipe pressure in chamber p then flows to chamber X, unseats check valve 53, and passes to the brake cylinders through port m in the cap and distributing valve body.

Q. 110.—What duty does the check valve 53 perform?

A.—When the brake cylinder and brake pipe pressures become equal, the check valve is forced to its seat by spring 54, thus preventing air in the brake cylinders from flowing back into the brake pipe.

Q. 111.—What takes place when a release is made?

A.—Piston 26 is moved back to *release* position, spring 55 forces graduating stem 50 and emergency valve 48 back to the position shown.

Q. 112.—Are there any other differences in the operation of the distributing valve having this cap?

A.—No; in all other respects the operation of the distributing valve is the same as described under the heading "No. 6 Distributing Valve With Plain Cylinder Cap."

THE B-6 FEED VALVE

Q. 113.—How does the B-6 feed valve differ from that used with former automatic brake equipments?

A.—The B-6 feed valve is made adjustable for either high or low brake pipe pressure and can easily be changed from one to the other. Otherwise, except for improvements in the mechanical design of the valve, it is the same as that used with former equipments.

Q. 114.—How is the change in adjustment accomplished?

A.—The adjustment nut is provided with a hand wheel, having a lug, working between two adjustable stops on the body of the valve. These stops are adjusted for the high and low brake pipe pressure which it is desired to carry and the change of pressure from one to the other is accomplished by simply turning the hand wheel from one stop to the other.

Q. 115.—Where is the feed valve located?

A.—On a bracket interposed between the main reservoir and feed valve pipes.

Q. 116.—Why is this bracket used?

A.—To support the valve and permit it to be easily removed and replaced.

Q. 117.—What are the essential working parts of the feed valve?

A.—The supply valve and actuating piston, the regulating valve, diaphragm, regulating spring, and supply valve piston spring.

Q. 118.—Explain the general arrangement of the feed valve?

A.—The feed valve consists of two sets of parts designated as the supply parts and the regulating parts. The supply parts, which control the flow of air through the valve, consist of the supply valve 9, and its spring 10, supply valve piston 8, and supply valve spring piston 6. The regulating parts consist of the regulating valve 12, regulating valve spring 13, diaphragm 14, diaphragm spindle 16, and regulating spring 17.

Q. 119.—What is the normal position of this valve?

A.—Closed.

Q. 120.—Explain the duty of the various operative parts.

A.—Supply valve 9 is for the purpose of opening and closing port c in its seat. Piston 8 is for the purpose of moving the supply valve 9. Spring 6 is for the purpose of moving the piston and closing the supply valve when the pressures have equalized on both sides of piston 8.

Q. 121.—What are the duties of the regulating parts?

A.—To control the action of the supply valve piston and supply valve when opening and closing the supply port c in the seat.

Q. 122.—Explain the operation and flow of air through the feed valve when open.

A.—Air entering through port a from the main reservoir is free to pass into the supply valve chamber B, causing the supply valve piston 8 to be moved to the left, compressing piston spring 6, by which movement the supply valve 9 uncovers port c in the valve seat, thereby permitting air to pass directly through ports c and dd to the feed valve pipe at the same time air is passing by the supply valve piston 8, which is not an airtight fit, to chamber G, thence through port hH by the regulating valve 12, and through port K to diaphragm chamber L, and on through ports edd to the feed valve pipe.

Q. 123.—What will cause a valve to close and stop the flow of air from the main reservoir to feed valve pipe?

A.—When the pressure in the feed valve pipe and chamber L slightly exceeds the tension of the regulating spring 17, the diaphragm 14 will yield and allow regulating valve 12 to move to its seat, closing port K, and preventing the flow of air from chamber G. As the air continues to leak by supply valve piston 8, it will equalize the pressure on both sides of the piston and allow supply valve piston spring 6, which was previously compressed, to react and move the piston and supply valve, closing port c in the supply valve seat.

Q. 124.—With the feed valve closed, and the pressure equalized on each side of the supply valve piston, what will cause it to open to supply the feed valve pipe when the pressure has been reduced?

A.—Diaphragm chamber L is always in direct communication with the feed valve pipe; therefore, any reduction in feed valve pipe pressure reduces the pressure in chamber L, which allows the tension of the regulating spring to overcome the diminished air pressure in chamber L, and force the diaphragm 14 to the left. This unseats the regulating valve 12, permitting the accumulated air pressure in chamber G to escape to the feed valve pipe through ports hH and through port K, diaphragm chamber L and ports edd. The equilibrium of pressure on the two sides of the supply valve piston now being destroyed, the main reservoir pressure which is present in supply valve chamber B forces the supply valve piston 8 to the left, which moves the supply valve 9 with it, opening port c and again permitting the air to pass to the feed valve pipe until the pressure has been restored to the proper amount.

Q. 125.—The supply valve then maintains practically a wide open port until maximum pressure is obtained?

A.—Yes; and when maximum pressure is obtained, the supply valve closes the supply port quickly.

C-6 REDUCING VALVE

Q. 126.—What is the difference in the construction and operation of the C-6 reducing valve and the B-6 feed valve?

A.—The only difference between it and the B-6 feed valve just described is in the convenience of adjustment, the C-6 reducing valve having the ordinary adjusting nut and cap nut used on former types of feed valves instead of the hand adjusting wheel used with the B-6 feed valve. It is called a "reducing valve" simply to distinguish it from the B-6 feed valve.

SF-4 PUMP GOVERNOR

Q. 127.—Where is the SF-4 pump governor located?

A.—In the pipe supplying steam to the air compressor.

Q. 128.—Explain the general arrangement of the pump governor.

A.—It consists of a standard steam portion, with Siamese fitting, and two diaphragm portions.

Q. 129.—How are these diaphragm portions designated?

A.—That having two pipe connections the *excess pressure head* and that having a single pipe connection the *maximum pressure head.*

Q. 130.—What are th pipe connections of the governor?

A.—B, to the boiler; P, the air compressor; MR, main reservoir; AB, the automatic brake valve; FVP, the feed valve pipe; W, waste pipe.

Q. 131.—When does the excess pressure head govern the operation of the air compressor?

A.—At all times when the automatic brake valve handle is in *release*, *running* or *holding* positions.

Q. 132.—When does the maximum pressure head govern the operation of the air compressor?

A.—During the time the automatic brake valve handle is in *lap*, *service*, or *emergency* positions.

Q. 133.—Explain the flow of steam through the governor.

A.—Steam enters at B, passes by steam valve 5 to the connection P, and on to the air compressor.

Q. 134.—With the automatic brake valve handle in *release*, *running* or *holding* position, what pressures act on the diaphragm 28 of the excess pressure head?

A.—Air from the main reservoir flows through the automatic brake valve to the connection marked ABV, to chamber d under diaphragm 28. Air from the feed valve pipe enters at connection FVP and flows to chamber f above diaphragm 28. In addition to this, regulating spring 27 also acts upon the upper side of the diaphragm.

Q. 135.—What is the adjustment of this spring?

A.—About 20 pounds.

Q. 136.—What total pressure is therefore acting upon the upper side of diaphragm 28?

A.—Whatever pressure the feed valve pipe may have, plus the tension of the regulating spring 27.

Q. 137.—What pressure in chamber d below diaphragm 28 will be required to overcome that acting on the upper side of the diaphragm?

A.—A pressure slightly higher than that in the feed valve pipe plus the spring pressure. For example, with a pressure of 70 pounds in the feed valve pipe, about 90 pounds pressure below diaphragm 28 will be required to overcome that acting upon the upper side of the diaphragm.

Q. 138.—How does a variation in feed valve adjustment affect the governor?

A.—When the feed valve adjustment is changed from one amount to another as where the locomotive is used alternately in high speed brake and ordinary service, the excess pressure head of the governor automatically changes the main reservoir pressure so as to maintain the same excess pressure (20 pounds).

Q. 139.—Why is this of advantage?

A.—Because it insures that the main reservoir pressure will always be 20 pounds higher than that of the feed valve pipe.

Q. 140.—Explain the operation of the governor when main reservoir pressure in chamber d below diaphragm 28 becomes slightly higher than that acting on top of the diaphragm.

A.—Diaphragm 28 will rise, unseat its pin valve 33, and allow air to flow to chamber b above the governor piston 6, forcing the latter down, compressing piston spring 9 and restricting the flow of steam past steam valve 5 to a point where the compressor will just supply the leakage in brake system.

Q. 141.—How long will the flow of steam through the governor be restricted in this manner?

A.—Until main reservoir pressure in diaphragm chamber d becomes reduced slightly below the combined spring and air pressure in chamber f above the diaphragm, which will then force diaphragm down, seating its pin valve.

Q. 142.—How does this affect the flow of steam through the governor?

A.—As chamber b is always open to the atmosphere through the small vent port c, the air pressure in chamber b above the governor piston 6 will then escape to the atmosphere and allow piston spring 9 and the steam pressure below valve 5 to raise it and the governor piston 6.

Q. 143.—With the automatic brake valve handle in *release*, *running* or *holding* position, does the maximum pressure head operate?

A.—No; as during this time its diaphragm pin valve remains seated.

Q. 144.—To what is chamber a in the maximum pressure head always connected?

A.—To the main reservoir.

Q. 145.—When does the maximum pressure head of the governor control the operation of the compressor?

A.—When the automatic brake valve handle is in *lap*, *service* or *emergency* position, or when the main reservoir cut-out cock is closed.

Q. 146.—With the automatic brake valve handle in *lap*, *service* or *emergency* position, or when the main reservoir cut-out cock is closed, what pressures act on the diaphragm 20 of the maximum pressure head?

A.—Main reservoir pressure which flows directly to chamber a on the under side of diaphragm 20 and the pressure of regulating spring 19 on the upper side.

Q. 147.—What is the adjustment of spring 19?

A.—Spring 19 is adjusted to the maximum pressure which is desired in the main reservoirs.

Q. 148.—Explain the operation of the governor when main reservoir pressure in chamber a exceeds the tension of spring 19.

A.—When main reservoir pressure in chamber a slightly exceeds the adjustment of spring 19, diaphragm 20 will rise, unseat its pin valve 33, and allow air to flow into chamber b above the governor piston, forcing it down, compressing its spring 9 and restricting the flow of steam past steam valve 5 to a point where the compressor will just supply the leakage in brake system.

Q. 149.—How long will the flow of steam through the governor be restricted in this manner?

A.—When main reservoir pressure in chamber *a* becomes slightly reduced, the spring 19 forces diaphragm 20 down, seating its pin valve. As chamber *b* is always open to the atmosphere through the small vent port *c*, the pressure in chamber *b* above the governor piston 6 will then escape to the atmosphere and allow the piston spring 9 and steam pressure below valve 5 to raise the valve and governor piston to the position shown.

Q. 150.—Is the maximum pressure head of the governor in any way controlled by the automatic brake valve?

A.—No; as the chamber *a* below the diaphragm is in no way connected to the brake valve.

Q. 151.—With the automatic brake valve handle in *lap*, *service* or *emergency* positions or when the main reservoir cut-out cock is closed, why does not the excess pressure head operate instead of the maximum pressure head?

A.—Because under these conditions, communication from the main reservoir to chamber *d* is cut off by the brake valve and at the same time connection from the feed valve pipe to chamber *f* above diaphragm 28 still remains open, so that the combined air and spring pressure on top of the diaphragm holds the pin valve to its seat, rendering the excess pressure head inoperative.

Q. 152.—Under ordinary running conditions, why is only a moderate excess pressure desirable?

A.—Because most of the time the automatic brake valve handle is in *running* position (keeping the brakes charged), but little excess pressure is needed and the governor regulates the main reservoir pressure to about 20 pounds above the brake pipe pressure, thus relieving the compressor of unnecessary work.

Q. 153.—When an application of the brakes is made, why is the higher excess pressure of advantage?

A.—To insure a prompt release of the brakes and recharge of the system.

DEAD ENGINE FIXTURES.

Q. 154.—What are the parts composing the dead engine fixtures?

A.—A ⅜-inch pipe connecting the brake pipe and main reservoir pipe, a combined strainer and check valve with choke fitting, and a ⅜-inch cut-out cock.

Q. 155.—What is the purpose of the "dead engine" feature of the "ET" equipment?

A.—To enable the compressor on a "live" engine to charge the main reservoir on a "dead" engine, so that the brake on the dead engine may be operated with the other brakes in the train.

Q. 156.—How is this done?

A.—Air from the main reservoir of the live engine passes through the brake pipe and dead engine fixtures to the main reservoirs of the dead engine.

Q. 157.—When is this apparatus used?

A.—Only when the air compressor on the locomotive is inoperative.

Q. 158.—Should the cut-out cock always be closed except when the compressor is inoperative?

A.—Yes.

Q. 159.—Describe the flow of air through the combined strainer and check valve.

A.—With the cut-out open, air from the brake pipe enters at BP, passes through the curled hair strainer, lifts check valve 4, held to its seat by a strong spring 2, passes through the choke bushing, and out at MR to the main reservoir pipe.

Q. 160.—Why is the "strong" spring 2 used in this valve?

A.—This spring over the check valve insures the valve seating and keeps the main reservoir pressure somewhat lower than the brake pipe pressure, yet assures ample pressure to operate the locomotive brakes.

Q. 161.—What is the object of the choke fitting?

A.—It prevents a sudden drop in brake pipe pressure and the application of the brakes in the train, as might otherwise occur with uncharged main reservoirs cut into a charged brake pipe or if for any reason the main reservoir pressure was lower than the brake pipe pressure.

Q. 162.—How can the maximum brake cylinder pressure be regulated on a dead engine?

A.—By the adjustment of the safety valve on the distributing valve.

Q. 163.—Can the brake on a dead engine be controlled with the independent brake valve the same as on a live engine?

A.—Yes, if it becomes necessary.

Q. 164.—When the dead engine feature is used, in what position should the automatic and independent brake valve handles be carried?

A.—*Running* position.

Q. 165.—What should be the position of the double heading cock?

A.—Closed.

Q. 166.—Is it sometimes desirable to keep the braking power of a locomotive below the standard?

A.—Yes; when there is no water in the boiler.

Q. 167.—How is this done?

A.—By adjusting the safety valve on the distributing valve to the maximum brake cylinder pressure which is desired in the locomotive brake cylinders.

AIR GAUGES.

Q. 168.—How many and what type of gauges are used in connection with the "ET" equipment?

A.—Two duplex gauges, designated: No. 1, large duplex air gauge; No. 2, small duplex air gauge. (See Figs. 1-A and 1-B.)

Q. 169.—What pressures are indicated by gauge No. 1?

A.—Red hand, main reservoir pressure; black hand, equalizing reservoir pressure.

Q. 170.—What pressures are indicated by gauge No. 2?

A.—Red hand, brake cylinder pressure; black hand, brake pipe pressure.

Q. 171.—Which gauge hand shows the amount of reduction being made during a service application of the brakes?

A.—Black hand, gauge No. 1.

Q. 172.—Why, then, is the black hand of gauge No. 2 necessary?

A.—To show brake pipe pressure when engine is second in double heading or a helper.

Q. 173.—What pressure is indicated by the red hand of gauge No. 2 when operating the automatic or independent brake valve?

A.—Brake cylinder pressure.

CUT-OUT COCKS.

Q. 174.—What provision is made for cutting off the main reservoirs from the brake system?

A.—The main reservoir cut-out cock in the main reservoir pipe.

Q. 175.—What takes place when this cock is closed?

A.—The flow of air from the main reservoirs is cut off and the air in the brake system back of it is exhausted to the atmosphere.

Q. 176.—When this cock is closed can air flow from the main reservoirs to any part of the system?

A.—Yes; to the maximum pressure head of the pump governor.

Q. 177.—Why is this necessary?

A.—To provide for the automatic control of the compressor when the cut-out cock is temporarily closed.

Q. 178.—What provision is made for cutting out the driver brake?

A.—A ¾-inch cut-out cock located in the pipe leading from the distributing valve to the driver brake cylinders.

Q. 179.—What provision is made for cutting out the tender brake?

A.—A ¾-inch cut-out cock located in the pipe between the distributing valve and the hose connection leading to the tender brake cylinder.

Q. 180.—What difference is there between this cock and the ¾-inch cocks generally used?

A.—It has a choke fitting.

Q. 181.—Why is this choke fitting used?

A.—To prevent a loss of driver and truck brake cylinder pressure in the event of a hose or tender brake cylinder pipe bursting.

Q. 182.—Is there another cock with choke fitting sometimes used in connection with this apparatus?

A.—Yes; when a truck brake is used a ½-inch cock is located in the pipe leading from the distributing valve to the truck brake cylinder with choke fitting.

Q. 183.—For what purpose is the ¾-inch cut-out cock in the main reservoir supply pipe to the distributing valve?

A.—To cut off the supply of air from the main reservoirs to the distributing valve to permit of inspection and repairs.

Q. 184.—For what purpose is the 1-inch double heading cock underneath the brake valve?

A.—To cut off the flow from the automatic brake valve to the brake pipe or vice versa.

Q. 185.—What is the purpose of the brake pipe air strainer?

A.—To prevent foreign matter entering the distributing valve, which might seriously interfere with its proper operation.

AIR SIGNAL SYSTEM.

Q. 186.—From what source is the supply of air to the signal system obtained with the "ET" equipment?

A.—From the reducing valve pipe between the reducing valve and the independent brake valve, as shown in Figs. 1-A and 1-B.

Q. 187.—Why is this supply taken from the reducing valve pipe?

A.—That the one reducing valve may govern the pressure for both the independent brake valve and the signal system.

Q. 188—What device is interposed between the reducing valve pipe and the air signal pipe?

A.—A combined strainer and check valve.

Q. 189.—Why is the strainer necessary?

A.—To protect the check valve and signal system from foreign matter.

Q. 190.—Why is the check valve employed?

A.—To prevent a back flow of air from the signal pipe to the reducing valve pipe.

Q. 191.—In what way does this combined strainer and check valve differ from that used with the dead engine fixtures?

A.—Only in the tension of the check valve spring.

GENERAL OPERATION OF THE No. 6 EQUIPMENT.

Note.—Details of construction and operation of the various devices will be found under their respective headings.

Q. 192.—What is the proper position of the brake valve handles and cut-out cocks before starting the compressor?

A.—The automatic and independent brake valve handles in *running* position all cut-out cocks must be open, except the ⅜-inch cut-out cock in the dead engine connection and the angle and stop cocks at the front and rear end of the locomotive.

Q. 193.—Explain the charging of the "ET" equipment.

A.—While the compressor is operating, the main reservoir pressure continues to rise until it reaches the point for which the governor is adjusted. The governor then automatically stops the compressor. From the main reservoirs air flows through the main reservoir pipe to the chamber above the application valve of the distributing valve. It also flows to the feed valve which reduces the pressure of the air to that carried in the brake pipe. The air at this reduced pressure flows through the automatic brake valve to the brake pipe and thence through the branch pipe and distributing valve to the pressure chamber, charging it up to brake pipe pressure. Air also flows from the main reservoirs through the reducing valve to the independent brake valve and air signal system.

Q. 194.—What must be done to make an automatic service application of the brake?

A.—Move the automatic brake valve handle to *service* position.

Q. 195.—How does this apply the brake?

A.—It starts a reduction of brake pipe pressure which causes the distributing valve to operate so as to allow air to flow from the main reservoirs into the brake cylinders.

Q. 196.—How is the application of the brake limited to any desired cylinder pressure?

A—By returning the automatic brake valve handle to *lap* position.

Q. 197.—What must be done to make an emergency application of the brakes?

A.—Move the automatic brake valve handle to *emergency* position.

Q. 198.—How does an emergency application of the brake differ from a service application?

A.—Brake pipe reduction takes place more rapidly, brake cylinder pressure rises more quickly and a higher brake cylinder pressure is obtained than in service applications.

Q. 199.—In what position should the automatic brake valve handle be placed to release the locomotive brake?

A.—*Running* position.

Q. 200.—Is there any position besides *running* position in which the locomotive brake can be released by the use of the automatic brake valve?

A.—No.

Q. 201—Can the locomotive brake be applied otherwise than by using the automatic brake valve?

A.—Yes; by the independent brake valve.

Q. 202.—In what position should the independent brake valve handle be placed to apply the locomotive brakes?

A.—*Application* position.

Q. 203.—How does this apply the brake?

A.—It allows air to flow from the reducing valve through the independent brake valve to the distributing valve, causing it to operate and allow air to flow from the main reservoirs into the brake cylinders at a reduced pressure.

Q. 204.—Is the operation of the train brakes affected in any way by the independent application of the locomotive brakes?

A.—No.

Q. 205.—How is the independent application of the locomotive brake limited to any desired cylinder pressure?

A.—By returning the independent brake valve handle to *lap* position.

Q. 206.—How can the locomotive brake be released by the independent brake valve?

A.—(a) If the automatic brake valve handle is in *running* position, move the independent brake valve handle to *running* position.

(b) If the automatic brake handle is *not* in *running* position, the independent brake valve handle must be moved to *release* position.

Q. 207.—Can the locomotive brake be released without in any way interfering with the train brakes under any and all conditions?

A.—Yes; by placing the independent brake valve handle in *release* position.

TESTING AND OPERATING THE "ET" EQUIPMENT.
TESTING LOCOMOTIVE BRAKE.

Q. 208.—Preparatory to making a test of the brake, what should be done?

A.—Blow out the brake pipe and signal pipe by opening and closing quickly a number of times the angle and stop cocks, both at the pilot and rear of the tender.

Q. 209.—Why is this done?

A.—To remove scale and other foreign matter that may be in the brake and signal pipes.

Q. 210.—What observations should the engineer make before taking the engine to the train?

A.—He should observe by the gauges that the proper pressures are present in different parts of the system. This will show that the regulating devices (governors, feed valves, etc.) are properly adjusted. He should also observe that the brake is in proper condition generally.

Q. 211.—What test should then be made?

A.—The brake should be applied and released with both the automatic and independent brake valves, to determine if the brake is in proper operative condition.

MANIPULATION OF LOCOMOTIVE AND TRAIN BRAKES.

Q. 212.—What is the proper position of the automatic and independent brake valve handles when not being operated?

A.—*Running* position.

Q. 213.—After attaching the engine to the train, in what position should the automatic brake valve be carried while charging the train brakes?

A.—*Release* position.

Q. 214.—How long should the brake valve handle be left in this position?

A.—Until the brake pipe system is charged to the pressure to be carried.

Q. 215.—How should the automatic brake valve be handled when testing the brakes?

A.—A full service application of the brakes should be made and the handle then moved to *lap* position.

Q. 216.—How should the brakes be released?

A.—Place the brake valve handle in *release* position for the proper length of time, then return it to *running* position, leaving it there.

Q. 217.—If the brakes apply in emergency from an unknown cause, while the train is running, what should be done?

A.—Move automatic brake valve handle quickly to *emergency* position and leave it there until train stops.

Q. 218.—Why is this done?

A.—To insure the brakes remaining applied and to prevent loss of main reservoir pressure.

Q. 219.—What must be done in the event of sudden danger?

A.—Move the automatic brake valve handle quickly to *emergency* position and leave it there until the train stops and the danger is past.

Q. 220.—With brakes applied in emergency, would anything be gained by moving the independent brake valve handle to *application* position?

A.—No. Because in an application of this kind the application cylinder pressure is higher than the maximum pressure obtainable with the independent brake.

Q. 221.—If, in making a stop, the driving wheels slide, can they be released?

A.—Yes; by placing the independent brake valve handle in *release* position and holding it there until the wheels again revolve, reapplying the brakes, if desired, with this brake valve.

Q. 222.—In the event of releasing and reapplying the locomotive brake in this manner, in what position should the independent brake valve handle be left after the application is made?

A.—*Running* position.

Q 223.—Why?

A.—Because if left in any other position, the locomotive brake can not be released by the automatic brake valve.

Q. 224.—Does the releasing and reapplying of the engine and tender brakes with the independent brake valve in this way have any effect on the train brakes?

A.—No; as the operation of the independent brake valve does not interfere with the train brakes.

Q. 225.—In making a service application, how should the automatic brake valve be handled?

A.—The same as with the older types of brake valves.

Q. 226.—In making the first release of a two-application stop, how should the brake valve be handled?

A.—(a) With short passenger trains, release the brakes by moving the brake valve handle to *running* position a sufficient length of time to start the locomotive and train brakes releasing, then to *lap* position.

(b) With the long passenger trains the brake valve handle should be moved to *release* position for about three seconds to start the train brakes releasing, then to *running* position to partly release the locomotive brake, then to *lap*.

Q. 227.—In making the final release of a two-application stop, how should the automatic brake valve be handled?

A.—(a) With short passenger trains, release the brakes just before coming to a stop, by moving the brake valve handle to *running* position and leaving it there.

(b) With long passenger trains, the brakes should be held applied until the train stops.

Q. 228.—In making a release after a one-application stop, how should the brake valve be handled?

A.—The same as a final release of a two-application stop, as just explained.

Q. 229.—Why is it necessary to move the automatic brake valve handle promptly to *running* position after going to *release* in releasing the brakes?

A.—Because, with the brake valve in *release* position, the locomotive brake is held applied.

Q. 230.—What is the only position of the automatic brake valve handle which will permit the release of both the locomotive and train brakes together?

A.—*Running* position.

Q. 231.—Is there any other position besides *running* position, which will release train brakes?

A.—Yes; *release* position and *holding* position.

Q. 232.—Is there any other than running position in which the locomotive brake can be released by the automatic brake valve?

A.—No.

Q. 233.—Can the locomotive brake always be released by placing the automatic brake valve handle in *running* position?

A.—No.

Q. 234.—Why?

A.—Because, if the independent brake valve handle is not in *running* position, the locomotive brake can not be released by the automatic brake valve.

Q. 235.—If the driving wheels pick up and slide while making a stop, what should be done?

A.—Release with the independent brake valve.

Q. 236.—In handling a light locomotive, which brake valve should be used?

A.—The independent brake valve.

Q. 237.—For a gradual application of the locomotive brake, how should the independent brake valve be used?

A.—Place the brake valve handle in *slow application* position until the brake is sufficiently applied; then return it to *lap* position.

Q. 238.—How operated if a quick application of the locomotive brake is desired?

A.—Place the independent brake handle in quick application position until the brake is sufficiently applied, then return it to *lap* position.

Q. 239.—Should the independent brake valve be used in completing a train stop?

A.—No.

Q. 240.—Why?

A.—Because, to apply the locomotive brake with the train brakes released, will cause slack to run in and produce shocks.

Q. 241.—In case of emergency, should the independent brake valve be used on a light locomotive?

A.—No; in *all* cases of emergency, move the *automatic* brake valve handle to *emergency* position.

Q. 242.—Why?

A.—Because a considerably higher brake cylinder pressure is obtained than would be possible with the use of the independent brake valve.

Q. 243.—How can the locomotive brake always be released, regardless of the position either brake handle may be in?

A.—By placing the independent brake valve handle in *release* position.

Q. 244.—How can the locomotive brake be held applied while releasing the train brakes?

A.—By moving the automatic brake valve handle to either *release* or *holding* positions.

Q. 245.—Can this be done in any other way?

A.—Yes; by placing the independent brake valve handle in *lap* position.

Q. 246.—Why should not the independent brake valve be used for this purpose?

A.—First, because it is better to use the automatic brake valve alone instead of in conjunction with the independent brake valve. Second, because if the independent brake valve is used for this purpose, it may be left in *lap* position by mistake and the proper operation of the brakes by the automatic brake valve interfered with.

Q. 247.—Why should the automatic brake valve handle never be left in *lap* position except while bringing the train to a stop?

A.—Because, if the handle is felt in *lap* position when the brakes are not applied, brake pipe leakage may materially reduce the brake pipe and auxiliary reservoir pressures, so that full braking power can not be obtained and because the driver brakes are likely to apply, as the outlet from the application chamber is closed.

Q. 248.—If, after a brake application, the automatic brake valve handle is moved to *release* position and returned to *lap* position, what will be the result?

A.—The locomotive brake will remain applied.

Q. 249.—What is the advantage of having the locomotive brake remain applied under these conditions?

A.—It would serve as a warning in case of neglect to move the handle to the proper position.

Q. 250.—Would anything be gained by moving the automatic brake valve handle to *release* position for a short time just before making an application of the brakes?

A.—No; this should never be done.

Q. 251.—Why?

A.—Because by placing the automatic brake valve handle in *release* position the brake pipe will be charged higher than the pressure in the auxiliary reservoirs; consequently, the brakes can not be applied until after this difference in pressure has been drawn off.

FREIGHT BRAKING.

Q. 252.—What feature of the No. 6 "ET" equipment is of particular advantage in handling trains on long, descending grades?

A.—The ability to handle the locomotive brake with or entirely independent of the train brakes.

Q. 253.—What is gained by this?

A.—The locomotive and train brakes can be alternated without interfering with each other.

Q. 254.—With all the brakes applied, can the locomotive brake be released without releasing the train brakes?

A.—Yes.

Q. 255.—How can this be done?

A.—By placing the handle of the independent brake valve in *release* position, holding it there until the brake is released.

Q. 256.—After releasing in this manner, where should the handle of the independent brake valve be placed?

A.—*Running* position.

Q. 257.—If it is then desired to release the train brakes and recharge the reservoirs, and reapply the locomotive brakes, in order to assist the retaining valves, in holding the train, how can this be accomplished?

A.—Place the independent brake valve handle in *application* position until the desired locomotive brake cylinder pressure is obtained, then return it to *running* position, then move the automatic brake valve handle to *release* position and leave it there until the train is charged.

Q. 258.—What is the maximum pressure obtainable in the brake pipe under these conditions?

A.—As the excess pressure head of the duplex governor will be in control, the maximum pressure obtainable will be twenty pounds above that ordinarily carried in the brake pipe.

Q. 259.—When reapplying the train brakes, how can excessive locomotive brake cylinder pressure be prevented?

A.—By partially releasing the locomotive brake with the independent brake valve before reapplying the train brakes.

Q. 260.—How can the overheating of driving wheel tires be prevented?

A.—By either holding the independent brake valve handle in *release* position when making an automatic application or by releasing immediately with the independent brake valve after the automatic application.

Q. 261.—When releasing the brakes on a freight train when in motion, should the automatic brake valve be handled in the same manner as with passenger trains?

A.—No; the brake valve handle should be moved to *release* position and allowed to remain there for a period of time, according to the length of the train, but not to exceed twenty seconds.

Q. 262.—Why should this be done?

A.—To insure a proper release of the train brakes and hold the locomotive brake applied, thus preventing the slack of the train running out.

Q. 263.—In making releases on long trains, after brake valve handle has been returned to *running* position, should it again be moved to *release* position for an instant?

A.—Yes; after being in *running* position for about three seconds.

Q. 264.—Why?

A.—Because in making such a release some of the head brakes may have been overcharged and may reapply.

BROKEN PIPES.

Q. 265.—What would be the result if the brake pipe branch to the distributing valve broke off?

A.—The locomotive and train brakes would apply.

Q. 266.—What should be done if this happens on the road?

A.—Plug the end leading from the brake pipe; release the locomotive brake by placing the independent brake valve handle in *release* position and proceed.

Q. 267.—Would it be possible to use the locomotive brake in this case?

A.—Yes; with the independent brake valve, always using *release* position to release the brake.

Q. 268.—What would be the result if any of the pipe connections between the distributing valve and the brake cylinders broke off?

A.—It would permit a constant escape of air when the brake is applied, and may cause the release of one or more of the locomotive brake cylinders, depending on where the break occurs.

Q. 269.—What should be done in a case of this kind?

A.—If the pipe can not be repaired, close the cut-out cock in the pipe leading to the broken pipe. If breakage occurs next to the distributing valve reservoir, close the cut-out cock in the distributing valve supply pipe.

Q. 270.—What would be the effect if the supply pipe to the distributing valve broke off?

A.—It would permit main reservoir pressure to escape and prevent the use of the locomotive brake.

Q. 271.—What should be done?

A.—If repairs can not be made to the pipe, the cut-out cock in the supply pipe should be closed, or the pipe plugged.

Q. 272.—What would be the effect if the application cylinder pipe to the distributing valve broke off?

A.—It would be impossible to apply the locomotive brake.

Q. 273.—What should be done?

A.—The connection to the distributing valve should be plugged and the brake could then be applied, but with the automatic brake valve only.

Q. 274.—With this opening plugged and the brake automatically applied, can it be released with the independent brake valve?

A.—No. It can only be released by placing the automatic brake valve handle in *running* position.

Q. 275.—If the release pipe to the distributing valve breaks off, what would be the effect?

A.—It would cut out the holding feature of the automatic brake valve.

Q. 276.—With this pipe broken off, would it interfere with the independent operation of the brake?

A.—Yes; if an independent application were made and the equalizing parts of the distributing valve were in release position, it would allow the independent brake to release when the independent valve was moved to lap position.

Q. 277.—With this pipe broken off and the brakes automatically applied, can they be released with the independent brake valve?

A.—Yes.

Q. 278.—Should any delay be occasioned by the breaking off of this pipe?

A.—No. Proceed and operate the brake with the automatic brake valve, but without attempting to use the holding feature.

Q. 279.—What would be the effect if the pipe connection to the spring chamber of the excess pressure head of the pump governor broke off?

A.—The compressor would not operate when the main reservoir pressure was about 40 pounds or over.

Q. 280.—What should be done in this case?

A.—Plug the broken pipe and place a blind gasket in the pipe leading to the chamber below the diaphragm of the excess pressure head.

Q. 281.—What should be done if the pipe connection leading to the chamber below the diaphragm of the excess pressure head breaks off?

A.—Plug the broken pipe and proceed.

Q. 282.—With the lower pipe to the excess pressure head plugged or with both pipes plugged, what would control the compressor?

A.—The maximum pressure head.

Q. 283.—What should be done in the event of the pipe connection to the maximum pressure head breaking off?

A.—Plug the pipe.

Q. 284.—What would control the compressor?

A.—The excess pressure head.

Q. 285.—In such a case, would the excess pressure head control the compressor at all times?

A.—No; only with the automatic brake valve handle in *release*, *running*, or *holding* positions.

Q. 286.—What would happen if the handle were left in *lap*, *service*, or *emergency* positions or it became necessary to close the main reservoir cut-out cock for any length of time?

A.—The governor then being out of commission, the compressor will continue to run until air pressure and steam pressure become approximately equal.

Q. 287.—What precaution should be taken with the governor out of commission in this way?

A.—Compressor should be throttled so that too high a main reservoir pressure could not be obtained and in case of main reservoir cock being closed compressor should be shut off.

Q. 288.—What should be done if the equalizing reservoir pipe breaks off?

A.—Plug the equalizing reservoir pipe to the brake valve and the service exhaust opening. The brakes should then be applied in service by a careful use of the *emergency* position.

Q. 289.—Why should extreme care be used when operating the brake valve in this manner?

A.—To avoid causing quick action and to prevent the head brakes "kicking" off when returning to *lap* position.

ROUNDHOUSE INSPECTOR'S TEST.

GENERAL.

Q. 290.—What are the objects of these tests?

A.—To determine the condition of the detail parts of the "ET" equipment.

Q. 291.—What should be done by the roundhouse air brake inspector when testing the brakes preparatory to turning out the engine on the road?

A.—The following cocks must be closed: The drain cocks in the main reservoirs, the brake pipe angle cocks and the signal pipe cut-out cocks at each end of the locomotive, and the ⅜-inch cut-out cock in the dead engine pipe.

The following cocks must be opened: Main reservoir cut-out cock, distributing valve cut-out cock, the double-heading cock and cut-out cocks in the brake cylinder pipes.

Both the automatic and independent brake valve handles should be in *running* position before starting the compressor.

Q. 292.—When the locomotive brake system has become fully charged what should first be done?

A.—Blow out the brake pipe and signal pipe by opening and closing quickly a number of times the angle and stop cocks, both at the pilot and rear of the tender.

Q. 293.—Why is this done?

A.—To remove scale and other foreign matter that may be in the brake and signal pipes.

Q. 294.—What pressure should there be in the brake pipe and distributing valve before testing the brake?

A.—The standard brake pipe pressure for the service in which the locomotive is to be used.

Q. 295.—What are the parts that should be tested first?

A.—The air gauges.

Q. 296.—What method should be employed to test the air gauges?

A.—Use a test gauge that is known to be correct. This gauge should be coupled to the front or to the rear brake pipe hose; then with system charged and automatic brake valve in *release* position, note if main reservoir, equalizing reservoir and brake pipe pressures as indicated by the air gauges correspond with the pressure indicated on the test gauge.

Q. 297.—How should the brake cylinder gauge be tested?

A.—Connect the test gauge to the brake cylinder, make a brake application, and see that the brake cylinder gauge registers with the test gauge.

Q. 298.—What test should follow the gauge test?

A.—A test of the pump governor.

Q. 299.—How should this test be made?

A.—Place the automatic brake valve handle in *running* position. In this position main reservoir pressure should register 20 pounds higher than that in the brake pipe. Then place the handle in *lap* position. In this position the main reservoir pressure should register the maximum pressure standard on the road for the class of service to which the engine is assigned.

Q. 300.—What should next be done?

A.—The feed valve should be tested.

Q. 301.—How should the feed valve be tested?

A.—Place the automatic brake valve handle in *running* position to see that the feed valve regulates the brake pipe pressure to the proper standard.

Q. 302.—What test should follow the feed valve test?

A.—A test of the automatic rotary valve for leakage.

Q. 303.—How should this be tested?

A.—Make a 20-pound service reduction, place the handle on *lap* position and close the double-heading cut-out cock under the brake valve. Harmful rotary valve leakage will be denoted in a few seconds by a material increase of pressure in the equalizing reservoir (shown as gauge), or by the equalizing piston lifting.

Q. 304.—Would any other defect cause the equalizing piston to lift?

A.—Yes; a leak from the equalizing reservoir, which will be shown on the gauge, will cause this. If the piston lifts, due to a rotary valve leak, however, the gauge hand does not fall.

Q. 305.—What should next be done?

A.—The locomotive brake pipe should be tested for leakage.

Q. 306.—How should test be made for brake pipe leakage?

A.—Charge the brake pipe and system to maximum pressure, then make a 5-pound service application and observe the fall in brake pipe pressure as indicated by the *brake pipe gauge*, not by the equalizing reservoir gauge.

Q. 307.—What should the limit of this leakage be?

A.—It should not exceed 5 pounds per minute.

Q. 308.—What test should be made to determine if the brake is in good order?

A.—Apply the brake by making a full service application with the automatic brake valve, and if it applies properly, release by placing the automatic brake valve handle in *running* position and note if the brake shoes properly clear the wheels and the cylinder pistons return to the end of the cylinder.

Q. 309.—What other test should be made?

A.—Apply the brake with the independent brake valve, noting that a full application (45 pounds) is registered by the red hand of the small air gauge and that the hand returns to zero when the brake is fully released.

Q. 310.—With the independent brake valve handle in *quick application* position how long should it take to get 45 pounds cylinder pressure?

A.—From two to four seconds.

Q. 311.—How long should it then take from the time the independent brake valve handle is placed in *release* position until the flow of air from the application chamber at the brake valve ceases?

A.—From two to three seconds.

Q. 312.—What should be observed regarding piston travel?

A—That the piston travel is only sufficient to give proper brake shoe clearance.

Q. 313.—What is usually about the proper piston travel?

A.—Driver brakes about four inches; engine truck brake about six inches, and tender brake about seven inches standing travel.

Q. 314.—Why is too long piston travel objectionable?

A.—It may cause a loss of the brake due to the piston striking the head or levers fouling, which will lengthen the time of release of the brake and cause a waste of air.

PUMP GOVERNOR TEST.

Q. 315.—Before adjusting the pump governor, what should be observed?

A.—That all air pipe connections are tight and that the vent port and drain port are open.

Q. 316.—What would be the effect of a stopped-up vent port?

A.—There might be a considerable drop in main reservoir pressure before the compressor would start.

Q. 317.—If, in addition to a stopped-up vent port, either diaphragm pin valve were leaking, what would be the effect?

A.—The compressor would not operate when the main reservoir pressure was about 40 pounds or over.

Q. 318.—What would be the effect of a stopped-up drain port?
A.—The governor would not shut off the compressor.

Q. 319.—If, with the handle of the automatic brake valve in *running* position, the main reservoir and brake pipe pressures do not stand 20 pounds apart, where is the trouble?
A.—In the adjustment of the excess pressure head of the pump governor.

Q. 320.—What should then be done?
A.—The excess pressure head of the pump governor should be properly adjusted.

Q. 321.—Before commencing to adjust the excess pressure head, what is it important to note?
A.—First, that the maximum pressure head is adjusted higher than the standard main reservoir pressure to be carried with the handle of the brake valve in *running* position. Second, that the air brake pressure is known to be correct. Third, that there is no obstruction either in the main reservoir connection to the chamber under the diaphragm of the excess pressure head or in the pipe connection to the spring chamber.

Q. 322.—How should the adjustment of the excess pressure head be made?
A.—Remove the cap nut from the excess pressure head and screw the regulating nut up or down, as may be required.

Q. 323.—With the automatic brake valve handle in *lap* position, if the main reservoir pressure varies from the maximum employed on the road, where is the trouble?
A. In the maximum pressure governor head.

Q. 324.—If such variation exists, what should be done?
A.—The maximum head should be properly adjusted.

Q. 325.—In case of a steady blow of air from the vent port when the compressor is operating, where is the trouble?
A.—A leak past the seat of one or both of the diaphragm pin valves.

FEED VALVE TEST.

Q. 326.—How should the B-6 feed valve be tested?
A.—With brake released and system charged to standard pressure, open the angle cock at the rear of the tender sufficiently to represent a brake pipe leakage of from 7 to 10 pounds per minute and observe the brake pipe gauge pointer.

Q. 327.—With this amount of brake pipe leakage, what should the brake pipe gauge pointer do?
A.—It should fluctuate.

Q. 328.—What does this fluctuation of the gauge pointer indicate?
A.—The opening and closing of the supply valve of the feed valve.

Q. 329.—If the gauge hand does not fluctuate, what does it indicate?

A.—That the supply valve piston is too loose a fit, and that the brake pipe leakage is being supplied past this piston and the regulating valve.

Q. 330.—How much variation should there be between the opening and closing of the feed valve supply valve?

A.—Not more than 2 pounds.

Q. 331.—If the variation is more than 2 pounds, what does it indicate?

A.—Undue friction of the parts or a sticky or dirty condition of the operating parts of the valve, causing insufficient opening past the piston.

Q. 332.—If the feed valve charges the brake pipe to a pressure higher than that for which it is adjusted, what does it indicate?

A.—That the piston has been made too tight a fit by oil or water.

Q. 333.—If the feed valve charges the brake pipe too slowly when nearing its maximum, what does it indicate?

A.—Either a loose fitting piston or a gummy condition of the regulating valve.

REDUCING VALVE TEST.

Q. 334.—How should the C-6 reducing valve be tested?

A.—First, with the system charged to standard pressure, fully apply the independent brake (handle in *slow application* position), and note the amount of brake cylinder pressure obtained.

Q. 335.—What should this pressure be?

A.—Forty-five pounds.

Q. 336.—If, in this test, the brake cylinder pressure is other than 45 pounds, what does it indicate?

A.—A leaky supply valve, a leaky regulating valve, or that the reducing valve is out of adjustment.

Q. 337.—After completing the test, what next should be done?

A.—Release the brake and make an application in *quick application* position.

Q. 338.—How can the reducing valve be tested for sensitiveness?

A.—By applying a test gauge to the signal line hose, and produce a leakage of from 7 to 10 pounds per minute in the signal line pipe and note the fluctuation of the gauge pointer.

Q. 339.—What is important in making this test?

A.—It must be known that the combined strainer and check valve is in a condition to permit a free flow of air through it.

Q. 340.—What other diseases might affect the operation of the reducing valve?

A.—Those given in questions 329 to 333 for the feed valve.

AUTOMATIC BRAKE VALVE TEST.

Q. 341.—What should be observed concerning the automatic brake valve?

A.—That all its pipe connections are tight and that the handle moves freely between its various positions and that the handle latch and its spring are in good condition.

Q. 342.—If the handle does not operate easily, what are the probable causes?

A.—A dry rotary valve seat, a dry rotary valve key gasket or a dry handle latch.

Q. 343.—What should be done?

A.—Rotary valve and seat, rotary valve key and handle latch should be properly lubricated.

Q. 344.—What is the proper method of lubricating the valve and seat?

A.—Close the double-heading cock under the brake valve, then the main reservoir cut-out cock and after the air pressure has escaped, remove the oil plug in the valve body and fill the oil hole with valve oil.

Q. 345.—After filling the oil hole and before replacing the oil plug, what should be done?

A.—The handle should be moved a few times between *release* and *emergency* positions to permit the oil to work in between the rotary valve and its seat. The oil hole should then be refilled and the oil plug replaced.

Q. 346.—How should the rotary valve key and gasket be lubricated?

A.—Remove the cap nut from the rotary valve key and fill the oil hole.

Q. 347.—Before replacing the cap nut, what should be done?

A.—Push down on the key and rotate the handle a few times between *release* and *emergency* positions; then refill the oil hole and replace the cap nut.

Q. 348.—If the handle latch becomes dry, what should be done?

A.—Lubricate the sides of the latch and the notches on the quadrant.

Q. 349.—If, with the handle in *release, running, holding* or *lap* positions, there is a leak at the brake pipe service exhaust, what does it indicate?

A.—That the equalizing piston valve is unseated, probably due to foreign matter.

Q. 350.—How can this leak usually be stopped?

A.—By closing the double-heading cut-out cock under the brake valve, making a heavy service application and returning the brake valve handle to *release* position. This will cause a heavy blow at the service exhaust fitting and usually remove the foreign matter and allow the valve to seat.

Q. 351.—With the handle of the automatic brake valve in *service application* position, brake pipe pressure 70 pounds, how long should it take to reduce the equalizing reservoir pressure 20 pounds?

A.—From 6 to 7 seconds.

Q. 352.—From a brake pipe pressure of 110 pounds, how long should it take?

A.—From 5 to 6 seconds.

Q. 353.—In case the equalizing reservoir pressure reduces considerably faster than the time given, what is the probable cause?

A.—Either an enlarged preliminary exhaust port, leakage past the rotary valve, seat, lower gasket, or in the equalizing reservoir and its connections to the brake valve or gauge

Q. 354.—If the reduction is materially slower than the figures given, what is probably the cause?

A.—A partial stoppage of the preliminary exhaust port or leakage into the equalizing reservoir.

Q. 355.—How should test be made for a leaky rotary valve?

A.—By placing the brake valve handle in *service* position and allowing it to remain there until the brake pipe gauge pointer drops to zero; then close the double-heading cock under the brake valve and place the brake valve handle on *lap*. If a blow starts at the brake pipe exhaust, it indicates a leak by the rotary valve into the brake pipe; if an increase of pressure is noted on the equalizing resevoir gauge it indicates a leak past the rotary valve or body gasket into the chamber above the equalizing piston and reservoir.

Q. 356.—During this test, if an increase of brake cylinder pressure results or the safety valve blows intermittently, what does it indicate?

A.—A leak by the rotary valve into the application cylinder of the distributing valve.

Q. 357.—With the brake valve handle on *lap* position after making a service application, if the brake pipe service exhaust continues to blow and the air gauge indicates a fall in pressure in both the equalizing reservoir and brake pipe, where should the trouble be looked for?

A.—In the equalizing reservoir and its connections, both to the brake valve and to the air gauge, and also the inner tube of the gauge.

INDEPENDENT BRAKE VALVE TEST.

Q. 358.—What are the important things to observe in connection with the independent brake valve?

A.—That no external leakage exists in the brake valve or its pipe connections and that the handle and return spring work freely and properly.

Q. 359.—What can cause the handle to move hard?

A.—Lack of lubrication on the rotary valve and seat, rotary valve key and gasket or handle latch, same as with the automatic brake valve.

Q. 360.—What should be done to make the handle move freely?

A.—Follow the same recommendations as prescribed for the automatic brake valve.

Q. 361.—Should the handle continue to work hard after the parts have been lubricated, where is the trouble?

A.—Probably something is wrong with the return spring or its housing.

Q. 362.—How should test for leaky rotary valve be made?

A.—Make a partial independent application of the brakes, place the handle on lap, and note if brake cylinder pressure increases gradually to the limit of adjustment of the reducing valve.

Q. 363.—Should the handle fail to automatically return to *running* position or to *slow application* position, what is the probable cause?

A.—Too much friction of the moving parts or a weak or broken return spring.

DISTRIBUTING VALVE TEST.

Q. 364.—With the system charged to standard pressure, if a 5-pound service reduction in brake pipe pressure fails to apply the locomotive brake, what is the probable cause?

A.—Excessive friction in one or more of the operative parts of the distributing valve.

Q. 365.—How should the test be made to determine which of the operating parts caused the trouble?

A.—By recharging and then making a slow independent application. If the brake applies properly, the indications are that the trouble is in the equalizing portion of the distributing valve; if it does not, the indications are that it is in the application portion.

Q. 366.—How frequently should the distributing valve be cleaned and oiled?

A.—At least every six months.

Q. 367.—What part of the distributing valve should be lubricated?

A.—All operating parts.

Q. 368.—If water is found in the distributing valve, what is usually the cause?

A.—Improper piping on the locomotive; not sufficient length of radiating pipe between the compressor and reservoirs.

Q. 369.—How should the equalizing piston, slide valve and **graduating** valve be removed from the distributing valve?

A.—Remove the equalizing cylinder cap and carefully pull out the piston and valves so as not to injure them.

Q. 370.—How should the application piston, application valve and exhaust valve be removed?

A.—First take off the application valve cover and remove the valve, then take out the application valve pin, after which the application cylinder cover should be removed and the piston and exhaust valve carefully pulled out.

Q. 371.—Must the application valve pin always be removed before attempting to take out the application piston and exhaust valve?

A.—Yes; if this is not done, damage will result, as the piston *can not* be taken out unless the pin is removed.

Q. 372.—With the valves removed from the distributing valve, what should be done?

A.—Air should be blown through the ports and passages to remove any foreign matter.

Q. 373.—Before assembling the parts, what should be done?

A.—All seats and bushings should be thoroughly cleaned and carefully examined to see that no lint is on the seats.

Q. 374.—What else should be given attention?

A.—The feed groove in the equalizing piston bushing should be carefully cleaned out.

Q. 375.—What should be the resulting brake cylinder pressure from a 10-pound brake pipe reduction?

A.—About 25 pounds.

Q. 376.—For each pound reduction of brake pipe pressure, what should be the resulting brake cylinder pressure?

A.—About 2½ pounds.

Q. 377.—If, after a partial service application has been made and the brake valve lapped, the brake cylinder pressure continues to increase, what are the causes?

A.—The most probable cause is brake pipe leakage. Others may be a leak past the automatic rotary valve, the independent rotary valve, the equalizing valve, or the graduating valve in the distributing valve.

Q. 378.—What brake pipe pressure should be used when testing the "ET" equipment?

A.—Seventy pounds.

Q. 379.—Why?

A.—With 70 pounds brake pipe pressure the point of equalization is below the adjustment of the safety valve. With 110 pounds pressure the point of equalization is above the adjustment of the safety valve and therefore leakage could not be so easily discovered.

Q. 380.—How is the source of leaks determined?

A.—By making a partial service application and observe to what figure the brake cylinder pressure rises. If it increases to 50 pounds and remains constant, it indicates brake pipe leakage.

Q. 381.—If the increase in the brake cylinder pressure is due to a leaky rotary in the automatic brake valve, how may it be detected?

A.—The brake cylinder pressure will increase up to the limit of adjustment of the safety valve, causing it to blow.

Q. 382.—If brake cylinder pressure increases to 45 pounds and stops, where may the trouble be looked for?

A.—In the independent brake valve, due to a leaky rotary.

Q. 383.—With the safety valve removed and the brake applied with a partial service application, if a continuous leak exists at the safety valve connection to the distributing valve, what would probably be the cause?

A.—A leaky graduating or equalizing valve.

Q. 384.—If the equalizing valve leaks, how can it be detected?

A.—By a steady discharge of air through the exhaust port of the automatic brake valve when the handle of both this brake valve and the independent brake valve is in *running* position.

Q. 385.—If, with a service application there is an intermittent blow at the brake cylinder exhaust port, what does it indicate?

A.—A leaky application valve, provided the application cylinder and the application cylinder pipe is tight.

Q. 386.—What indicates exhaust valve leakage?

A.—A continuous discharge of air from the exhaust port when the brake is applied.

Q. 387.—If after a service application the equalizing piston, slide valve and graduating valve move to release position because of graduating valve leakage, will the locomotive release?

A.—On the engine from which the brakes are being operated the locomotive brake will not release, but on the second engine in double-headers or helpers with the brake valves cut out (double-heading cock closed) the locomotive brake will release.

Q. 388.—Why does not the brake release on the locomotive from which the brakes are being operated?

A.—Because under these conditions the automatic brake valve is on *lap;* consequently the air can not exhaust from the application chamber.

Q. 389.—Why will the brake release on the second locomotive or helper?

A.—Because the release pipe is open to the atmosphere.

Q. 390.—If the brake released after an automatic application, when the handle is placed in *release* or *holding* position, but remains applied after an independent application, where would you look for the trouble?

A.—It is caused by a leak from the distributing valve release pipe, between the automatic and the independent brake valves.

Q. 391.—If the brake releases after an independent application, but remains applied after an automatic application, what would cause the trouble?

A.—A leak in the distributing valve release pipe between the distributing valve and the independent brake valve.

Q. 392.—If the brake releases after either an automatic or an independent application, what would cause the trouble?

A.—A leak from the application cylinder pipe or past the application cylinder cap gasket.

Q. 393.—How would a weak or broken application piston graduating spring be detected?

A.—If this spring becomes weak or broken, the application portion of the distributing valve would not be as sensitive to graduation.

Q. 394.—How should test for leakage in the application cylinder pipe be made?

A.—Make a *service* application of the brake, lap the handle and note if the brake remains applied. If it does not, it indicates that the application cylinder pipe or possibly that the application cylinder cap gasket is leaking.

Q. 395.—To determine if the release pipe is leaking, how should test be made?

A.—Make a service application of the brake with the automatic brake valve. If the brake remains applied with handle in *lap* position but releases when handle is returned to *holding*, it indicates release pipe leakage.

Q. 396.—If the brake cylinder pressure does not remain at that to which it is applied, what is the cause?

A.—Leakage from application chamber, application cylinder or their pipe connections.

BRAKE CYLINDER LEAKAGE TEST.

Q. 397.—Can brake cylinder leakage be readily determined with "ET" equipment?

A.—Yes.

Q. 398.—How?

A.—By noting the number of strokes which the compressor makes in a given period of time. Then apply the brake with the independent brake valve and after the compressor has restored the main reservoir pressure again note the number of strokes. The difference in the number of strokes indicates the amount of leakage in the brake cylinders.

Q. 399.—Is there any other method of determining brake cylinder leakage?

A.—Yes; apply the brake with the independent brake valve, then close the cut-out cock in the distributing valve supply pipe and observe the brake cylinder gauge. The gauge will indicate the amount of leakage from the brake cylinders.

Q. 400.—Can it be determined which of the brake cylinders is leaking?

A.—Yes.

Q. 401.—How?

A.—Apply the brake with the independent brake valve and close the cut-out cock in the distributing valve supply pipe, then close the cut-out cocks in the pipes leading to the truck brake cylinder, driver brake cylinder and tender cylinder in order, noting the gauge after each cock is closed.

SAFETY VALVE TEST.

Q. 402.—What attention should be given the E-6 safety valve?

A.—It should be noted that the safety valve is screwed properly in place, that the cap nut is screwed down on the regulating nut, making an air-tight joint with the body, and that all vent holes and ports are open.

Q. 403.—If the cap nut is not screwed down properly, what would be the effect?

A.—The valve and its stem would have too much lift and the leakage of air around the threads of the regulating nut to the atmosphere would interfere with its proper operation.

Q. 404.—How should the safety valve be tested to determine if it is properly adjusted?

A.—Make an emergency application of the brake, allowing the handle to remain in *emergency* position, and note if the proper brake cylinder pressure is obtained.

Q. 405.—What brake pipe pressure should be used when testing the safety valve?

A.—One hundred pounds.

Q.. 406.—Within what limits should the safety valve limit the locomotive brake cylinder pressure?

A.—Between 68 and 70 pounds.

Q. 407.—If the safety valve is adjusted at 68 pounds, and the pressure increases above 70 pounds, what would be the cause?

A.—The holes leading from the spring chamber of the valve are restricted or the piston valve has worn loose.

Q. 408.—If the safety valve permits the pressure to reduce considerably below 68 pounds before closing, what would be the trouble?

A.—The holes leading from the spring chamber of the valve have been enlarged or gum or dirt has made the piston valve too close a fit.

Q. 409.—Within what limits should the safety valve limit the locomotive brake cylinder pressure for ordinary service applications (110 pounds brake pressure)?

A.—Between 65 and 70 pounds.

AIR SIGNAL SUPPLY SYSTEM TEST.

Q. 410.—In testing the air signal, what should first be done?
A.—The signal pipe should be charged and all stop cocks, joints and unions carefully examined for leakage.

Q. 411.—How can it be determined whether the proper pressure is being carried in the signal line?
A.—By attaching a test gauge to the signal line hose.

Q. 412.—What would a too high signal pipe pressure indicate?
A.—That the reducing valve was improperly adjusted or was leaking.

Q. 413.—What effect might this have?
A.—In combination with a leaky signal line it might cause the signal whistle to blow when an independent application of the brake is made.

Q. 414.—How can reducing valve leakage be determined?
A.—By making a signal pipe reduction and noting if the pressure gradually increases after the standard maximum signal pipe pressure has been attained.

Q. 415.—With a reasonably tight signal pipe, if the whistle blows when an independent application of the brake is made, what would be the cause?
A.—A leaky valve in the combined strainer and check valve.

Q. 416.—If, in charging up the signal pipe the test gauge indicates a too slow increase of pressure, where should the trouble be looked for?
A.—Probably an obstruction in the strainer or choke fitting or a loose fitting feed valve piston.

Q. 417.—If, with the signal system of the locomotive fully charged, the signal whistle blows, what is the probable cause?
A.—Leakage in the signal system and a sluggishly operating reduction valve.

The New York B-3 Locomotive Brake Equipment

This locomotive brake equipment is known as the B-3 equipment, and is arranged in four different schedules to cover the general requirements of railroad service.

Schedule B-3 is for engines in passenger or freight service, where but one brake pipe pressure is used. Both pump governor and pressure controller have single regulating heads, which should be adjusted for the standard brake pipe and main reservoir pressure.

Schedule B-3S is for switch engines only. A single pump governor and single pressure controller are used. The controller is set to give a brake pipe pressure of 70 pounds and the pump governor for 90 pounds main reservoir pressure, for ordinary switching service. However, when the engine is used for passenger switching service, and handles trains that are using 110 pounds brake pipe pressure, the pump governor should be adjusted to 110 pounds main reservoir pressure. When handling a train using the high pressure, close cock No. 2 between the regulating and supply portions of the controller. This renders the controller inoperative, allowing the main reservoir pressure of 110 pounds to pass to the brake valve and brake pipe, so that trains using the high speed brake can be handled without delay without the necessity of carrying additional apparatus. A quick release valve is furnished with this schedule, to be placed in the straight air pipe, so that the brakes can be released quickly, permitting quicker movement. The divided reservoir and accelerator valve are not furnished with this schedule. The supplementary reservoir is substituted for the divided reservoir.

Schedule B-3HP is for freight service where heavily loaded trains are handled on heavy grades, or loads handled down grades and empties up. Both regulating portions of the pump governor and pressure controller are duplex, so that pressures of 70 and 90 pounds can be carried in the brake pipe and 90 and 110 pounds in the main reservoir for the ordinary brake pipe pressure and the high pressure control.

For the operation of these duplex regulating portions, three-way cocks are provided, being connected as shown in the piping diagram. To operate these cocks, turn the handle in line with the pipe leading to the regulating head to be used, high or low pressure as desired. This will cut in the head to regulate the supply portion, and cut off the pressure to the one not in use.

Schedule B-3HS is the high speed brake. It includes the duplex pressure controller and the duplex pump governor. The regulating

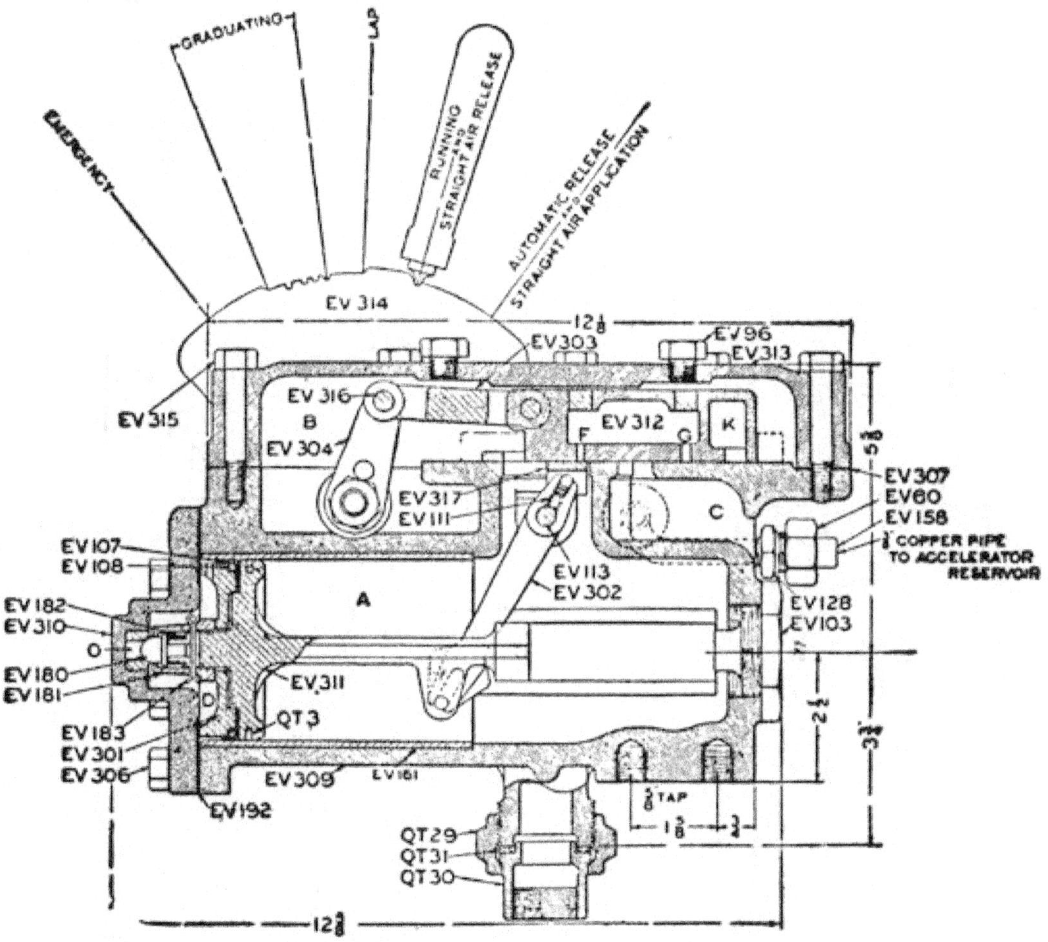

ENGINEMEN'S MANUAL

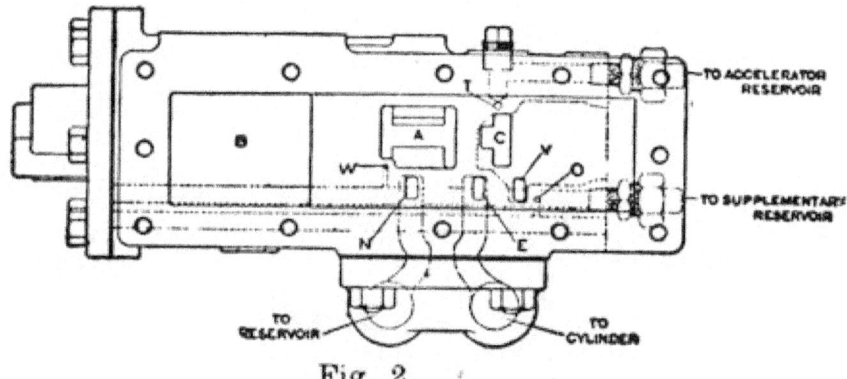

Fig. 1.

Fig. 2.

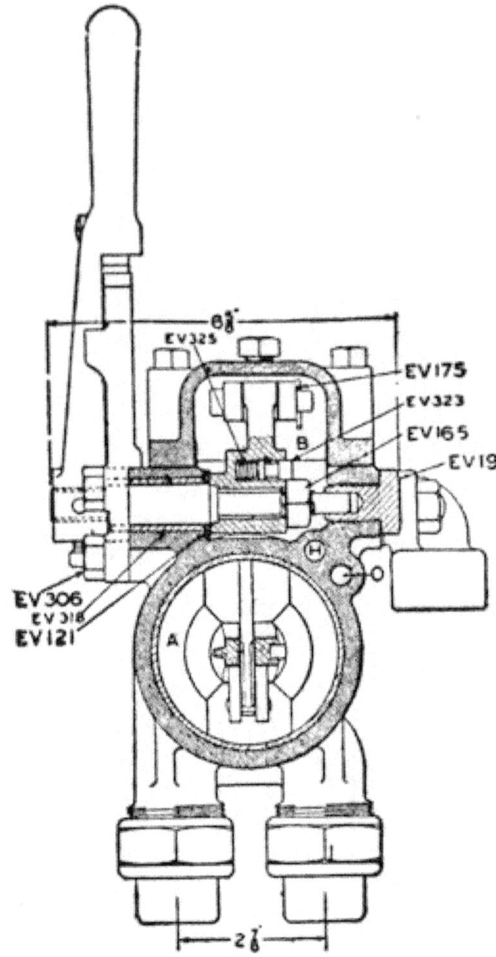

384 ENGINEMEN'S MANUAL

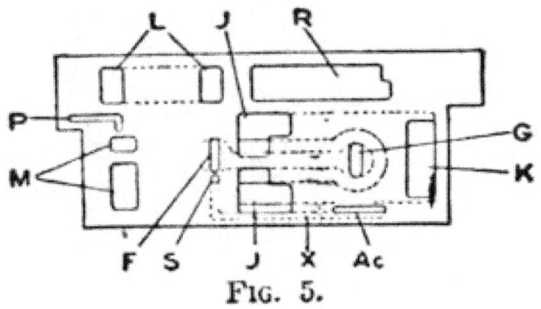

FIG. 3.

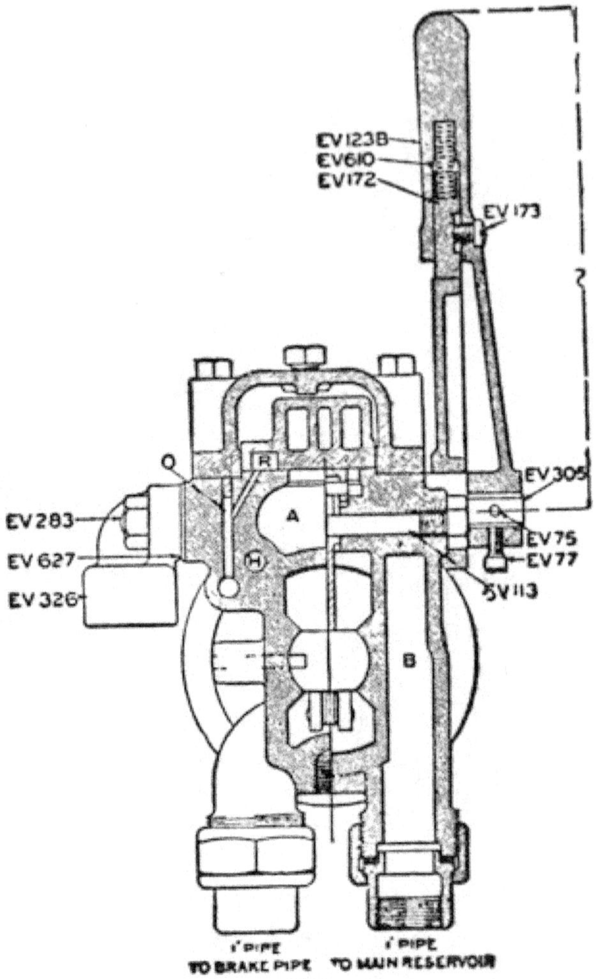

FIG. 4.

FIG. 5.

heads of the pressure controller should be adjusted to 70 pounds and 110 pounds for brake pipe pressure, and the pump governor heads adjusted to 90 pounds and 130 pounds for the main reservoir pressure. A union four-way cock is used with the regulating heads of the pressure controller. This is a special cock with a connection to each regulating top, one to the supply pipe between the controller and brake valve, and one to the pipe between the brake valve and accelerator reservoir. When the handle of the four-way cock is in the position to operate the regulating head adjusted to 110 pounds brake pipe pressure, a small port in the accelerator reservoir connection is brought into communication with a port to the atmosphere. The object of this port is to prevent more than the usual predetermined reduction of brake pipe air, obtained in the graduating notches, taking place with 110 pounds pressure. A union three-way cock connected to the main reservoir and pump governor regulating tops is used to change the main reservoir pressures.

This equipment is an improvement on former equipments. It not only includes all necessary features for the automatic brake, but also a straight air brake for the locomotive and tender, all operated by the automatic brake valve, without any additional positions.

Some of the notable improvements incorporated in the B-3 brake valve, which will be appreciated by those who come in contact with it, are: The use of tap bolts instead of screws to fasten the valve cover to the body; port O is cored in the valve body instead of being drilled through the cover; the projection for centering the piston packing leather EV 107 is on the piston instead of on the follower. A new packing leather can now be applied without removing the piston from the brake valve. It is only necessary to remove the back cap and the piston follower.

MANIPULATION.

To apply the automatic brakes on the locomotive and train, move the handle of the brake valve to the graduating notch necessary to make the required brake pipe reduction.

To release both locomotive and train brakes, move the handle to running and straight air release position.

To release the train brakes and hold the locomotive brakes set, move the handle to automatic release and straight air application position.

To apply the locomotive brakes (straight air), move the handle to full automatic release and straight air application position.

To release the locomotive brakes move the handle to running and straight air release position.

To apply the brakes in an emergency, move the handle quickly to emergency position and leave it there until the train stops.

In case the automatic brakes are applied by the bursting of a hose, the train parts, or a conductor's valve is opened, place the handle in lap position to retain the main reservoir pressure.

To graduate off or entirely release the locomotive brakes while holding the train brakes applied, use the lever safety valve to make the required reduction.

The handle of the brake valve will be found to work freely and easily at all times, as the pressure on the main slide valve does not exceed the maximum brake pipe pressure.

The cylinder gauge will show at all times the pressure in the locomotive brake cylinder and should be observed in brake manipulations.

Where there are two or more locomotives in a train, cut-out cock No. 1 should be turned to close the brake pipe and the brake valve handle carried in running and straight air release position on all locomotives except the one from which the brakes are operated.

In case it becomes necessary to cut out the straight air brake, close cut-out cock No. 3, located in the straight air pipe.

To cut out the automatic brake on the engine, close cut-out cock No. 6, located in the pipe connecting the triple valve with the double check valve. By locating the cut-out cock at this point the auxiliary reservoir will remain charged if the brake is cut out, and can be cut in immediately should it be so desired. This cut-out cock and also cut-out cock No. 3 are special; they are of the three-way pattern and when turned off drain the pipes leading to the double check valve, which insures the check valve remaining seated in the direction of the closed cock.

The main reservoir cock No. 4 is to cut off the supply of air when removing any of the apparatus except the governor.

The straight air controller is to limit the pressure in the driver, truck and tender brake cylinders for the straight air brake, and should be adjusted to 40 pounds pressure.

QUESTIONS AND ANSWERS ON B-3 "HS" LOCOMOTIVE BRAKE

Q.—On what is this type of brake designed to operate?
A.—On locomotives in passenger service.

Q.—What are some of the advantages of the B3-HS type of brake over the older style equipment?
A.—But one engineer's brake valve is used to operate either the automatic or straight air brake on the locomotive; only maximum brake pipe pressure enters the brake valve, thereby preventing any possibility of overcharging the brake pipe, also reducing the friction between the slide valve and its seat; the brake valve is assisted by the accelerator valve, in reducing the brake pipe pressure on long trains; the high speed controller valve takes the place of the compensating valve, also enables the engineer to partially or wholly release the driver and truck brakes without releasing the train brakes; the locomotive brake will not release, on account of brake cylinder leakage, when the brake valve is in the fifth service notch or in emergency position.

Q.—Name the different parts of the equipment, and state briefly their duties.
A.—1. The air pump; to compress the air used on the locomotive and cars.

2. The duplex pump governor; to control the pump when the desired pressure is obtained in the main reservoir.

3. The main reservoir; in which to store a large volume of air for the prompt charging and recharging of the brakes, and to collect the moisture and dirt in the air.

4. The main reservoir cut-out cock; which, when closed, cuts off the communication between the main reservoir and the brake system.

5. The engineer's brake valve; to operate the straight air on the locomotive, and the automatic brake on both locomotive and train.

6. The divided reservoir; to furnish the proper volume of air in chamber D of the brake valve, also a reservoir which is used in conjunction with the accelerator valve.

7. The pressure controller; to control the pressure in the slide valve chamber of the brake valve.

8. The accelerator valve; to assist the brake valve in reducing the brake pipe pressure on long trains, when a service application of the brake is made.

9. The ¾-inch pressure controller; to control the maximum straight air pressure.

10. The high speed controller; acts as a safety valve to all brake cylinders on the locomotive to which it is connected, also provides a means of partially or wholly releasing the locomotive brake independent of the train brake.

11. The auxiliary reservoirs; in which a supply of compressed air is stored to operate the brakes on the locomotive.

12. The triple valves; to admit air to and exhaust it from the brake cylinders, and to control the flow of air to and from the auxiliary reservoirs. The above, with the necessary gauges, strainers, cylinders, cut-out cocks, hose couplings and piping make up the B3 equipment.

Q.—Commencing at the air pump name the different pipes and their connections.

A.—Discharge pipe; to connect the pump and first main reservoir.

Connecting pipe; to connect the two main reservoirs.

Main reservoir pipe; to connect the second main reservoir to the pump governor, straight air pipe, brake valve, through the 1¼-inch pressure controller. This pipe also furnishes air to the connections of all other air-operated appliances on the locomotive.

Pressure controller pipe; to connect the pressure controller with the slide valve chamber in the brake valve, and to the regulating portion of the 1¼-inch pressure controller.

Brake cylinder pipe; connects the brake valve through the straight air side of the double check with the brake cylinders on the locomotive, also with the regulating portion of the ¾-inch pressure controller, and the triple valves, through the automatic side of the double check, with the brake cylinders.

The high speed controller pipe; connects the high speed controller with both the automatic and straight air sides of the double check to the driver and truck brake cylinders, and the straight air side of the double check to the tender brake cylinder.

The supplementary reservoir pipe; to connect the supplementary reservoir with chamber D in the brake valve.

The accelerator valve pipe; to connect the accelerator valve with the brake pipe.

The accelerator reservoir pipe; to connect the accelerator reservoir with the brake valve.

The brake pipe; to connect the brake valve with all operating triple valves on both locomotive and train.

Auxiliary reservoir pipe; to connect the triple valves, with their respective auxiliaries.

B-3 LOCOMOTIVE BRAKE

Q.—What type of brake valve is used with this equipment?
A.—The B-3 is of the slide valve type.
Q.—What are the duties of the main slide valve?
A.—The main slide valve forms a dividing between the main reservoir supply and the various parts of the equipment charged with air, and, in its various positions, connects these parts with the atmosphere.
Q.—What are the duties of the graduating valve?
A.—The duties of the graduating valve are to close the opening in the exhaust port, made by the movement of the main slide valve, in a service application of the brake.
Q.—Name the different positions of the brake valve.
A.—Automatic release, and straight air application; running and straight air release; lap; service, subdivided into five graduating notches; and emergency positions.
Q.—What is the object of having the straight air port open to the brake cylinders when an automatic application of the brake is made?
A.—When the fifth notch is used, generally speaking, the train has no great distance in which to complete the stop, therefore, to insure full braking pressure on the locomotive, regardless of piston travel or brake cylinder leakage, this feature is used.
Q.—What is the object of the divided reservoir?
A.—To secure the proper movement of the piston in service applications of the brake, it is necessary to have a greater volume of air behind the piston than that found in Chamber D, therefore, to increase this volume, the small chamber in the divided reservoir is added to it by both chambers being connected by piping. The larger chamber is used in connection with the accelerator valve.
Q.—Is this type of reservoir used in all the different schedules of the B-3 equipment?
A.—No; it is used only when the accelerator valve is part of the equipment.

PRESSURE CONTROLLER

Q.—How is the brake pipe pressure regulated with this equipment?
A.—As the maximum brake pipe pressure is controlled by the pressure in chamber B of the brake valve, and as this pressure is, in turn, controlled by the pressure controller, it may be said that the brake pipe pressure is regulated by the pressure controller.

Q.—Does the pressure controller then take the place of the feed valve or excess pressure valve as used with other types of brake valves?

A.—Yes; the pressure controller may be considered a part of the brake valve.

Q.—Where is the pressure controller located?

A.—In the pipe between the main reservoir and the brake valve, and is generally located inside the cab.

Q.—Of what does the pressure controller consist?

A.—Generally it is in two parts, known as the regulating portion and supply portion, with a pipe connection between them. Where it is desired, the regulating portion may be attached direct to the supply portion.

Q.—What pressure is found below the diaphragm of the regulating portion?

A.—Pressure controller pipe pressure.

Q.—What pressure is found in the supply portion of the pressure controller?

A.—Main reservoir pressure enters as far as the valve PG 166, while on the other side of this valve the pressure is the same as that in the main slide valve chamber of the brake valve.

Q.—How is the brake pipe pressure regulated?

A.—By screwing the regulating nut up or down, as may be required.

Q.—What is the object of the duplex or double top regulating portion?

A.—This is simply for a matter of convenience, where the brake pipe pressure is changed from one standard pressure to that of another, while the train is en route, or where the engine may be running in two different classes of service.

Q.—At what pressure are these tops usually adjusted?

A.—On engines in passenger service the low pressure top is generally adjusted at 70 pounds, and the high pressure top at 110 pounds.

Q.—How are the regulating portions of the duplex controller cut in and cut out?

A.—By means of a four-way cock, which is connection to both of the regulating tops, when one top is cut in the other cut out. This cock also has a connection to accelerator reservoir.

Q.—What do the letters L, H, and R cast on a four-way cock indicate?

A.—L indicates the low pressure position, H the high pressure position, R the accelerator reservoir connection.

Q.—How is the four-way cock operated?

A.—By turning the handle to have it point toward L for low pressure, and H for high pressure.

Q.—What is the purpose of the hand wheel?

A.—By screwing up on the hand wheel, the valve will be held from its seat, and main reservoir air will be free to flow to the brake pipe until the pressure equalizes.

Q.—When should the hand wheel be used?

A.—Whenever the pressure controller, through some defect, fails to furnish the proper pressure in the brake pipe, or when it is desired to carry the same pressure in the brake pipe as that in the main reservoir, as in braking trains on heavy grades, where the higher pressure is required.

Q.—Can a sticking brake be released by screwing up on the hand wheel?

A.—Yes, it may; but in releasing a stuck brake in this way the brake pipe will become overcharged, which may cause the brakes to reapply; therefore, it may be said to be bad practice to release a stuck brake by screwing up on the hand wheel.

Q.—What is the purpose of port x in the supply portion of the control valve?

A.—To exhaust any air that may leak into the chamber under the piston.

ACCELERATOR VALVE

Q.—What is the purpose of the accelerator valve?

A.—The accelerator valve is for the purpose of accelerating or hastening the discharge of air from the brake pipe when a service application of the brake is being made on a long train; in other words, it is to assist the brake valve in reducing the brake pipe pressure.

Q.—Why is it necessary to accelerate or hasten the reduction of brake pipe pressure on a long train?

A.—When a service application of the brake is being made, the pressure toward the rear end of train will drop so slowly that the air from the auxiliary reservoirs may flow back into the brake pipe, increasing the volume that has to be discharged from the brake pipe, and where this condition exists it means that many of the brakes at or near the rear of the train will not apply, due to the fact that a sufficient difference in pressure between the brake pipe and the auxiliary reservoir cannot be created to move the triple valves to application position, and it is for this reason that the accelerator valve is used, as by hastening the drop of brake pipe pressure a greater number of brakes may apply.

Q.—Is there any other cause for brakes failing to apply due to a large volume and slow reduction?

A.—When making a service application of the brake, the air from the auxiliary reservoir cannot flow to the brake cylinder any faster than the brake pipe pressure can be reduced at the brake valve; therefore, with long trains, where the reduction of brake pipe pressure is slow, the air may flow from the auxiliary reservoir so slowly that it may pass through the leakage grooves to the atmosphere and not apply the brakes.

Q.—To what is the accelerator valve attached?
A.—To the accelerator reservoir.
Q.—What pipe connections are there to the accelerator reservoir?
A.—There is but one pipe leading from the accelerator reservoir, which goes to the engineer's brake valve; this pipe is teed and a connection goes to the four-way cock.
Q.—What length of train is necessary to obtain action of the accelerator valve?
A.—About eight cars.
Q.—How long after the brake valve is placed in one of the graduating notches before the accelerator valve will operate?
A.—About four seconds.
Q.—How soon does it close, after the exhaust is closed, at the brake valve?
A.—About four seconds.

HIGH SPEED CONTROLLER

Q.—What is the purpose of the high speed controller?
A.—It acts as a safety valve to the driver, truck, and tender brake cylinders in straight air applications, and to the driver and truck brake cylinders in an automatic application; also provides a means of releasing the driver and truck brakes independent of the train brake following an automatic application of the brake.
Q.—Of what does the high speed controller consist?
A.—It consists of a cylinder containing a double faced piston having leather seats on each face; this piston is attached to a stem or valve, which has two annular grooves, one large and one small. The upper portion consists of a cap nut, regulating nut, regulating spring, regulating spring stem, lever handle, and valve.
Q.—What pressure is found in the chamber at the right of the piston?
A.—Brake pipe pressure.
Q.—What pressure is found in the chamber at the left of the piston?
A.—Brake cylinder pressure.
Q.—Explain the operation of the high speed controller, when a service application of the brake is made.
A.—Brake pipe air, which enters the controller at the connection, forces the piston to the left, bringing the large annular opening in valve over the opening from the brake cylinder connection, thus allowing the brake cylinder air to flow through the large annular groove and port G to the under side of valve, which is being held to its seat by the tension of the regulating spring. If the cylinder pressure becomes greater than that for which the controller is adjusted, the valve will be raised from its seat, and brake cylinder air will

escape to the atmosphere until the pressure is reduced slightly below that for which the controller is adjusted. Where the brake cylinder pressure remains below the adjustment of the controller, there is no movement of the parts.

Q.—Explain the operation when an emergency application is made.

A.—When an emergency application is made, the brake pipe pressure is reduced quite low, or probably to zero; this drops the pressure on the right or brake pipe side of the double faced piston, and the brake cylinder pressure forming on the left or brake cylinder side of the piston will force it to the right, bringing the small annular opening in the valve over the opening to the brake cylinder connection; this allows the brake cylinder air to flow through the small annular opening and port G to the under side of the valve; when the brake cylinder pressure becomes greater than that for which the controller is adjusted, the valve will rise, and the brake cylinder air will escape to the atmosphere gradually, until the pressure is reduced slightly below that for which the controller is adjusted—thus retaining the higher brake cylinder pressure for a greater length of time.

Q.—At what pressure should the controller be adjusted?
A.—At 53 pounds.

Q.—Explain how the driver and truck brake may be partially or wholly released, independent of the train brake.

A.—By pressing down the handle, the spring pressure is removed from the top of valve *RV 133;* this permits the brake cylinder pressure to raise the valve and the air to flow to the atmosphere, releasing it all or in part, as desired.

STRAIGHT AIR BRAKE

Q.—What brakes are operated by the straight air?
A.—The locomotive brakes only.

Q.—Why is this called the straight air?
A.—Because the air used comes from the main reservoir direct, and is not dependent on the movement of triple valves or other similar devices for the application or release of the brake.

Q.—How is the straight air applied?

A.—By placing the combined automatic and straight air brake valve in application position; N, to which is connected the straight air pipe carrying main reservoir air, is opened through passage L in the slide valve to E, to which is connected the pipe leading to the straight air side of the double check valve, and on to the locomotive brake cylinders.

Q.—What should be the maximum pressure developed with this brake?
A.—About 40 pounds.

Q.—How is this pressure regulated?
A.—By the ¾-inch pressure controller.

Q.—Can the straight air brake be graduated on and off?

A.—Yes, the brake may be graduated on by moving the brake valve to application position and back to *straight air lap* position, which is about halfway between automatic release and running positions, and by moving between straight air lap and running position, the brake may be graduated off.

Q.—If, after applying the straight air, the brake valve handle is placed in positive lap position, will the brake stay set?

A.—No.

Q.—How is this brake released?

A.—When the brake valve is placed in running and straight air released position, port E, which leads to the brake cylinders, is connected with port V, which leads to the exhaust, thus allowing any air in the brake cylinders to escape to the atmosphere.

Q.—Does the variation of piston travel affect the pressure developed with this brake?

A—No.

Q.—Will the brake release with ordinary brake cylinder leakage?

A—No; if the brake valve is left in application position, air will continue to flow to the brake cylinders as fast as it leaks away.

DEFECTS AND REMEDIES

Q.—The B-3 brake valve is supposed to make a brake pipe reduction corresponding to the notch the handle is placed in, and then automatically move to lap position; if it does not do this, where would you look for the trouble?

A.—Would look for a leak from chamber D or the supplementary reservoir.

Q.—If there be no leak from chamber D or the supplementary reservoir to the atmosphere, and the valve failed to automatically lap, where might the trouble be?

A.—The fact that the brake valve fails to automatically lap or close the service exhaust port, indicates a leakage of air from chamber D and the supplementary reservoir, and if the leakage is not to the atmosphere, then it may be past the piston *EV 311* into chamber A and the brake pipe, or may be through the partition of the divided reservoir, which would mean that chamber D and supplementary reservoir air would be leaking into the accelerator reservoir. Great care should be taken to see that there be no leakage from this chamber; as its volume is small, the pressure, therefore, is affected by even light leakage.

Q.—What effect will a leak from chamber D or the supplementary reservoir have, brakes released, valve in running position?

A.—As the air in chamber D and the supplementary reservoir comes from the brake pipe, this, then, would be a brake pipe leak, and have no effect other than to increase the work of the pump.

Q.—If the brake valve fails to automatically lap the service exhaust port, following a service application of the brake, what should be done?

A.—The brake valve handle should be moved slowly back to positive lap position, when the desired reduction is made.

Q.—If the brake valve is returned quickly to positive lap position, what would be the effect?

A.—If the brake pipe exhaust is closed quickly, there is a tendency for the brakes to release on the head end of the train.

Q.—If the pipe connecting the supplementary reservoir and the brake valve breaks, what should be done?

A.—Plug the broken pipe towards the brake valve, and when making a service application of the brake the valve will have to be returned to positive lap position when the desired reduction is made.

Q.—How will the engineman know when the brake valve is failing to automatically lap?

A.—By noting if the brake pipe reduction corresponds with the reduction that should be obtained in the notch in which the handle is placed.

Q.—What reduction should be obtained in the different service notches, with a 70-pound brake pipe pressure; with a 110-pound?

A.—The following table shows the total reduction obtained as the handle is moved to the different notches, also the reduction as the handle is moved to each notch.

		70 lbs.	110 lbs.
1.	Service graduating notch	5-5	6-6
2.	Service graduating notch	8-3	10-4
3.	Service graduating notch	11-3	14-4
4.	Service graduating notch	16-5	21-7
5.	Service graduating notch	23-7	30-9

Q.—What will cause a blow at the brake pipe exhaust port when the brake valve is in release, running, or lap position?

A.—A leaky main slide valve, vent valve, or a leak through the partition in the double chamber reservoir; leakage past the double-seated valve in the high pressure controller, will cause a blow when the brake valve is in running or lap position; a leaky graduating valve will cause a blow when the brake valve is in automatic lap position.

Q.—How would you test for main slide valve leaking?

A.—First exhaust all the air from the system, then place the brake valve in lap position, then start the pump, next open the angle cock at the rear of tender, and if air is found here the valve is leaking. Generally speaking, if there be a continuous blow in all positions, the slide valve is leaking.

Q.—Where is the trouble when the brake valve will automatically move to lap position with a lone engine, and fails to do so when coupled to a train?

A.—This is caused by leakage of chamber D and supplementary reservoir air past the piston $EV\ 311$ into chamber A and the brake pipe, and the action may be accounted for in the following: with the engine alone, the brake pipe volume is small, and its pressure is reduced quite rapidly, thereby creating a difference in pressures in chambers A and D, which causes the piston *EV 311* to move, which, in turn, moves the graduating valve to lap position, closing the exhaust. But when coupled to a train, where the brake pipe volume is larger, the drop in pressure will be slower, giving the air in chamber D time to leak by the piston *EV 311*, keeping the pressures equal on both sides of the piston, therefore the piston will not move the graduating valve to lap position.

Q.—Where would you look for the trouble if there were a constant blow at the accelerator valve exhaust?

A.—Would look for a leak past the slide valve.

Q.—When making a service application of the brake, the accelerator valve is not supposed to operate on trains of less than eight cars, but if it does, where would you look for the trouble?

A.—This may be caused by the port *S* in the piston or the port in the four-way cock being stopped up, or the spring too weak or broken.

Q.—If port *S* in the piston *RV 65* or the exhaust port in the four-way cock were stopped up, what effect whould it have on the brake pipe reduction when making a service application of the brake?

A.—The accelerator valve would cause a greater reduction than should be obtained for the notch in which the brake valve is placed.

Q.—Where might the trouble be if the maximum brake pipe pressure is not obtained?

A.—The regulating portion may be improperly adjusted, the relief port *C* stopped up, or the diaphragm valve leaking.

Q.—How can you tell if the diaphragm valve is leaking?

A.—There will be a continuous blow at the relief port *C*.

Q.—What will cause the brake pipe pressure to vary, when the brake is not being used?

A.—This is caused by sluggish action of the pressure controller.

Q.—If the pipe leading to the regulating tops of the pressure controller broke, how would it affect the controller, and what should be done?

A.—If this pipe breaks, the controller will not regulate the brake pipe pressure, that is, main reservoir pressure would be had in the brake pipe; the broken pipe should be plugged to prevent the waste of air and the pump governor adjusted to the pressure desired in the brake pipe.

Q.—What would be the effect of a leak past the seat, on the brake cylinder side, of the high speed controller?

A.—Brake pipe air would leak to the brake cylinders, causing a build up of pressure, if the brake was set; and if released, would cause a blow at the triple valve or the straight air exhaust ports.

Q.—What would be the effect of a leak past the seat, on the brake pipe side, of the high speed controller?

A.—The brake cylinder pressure would leak into the brake pipe any time the brake pipe pressure becomes less than that in the brake cylinders.

Questions and Answers on the "K" Triple Valve

Q.—On what car equipment is this type of triple valve used?
A.—On freight cars.

Q.—What are the duties of the triple valve?
A.—To control the flow of air from the brake pipe to the auxiliary reservoir, when charging the brake; to regulate the flow, and measure the amount of auxiliary reservoir air to the brake cylinders when applying the brake, and to create a communication from the brake cylinders to the atmosphere when releasing the brake.

These functions are found in the different types of triple valves.

Q.—Are there any additional features found in the K type of valve?
A.—Yes, there has been added what is known as quick service, retarded release and uniform recharge features, which are not found in the F-36 or the H-49 Westinghouse triple valves.

Q.—What is meant by the quick service feature?
A.—When a service application of the brake is made at the brake valve each triple valve will move to what is known as quick-service position, in which position a small port is open from the brake pipe to the brake cylinder, which permits the brake pipe air to flow to the brake cylinder, thereby making a local brake pipe reduction, causing a somewhat rapid and uniform drop of pressure throughout the train.

Q.—Is this somewhat rapid drop of brake pipe pressure necessary for the proper operation of the brakes throughout the train?
A.—Yes, especially on a long train.

Q.—Why?
A.—When making a service application of the brake the triple valves are moved to application position by a reduction of brake pipe pressure; and with the older type of triple valves this reduction was made at the brake valve only; therefore, the rate of reduction was governed by the opening of the brake pipe exhaust port in the brake valve and length of train. Where the train was long, the drop in pressure was necessarily slow, thus allowing the air in the auxiliary reservoirs to flow back to the brake pipe, through the feed groove in the triple valve, keeping the pressure the same on both sides of the triple piston and thus fail to move the triple to application position and apply the brake. Again, when the rate of reduction is slow, the triple valves may move to application position, but as the auxiliary reservoir air can not

flow to the brake cylinders any faster than the brake pipe pressure is being reduced, the air from the auxiliary flows to the brake cylinders so slowly that it passes through the leakage grooves, or past the packing leather to the atmosphere, and does not move the brake piston, therefore fails to set the brake. However, with the quick-service port, taking air from the brake pipe on each car, the pressure is reduced rapidly and uniformly, thus insuring the brakes applying throughout the train.

Q.—What is meant by the uniform release feature?

A.—When a release of the brakes is being made, and the triple valves move to retarded release position, the exhaust port from the brake cylinder to the atmosphere is partly closed, thereby making the exhaust of the brake cylinder air slower than when the triple valve moves to normal release position. Retarded release may be obtained on about the first thirty cars in the train, and as the brakes on the head end of the train commence to release first, the result is practically a uniform release of the entire train, which lessens the danger of parting the train when making a release of the brakes without stopping.

Q.—What is meant by uniform recharge?

A.—When releasing the brakes on a train the brake valve is placed in release position, which causes the brake pipe pressure at the head end of the train to rise rapidly above the pressure in the auxiliary reservoir, while the pressure on the rear portion of the train rises slowly.

This causes the triple valves on the head portion of the train to move to what might be termed retarded recharge position, in which position the opening in the triple valve from the brake pipe to the auxiliary reservoir is small; this retards the flow of brake pipe air to the auxiliary reservoir, thus delaying, or rather lengthening the time of their recharge. The triples on the rear portion of the train, due to the slow rise of brake pipe pressure, are moved to normal release position, in which there is a large opening from the brake pipe to the auxiliary reservoir, and it is this difference in the size of the charging ports that brings about a more uniform recharge of the auxiliary reservoirs throughout the train.

Q.—What is the advantage of uniform recharge?

A.—In recharging the brakes of a train, where it is done uniformly there is less tendency for the head brakes to reapply, when the brake valve is moved from release to running position, which is quite likely to occur, if the auxiliary reservoirs on the head portion of the train are overcharged. Uniform recharge will also bring about a more even distribution of the brake power following the first application of the brake.

Q.—How many sizes of K triple valves are there?

A.—Two, K-1 and K-2.

Q.—Why are two sizes of K valves used?

A.—The K-1 valve is used with an eight-inch brake cylinder, for cars weighing from 22,000 pounds to 37,000; the K-2 valve, with ten-inch brake cylinder, for cars weighing from 37,000 pounds to 58,000 pounds. The K-1 valve may be used in place of the F-36 and the K-2 valve in place of the H-49.

Q.—How may the K-1 valve be distinguished from the K-2 valve?

A.—Each valve is marked on the side, with its designating number; and again the K-2 valve has three bolt holes, while the K-1 has but two, in the reservoir flange.

Q.—Name the different parts of the triple valve.

A.—Referring to the numbered parts in Figure 1:

Q.—Name the different ports in the K-1 triple valve, and state their purpose.

A.—Port r is the brake cylinder port, and it is through this port that the auxiliary reservoir air passes to the brake cylinder when making either a service or emergency application of the brake. Port y is the quick-service port, and it is through this port that the brake pipe air flows to the brake cylinder, when the triple valve moves to quick-service position. Port p is the exhaust port, through which the air from the brake cylinder escapes to the atmosphere when releasing the brake. Port Z is the service port, through which the auxiliary reservoir air passes on its way through port r to the brake cylinder in a service application of the brake. Port s is the emergency port, and through this port auxiliary reservoir air passes on its way to port r and the brake cylinder, in an emergency application of the brake. Port t is an emergency port and leads from the seat of the main slide valve to the chamber above the emergency piston, and it is through this port that the auxiliary reservoir air passes to the top of the emergency piston, when an emergency application of the brake is made. Port q and o when connected by the cavity v in the graduating valve, as in quick-service position, connects port y with port t.

Q.—How many different positions has the K triple valve?

A.—Seven.

Q.—Name the different positions.

A.—Full release and charging position, quick-service position, full-service position, quick-service lap position, full-service lap position, retarded release and charging position and emergency position.

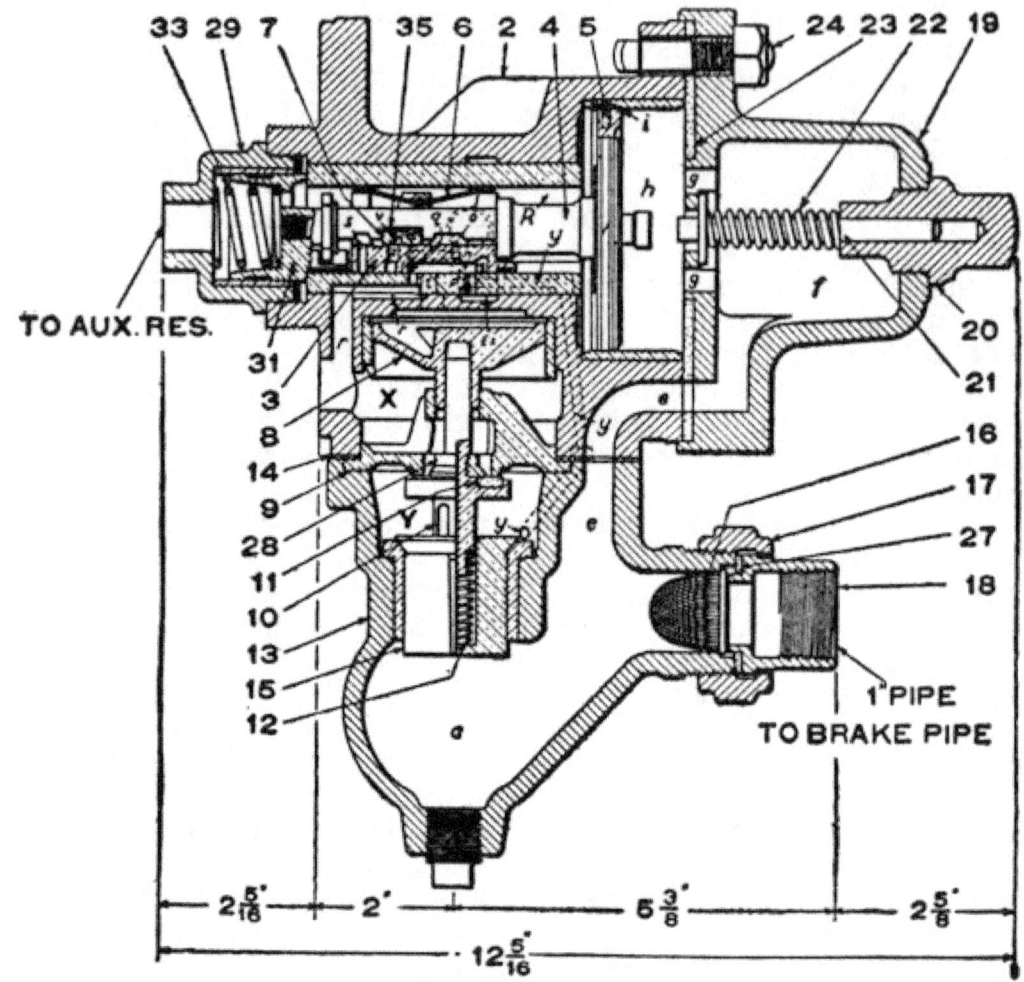

K-1 Triple Valve Actual. Section View

NAMES OF PARTS

- 2 Valve Body.
- 3 Slide Valve.
- 4 Main Piston.
- 5 Piston Ring.
- 6 Slide Valve Spring.
- 7 Graduating Valve.
- 8 Emergency Piston.
- 9 Emergency Valve Seat.
- 10 Emergency Valve.
- 11 Emergency Valve Rubber Seat.
- 12 Check Valve Spring.
- 13 Check Valve Case.
- 14 Check Valve Case Gasket.
- 15 Check Valve.
- 16 Air Strainer.
- 17 Union Nut.
- 18 Union Swivel.
- 19 Cylinder Cap.
- 20 Graduating Stem Nut.
- 21 Graduating Stem.
- 22 Graduating Spring.
- 23 Cylinder Cap Gasket.
- 24 Bolt and Nut.
- 27 Union Gasket.
- 28 Emergency Valve Nut.
- 29 Retarding Device Body.
- 31 Retarding Stem.
- 33 Retarding Spring.
- 35 Graduating Valve Spring.

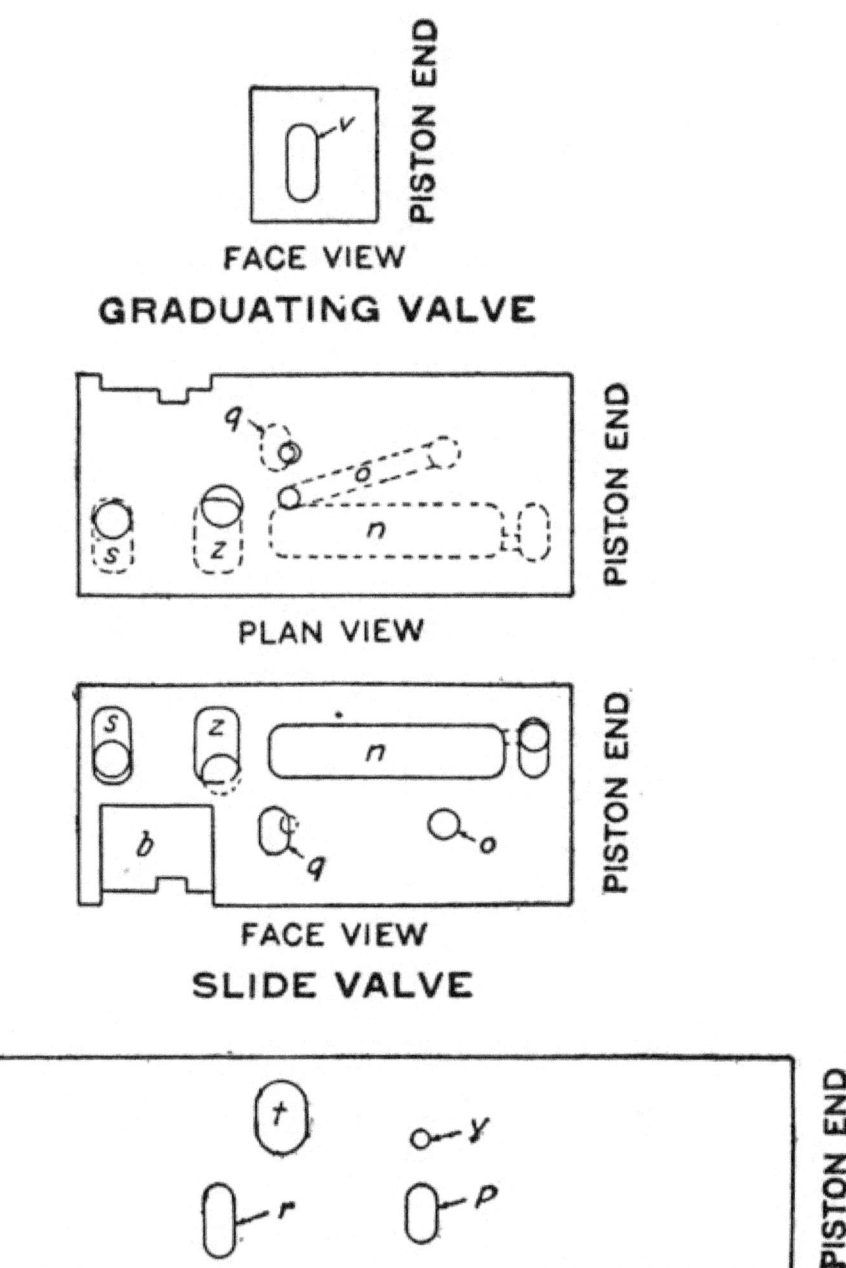

Graduating Valve, Slide Valve and Slide Valve Seat,
K-1 Triple Valve.

Q.—Is there any difference in the method in the charging of the auxiliary reservoir, where the K-2 triple valve is used?

A.—Yes. With the K-2 triple valve in addition to the air passing through the feed groove i, there is a port in the slide valve which stands directly over port y in the valve seat, when the triple valve is in full release and charging position. Through this port brake pipe air from chamber Y may flow to the slide valve chamber and on to the auxiliary reservoir; thus charging the auxiliary reservoir through two ports.

Q.—Are the feed grooves the same size in the K-1 and K-2 triple valves?

A.—Yes.

Q.—With feed groove I the same size in the K-1 and K-2 valves, will not the auxiliary reservoir of the K-2 valve charge quicker, due to air feeding through two ports, than the auxiliary reservoir of the K-1 valve, which is charged through one port only?

A.—No; as the K-2 triple valve is used with an auxiliary reservoir much larger than that used with the K-1 valve; and these ports are so proportioned that each triple valve will charge its auxiliary reservoir in the same length of time.

Q.—Is the auxiliary reservoir charged through the two ports of the K-2 triple valve when in retarded release position?

A.—No; in this position the slide valve blanks port y and all air going to the auxiliary reservoir must pass through the feed groove i the same as with the K-1 valve; in other words, the K-2 valve charges its auxiliary reservoir through one port only, when in retarded release position.

Q.—As the feed groove I is the same size in the K-1 and K-2 valves and the auxiliary reservoir used with the K-1 valve much smaller than the one used with the K-2, will not the auxiliary reservoir of the K-1 valve charge much quicker than that of the K-2?

A.—No; as when the triple valves are in retarded release position the shoulder on the left or auxiliary side of the triple piston comes in contact with the slide valve bushing, closing the opening to the slide valve chamber except the feed groove in the shoulder of the piston, and therefore it is this groove that regulates the flow of air to the auxiliary reservoir when the triple valve is in retarded release position. The feed groove in K-2 valve is larger than that in the K-1, therefore both auxiliary reservoirs are charged in the same time.

Q.—What other benefits are obtained by retarding the recharge of the auxiliary reservoirs on the forward portion of the train?

A.—This retarded recharge of the auxiliaries on the head end of the train permits a greater volume of air to flow to the rear of the train, thus securing a more prompt rise of brake pipe pressure in this part of the train, thereby insuring a more prompt release and recharge of the rear brakes.

Q.—With these different new features, will the K valves work in harmony with the older type of valves?

A.—Yes; not only work in harmony, but will assist the older type of valves to perform properly in both the application and release of the brake.

Q.—With the triple valve in quick-service position, is the service port Z fully open to the brake cylinder port r?

A.—No; just a sufficient opening is made in the port to allow auxiliary-reservoir air to reduce by passing to the brake cylinder as fast as the pressure is reducing in the brake pipe, as it will be understood that if the auxiliary reservoir pressure reduced more rapid than that in the brake pipe, the triple valve would move to lap position.

Q.—How is the triple valve affected by the brake pipe pressure dropping more quickly than that in the auxiliary reservoir through the partially open service port Z?

A.—If the brake pipe pressure reduced more rapidly than that in the auxiliary reservoir, as with short trains, or where heavy brake pipe leakage is found, the higher auxiliary reservoir pressure will cause the triple piston 4 to move farther to the right, slightly compressing the graduating spring 22, and move the slide valve 3 to full service position.

Q.—With the brake pipe pressure being reduced at the brake valve and each triple valve when in quick-service position, taking air from the brake pipe, is there not danger of the brake pipe pressure being reduced so rapidly as to cause undesired quick action of the brakes?

A.—No; for as explained in replying to the preceding question, when there is a rapid drop in brake pipe pressure the triple valves move to full service position, thereby closing the quick-service ports, thus delaying the drop in brake pipe pressure.

Q.—Will the brake pipe air flowing through the quick-service ports to the chamber above the emergency piston create sufficient pressure to move the piston down and cause quick action?

A.—No; as the fit of the emergency piston in its cylinder is such that the brake pipe air coming through the small quick-service ports can pass by the piston to chamber X and the brake cylinder as rapidly as it enters the chamber above the piston, therefore no pressure is developed above the piston.

Q.—When making a service application of the brake, how long will the triple valve remain in either of its service positions?

A.—Just so long as the auxiliary reservoir pressure is greater than that in the brake pipe, the triple valve will remain in service position, and auxiliary reservoir air will flow to the brake cylinder, until the pressure in the auxiliary reservoir and brake cylinder have equalized.

Q.—How many positions of lap are there?

A.—Two, quick-service lap and full-service lap.

Q.—What is the difference between quick-service lap and full-service lap positions?

A.—In quick-service lap position, the quick-service ports o and q in the slide valve are still in register with the quick-service ports y and t in the seat; while in full-service lap the ports y and t are closed by the slide valve 3.

Q.—How much of a reduction is necessary to set the brakes in full?

A.—Twenty pounds.

Q.—Why?

A.—The size of the auxiliary reservoir is so proportioned to the size of the brake cylinder, that with a pressure of 70 pounds in the auxiliary reservoir, and eight-inch piston travel, the auxiliary pressure will equalize into the brake cylinder at 50 pounds; in other words, 20 pounds from the auxiliary reservoir will make 50 pounds in the brake cylinder, and leave 50 pounds in the auxiliary reservoir, thus causing equalization.

Q.—Will the exhaust at the brake valve be as long, for a given reduction, when operating a train of K triple valves as with the older type of valves?

A.—No; the length of the exhaust will be only about one-half.

Q.—Explain how the brakes are released.

A.—To release the brakes the brake-valve handle is placed in release position, creating a large and direct opening from the main reservoir to the brake pipe, causing a rise of pressure in the brake pipe throughout the train. When the pressure on the brake pipe side of the triple piston is sufficient to overcome the auxiliary reservoir pressure, and the friction of the triple piston 4 and slide valve 3, the triple valve will move to one of its release positions.

Q.—How many release positions has the K triple valve?

A.—Two: Full release and retarded release positions.

Q.—When making a release of the brakes, which of its release positions will it assume?

A.—This depends entirely on how the brake pipe pressure is increased in relation to the auxiliary reservoir pressure. If the rate of increase be slow, as, for example, on the rear portion of a long train, the triple valve will move to full release position; however, in the forward portion of the train, where the brake pipe pressure builds up more rapidly than the auxiliary reservoirs can recharge, the triple valves will move to retarded release position.

Q.—Explain why the triple valves on the rear portion of the train move to full release position, while those on the forward portion move to retarded release position.

A.—When the brake pipe pressure, in chamber h, has been increased sufficient to overcome the auxiliary reservoir pressure and the friction of the triple piston 4, and slide valve 3, these parts will move to the left until the end of the piston stem and slide valve strike the retarding stem 31, which stops their movement, holding the triple in full release and charging position. However, if the brake pipe pressure builds up more rapidly than the auxiliary reservoirs can recharge, an excess of pressure will build up in chamber *h*, over that in the auxiliary reservoirs, and will cause the triple piston to move farther to the left, compressing the retarding spring 33 until the shoulder on the left or auxiliary side of the triple piston strikes the slide valve bushing. Therefore if the rise of brake pipe pressure be slow, the triple valve will move to full release and charging position; if quick, the triple valve will move to retarded release position.

Q.—What difference in pressure is required between the brake pipe and auxiliary reservoir to compress the retarding spring 33, and cause the triple valve to move to retarded release position?

A.—About three pounds.

Q.—When releasing the brakes on a train of fifty cars or more, with the brake valve in release position, how far back in the train will the triple valves move to retarded release position?

A.—Retarded release may be had on about the first thirty cars in the train.

Q.—Why can retarded release be had on the first thirty cars only; why not on the entire train?

A.—Because it is impossible, with a long train, to raise the brake pipe pressure three pounds above the auxiliary reservoir pressure on more than the first thirty cars in the train.

Q.—What prevents as prompt a rise of pressure on the rear portion of a long train as on the head portion?

A.—This is caused by the frictional resistance offered to the flow of the air through the angle cocks, cut-out cocks, hose couplings and the brake pipe.

Q.—When releasing the brakes on a long train without stopping, and with K triple valves on the head portion of the train, can the release be made with greater safety, and at lower speed, than with the older type of triple valves?

A.—Yes; as with the K triple valves we have the benefit of the retarded release on the first thirty cars, which will hold the slack bunched, while the brakes on the rear portion are releasing.

Q.—Is there as much air used in handling a train equipped with K triple valves as with a similar train equipped with the older type of triple valves?

A.—No; as a portion of the brake pipe air goes to the brake cylinders, therefore not requiring as heavy a reduction to obtain the same braking power as with the older type of valves. The great saving of air, however, is brought about by the prompt and uniform application of all brakes throughout the train.

Q.—What increase of brake cylinder pressure is obtained, due to brake pipe air going to the brake cylinder through the quick-service ports?

A.—The pressure equalizes at about one pound higher than that obtained with the older type of triple valve.

Q.—Is the quick-service feature operative on short trains?

A.—No; whenever the brake pipe pressure can be reduced at the brake valve faster than the auxiliary reservoir air can flow to the brake cylinder through the partly opened brake cylinder port obtained in quick-service position, the triple valve will move to full service position, thereby cutting out the quick-service feature.

Q.—How should a stuck brake be bled off?

A.—By opening the auxiliary reservoir release valve until a discharge of air is heard at the retainer.

Q.—What will be the effect if the release valve is held open some time after the discharge is heard at the retainer?

A.—The triple valve will move to retarded release position, therefore be more slow in releasing.

Q.—When using a 70-pound brake pipe pressure, what pressure is developed in the brake cylinder in an emergency application?

A.—About 60 pounds.

Q.—When making an emergency application of the brake, is the air taken from the brake pipe to the brake cylinders at the same rate as when making a quick-service application?

A.—No. In an emergency application the brake pipe air is free to flow through a large and what might be termed direct opening to the brake cylinder, raising the pressure quickly, and at the same time causing a sudden drop of pressure in the brake pipe; this sudden reduction starts the next triple, and that starts the next, and so on throughout the train. Therefore, if from any cause one triple valve goes into quick action, all will follow.

Q.—What is the time required to apply the brakes in quick action throughout a train of 50 cars?

A.—About three seconds.

Q.—How are brakes released after an emergency application?

A.—They are released in the same manner as after a service application but require longer time, owing to the high auxiliary reservoir pressure, and the low brake pipe pressure.

Q.—What causes the triple valve to work quick-action when a service reduction is made?

A.—Generally speaking, this is caused by high friction of the triple piston and slide valve.

Q.—How will a weak or broken graduating spring affect the operation of the triple valve?

A.—The effect produced by a weak or broken graduating spring depends on the length of the train, or, to be more correct, on the rate at which the brake pipe pressure is being reduced. The duty of this spring is to prevent the parts of the triple valve from moving past service position during a service reduction of the brake pipe pressure. If the spring be broken or is too weak to stop the parts at service position, and if the train be short, say six cars or less, the triple valve will move to emergency position, applying the brakes in quick action. However, with a long train, the graduating spring may be weak or broken; in fact, it may be removed, and the brakes will not work quick action. The reason for this is as follows: When a service reduction is made, the graduating valve opens a port in the slide valve, and when the slide valve moves so that the service port registers with the brake cylinder port in the seat, the auxiliary reservoir air begins to discharge to the brake cylinder. Now, whether the parts will remain in service position, or move to emergency position, depends on whether the brake pipe or auxiliary reservoir pressure reduces the more quickly. With a short train, say six cars or less, the brake pipe volume is comparatively small, and its pressure can be reduced at the brake valve at a much greater rate than the auxiliary reservoir pressure can be reduced to the brake cylinder through the service port Z, and as soon as a sufficient difference in pressure is formed the triple piston and slide valve will move to emergency position, causing undesired quick action. However with a long train, where the brake pipe volume is large, its pressure cannot be reduced through the exhaust port of the brake valve as fast as the auxiliary reservoir pressure can be reduced to the brake cylinder through the service port Z; therefore, the pressure on both sides of the triple piston will remain about the same, and a sufficient difference of pressure is not obtained to move the parts to emergency position.

Q.—What will cause a blow at the triple valve exhaust port?

A.—A leaky check valve, a leaky case gasket, a leaky emergency valve, a leaky slide valve, a leaky triple valve body gasket, or a leak in the induction tube.

Q.—Where does the air come from when a blow exists at the triple exhaust port?

A.—It may be from the brake pipe or the auxiliary reservoir, depending on what is at fault.

Q.—Name the parts that would cause an auxiliary reservoir leak.

A.—A leaky slide valve, a leaky induction tube, or a leaky triple valve body gasket.

Q.—Name the parts that would cause a leak from the brake pipe.

A.—Check valve case gasket or an emergency valve.

Q.—How would you test to determine whether the leakage was coming from the brake pipe or auxiliary reservoir?

A.—First charge the brake, then close the cut-out cock in the cross-over pipe; if the brake applies, it indicates that the leak is coming from the brake pipe, and would be a leak past the emergency valve 10 or the check valve case gasket 14. If the brake does not apply, the leak is in the auxiliary reservoir.

Q.—How would you test for a leaky slide valve?

A.—A leaky slide valve will generally cause a blow at the exhaust port of the triple valve, regardless of whether the brake is set or released, as in either position the exhaust cavity in the face of the slide valve 3 is over the exhaust port p in the seat of the valve, therefore any air leaking into the exhaust cavity will be free to go out the exhaust port, thus causing a blow. With a leaky slide valve, there is a tendency for the brake to release, since it is auxiliary reservoir pressure that is being reduced.

Q.—How would you test for a leaky emergency valve?

A.—When an emergency valve leaks, air passes from the brake pipe to the brake cylinder through chamber Y. If the triple valve is in release position the air leaking past the emergency valve will escape to the atmosphere through the exhaust port; if the brake is set, this air can not escape, but will go to the brake cylinder, and the brake pipe and brake cylinder pressure will equalize, and apply the brake on this car hard; that is, with a long train, where the brake pipe volume is comparatively great, the brake cylinder pressure obtained will be so high that the wheels on this car will, no doubt, be slid. Also in the release of the train brake, this brake will in all probability stick, due to the high equalization of the auxiliary reservoir and the brake cylinder pressure.

Q.—What may sometimes be done to overcome the trouble of air leaking past an emergency valve?

A.—A light tap on the outside of the triple valve, or making an emergency application of the brake on the car having the defective valve, will sometimes cause the emergency valve to seat properly and stop the blow.

Q.—If the blow cannot be stopped in the manner just described, what should be done?

A.—The brake should be cut out.

Q.—How would you cut out a brake?

A.—By closing the cut-out cock in the cross-over pipe and bleeding the auxiliary reservoir.

Q.—How will a leaky check-valve case gasket affect the brake cylinder pressure?

A.—Much the same as a leak past the emergency valve.

Q.—How will a leaky induction tube or triple valve body gasket affect the brake cylinder pressure?

A.—As both of these are auxiliary reservoir leaks, the tendency will be to first raise the brake cylinder pressure, and later cause the brake to release.

Q.—Will a leak past the graduating valve cause a blow at the triple valve exhaust port?

A.—No.

Q.—How will a leaky graduating valve affect the operation of the triple valve?

A.—The triple will not be affected in release position as the service port Z is now closed by the slide valve seat, therefore it will make no difference whether the service port is open or closed by the graduating valve. However, after a partial service application when the triple valve has moved to lap position, a leak past the graduating valve will allow the auxiliary reservoir air to pass through the service port Z and brake cylinder port r to the brake cylinder, thus applying the brake harder, and at the same time reducing auxiliary reservoir pressure. This reduction of auxiliary reservoir pressure has a tendency to release the brake; whether or not it releases depends on the amount of brake pipe leakage, and the leakage past the triple piston packing ring. If this leakage be greater than that of the graduating valve, the brake will stay set; if not, the brake will release.

Westinghouse Eleven-Inch Pump*

QUESTIONS AND ANSWERS

Q.—Why is this called an 11-inch pump?
A.—Because both steam and air cylinders are 11 inches in diameter.

Q.—What is the length of stroke?
A.—Twelve inches.

Q.—Explain the operation of steam end of pump.
A.—When steam is first turned on it passes through the governor and enters the pump at the connection marked "steam inlet," and flows through the passage a to the chamber A, above the main valve 83 and between the two pistons 77 and 79, also through passage e to chamber C, in which is reversing valve 72. The area of the piston 77 being so much greater than that of 79, the steam moves these pistons to the right, carrying the slide valve 83 with them to the position shown in Fig. 1. Steam in chamber A is now free to pass through port b to the lower end of the cylinder, under piston 65, thus forcing this piston upward. Any steam that might be above this piston is free to pass through port c, the exhaust cavity B of the slide valve, and port b to the exhaust.

Q.—How is the action of the pump reversed?
A.—The main piston 65 is now being forced upward by the steam pressure, and just before it reaches the end of its stroke, the reversing plate 69, which is attached to the top of the steam piston 65, engages the shoulder j on the reversing rod 71, lifting the rod. As the rod is lifted, the reversing valve 72 is carried to its upper position, as shown in Fig. 2. In this position of the reversing valve, live steam from chamber C is free to flow through port g to chamber D, at the right of piston 77; thus the pressures on the two sides of this piston are equalized or balanced. Steam pressure acting on the right side of piston 79—the chamber at the left of the piston being open to the exhaust at all times—forces the piston to left, drawing with it piston 77 and main valve 83, to the position shown in Fig. 2.

---

*What is said of the eleven-inch also applies to the nine and one-half inch pump, as there is no difference in the working of the two pumps.

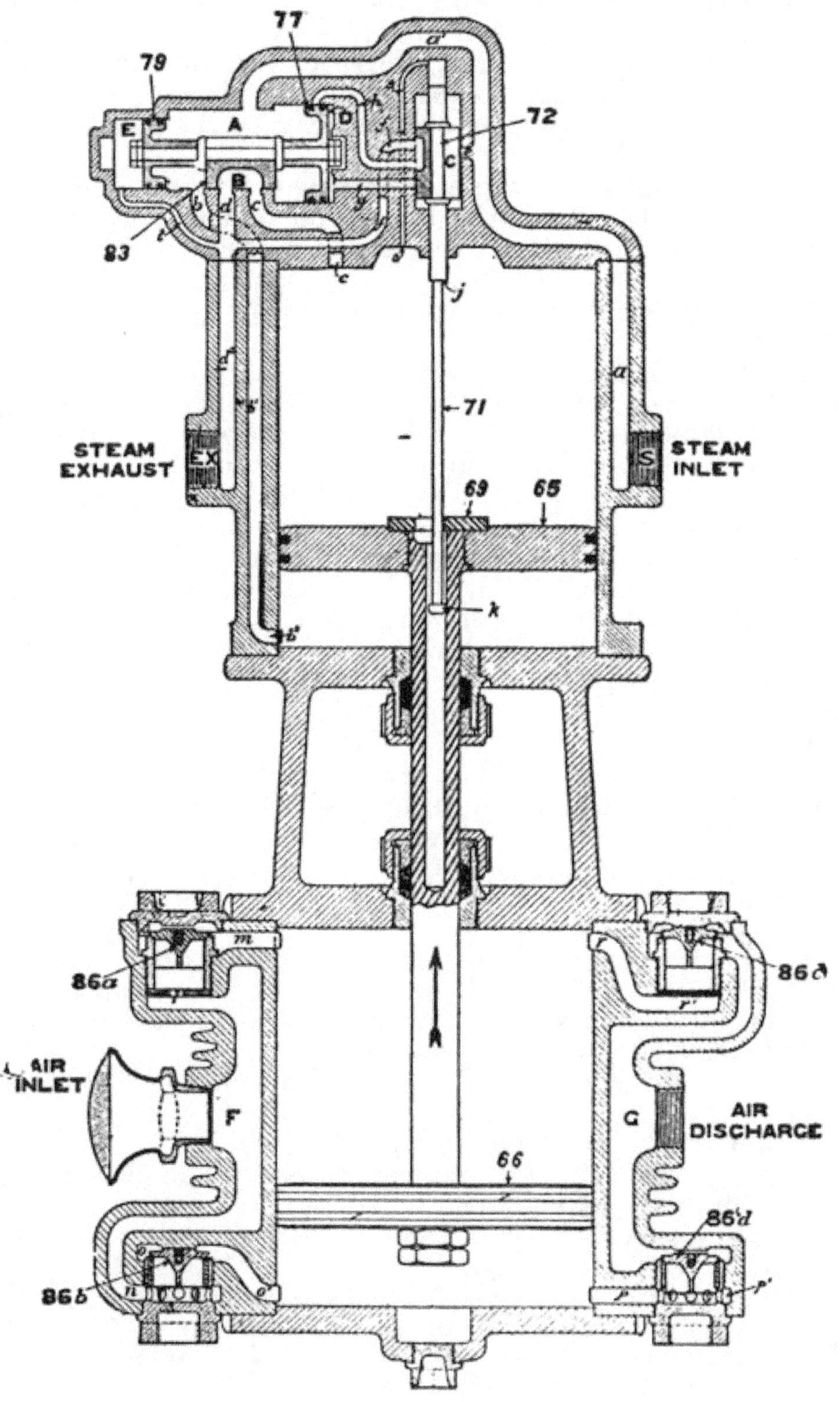

Fig. 1. Up Stroke.

Q.—When the main valve moves to the left, what takes place?

A.—When the main valve 83 is moved to the position shown in Fig. 2, steam is admitted from chamber A through port c to the upper end of the steam cylinder, above piston 65, forcing it downward; at the same time the steam below the piston is exhausted to the atmosphere through port b, exhaust cavity B in the main valve, and port d to the exhaust.

When piston 65 about completes its down stroke, reversing plate 69 engages the button k on the lower end of the reversing rod 71, pulling it and the reversing valve down to the position shown in Fig. 1.

Q.—The reversing valve being moved to its lower position, what takes place?

A.—In this position of the reversing valve, port g leading to the chamber D is closed, thus cutting off the supply of steam to this chamber; at the same time ports h and f are connected through a cavity in the reversing valve, allowing the steam in Chamber D to escape to the exhaust. This unbalances the pressure upon the two sides of piston 77, and the main valve will again move to the right.

Q.—Describe the action of the air end of the pump.

A.—As piston 66 moves upward, a partial vacuum is formed beneath it; atmospheric pressure will then raise the lower receiving valve 86b, and fill the lower end of the cylinder with air at about atmospheric pressure; at the same time the air above the piston is compressed and forced past the upper discharge valve 86c, through passage G to the main reservoir. On the down stroke of the piston the action is the same, only that air is taken into the upper end of the cylinder through the upper receiving valve 86a, and discharged to the main reservoir past the lower discharge valve 86d.

Q.—What should be the lift of the air valves?

A.—The air valves in all Westinghouse pumps should have the same lift; namely $\frac{3}{32}$ of an inch.

Q.—What is meant by the lift of the air valves?

A.—The distance the valves may be raised from their seat.

Q.—If the valves have too much lift what will be the result?

A.—Will cause the pump to pound.

Q.—At what speed should the pump be run to obtain the best results?

A.—At 100 or 120 single strokes per minute.

Q.—What are some of the common causes for the pump stopping?

A.—Lack of lubrication, bent or broken reversing rod, loose or worn reversing plate, nuts on air end of piston coming off, defective pump governor.

Q.—What will cause the piston to make an uneven stroke?

A.—This may be caused by broken, stuck open, or stuck shut air valves, or valves not having proper lift. Where the piston short-strokes it is generally caused by overlubrication of the steam end.

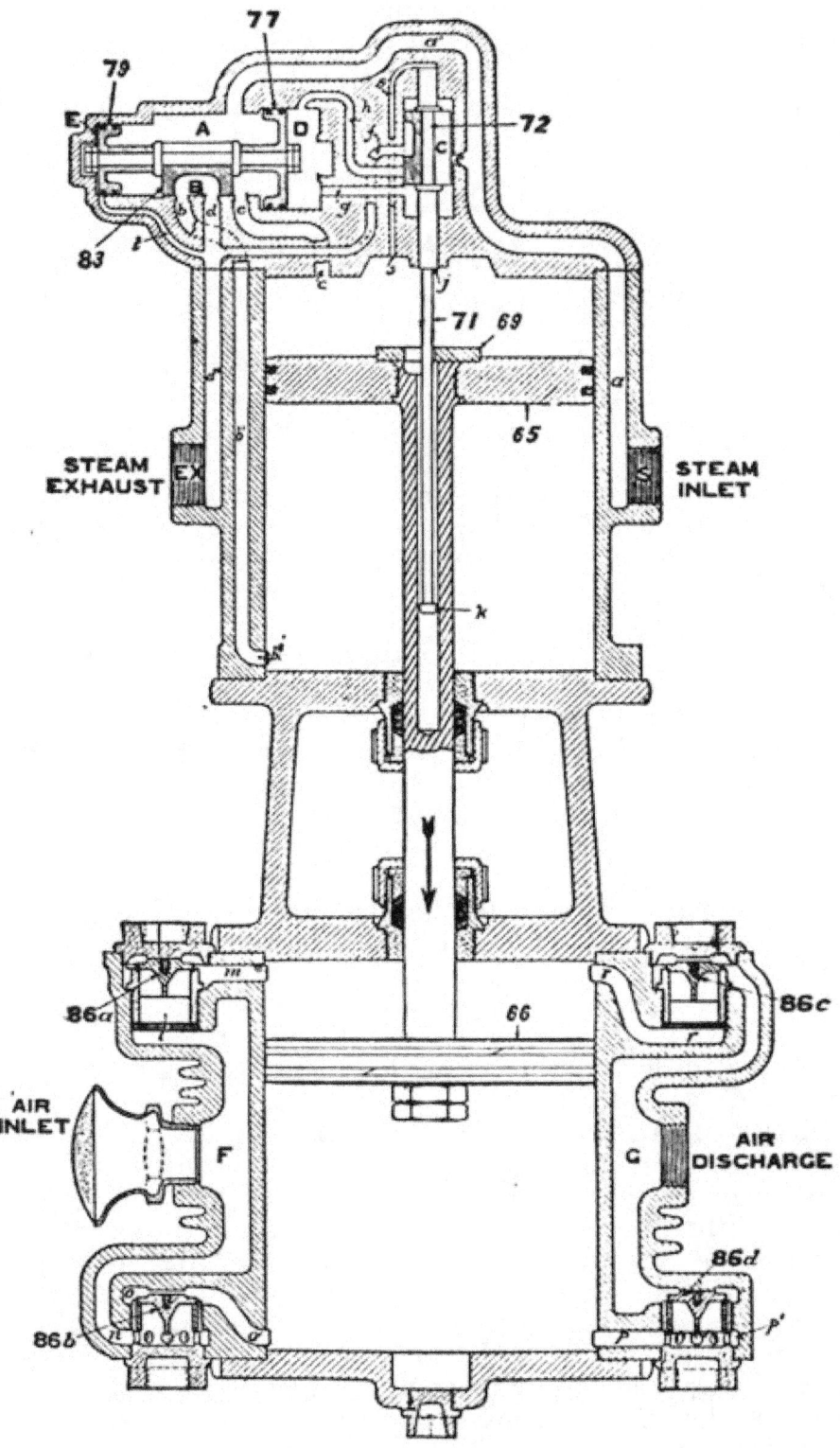

Fig. 2. Down Stroke.

Q.—What will cause an air pump to run hot?

A.—The overheating of a pump may be due to one of the following causes: running at high speed; working against high pressure; packing rings in air piston badly worn; defective air valve; air passages in pump or air discharge pipe partially stopped up; leaky piston rod packing.

Q.—What will cause the air pump to run slow?

A.—This may be caused by leaky packing rings in the air piston; discharge valves leaking, or air passages partially stopped up. A defective pump governor may also cause the pump to run slow.

Q.—What will cause the pump to run very fast and heat, and not compress any air?

A.—This may be caused by the strainer becoming clogged with ice or dirt, preventing air entering the cylinder.

Q.—If, when steam is first turned on, the piston makes a stroke up and stops, where would you look for the trouble?

A.—The shoulder j on the reversing rod may be worn; the opening in the reversing plate 69 may be too large to engage the shoulder on the reversing rod; loose reversing plate studs preventing the piston traveling far enough to reverse the pump, or the main valve stuck in its position at the right.

Q.—If the piston makes a stroke up and a stroke down and stops, where is the trouble?

A.—This may be caused by a loose reversing plate 69, or the button k on the lower end of the reversing rod worn or broken off, or the nuts off the piston rod in the air end of the pump, or the main valve stuck in its position at the left.

Q.—If a receiving valve breaks or sticks open, how may it be located?

A.—The air will flow back to the atmosphere as the piston moves toward the defective valve and may be detected by holding the hand over the strainer.

Q.—If a discharge valve breaks or sticks open, how may it be located?

A.—The piston will make a quick stroke from and a slow stroke toward the defective valve.

Q.—What will cause the piston to make a quick up stroke?

A.—This may be caused by a broken or stuck open upper receiving or lower discharge valve.

Q.—How will this cause the piston to make a quick up stroke?

A.—In the case of an upper receiving valve, air would be drawn into the cylinder on the down stroke, but would blow back to the atmosphere on the up stroke; therefore the piston, having no work to do, will move quickly. If the lower discharge valve were at fault main reservoir air would flow back under the piston, causing a quick up stroke, as the main reservoir pressure would assist the steam pressure in the movement of the piston; the down stroke, however, would be slow, as the piston would have to work against main reservoir pressure from the beginning of the stroke. No air would be taken into the pump on the up stroke.

Q.—What will cause the piston to make a quick down stroke?
A.—Lower receiving or upper discharge valve broken or stuck open.

Q.—Where piston rod packing is blowing bad, what may be done to stop it?
A.—Piston rod packing blowing generally indicates lack of lubrication, and by cleaning and oiling the swab the trouble may be overcome. However, there are times when leakage by the packing is so great that the oil is blown off the swab as fast as it is applied, therefore is of no value in lubricating the parts. Where this condition exists, a little hard grease wrapped up in an old flag and tied around the piston rod would insure its being lubricated.

Q.—How often should the air end of the pump be oiled?
A.—No fixed rule can be given as so much depends on the condition of the pump, as well as the amount of work required; but in any case it should be used sparingly.

Q.—Should oil be introduced through the strainer?
A.—No; as oiling in this manner has a tendency to gum up the air passages and air valves.

Q.—If the pump stops, how can you tell if the pump governor is responsible for the trouble?
A.—By opening the drain cock in the steam passage between the governor and the pump: if steam flows freely, the trouble is in the pump; if not, it is in the governor.

Q.—How may a pump often be started when it stops?
A.—By closing the steam throttle for a few seconds, then opening it quickly; if this does not start it, try tapping the main valve chamber. This will usually overcome the trouble where the pump stops on account of lack of lubrication.

Q.—What will cause the pump to short stroke or dance?
A.—Too much oil in the steam end, or bent reversing rod.

WESTINGHOUSE CROSS-COMPOUND PUMP QUESTIONS AND ANSWERS

Q.—What is meant by a cross-compound pump?
A.—This means that both the steam and air are compounded; that is, the steam is used the second time before it is exhausted, while the air is compressed the second time before it is forced into the main reservoir.

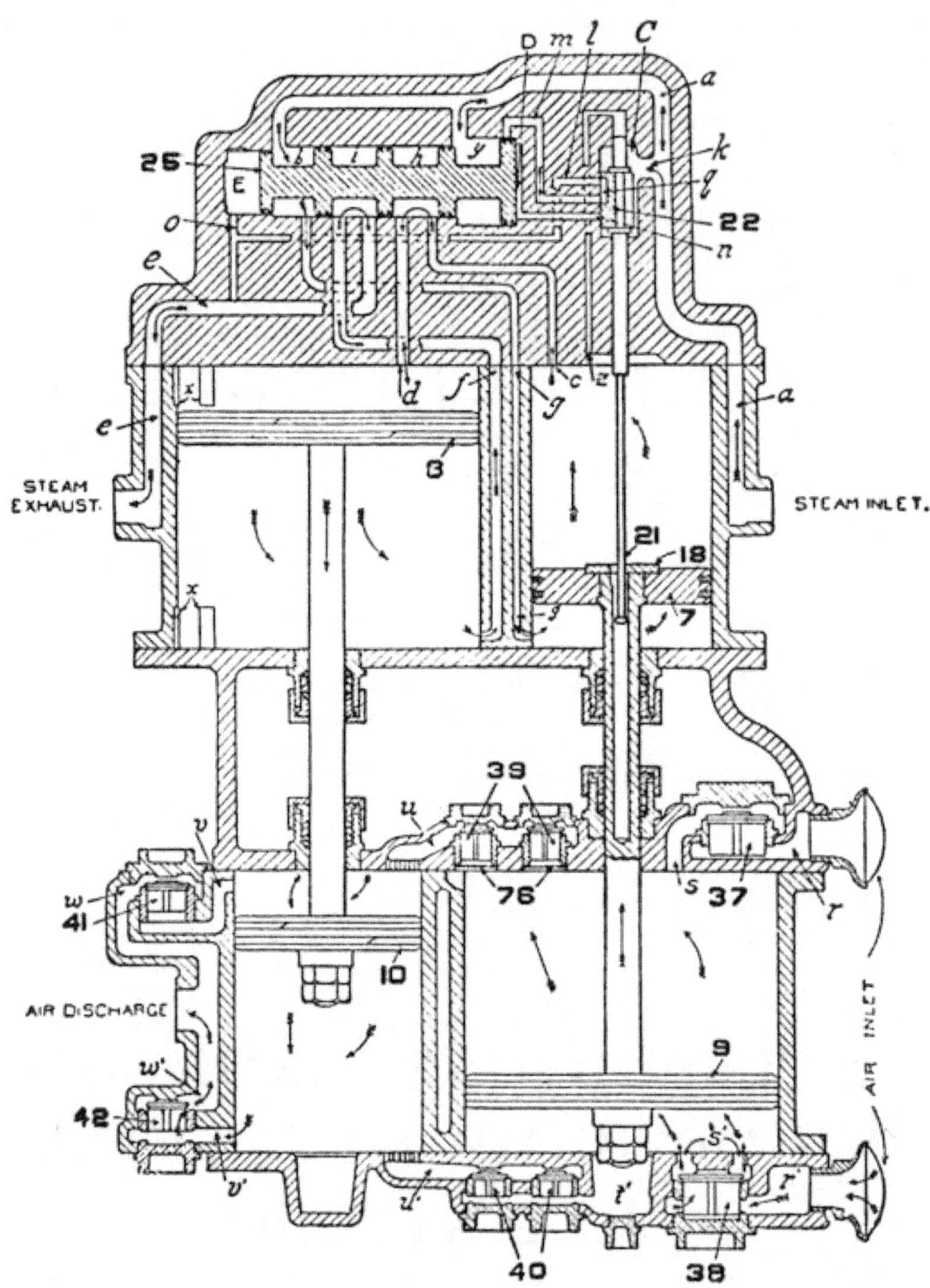

Fig. 1. Diagram of 8½-Inch Cross Compound Compressor. The High Pressure Steam (Low Pressure Air) Piston on its Upward Stroke

Q.—Is the valve gear of the cross-compound pump similar to that of the 9½ and 11-inch pumps?

A.—Yes.

Q.—Is a slide valve used to distribute the steam the same as in the 9½ and 11-inch pumps?

A.—No; a piston type of valve is used, consisting of three piston heads, which control the flow of steam to and from both cylinders.

Q.—How many cylinders has the cross-compound?

A.—Four; two steam cylinders and two air cylinders.

Q.—Name the different cylinders.

A.—High and low pressure steam cylinders; low and high pressure air cylinders.

Q.—What is the diameter of the different cylinders?

A.—The high pressure steam cylinder is 8½ inches; low pressure steam cylinder, 14½ inches; low pressure air cylinder, 14½ inches; high pressure air cylinder, 9 inches.

Q.—What is the length of stroke?

A.—Twelve inches.

Q.—How are the cylinders located?

A.—The low pressure air cylinder is under the high pressure steam cylinder and the high pressure air cylinder is under the low pressure steam cylinder.

Q.—Explain the operation of the steam end of the pump.

A.—When steam is turned on, it first passes through the governor and enters the pump at the connection marked "steam inlet" (see Fig. 1), then flows through passage a to the reversing valve, chamber C, and on to the main valve chambers B and Y. The steam pressure acting on the inner faces of the two outer pistons—the differential pistons—causes the main valve to move to the right, due to the piston at the right being the larger. In this position of the main valve, port g, which leads to the lower end of the high pressure steam cylinder, is open to chamber b, thus admitting live steam to the under side of the high pressure steam piston, causing it to make an upward stroke. As the piston about completes its up stroke, the reversing plate 18 engages the shoulder on the reversing rod 21, moving the rod and reversing valve 22 to their upper position. This movement of the reversing valve closes port m and opens port n, thus admitting live steam to chamber D, and against the outer face of the large piston of the differential pistons. This balances the pressure on the two sides of this piston, and the pressure acting on the inner face of the small piston causes the main valve to move to the left. (See Fig. 2.)

In moving, the left port c, which leads to the upper end of the high pressure cylinder, is connected to chamber y, admitting live steam above the piston. In the meantime the steam beneath the high pressure piston can flow back through port g, which is now connected to port f through chamber 1 to the lower end of the low pressure steam cylinder, where it becomes the working pressure of

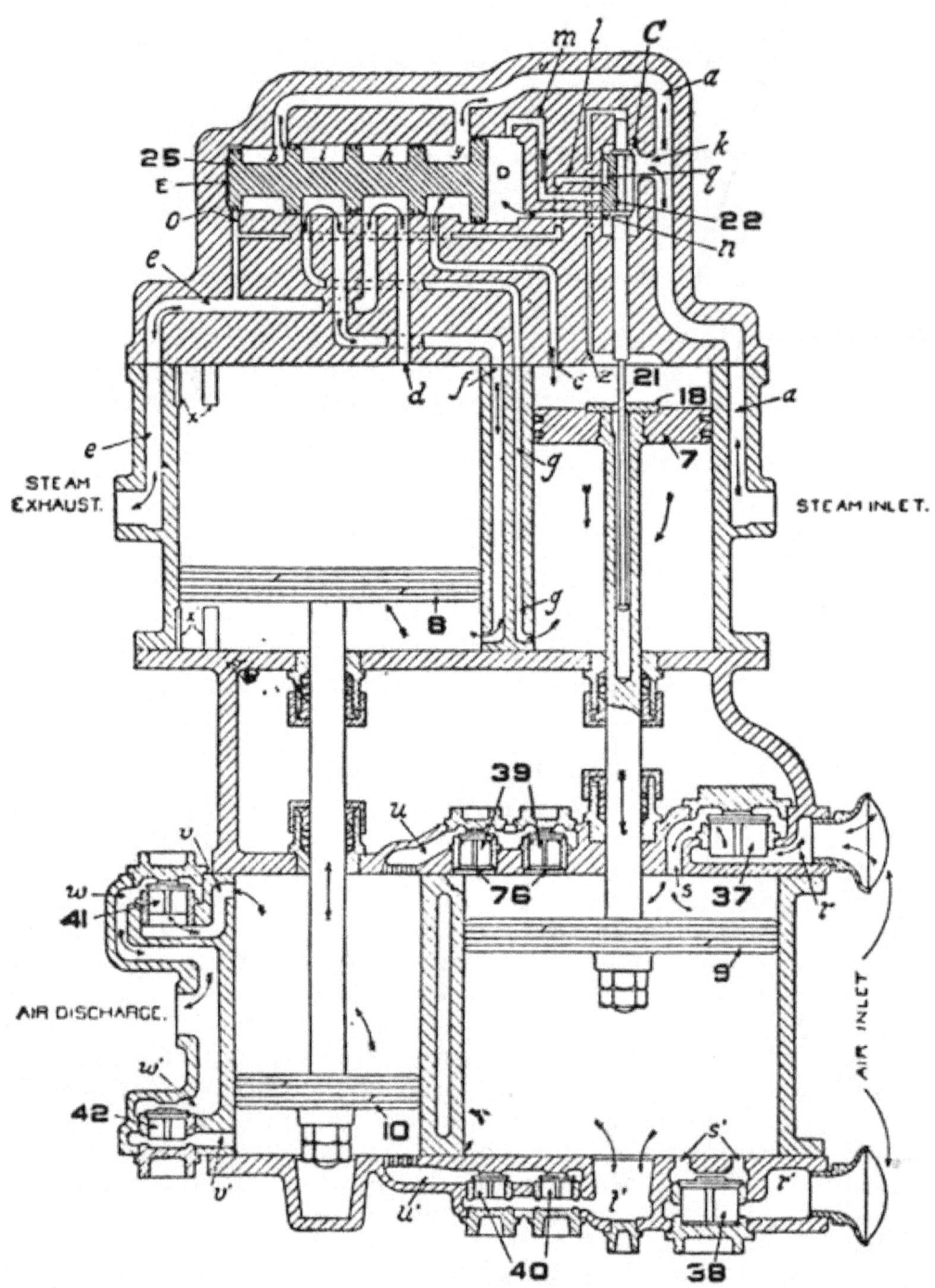

Fig. 2. Diagram of 8½-Inch Cross Compound Compressor. The High Pressure Steam (Low Pressure Air) Piston on its Downward Stroke

this cylinder, causing this piston to move upward; the upper end of this cylinder is now open to exhaust through port d, chamber h and port e. As the high pressure steam piston about completes its downward stroke, the reversing plate 18 engages the button on the lower end of the reversing rod 21, moving the rod and valve 22 to their lower position. The reversing valve being in its lower position, as shown in Fig. 1, closes port n, thus cutting off the supply of steam to chamber D, and at the same time connecting this chamber with the exhaust through port m, cavity q, in the face of the valve and port o, thus removing the pressure against the outer face of the large piston, allowing the main valve to again move to the right, thereby connecting the upper end of the high pressure cylinder with the upper end of the low pressure cylinder through port c, chamber h and port d; the lower end of the low pressure cylinder is now open to the exhaust through port f, chamber i and port e. Thus it will be seen that the steam used in the high pressure cylinder comes direct from the boiler while the steam used in the low pressure cylinder is that exhausted from the high pressure cylinder; hence the term "compound pump."

Q.—Is the low pressure steam piston in any way connected with the valve gear of the pump?

A.—No; this is simply a floating piston and depends entirely on the exhaust steam from the high pressure steam cylinder for its steam supply.

Q.—What effect has the working pressure of the low pressure cylinder on the high pressure piston?

A.—In this, as in all compound engines, the working pressure of the low pressure cylinder is back pressure on the high pressure piston.

Q.—Can the steam end of this pump, like the compound locomotive, be operated as a simple engine?

A.—No, it can not.

Q.—Will low steam pressure affect the operation of this pump?

A.—This pump is so designed that to obtain what might be termed the proper maximum speed it is necessary to have a steam pressure not less than fifty or sixty pounds greater than air pressure desired.

Q.—How many air valves are used in a cross-compound pump?

A.—Ten; four receiving, four intermediate discharge and two final discharge valves.

Q.—What are the duties of the different air valves?

A.—The receiving valves admit the air to the pump from and prevent its return to the atmosphere; the intermediate discharge valves permit the air to pass from the low pressure cylinder to the high pressure air cylinder, and prevent its return to the low pressure cylinder; the final discharge valves permit the air to pass from the high pressure air cylinders to the main reservoir and prevent its return.

Q.—Are the air valves all one size?

A.—No; the receiving and final discharge are one size, and of the size used in the 11-inch pump, while the intermediate discharge valves are one size, and of the size used in the 9½-inch pump.

Q.—What is the lift of the different air valves?

A.—The air valves in all Westinghouse pumps have the same lift, namely, 3/32 of an inch.

Q.—Explain the operation of the air end.

A.—When the low pressure air piston moves upward it creates a partial vacuum beneath it, and atmospheric pressure raises the lower receiving valves and fills the lower end of the cylinder with air at about atmospheric pressure. At the same time the air above the piston is being compressed and forced past the upper intermediate discharge valves to the upper end of the high pressure air cylinder, on top of the high pressure air piston, which is now moving downward. The air beneath the high pressure air piston is also being compressed and forced past the lower final discharge valve to the main reservoir. On the down stroke of the low pressure air piston air is taken in from the atmosphere through the upper receiving valves, while the air beneath the piston is being forced past the lower intermediate discharge valves to the high pressure air cylinder; and the air above the high pressure piston is being forced past the upper final discharge valve to the main reservoir.

Q.—At what pressure does the low pressure piston deliver air to the high pressure cylinder?

A.—At about forty pounds.

Q.—Does this air pressure assist the low pressure steam piston in doing its work?

A.—Yes; the air pressure coming from the low pressure air cylinder acts in conjunction with the steam pressure on the low pressure steam piston in moving the high pressure air piston.

Q.—How should an air pump be started?

A.—The pump should be started slow, with the drain cocks open to allow the water of condensation to escape; and as no provision is made in the steam end to cushion the pistons at the end of their stroke, it should be allowed to work slowly until a pressure of thirty or forty pounds is accumulated in the main reservoir; so the pistons having to work against this pressure will be cushioned at the end of each stroke. After the pump is warm, the drain cocks should be closed, and the throttle opened sufficiently to run the pump at the proper speed.

Q.—At what speed should the pump be run to obtain the best results?

A.—At 100 to 120 single strokes per minute.

Q.—How should the pump be lubricated?

A.—After the water has worked out of the pump, the lubricator should be started and allowed to feed freely until eight or ten drops has passed to the pump; the feed should then be reduced to an amount for proper lubrication.

Q.—How much oil should be fed to the air cylinders?

A.—No fixed rule can be given, as so much depends on the service required and condition of the pump; but in any case it should be used sparingly.

Q.—Does the low pressure air cylinder require as much oil as the high pressure cylinder?

A.—The low pressure air cylinder does not require as much oil, as it is constantly receiving cool air from the atmosphere, and compresses it to a pressure of about forty pounds only; therefore but little heat is created, which means but little oil is required, whereas the air in the high pressure air cylinder has to be compressed to a pressure equal to that carried in the main reservoir, and as the air this cylinder receives is compressed air from the low pressure air cylinder, the temperature will be much higher, therefore will require lubricating oftener.

Q.—What kind of oil should be used in the steam and air cylinders and on the swab?

A.—Valve oil.

Q.—Why not use engine oil?

A.—Engine oil might be used, were it not that its burning point is below the working temperature of the cylinders of the pump.

Q.—What means are provided for oiling the air end of the pump?

A.—Oil cups are generally provided, some of which are automatic in action, while others have to be operated by hand. A device now in common use, known as the Air Cylinder Lubricator, furnishes a practical and efficient means of securing proper lubrication. This device is connected to the oil reservoir of the main lubricator at one end, and to the air cylinder of the pump at the other, and consists of three parts, a sight feed attachment to regulate the amount of oil to the pump; an emergency valve to throttle the pressure from the main lubricator to the sight feed valve, and to cut off the oil completely when not in use; and a check valve at the pump connection to prevent the compressed air entering the oil pipe. To operate the lubricator, first open the emergency throttle about one-half turn and then close it; the sight feed valve should be opened sufficiently to permit from five to eight drops of oil to pass to the pump. This lubricator must not be treated as a lubricator for continuous feeding, but must be employed as a valve for use only when it becomes necessary to feed a few drops of oil to the pump.

Q.—What are some of the common causes for the pump stopping?

A.—Lack of lubrication, bent or broken reversing rod, loose or worn reversing plate, nuts on air end of pistons coming off, final discharge valve broken or stuck open, packing rings in main valve piston breaking and catching in steam ports and defective pump governor.

Q.—What causes the piston to make an uneven stroke?

A.—This may be caused by broken or stuck open air valves, or valves not having the proper lift. Where the piston "short-strokes," it is generally caused by overlubrication of the steam end.

Q.—What are some of the causes for the pump running hot?

A.—The overheating of a pump may be due to one of the following causes: Running at high speed; working against high pressure; packing rings in air pistons badly worn; air cylinders worn, defective air valves; air passages in pump or air discharge pipe partially stopped up; leaky piston rod packing.

Q.—What will cause the air pump to run slow?

A.—This may be caused by leaky packing rings in the air pistons; final discharge valves leaking, or air passages partially stopped up. A defective pump governor may also cause the pump to run slow.

Q.—What will cause the pump to run very fast and not compress any air?

A.—This may be caused by the strainer becoming clogged with ice or dirt, preventing air entering the cylinder.

Q.—If, when steam is first turned on, the high pressure steam piston makes a stroke up and stops, and the low pressure steam piston does not move, where would you look for the trouble?

A.—The shoulder on the reversing rod may be worn; the opening in the reversing plate too large to engage the shoulder on the reversing rod; loose reversing plate studs preventing the piston traveling far enough to reverse the pump, or the main valve stuck in its position at the right.

Q.—If the high pressure steam piston makes a stroke up and a stroke down, and the low pressure steam piston makes a stroke up and both pistons stop, where would you look for the trouble?

A.—This may be caused by a loose reversing plate, or the button on the lower end of the reversing rod worn or broken off, or the nuts off the low pressure piston rod in the air end of the pump, or the main valve stuck in its position at the left.

Q.—If a receiving valve breaks or sticks open, how may it be located?

A.—The air will flow back to the atmosphere as the piston moves toward the defective valve, and may be located by holding the hand over the strainer.

Q.—If a receiving valve breaks, what may be done?

A.—Remove the broken valve, blocking the opening made by its removal, and as there are two upper and two lower receiving valves, the pump will now take air through the other valve.

Q.—If an intermediate discharge valve breaks or sticks open, how may it be located?

A.—No air will be taken into the pump, as the piston moves from the defective valve and this may be detected by holding the hand over the strainer.

Q.—If an intermediate discharge valve breaks, what may be done?

A.—Remove the broken valve, blocking the opening made by

its removal, and as there are two upper and two lower intermediate discharge valves the air will now pass from the low pressure cylinder to the high pressure cylinder through the other valve.

Q.—If a final discharge valve breaks or sticks open, what effect will it have on the pump?

A.—Will cause the pump to stop when the main reservoir pressure is in excess of forty pounds.

Q.—How would you test for a defective final discharge valve?

A.—To test for this defect, bleed the main reservoir pressure below forty pounds, and if the pump starts it indicates a defective discharge valve.

Q.—If a final discharge valve breaks, what may be done?

A.—As the receiving valves are the same size, the broken final discharge valve may be replaced by one of the receiving valves, blocking the opening made by the removal of the receiving valve.

Q.—What will cause the low pressure air piston to make a quick up stroke?

A.—This may be caused by a broken or stuck open upper receiving valve or lower intermediate discharge valve.

Rules and Instructions for Inspection and Testing of Steam Locomotives and Tenders

IN ACCORDANCE WITH THE ACT OF MARCH 4, 1915, AMENDING THE ACT OF FEBRUARY 17, 1911.

101. The railroad company will be held responsible for the general design, construction, and maintenance of locomotives and tenders under its control.

102. The mechanical officer in charge at each point where repairs are made, will be held responsible for the inspection and repair of all parts of locomotives and tenders under his jurisdiction. He must know that inspections are made as required and that the defects are properly repaired before the locomotive is returned to service.

103. The term "inspector" as used in these rules and instructions means, unless otherwise specified, the railroad company's inspector.

104. Each locomotive and tender shall be inspected after each trip, or day's work, and the defects found reported on an approved form to the proper representative of the company. This form shall show the name of the railroad, the initials and number of the locomotive, the place, date, and time of the inspection, the defects found, and the signature of the employe making the inspection. The report shall be approved by the foreman, with proper written explanation made thereon for defects reported which were not repaired before the locomotive is returned to service. The report shall then be filed in the office of the railroad company at the place where the inspection is made.

ASH PANS

105. Ash pans shall be securely supported and maintained in safe and suitable condition for service.

Locomotives built after January 1, 1916, shall have ash pans supported from mud rings or frames. Locomotives built prior to

January 1, 1916, which do not have the ash pans supported from mud rings or frames shall be changed when the locomotive receives new fire-box.

The operating mechanism of all ash pans shall be so arranged that it may be safely operated, and maintained in safe and suitable condition for service.

No part of ash pan shall be less than 2½ inches above the rail.

BRAKE AND SIGNAL EQUIPMENT

106. It must be known before each trip that the brakes on locomotives and tender are in safe and suitable condition for service; that the air compressor or compressors are in condition to provide an ample supply of air for the service in which the locomotive is put; that the devices for regulating all pressures are properly performing their functions; that the brake valves work properly in all positions; and that the water has been drained from the air brake system.

107. *Compressors.* The compressor or compressors shall be tested for capacity by orifice test as often as conditions may require, but not less frequently than once each three months.

The diameter of orifice, speed of compressor, and the air pressure to be maintained for compressors in common use are given in the following table:

MAKE	Size compressor	Single strokes per minute	Diameter of orifice, inches	Air pressure maintained pounds
Westinghouse	9½	120	11/16	60
Do	11	100	7/16	60
Do	8½cc	100	7/16	60
New York	2a	120	7/16	60
Do	6a	100	11/16	60
Do	5b	100	11/16	60

For diagram of orifice see figure No. 14.

This table shall be used for altitudes to and including 1,000 feet. For altitudes over 1,000 feet the speed of compressor may be increased 5 single strokes per minute for each 1,000 feet increase in altitude.

108. *Testing main reservoirs.* Every main reservoir before being put into service, and at least once each twelve months thereafter, shall be subjected to hydrostatic pressure not less than 25 per cent above the maximum allowed air pressure.

The entire surface of the reservoir shall be hammer tested each time the locomotive is shopped for general repairs, but not less frequently than once each eighteen months.

109. *Air gauges.* Air gauges shall be so located that they may be conveniently read by the engineer from his usual position in the cab. Air gauges shall be tested at least once each three months, and also when any irregularity is reported.

Air gauges shall be compared with an accurate test gauge or dead weight tester, and gauges found incorrect shall be repaired before they are returned to service.

110. *Time of cleaning.* Distributing or control valves, reducing valves, triple valves, straight-air double-check valves, dirt collectors, and brake cylinders shall be cleaned, and brake cylinders lubricated as often as conditions require to maintain them in a safe and suitable condition for service, but not less frequently than once each six months.

111. *Stenciling dates of tests and cleaning.* The date of testing or cleaning, and the initials of the shop or station at which the work is done, shall be legibly stenciled in a conspicuous place on the parts, or placed on a card displayed under glass in the cab of the locomotive, or stamped on metal tags. When metal tags are used, the height of letters and figures shall be not less than three-eighths inch, and the tags located as follows:

One securely attached to brake pipe near automatic brake valve, which will show the date on which the distributing valve, control valve or triple valves, reducing valves, straight-air double-check valves, dirt collectors, and brake cylinders were cleaned and cylinders lubricated.

One securely attached to air compressor steam pipe, which will show the date on which the compressor was tested by orifice test.

One securely attached to the return pipe near main reservoir, which will show the date on which the hydrostatic test was applied to main reservoirs.

112. *Piston travel.* The minimum piston travel shall be sufficient to provide proper brake shoe clearance when the brakes are released.

The maximum piston travel when locomotive is standing shall be as follows:

	Inches.
Cam type of driving-wheel brake	3½
Other forms of driving-wheel brake	6
Engine-truck brake	8
Tender brake	9

113. *Foundation brake gear.* Foundation brake gear shall be maintained in a safe and suitable condition for service. Levers, rods, brake beams, hangers, and pins shall be of ample strength, and shall not be fouled in any way which will affect the proper

operation of the brake. All pins shall be properly secured in place with cotters. split keys, or nuts. Brake shoes must be properly applied and kept approximately in line with the tread of the wheel.

No part of the foundation brake gear of the locomotive or tender shall be less than 2½ inches above the rails.

114. *Leakage.* Main reservoir leakage; leakage from main reservoir and related piping shall not exceed an average of three pounds per minute in a test of three minutes' duration, made after the pressure has been reduced 40 per cent below maximum pressure.

Brake pipe leakage shall not exceed five pounds per minute.

Brake cylinder leakage. With a full service application from maximum brake pipe pressure, and with communication to the brake cylinders closed, the brakes on the locomotive and tender shall remain applied not less than five minutes.

115. *Train signal system.* The train signal system, when used, shall be tested and known to be in safe and suitable condition for service before each trip.

CABS, WARNING SIGNALS, AND SANDERS

116. *Cabs.* Cabs shall be securely attached or braced and maintained in a safe and suitable condition for service. Cab windows shall be so located and maintained that the enginemen may have a clear view of track and signals from their usual and proper positions in the cab.

Road locomotives used in regions where snowstorms are generally encountered shall be provided with what is known as a "clear vision" window, which is a window hinged at the top and placed in the glass in each front cab door or window. These windows shall be not less than five inches high, located as nearly as possible in line of the enginemen's vision, and so constructed that they may be easily opened or closed.

Steam pipes shall not be fastened to the cab. On new construction or when renewals are made of iron or steel pipe subject to boiler pressure in cabs, it shall be what is commercially known as double-strength pipe, with extra heavy valves and fittings.

117. *Cab aprons.* Cab aprons shall be of proper length and width to insure safety. Aprons must be securely hinged, maintained in a safe and suitable condition for service, and roughened, or other provision made, to afford secure footing.

118.

119. *Cylinder cocks.* Necessary cylinder cocks operative from cab of locomotive, shall be provided and maintained in a safe and suitable condition for service.

120. *Sanders.* Locomotives shall be equipped with proper sanding apparatus, which shall be maintained in safe and suitable condition for service, and tested before each trip. Sand pipes must be securely fastened in line with the rails.

121. *Whistle.* Each locomotive must be provided with a suitable steam whistle, so arranged that it may be conveniently operated by the engineer.

DRAW GEAR AND DRAFT GEAR

122. *Draw gear between locomotive and tender.* The draw gear between the locomotive and tender, together with the pins and fastenings, shall be maintained in safe and suitable condition for service. The pins and drawbar shall be removed and carefully examined for defects not less frequently than once each three months. Suitable means for securing the drawbar pins in place shall be provided. Inverted drawbar pins shall be held in place by plate or stirrup.

Two or more safety bars or safety chains of ample strength shall be provided between locomotive and tender, maintained in safe and suitable condition for service, and inspected at the same time draw gear is inspected.

Safety chains or safety bars shall be of the minimum length consistent with the curvature of the railroad on which the locomotive is operated.

Lost motion between locomotives and tenders not equipped with spring buffers shall be kept to a minimum, and shall not exceed one-half inch.

When spring buffers are used between locomotive and tender the springs shall be applied with not less than three-fourths inch compression, and shall at all times be under sufficient compression to keep the chafing faces in contact.

123. *Chafing irons.* Chafing irons of such radius as will permit proper curving shall be securely attached to locomotive and tender, and shall be maintained in condition to permit free movement laterally and vertically.

124. *Draft gear.* Draft gear and attachments on locomotives and tenders shall be securely fastened, and maintained in safe and suitable condition for service.

DRIVING GEAR

125. *Crossheads.* Crossheads shall be maintained in a safe and suitable condition for service, with not more than one-fourth inch vertical or five-sixteenths inch lateral play between crossheads and guides.

126. *Guides.* Guides must be securely fastened and maintained in a safe and suitable condition for service.

127. *Pistons and piston rods.* Piston and piston rods shall be maintained in safe and suitable condition for service. Piston rods shall be carefully examined for cracks each time they are removed, and shall be renewed if found defective.

All piston rods applied after January 1, 1916, shall have the date of application, original diameter, and kind of material legibly stamped on or near the end of rod.

128. *Rods, main and side.* Cracked or defective main or side rods shall not be continued in service.

Autogenous welding of broken or cracked main and side rods not permitted.

Bearings and bushings shall so fit the rods as to be in a safe and suitable condition for service, and means be provided to prevent bushings turning in rod. Straps shall fit and be securely bolted to rods.

The total amount of side motion of rods on crank pins shall not exceed one-fourth inch.

Locomotives used in road service. The bore of main rod bearings shall not exceed pin diameters more than three thirty-seconds inch at front or back end. The total lost motion at both ends shall not exceed five thirty-seconds inch.

The bore of side rod bearings shall not exceed pin diameters more than five thirty-seconds inch on main pin, nor more than three-sixteenths inch on other pins.

Locomotives used in yard service. The bore of main rod bearings shall not exceed pin diameters more than one-eighth inch at front end or five thirty-seconds inch at back end.

The bore of side rod bearings shall not exceed pin diameter more than three-sixteenths inch.

Oil and grease cups shall be securely attached to rods, and grease cup plugs shall be equipped with suitable fastenings.

LIGHTS

129 (a). *Locomotives used in road service.* Each locomotive used in road service between sunset and sunrise shall have a headlight which will enable persons with normal vision in the cab of the locomotive, under normal weather conditions, to see a dark object the size of a man for a distance of 1,000 feet or more ahead of the locomotive; and such headlights must be maintained in good condition.

(b). Locomotives used in road service, which are regularly required to run backward for any portion of their trip, except to pick up a detached portion of their train, or in making terminal movements, shall have on the rear a headlight which will meet the foregoing requirements.

(c) Nothing in the foregoing rules shall prevent the use of a device whereby the light may be diminished in yards and at stations to an extent that will enable the person or persons operating the locomotive to see a dark object the size of a man for a distance of 300 feet or more ahead of the locomotive under the same conditions as set forth above.

(d) When two or more locomotives are used in the same train, the leading locomotive only will be required to display a headlight.

130. *Classification lamps.* Each locomotive used in road service shall be provided with such classification lamps as may be required by the rules of the railroad company operating the locomotive. When such classification lamps are provided they shall be kept clean and maintained in safe and suitable condition for service.

131. *Locomotives used in yard service.* Each locomotive used in yard service between sunset and sunrise shall have two headlights, one located on the front of the locomotive and one on the rear, each of which will enable persons with normal vision, in the cab of the locomotive, under normal weather conditions, to see a dark object the size of a man for a distance of 300 feet or more; and such headlights must be maintained in good condition.

132. *Cab lights.* Each locomotive used between sunset and sunrise shall have cab lamps which will provide sufficient illumination for the steam, air, and water gauges to enable the enginemen to make necessary and accurate readings from their usual and proper positions in the cab. These lights shall be so located and constructed that the light will shine only on those parts requiring illumination. Locomotives used in road service shall have an additional lamp conveniently located to enable the persons operating the locomotive to easily and accurately read train orders and time-tables, and so constructed that it may be readily darkened or extinguished.

RUNNING GEAR

133. *Driving, trailing, and engine truck axles.* Driving, trailing, and engine truck axles with any of the following defects shall not be continued in service:

Bent axle; cut journals that cannot be made to run cool without turning; seamy journals in steel axles; transverse seams in iron axles, or any seams in iron axles causing journals to run hot, or unsafe on account of usage, accident, or derailment; driving, trailing, or engine truck axles more than one-half inch under original diameter, except for locomotives having all driving axles of the same diameter, when other than main driving axles, may be worn three-fourths inch below the original diameter.

The date applied, the original diameter of the journal, and the kind of material shall be legibly stamped on one end of each driving axle, trailing truck axle, and engine truck axle applied after January 1, 1916.

134. *Tender truck axles.* The minimum diameters of axles for various axle loads shall be as follows:

AXLE LOAD	Minimum diameter of Journal, inches	Minimum diameter of wheel seat, inches	Minimum diameter of center, inches
50,000 pounds	$5\frac{1}{2}$	$7\frac{3}{8}$	$6\frac{1}{16}$
38,000 pounds	5	$6\frac{3}{4}$	$5\frac{1}{8}$
31,000 pounds	$4\frac{1}{2}$	$6\frac{1}{4}$	$5\frac{3}{16}$
22,000 pounds	$3\frac{3}{4}$	5	$4\frac{3}{8}$
15,000 pounds	$3\frac{1}{4}$	$4\frac{5}{8}$	$3\frac{7}{8}$

135. Tender truck axles with any of the following defects shall not be continued in service:

Bent axle; cut journals that cannot be made to run cool without turning; seamy journals in steel axles, or transverse seams in journals of iron axles, or unsafe on account of usage, accident, or derailment; collars broken or worn to one-fourth inch or less in thickness; fillet in back shoulder worn out.

136. *Crank pins.* Crank pins shall be securely applied. Shimming or prick punching crank pins will not be allowed. All crank pins applied after January 1, 1916, shall have the date applied and kind of material used legibly stamped on end of pin.

Crank pin collars and collar bolts shall be maintained in a safe and suitable condition for service.

137. *Driving boxes.* Driving boxes shall be maintained in a safe and suitable condition for service. Broken and loose bearings shall be renewed. Not more than one shim may be used between box and bearing.

138. *Driving box shoes and wedges.* Driving box shoes and wedges shall be maintained in a safe and suitable condition for service.

139. *Frames.* Frames, deck plates, tailpieces, pedestals, and braces shall be maintained in a safe and suitable condition for service, and shall be cleaned and thoroughly inspected each time the locomotive is in shop for heavy repairs.

140. *Lateral motion.* The total lateral motion or play between the hubs of the wheels and the boxes on any pair of wheels shall not exceed the following limits:

                                                               Inches.
For engine truck wheels (trucks with swing centers)...... 1
For engine truck wheels (trucks with rigid centers)....... 1½
For trailing truck wheels 1
For driving wheels (more than one pair).................... ¾

These limits may be increased on locomotives operating on track where the curvature exceeds 20 degrees when it can be shown that conditions require additional lateral motion.

The lateral motion shall in all cases be kept within such limits that the driving wheels, rods, or crank pins will not interfere with other parts of the locomotive.

141. *Pilots.* Pilots shall be securely attached, properly braced, and maintained in a safe and suitable condition for service.

The minimum clearance of pilot above the rail shall be three inches, and the maximum clearance six inches.

142. *Spring rigging.* Springs and equalizers shall be arranged to insure the proper distribution of weight to the various wheels of the locomotive, maintained approximately level, and in a safe and suitable condition for service.

Springs or spring rigging with any of the following defects shall be renewed or properly repaired:

One long leaf or two or more shorter leaves broken.

Springs with leaves working in band.

Broken coil springs.

Broken driving box saddle, equalizer, hanger, bolt, or pin.

143. *Trucks, leading and trailing.* Trucks shall be maintained in safe and suitable condition for service. Center plates shall fit properly, and the male center plate shall extend into the female center plate not less than three-fourths inch. All centering devices shall be properly maintained.

A suitable safety chain shall be provided at each front corner of all four-wheel engine trucks.

All parts of trucks shall have sufficient clearance to prevent them from seriously interfering with any other part of the locomotive.

144. *Wheels.* Wheels shall be securely pressed on axles. Prick punching or shimming the wheel fit will not be permitted. The diameter of wheels on the same axle shall not vary more than three thirty-seconds inch.

Wheels used on standard gauge track will be out of gauge if the inside gauge of flanges, measured on base line, is less than 53 inches or more than 53⅜ inches.

The distance back to back of flanges of wheels mounted on the same axle shall not vary more than one-fourth inch.

145. *Cast iron or cast steel wheels.* Cast iron or cast steel wheels with any of the following defects shall not be continued in service:

Slid flat. When the flat spot is 2½ inches or over in length; or if there are two or more adjoining spots each 2 inches or over in length.

Broken or chipped flange. If the chip exceeds 1½ inches in length and one-half inch in width.

Broken rim. If the tread, measured from the flange at a point five-eighths inch above the tread, is less than 3¾ inches in width.

Shelled out. Wheels with defective treads on account of cracks or shell out spots 2½ inches or over, or so numerous as to endanger the safety of the wheel.

Brake burn. Wheels having defective tread on account of cracks or shelling out due to heating.

Seams one-half inch long or over, at a distance of one-half inch or less from the throat of the flange, or seams 3 inches or more in length, if such seams are within the limits of 3¾ inches from the flange, measured at a point five-eights inch from the tread.

Worn flanges. Wheels on axles with journals 5 inches by 9 inches or over with flanges having flat vertical surfaces extending seven-eighths inch or more from the tread, or flanges 1 inch thick or less gauged at a point three-eighths inch above tread. Wheels on axles with journals less than 5 inches by 9 inches with flanges having flat vertical surfaces extending 1 inch or more from the tread, or flanges fifteen-sixteenths inch thick or less, gauged at a point three-eighths inch above the tread.

Tread worn hollow. If the tread is worn sufficiently hollow to render the flange or rim liable to breakage.

Burst. If the wheel is cracked from the wheel fit outward.

Cracked tread, cracked plate, or one or more cracked brackets.

Wheels out of gauge.

Wheels loose on axle.

NOTE.—The determination of flat spots, worn flanges, and broken rims shall be made by a gauge as shown in figure 8, and its application to defective wheels as shown in figures 9, 10, 11, 12, and 13.

146. *Forged steel or steel tired wheels.* Forged steel or steel tired whels with any of the following defects shall not be continued in service:

Loose wheels; loose, broken, or defective retaining rings or tires; broken or cracked hubs, plates, spokes, or bolts.

Slid flat spot 2½ inches or longer; or, if there are two or more adjoining spots, each 2 inches or longer.

Defective tread on account of cracks or shelled out spots 2½ inches or longer, or so numerous as to endanger the safety of the wheel.

Broken flange.

Flange worn to fifteen-sixteenths inch or less in thickness, gauged at a point three-eighths inch above the tread, or having flat vertical surface 1 inch or more from tread; tread worn five-sixteenths inch; flange more than 1½ inches from tread to top of flange, or thickness of tires or rims less than shown in figures 4, 5, 6, and 7.

Wheels out of gauge.

147. *Driving and trailing wheels.* Driving and trailing wheel centers with divided rims shall be properly fitted with iron or steel filling blocks before the tires are applied, and such filling blocks shall be properly maintained. When shims are inserted between the tire and the wheel center, not more than two thicknesses of shims may be used, one of which must extend entirely around the wheel.

148. Driving wheel counterbalance shall be maintained in a safe and suitable condition for service.

149. Driving and trailing wheels with any of the following defects shall not be continued in service:

Driving or trailing wheel centers with three adjacent spokes, or 25 per cent of the spokes in wheel broken.

Loose wheels; loose, broken, or defective tires or tire fastenings; broken or cracked hubs, or wheels out of gauge.

150. *Driving and trailing wheel tires.* The minimum height of flange for driving and trailing wheel tires, measured from tread, shall be 1 inch for locomotive used in road service, except for locomotives originally constructed for plain tires, when the minimum height of flange on one pair of wheels may be seven-eighths inch.

The minimum height of flange for driving wheel tires, measured from tread, shall be seven-eighths inch for locomotives used in switching service.

The maximum taper for tread of tires from throat of flange to outside of tire, for driving and trailing wheels for locomotives used in road service, shall be one-fourth inch, and for locomotives used in switching service five-sixteenths inch.

The minimum width of tires for driving and trailing wheels of standard gauge locomotives shall be 5½ inches for flanged tires, and 6 inches for plain tires.

The minimum width of tires for driving and trailing wheels of narrow gauge locomotives shall be 5 inches for flanged tires, and 5½ inches for plain tires.

When all tires are turned or new tires applied to driving and trailing wheels, the diameter of the wheels on the same axle, or in the same driving wheel base, shall not vary more than three thirty-seconds inch. When a single tire is applied the diameter must not vary more than three thirty-seconds inch from that of the opposite wheel on the same axle. When a single pair of tires is applied the diameter must be within three thirty-seconds inch of the average diameter of the wheels in the driving wheel base to which they are applied.

Driving and trailing wheel tires with any of the following defects shall not be continued in service:

Slid flat spot 2½ inches or more in length; flange fifteen-sixteenths inch or less in thickness, gauged at a point three-eighths inch above the tread, or having flat vertical surface one inch or more from tread; tread worn hollow five-sixteenths inch on locomotives used in road service, or three-eighths inch on locomotives used in switching service; flange more than 1½ inches from tread to top of flange. (See figures 1, 2, and 3.)

NOTE.—The determination of flat spots and worn flanges shall be made by a gauge as shown in figure 8, and its application to defective tires as shown in figures 9, 10, and 11.

151. *Minimum thickness for driving wheel and trailer tires on standard and narrow gauge locomotives:*

Weight per axle (weight on drivers divided by number of pairs of driving wheels).	Diameter of wheel center, inches	Minimum thickness, service limits	
		Road service, inches	Switching service, inches
30,000 pounds and under	44 and under	1 1/4	1 1/8
	Over 44 to 50	1 5/16	1 3/16
	Over 50 to 56	1 3/8	1 1/4
	Over 56 to 62	1 7/16	1 5/16
	Over 62 to 68	1 1/2	--------
	Over 68 to 74	1 9/16	--------
	Over 74	1 5/8	--------
Over 30,000 to 35,000 pounds	44 and under	1 5/16	1 3/16
	Over 44 to 50	1 3/8	1 1/4
	Over 50 to 56	1 7/16	1 5/16
	Over 56 to 62	1 1/2	1 3/8
	Over 62 to 68	1 9/16	--------
	Over 68 to 74	1 5/8	--------
	Over 74	1 11/16	--------
Over 35,000 to 40,000 pounds	44 and under	1 3/8	1 1/4
	Over 44 to 50	1 7/16	1 5/16
	Over 50 to 56	1 1/2	1 3/8
	Over 56 to 62	1 9/16	1 7/16
	Over 62 to 68	1 5/8	--------
	Over 68 to 74	1 11/16	--------
	Over 74	1 3/4	--------
Over 40,000 to 45,000 pounds	44 and under	1 7/16	1 5/16
	Over 44 to 50	1 1/2	1 3/8
	Over 50 to 56	1 9/16	1 7/16
	Over 56 to 62	1 5/8	1 1/2
	Over 62 to 68	1 11/16	--------
	Over 68 to 74	1 3/4	--------
	Over 74	1 13/16	--------
Over 45,000 to 50,000 pounds	44 and under	1 1/2	1 3/8
	Over 44 to 50	1 9/16	1 7/16
	Over 50 to 56	1 5/8	1 1/2
	Over 56 to 62	1 11/16	1 9/16
	Over 62 to 68	1 3/4	--------
	Over 68 to 74	1 13/16	--------
	Over 74	1 7/8	--------
Over 50,000 to **55,000 pounds**	44 and under	1 9/16	1 7/16
	Over 44 to 50	1 5/8	1 1/2
	Over 50 to 56	1 11/16	1 9/16
	Over 56 to 62	1 3/4	1 5/8
	Over 62 to 68	1 13/16	--------
	Over 68 to 74	1 7/8	--------
	Over 74	1 15/16	--------
Over 55,000 pounds	44 and under	1 5/8	1 1/2
	Over 44 to 50	1 11/16	1 9/16
	Over 50 to 56	1 3/4	1 5/8
	Over 56 to 62	1 13/16	1 11/16
	Over 62 to 68	1 7/8	--------

When retaining rings are used, measurements of tires to be taken from the outside circumference of the ring, and the minimum thickness of tires may be as much below the limits specified above as the tires extend between the retaining rings, provided it does not reduce the thickness of the tire to less than $1\frac{1}{8}$ inches from the throat of flange to the counterbore for the retaining ring.

The minimum thickness for driving wheel tires shall be 1 inch for locomotives operated on track of 2-foot gauge.

TENDERS

152. *Tender frames.* Tender frames shall be maintained in a safe and suitable condition for service.

The difference in height between the deck on the tender and the cab floor or deck on the locomotive shall not exceed $1\frac{1}{2}$ inches.

The minimum width of the gangway between locomotive and tender, while standing on straight track, shall be 16 inches.

153. *Feed water tanks.* Tanks shall be maintained free from leaks, and in safe and suitable condition for service. Suitable screens must be provided for tank wells or tank hose.

Not less frequently than once each month the interior of the tank shall be inspected, and cleaned if necessary.

Top of tender behind fuel space shall be kept clean, and means provided to carry off waste water. Suitable covers shall be provided for filling holes.

154. *Oil tanks.* The oil tanks on oil burning locomotives shall be maintained free from leaks. An automatic safety cutout valve, which may be operated by hand from inside and outside of cab, shall be provided for the oil supply pipe.

155. *Tender trucks.* Tender truck center plates shall be securely fastened, maintained in a safe and suitable condition for service, and provided with a center pin properly secured. When shims are used between truck center plates, the male center plate must extend into the female center plate not less than three-fourths inch.

Truck bolsters shall be maintained approximately level.

When tender trucks are equipped with safety chains, they shall be maintained in a safe and suitable condition for service.

Side bearings shall be maintained in a safe and suitable condition for service.

Friction side bearings shall not be run in contact.

The maximum clearance of side bearings on rear truck shall be three-eighths inch, and if used on front truck three-fourths inch, when the spread of side bearings is 50 inches. When the spread of the side bearings is increased, the maximum clearance may be increased in proportion.

THROTTLE AND REVERSING GEAR

156. *Throttles.* Throttles shall be maintained in safe and suitable condition for service, and efficient means provided to hold the throttle lever in any desired position.

157. *Reversing gear.* Reversing gear, reverse levers, and quadrants shall be maintained in a safe and suitable condition for service. Reverse lever latch shall be so arranged that it can be easily disengaged, and provided with a spring which will keep it firmly seated in quadrant. Proper counterbalance shall be provided for the valve gear.

158. Upon application to the Chief Inspector, modification of these rules, not inconsistent with their purpose, may be made for roads operating less than five locomotives, if an investigation shows that conditions warrant it.

FILING REPORTS

159. *Report of inspection.* Not less than once each month and within 10 days after inspection a report of inspection, Form No. 1, size 6 by 9 inches, shall be filed with the United States Inspector in charge for each locomotive used by a railroad company; and a copy shall be filed in the office of the chief mechanical officer having charge of the locomotive.

160. A copy of the monthly inspection report, Form No. 1, or annual inspection report, Form No. 3, properly filled out, shall be placed under glass in a conspicuous place in the cab before the locomotive inspected is put into service.

161. Not less than once each year, and within 10 days after required tests have been completed, a report of such tests, showing general condition of the locomotive, shall be submitted on form No. 3, size 6 by 9 inches, and filed with the United States Inspector in Charge, and a copy shall be filed in the office of the chief mechanical officer having charge of the locomotive. The monthly report will not be required for the month in which this report is filed.

Form No. 3 should be printed on yellow paper.

NOTE.—Samples of Forms Nos. 1 and 3, indicating exact size, color, weight, and grade of paper, will be furnished on application.

ACCIDENT REPORTS

162. In the case of an accident resulting from failure, from any cause, of a locomotive or tender, or any appurtenances thereof, resulting in serious injury or death to one or more persons, the carrier owning or operating such locomotive shall immediately transmit by wire to the Chief Inspector, at his office in Washington, D. C., a report of such accident, stating the nature of the accident, the place at which it occurred, as well as where the locomotive may be inspected, which wire shall be immediately confirmed by mail, giving a full detailed report of such accident, stating, so far as may be known, the cause and giving a complete list of the killed or injured.

NOTE.—Locomotive boilers and their appurtenances will be inspected in accordance with the order of the Commission, dated June 2, 1911.

Safety appliances on locomotives will be inspected in accordance with the order of the Commission, dated March 13, 1911.

Form No. 1.   MONTHLY LOCOMOTIVE INSPECTION AND REPAIR REPORT.

..............., 191 .

Locomotive { Number..............
            { Initial...............

.......................Company.

In accordance with the act of Congress approved February 17, 1911, as amended March 4, 1915, and the rules and instructions issued in pursuance thereof and approved by the Interstate Commerce Commission, all parts of locomotive No............, including the boiler and appurtenances, were inspected on ...., 191 , at ...., and all defects disclosed by said inspection have been repaired, except as noted on the back of this report.

1. Steam gauges tested and left in good condition on ...., 191 .
2. Safety valves set to pop at ...... pounds, ... pounds, ... pounds on ...., 191 .
3. Were both injectors tested and left in good condition?
4. Were steam leaks repaired?
5. Condition of brake and signal equipment,
6. Condition of draft gear and draw gear,
7. Condition of driving gear,
8. Condition of running gear,
9. Condition of tender,
I certify that the above report is correct.

.... Inspector.

10. Was boiler washed and gauge cocks and water glass cock spindles removed and cocks cleaned?
11. Were steam leaks repaired?
12. Condition of staybolts and crown stays,
13. Number of staybolts and crown stays renewed,
14. Condition of flues and fire-box sheets,
15. Condition of arch and water bar tubes, if used,
16. Were fusible plugs removed and cleaned?
17. Date of previous hydrostatic test, ..., 191 .
18. Date of removal of caps from flexible staybolts.

I certify that the above report is correct.

.... Inspector.

State of .... } ss:
County of .... }

Subscribed and sworn to before me this........ day of............, 191 , by .... Inspectors of the ....Company.

.... Notary Public.

The above work has been performed and the report approved.

.... Officer in charge.

Form No. 2.

Locomotive { Number..........
             { Initial ....

..............................Railroad.

LOCOMOTIVE INSPECTION REPORT

INSTRUCTIONS.—Each locomotive and tender must be inspected after each trip or day's work and report made on this form, whether needing repairs or not. Proper explanation must be made hereon for failure to repair any defects reported, and the form approved by foreman, before the locomotive is returned to service.

Inspected at.........., time .... m. Date ...., 191..

Repairs needed:

....
....
....
....
....
....
....

Condition of injectors................. Water glass..........
Condition of gauge cocks.............. Brakes..............
Condition of piston rod and valve stem packing................
Safety valve lifts at........pounds. Seats at........pounds.
Main reservoir pressure, ... pounds. Brake pipe pressure, ...pounds.

(Signature) ....,
(Occupation) ....

The above work has been performed, except as noted, and the report is approved.

..........................,
Foreman.

NOTE.—Additional items may be added to this form if desired.

Form No. 3.   ANNUAL LOCOMOTIVE INSPECTION AND REPAIR REPORT.

..................., 191 .

Locomotive { Number............
{ Initial.............

.... Company.

In accordance with the act of Congress approved February 17, 1911, as amended March 4, 1915, and the rules and instructions issued in pursuance thereof and approved by the Interstate Commerce Commission, all parts of locomotive No......., including the boiler and its appurtenances, were inspected on..........., 191 , at ...., and all defects disclosed by said inspection have been repaired, except as noted on the back of this report.

1. Date of previous hydrostatic test, ..., 191 .
2. Date of previous removal of caps from flexible stay bolts, ..., 191 .
3. Date of previous removal of flues, ..., 191 .
4. Date of previous removal of all lagging, ..., 191 .
5. Hydrostatic test pressure of ....pounds was applied.
6. Were caps removed from all flexible staybolts? ....
7. Were all flues removed? .... Number...........
8. Condition of interior of barrel, ...
9. Was all lagging removed? ....
10. Condition of exterior of barrel, ...
11. Was boiler entered and inspected? ....
12. Was boiler washed? Water glass cocks and gauge cocks cleaned? ....
13. Condition of crown stays and staybolts, ...
14. Condition of sling stays and crown bars, ...
15. Condition of fire-box sheets and flues, ...
16. Condition of arch tubes,...... Water-bar tubes, ...
17. Condition of throat braces, ...
18. Condition of back head braces, ...
19. Condition of front flue sheet braces, ...
20. Were fusible plugs removed and cleaned? ....

21. Were steam leaks repaired? ....
I certify that the above report is correct.

...................................., Inspector.

22. Were steam gauges tested and left in good condition? ....
23. Safety valves set to pop at ..... pounds, ... pounds, ... pounds.
24. Were both injectors tested and left in good condition? ....
25. Were steam leaks repaired? ....
26. Hydrostatic test of ..... pounds applied to main reservoirs.
27. Condition of brake and signal equipment, ...
28. Were drawbar and drawbar pins removed and inspected?
29. Condition of draft gear and draw gear, ...
30. Condition of driving gear, ...
31. Condition of running gear, ...
32. Condition of tender, ...

...................................., Inspector.

I certify that the above report is correct.

State of ....} ss:
County of ....}

Subscribed and sworn to before me this...... day of............., 191 , by ....Inspectors of the ....Company.

...., Notary Public.

The above work has been performed and the report is approved.

....Officer in charge.

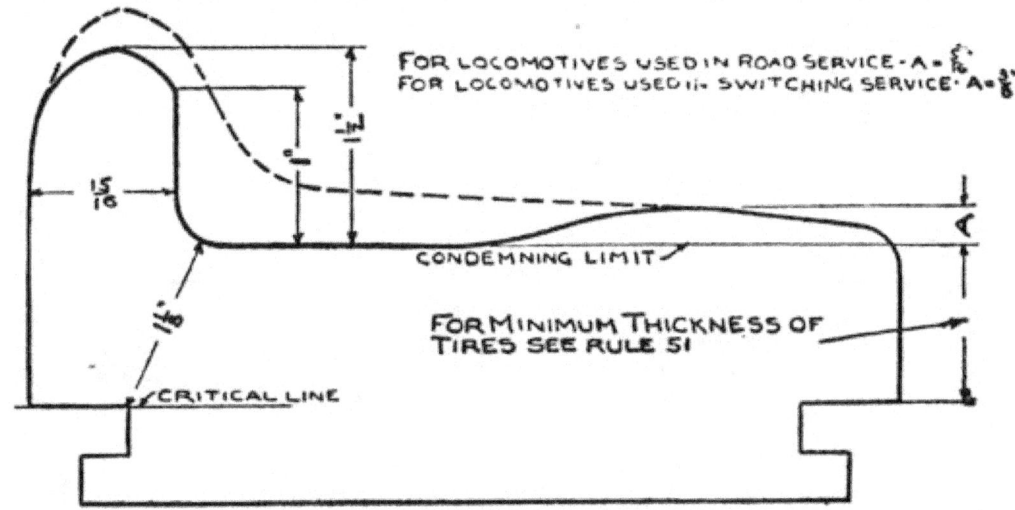

Fig. 1.—STEEL TIRE.

Retaining ring fastening. Driving and trailing wheels.

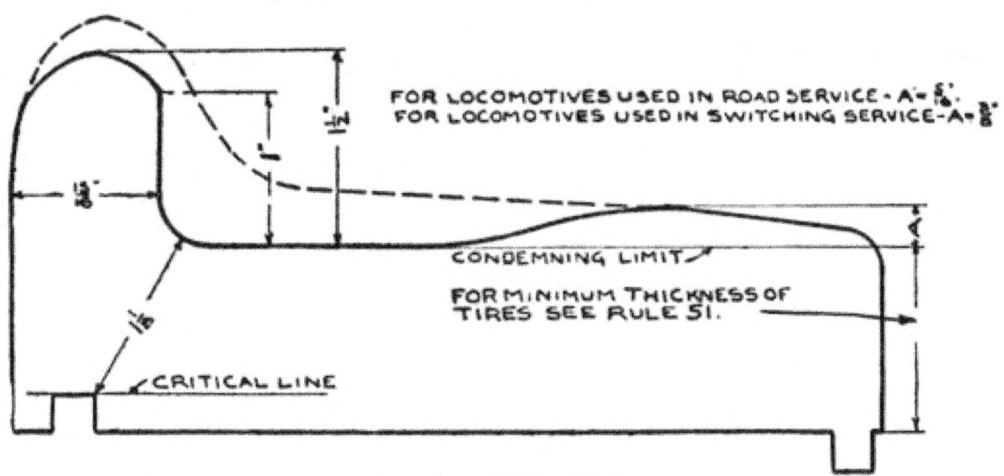

Fig. 2.—STEEL TIRE.

Shrinkage fastening with shoulder and retaining segments. Driving and trailing wheels.

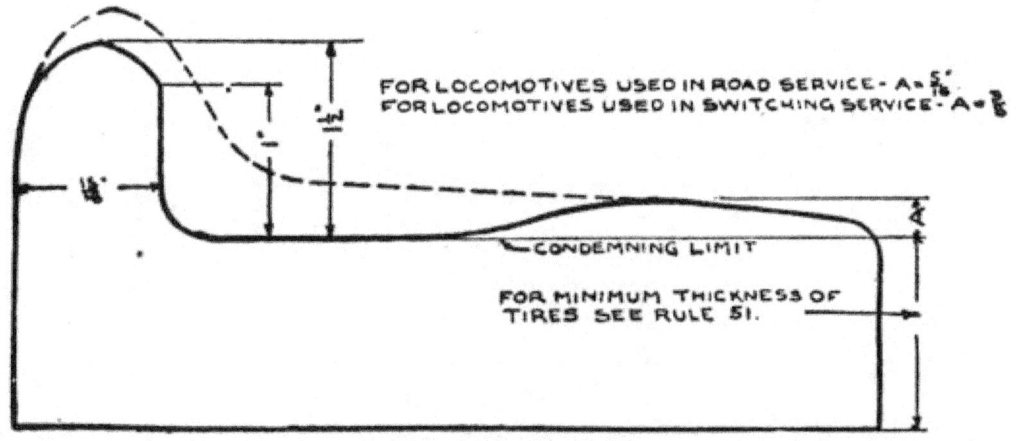

Fig. 3.—STEEL TIRE.

Shrinkage fastening. Driving and trailing wheels.

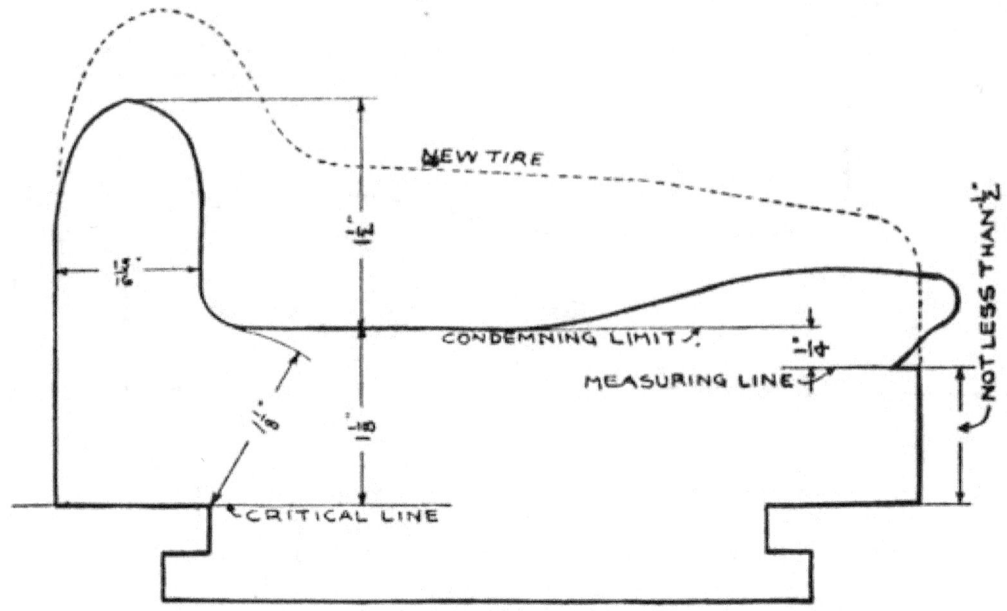

Fig. 4.—STEEL TIRE.

Retaining ring fastening. Minimum thickness for steel tires. Engine and tender truck wheels. (See Rule 46.)

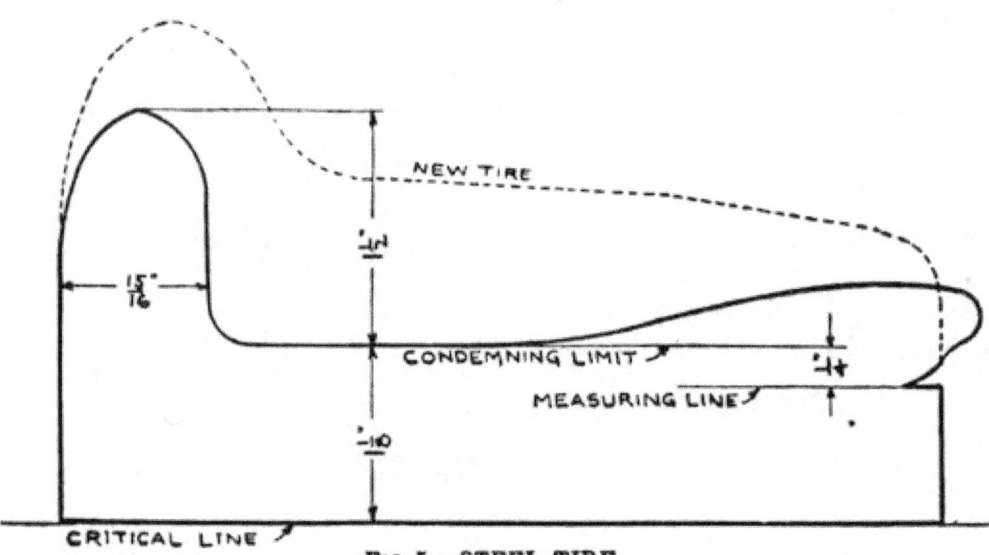

Fig. 5.—STEEL TIRE.

Shrinkage fastening only. Minimum thickness for steel tires. Engine and tender truck wheels. (See Rule 46.)

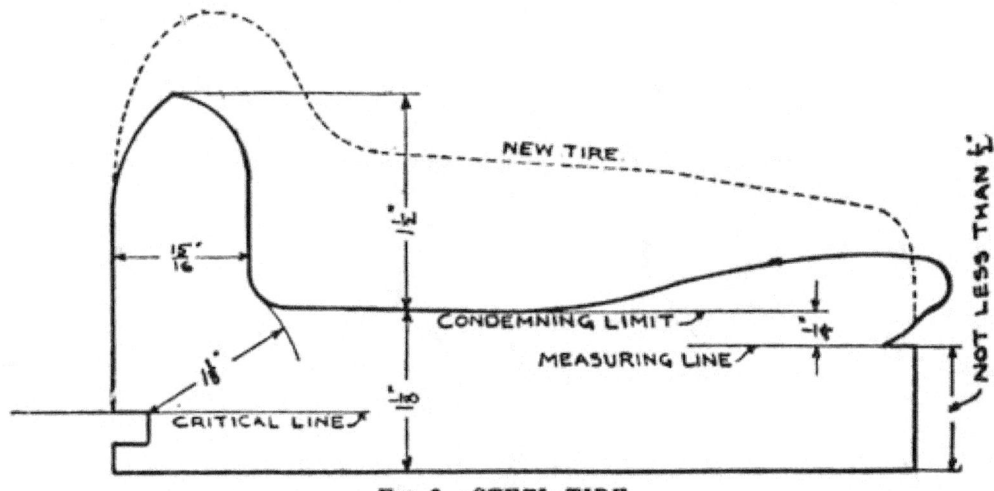

Fig. 6.—STEEL TIRE.

Retaining ring fastening. Minimum thickness for steel tires. Engine and tender truck wheels. (See Rule 46.)

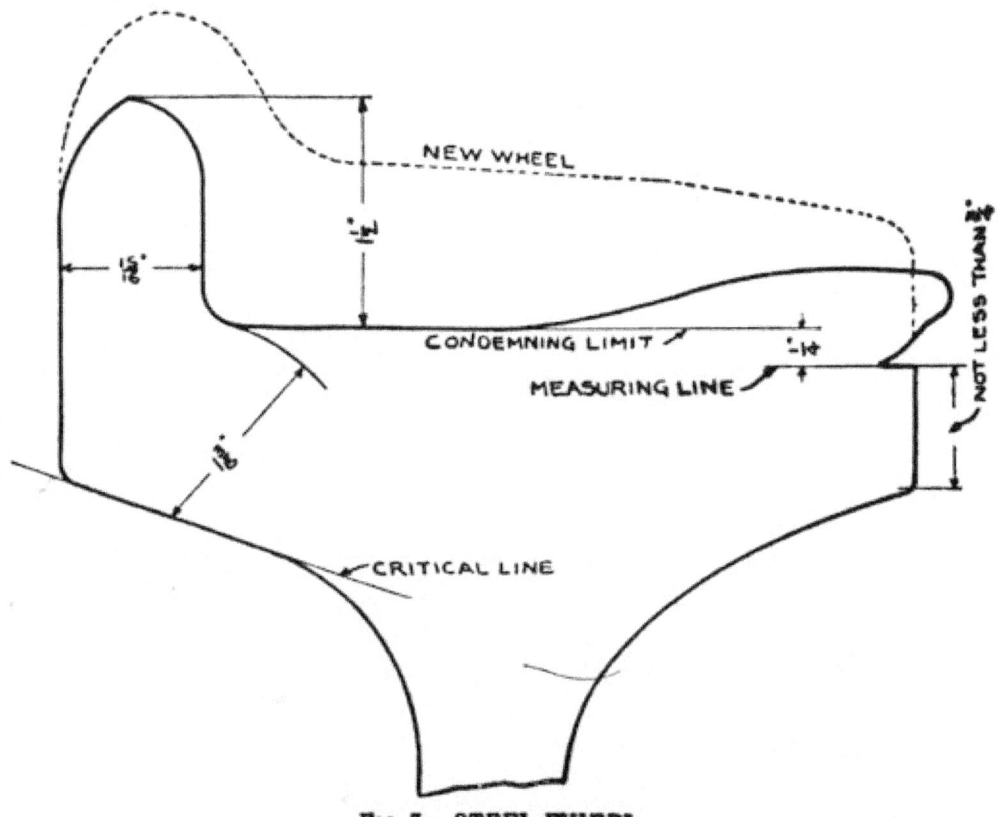

Fig. 7.—STEEL WHEEL.

Minimum thickness of rim. Engine and tender truck wheels. (See Rule 46.)

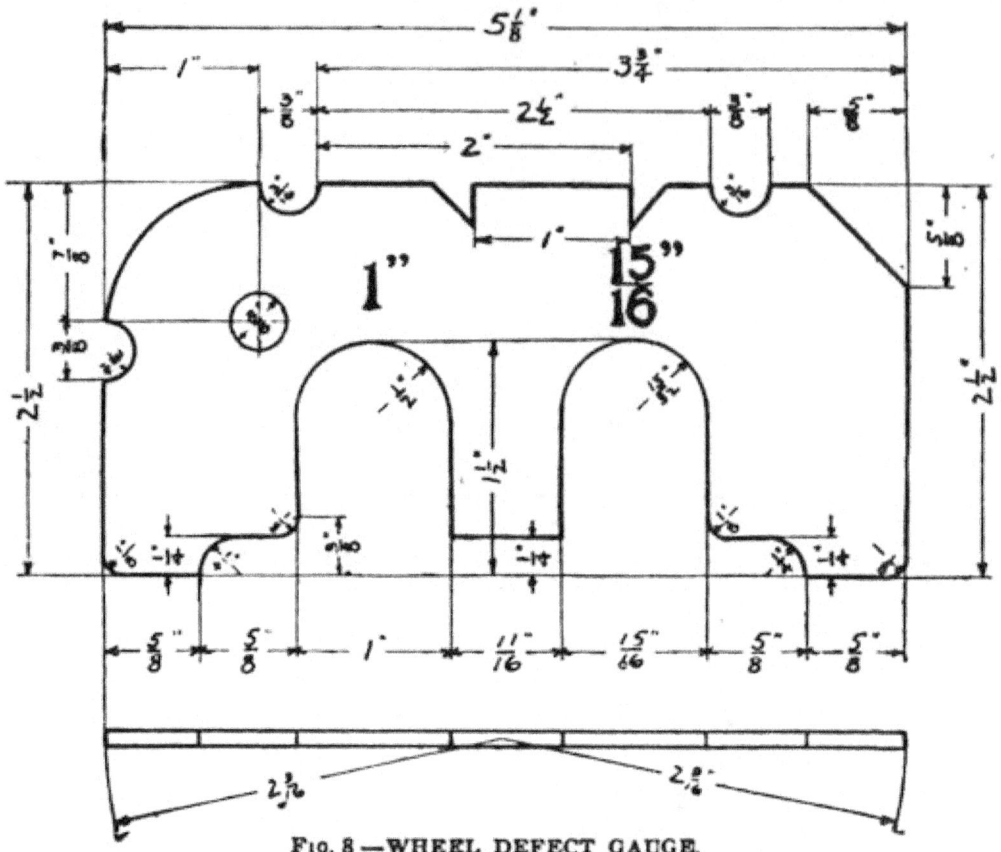

Fig. 8.—WHEEL DEFECT GAUGE.

This gauge to be used in determining flat spots, worn flanges, and broken rims.
(See Rules 45, 46, and 50.)

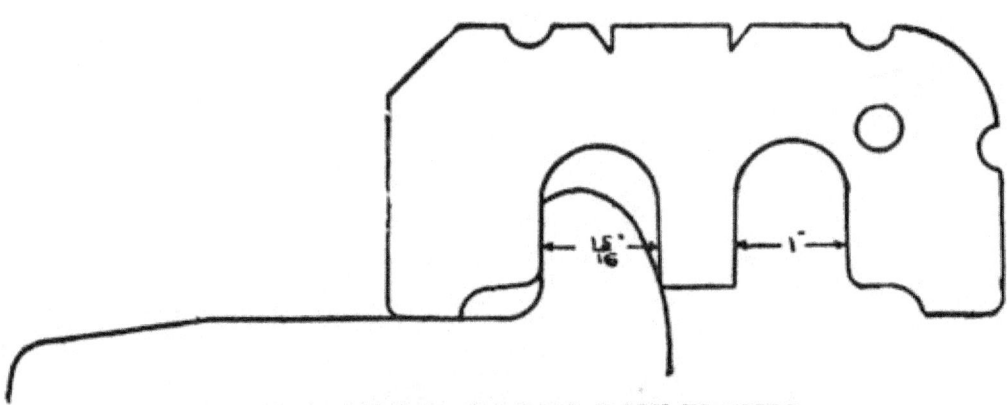

Fig. 9.—METHOD OF GAUGING WORN FLANGES.

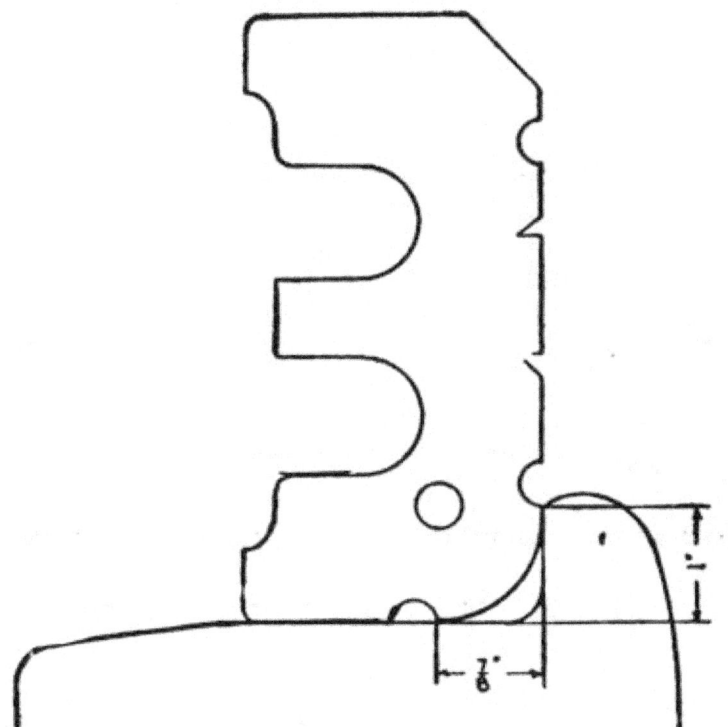

Fig. 10.—METHOD OF GAUGING WORN FLANGES.

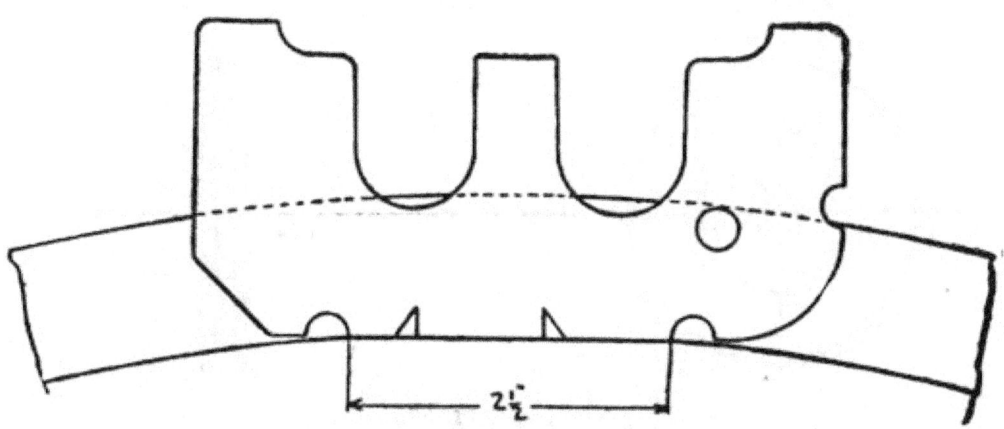

Fig. 11.—METHOD OF GAUGING SHELLED AND FLAT SPOTS.

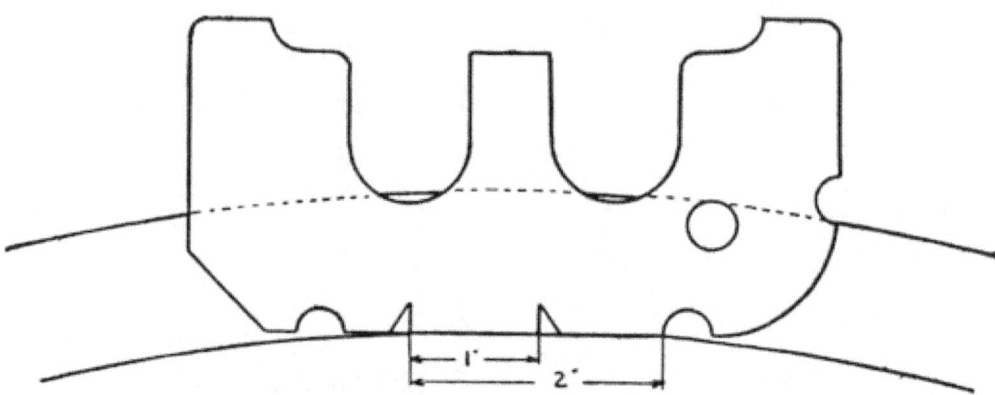

Fig. 12.—METHOD OF MEASURING FLAT SPOTS OF ONE AND TWO INCHES.

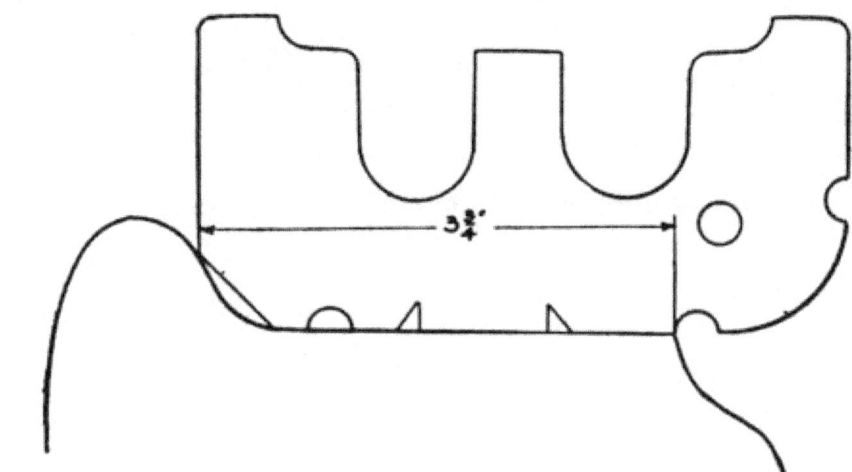

Fig. 13.—METHOD OF GAUGING BROKEN RIMS.

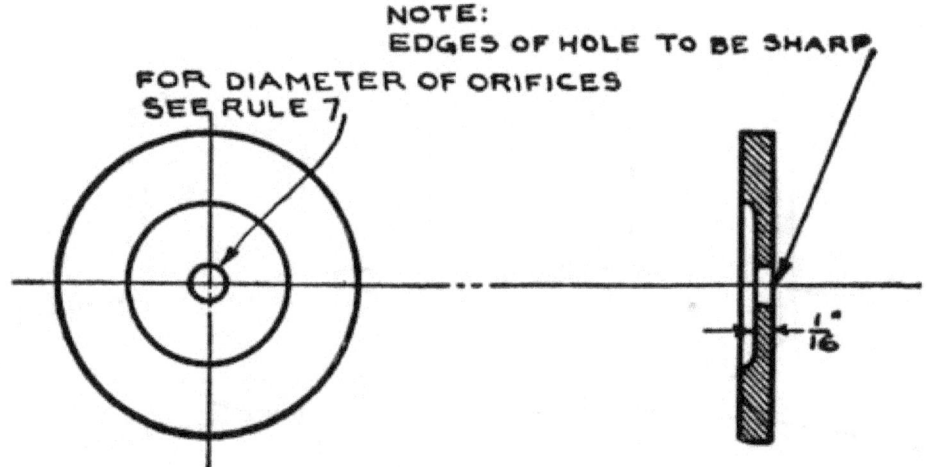

Fig. 14.—ORIFICE.

Safety Appliance Standards for Locomotives, as fixed by order of the Commission Dated March 13, 1911.

STEAM LOCOMOTIVES USED IN ROAD SERVICE
TENDER SILL-STEPS

Number:
  Four (4) on tender.

Dimensions:
  Bottom tread not less than eight (8) by twelve (12) inches, metal.
  [*May have wooden treads.*]
  If stirrup-steps are used, clear length of tread shall be not less than ten (10), preferably twelve (12), inches.

Location:
  One (1) near each corner of tender on sides.

Manner of application:
  Tender sill-steps shall be securely fastened with bolts or rivets.

PILOT SILL-STEPS

Number:
  Two (2).

Dimensions:
  Tread not less than eight (8) inches in width by ten (10) inches in length, metal.
  [*May have wooden treads.*]

Location:
  One (1) on or near each end of buffer-beam outside of rail and not more than sixteen (16) inches above rail.

Manner of application:
  Pivot sill-steps shall be securely fastened with bolts or rivets.

PILOT-BEAM HANDHOLDS

Number:
  Two (2).

Dimensions:
  Minimum diameter, five-eighths (5/8) of an inch, wrought iron or steel.
  Minimum clear length, fourteen (14), preferably sixteen (16), inches.
  Minimum clearance, two and one-half (2½) inches.

Location:
  One (1) on each end of buffer-beam.

[*If uncoupling-lever extends across front end of locomotive to within eight (8) inches of end of buffer-beam, and is seven-eighths (7/8) of an inch or more in diameter, securely fastened, with a clearance of two and one-half (2½) inches, it is a handhold.*]

Manner of application:
    Pilot-beam handholds shall be securely fastened with bolts or rivets.

SIDE-HANDHOLDS

Number:
    Six (6).

Dimensions:
    Minimum diameter, if horizontal, five-eighths (5/8) of an inch; if vertical, seven-eighths (7/8) of an inch, wrought iron or steel.
    Horizontal, minimum clear length, sixteen (16) inches. Vertical, clear length equal to approximate height of tank.
    Minimum clearance two (2), preferably two and one-half (2½), inches.

Location:
    Horizontal or vertical: If vertical, one (1) on each side of tender within six (6) inches of rear or on corner, if horizontal, same as specified for "Box and other house cars."
    One (1) on each side of tender near gangway; one (1) on each side of locomotive at gangway; applied vertically.

Manner of application:
    Side-handholds shall be securely fastened with not less than one-half (½) inch bolts or rivets.

REAR-END HANDHOLDS

Number:
    Two (2).

Dimensions:
    Minimum diameter, five-eighths (5/8) of an inch, wrought iron or steel.
    Minimum clear length, fourteen (14) inches.
    Minimum clearance two (2), preferably two and one-half (2½), inches.

Location:
    Horizontal: One (1) near each side of rear end of tender on face of end-sill. Clearance of outer end of handhold shall be not more than sixteen (16) inches from side of tender.

Manner of application:
    Rear-end handholds shall be securely fastened with not less than one-half (½) inch bolts or rivets.

UNCOUPLING-LEVERS

Number:
> Two (2) double levers, operative from either side.

Dimensions:
> Rear-end levers shall extend across end of tender with handles not more than twelve (12), preferably nine (9), inches from side of tender with a guard bent on handle to give not less than two (2) inches clearance around handle.

Location:
> One (1) on rear end of tender and one (1) on front end of locomotive. Handles of front-end levers shall be not more than twelve (12), preferably nine (9), inches from ends of buffer-beam, and shall be so constructed as to give a minimum clearance of two (2) inches around handle.

Manner of application:
> Uncoupling-levers shall be securely fastened with bolts or rivets.

COUPLERS

Locomotives shall be equipped with automatic couplers at rear of tender and front of locomotive.

STEAM LOCOMOTIVES USED IN SWITCHING SERVICE

FOOTBOARDS

Number:
> Two (2) or more.

Dimensions:
> Minimum width of tread, ten (10) inches, wood.
> Minimum thickness of tread, one and one-half (1½), preferably two (2), inches.
> Minimum height of backstop, four (4) inches above tread.
> Height from top of rail to top of tread, not more than twelve (12) nor less than nine (9) inches.

Location:
> Ends or sides.
> If on ends, they shall extend not less than eighteen (18) inches outside of gauge of straight track, and shall be not more than twelve (12) inches shorter than buffer-beam at each end.

Manner of application:
> End footboards may be constructed in two (2) sections, *provided* that practically all space on each side of coupler is filled; each section shall be not less than three (3) feet in length.
> Footboards shall be securely bolted to two (2) one (1) by four (4) inches metal brackets, *provided* footboard is not cut or notched at any point.

If footboard is cut or notched or in two (2) sections, not less than four (4) one (1) by three (3) inches metal brackets shall be used, two (2) located on each side of coupler. each bracket shall be securely bolted to buffer-beam, end-sill or tank-frame by not less than two (2) seven-eighths (⅞) inch bolts.

If side footboards are used, a substantial handhold or rail shall be applied not less than thirty (30) inches nor more than sixty (60) inches above tread of footboard.

SILL-STEPS

Number:
Two (2) or more.

Dimensions:
Lower tread of step shall be not less than eight (8) by twelve (12) inches, metal.
[*May have wooden treads.*]
If stirrup-steps are used, clear length of tread shall be not less than ten (10), preferably (12), inches.

Location:
One (1) or more on each side at gangway secured to locomotive or tender.

Manner of application:
Sill-steps shall be securely fastened with bolts or rivets.

END-HANDHOLDS

Number:
Two (2).

Dimensions:
Minimum diameter, one (1) inch, wrought iron or steel.
Minimum clearance, four (4) inches, *except* at coupler casting or braces, when minimum clearance shall be two (2) inches.

Location:
One (1) on pilot buffer-beam; one (1) on rear end of tender, extending across front end of locomotive and rear end of tender. Ends of handholds shall be not more than six (6) inches from ends of buffer-beam or end-sill, securely fastened at ends.

Manner of application:
End-handholds shall be securely fastened with bolts or rivets.

SIDE-HANDHOLDS

Number:
Four (4).

Dimensions:
Minimum diameter, seven-eighths (⅞) of an inch, wrought iron or steel.

Clear length equal to approximate height of tank.

Minimum clearance, two (2), preferably two and one-half (2½), inches.

Location:

Vertical. One (1) on each side of tender near front corner; one (1) on each side of locomotive at gangway.

Manner of application:

Side-handholds shall be securely fastened with bolts or rivets.

UNCOUPLING-LEVERS

Number:

Two (2) double levers, operative from either side.

Dimensions:

Handles of front-end levers shall be not more than twelve (12), preferably nine (9), inches from ends of buffer-beam, and shall be so constructed as to give a minimum clearance of two (2) inches around handle.

Rear end levers shall extend across end of tender with handles not more than twelve (12), preferably nine (9), inches from side of tender, with a guard bent on handle to give not less than two (2) inches clearance around handle.

Location:

One (1) on rear end of tender and one (1) on front end of locomotive.

HANDRAILS AND STEPS FOR HEADLIGHTS

Switching locomotives with sloping tenders with manhole or headlight located on sloping portion of tender shall be equipped with secure steps and handrail or with platform and handrail leading to such manhole or headlight.

END-LADDER CLEARANCE

No part of locomotive or tender *except* draft rigging, coupler and attachments, safety-chains, buffer-block, foot-board, brake pipe, signal pipe, steam-heat pipe or arms of uncoupling lever shall extend to within fourteen (14) inches of a vertical plane passing through the inside face of knuckle when closed with horn of coupler against buffer-block or end sill.

COUPLERS

Locomotives shall be equipped with automatic couplers at rear of tender and front of locomotive.

SPECIFICATIONS COMMON TO ALL STEAM LOCOMOTIVES

HAND-BRAKES

Hand-brakes will not be required on locomotives nor on tenders when attached to locomotives.

If tenders are detached from locomotives and used in special service, they shall be equipped with efficient hand-brakes.

RUNNING-BOARDS

Number:
Two (2).
52914°—16——6.

Dimensions:
Not less than ten (10) inches wide. If of wood, not less than one and one-half (1½) inches in thickness; if of metal, not less than three-sixteenths ($\frac{3}{16}$) of an inch, properly supported.

Location:
One (1) on each side of boiler extending from cab to front end near pilot-beam.
[*Running boards may be in sections. Flat top steamchests may form section of running board.*]

Manner of application:
Running boards shall be securely fastened with bolts, rivets or studs.

Locomotives having Wooten type boilers with cab located on top of boiler more than twelve (12) inches forward from boiler head shall have suitable running-boards running from cab to rear of locomotive, with handrailings not less than twenty (20) nor more than forty-eight (48) inches above outside edge of running boards, securely fastened with bolts, rivets or studs.

HANDRAILS

Number:
Two (2) or more.

Dimensions:
Not less than one (1) inch in diameter, wrought iron or steel.

Location:
One on each side of boiler extending from near cab to near front end of boiler and extending across front end of boiler, not less than twenty-four (24) nor more than sixty-six (66) inches above running board.

Manner of application:
Handrails shall be securely fastened to boiler.

TENDERS OF VANDERBILT TYPE

Tenders known as the Vanderbilt type shall be equipped with running boards; one (1) on each side of tender not less than ten (10) inches in width and one on top of tender not less than forty-eight (48) inches in width, extending from coal space to rear of tender.

There shall be a handrail on each side of top running board, extending from coal space to rear of tank, not less than one (1) inch in diameter and not less than twenty (20) inches in height above running board from coal space to manhole.

There shall be a handrail extending from coal space to within twelve (12) inches of rear of tank, attached to each side of tank above side running board, not less than thirty (30) nor more than sixty-six (66) inches above running board.

There shall be one (1) vertical end handhold on each side of Vanderbilt type of tender, located within eight (8) inches of rear of tank extending from within eight (8) inches of top of end-sill to within eight (8) inches of side handrail. Post supporting rear end of side running board if not more than two (2) inches in diameter and properly located, may form section of handhold.

An additional horizontal end handhold shall be applied on rear end of all Vanderbilt type of tenders which are not equipped with vestibules. Handhold to be located not less than thirty (30) nor more than sixty-six (66) inches above top of end-sill. Clear length of handhold to be not less than forty-eight (48) inches.

Ladders shall be applied at forward ends of side running boards.

HANDRAILS AND STEPS FOR HEADLIGHTS

Locomotives having headlights which can not be safely and conveniently reached from pilot beam or steam chests shall be equipped with secure handrails and steps suitable for the use of men in getting to and from such headlights.

A suitable metal end or side ladder shall be applied to all tanks more than forty-eight (48) inches in height, measured from the top of end-sill, and securely fastened with bolts or rivets.

COUPLERS

Locomotives shall be equipped with automatic coupler at rear of tender and front of locomotive.

NOTE.—Prescribed standard height of drawbars: Standard gauge railroads—maximum 34½, minimum 31½ inches; narrow gauge railroads—maximum 26, minimum 23 inches; 2-foot gauge railroads—maximum 17½, minimum 14½ inches.

Index

	Page
Air Pump Running Hot, Reasons for	294
Arithmetic, Handy Rules in	16
Axles	161
Baker Valve Gear	103
Boilers	140
British Thermal Unit	17
B-3 Locomotive Brake	389
B-3 Manipulation	385
Classification of Locomotives	18
Combustion	4
Definition of Technical Terms	14
Draft Appliances	147
Electric Headlights	54
Engine Failure, What Constitutes an	19
Engine Failures and Breakdowns	136
Handling of Freight Trains	292
Injectors	150
"K" Triple Valves	397
Linstroms Improved Eccentric	182
Locomotive and Adhesion, The	136
Lubricators	157
Mallet Locomotives	38
Mallet Locomotives, Breakdowns	42
Mallet Locomotives, Operating Rules	42
Mechanical Problems	16
Mikado Type Locomotives	24
Nathan Bull's-Eye Lubricator	64
Nathan Simplex Injector	67
No. 6 "ET" Locomotive Brake Equipment	322
"PC" Passenger Brake Equipment	298
"Piston Travel," Definition of the Term	296
Pounds in Locomotives	20
Progressive Examination—	
First Year	192
Second Year	205
Third Year	226
Pyle-National Electric Headlight	49
Questions and Answers on—	
Air Brake, First Year	203
Air Brake, Second Year	215
Air Brake, Third Year	276

Questions and Answers—Continued.

Air Brake, New York	284
Air Pump	276
Axles	161
B-3 Equipment	387
B-3 "HS" Locomotive Brake	387
Baker Valve Gear	117
Boilers	140
Combustion	7
Compound Locomotives, Third Year's Examination	264
Draft Appliances	147
Duplex Air Pump	284
Electric Headlights	273
Electric Headlights, Pyle-National	54
Electric Headlights in General	59
Electric Headlights, Schroeder	32
Engine Failures and Breakdowns	136
Engineers Brake and Equalizing Discharge Valve	280
Frames	161
Guides	167
Injectors	150
"LT" Equipment	286
Locomotive and Adhesion	136
Lubricators	158
Lubrication, Third Year's Examination	271
Mallet Locomotives	38
Oil-Burning Locomotives	220
"PC" Passenger Brake Equipment	307
Control Valve	310
Compartment Reservoir	310
Pump Governor	278
Rods	167
Southern Valve Gear	125
Tires	161
Triple Valve	283
Trucks	161
Valves and Valve Gear	172
Walschaert Valve Gear	80
Westinghouse Eleven-inch Pump	409A
Wheels	161
No. 6 "ET" Equipment—	
Air Gauges	358
Air Signal Supply System Test	381
Air Signal System	359
Automatic Brake Valve Test	374
B-6 Feed Valve	351
Brake Cylinder Leakage Test	379
Broken Pipes	367
C-6 Reducing Valve	353

Questions and Answers—Continued.
    No. 6 "ET" Equipment—Continued.

Cut-out Cocks	358
Dead Engine Fixtures	356
Distributing Valve Test	376
Feed Valve Test	372
Freight Braking	365
General Operation	360
H-6 Automatic Brake Valve	339
Independent Brake Valve Test	375
Manipulation of Locomotive and Train Brakes	362
No. 6 Distributing Valve with Plain Cylinder Cap	344
Parts of Equipment	337
Pump Governor Test	371
Quick Action Cylinder Cap	350
Reducing Valve Test	373
Roundhouse Inspector's Test	369
S-6 Independent Brake Valve	342
SF-4 Pump Governor	353
Safety Valve	349
Safety Valve Test	380
Testing and Operating	361
Rules and Instructions for Inspection and Testing of Steam Locomotives and Tenders	410
"Running Travel," Definition of the Term	296
"Standing Travel," Definition of the Term	296
Safety Appliance Standards for Locomotives, as fixed by order of the Commission Dated March 13, 1911	435
Schroeder Electric Headlight	28
Sellers Injector	69
Slide Valves, The Allen-Richardson	71
Southern Locomotive Valve Gear	122
Steam	1
Steam, The Theory of Superheating	2
Superheaters, Schmidt	127
Superheaters, Dont's on	135
Technical Terms, Definition of	14
Triplex Articulated Compound Locomotive	45
Valves and Valve Gear	172
Walschaert Valve Gear	73
General Instructions for	77
Instructions for Erecting and Setting the	78
Helmholtz Modification	79
Westinghouse Eleven-inch Pump	409A

1. Headlight.
2. Headlight Bracket.
3. Number Plate.
4. Smoke-box Front.
5. Smoke-box Front Door.
6. Signal Lamp Bracket.
7. Running Board Step.
8. Running Board Step Bracket.
9. Bumper Brace.
10. Truck Center Bolt.
11. Truck Center Bolt Nut.
12. Truck Center Pin.
13. Bumper Bracket.
14. Flag Socket.
15. Uncoupling Arm.
16. Uncoupling Lever.
17. Drawhead.
18. Coupling.
19. Pilot Bar.
20. Pilot.
21. Pilot Nosing.
22. Pilot Brace.
23. Pilot Bracket.
24. Front Bumper Beam.
25. Bumper Step.
26. Bumper Step.
27. Truck Swing Frame.
28. Truck Swing Bolster.
29. Truck Pedestal.
30. Truck Swing Link.
31. Truck Spring.
32. Truck Pedestal Thimble.
33. Truck Radius Bar Brace.
34. Truck Axle.
35. Truck Wheel.
36. Piston Head.
37. Piston Rod Extension.
38. Piston Rod Extension Guide.
39. Piston Rod Extension Guide Bracket.
40. Piston Packing Rings.
41. Cylinder.
42. Front Cylinder Head.
43. Back Cylinder Head.
44. Cylinder Cock.
45. Cylinder Cock Lifting Rod.
46. Cylinder Casing.
47. Cylinder Head Vacuum Valve.
48. Piston Rod Extension Guide Cover.
49. Piston Valve Body.
50. Piston Valve Stem.
51. Piston Valve Packing Rings.
52. Piston Valve Bushing.
53. Front Piston Valve Casing.
54. Pack Piston Valve Casing and Guide Support.
55. Live Steam Space.
56. Exhaust Steam Space.
57. Steam Port.
58. Cylinder Saddle.
59. Exhaust Passage.
60. Longtitudinal Equalizer.
61. Equalizer Fulcrum.
62. Equalizer Fulcrum Pin.
63. Link Motion Union Link.
64. Link Motion Combination Lever.
65. Link Motion Radius Bar.
66. Link Motion Radius Bar Hanger.
67. Link.
68. Link Bracket.
69. Eccentric Rod.
70. Eccentric Crank.
71. Crosshead.
72. Crosshead Arm.
73. Wrist Pin.
74. Top Guide.
75. Bottom Guide.
76. Valve Rod Guide.
77. Forward Springs and Truck Equalizer Hanger.
78. Driver Spring Band.
79. Driver Spring.
80. Driving Spring Saddle.
81. Spring Hanger.
82. Driving Spring Equalizer.
83. Wrist Pin Bearing Key.
84. Guide Yoke.
85. Spring Equalizer.
86. Guide Bearer Bracket.
87. Equalizer Fulcrum.
88. Spring Hanger Key.
89. Sand Pipe.
90. Guide Yoke Step.
91. Driver Brake Cylinder.
92. Driver Brake Cylinder Lever.
93. Driver Brake Pull Angle.
94. Driver Brake Adjusting Block.
95. Driver Brake Adjusting Screw.
96. Driver Brake Shoe.
97. Driver Brake Shoe Hanger.
98. Driver Brake Pull Rod.
99. Driver Brake Hanger Bracket.
100. Frame Brace.
101. Main Driving Rod.
102. Forward Side Rod.
103. Intermediate Side Rod.
104. Back Side Rod.
105. Main Crank Pin.
106. Forward Crank Pin.
107. Intermediate Crank Pin.
108. Back Crank Pin.
109. Forward Side Rod Pin.
110. Back Side Rod Knuckle.
111. Main Rod Bearing.
112. Main Rod Strap Bolts.
113. Eccentric Pin.
114. Frame Brace.
115. Driving Axle.
116. Driving Axle Key.
117. Main Frame.
118. Main Rod Strap.
119. Frame Pedestal Cap.

MIKADO OR 2-8-2 TYPE OF LOCOMO

120. Frame Brace.	135. Trailing Truck Equalizer Spring Hanger.
121. Foot Plate.	136. Trailing Truck Spring Hanger Seat.
122. Chafing Block.	137. Trailing Truck Equalizer Spring.
123. Chafing Plate.	138. Trailing Truck Equalizer.
124. Driving Tire.	139. Journal Box Trailing.
125. Driving Wheel Center.	140. Ash Pan Dumping Cylinder.
126. Main Driving Counterbalance.	141. Ash Pan Dumping Cylinder Rod.
127. Intermediate Driver Counterbalance.	142. Ash Pan Slide.
128. Journal Box Driving.	143. Ash Pan Slide Guide.
129. Eccentric Rod Link Pin.	144. Ash Pan Slide Connections.
130. Trailing Axle.	145. Ash Pan Slide Connections Arm.
131. Trailing Wheel Center.	146. Ash Pan Dumping Cylinder Rod Extension.
132. Trailing Tire.	147. Ash Pan Slide Connection Arm Bracket.
133. Trailing Truck Pedestal Thimble.	148. Trailing Truck Equalizer Spring Seat.
134. Trailing Truck Spring.	149. Grate Shaker Cylinder Support.
	150. Brake Shoe Hanger Support.
	151. Frame Extension.
	152. Smoke-box Ring.
	153. Smoke-box Shell.
	154. Smokestack.
	155. Smokestack Projection.
	156. Smokestack Petticoat.
	157. Headlight Step.
	158. Perforated Deflector or Smoke-box Netting.
	159. Deflecting Plate Bottom.
	160. Superheater Damper
	161. Superheater Damper
	162. Steam Pipe.
	163. Deflecting Plate Bac
	164. Exhaust Nozzle.
	165. Exhaust Pipe.
	166. Steam Pipe Casing.
	167. Steam Pipe Casing
	168. Superheater Damper Feed Pipe.
	169. Superheater Tee He Ground Flange.
	170. Superheater Tee He
	171. Superheater Tubes.
	172. Superheater Return Front Connections.

LOCOMOTIVE

Superheater Damper.
Superheater Damper Cylinder.
Steam Pipe.
Deflecting Plate Back.
Exhaust Nozzle.
Exhaust Pipe.
Steam Pipe Casing.
Steam Pipe Casing Flange.
Superheater Damper Cylinder Feed Pipe.
Superheater Tee Head. Ground Flange.
Superheater Tee Head.
Superheater Tubes.
Superheater Return Bend Front Connections.

173. Superheater Damper Cylinder Counter Weight.
174. Front Tube Sheet.
175. Dry Pipe Stiffening Ring.
176. Dry Pipe Sleeve.
177. Dry Pipe.
178. Sand Dome.
179. Sand Dome Cap.
180. Main Sand Pipe.
181. Sand Box.
182. Sand Box Step.
183. Front Tube Sheet Brace.
184. Front Course of Boiler Shell.
185. Bell.
186. Bell Stand.
187. Boiler Lagging.
188. Boiler Casing or Jacketing.

189. Boiler Course Intermediate.
190. Superheater Pipe Supports.
191. Boiler Tube.
192. Boiler Check Valve.
193. Injector Delivery Pipe.
194. Intermediate Check Valve.
195. Injector Delivery Pipe Support.
196. Reverse Spring Casing.
197. Reverse Spring Rod.
198. Reverse Shaft.
199. Reverse Shaft Crank.
200. Reverse Shaft Reach Rod.
201. Reverse Shaft Reach Rod Support.
202. Running Board Bracket.
203. Reservoir Hanger.
204. Main Reservoir.

205. Boiler Waist Sheet.
206. Boiler Waist Sheet Angle.
207. Washout Flange and Cap.
208. Grate Shaker Lever.
209. Grate Shaker Lever Fulcrum.
210. Grate Shaker Cylinder Connection Rod.
211. Grate Shaker Bracket.
212. Grate Shaker Cylinder.
213. Handrail.
214. Handrail Post.
215. Dry Pipe Elbow.
216. Dry Pipe Bracket.
217. Throttle Casing.
218. Throttle Valve.
219. Throttle Valve Stem.
220. Throttle Valve Bell Crank.

- Throttle Stem.
- Superheater Boiler Flues.
- Superheater Return Bends Rear.
- Back Tube Sheet.
- Reverse Shaft Reach Rod Guide and Casing.
- Running Board.
- Fire-box Throat Sheet Brace.
- Throat Sheet.
- Mud Ring.
- Arch Tube.
- Brick Arch.
- Stay Bolts.
- Reach Rod Guide Screw Connection.
- Reversing Gear Screw Guide.

235. Reversing Screw.
236. Reversing Gear Support.
237. Reversing Gear Hand Wheel.
238. Reversing Gear Catch.
239. Safety Valves.
240. Safety Valve Casing.
241. Roof Sheet.
242. Expansion Stay Bolts.
243. Longitudinal Brace.
244. Back Head Angle Brace.
245. Crown Sheet.
246. Whistle Connecting Rod Front.
247. Whistle Bell Crank.
248. Whistle Bell Crank Bracket.
249. Whistle Connecting Rod Rear.
250. Whistle Operating Lever.
251. Whistle Operating Lever Bracket.
252. Throttle Stem Bracket.
253. Throttle Stuffing Box.
254. Throttle Lever.
255. Throttle Lever Quadrant.
256. Throttle Lever Fulcrum.
257. Throttle Lever Latch.
258. Water Gauge.
259. Air Gauge.
260. Steam Gauge.
261. Gauge Stand.
262. Steam Gauge Goose Neck.
263. Injector.
264. Injector Steam Pipe.
265. Injector Steam Valve.
266. Injector Suction Pipe.
267. Injector Overflow Pipe.
268. Injector Suction Pipe Support.
269. Injector Suction Pipe Valve.
270. Injector Suction Pipe Strainer.
271. Cab Ventilator Cover.
272. Cab Ventilator.
273. Cab Roof.
274. Cab Roof Overhang.
275. Cab Back.
276. Cab Bracket.
277. Cab Handle.
278. Cab Seat.
279. Cab Window.
280. Back Head.
281. Back Sheet of Fire-box.
282. Fire-box Opening.
283. Fire-box Door.
284. Dead Grate.
285. Rocking Grate.
286. Rocking Grate Connecting Rods.
287. Dome Casing.
288. Dome Cap.
289. Dome.
290. Dome Stiffening Ring.
291. Dome Boiler Course.
292. Ash Pan.
293. Ash Pan Hopper.
294. Piston Rod.
295. Piston Valve Rod Extension Guide.
296. Piston Valve Rod Guide Bracket.
297. Radius Bar.
298. Radius Bar Cross-tie.
299. Guide Bearer.
300. Whistle.
301. Radial Stay Bolts.
302. Fire-box.
303. Combustion Chamber.

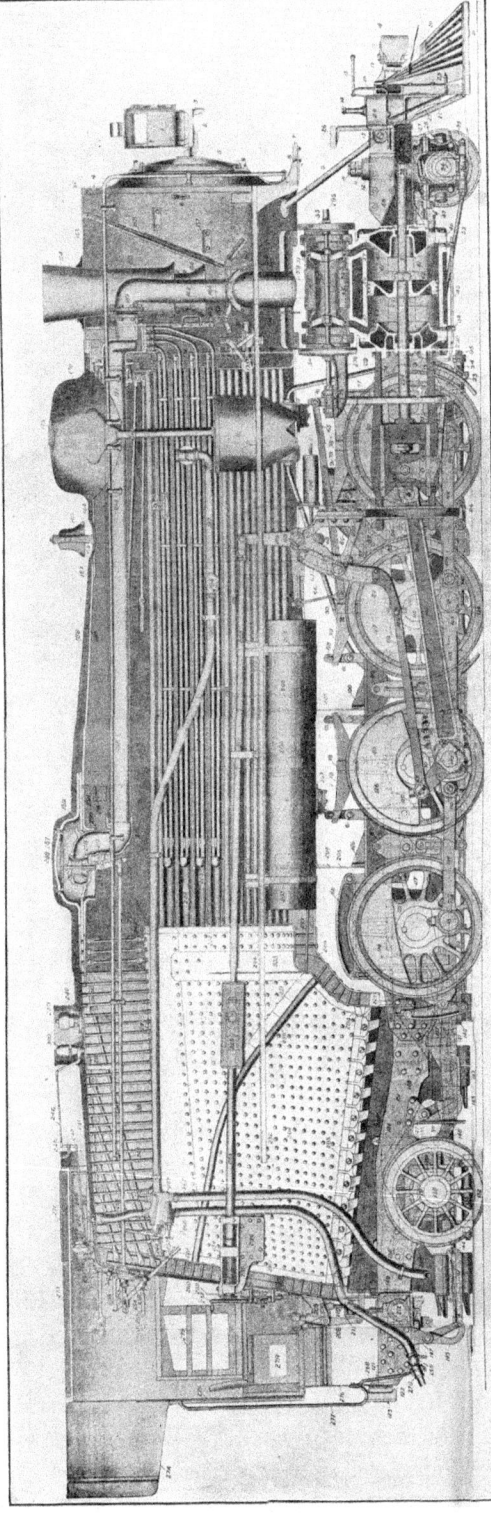

MIKADO OR 2-8-2 TYPE OF LOCOMOTIVE

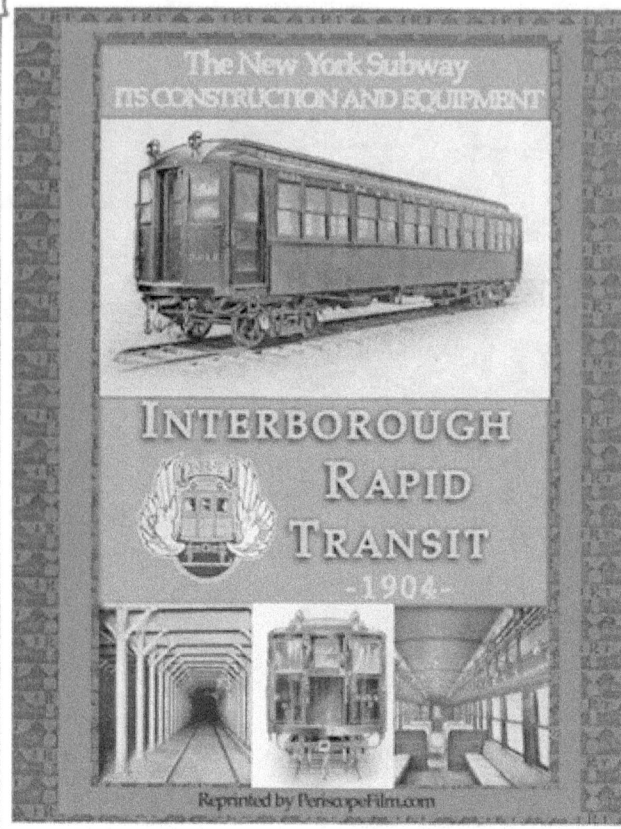

On October 27, 1904, the Interborough Rapid Transit Company opened the first subway in New York City. Running between City Hall and 145th Street at Broadway, the line was greeted with enthusiasm and, in some circles, trepidation. Created under the supervision of Chief Engineer S.L.F. Deyo, the arrival of the IRT foreshadowed the end of the "elevated" transit era on the island of Manhattan. The subway proved such a success that the IRT Co. soon achieved a monopoly on New York public transit. In 1940 the IRT and its rival the BMT were taken over by the City of New York. Today, the IRT subway lines still exist, primarily in Manhattan where they are operated as the "A Division" of the subway. Reprinted here is a special book created by the IRT, recounting the design and construction of the fledgling subway system. Originally created in 1904, it presents the IRT story with a flourish, and with numerous fascinating illustrations and rare photographs.

Originally written in the late 1900's and then periodically revised, A History of the Baldwin Locomotive Works chronicles the origins and growth of one of America's greatest industrial-era corporations. Founded in the early 1830's by Philadelphia jeweler Matthais Baldwin, the company built a huge number of steam locomotives before ceasing production in 1949. These included the 4-4-0 American type, 2-8-2 Mikado and 2-8-0 Consolidation. Hit hard by the loss of the steam engine market, Baldwin soldiered on for a brief while, producing electric and diesel engines. General Electric's dominance of the market proved too much, and Baldwin finally closed its doors in 1956. By that time over 70,500 Baldwin locomotives had been produced. This high quality reprint of the official company history dates from 1920. The book has been slightly reformatted, but care has been taken to preserve the integrity of the text.

NOW AVAILABLE AT
WWW.PERISCOPEFILM.COM